Algorithms and Applications of Machine Learning Techniques for Healthcare

Algorithms and Applications of Machine Learning Techniques for Healthcare

Guest Editor

Edward Rolando Núñez-Valdez

MDPI

Basel • Beijing • Wuhan • Barcelona • Belgrade • Novi Sad • Cluj • Manchester

Guest Editor
Edward Rolando Núñez-Valdez
Department of Computer Science
University of Oviedo
Oviedo
Spain

Editorial Office
MDPI AG
Grosspeteranlage 5
4052 Basel, Switzerland

This is a reprint of the Special Issue, published open access by the journal *Algorithms* (ISSN 1999-4893), freely accessible at: https://www.mdpi.com/journal/algorithms/special_issues/1J56DYHD13.

For citation purposes, cite each article independently as indicated on the article page online and as indicated below:

Lastname, A.A.; Lastname, B.B. Article Title. *Journal Name* **Year**, *Volume Number*, Page Range.

ISBN 978-3-7258-6506-2 (Hbk)
ISBN 978-3-7258-6507-9 (PDF)
https://doi.org/10.3390/books978-3-7258-6507-9

Contents

About the Editor

Edward Rolando Núñez-Valdez

Edward Rolando Núñez-Valdez is affiliated with the Department of Computer Science at the University of Oviedo, Spain, where he works as a researcher and associate professor in computer science and artificial intelligence. His academic background includes a Ph.D. in Computer Engineering, complemented by graduate training in software engineering and innovation, as well as a bachelor's degree in computer science. His research focuses on artificial intelligence, machine learning, recommender systems, health informatics, sentiment analysis, and natural language processing. Throughout his career, he has participated in multiple national and international research projects, collaborated with software development companies and IT consulting firms, and published his work in recognized international journals and conferences. He is officially accredited as a scientific researcher in the National Career of Researchers in Science, Technology, and Innovation by the Ministry of Higher Education, Science, and Technology of the Dominican Republic.

Preface

Improving human health and ensuring equitable access to high-quality healthcare remain major challenges for modern societies. In this context, advances in digital technologies have opened new opportunities to support disease prevention, diagnosis, and treatment, as well as to enhance the efficiency of healthcare systems. Among these technologies, machine learning has attracted increasing attention due to its ability to extract meaningful patterns from large-scale data and to support decision-making in complex environments.

Over the past decade, research at the intersection of machine learning and healthcare has grown significantly, leading to innovative approaches in areas such as computer-assisted diagnosis, clinical workflow automation, personalized treatments, and telemedicine. Despite these advances, the effective translation of research outcomes into real clinical practice is still limited and faces substantial technical, ethical, and organizational challenges.

The aim of this Reprint is to present a consolidated and up-to-date overview of the state of the art in machine learning for healthcare by bringing together contributions that address both methodological developments and real-world applications. By doing so, this collection seeks to stimulate collaboration between researchers and healthcare professionals and to promote the development of solutions that support a more effective and responsible integration of machine learning technologies into healthcare systems.

Edward Rolando Núñez-Valdez
Guest Editor

algorithms

MDPI

Editorial

Special Issue on Algorithms and Applications of Machine Learning Techniques for Healthcare

Edward Rolando Núñez-Valdez

Department of Computer Science, University of Oviedo, 33007 Oviedo, Spain; nunezedward@uniovi.es

1. Introduction

Machine learning, as a core subfield of artificial intelligence, enables computational systems to learn from data and emulate aspects of intelligent human behavior. Its effectiveness has already been demonstrated across a wide range of domains, including virtual personal assistants [1,2], autonomous systems [3,4], intelligent surveillance [5,6], recommendation platforms [7,8], and early warning and alert mechanisms [9,10]. These successful applications illustrate the transformative potential of machine learning and its growing impact on everyday life.

Building on these advances, machine learning has emerged as a key enabling technology in modern healthcare. Its capacity to analyze large and complex datasets has driven significant progress in areas such as clinical decision support [11], disease diagnosis [12], patient monitoring [13], and personalized medicine [14]. As healthcare systems worldwide face increasing demands for efficiency, accuracy, and accessibility, machine learning-based solutions offer promising tools to support clinicians and improve patient outcomes.

Despite the growing body of research, the integration of machine learning techniques into real-world healthcare environments remains limited. Challenges related to data quality, model interpretability, ethical considerations, and clinical validation continue to hinder widespread adoption. In response, this Special Issue aims to advance the state of the art in machine learning for healthcare by presenting recent research that addresses both methodological innovation and practical application.

2. Overview of Contents

This Special Issue brings together seventeen peer-reviewed articles that were carefully evaluated and selected for publication by expert reviewers. The main contributions of the accepted papers are summarized below.

The first article focuses on improving the efficiency and accuracy of skin cancer diagnosis through machine learning techniques. The authors propose an integrated approach that combines feature reduction and ensemble learning with deep neural networks, enabling reliable classification of skin lesions as malignant or benign. Experimental results on widely used dermatological datasets demonstrate the effectiveness of the proposed method, highlighting its potential to reduce diagnostic costs, minimize reliance on medical expertise, and support faster decision-making in clinical practice.

The second article presents a comprehensive review of machine learning models based on wearable device data for predicting and monitoring symptoms of major depressive disorder. Focusing primarily on wrist-worn devices, the article highlights the clinical potential of these approaches for treatment monitoring, early intervention, and preventive care. At the same time, it critically discusses current limitations related to methodological heterogeneity, reproducibility, and generalizability, emphasizing the need for standardized evaluation frameworks and more robust study designs to enable reliable clinical adoption.

The third article addresses the challenge of noise degradation in low-dose computed tomography imaging, a key limitation that affects diagnostic accuracy despite reduced radiation exposure. The authors propose a vision transformer-based denoising model enhanced with an attention mechanism designed to preserve edges and fine anatomical structures. Evaluations across multiple datasets and comparisons with state-of-the-art approaches demonstrate the robustness and efficiency of the proposed method, highlighting its potential for improving image quality in low-dose CT while maintaining clinical and computational feasibility.

The fourth contribution tackles the challenge of data scarcity and bias in artificial intelligence models for colorectal cancer detection. The authors propose a novel data augmentation strategy based on text-to-image synthesis using fine-tuned generative models to produce realistic synthetic colonoscopy images. By demonstrating improvements in both classification and segmentation tasks, the study highlights the potential of AI-generated medical data to enhance model robustness, reduce bias, and support more reliable and inclusive colorectal cancer detection in clinical practice.

The fifth article examines the security and reliability of deep learning models in healthcare, addressing critical vulnerabilities that threaten patient safety and trust in AI-driven systems. Focusing on breast cancer detection, the study presents a unified framework for evaluating the impact of multiple attack scenarios, including adversarial, evasion, and data poisoning attacks. By quantitatively assessing post-attack performance degradation, the contribution highlights the importance of systematic vulnerability analysis and provides valuable insights toward the development of more resilient and trustworthy AI solutions for healthcare applications.

The sixth article explores the use of foundation models for semantic segmentation in medical imaging, aiming to simplify and accelerate the segmentation process for clinical use. By leveraging the video segmentation capabilities of the Segment Anything Model 2, the authors propose an approach that dramatically reduces the need for user prompts while maintaining competitive segmentation accuracy. The results demonstrate that large pre-trained models can offer efficient and accessible alternatives to task-specific deep learning solutions, lowering technical and resource barriers for advanced medical image segmentation.

The seventh contribution explores the application of machine learning for early prediction of Acute Aortic Syndrome using large-scale emergency department data. By integrating extensive clinical records and evaluating multiple classifiers and feature selection strategies, the study achieves exceptionally high predictive performance. The results highlight the potential of data-driven models to support early detection of life-threatening cardiovascular conditions and to inform future research in emergency medicine.

The eighth contribution applies machine learning techniques to analyze and forecast cancer trends in Canada using large-scale epidemiological data. By combining traditional statistical models with deep learning approaches, the study provides accurate projections of cancer incidence across regions, genders, and age groups. The findings offer valuable insights for public health planning and policy-making, demonstrating the potential of hybrid machine learning models to support data-driven decision-making in cancer prevention and healthcare resource allocation.

The nineth article provides a comprehensive review of advanced signal processing techniques for structural health monitoring, with a particular focus on time–frequency analysis, adaptive decomposition, and deconvolution methods. By systematically discussing classical and modern approaches for analyzing nonlinear and non-stationary signals, the

https://doi.org/10.3390/a19010053

study offers valuable insights into their applicability for condition monitoring and fault diagnosis. This contribution serves as a useful reference for researchers seeking to apply data-driven and machine learning-oriented techniques to complex monitoring problems in healthcare-related and engineering system.

The tenth article addresses the need for reliable diagnostic tools during the COVID-19 pandemic by proposing an advanced hybrid deep learning model for SARS-CoV-2 detection from computed tomography images. The study introduces a unified architecture that combines convolutional and graph-based feature extraction with vision transformer-based classification, enabling a rich representation of both local and global image patterns. Experimental results demonstrate superior diagnostic performance compared to existing approaches, highlighting the effectiveness of hybrid neural architectures for medical imaging tasks and their potential applicability beyond COVID-19 diagnosis.

The eleventh article investigates the interpretability of convolutional neural networks for glaucoma prediction using Shapley value-based explanations. To address the high computational cost of Shapley methods, the authors propose a discretization strategy that partitions medical images into clinically meaningful regions, enabling more efficient explanation generation. The study reveals important insights into the limitations of current explainability approaches, highlighting potential mismatches between model reasoning and clinical expectations, and raising critical considerations for the trustworthy deployment of deep learning models in ophthalmology.

The twelfth article focuses on automated hippocampal segmentation from brain MRI to support accurate brain-age estimation and early detection of neurodegenerative processes. Leveraging a self-configuring deep learning framework, the proposed pipeline enables reliable extraction of hippocampal volumes from high-resolution imaging data. By integrating neuroanatomical knowledge with data-driven learning, this contribution highlights the role of advanced segmentation models as a foundation for predictive neuroscience and early risk assessment in aging-related conditions.

The thirteenth article addresses the challenge of segmenting pigmented skin lesions with ambiguous or poorly defined borders, a common limitation in melanoma analysis. The authors propose a region-based segmentation framework that redefines lesion boundaries and leverages superpixel representations combined with transformer-based embeddings and spatial context modeling. By integrating local and global information, the approach significantly improves segmentation performance in challenging border regions, demonstrating the potential of structured, region-level representations to enhance computer-assisted diagnosis in dermatology and related medical imaging tasks.

The fourteenth article examines the effects of Iyengar yoga postures on autonomic nervous system activity using multimodal data collected from wearable sensors. By applying interpretable machine learning models, the study reveals that even subtle postural variations and micro-movements can induce measurable autonomic responses. The findings highlight the relevance of fine-grained physiological and kinematic features for understanding mind–body practices and suggest new opportunities for personalized biofeedback and data-driven yoga-based health interventions.

The fifteenth article evaluates the effectiveness of an educational intervention designed to improve evidence-based management of benign paroxysmal positional vertigo in clinical practice. Using interrupted time series analysis, the study demonstrates significant and sustained improvements in the use of recommended diagnostic and therapeutic maneuvers following the intervention. The findings highlight the value of targeted educational strategies for enhancing clinical adherence to best practices, while also indicating that additional measures may be required to reduce unnecessary imaging in routine care.

https://doi.org/10.3390/a19010053

The sixteenth article presents a real-time deep learning framework for pneumonia detection from chest X-ray images, emphasizing both diagnostic accuracy and model interpretability. Built on a YOLO-based architecture and enhanced with targeted preprocessing and visual explanation techniques, the proposed approach enables precise localization of clinically relevant features while maintaining high computational efficiency. The results demonstrate strong performance across multiple datasets and highlight the importance of explainable and robust AI solutions for supporting reliable clinical decision-making in respiratory disease diagnosis.

The seventeenth article addresses the scalability challenges of record linkage by combining large language models with traditional blocking strategies. By integrating semantic capabilities of LLMs with efficient data partitioning, the proposed approach significantly reduces computational costs while simultaneously improving matching accuracy. The results underscore the continued relevance of classical data integration techniques and demonstrate how they can be effectively enhanced through modern machine learning models for large-scale, real-world applications, including healthcare data management.

3. Conclusions

The research presented in this Special Issue reflects the breadth and maturity of current efforts at the intersection of machine learning and healthcare. The collected contributions span a wide range of applications, methodologies, and clinical contexts, highlighting both technological advances and practical considerations such as efficiency, interpretability, robustness, and security. Together, these works not only demonstrate the transformative potential of machine learning in healthcare but also underscore the challenges that must be addressed to enable reliable and responsible real-world adoption. We hope this Special Issue will inspire further research, interdisciplinary collaboration, and innovation, contributing to the continued advancement of intelligent healthcare systems.

Funding: This research received no external funding.

Acknowledgments: I would like to express my sincere gratitude to all the authors and reviewers for their valuable contributions and commitment, which were essential to the success of this Special Issue. I also extend my special thanks to the Editor-in-Chief of this journal for the opportunity and trust placed in us to curate this Special Issue.

Conflicts of Interest: The author declares no conflicts of interest.

References

1. Tulshan, A.S.; Dhage, S.N. Survey on virtual assistant: Google assistant, Siri, Cortana, Alexa. In *Communications in Computer and Information Science*; Springer: Singapore, 2019; Volume 968.
2. Shirkande, S.T.; Nagnath, D.P.; Ganesh, K.A.; Santosh, S.V.; Sunil, S.T. Comprehensive Survey on Healthcare Virtual Assistants: Leveraging Natural Language Processing for Predictive Insights. *Int. J. Adv. Comput. Theory Eng.* **2024**, *13*, 39–44. [CrossRef]
3. Nascimento, A.M.; Vismari, L.F.; Molina, C.B.S.T.; Cugnasca, P.S.; Camargo, J.B.; De Almeida, J.R.; Inam, R.; Fersman, E.; Marquezini, M.V.; Hata, A.Y. A Systematic Literature Review about the Impact of Artificial Intelligence on Autonomous Vehicle Safety. *IEEE Trans. Intell. Transp. Syst.* **2020**, *21*, 4928–4946. [CrossRef]
4. Sadaf, M.; Iqbal, Z.; Javed, A.R.; Saba, I.; Krichen, M.; Majeed, S.; Raza, A. Connected and Automated Vehicles: Infrastructure, Applications, Security, Critical Challenges, and Future Aspects. *Technologies* **2023**, *11*, 117. [CrossRef]
5. Bresniker, K.; Gavrilovska, A.; Holt, J.; Milojicic, D.; Tran, T. Grand challenge: Applying artificial intelligence and machine learning to cybersecurity. *Computer* **2019**, *52*, 45–52. [CrossRef]
6. Mohamed, N. Artificial intelligence and machine learning in cybersecurity: A deep dive into state-of-the-art techniques and future paradigms. *Knowl. Inf. Syst.* **2025**, *67*, 6969–7055. [CrossRef]
7. Portugal, I.; Alencar, P.; Cowan, D. The use of machine learning algorithms in recommender systems: A systematic review. *Expert Syst. Appl.* **2018**, *97*, 205–227. [CrossRef]

https://doi.org/10.3390/a19010053

8. de Campos, L.M.; Fernández-Luna, J.M.; Huete, J.F.; Ribadas-Pena, F.J.; Bolaños, N.; de Campos, L.M.; Fernández-Luna, J.M.; Huete, J.F.; Ribadas-Pena, F.J.; Bolaños, N. Information Retrieval and Machine Learning Methods for Academic Expert Finding. *Algorithms* **2024**, *17*, 51. [CrossRef]
9. Tiggeloven, T.; Pfeiffer, S.; Matanó, A.; van den Homberg, M.; Thalheimer, L.; Reichstein, M.; Torresan, S. The role of artificial intelligence for early warning systems: Status, applicability, guardrails, and ways forward. *iScience* **2025**, *28*, 113689. [CrossRef] [PubMed]
10. MacIntyre, C.R.; Chen, X.; Kunasekaran, M.; Quigley, A.; Lim, S.; Stone, H.; Paik, H.Y.; Yao, L.; Heslop, D.; Wei, W.; et al. Artificial intelligence in public health: The potential of epidemic early warning systems. *J. Int. Med. Res.* **2023**, *51*, 03000605231159335. [CrossRef] [PubMed]
11. Kim, S.Y.; Kim, D.H.; Kim, M.J.; Ko, H.J.; Jeong, O.R. XAI-Based Clinical Decision Support Systems: A Systematic Review. *Appl. Sci.* **2024**, *14*, 6638. [CrossRef]
12. Ghaffar Nia, N.; Kaplanoglu, E.; Nasab, A. Evaluation of artificial intelligence techniques in disease diagnosis and prediction. *Discov. Artif. Intell.* **2023**, *3*, 5. [CrossRef] [PubMed]
13. Shaik, T.; Tao, X.; Higgins, N.; Li, L.; Gururajan, R.; Zhou, X.; Acharya, U.R. Remote patient monitoring using artificial intelligence: Current state, applications, and challenges. *Wiley Interdiscip. Rev. Data Min. Knowl. Discov.* **2023**, *13*, e1485. [CrossRef]
14. Wu, Y.; Li, L.; Xin, B.; Hu, Q.; Dong, X.; Li, Z. Application of machine learning in personalized medicine. *Intell. Pharm.* **2023**, *1*, 152–156. [CrossRef]

https://doi.org/10.3390/a19010053

algorithms

MDPI

Article

Efficient Record Linkage in the Age of Large Language Models: The Critical Role of Blocking

Nidhibahen Shah [1], Sreevar Patiyara [2], Joyanta Basak [1], Sartaj Sahni [3], Anup Mathur [4], Krista Park [4] and Sanguthevar Rajasekaran [1,*]

1 School of Computing, University of Connecticut, 371 Fairfield Way, Storrs, CT 06269, USA; nidhibahen.shah@uconn.edu (N.S.)
2 CS Department, Purdue University, 305 N. University St., West Lafayette, IN 47907, USA
3 CISE Department, University of Florida, Gainesville, FL 32611, USA
4 U.S. Census Bureau, 4600 Silver Hill Road, Washington, DC 20233, USA
* Correspondence: sanguthevar.rajasekaran@uconn.edu

Abstract: Record linkage is an essential task in data integration in the fields of healthcare, law enforcement, fraud detection, transportation, biology, and supply chain management. The problem of record linkage is to cluster records from various sources such that each cluster belongs to a single entity. Scalability in record linking is limited by the large number of pairwise comparisons required. Blocking addresses this challenge by partitioning data into smaller parts, substantially reducing the computational cost. With the advancement of Large Language Models (LLMs), there are several possibilities to improve record linkage by leveraging their semantic understanding of textual attributes. LLM-based record linkage algorithms in the literature have very large runtimes. In this paper, we show that the employment of blocking can result in significant improvements not only in the runtime but also in the accuracy. Specifically, we propose a record linkage algorithm that combines LLMs with blocking. Experimental evaluation demonstrates that our algorithm achieves lower runtimes while simultaneously improving F1 scores compared to the approaches relying solely on LLMs. These findings demonstrate the importance of blocking even in the era of advanced machine learning models.

Keywords: record linkage; blocking; large language models

1. Introduction

Record linkage is a fundamental task in data integration [1]. It refers to the process of clustering the input records in such a way that each cluster of records belongs to one and only one entity. It plays a crucial role in the fields of healthcare, E-commerce, transportation, law enforcement, and biology. In a typical application of interest, there will be multiple datasets where each dataset has records pertaining to entities. A record can be thought of as a set of attributes. Possible attributes include first name, last name, age, gender, address, Social Security Number, and date of birth. For example, in the healthcare domain, each provider has a dataset of records belonging to individuals that they cater to. Our approach leverages the structural specificity of domains like healthcare, where attributes such as patient name and date of birth facilitate effective block information.

The record linkage problem is challenging due to various factors such as the absence of a global key across different datasets, missing values, presence of errors of different kinds, schema and granularity, the use of different formats, and longer runtimes. However, one of the central challenges of record linkage is scalability. As data increases in size

 https://doi.org/10.3390/a18110723

and complexity, the number of record pair comparisons performed by the brute force algorithm increases quadratically. To address this challenge, blocking has been introduced. Blocking partitions data into smaller parts based on shared characteristics. Pairwise record comparisons are performed only within the individual parts. Over the years, various blocking strategies have been introduced. In our prior work, we have introduced Soundex blocking [2] and Double Metaphone Blocking [3] techniques.

The advancements in Large Language Models (LLMs) [4] have opened new opportunities for record linkage. With the ability to capture contextual relationships and semantic meaning in texts, LLMs [5] are well suited for identifying potential matches across databases [6,7]. Related work includes studies like HomLLM [8], which leverages semantic homology relationships for fine-grained bird image classification using Large Language Models, HPCTrans [9], which employs heterogeneous plumage cue-aware texton correlation representation for fine-grained bird image classification via transformers, and DSR-Net [10], which uses distinct selective rollback queries for road crack detection with detection transformers. However, the computational demands of LLMs are non-trivial and applying them to all possible record pairs, especially in large datasets, is impractical and a time-consuming process. To overcome this challenge, we have integrated blocking techniques with LLMs to improve the performance of linking records across datasets. Our method uniquely combines blocking techniques with LLMs to achieve significant scalability and efficiency gain, enabling the processing of large-scale datasets with reduced computational overhead compared to traditional methods. This paper establishes that blocking remains a critical enabler of efficient record linkage in the era of LLMs.

2. Related Work

The literature on record linkage categorizes algorithms into two types: (1) deterministic and (2) probabilistic [11]. The primary distinction lies in how the distance is computed between the record pairs—deterministically using fixed rules or probabilistically. A classical probabilistic algorithm was introduced by Fellegi and Sunter [12]. They assumed independence among record pairs but do not incorporate transitivity or other global constraints. For instance, consider two records $R_1 = a_1^1, a_2^1, \ldots, a_q^1$ and $R_2 = a_1^2, a_2^2, \ldots, a_q^2$. Here, q is the number of attributes and the a_i^j's are attribute values.

Fellegi and Sunter's [12] algorithm computes the distance d_i between a_i^1 and a_i^2 for every $1 \leq i \leq q$ and composes $d_1, d_2, \ldots, d_q$ to arrive at a distance between R_1 and R_2. The Bayesian approach underpins their probabilistic model with a blocking step to reduce the computational overhead. However, the algorithm can only link two datasets at a time and often struggles with large and complex data.

Sadinle and Fienberg [13] proposed an extension of this model to support multiple datasets, though scalability remains a challenge. In practice, tools such as FastLink [14] which is developed around Fellegi and Sunter's model, have been widely adopted. More recently, SPLINK [15] has also emerged as a faster implementation. However, when applied to modern large-scale datasets, both systems exhibit limitations in accuracy and runtime efficiency.

Deterministic approaches, such as those implemented in FEBRL [16,17], rely on predefined similarity metrics like edit distance, q-gram distance, and Hausdorff distance. FEBRL often under-performs on both accuracy and runtime compared to most recent deterministic algorithms. Despite some improvements, there remains a considerable scope for advancing scalability and accuracy in record linkage. Record linkage has long been recognized as vital in medical and healthcare fields. For example, in 1900, Alexander Graham Bell [18] combined genealogical and administrative records, such as marriage and census data, to study familial patterns of deafness.

Similarly, in 1929, R.A.Fisher [19] integrated public records with family data for human genetics research. Since then, record linkage has been widely adopted in the biomedical field. In one study, Victor and Mera [20] linked patient and healthcare provider records across time and geographic regions using a mix of exact and probabilistic algorithms. Their dataset was drawn from insurance claim databases and included 52 million records representing over 20 million individuals. Their algorithm involved three key steps: data standardization, weight estimation, and matching. Its effectiveness was validated through divergent, convergent, and criterion validity tests.

The authors of the paper [21] emphasize the shift in healthcare from institution-centered to consumer-centered care, nothing that accurate patient identification is crucial for effective healthcare reform and delivering fast, safe, and high-quality care. They proposed an algorithm to identify exact and approximate duplicate medical identity records. The algorithm has three steps: data standardization, matching similar record pairs, and creating clusters of related records. When applied to a dataset of 300,000 records, it identified 240,000 unique clusters.

Padmanabhan, Carty, and other authors [22] described the record linkage approach used by NHS Digital and the Clinical Practice Research Datalink in England. CPRD routinely links primary care data with various health-related datasets, facilitating comprehensive health research. A significant application of record linkage in biomedicine involves connecting genealogical records with morbidity, mortality, and medical data. The linkage aids in identifying the genetic basis of diseases and understanding how patients with different genetic profiles respond to treatments [23].

Most record linkage algorithms have a quadratic time complexity relative to total number of records across datasets. To address this, indexing techniques have been developed to reduce computational demands by filtering out clearly dissimilar record pairs [24]. Another method, blocking, groups records into potentially overlapping blocks, limiting comparisons to records within the same block. Additionally, filtering techniques identify similar record pairs based on similarity threshold under specific metrics. A recent survey on blocking and filtering methods is available in [25]. A key challenge in record linkage lies in the large number of record pairs to be processed. Blocking reduces the number of record pair comparisons by partitioning records into blocks. Pairwise record comparisons are performed only within the blocks.

Numerous blocking strategies can be found in the literature. The Sorted Neighborhood Method [1] sorts records by a key and only compares those within a sliding window. Canopy clustering [1] uses similarity metrics to create overlapping canopies. Token-based blocking is particularly effective for noisy or short strings.

Phonetic encodings are also widely adopted. Soundex [26], one of the earliest phonetic algorithms, maps names with similar pronunciations to the same code. Soundex was first developed by [26] in 1918 and it was first employed by the United States Census Bureau to categorize names for statistical purposes. According to the National Archives, the Soundex index is a method of coding surnames (last names) based on their pronunciation rather than their spelling. Surnames with similar sounds, such as "SMITH" and "SMYTH", are assigned the same code, allowing them to be grouped together [26]. The Soundex generates one code for each provided name. However, this approach carries a risk of errors, as phonetically similar names may refer to different entities. In our approach, the probability of such errors is reduced, as blocking and clustering does not rely solely on first- and last-name comparisons. We incorporate other attributes such as date of birth and address which are evaluated using a pairwise matching process using the LLaMA3 and BERT model. Even if the error occurs during blocking due to similar phonetic codes, records are unlikely to cluster together as other attributes differ significantly. Recently, Soundex blocking [2] has been proposed as a novel candidate generation approach that demonstrates improved runtime and F1 score compared to traditional blocking approaches.

Double Metaphone generates two phonetic codes per string to better capture the alternative pronunciations. The Double Metaphone algorithm, which was introduced by Philips [27], generates two codes per name: primary and secondary and handles names in a better way for variations like "Kline" and "Cline". The Double Metaphone is widely adopted as it works well with different languages and catches more phonetic matches than Soundex. Previous studies have used Double Metaphone for matching names in historical records, indicating that it outperforms older methods in accuracy [28]. Another work applied Double Metaphone to customer data deduplication, proving that it can handle noisy real-world data like typographical errors and abbreviations [29]. Double Metaphone has also been used beyond simple pairwise matching. In healthcare, Double Metaphone is part of systems that link patient records across hospitals, where names might vary due to some transcription errors [30]. It has been used in search systems, tweaking it to rank similar-sounding terms for fuzzy queries [31]. However, these studies typically focus on comparing two records at a time and Double Metaphone is used for measuring similarity only. There is one study that tried to use Double Metaphone for clustering by precomputing codes for all records. However, it did not do well for large-scale datasets due to memory and time costs [32].

Blocking tackles the problem of speed in record linkage by dividing the dataset into small groups or blocks, thereby reducing the number of comparisons required and hence reducing the runtime. Standard blocking uses attributes like first name or zip code to create blocks [12]. Using Double Metaphone for approximate string matching in databases (but only as a preprocessing step, not as a full blocking strategy) was considered in [33].

Ref. [34] applied Double Metaphone to link encrypted records. The codes were used to group data securely. However, the focus was privacy, not speed. Shah introduced Double Metaphone Blocking [3] for record linkage, showing that it achieves higher F1 scores and faster runtimes compared to state-of-the-art blocking methods. The emergence of Large Language Models (LLMs) has opened new opportunities for record linkage. Systems such as DeepMatcher [35] and Ditto [36] demonstrate that pre-trained transformer models significantly outperform classical methods in record linkage tasks.

Recent studies show that fine-tuned LLMs can be generalized across domains. Moreover, generative models are being explored for explainable linkage decisions. However, LLMs face several limitations, such as scalability issues, calibration changes, and performance degradation in noisy or real-world datasets compared to curated benchmarks. To further contextualize our approach, we integrate insights from recent foundational works. Choi et al. [37] propose a multi-stage explainable clustering pipeline with network-based visualization, complementing our focus on interpretable analysis of high-dimensional records.

3. Methodology

Building on our prior works, we recognize that blocking is an important enabler of scalability in the record linkage process. Blocking reduces the number of record pair comparisons. The recent advancement of LLMs provides an opportunity to learn semantic similarity between the records. We have explored the combined impact of blocking and LLMs using the framework shown in Figure 1. Algorithm 1 also provides more details on our framework. The workflow is divided into the following steps.

Algorithm 1: Integrated Blocking-LLM Record Linkage

Input : Dataset D, Training Dataset D_{train}, Attribute Criteria
Output: Set of matched record pairs

begin
  /* Train LLM for pair classification */
  Model $M \leftarrow$ FineTuneLLM(D_{train}) ; // e.g., LLaMA3.1 or BERT, instruct-tuned
  /* Generate blocks with attribute-based blocking */
  SelectedAttrs $\leftarrow$ SelectAttributes(D, Criteria) ; // e.g., name, address, gender, DOB
  Blocks $B = \{B_1, B_2, \ldots, B_n\} \leftarrow$ BlockData(D, SelectedAttrs);
  ; // $\bigcup_{i=1}^{n} B_i = D$, similar attribute values per block
  /* Match pairs within blocks using LLM */
  MatchedPairs $\leftarrow \emptyset$;
  foreach *block B_i in B* **do**
    Pairs $\leftarrow$ GeneratePairs(B_i);
    foreach *pair (r_a, r_b) in Pairs* **do**
      Prediction $\leftarrow$ Classify(M, (r_a, r_b));
      if *Prediction = match* **then**
        MatchedPairs $\leftarrow$ MatchedPairs $\cup \{(r_a, r_b)\}$;
      end
    end
  end
  return *MatchedPairs*;
end

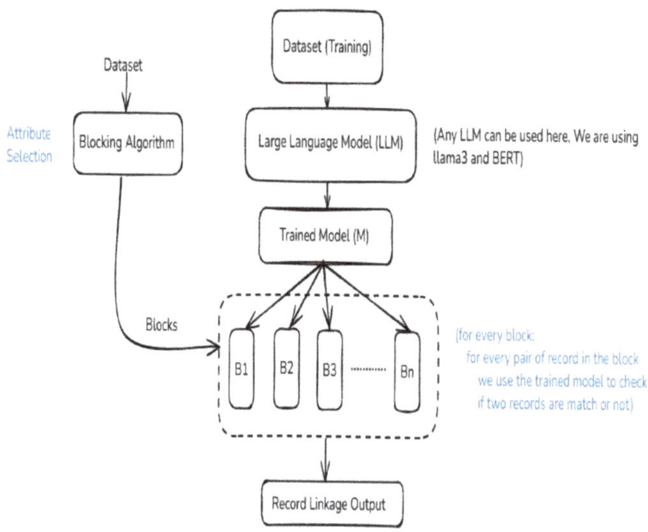

Figure 1. Workflow for record linkage using blocking and LLMs.

3.1. Dataset Preparation

The process begins with the selection of a dataset that has to be linked. In our experiments, we use six different datasets. All these datasets contain different attributes.

Each dataset varies in size, structure, and attribute composition. Each dataset contains a unique set of identifying attributes such as names, address, date of birth, and other demographic fields. Prior to training, we standardize the data formats and normalize string representations such as converting to lower case, handling the missing values. This preprocessing step ensures consistency across datasets.

3.2. Blocking Algorithm

Not all the attributes are important for the linkage task. Therefore, using an attribute selection algorithm [38], we choose a subset of the attributes for blocking. Attributes such as name, address, gender, and date of birth get selected often as they carry the most semantic weight in determining whether two records match or not. Based on the selected attributes, the blocks are generated. We employ a k-mer-based attribute selection algorithm as described in [38]. This algorithm is critical for reducing the comparison space in record linkage by grouping similar records into blocks based on selected attributes, such as name or address. The algorithm operates in two stages: deduplication and k-mer-based blocking. First, the input dataset is deduplicated to remove identical records, ensuring computational efficiency by avoiding redundant record pair comparisons. Next, for the chosen blocking attribute (e.g., name), the algorithm generates k-mer sub strings of length k. Each k-mer serves as a blocking key, and records are grouped into blocks if they share the same k-mer. Each block contains records that share similar attribute values. Formally, let D denote the dataset and f be the blocking function. The dataset is partitioned into blocks:

$$B = \{B_1, B_2, \ldots, B_n\}, \bigcup_{i=0}^{n} B_i = D \tag{1}$$

Each B_i is then processed independently, thereby improving the scalability while maintaining a high likelihood of retaining the true matches.

3.3. LLM Training

In parallel with blocking, we use a training dataset to train the LLM models. Here, we use the LLaMA3.1 8B Instruct model, [39] which has 8 billion parameters, and the BERT-based uncased model [40], which has 110 million parameters, for training. LLaMA3.1 is a state-of-the-art instruction-tuned model known for its strong contextual reasoning ability. BERT is a bidirectional transformer pre-trained on large text repositories widely used for entity matching. Related work includes works such as LDCNet [41], which focuses on limb direction cue-aware networks for adaptable human pose estimation in industrial behavioral biometrics systems, EHPE [42], which utilizes skeleton cue-based Gaussian coordinate encoding for efficient human pose estimation, and TransIFC [43], which employs invariant cue-aware feature concentration learning for efficient fine-grained bird image classification. Both models are fine-tuned to classify whether a given pair of record is a match or non-match. The training data consists of record pairs labeled according to the ground truth linkages. Once the training is completed, we obtain the trained model M. The separate models are fine-tuned for each dataset in our experiments. Here are the fine-tuning details for the Llama3 model:

- Model loading: the base model is loaded from "unsloth/Meta-Llama-3.1-8B-Instruct-bnb-4bit" with quantization to reduce memory usage. The maximum sequence length is set to 2048 tokens.
- Parameter Efficient Fine-Tuning setup: LoRA(Low Rank Adaptation) is applied with rank (r = 16), alpha = 16, and dropout = 0.

- Training Configuration: Uses Supervised Fine-Tuning trainer from TRL library. Per device batch size = 2. Optimizer "adamw8bit" with learning rate = 2×10^{-4}, weight decay = 0.01.

Below are the fine-tuning details for the BERT model.

- Tokenizer and Model loading: tokenizer and model loaded from "bert-base-uncased" with number of labels = 2
- Training Configuration: batch size per device = 4, gradient accumulation steps = 8, learning rate = 2×10^{-5}, weight decay = 0.01.

3.4. Pairwise Matching Within the Blocks

Once the LLM-based model M is trained, it is applied to each block. For each block B_i, the model evaluates all possible record pairs within that block $(r_a, r_b) \in B_i$. The trained model outputs if it is a match or not. This step reduces the number of record pair comparisons as the comparison is performed within each block and not the whole dataset. By performing the pairwise comparisons within blocks rather than across the entire dataset, this approach significantly reduces computational complexity while maintaining high recall. The blocking step ensures that only records with a high likelihood of referring to the same entity are compared. This minimizes the redundant or irrelevant comparisons. Furthermore, the model's predictions allow us to capture subtle semantic similarities between attributes.

3.5. Record Linkage Output

Finally, the decision from all blocks are aggregated into record linkage output. This output identifies all record pairs that the model classified as matches. For graph construction, each positive pair forms an edge in the undirected graph, with records as nodes. Cluster inference then applies transitive closure to connect all nodes linked by paths of matches. As a simple example, given records $R1$, $R2$, and $R3$, if $R1 - R2$ is a match and $R2 - R3$ is a match, then the final cluster is $R1, R2, R3$.

4. Experimental Setup

We conducted our experiments using two computing environments:

- NVIDIA TITAN RTX GPU with an AMD Ryzen Threadripper 2950X 16-Core Processor. All experiments with Llama3.1 were performed on this environment.
- NVIDIA TITAN XP GPU (11.896 GB memory) with an Intel(R) Core(TM) i5-8400 CPU @ 2.80GHz. BERT experiments were performed with this environment.

These configurations enabled us to efficiently train and evaluate LLaMA3 and BERT across multiple datasets.

4.1. Datasets

To evaluate the robustness of our proposed algorithm, we conducted experiments with six datasets: FEBRL, DS, OCR, Phonetic, Typo, and North Carolina Voter Dataset. These datasets vary in size, structure, and types of noise, which allows us to test the generalization of our approach.

- FEBRL (Freely Extensible Biomedical Record Linkage): FEBRL [17] is perhaps the most widely used dataset for record linkage tasks. It consists of synthetically generated records, with introduction of errors such as misspellings, missing values, and typographical variations to simulate real-world scenarios. There are multiple versions of FEBRL available, such as febrl-1 through febrl-4. Each of them varies in size and error distribution. In our experiment, we used the febrl-4 dataset provided by recordlinkage

package in Python. This contains two datasets to be linked along with the ground truth mapping of true matches.The febrl-4 dataset comprises 10,000 records in total: 5000 original records and 5000 duplicates, with exactly one duplicate per original to provide a controlled 1:1 matching structure and ground truth labels for evaluation. The attributes include first name, last name, address, suburb, date of birth, and Social Security ID. The duplicates incorporate realistic error types to mimic the data quality issues in real-world datasets. We selected febrl-4 over other versions like febrl-1 with 1000 records or febrl-3 with 3000 records due to its large-scale controlled duplicate structure.
- DS Dataset: To evaluate our algorithms, we utilized real-world data sourced from the Social Security Death Master File, provided by SSDMF.INFO [44]. Each record includes the following attributes: Social Security Number, last name, first name, date of birth, and date of death. To simulate realistic errors, we employed a modified version of the FEBRL dataset generator program to introduce variations into the data.
- OCR (Pseudopeople Dataset): This dataset is generated from the Pseudopeople library from Census, which generates large-scale simulated populations. It contains slightly over 10 million records of people in the state of Michigan. In this variant, 10% OCR errors were introduced in the first name and last name attributes, simulating character recognition mistakes.
- Phonetic (Pseudopeople Dataset): Similarly generated from the Pseudopeople library, this dataset introduces 10% phonetic errors in the first name and last name fields. These errors capture common variations in spellings due to phonetic similarities such as Smith vs Smyth. This makes it necessary to evaluate phonetic-based records linkage approaches.
- Typo (Pseudopeople Dataset): This dataset introduces 10% typographical errors in the first name and last name attributes. These types of errors are commonly observed in administrative databases.
- North Carolina Voter Dataset (NCV): The NCV [45] dataset contains five files, each containing one million voter records. Each file is source-consistent, meaning that within each file, there is only one record per entity. However, individuals may appear across multiple files. Some entities may be present in all the five files, others in two or three files, and some in only one file. This dataset is used in multi-source record linkage.

4.2. Evaluation Metrics

This study employs two primary metrics to evaluate performance of the proposed method. The first metric is the F1 score, a widely used measure for assessing the accuracy of binary classification tasks, such as record linkage. The F1 score combines precision and recall into a single value, providing a balanced evaluation of the model's ability to correctly identify true positive matches while minimizing both false positives and false negatives. A higher F1 score indicates a better performance. Mathematically, the F1 score is defined as follows:

$$F1 = 2 * (Precison \times Recall)/(Precision + Recall) \tag{2}$$

The second metric is runtime, which is particularly important in the context of record linkage involving large datasets. Runtime reflects the computational efficiency of the method, with lower runtime indicating faster and more efficient processing.

4.3. Implementation Detail

Our implementation was developed in Python 3.10 on Ubuntu 22.04.5 LTS (GNU/Linux 5.15.0-153-generic X86_64). The following key libraries and frameworks were used:

- PyTorch with CUDA 12.2 for LLM training and interface.
- Transformers (Hugging Face) for loading and fine-tuning the LLaMA3 model.
- Unsloth library for efficient model loading and handling.
- tqdm for progress tracking and runtime monitoring.
- recordlinkage for dataset preparation and benchmark record linkage tasks.
- scikit-learn for computing evaluation metrics.

The LLaMA3 model was trained on the above datasets. Blocking was applied using our attribute-based blocking function. It generates candidate record pairs within each block. These pairs were formatted as textual sequences and classified using the trained LLaMA3 model. The model leveraged a context length of 2048 tokens with 4-bit quantization via Unsloth to reduce memory footprint. Quantization has several potential impacts on performance. It lowers memory usage and speeds up computation by using fewer bits to represent weights and activation, which is great for efficiency, especially on resource-limited devices. In parallel, a BERT-based uncased model was trained for sequence classification. Training data was first transformed into instruct-input-output format, where each record pair was wrapped as: Instruction: "Determine if these records match:", Input: "<record pair text>", Output: "<label:match / not a match>". The dataset was tokenized using BERT's tokenizer with truncation and padding, and labels were mapped to binary classes. Fine-tuning was performed using the Hugging Face Trainer API with the following configurations:

- Batch size: 4 per device
- Gradient accumulation: 8 steps
- learning rate: 2×10^{-5}
- Number of epochs: 1
- Mixed-precision training: fp16
- Weight decay: 0.01

The hyperparameters listed were selected based on a combination of standard practices from the literature. Specifically, values such as learning rate 2×10^{-5}, batch size 4, and number of epochs 1 align with recommended settings for fine-tuning transformer models like BERT and LLaMA3 as documented in Hugging Face guidelines. The 8 steps of gradient accumulation and mixed precision training fp16 were chosen to optimize memory usage and training stability. The evaluation was performed using standard classification metrics like precision, accuracy, recall, and F1 score. After training, the model tokenizers were saved for inference. For both LLaMA3 and BERT, the inference process follows a common pipeline. First, we preprocess the dataset by performing deduplication, blocking, and candidate pair generation. Each candidate pair within the block is then passed to the model in the textual form, where the model evaluates whether two records represent the same entity. In the case of BERT, this is achieved through a sequence classification head that outputs the probability of match and non-match. This means at the test time, we tokenize the candidate pair, feed it to the fine-tuned BERT model, and use the output probabilities to decide if it is a match. For LLaMA3, we use an instruction-tuned prompting setup, where the model is asked to determine if two sequences correspond to the same entity. Regardless of the model, the outputs are converted into binary decisions, which are then used to identify the linked records. Finally, the predictions are compared against the ground truth to compute the evaluation metrics.

5. Results and Discussion

The experiments demonstrate that our approach results in a substantial improvement in F1 scores when we incorporate blocking with LLaMA3 and BERT models for record linkage tasks across six different datasets. This is shown in Table 1. We maintained the total number of record pair comparisons at approximately 2 million for each dataset. For

LLaMA3, blocking elevated F1 scores significantly. For the FEBRL data, F1 score increases from 91.24% to 96.03%; for DS data, the increase is from 77.65% to 88.48%; for OCR data, the F1 score improves drastically from 9.20% to 94.28%. For phonetic and Typo datasets the improvements are from 16.03% to 93.39% and from 38.02% to 94.24%, respectively. For NCV data, the F1 score improves slightly from 93.29% to 99.73%. With BERT, we also saw similar improvements as shown in Table 2. These results highlight the effectiveness of blocking in boosting the accuracy of LLM-based record linkage.

Table 1. F1 score comparison for LLaMA3.1 8B Instruct.

Dataset	Blocking	No Blocking
FEBRL	96.03%	91.24%
DS	88.48%	77.65%
OCR	94.28%	9.20%
Phonetic	93.39%	16.03%
Typo	94.24%	38.02%
NCV	99.73%	93.29%

Table 2. F1 score comparison for BERT-based uncased.

Dataset	Blocking	No Blocking
FEBRL	100.00%	100.00%
DS	89.57%	100.00%
OCR	94.12%	13.63%
Phonetic	93.91%	22.67%
Typo	94.12%	45.09%
NCV	98.32%	50.23%

For the DS dataset in BERT, we can see that the F1 score with blocking is lower than non-blocking. These variation stem from dataset specific characteristics and trade-offs inherent in the blocking approach, which balances efficiency with recall. For the DS dataset, the drop in F1 score with blocking indicates a minor recall loss due to the partitioning. On the other hand, for NCV, the improvement with blocking highlights precision gain in noisy data.

A significant achievement of the study is the remarkable reductions in the runtimes as show in Tables 3 and 4 that we obtain through blocking. Our methodology enhances the practicality of LLM applications. For LLaMA3, the runtime decreased dramatically. For FEBRL, the runtime drops from 18:13:53 h to 1:24:10; for OCR, from 73:52:18 h to 0:05:35 min, and for phonetic, from 73:52:18 h to 0:06:19 min. For NCV, the runtime reduces from 70:51:55 h to 0:19:02 min. BERT also benefited from blocking. For FEBRL data, the runtime reduces from 7:37:02 h to 0:40:10 min. For OCR data, the runtime reduces from 39:51:00 h to 0:02:52 min. For phonetic data, the time reduces from 39:44:20 h to 0:03:19 min. For typo data, the reduction is from 39:14:08 h to 0:03:02 min and for the NCV data, the runtime reduces from 21:21:05 h to 0:05:49 min.

Figure 2 visualizes the improvements in F1 scores. The log-scale chart in Figure 3 displays the reductions in runtimes corresponding to the six different datasets for which experiments were performed. These experiments demonstrate that using blocking with LLM not only maintains high F1 scores but also significantly improves the runtime performance. Thus, blocking is indispensable in the context of large-scale record linkage tasks.

Table 3. Runtime comparison for LLaMA3.1 8B Instruct.

Dataset	Blocking (Hours)	No Blocking (Hours)
FEBRL	1:24:10	18:13:53
DS	0:07:37	18:14:09
OCR	0:05:35	73:58:48
Phonetic	0:06:19	73:52:18
Typo	0:05:31	74:38:55
NCV	0:19:02	70:51:55

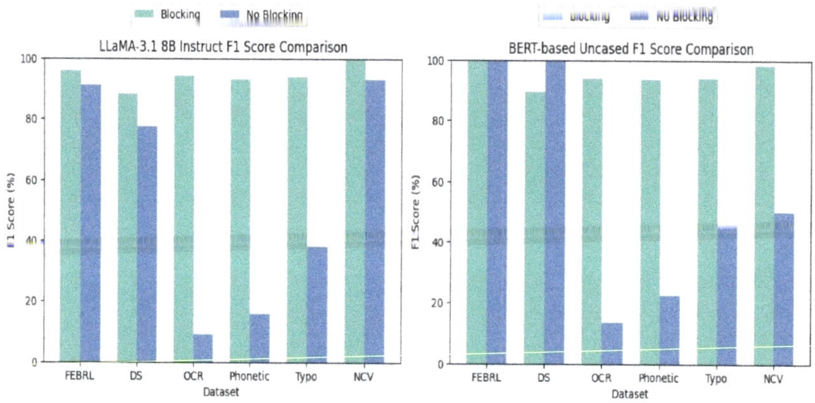

Figure 2. F1 score comparison for LLaMA3 and BERT.

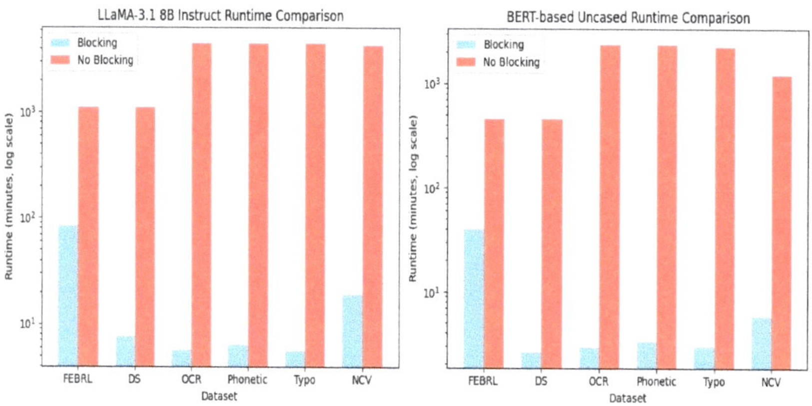

Figure 3. Runtime comparison for LLaMA3 and BERT.

Table 4. Runtime comparison for BERT-based uncased.

Dataset	Blocking (Hours)	No Blocking (Hours)
FEBRL	0:40:10	7:37:02
DS	0:02:35	7:37:02
OCR	0:02:52	39:51:00
Phonetic	0:03:19	39:44:20
Typo	0:03:02	39:14:08
NCV	0:05:49	21:21:05

6. Conclusions and Future Work

The research conclusively demonstrates that integrating blocking with LLMs significantly enhances both F1 scores and runtime efficiency in the record linkage tasks across diverse datasets. These results reveal substantial improvements in accuracy when blocking is employed. Also, there is a remarkable reduction in processing times. This dual benefit indicates the robustness of the blocking approach, making it a valuable technique for improving LLMs' performance in record linkage applications.

For future work, integration of blocking with other advanced LLM models can be investigated. Various blocking strategies can be explored with LLMs. This could further optimize the performance. To further enhance the contribution of this study, we plan to extend our work in several directions. We aim to validate our method on large-scale, real-world datasets, such as enterprise CRM [46] and healthcare EHR [47] systems. Additionally, we will explore advanced blocking strategies, such as Soundex blocking, Double Metaphone Blocking, and super blocking, to evaluate their impact on efficiency and scalability in record linkage tasks. To provide a more comprehensive evaluation of our approach, we plan to incorporate comparisons with state-of-the-art record linkage systems like Ditto and DeepMatcher.

Author Contributions: Conceptualization, N.S., S.R.; methodology, N.S., S.S., S.R.; software, N.S., S.P.; validation, N.S., S.P., J.B., S.S., A.M., K.P., S.R.; formal analysis, S.R., S.S.; investigation, S.R., S.S.; resources, A.M., K.P.; data curation, N.S., S.P., J.B.; writing—original draft preparation, N.S., S.P., S.R.; writing—review and editing, N.S., S.R., A.M., K.P.; visualization, N.S.; supervision, S.R., S.S.; project administration, A.M., K.P.; funding acquisition, S.R. All authors have read and agreed to the published version of the manuscript.

Funding: This work was partially supported by the United States Census Bureau under Award Number CB21RMD0160003. The content is solely the responsibility of the authors and does not necessarily represent the official views of the US Census Bureau.

Data Availability Statement: The code and datasets used in this study are available in the GitHub repository https://github.com/Nidhibahenshah/LLM-with-Blocking (accessed on 24 September 2025).

Acknowledgments: The authors would like to extend their heartfelt gratitude to Kenneth Haase, Daniel Weinberg, Rebecca Steorts, Haley S. Hunter-Zinck, Wendy L. Martinez, and Jennifer Hutnick for their invaluable discussions and constructive feedback, which greatly enriched this research.

Conflicts of Interest: The authors declare no conflicts of interest. The funders had no role in the design of the study; in the collection, analyses, or interpretation of data; in the writing of the manuscript; or in the decision to publish the results.

Abbreviations

The following abbreviations are used in this manuscript:

LLM	Large Language Model
FEBRL	Freely Extensible Biomedical Record Linkage
NCV	North Carolina Voter dataset

References

1. Papadakis, G.; Ioannou, E.; Thanos, E.; Palpanas, T. *Four Generations of Entity Resolution*; Springer: Berlin/Heidelberg, Germany, 2021.
2. Shah, N.; Soliman, A.; Basak, J.; Sahni, S.; Haase, K.; Mathur, A.; Park, K.; Weinberg, D.; White, J.; Rajasekaran, S. The Soundex Blocking: A Novel Blocking Approach for Record Linkage. In Proceedings of the 2024 IEEE International Conference on Big Data (BigData), Washington, DC, USA, 15–18 December 2024; pp. 4039–4047. [CrossRef]

3. Shah, N.; Basak, J.; Sahni, S.; Mathur, A.; Park, K.; Weinberg, D.; Rajasekaran, S. Double Metaphone Blocking: An Innovative Blocking Approach to Record Linkage. In *International Symposium on Bioinformatics Research and Applications*; Springer Nature: Singapore, 2025; pp. 139–150.
4. Vaswani, A.; Shazeer, N.; Parmar, N.; Uszkoreit, J.; Jones, L.; Gomez, A.N.; Kaiser, Ł.; Polosukhin, I. Attention Is All You Need. *Adv. Neural Inf. Process. Syst.* **2017**, *30*, 5998–6008.
5. Radford, A.; Narasimhan, K.; Salimans, T.; Sutskever, I. Improving Language Understanding by Generative Pre-Training. In Proceedings of the 2018 OpenAI Workshop, San Francisco, CA, USA, 24 September 2018; pp. 1–12.
6. Chu, Z.; Ni, S.; Wang, Z.; Feng, X.; Li, C.; Hu, X.; Xu, R.; Yang, M.; Zhang, W. History, Development, and Principles of Large Language Models-An Introductory Survey. *arXiv* **2024**, arXiv:2402.06853. [CrossRef]
7. Xhst. Unstructured Record Linkage Using Siamese Networks and Large Language Models (LLMs). Available online: https://github.com/Xhst/ml-record-linkage (accessed on 24 September 2025).
8. Liu, M.; Roy, S.; Li, W.; Zhong, Z.; Sebe, N.; Ricci, E. Democratizing Fine-grained Visual Recognition with Large Language Models. In Proceedings of the Twelfth International Conference on Learning Representations, Vienna, Austria, 7–11 May 2024. Available online: https://openreview.net/forum?id=c7DND1iIgb (accessed on 8 October 2025).
9. Liu, H.; Zeng, S.; Deng, L.; Liu, T.; Liu, X.; Zhang, Z.; Li, Y.-F. HPCTrans: Heterogeneous Plumage Cues-Aware Texton Correlation Representation for FBIC via Transformers. *IEEE Trans. Circuits Syst. Video Technol.* 2025, *in press*. [CrossRef]
10. Deng, Y.; Ma, J.; Wu, Z.; Wang, W.; Liu, H. DSR-Net: Distinct Selective Rollback Queries for Road Cracks Detection with Detection Transformer. *Digit. Signal Process.* **2025**, *164*, 105266. [CrossRef]
11. Enamorado, T.; Fifield, B.; Imai, K. Using a Probabilistic Model to Assist Merging of Large-Scale Administrative Records. *Am. Polit. Sci. Rev.* **2019**, *113*, 404–422. [CrossRef]
12. Fellegi, I.P.; Sunter, A.B. A Theory for Record Linkage. *J. Am. Stat. Assoc.* **1969**, *64*, 1183–1210. [CrossRef]
13. Sadinle, M.; Fienberg, S. A Generalized Fellegi-Sunter Framework for Multiple Record Linkage with Application to Homicide Record Systems. *J. Am. Stat. Assoc.* **2013**, *108*, 385–397. [CrossRef]
14. Enamorado, T.; Fifield, B.; Imai, K. *FastLink: Fast Probabilistic Record Linkage with Missing Data. R Package, Version 0.6.1*; CRAN: Vienna, Austria, 2019. Available online: https://CRAN.R-project.org/package=fastLink (accessed on 24 September 2025).
15. Ministry of Justice (MoJ). *Splink: MoJ's Open Source Library for Probabilistic Record Linkage at Scale. Version 1.0*; GitHub: London, UK, 2021. Available online: https://github.com/moj-analytical-services/splink (accessed on 24 September 2025).
16. Christen, P.; Churches, T. FEBRL—Freely Extensible Biomedical Record Linkage. In *Joint Computer Science Technical Report Series (Online)*; TRCS-02-05; Australian National University, Department of Computer Science: Canberra, Australia, 2002.
17. FEBRL. Available online: http://sourceforge.net/projects/febrl/ (accessed on 24 September 2025).
18. Bell, A.G. The Deaf. In *Special Reports: The Blind and the Deaf*; U.S. Department of Commerce and Labor, Bureau of the Census, Eds.; U.S. Government Printing Office: Washington, DC, USA, 1900.
19. Box, J.F. *R.A. Fisher, the Life of a Scientist*; Wiley: New York, NY, USA, 1978.
20. Victor, T.W.; Mera, R.M. Record Linkage of Healthcare Insurance Claims. *Stud. Health Technol. Inform.* **2001**, *84*, 1409–1413.
21. Sauleau, E.A.; Paumier, J.P.; Buemi, A. Medical Record Linkage in Health Information Systems by Approximate String Matching and Clustering. *BMC Med. Inform. Decis. Mak.* **2005**, *5*, 32. [CrossRef]
22. Padmanabhan, S.; Carty, L.; Cameron, E.; Ghosh, R.E.; Williams, R.; Strongman, H. Approach to Record Linkage of Primary Care Data from Clinical Practice Research Datalink to Other Health-Related Patient Data: Overview and Implications. *Eur. J. Epidemiol.* **2019**, *34*, 91–99. [CrossRef]
23. Kim, D.; Labkoff, S.; Holliday, S.H. Opportunities for Electronic Health Record Data to Support Business Functions in the Pharmaceutical Industry—A Case Study from Pfizer, Inc. *J. Am. Med. Inform. Assoc.* **2008**, *15*, 581–584. [CrossRef]
24. Christen, P. A Survey of Indexing Techniques for Scalable Record Linkage and Deduplication. *IEEE Trans. Knowl. Data Eng.* **2012**, *24*, 1537–1555. [CrossRef]
25. Papadakis, G.; Skoutas, D.; Thanos, E.; Palpanas, T. Blocking and Filtering Techniques for Entity Resolution: A Survey. *ACM Comput. Surv.* **2020**, *53*, 31. [CrossRef]
26. Odell, M.; Russell, R. The Soundex Coding System. U.S. Patent US1261167A, 9 April 1918; p. 9.
27. Philips, L. The Double Metaphone Search Algorithm. *C/C++ Users J.* **2000**, *18*, 38–43.
28. Christen, P. A Comparison of Phonetic Encoding Algorithms for Historical Name Matching. In Proceedings of the 15th ACM International Conference on Information and Knowledge Management (CIKM), Arlington, VA, USA, 6–11 November 2006; Association for Computing Machinery: New York, NY, USA, 2006; pp. 123–130.
29. Talburt, J.R.; Zhou, Y. Entity Resolution Using Double Metaphone in Commercial Datasets. In Proceedings of the IEEE International Conference on Information Reuse and Integration (IRI), Las Vegas, NV, USA, 4–6 August 2010; pp. 89–94.
30. Ong, T.C.; Mannino, M.V.; Schilling, L.M. Improving Record Linkage with Phonetic Algorithms in Healthcare. *J. Biomed. Inform.* **2014**, *48*, 45–53.

31. Behm, A.; Ji, S.; Li, C.; Lu, J. Fuzzy Search with Double Metaphone for Approximate Matching. In Proceedings of the 25th IEEE International Conference on Data Engineering (ICDE), Shanghai, China, 29 March–2 April 2009; pp. 456–461.
32. Hassanzadeh, O.; Chiang, F.; Miller, R.J. Clustering Records with Double Metaphone: A Scalability Study. In Proceedings of the 16th International Conference on Database Systems for Advanced Applications (DASFAA), Hong Kong, China, 22–25 April 2011; pp. 201–208.
33. Gravano, L.; Ipeirotis, P.G.; Jagadish, H.V.; Koudas, N.; Muthukrishnan, S.; Srivastava, D. Approximate String Joins with Double Metaphone in Databases. *VLDB J.* **2003**, *12*, 345–364.
34. Karakasidis, A.; Verykios, V.S. Privacy-Preserving Record Linkage Using Phonetic Codes. In Proceedings of the 13th Panhellenic Conference on Informatics (PCI), Corfu, Greece, 10–12 September 2009; pp. 101–106.
35. Mudgal, S.; Li, H.; Ko, T.; Srivastava, A.; Wang, R.; Mitra, S.; Srivatsa, S.; Popa, R.A.; Elmore, A.J.; Halevy, A. Deep Learning for Entity Matching: A Design Space Exploration. In Proceedings of the 2018 International Conference on Management of Data (SIGMOD'18), Houston, TX, USA, 10–15 June 2018; pp. 19–34. [CrossRef]
36. Li, Y.; Li, J.; Suhara, Y.; Doan, A.; Tan, W.-C. Deep Entity Matching with Pre-Trained Language Models. *Proc. VLDB Endow.* **2020**, *14*, 50–58. [CrossRef]
37. Choi, I.; Koh, W.; Koo, B.; Kim, W.C. Network-based exploratory data analysis and explainable three-stage deep clustering for financial customer profiling. *Eng. Appl. Artif. Intell.* **2024**, *128*, 107378. [CrossRef]
38. Deo, N.; Rajasekaran, S.; Kamel, R. Identifying Suitable Attributes for Record Linkage using Association Analysis. In Proceedings of the 2023 IEEE International Conference on Big Data (BigData), Sorrento, Italy, 15–18 December 2023; pp. 5753–5760.
39. Meta AI. *LLaMA 3.1 8B Instruct Model*, Version 3.1; Meta: Menlo Park, CA, USA, 2024. Available online: https://huggingface.co/meta-llama/Llama-3.1-8B-Instruct (accessed on 24 September 2025).
40. Devlin, J.; Chang, M.-W.; Lee, K.; Toutanova, K. BERT: Pre-training of Deep Bidirectional Transformers for Language Understanding. *arXiv* **2019**, arXiv:1810.04805. [CrossRef]
41. Liu, T.; Liu, H.; Yang, B.; Zhang, Z. LDCNet: Limb Direction Cues-Aware Network for Flexible Human Pose Estimation in Industrial Behavioral Biometrics Systems. *IEEE Trans. Ind. Informat.* **2023**, *20*, 8068–8078. [CrossRef]
42. Liu, H.; Liu, T.; Chen, Y.; Zhang, Z.; Li, Y.-F. EHPE: Skeleton Cues-Based Gaussian Coordinate Encoding for Efficient Human Pose Estimation. *IEEE Trans. Multimed.* **2022**, *26*, 8464–8475. [CrossRef]
43. Liu, H.; Zhang, C.; Deng, Y.; Xie, B.; Liu, T.; Li, Y.-F. TransIFC: Invariant Cues-Aware Feature Concentration Learning for Efficient Fine-Grained Bird Image Classification. *IEEE Trans. Multimed.* **2023**, *27*, 1677–1690. [CrossRef]
44. SSDMF Homepage. Available online: http://ssdmf.info/download.html (accessed on 24 September 2025).
45. North Carolina State Board of Elections (NCSBE). Voter Registration Data. Available online: https://www.ncsbe.gov/results-data/voter-registration-data (accessed on 24 September 2025).
46. Revinate Engineering. CRM Data Pipeline Record Linkage (Part I). In *Revinate Engineering Blog (Online)*; Revinate: San Francisco, CA, USA, 2016. Available online: https://underthehood.meltwater.com/blog/2020/06/29/the-record-linking-pipeline-for-our-knowledge-graph-part-1/ (accessed on 9 October 2025).
47. Adler-Milstein, J.; Jha, A.K. Health Information Exchange among U.S. Hospitals: Who's In, Who's Out, and What Are the Implications? *Health Aff.* **2017**, *36*, 1420–1428. [CrossRef]

algorithms

MDPI

Article

An Explainable YOLO-Based Deep Learning Framework for Pneumonia Detection from Chest X-Ray Images

Ali Ahmed [1,*], Ali I. Siam [2,3], Ahmed E. Mansour Atwa [4], Mohamed Ahmed Atwa [5], Elsaid Md. Abdelrahim [6,*] and El-Sayed Atlam [7,8]

1 Information Technology Department, Faculty of Computers and Information, Menoufia University, Shebin El-Kom 32511, Egypt
2 College of Arts and Science, Umm Al Quwain University, Umm Al Quwain 536, United Arab Emirates; drali.siam@uaqu.ac.ae
3 Department of Embedded Network Systems Technology, Faculty of Artificial Intelligence, Kafrelsheikh University, Kafr El-Sheikh 33516, Egypt
4 Electronics and Communication Department, College of Engineering and Computer Science, Mustaqbal University, Buraydh 51411, Saudi Arabia; ecs.ec.head@uom.edu.sa
5 Faculty of Medicine Kasr Al-Ainy, Cairo University, Giza 12613, Egypt; mo_atwa2022@students.kasralainy.edu.eg
6 Computer Science Department, College of Science, Northern Border University, Arar 91431, Saudi Arabia
7 Department of Computer Science, College of Computer Science and Engineering, Taibah University, Yanbu 46421, Saudi Arabia; satlam@taibahu.edu.sa or satlam@yahoo.com
8 Computer Science Department, Faculty of Science, University of Tanta, Tanta 31527, Egypt
* Correspondence: ali.ahmed@ci.menofia.edu.eg (A.A.); elsaid.abdelrahim@nbu.edu.sa (E.M.A.)

Abstract: Pneumonia remains a serious global health issue, particularly affecting vulnerable groups such as children and the elderly, where timely and accurate diagnosis is critical for effective treatment. Recent advances in deep learning have significantly enhanced pneumonia detection using chest X-rays, yet many current methods still face challenges with interpretability, efficiency, and clinical applicability. In this work, we proposed a YOLOv11-based deep learning framework designed for real-time pneumonia detection, strengthened by the integration of Grad-CAM for visual interpretability. To further enhance robustness, the framework incorporated preprocessing techniques such as Contrast Limited Adaptive Histogram Equalization (CLAHE) for contrast improvement, region-of-interest extraction, and lung segmentation, ensuring both precise localization and improved focus on clinically relevant features. Evaluation on two publicly available datasets confirmed the effectiveness of the approach. On the COVID-19 Radiography Dataset, the system reached a macro-average accuracy of 98.50%, precision of 98.60%, recall of 97.40%, and F1-score of 97.99%. On the Chest X-ray COVID-19 & Pneumonia dataset, it achieved 98.06% accuracy, with corresponding high precision and recall, yielding an F1-score of 98.06%. The Grad-CAM visualizations consistently highlighted pathologically relevant lung regions, providing radiologists with interpretable and trustworthy predictions. Comparative analysis with other recent approaches demonstrated the superiority of the proposed method in both diagnostic accuracy and transparency. With its combination of real-time processing, strong predictive capability, and explainable outputs, the framework represents a reliable and clinically applicable tool for supporting pneumonia and COVID-19 diagnosis in diverse healthcare settings.

Keywords: pneumonia detection; YOLOv11; chest X-ray imaging; deep learning; explainable AI; Grad-CAM; COVID-19

1. Introduction

Pneumonia continues to be a major contributor to global illness and mortality, particularly affecting vulnerable groups such as children under five and the elderly. The World Health Organization (WHO) estimates that the disease causes more than 2.5 million deaths each year, underscoring the urgent demand for timely and reliable diagnostic methods. Chest X-ray imaging remains a widely used and cost-effective approach for detecting pneumonia; however, conventional assessments depend heavily on radiologists' expertise, which can introduce variability and subjectivity in interpretation, especially in settings with limited medical resources [1]. To address these challenges, automatic pneumonia detection systems have gained significant attention due to their potential to provide consistent, rapid, and scalable diagnostic support. Early automated detection not only assists clinicians in decision-making but also alleviates the burden on healthcare systems and improves patient outcomes [2]. Nevertheless, traditional computer-aided diagnosis (CAD) systems often depend on handcrafted features and shallow classifiers, which tend to be limited in their capacity to generalize across varied imaging conditions and patient populations [3–5].

In recent years, deep learning (DL) has emerged as a transformative technique for medical image analysis, offering notable improvements in robustness and detection accuracy. Convolutional Neural Networks (CNNs), in particular, have shown remarkable success in automatically learning complex visual representations from raw image data, thus removing the need for manual feature extraction [6–8]. Within DL-based object detection frameworks, the You Only Look Once (YOLO) model is especially notable for its ability to achieve real-time analysis with high precision [9,10], positioning it as a strong approach for pneumonia detection in chest X-ray imaging [11].

Despite the impressive performance of deep learning models, a major concern in clinical applications is their lack of transparency. To gain trust from healthcare professionals, it is essential that such models provide explainable results that clarify the reasoning behind predictions. Hence, integrating explainable AI (XAI) techniques into DL-based pneumonia detection frameworks is critical for fostering clinical acceptance and ensuring ethical, interpretable diagnostics [12,13].

This article presents an explainable YOLO-based framework tailored for pneumonia detection from chest X-ray images. The proposed approach combines the detection strength of YOLO with post hoc explainability techniques to provide not only accurate diagnoses but also visual justifications, thereby enhancing transparency and clinical usability.

The proposed framework leverages the latest YOLOv11 architecture, which provides notable improvements in detection accuracy and efficiency compared to earlier YOLO versions. Its enhanced feature extraction and anchor-free detection mechanisms make it particularly effective for identifying small, low-contrast abnormalities in chest X-rays. These capabilities allow for more precise localization of pneumonia and COVID-19–related opacities, supporting both diagnostic accuracy and clinical interpretability.

The contribution of this work can be summarized as follows:

1. Proposed a novel pneumonia detection system combining YOLOv11 for real-time object detection with Grad-CAM for visual interpretability.
2. Employed Grad-CAM to generate diagnostic heatmaps, enabling clinicians to visualize the critical regions influencing the model's predictions, hereby enhancing explainability and trust in AI-assisted decision-making.
3. Applied a robust preprocessing pipeline including CLAHE-based contrast enhancement, region-of-interest (ROI) extraction, and lung segmentation to improve feature localization and reduce background noise.

4. Validated the proposed framework using two public benchmark datasets called COVID-19 Radiography Database and Chest X-ray COVID-19 & Pneumonia Dataset) to ensure performance generalizability across diverse clinical cases.
5. Conducted a comparative analysis with state-of-the-art models, showing competitive or superior performance in terms of well-known evaluation metrics.

The structure of the study is as follows: Section 2 reviews the most recent developments in pneumonia detection. Section 3 introduces the proposed explainable YOLO-based framework for detecting pneumonia from chest X-ray images. Section 4 details the experimental results obtained using the proposed models, along with a performance evaluation compared to the latest related studies. Finally, Section 5 summarizes the main contributions of this work and outlines potential directions for future improvements.

2. Literature Review

This section provides a comprehensive overview of the most relevant and up-to-date research efforts in this domain, focusing on different model architectures, datasets, classification strategies, and performance metrics. Emphasis is placed on the comparative analysis of traditional transfer learning, hybrid deep learning methods, and custom-designed CNNs for pneumonia and COVID-19 diagnosis. The goal is to identify the strengths, limitations, and trends in current methodologies to better position the proposed explainable YOLO-based framework within the existing body of work.

2.1. Hybrid Deep Learning Models

Hybrid models that combine multiple architectures or integrate machine learning classifiers with deep learning feature extractors have gained attention for their performance enhancements. Abdullah et al. [14] proposed a hybrid CNN model combining VGG16 and VGG19 with average pooling for feature fusion and a dense neural network for classification. Trained on the COVID-19 Radiography Database, this model achieved 92% accuracy. Despite improvements over individual CNNs, class imbalance and overfitting risks were noted. Aslan et al. [15] integrated ANN-based lung segmentation with features from eight CNN models (e.g., DenseNet201, ResNet50), classifying with SVMs and other ML algorithms. Their model reached 96.29% accuracy. The approach, though accurate, incurred significant computational costs due to Bayesian optimization. Lakshmi et al. [16] adopted a Bayesian-optimized SVM with deep features extracted from models like AlexNet and ResNet50, achieving 96.20% accuracy. While promising, the approach's processing time and overfitting risk limited real-time application.

2.2. Transfer Learning Approaches and Custom CNN Architectures

Transfer learning using pre-trained CNN architectures has become a dominant approach, especially in scenarios with limited medical image datasets. Singh et al. [17] and El Houby [18] used ResNet50 and VGG19, respectively, achieving up to 97% accuracy. El Houby applied contrast enhancement techniques like CLAHE and histogram equalization for improved feature visibility. Chakravarthy et al. [19] used the SEA-ResNet50 model, attaining 97.50% accuracy in binary classification and employing explainable AI for interpretability. Srinivas et al. [20] fused InceptionV3 and VGG16, attaining 98% accuracy, though the model's robustness on unseen data remains uncertain. Researchers have also designed custom CNNs tailored to pneumonia detection tasks. Ullah et al. [21] proposed CovidDetNet using a custom CNN structure incorporating batch and cross-channel normalization. It achieved 98.40% accuracy but faced limitations due to limited dataset variety. P. Szepesi and L. Szilágyi [22] optimized a lightweight CNN for pediatric pneumonia detection using dropout layers, achieving up to 97.76% accuracy. However, model applicability in clinical environments remains uncertain. F. Bayram and A. Eleyan [23] proposed a DL approach using a 3-stream fusion-based CNN model trained on a large US clinical dataset of chest X-ray images, achieving an accuracy of 97.76%. Their methodology involved extracting features from grayscale X-ray, LBP, and HOG images, then concatenating these features for classification, validated through fivefold cross-validation.

2.3. Federated Learning

To preserve patient data privacy while leveraging distributed training, federated learning (FL) has been explored. Naz et al. [24] applied FL with ResNet50, achieving up to 98% accuracy on both IID and non-IID distributions using the COVID-19 Radiography Database. However, model convergence and parameter tuning posed challenges in large-scale deployments. A. Kareem et al. [25] demonstrated the use of a federated learning framework to ensure data privacy, enabling collaboration between hospitals and medical institutes for model training using real-time datasets while preserving privacy and achieving high accuracy. A. Mabrouk et al. [26] proposed an Ensemble Federated Learning (EFL) framework for pneumonia detection from chest X-ray images, enabling multiple hospitals to train local CNN models (DenseNet, ResNet, MobileNet) on private data, form local ensembles, and share only model parameters with a central server for aggregation into a global ensemble. Experiments on a chest X-ray dataset achieved an accuracy of about 96.63%, highlighting the framework's ability to enhance diagnostic performance while maintaining patient data privacy.

2.4. YOLO-Based Detection Models

The YOLO architecture has been a popular choice for its real-time object detection capability. Munna et al. [27] compared YOLOv3, YOLOv4, and YOLOv6 for pneumonia detection, with YOLOv6 performing best. Despite their effectiveness, the models required further tuning for clinical deployment. Yao [28] enhanced YOLOv3 with MaskFPN and dilated convolutions, achieving 83.70% AP. Nevertheless, the localization of subtle lesions remained challenging. Telaumbanua [29] applied YOLOv11 with standard preprocessing (resizing, normalization), achieving 91.24% accuracy. The model's strength lies in its balance of sensitivity and specificity, though dataset limitations hinder generalization. Zhao [30] improved Fast-YOLO with the FASPA attention mechanism, using over 14,000 re-annotated images. This model excelled in both accuracy and speed, which is critical for real-time settings. Xie et al. [31] optimized YOLO for robustness by incorporating modules like DCNv2 and DynamicConv, attaining a mAP of 97.80%. Despite strong performance, interpretability was a noted limitation.

2.5. Alternative Techniques and Exploratory Models

Several studies have pursued alternative deep learning or preprocessing approaches to boost classification accuracy. Zhang [32] introduced NSEC-YOLO, incorporating adaptive noise suppression and global perception aggregation, achieving state-of-the-art accuracy and inference speed. Hameed et al. [33] proposed a steganography-based framework for medical data embedding, which, while outside classification, highlights security considerations in image-based AI systems. Das et al. [34] used U-Net and W-Net for segmentation and classification, achieving 97.50% F1-score. Their approach performed well but was sensitive to image quality and data diversity. Kailasam and Balasubramanian [35] combined CNNs and YOLO for pneumonia detection with an 83% accuracy. However, generalization and interpretability remained problematic. Accurate lung segmentation enhances the model's focus on relevant anatomical regions. Nguyen et al. [36] combined YOLOv5s-based lung segmentation with Faster R-CNN and YOLOv5s for detecting five thoracic abnormalities. YOLOv5s surpassed Faster R-CNN in both speed and accuracy but struggled with small anomalies and hyperparameter tuning. H. M. Balaha et al. [37] introduced an Archimedes Optimization Algorithm (AOA)-guided framework for hyperparameter optimization in medical image segmentation. The methodology follows four stages: population initialization, fitness function evaluation, population updating, and results logging, where AOA optimizes hyperparameters such as activation functions, loss functions, optimizers, and batch sizes. The results showed high segmentation performance, with the R2 U-Net 2D model achieving 95.70% accuracy on the BUSI dataset and the V-Net model achieving 99.20% accuracy on the COVID-19 dataset.

The literature highlights several key trends: hybrid models and transfer learning dominate accuracy benchmarks; YOLO-based models excel in speed and localization; and interpretability is increasingly important, particularly in healthcare applications. However, challenges remain in achieving model generalization, real-time deployment, and explainability. The proposed YOLOv11-based framework addresses these gaps by combining efficient object detection with post hoc interpretability (Grad-CAM), offering a balanced solution suitable for clinical use. Table 1 summarizes the most recent work related to pneumonia detection.

Table 1. Summary of pneumonia detection related work.

Ref.	Year	Dataset (# Images)	Model Used	Classification Type	Performance
[14]	2024	COVID-19 Radiography Database (9220 images)	Hybrid CNN (VGG16 + VGG19) + Avg Pooling	Binary	Accuracy: 92.00%
[31]	2025	Re-annotated images from MIMIC-CXR dataset (4194 images)	Fast-YOLO	Multi-class	Precision 95.20%, Recall 94.90%
[38]	2020	COVID-19 Radiography Database (5856 images)	AlexNet	Binary, 3-class, 4-class	Accuracy: 99.16%, 94.00%, 93.42%
[39]	2022	COVID-19 Radiography Database (21,000 images)	EfficientNetB1, MobileNetV2, NasNetMobile	4-class	Accuracy: 96.13%
[40]	2023	COVID-19 Radiography Database, Chest X-ray (COVID-19 & Pneumonia), Other (25,000 images)	ResNet-50, VGG-19, AlexNet, MobileNet	Multi-center	Accuracy: 99.54%, 95.90%, 83.00%
[41]	2022	COVID-19 Radiography Database, Chest X-ray (COVID-19 & Pneumonia) (26,009 images)	CNN + ALO + NB/SVM/KNN/DT	Multi-class	Accuracy: 99.63%
[42]	2024	COVID-19 Radiography Database, Chest X-ray (COVID-19 & Pneumonia) (images)	VGG16, InceptionResNetV2, Custom CNN	Multiclass	Accuracy: 97.00%, 96.00%, 93.00%
[43]	2024	Chest X-ray (COVID-19 & Pneumonia) (6432 images)	CNN, Customized CNN (CCNN)	Multi-class	Accuracy: 95.62%
[44]	2022	Mendeley (5000 images)	U-Net, EfficientNetB1, XGBoost, RFE	Multi-class	Accuracy: 97.60%

3. Methodology

This section describes the proposed pneumonia detection framework based on YOLOv11 and Grad-CAM. The overall workflow includes image preprocessing, lung region segmentation, model training, and explainable visualization. The proposed detection framework is built upon the YOLOv11 architecture, which introduces several improvements over previous YOLO versions such as YOLOv8 and YOLOv10. YOLOv11 incorporates an enhanced backbone and feature pyramid (PAN-FPN) structure for more effective multi-scale feature extraction, improving sensitivity to small and low-contrast lesions common in medical images. It also adopts anchor-free detection with dynamic label assignment, reducing localization errors and improving training stability. The integration of efficient attention mechanisms and decoupled head design further enhances feature representation and object classification accuracy. These architectural advancements enable YOLOv11 to achieve faster convergence, higher precision, and improved localization, making it particularly well suited for accurate and reliable pneumonia detection in chest X-rays.

The proposed framework for pneumonia detection, as shown in Figure 1, integrates a real-time object detection model (YOLO) with explainable AI techniques to provide both accurate localization of infected lung regions and interpretable results that can aid clinical decision-making. The framework comprises a structured pipeline with several key stages, from input image acquisition to final explainable prediction. Algorithm 1 outlines the complete methodology used in this study for pneumonia detection and explainability using the YOLOv11 model.

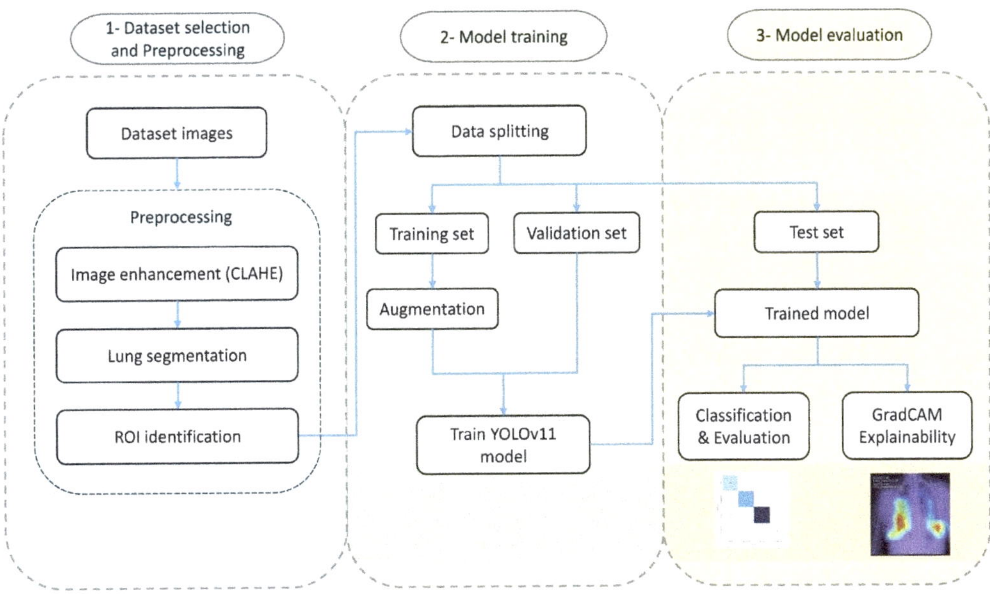

Figure 1. The proposed pneumonia detection framework.

To enhance the diagnostic effectiveness of chest X-ray images, a series of preprocessing steps were applied. Publicly available datasets containing Normal, COVID-19, and Pneumonia cases were utilized, with preprocessing focused on improving image clarity and reducing noise. CLAHE was employed to highlight key structures such as lung textures and opacities, thereby improving visibility of clinically significant features. Segmentation was then performed to isolate the lung fields, ensuring that the model focused on relevant regions while excluding surrounding background areas. This process not only reduced false activations but also enhanced the accuracy of Grad-CAM heatmap generation by localizing the areas most responsible for prediction. To further increase robustness, the segmented images underwent data augmentation before training. Transformations such as random rotations, scaling, and brightness variations were applied to simulate real-world imaging variability. These augmentations strengthened the model's ability to generalize across diverse clinical conditions and reduced overfitting.

Algorithm 1: Pneumonia Detection and Explainability using YOLOv11.

```
Input: Chest X-ray image dataset
Output: Classification results and Grad-CAM heatmaps
BEGIN
1. Dataset Selection and Preprocessing
   1.1 Load Dataset Images
   1.2 FOR each image in DatasetImages DO
      a. Apply ImageEnhancement(image) using CLAHE
      b. Perform LungSegmentation(image)
      c. Identify RegionOfInterest(image)
      d. Pass preprocessed image to pipeline
      END FOR
2. Model Training
   2.1 Split the preprocessed dataset into:
      - TrainingSet
      - ValidationSet
      - TestSet
   2.2 Apply Data Augmentation on TrainingSet
   2.3 Train YOLOv11 model:
      Model ← TrainYOLOv11(TrainingSet, ValidationSet)
3. Model Evaluation
   3.1 Evaluate TrainedModel using TestSet
      Results ← Evaluate(Model, TestSet)
   3.2 FOR each test image in TestSet DO
      a. Predict class using TrainedModel
      b. Apply Grad-CAM to generate heatmap
      c. Overlay heatmap on test image
      END FOR
   3.3 Display and Save:
      - Classification Results
      - Confusion Matrix
      - Grad-CAM Visualizations
END
```

The processed and augmented images were then introduced into the YOLOv11 framework, selected for its real-time performance and strong detection accuracy. YOLO divides the image into a grid, predicting bounding boxes and class probabilities simultaneously, which enables effective pneumonia detection and localization. For interpretability, Grad-CAM was integrated into the framework to generate class-specific heatmaps that highlight areas of the lungs most influential to the model's predictions. These visual explanations support clinical validation by confirming that the system is attending to medically relevant regions rather than irrelevant patterns.

The final stage involves training and evaluating the model on two separate benchmark datasets: (1) COVID-19 Radiography Database and (2) Chest X-ray COVID-19 & Pneumonia Database. These datasets provide diverse imaging conditions and disease classes to ensure generalizability. Performance metrics such as accuracy, precision, recall, F1-score, and confusion matrices are computed to assess the effectiveness of the detection framework.

3.1. Dataset Description

3.1.1. Dataset 1: COVID-19 Radiography Database

The first dataset is the COVID-19 Radiography Database, compiled and made publicly available by Tawsifur Rahman et al. on Kaggle [45]. This dataset comprises over 21,000 posterior–anterior (PA) view chest X-ray images divided into four categories: COVID-19 (3616 images), Normal (10,192 images), Lung Opacity (6012 images), and Viral Pneumonia (1345 images). The images are stored in JPEG format and annotated by clinical professionals. This dataset is widely recognized in the research community for its high-quality annotations and balanced representation of respiratory classes, making it suitable for both binary and multiclass classification tasks.

3.1.2. Dataset 2: Chest X-Ray (COVID-19 & Pneumonia)

The second dataset is the Chest X-ray (COVID-19 & Pneumonia) dataset, curated by Prashant Mohan and available on Kaggle [46]. It contains a total of 6432 chest X-ray images, categorized into three diagnostic classes: COVID-19 (1252 images), Pneumonia (3427 images), and Normal (1753 images). All images are in JPEG format and primarily captured in PA orientation. This dataset is particularly useful due to its balanced structure and clinical relevance in detecting COVID-19 and pneumonia symptoms from radiographic features. Its compact size and well-separated class structure make it ideal for rapid model prototyping and benchmarking.

Both datasets were used independently and not combined. Each dataset was divided into 70% training, 15% validation, and 15% testing subsets, ensuring that no image was repeated across the splits. As neither dataset includes patient identifiers, splitting was performed strictly at the image level to prevent overlap between subsets. According to their official Kaggle documentation, the COVID-19 Radiography Database was curated by medical experts, with duplicate and low-quality images removed during dataset preparation, while the Chest X-ray (COVID-19 & Pneumonia) Dataset was manually reviewed and balanced to eliminate duplicates and ensure representative class coverage. These properties help minimize data leakage and support a fair and reliable evaluation of the proposed model.

3.2. Data Preprocessing

Although the datasets used in this study provide only image-level diagnostic labels (i.e., COVID-19, Pneumonia, and Normal) without bounding box annotations, our framework is designed as a weakly supervised detection system, rather than a conventional object detector, that leverages YOLOv11's localization capability. Therefore, it was not trained with manually annotated bounding boxes. Furthermore, our YOLOv11-based model was employed in a detection mode where each image was associated with the corresponding label.

CLAHE is an advanced image enhancement technique used to improve the contrast of images, particularly in medical imaging and low-contrast environments [47]. Unlike traditional histogram equalization that applies to a global contrast adjustment, CLAHE operates on small regions called tiles (usually 8×8 or 16×16 pixels), applying histogram equalization within each tile to enhance local details. To prevent noise amplification in nearly uniform regions, CLAHE introduces a contrast limiting step by clipping the histogram at a predefined threshold before redistributing the excess pixels. Mathematically, for a tile with intensity levels I(x, y), the transformation function T(i) is given by the cumulative distribution function (CDF) of the clipped and normalized histogram H(i):

$$T(i) = \frac{1}{M \times N} \sum_{j=0}^{i} H_{clipped}(j) \quad (1)$$

where $M \times N$ is the number of pixels in the tile, and $H_{clipped}(j)$ is the clipped histogram count for gray level j. To avoid abrupt changes between tiles, CLAHE uses bilinear interpolation to merge neighboring tiles. This technique has proven effective in enhancing medical images such as MRI, CT, and ECG visualizations, by revealing subtle features while minimizing noise amplification.

According to the proposed framework, the preprocessing pipeline, as demonstrated in Figure 2, began with the application of CLAHE, which significantly improved local contrast and visibility of critical lung features. This enhancement is vital in radiographic imaging, where subtle opacities can indicate pathological changes. Following enhancement, the framework incorporated ROI identification to direct attention toward the lung areas, effectively minimizing background interference. Additionally, lung segmentation was performed to further isolate the anatomical zones of interest, ensuring that subsequent predictions and explanations pertain strictly to lung regions. This segmentation step also lays the groundwork for meaningful application of Grad-CAM visualizations.

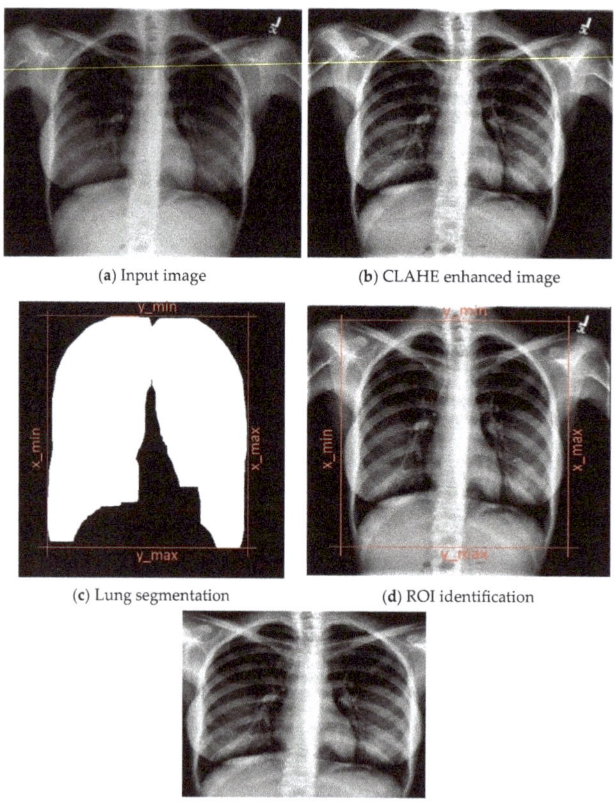

(a) Input image (b) CLAHE enhanced image

(c) Lung segmentation (d) ROI identification

(e) Output image

Figure 2. Preprocessing steps with an image sample.

3.3. YOLOv11 Model Architecture

The YOLOv11 model architecture represents an advanced iteration in the YOLO family, designed to enhance real-time object detection by improving speed, accuracy, and feature representation. The architecture of YOLOv11 model is shown in Figure 3. It incorporates a refined backbone network for efficient feature extraction, typically built on a modified CSP (Cross Stage Partial) structure to reduce computational cost while preserving gradient flow. The neck of the model employs a combination of PANet (Path Aggregation Network) and attention mechanisms to fuse multi-scale features, facilitating the detection of small and overlapping objects, particularly beneficial in medical imaging tasks like pneumonia detection from chest X-ray images. Furthermore, YOLOv11 introduces an optimized anchor-free head that improves bounding box regression and classification performance, thus delivering state-of-the-art results in various object detection benchmarks. This version emphasizes lightweight computation, making it suitable for edge deployments in healthcare applications where latency and resource constraints are critical [48,49].

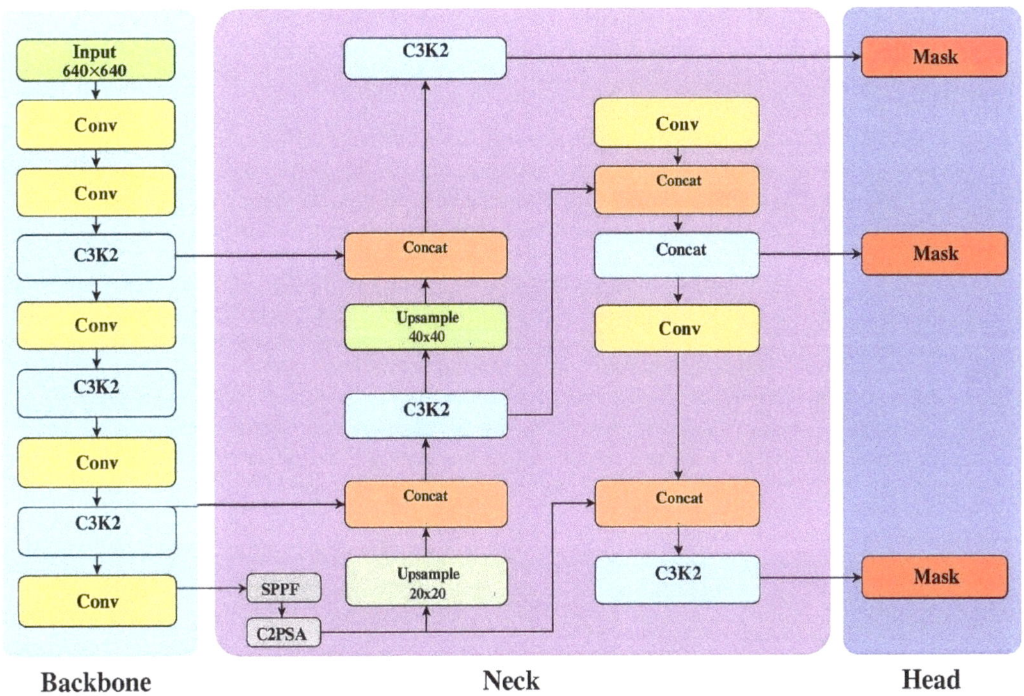

Figure 3. YOLOv11 architecture.

The experimental setup utilizes YOLOv11 model with the parameters listed in Table 2. This table outlines the key training parameters used for implementing the YOLOv11 model in the proposed pneumonia detection framework. The model was trained for 100 epochs using images resized to 520 × 520 pixels, with a batch size of 16 and three output classes (COVID-19, pneumonia, and normal). The optimizer was set to auto-select the best option, starting with an initial learning rate (lr0) of 0.01 and a momentum value of 0.937, while a patience parameter of 100 was applied to prevent overfitting by allowing early stopping when no further improvement was observed. These parameter choices were designed to balance computational efficiency, convergence stability, and classification performance, ensuring the model's robustness and suitability for real-time clinical applications.

Table 2. YOLOv11 model parameters used in the experiments.

Parameter	Value
Epochs	100
Image size	520 × 520
Patience	100
Batch Size	16
Number of classes	3
Optimizer	Auto
Initial Learning Rate (lr0)	0.01
Momentum	0.94

The YOLOv11 detection framework predicts a set of bounding boxes and class probabilities for each input image. Each detection output is represented as a vector $(x, y, w, h, P\_obj, P(c \mid obj))$, where (x, y) denote the center coordinates of the bounding box, w and h represent its width and height, P_{obj} is the objectness confidence indicating the probability that the box contains an object, and $P(c \mid obj)$ is the conditional class probability. The final detection confidence for each class is computed as $P_{obj} \times P(\mathrm{c} \mid \mathrm{obj})$.

The total loss function L used to optimize the YOLOv11 model is a multi-component objective that jointly minimizes errors in localization, objectness, and classification, expressed as:

$$\mathrm{L} = \lambda_{\mathrm{box}}\mathrm{L}_{\mathrm{box}} + \lambda_{\mathrm{obj}}\mathrm{L}_{\mathrm{obj}} + \lambda_{\mathrm{cls}}\mathrm{L}_{\mathrm{cls}} \quad (2)$$

where $\mathrm{L}_{\mathrm{box}}$ represents the bounding box regression loss based on Complete Intersection over Union (CIoU) to improve spatial accuracy, $\mathrm{L}_{\mathrm{obj}}$ is the binary cross-entropy loss for objectness prediction, and $\mathrm{L}_{\mathrm{cls}}$ is the classification loss for multi-class label prediction. The coefficients $\lambda_{\mathrm{box}}, \lambda_{\mathrm{obj}}, \lambda_{\mathrm{cls}}$ are weighting factors that balance the contributions of each component. This composite formulation ensures that the model simultaneously optimizes precise localization, reliable object detection, and accurate disease classification, which are crucial for robust medical image interpretation.

3.4. *Grad-CAM Method for YOLOv11 Model Explainability*

Grad-CAM, short for Gradient-weighted Class Activation Mapping, is a popular explainable AI method that provides visual interpretations of convolutional neural network predictions. It works by tracing the gradients of the target output back through the final convolutional layer to create heatmaps that highlight the most influential image regions. Unlike earlier methods, Grad-CAM can be applied to CNNs without modifying their structure, making it versatile across a wide variety of models. This capability is particularly useful in medical image analysis, where understanding why a diagnosis was made—such as in pneumonia detection from chest X-rays—builds trust in the system's decisions. The heatmaps offer intuitive, spatially aligned insights that help clinicians and researchers confirm that the network is attending to medically meaningful features rather than irrelevant patterns [50].

Grad-CAM is valuable not just for its technical role but for the clarity it brings to AI predictions. By overlaying heatmaps on chest X-rays, it visually points to the exact lung regions that guided the YOLOv11 model's decision. In pneumonia cases, for instance, the highlighted areas often correspond to classic signs such as consolidation or ground-glass opacities, showing that the model is focusing on clinically meaningful features rather than irrelevant background details. This level of transparency helps radiologists quickly see whether the AI's reasoning aligns with their own observations. In this way, Grad-CAM turns the model from a "black box" into a supportive diagnostic partner—building trust, encouraging clinical use, and reducing the risks of relying on unexplained predictions.

3.5. Model Evaluation Metrics

Model evaluation metrics are essential for assessing the effectiveness of machine learning and deep learning models, especially in classification tasks. The most common metrics are accuracy, precision, and recall (or sensitivity). These metrics are often derived from the confusion matrix, which summarizes predictions into true positives (TP), true negatives (TN), false positives (FP), and false negatives (FN) [51].

Precision: This metric quantifies the fraction of correctly identified positive cases relative to all instances predicted as positive. It indicates the reliability of the model's positive predictions, which is critical in medical diagnostics to minimize false alarms. High precision reflects a reduced likelihood of false positives. It can be mathematically expressed as:

$$Precision = \frac{TP}{TP + FP} \tag{3}$$

Here, TP denotes the count of correctly identified positive cases, while FP represents the count of incorrectly classified positive cases.

Recall: Commonly referred to as sensitivity or the true positive rate, this metric measures the model's effectiveness in accurately detecting all instances that belong to the positive class. It is especially crucial in health-related applications where missing a positive case (such as a pneumonia infection) can be critical. Recall is calculated as:

$$Recall = \frac{TP}{TP + FN} \tag{4}$$

where FN denotes the count of false negatives. A higher recall value indicates that the model is able to correctly identify the majority of true positive cases.

F1-Score: This metric represents the harmonic mean of precision and recall, offering a unified measure that captures the trade-off between them. This metric is especially valuable in scenarios with imbalanced class distributions or when minimizing both false positives and false negatives is critical. The F1-score is defined as:

$$F1\ Score = 2 \times \frac{Precision \times Recall}{Precision + Recall} \tag{5}$$

The metric is bounded between 0 and 1, where larger values correspond to superior performance.

Accuracy: This metric reflects the model's overall ability to correctly distinguish between positive and negative cases. Although it is often considered the most straightforward performance indicator, it may yield misleading interpretations when applied to imbalanced datasets. Accuracy is defined as:

$$Accuracy = \frac{TP + TN}{TP + TN + FP + FN} \tag{6}$$

where TN is true negatives. While useful, accuracy should be considered alongside other metrics in skewed class scenarios.

Confusion Matrix: A confusion matrix is a structured table that evaluates the performance of a classification model by comparing the actual classes with the predicted ones. It offers a detailed breakdown of prediction outcomes, differentiating between TP, FP, TN, and FN. In binary classification tasks, it is generally organized as follows:

	Predicted Positive	Predicted Negative
Actual Positive	TP	FN
Actual Negative	FP	TN

This matrix serves as a basis for calculating key evaluation metrics such as precision, recall, F1-score, and accuracy, thereby providing a holistic assessment of the model's performance and diagnostic reliability.

4. Results and Discussion

This section presents the experimental outcomes of the proposed explainable YOLOv11-based pneumonia detection framework and evaluates its performance using two benchmark chest X-ray datasets. The evaluation includes a detailed analysis of classification accuracy, precision, recall, and F1 score for each diagnostic category across both datasets. Additionally, the section showcases visual results, including prediction samples, confusion matrices, and Grad-CAM-based explanations, to demonstrate both the diagnostic capability and interpretability of the model. Comparative analysis with existing state-of-the-art approaches is also provided to highlight the relative strengths and unique contributions of the proposed framework.

4.1. Experimental Setup

Model training and evaluation were performed using the preprocessed datasets described in Section 3.1. Each dataset was already partitioned into training, validation, and testing subsets as outlined earlier, ensuring proportional class representation and strict separation between splits. All images were resized to 320 $\times$ 320 pixels to align with the YOLOv11 input dimensions. Data augmentation methods, such as random rotation and brightness adjustment, were applied to improve generalization and reduce overfitting. Model training was executed on a Kaggle environment using an NVIDIA Tesla P100 GPU with 16 GB of memory. Performance evaluation was based on standard metrics, including accuracy, precision, recall, F1-score, and confusion matrices, calculated on the test set after each training epoch.

4.2. Experimental Results Using Dataset 1

When trained and tested on the COVID-19 Radiography Database, the proposed YOLOv11-based pneumonia detection model achieved outstanding performance across all three classes—COVID-19, Normal, and Pneumonia. Figure 4 illustrates the model's learning behavior, with both training and validation loss steadily decreasing over successive epochs and training accuracy consistently improving, indicating effective convergence without signs of overfitting. The confusion matrix in Figure 5 confirms the high classification accuracy, with only a few misclassifications and strong sensitivity and specificity for each category. Visual examples in Figure 6 further validates these results, showing a close match between ground-truth labels (panel a) and the model's predictions (panel b). The high level of agreement across diverse chest X-ray samples highlights the framework's reliability and robustness in accurately distinguishing between COVID-19, normal, and pneumonia cases.

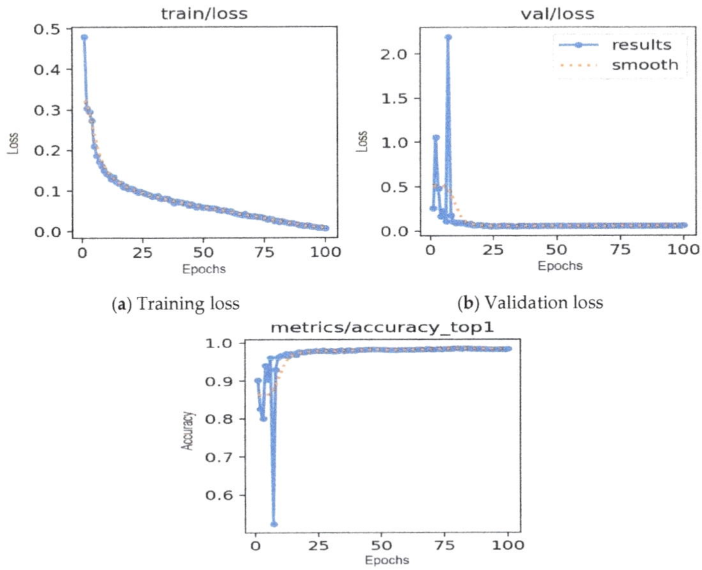

(**a**) Training loss (**b**) Validation loss

(**c**) Training accuracy

Figure 4. The model performance for Dataset 1.

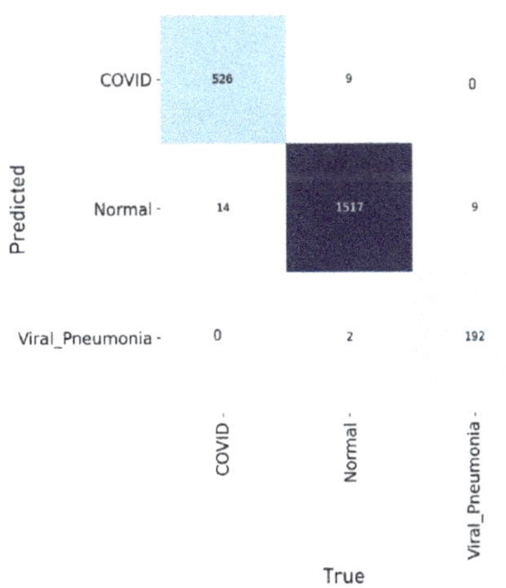

Figure 5. Confusion matrix of the proposed model using Dataset 1.

Table 3 summarizes the classification results of the YOLOv11-based model when tested on the COVID-19 Radiography dataset. The framework demonstrated consistently strong outcomes across all three categories—COVID-19, Normal, and Pneumonia—based on accuracy, precision, recall, and F1-score. Specifically, accuracy reached 98.98% for COVID-19, 98.50% for Normal, and 99.52% for Pneumonia. Precision was above 98% for every class, while recall values ranged from 97.41% for COVID-19 to 99.28% for Pneumonia. F1-scores also showed stability, with values of 97.86% (COVID-19), 98.89% (Normal), and 97.22% (Pneumonia). When macro-averaged, the framework achieved 98.96% accuracy, 98.60% precision, 97.40% recall, and a 97.99% F1-score, confirming reliable and balanced performance. Figure 7 offers a visual look into how the model makes its decisions, using Grad-CAM to generate heatmaps for sample chest X-rays from each class. In each example, the original image (top row) is paired with a Grad-CAM heatmap (bottom row), where warmer colors mark the region's most influential to the prediction. These highlighted lung areas closely match known pathological patterns, showing that the model's attention is focused on clinically relevant zones. Together, the solid numerical results in Table 3 and the clear visual explanations in Figure 7 demonstrate not only the accuracy of the YOLOv11-based framework but also its transparency—making it a promising tool for reliable and interpretable clinical use.

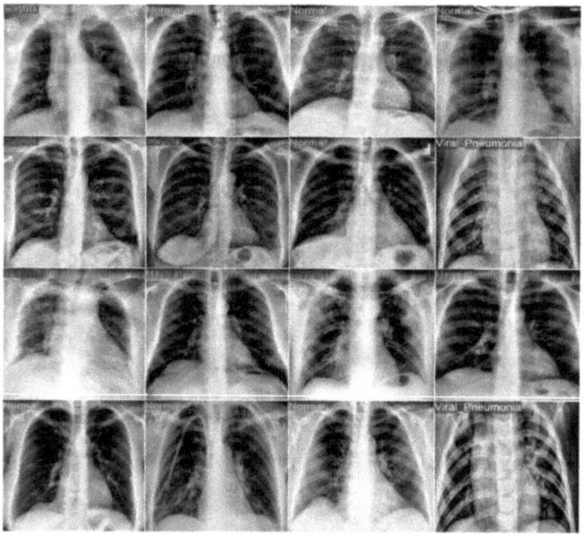

(a)

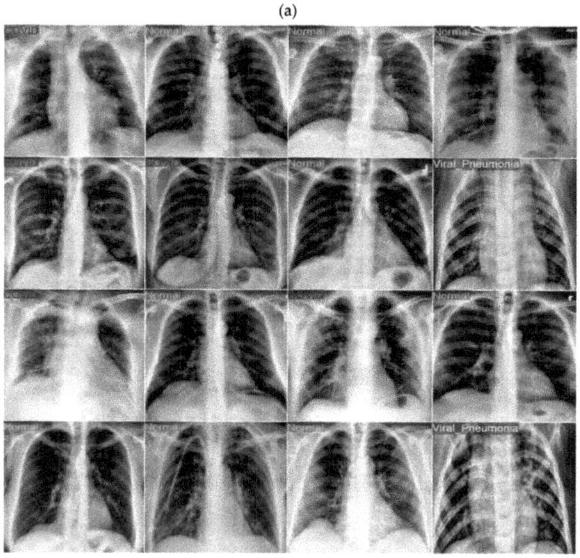

(b)

Figure 6. Samples of model predictions using Dataset 1, (**a**) True labels, and (**b**) Predicted labels.

Table 3. The performance metrics of the proposed model using the first dataset.

Class	Accuracy (%)	Precision (%)	Recall (%)	F1-Score (%)
VID	98.98%	98.32%	97.41%	97.86%
Normal	98.50%	98.51%	99.28%	98.89%
Pneumonia	99.52%	98.97%	95.52%	97.22%
Macro average	98.50%	98.60%	97.40%	97.99%

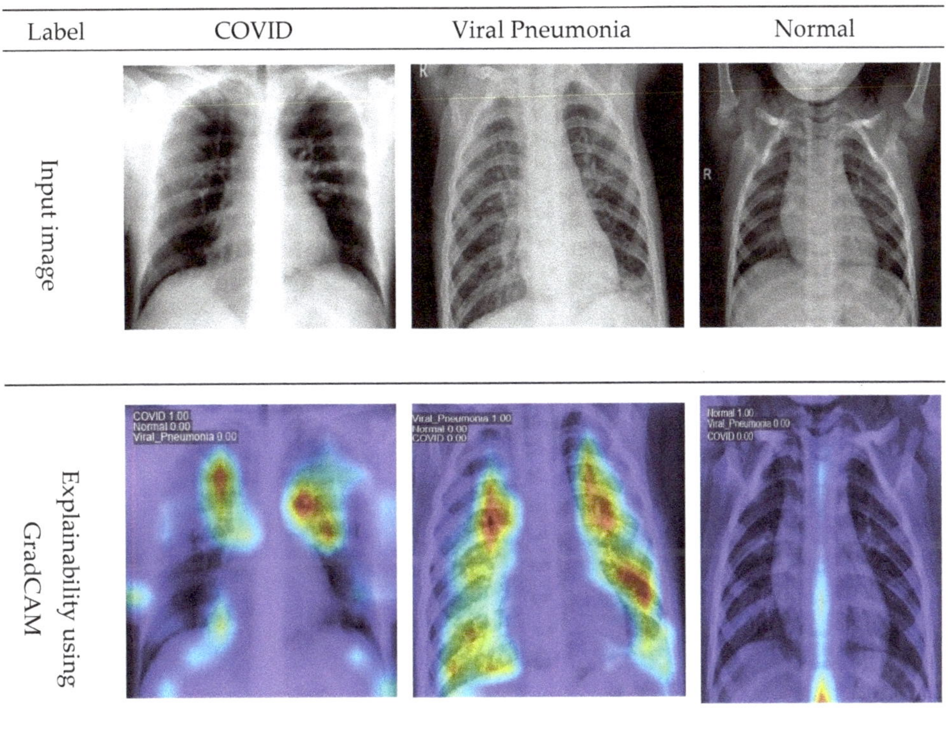

Figure 7. Samples from Dataset 1 after the model explainability using Grad-CAM (Red color: high contribution, to Blue color: no contribution).

4.3. Experimental Results Using Dataset 2

Using the second dataset (Chest X-ray COVID-19 & Pneumonia), the proposed YOLOv11 framework achieved consistently strong outcomes across all three classes. Figure 8a–c show the training behavior, where both training and validation losses steadily declined, and accuracy quickly rose above 98% before stabilizing—indicating effective convergence without evidence of overfitting. The confusion matrix in Figure 9 highlights only a small number of misclassifications: 20 Normal scans predicted as Pneumonia, 5 Pneumonia cases classified as Normal, and a single Pneumonia image mislabeled as COVID-19. This demonstrates clear class separation, particularly for COVID-19, which reached near-perfect accuracy. Figure 10 further illustrates this reliability, as predicted labels closely matched ground-truth annotations with minimal discrepancies.

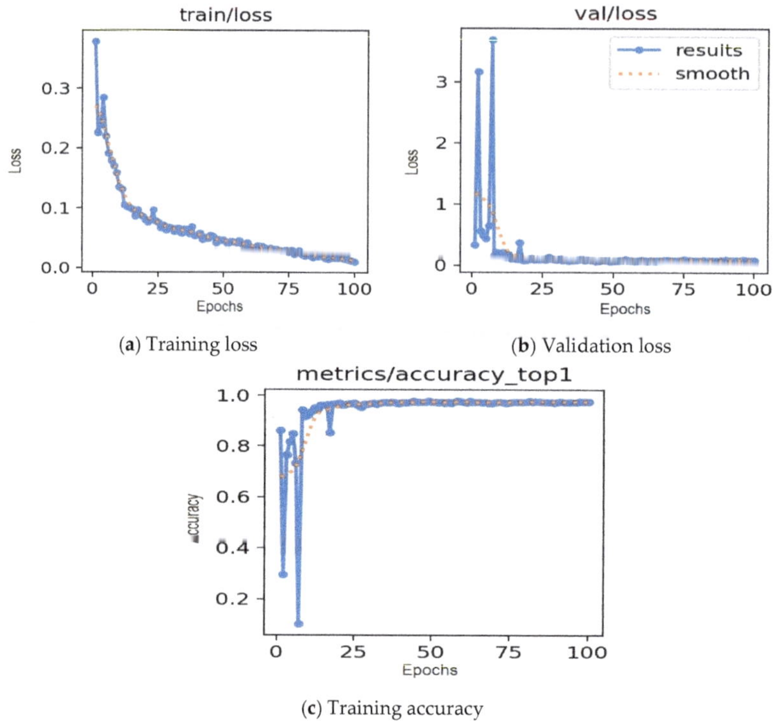

(**a**) Training loss

(**b**) Validation loss

(**c**) Training accuracy

Figure 8. The model performance using Dataset 2.

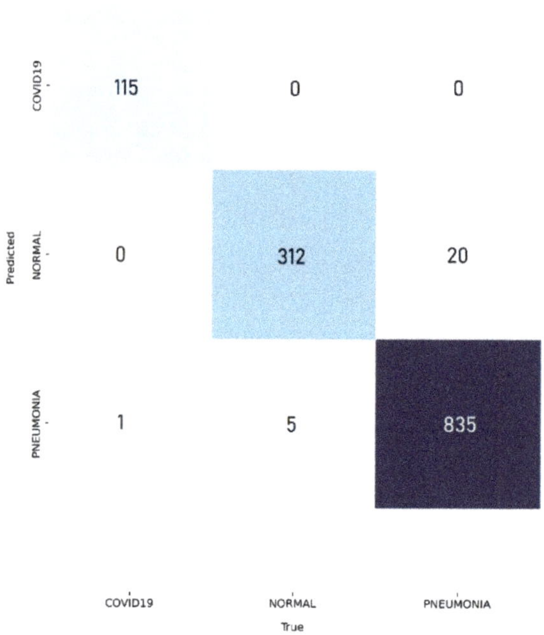

Figure 9. Confusion matrix of the proposed model using Dataset 2.

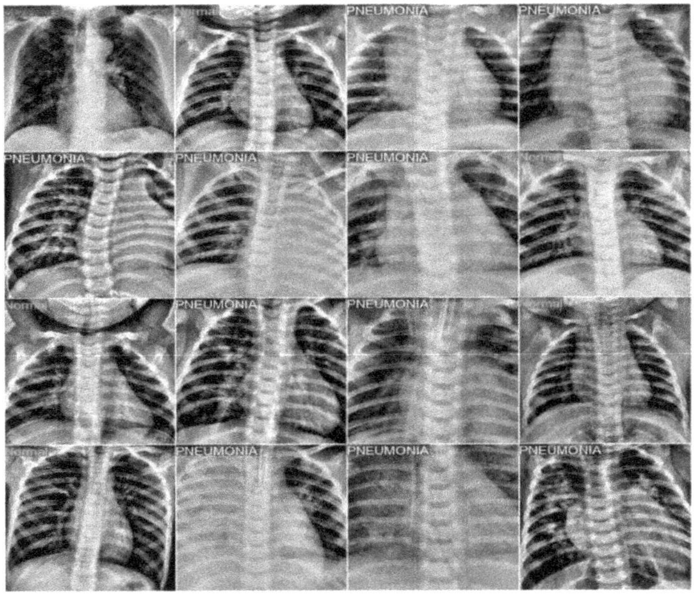

(**a**)

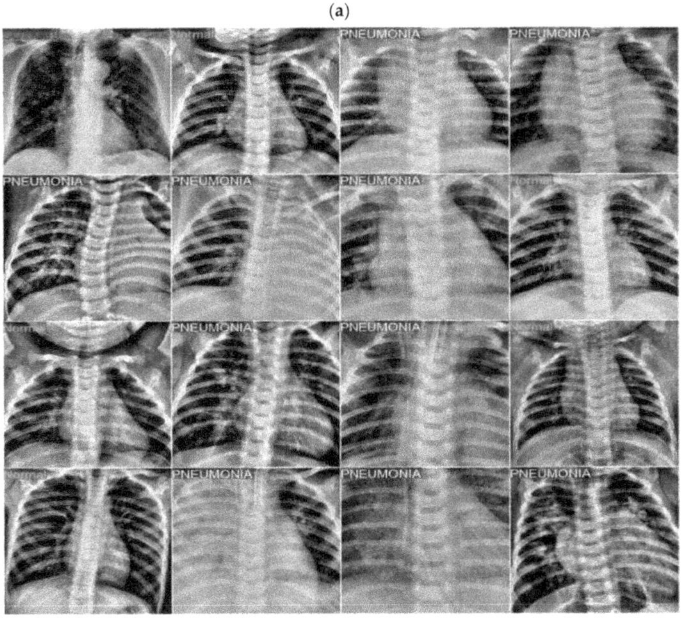

(**b**)

Figure 10. Samples of model predictions from Dataset 2: (**a**) True labels, and (**b**) Predicted labels.

The quantitative metrics are presented in Table 4. For COVID-19 detection, the framework delivered 99.92% accuracy, 100% precision, and an F1-score of 99.57%, confirming its high sensitivity and specificity for COVID-related pneumonia. The Normal and Pneumonia categories also achieved strong results, with accuracies of 98.06% and 97.98%. On average, across all three classes, the framework attained 98% accuracy, 97.76% precision, 98.41% recall, and 98.06% F1-score, verifying robust and balanced classification performance.

Table 4. The performance metrics of the proposed model using the second dataset.

Class	Accuracy (%)	Precision (%)	Recall (%)	F1-Score (%)
COVID	99.92%	100%	99.14%	99.57%
Normal	98.06%	93.98%	98.42%	96.15%
Pneumonia	97.98%	99.29%	97.66%	98.45%
Macro average	98%	97.76%	98.41%	98.06%

Figure 11 presents Grad-CAM–based visual explanations for representative samples from the second dataset, covering COVID-19, Pneumonia, and Normal cases. For each example, the original chest X-ray image is shown alongside its corresponding Grad-CAM heatmap, where warmer colors indicate areas with greater influence on the model's decision. The highlighted lung regions align closely with known pathological patterns, confirming that the framework focuses on clinically relevant zones when making predictions. This interpretability strengthens trust in the model's outputs and underscores its potential as a transparent and reliable tool for clinical use.

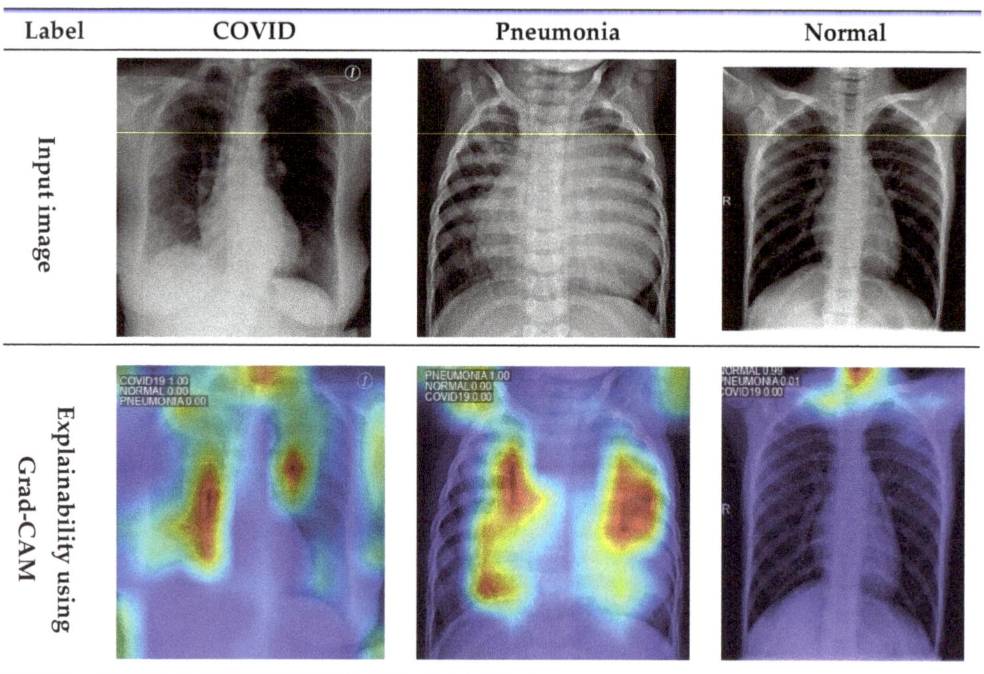

Figure 11. Samples from the second dataset after the model explainability using Grad-CAM method (Red color: high contribution, to Blue color: no contribution).

4.4. Comparative Performance Evaluation with Recently Related Work

Evaluating the YOLOv11-based pneumonia detection framework against existing state-of-the-art methods is necessary to demonstrate its clinical potential and relative advantages. Table 5 reports a comparison with several advanced models on the COVID-19 Radiography dataset, using four key performance indicators: accuracy, precision, recall, and F1-score. On this benchmark dataset, the proposed YOLOv11 system achieved a macro-average accuracy of 98.56%, precision of 98.6%, recall of 97.45%, and F1-score of

97.99%. These results position it among the best-performing approaches and highlight its competitiveness in pneumonia and COVID-19 classification tasks. It clearly outperformed models such as the hybrid DL + ML approach [14] (92% accuracy), VGG19 [18] (93.38% accuracy), and CNN [23] (97.76% accuracy). Even advanced combinations like Inception V3 with VGG16 [20], which reached 98% across all metrics, were slightly below or on par with YOLOv11. The YOLO-based approaches such as YOLOv3 with MaskFPN [28] and Fast-YOLO [31], demonstrated mixed performance. Yao's improved YOLOv3 achieved only 81% accuracy on the RSNA dataset, while Fast-YOLO reached strong precision (95.20%) and recall (94.90%).

Table 5. Performance evaluation against some related work.

Ref.	Dataset	Model	Accuracy (%)	Precision (%)	Recall (%)	F1-Score (%)
[14]	COVID-19 Radiography dataset	hybrid DL + ML	92%	93%	92%	92%
[15]	COVID-19 Radiography dataset	DenseNet201 + SVM	96.29%	96.42%	96.42%	94.53%
[16]	COVID-19 Radiography dataset	ResNet50 + SVM	96.20%	-	-	-
[17]	Labeled Optical Coherence Tomography (OCT) and Chest X-Ray Images for Classification + Chest X-Ray Images (Pneumonia)	Adopted-CNN and ResNet50	97%	-	-	-
[18]	COVID-19 Radiography dataset	VGG19	93.38%	94.12%	96%	95.05%
[20]	COVID-19 Radiography dataset	Inception V3 with VGG16	98%	98%	98%	98%
[21]	COVID-19 Radiography dataset	DL + SVM	98.40%	97%	96.66%	96.82%
[23]	COVID-19 Radiography dataset	CNN	97.76%	97.78%	97.76%	97.76%
[24]	COVID-19 Radiography dataset	Federated Learning (FL)	98%	98%	98%	98%
[28]	RSNA dataset	Yolov3 with MaskFPN	81%	-	-	-
[31]	Re-annotated images from MIMIC-CXR dataset	Fast-YOLO	-	95.20%	94.90%	-
Proposed	COVID-19 Radiography dataset	YOLOv11	98.50%	98.60%	97.45%	97.99%
	Chest X-ray (COVID-19 & Pneumonia)	YOLOv11	98%	97.76%	98.41%	98.06%

A major advantage of the proposed framework is its ability to perform real-time object detection, enabling rapid diagnostic support without sacrificing accuracy. In addition, the incorporation of Grad-CAM provides an interpretability component that is often lacking in comparable models, thereby enhancing user confidence and making the approach more appropriate for clinical environments where transparency is critical. The system also exhibited strong generalization when evaluated on the Chest X-ray COVID-19 & Pneumonia dataset, sustaining high performance with 98% accuracy, 97.76% precision, 98.41% recall, and 98.06% F1-score. Achieving consistent results across datasets with varying distributions demonstrates the robustness and adaptability of the YOLOv11-based method.

4.5. Discussion

The findings collectively demonstrate both the effectiveness and clinical promise of the proposed YOLOv11-based pneumonia detection framework, while also pointing to areas for future improvement. On both benchmark datasets, the model reached macro-average accuracies of 98.50% on the COVID-19 Radiography Dataset and 98% on the

Chest X-ray COVID-19 & Pneumonia dataset. These consistently high values confirm the framework's strong ability to recognize critical lung abnormalities, demonstrating competitive performance among state-of-the-art approaches. One of the notable strengths of this approach is the integration of Grad-CAM, which enhances interpretability by highlighting the lung regions most influential in the model's predictions.

The heatmaps shown in Figures 7 and 11 provide clear visual evidence that complements the numerical metrics, offering direct insight into the model's decision-making. For pneumonia and COVID-19 images, Grad-CAM highlighted areas corresponding to typical pathological signs such as consolidations, infiltrates, and ground-glass opacities. In contrast, normal chest radiographs showed only minimal activation within the lung fields, suggesting that the model focuses on medically meaningful features rather than irrelevant image patterns. This behavior establishes a clinically meaningful baseline, confirming that the framework focuses on medically relevant regions rather than spurious image artifacts. Collectively, these visual explanations support the validity of the diagnostic outputs and strengthen clinical trust in the framework's applicability. This not only improves transparency but also builds clinical trust, as radiologists can visually verify the AI's reasoning. Preprocessing steps like CLAHE and lung segmentation further improved the model's focus and robustness, while the YOLOv11 architecture allowed for real-time detection with low computational requirements—an important feature for deployment in settings with limited resources.

The work is not without limitations. The datasets used, although reliable, cover a limited range of patient demographics and imaging variations, which could affect how well the model generalizes to different clinical environments. In addition, Grad-CAM's usefulness depends on the model's own accuracy—if the model is wrong, the highlighted regions may be misleading. Still, the overall findings show that the framework is an effective, efficient, and interpretable approach to automated pneumonia detection, with clear potential for further improvement through more diverse datasets and broader testing across hospitals and imaging systems.

To ensure a fair comparison, all baseline models reproduced in this study were trained and evaluated using identical data splits, preprocessing, and augmentation procedures as the proposed YOLOv11 framework. This consistent setup guarantees that differences in performance reflect model capability rather than data or processing bias. For previously published methods whose raw data or code were unavailable, the reported results are presented as indicative comparisons only, since exact replication under the same experimental settings was not possible. Statistical tests such as DeLong for AUC were not applied due to the lack of prediction-level outputs from external studies; however, the consistent improvements across multiple metrics demonstrate the robustness and reliability of the proposed model.

4.6. Clinical Significance and Practical Implications

The clinical significance of this framework extends beyond mere high accuracy scores. The combination of real-time performance, high diagnostic precision, and explainable outputs makes the proposed system a practical and valuable tool in healthcare settings, particularly those with limited resources. The ability to accurately detect and localize pneumonia in real time can significantly reduce the time from imaging to diagnosis, enabling earlier treatment and potentially improving patient outcomes. In settings where access to experienced radiologists is limited, this automated system can provide a reliable second opinion or serve as an initial screening tool to prioritize critical cases. The integrated Grad-CAM visualizations are key for clinical trust and validation, as they allow healthcare professionals to visually confirm that the model's predictions are based on medically plausible evidence, thereby fostering greater acceptance of AI in clinical practice. This framework's robustness, demonstrated on two different public datasets, suggests its potential for widespread, effective deployment, addressing the global health challenge posed by pneumonia.

To further improve the generalization and robustness of the proposed framework, future work may integrate concepts from robust feature learning and resilient signal reconstruction. Recent studies on complex scene parsing and light-field image watermarking have demonstrated effective strategies for maintaining feature stability and signal integrity in noisy or distorted environments [52,53]. Incorporating such approaches could enhance the proposed model's adaptability to non-Gaussian noise and its applicability to multidimensional medical imaging scenarios.

5. Conclusions

Pneumonia remains a serious global health challenge, especially among vulnerable populations such as children and the elderly, where fast and accurate diagnosis can save lives. Traditional diagnostic methods, while valuable, often face practical challenges—ranging from subjective interpretation to limited access to expert radiologists, and an inability to provide instant results in resource-limited areas. This study introduced a new, explainable pneumonia detection framework that combines the real-time object detection power of YOLOv11 with Grad-CAM visualizations for interpretability. The system not only delivers high detection accuracy but also pinpoints infected lung regions, giving clinicians a clear and visual explanation for each prediction. Tested on two benchmark datasets, the framework consistently outperformed or matched leading methods, demonstrating both accuracy and robustness. Looking ahead, the approach could be made even more versatile by incorporating additional medical data such as CT scans or patient records, adapting it for use on mobile or edge devices for on-site diagnosis, and exploring federated learning for privacy-preserving collaboration between hospitals. While this work focused on pneumonia, the same framework could be extended to detect and differentiate other thoracic diseases, such as tuberculosis or lung cancer, making it a powerful tool for comprehensive chest disease screening. Future work could focus on expanding the model to detect multiple chest diseases, integrating clinical and multimodal data, enhancing explainability with advanced XAI methods, validating performance on larger and diverse datasets.

Author Contributions: Conceptualization, M.A.A. and A.E.M.A.; methodology, A.A., A.I.S. and A.E.M.A.; software, A.I.S.; validation, M.A.A.; formal analysis, A.E.M.A. and M.A.A.; investigation, A.A., A.I.S. and M.A.A.; resources, E.-S.A., E.M.A. and A.E.M.A.; data curation, A.I.S. and M.A.A.; writing—original draft preparation, A.E.M.A., A.A. and M.A.A.; writing—review and editing, A.E.M.A., E.M.A. and E.-S.A.; visualization, A.I.S. and A.A.; supervision, E.M.A. and E.-S.A.; project administration, E.-S.A. and A.A.; funding acquisition, E.M.A. All authors have read and agreed to the published version of the manuscript.

Funding: Deanship of Scientific Research at Northern Border University, Arar, KSA: NBU-FFR-2025-750 159-04.

Data Availability Statement: The datasets used in this work are publicly available at: https://www.kaggle.com/datasets/tawsifurrahman/covid19-radiography-database (accessed on 20 June 2025). https://www.kaggle.com/datasets/prashant268/chest-xray-covid19-pneumonia (accessed on 20 June 2025).

Acknowledgments: The authors extend their appreciation to the Deanship of Scientific Research at Northern Border 749 University, Arar, KSA for funding this research work through the project number "NBU-FFR-2025-750 159-04".

Conflicts of Interest: The authors declare that they have no conflicts of interest regarding this work.

References

1. World Health Organization. Available online: https://www.who.int/news-room/fact-sheets/detail/pneumonia (accessed on 1 May 2025).
2. Kermany, D.; Zhang, K.; Goldbaum, M. Labeled Optical Coherence Tomography (OCT) and Chest X-Ray Images for Classification. *Mendeley Data* **2018**, 2. [CrossRef]
3. Yanase, J.; Triantaphyllou, E. A systematic survey of computer-aided diagnosis in medicine: Past and present developments. *Expert Syst. Appl.* **2019**, *138*, 112821. [CrossRef]
4. El-Rashidy, N.; Sedik, A.; Siam, A.I.; Ali, Z.H. An efficient edge/cloud medical system for rapid detection of level of consciousness in emergency medicine based on explainable machine learning models. *Neural Comput. Appl.* **2023**, *35*, 10695–10716. [CrossRef] [PubMed]
5. Masmoudi, M.; Shakrouf, Y.; Omar, O.H.; Shikhli, A.; Abdalla, F.; Alketbi, W.; Alsyouf, I.; Cheaitou, A.; Jarndal, A.; Siam, A.I. Driver risk classification for transportation safety: A machine learning approach using psychological, physiological, and demographic factors with driving simulator. *Eng. Appl. Artif. Intell.* **2025**, *162*, 112585. [CrossRef]
6. Krizhevsky, A.; Sutskever, I.; Hinton, G.E. ImageNet classification with deep convolutional neural networks. *Commun. ACM* **2017**, *60*, 84–90. [CrossRef]
7. Abdelrahim, E.M.; Hashim, H.; Atlam, E.-S.; Osman, R.A.; Gad, I. TMS: Ensemble Deep Learning Model for Accurate Classification of Monkeypox Lesions Based on Transformer Models with SVM. *Diagnostics* **2024**, *14*, 2638. [CrossRef]
8. Siam, A.I.; Sedik, A.; El-Shafai, W.; Elazm, A.A.; El-Bahnasawy, N.A.; El Banby, G.M.; Khalaf, A.A.; El-Samie, F.E.A. Biosignal classification for human identification based on convolutional neural networks. *Int. J. Commun. Syst.* **2021**, *34*, e4685. [CrossRef]
9. Talaat, F.M.; El-Shafai, W.; Soliman, N.F.; Algarni, A.D.; El-Samie, F.E.A.; Siam, A.I. Real-time Arabic avatar for deaf-mute communication enabled by deep learning sign language translation. *Comput. Electr. Eng.* **2024**, *119*, 109475. [CrossRef]
10. Zayed, A.; Siam, A.I. A YOLO-based Deep Learning Approach for Vibration-based Rotating Shaft Imbalance Detection. *J. Eng. Res.* **2025**, *9*, 32. [CrossRef]
11. Redmon, J.; Divvala, S.; Girshick, R.; Farhadi, A. You Only Look Once: Unified, Real-Time Object Detection. In Proceedings of the 2016 IEEE Conference on Computer Vision and Pattern Recognition (CVPR), Las Vegas, NV, USA, 27–30 June 2016; IEEE: Piscataway, NJ, USA, 2016; pp. 779–788. [CrossRef]
12. Samek, W.; Wiegand, T.; Müller, K.-R. Explainable Artificial Intelligence: Understanding, Visualizing and Interpreting Deep Learning Models. *arXiv* **2017**, arXiv:arXiv:1708.08296.
13. Atwa, A.E.M.; Atlam, E.-S.; Ahmed, A.; Atwa, M.A.; Abdelrahim, E.M.; Siam, A.I. Interpretable Deep Learning Models for Arrhythmia Classification Based on ECG Signals Using PTB-X Dataset. *Diagnostics* **2025**, *15*, 1950. [CrossRef]
14. Abdullah, M.; Abrha, F.B.; Kedir, B.; Tagesse, T.T. A Hybrid Deep Learning CNN model for COVID-19 detection from chest X-rays. *Heliyon* **2024**, *10*, e26938. [CrossRef]
15. Aslan, M.F.; Sabanci, K.; Durdu, A.; Unlersen, M.F. COVID-19 diagnosis using state-of-the-art CNN architecture features and Bayesian Optimization. *Comput. Biol. Med.* **2022**, *142*, 105244. [CrossRef]
16. Lakshmi, M.; Das, R.; Manohar, B. A new COVID-19 classification approach based on Bayesian optimization SVM kernel using chest X-ray datasets. *Evol. Syst.* **2024**, *15*, 1521–1540. [CrossRef]
17. Singh, A.K.; Kumar, A.; Kumar, V.; Prakash, S. COVID-19 Detection using adopted convolutional neural networks and high-performance computing. *Multimedia Tools Appl.* **2024**, *83*, 593–608. [CrossRef] [PubMed]
18. El Houby, E.M.F. COVID-19 detection from chest X-ray images using transfer learning. *Sci. Rep.* **2024**, *14*, 11639. [CrossRef] [PubMed]
19. Chakravarthy, S.R.S.; Bharanidharan, N.; Vinothini, C.; Kumar, V.V.; Mahesh, T.R.; Guluwadi, S. Adaptive Mish activation and ranger optimizer-based SEA-ResNet50 model with explainable AI for multiclass classification of COVID-19 chest X-ray images. *BMC Med. Imaging* **2024**, *24*, 206. [CrossRef] [PubMed]
20. Srinivas, K.; Sri, R.G.; Pravallika, K.; Nishitha, K.; Polamuri, S.R. COVID-19 prediction based on hybrid Inception V3 with VGG16 using chest X-ray images. *Multimedia Tools Appl.* **2023**, *83*, 36665–36682. [CrossRef]
21. Ullah, N.; Khan, J.A.; Almakdi, S.; Khan, M.S.; Alshehri, M.; Alboaneen, D.; Raza, A. A Novel CovidDetNet Deep Learning Model for Effective COVID-19 Infection Detection Using Chest Radiograph Images. *Appl. Sci.* **2022**, *12*, 6269. [CrossRef]
22. Szepesi, P.; Szilágyi, L. Detection of pneumonia using convolutional neural networks and deep learning. *Biocybern. Biomed. Eng.* **2022**, *42*, 1012–1022. [CrossRef]
23. Bayram, F.; Eleyan, A. COVID-19 detection on chest radiographs using feature fusion based deep learning. *Signal Image Video Process.* **2022**, *16*, 1455–1462. [CrossRef]
24. Naz, S.; Phan, K.; Chen, Y.-P.P. Centralized and Federated Learning for COVID-19 Detection with Chest X-Ray Images: Implementations and Analysis. *IEEE Trans. Emerg. Top. Comput. Intell.* **2024**, *8*, 2987–3000. [CrossRef]
25. Kareem, A.; Liu, H.; Velisavljevic, V. A federated learning framework for pneumonia image detection using distributed data. *Health Anal.* **2023**, *4*, 100204. [CrossRef]

26. Mabrouk, A.; Redondo, R.P.D.; Elaziz, M.A.; Kayed, M. Ensemble Federated Learning: An approach for collaborative pneumonia diagnosis. *Appl. Soft Comput.* **2023**, *144*, 110500. [CrossRef]
27. Munna, M.S.; Chowdhury, R.; Siddiqee, A.M. A Comparative Study of YOLO Models for Pneumonia Detection. Available online: www.ijfmr.com (accessed on 1 May 2025).
28. Yao, S.; Chen, Y.; Tian, X.; Jiang, R.; Ma, S. An improved algorithm for detecting pneumonia based on YOLOv3. *Appl. Sci.* **2020**, *10*, 1818. [CrossRef]
29. Telaumbanua, P.; Fatihah, M.R.; Pratama Tarigan, A.; Afzalurrahmah, A. Deep Learning for Pneumonia Detection in Lung Diseases: Implementing YOLO11 Architecture. Available online: https://www.researchgate.net/publication/387020311_Deep_Learning_for_Pneumonia_Detection_in_Lung_Diseases_Implementing_YOLO11_Architecture (accessed on 1 May 2025).
30. Zhao, B.; Chang, L.; Liu, Z. Fast-YOLO Network Model for X-Ray Image Detection of Pneumonia. *Electronics* **2025**, *14*, 903. [CrossRef]
31. Xie, Y.; Zhu, B.; Jiang, Y.; Zhao, B.; Yu, H. Diagnosis of pneumonia from chest X-ray images using YOLO deep learning. *Front. Neurorobotics* **2025**, *19*, 1576438. [CrossRef]
32. Zhang, X.; Liu, L.; Yang, X.; Liu, L.; Peng, W. NSEC-YOLO: Real-time lesion detection on chest X-ray with adaptive noise suppression and global perception aggregation. *J. Radiat. Res. Appl. Sci.* **2025**, *18*, 101281. [CrossRef]
33. Hameed, M.A.; Hassaballah, M.; Abdelazim, R.; Sahu, A.K. A novel medical steganography technique based on Adversarial Neural Cryptography and digital signature using least significant bit replacement. *Int. J. Cogn. Comput. Eng.* **2024**, *5*, 379–397. [CrossRef]
34. Das, A.; Agarwal, R.; Singh, R.; Chowdhury, A.; Nandi, D. Automatic Detection of COVID-19 from Chest X-Ray Images Using Deep Learning Model. August 2024. Available online: http://arxiv.org/abs/2408.14927 (accessed on 1 May 2025).
35. Kailasam, R.; Balasubramanian, S. Deep Learning for Pneumonia Detection: A Combined CNN and YOLO Approach. *Human-Centric Intell. Syst.* **2025**, *5*, 44–62. [CrossRef]
36. Nguyen, H.T.; Nguyen, M.N.; Phung, L.D.; Pham, L.T.T. Anomalies Detection in Chest X-Rays Images Using Faster R-CNN and YOLO. *Vietnam. J. Comput. Sci.* **2023**, *10*, 499–515. [CrossRef]
37. Balaha, H.M.; Bahgat, W.M.; Aljohani, M.; Bamaqa, A.; Atlam, E.-S.; Badawy, M.; Elhosseini, M.A. AOA-guided hyperparameter refinement for precise medical image segmentation. *Alex. Eng. J.* **2025**, *120*, 547–560. [CrossRef]
38. Ibrahim, A.U.; Ozsoz, M.; Serte, S.; Al-Turjman, F.; Yakoi, P.S. Pneumonia Classification Using Deep Learning from Chest X-ray Images During COVID-19. *Cogn. Comput.* **2024**, *16*, 1589–1601. [CrossRef]
39. Khan, E.; Rehman, M.Z.U.; Ahmed, F.; Alfouzan, F.A.; Alzahrani, N.M.; Ahmad, J. Chest X-ray Classification for the Detection of COVID-19 Using Deep Learning Techniques. *Sensors* **2022**, *22*, 1211. [CrossRef]
40. Talaat, M.; Si, X.; Xi, J. Multi-Level Training and Testing of CNN Models in Diagnosing Multi-Center COVID-19 and Pneumonia X-ray Images. *Appl. Sci.* **2023**, *13*, 10270. [CrossRef]
41. Karim, A.M.; Kaya, H.; Alcan, V.; Sen, B.; Hadimlioglu, I.A. New Optimized Deep Learning Application for COVID-19 Detection in Chest X-ray Images. *Symmetry* **2022**, *14*, 1003. [CrossRef]
42. Mohan, G.; Subashini, M.M.; Balan, S.; Singh, S. A multiclass deep learning algorithm for healthy lung, Covid-19 and pneumonia disease detection from chest X-ray images. *Discov. Artif. Intell.* **2024**, *4*, 20. [CrossRef]
43. Fahad, N.; Ahmed, R.; Jahan, F.; Sadib, R.J.; Morol, M.K.; Al Jubair, M.A. MIC: Medical Image Classification Using Chest X-ray (COVID-19 & Pneumonia) Dataset with the Help of CNN and Customized CNN. In Proceedings of the 3rd International Conference on Computing Advancements, Dhaka, Bangladesh, 17–18 October 2024; ACM: New York, NY, USA, 2024; pp. 1007–1013. [CrossRef]
44. Lunagaria, M.; Katkar, V.; Vaghela, K. COVID-19 and Pneumonia Infection Detection from Chest X-Ray Images using U-Net, EfficientNetB1, XGBoost and Recursive Feature Elimination. *Int. J. Adv. Comput. Sci. Appl.* **2022**, *13*, 475–483. [CrossRef]
45. Rahman, T. COVID-19 Radiography Database. 2021. Available online: https://www.kaggle.com/datasets/tawsifurrahman/covid19-radiography-database (accessed on 1 May 2025).
46. Mohan, P. Chest X-Ray (COVID-19 & Pneumonia). 2021. Available online: https://www.kaggle.com/datasets/prashant268/chest-xray-covid19-pneumonia (accessed on 1 May 2025).
47. Zuiderveld, K. Contrast limited adaptive histogram equalization. In *Graphics Gems IV*; Academic Press Professional: San Diego, CA, USA, 1994; pp. 474–485.
48. Redmon, J.; Farhadi, A. YOLOv3: An Incremental Improvement. 2018. Available online: http://arxiv.org/abs/1804.02767 (accessed on 1 May 2025).
49. Wang, C.-Y.; Bochkovskiy, A.; Liao, H.-Y.M. YOLOv7: Trainable Bag-of-Freebies Sets New State-of-the-Art for Real-Time Object Detectors. In Proceedings of the 2023 IEEE/CVF Conference on Computer Vision and Pattern Recognition (CVPR), Vancouver, BC, Canada, 17–24 June 2023; IEEE: Piscataway, NJ, USA, 2023; pp. 7464–7475. [CrossRef]

50. Selvaraju, R.R.; Cogswell, M.; Das, A.; Vedantam, R.; Parikh, D.; Batra, D. Grad-CAM: Visual Explanations from Deep Networks via Gradient-Based Localization. In Proceedings of the 2017 IEEE International Conference on Computer Vision (ICCV), Venice, Italy, 22–29 October 2017; IEEE: Piscataway, NJ, USA, 2017; pp. 618–626. [CrossRef]
51. Miller, C.; Portlock, T.; Nyaga, D.M.; O'Sullivan, J.M. A review of model evaluation metrics for machine learning in genetics and genomics. *Front. Bioinform.* **2024**, *4*, 1457619. [CrossRef]
52. Liu, Y.; Wang, C.; Lu, M.; Yang, J.; Gui, J.; Zhang, S. From Simple to Complex Scenes: Learning Robust Feature Representations for Accurate Human Parsing. *IEEE Trans. Pattern Anal. Mach. Intell.* **2024**, *46*, 5449–5462. [CrossRef]
53. Wang, C.; Zhang, Q.; Wang, X.; Zhou, L.; Li, Q.; Xia, Z.; Ma, B.; Shi, Y.-Q. Light-Field Image Multiple Reversible Robust Watermarking Against Geometric Attacks. *IEEE Trans. Dependable Secur. Comput.* **2025**, *99*, 1–15. [CrossRef]

algorithms

MDPI

Article

Impact of an Educational Intervention on BPPV Management: An Interrupted Time Series Analysis

Erfan Arbab [1], Kalpdrum Passi [1,*] and Robert Ohle [2]

1 School of Engineering & Computer Science, Laurentian University, Sudbury, ON P3E 2C6, Canada; earbab@laurentian.ca

2 Department of Emergency Medicine, Health Science North Research Institute, Northern Ontario School of Medicine, Sudbury, ON P3E 5J1, Canada; rohle@hsnsudbury.ca

* Correspondence: kpassi@laurentian.ca

Abstract: This study evaluates the impact of an educational intervention aimed at improving the management of benign paroxysmal positional vertigo (BPPV) in a clinical setting. Interrupted Time Series (ITS) analysis was used to assess changes in the use of key diagnostic maneuvers—Dix–Hallpike and Supine Roll—as well as the treatment maneuver, Canalith Repositioning Maneuvers (CRM), and the use of CT scans. The intervention aimed to promote evidence-based practices and minimize unnecessary imaging. ITS models accounted for confounders such as history of BPPV and dizziness. The results showed significant improvements in the use of the Supine Roll and CRM maneuvers, with both immediate increases and sustained upward trends following the intervention. For the Dix–Hallpike maneuver, an initial increase was observed after the intervention; however, this effect was no longer statistically significant after adjusting for confounders, suggesting that the observed change may have been influenced by shifts in the patient population rather than the intervention itself. A positive long-term trend persisted. No significant reduction in CT scan usage was found. These findings demonstrate the intervention's effectiveness in enhancing adherence to recommended diagnostic and treatment practices for BPPV. However, they also suggest that reducing unnecessary imaging may require additional strategies beyond provider education.

Keywords: benign paroxysmal positional vertigo (BPPV); Interrupted Time Series (ITS); educational intervention; Dix–Hallpike maneuver; Supine Roll test; Canalith Repositioning Maneuver (CRM)

1. Introduction

Benign Paroxysmal Positional Vertigo (BPPV) is the most common peripheral vestibular disorder and a significant contributor to vertigo-related healthcare visits. Despite the availability of well-established diagnostic tests and effective treatment maneuvers, BPPV is frequently underdiagnosed or mismanaged in clinical settings. Improving the adherence of healthcare providers to evidence-based BPPV practices remains an important challenge.

This study evaluates the impact of an educational intervention on the use of BPPV diagnostic and treatment practices using Interrupted Time Series (ITS) analysis. The intervention was implemented across multiple healthcare settings and aimed to promote the use of positional maneuvers and reduce unnecessary imaging, particularly CT scans. To situate this work, we review the clinical background of BPPV, evidence on educational interventions in vertigo management, and the relevance of ITS methods in healthcare research.

1.1. Clinical Background on BPPV

BPPV is characterized by brief episodes of vertigo triggered by specific head movements, typically due to the displacement of otoconia into the semicircular canals [1,2]. The posterior canal is most commonly involved, though horizontal canal cases also occur. Diagnosis is made through bedside positional maneuvers such as the Dix–Hallpike test for posterior canal BPPV and the Supine Roll test for horizontal canal variants [3,4]. Treatment primarily involves canalith repositioning maneuvers (CRMs), including the Epley and Semont maneuvers, which have demonstrated high effectiveness [5].

Despite their simplicity and proven efficacy, these diagnostic and therapeutic techniques are underutilized in clinical practice. Instead, patients frequently undergo neuroimaging, especially head CT scans, which offer limited diagnostic value for BPPV but contribute to increased healthcare costs and radiation exposure [6]. This diagnostic gap highlights the need for provider-level interventions to align practice with established guidelines.

1.2. Interrupted Time Series in Healthcare Research

Interrupted Time Series (ITS) analysis is a quasi-experimental design well suited for evaluating the longitudinal impact of policy or practice interventions where randomized controlled trials are impractical. ITS uses segmented regression to estimate level and trend changes before and after an intervention, accounting for pre-existing trends and temporal structure [7,8].

ITS has been widely applied in healthcare settings to assess the effects of guideline implementation, public health campaigns, regulatory changes, and quality improvement initiatives [9–11]. Turner et al. and Ewusie et al. have highlighted the utility of ITS in detecting both immediate and gradual effects of complex interventions and emphasized the importance of model diagnostics such as autocorrelation, stationarity, and heteroscedasticity [12,13].

1.3. Prior ITS Applications to BPPV Management

Efforts to improve adherence to evidence-based protocols for BPPV have begun to emerge in clinical settings. A prominent example is the Emergency VESTibular Algorithm (EVESTA), developed by Neely et al. to standardize the diagnosis and management of BPPV in emergency departments [6]. Evaluated using an interrupted time series design, the intervention led to marked improvements in clinical practice, including a 27% increase in Dix–Hallpike testing, a 33% increase in repositioning maneuvers, a 30% reduction in vestibular suppressant use, and a 16% decrease in neuroimaging. Additionally, a sustained decline in BPPV-related admissions highlighted the program's broader clinical impact.

These findings underscore the value of structured implementation strategies and emphasize the importance of evaluating such interventions through rigorous longitudinal designs, such as interrupted time series analysis, which can assess both immediate and sustained effects across diverse clinical outcomes.

1.4. Study Rationale and Objectives

Building on this context, the present study investigates the effects of a real-world, multi-site intervention designed to improve BPPV management practices.

BPPV is a common yet frequently underdiagnosed cause of dizziness in emergency settings. Despite the availability of effective bedside assessments and repositioning maneuvers, clinical practices often rely on less effective or unnecessary diagnostic tools, such as head CT scans, contributing to delays, increased healthcare costs, and potential harm. Previous efforts to improve BPPV management have shown that structured clinical pathways can enhance the use of positional testing and treatments. However, most of these evaluations have been conducted in single centers with limited temporal scope and lack rigorous methodological designs.

This study aims to evaluate the impact of a structured educational intervention implemented across multiple hospital sites to improve adherence to evidence-based BPPV management.

To rigorously assess both the short- and long-term effects of this intervention, Interrupted Time Series (ITS) analysis was chosen as the evaluation framework. ITS is particularly well suited for detecting immediate changes while accounting for pre-existing trends, and for assessing whether improvements are sustained over time.

The study addresses the following objectives:

- Assess changes in the frequency of positional tests such as the Dix–Hallpike maneuver and Supine Roll test, and canalith repositioning maneuvers (CRMs);
- Examine trends in the use of computed tomography (CT) scans for patients presenting with vertigo;
- Apply segmented regression ITS models with appropriate statistical diagnostics to evaluate the immediate and sustained effects of the intervention.

By examining both behavioral and system-level outcomes using a robust quasi-experimental design, this research contributes to the evidence base on implementing sustainable practice change in emergency care for BPPV.

2. Materials and Methods

2.1. Study Design

This study employed an Interrupted Time Series (ITS) design to evaluate the impact of an educational intervention on the diagnosis and management of BPPV. ITS is a robust quasi-experimental method well-suited for situations where randomized controlled trials are not feasible. It allows for the assessment of both immediate and long-term intervention effects by analyzing outcome trends before and after implementation [10,11].

2.2. Setting and Data Sources

Data were obtained from three hospitals in Ontario, Canada: Health Sciences North (Sudbury), The Ottawa Hospital (Ottawa), and Thunder Bay Regional Health Sciences Centre (Thunder Bay). The dataset included 2015 patient records from emergency department visits between April 2018 and December 2022, spanning both pre-intervention (April 2018 to October 2021) and post-intervention (October 2021 to December 2022) periods. Each record comprised over 300 variables, including patient demographics, presenting symptoms, diagnostic procedures, treatment interventions, and discharge outcomes.

2.3. Educational Intervention

The intervention introduced a structured, guideline-based diagnostic and treatment algorithm aimed at improving adherence to best practices in BPPV management. It consisted of the following components:

- Educational Program: Comprehensive training sessions were delivered to emergency department providers. These sessions covered BPPV pathophysiology, diagnostic maneuvers (e.g., Dix–Hallpike and Supine Roll), and treatment techniques (e.g., Canalith Repositioning Maneuvers, CRMs).
- Algorithm Implementation: A standardized clinical pathway was introduced to encourage evidence-based diagnosis and treatment, reduce unnecessary CT imaging, and minimize inappropriate referrals.

- Support and Monitoring: Research assistants supported implementation across sites and conducted periodic audits to monitor adherence and address barriers.

2.4. Key Variables

2.4.1. Outcome Variables

The following binary indicators were assessed for each patient encounter:

- Dix-Hallpike Performed;
- Supine Roll Performed;
- Canalith Repositioning Maneuver (CRM) Performed;
- CT Scan Performed.

2.4.2. Time and Intervention Variables

- Date of Visit: Used to track time over the study period.
- Intervention Indicator: A binary variable distinguishing the pre- and post-intervention periods, with October 2021 as the start of the intervention.

2.4.3. Confounding Variables

Potential confounders included patient demographics and clinical characteristics such as age, sex, prior BPPV, symptoms (e.g., vertigo, dizziness, vomiting, unsteadiness), blood pressure, and relevant comorbidities (e.g., migraine, stroke). These were assessed using stepwise multivariable modeling and backward elimination.

2.5. Data Preprocessing

2.5.1. Merging and Cleaning

Data from pre- and post-intervention periods were merged. Variable formats were standardized, and missing values were interpreted as procedures not performed.

2.5.2. Standardization

Diagnostic test result values were harmonized ("positive"/"yes" treated as performed; "negative"/"no" still counted as performed). New binary outcome variables were created to indicate whether each maneuver or test was performed.

2.5.3. Handling Missing Data

Missing or blank values for CRM and CT variables were set to "no." For Dix–Hallpike and Supine Roll, performance was inferred from the presence of any result entry.

2.6. Sample Size and Time Aggregation

To enhance statistical power and account for temporal variability, outcome data were aggregated into bi-weekly intervals for analysis. This granularity balanced detail with model stability and avoided excessive noise from daily fluctuations.

Aggregation choices were informed by diagnostic comparisons across multiple configurations (e.g., weekly, bi-weekly, monthly; raw counts vs. proportions). Bi-weekly counts provided optimal fit based on criteria such as R-squared, Durbin–Watson statistics, Augmented Dickey–Fuller (ADF) stationarity tests, and White's test for heteroscedasticity.

Sample sizes were sufficient for ITS modeling, with a minimum of 12 intervals both pre- and post-intervention per outcome. Aggregated values reflected the number of procedures performed per interval (e.g., Dix–Hallpike, CRM, CT scan).

2.7. Statistical Analysis

Segmented regression models were used to estimate both level and slope changes in outcomes associated with the intervention [10,11]. The model was specified as:

$$Y_t = \beta_0 + \beta_1 \times \text{time}_t + \beta_2 \times \text{intervention}_t + \beta_3 \times \text{time\_after\_intervention}_t + e_t \quad (1)$$

where Y_t is the outcome at time t; β_0 is the baseline level; β_1 reflects the pre-intervention trend; β_2 captures the immediate post-intervention change; β_3 denotes trend change post-intervention; and e_t is the error term.

Data were analyzed at the bi-weekly level, as described in Section 2.6. A comprehensive set of diagnostic tests was conducted to ensure model validity, including tests for autocorrelation (Durbin–Watson, Breusch–Godfrey), stationarity (ADF), seasonality (STL decomposition), heteroscedasticity (Breusch–Pagan, White), residual normality (Shapiro–Wilk), and influential observations (Cook's Distance). Newey–West standard errors were applied where assumptions were violated [14–16].

2.8. Confounder Identification and Adjustment

To account for potential confounding factors, a stepwise regression strategy was applied during model development. The process involved:

- Baseline model: Included only the time and intervention indicators.
- Multivariable model: Incorporated all candidate confounders identified in Section 2.4.3 (e.g., age, sex, clinical symptoms, prior BPPV diagnosis).
- Backward elimination: Backward elimination was used to remove variables with limited predictive value, retaining only those with statistically significant associations at the 0.05 level [17].

This approach ensured that the final ITS models adequately adjusted for relevant clinical and demographic characteristics while avoiding overfitting.

3. Results

3.1. Overview

This section presents findings from the Interrupted Time Series (ITS) analysis, evaluating the impact of an educational intervention on key diagnostic and treatment practices for BPPV, including Dix–Hallpike and Supine Roll tests, Canalith Repositioning Maneuvers (CRM), and CT scan usage. The section integrates descriptive statistics, inferential ITS modeling results, box plots, and model diagnostics.

3.2. Descriptive Statistics and Boxplots

To understand baseline and post-intervention patterns in clinical practice, descriptive statistics were calculated for each outcome measure, and boxplots were constructed to visualize changes in central tendency and variability. The results below summarize shifts in test usage and imaging rates across the two study periods.

3.2.1. Dix–Hallpike Test

The average number of Dix–Hallpike maneuvers declined notably after the intervention. Pre-intervention values showed a mean of 27.58 (SD = 16.62, Median = 27), which dropped to a post-intervention mean of 10.53 (SD = 4.12, Median = 10). Figure 1 displays a boxplot including jittered bi-weekly data points illustrating this reduction in both frequency and variability.

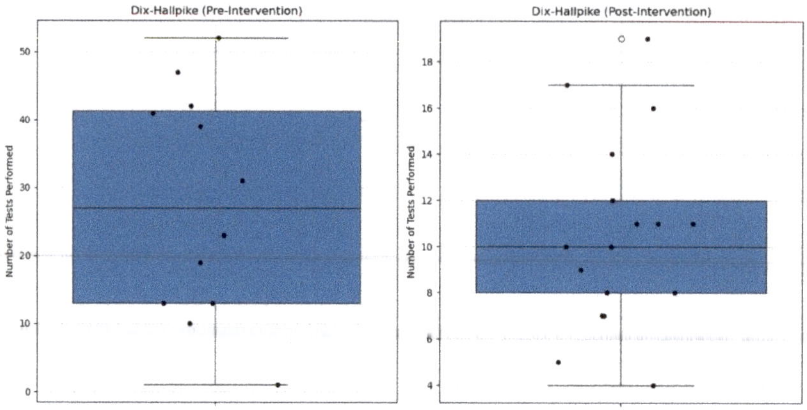

Figure 1. Boxplot of Dix–Hallpike maneuvers before and after the intervention. A notable reduction in both test frequency and variability was observed post-intervention.

3.2.2. Supine Roll Test

Use of the Supine Roll test decreased substantially post intervention. The mean fell from 19.67 (SD = 17.97) before the intervention to 5.75 (SD = 2.35) afterward. Figure 2 shows the corresponding boxplot, which includes jittered bi-weekly data points to illustrate the distribution and highlights lower post-intervention usage.

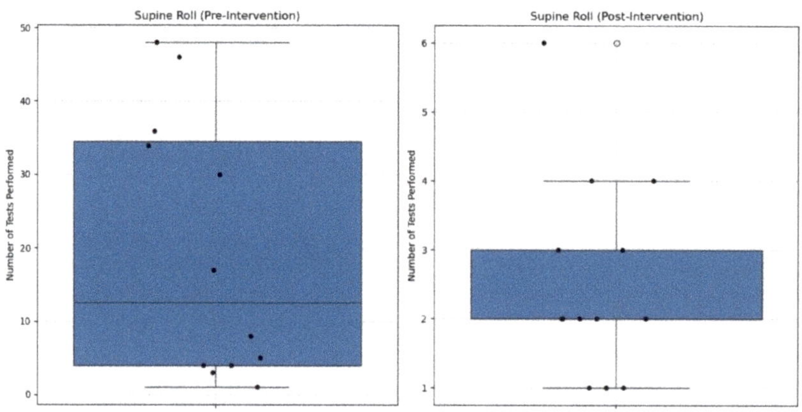

Figure 2. Boxplot of Supine Roll tests before and after the intervention. The test was used less frequently and with more consistency following the intervention.

3.2.3. Canalith Repositioning Maneuvers (CRM)

CRM usage remained relatively stable but showed a slight post-intervention increase. The mean rose from 7.17 (SD = 6.28) to 8.15 (SD = 5.03). Figure 3 presents the boxplot, including jittered bi-weekly data points, comparing pre- and post-intervention frequencies.

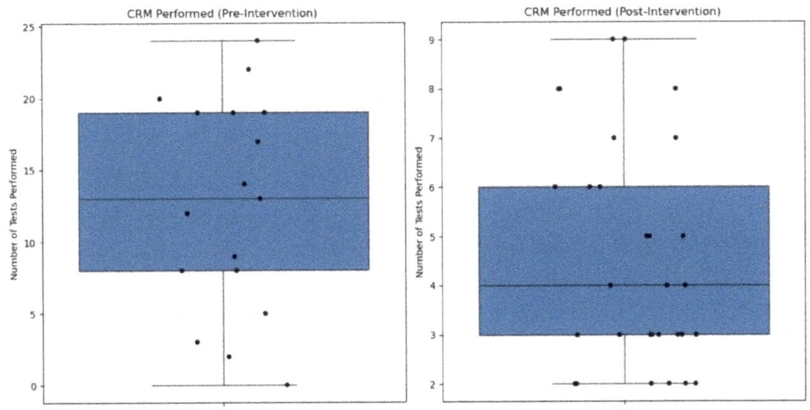

Figure 3. Boxplot of Canalith Repositioning Maneuvers (CRM) before and after the intervention. A slight increase in CRM usage was noted after the intervention.

3.2.4. CT Scan Utilization

CT scan use dropped marginally following the intervention, with the mean declining from 54.25 (SD = 17.10) to 51.62 (SD = 10.82). Figure 4 illustrates this modest change in imaging frequency using a boxplot that includes jittered bi-weekly data points.

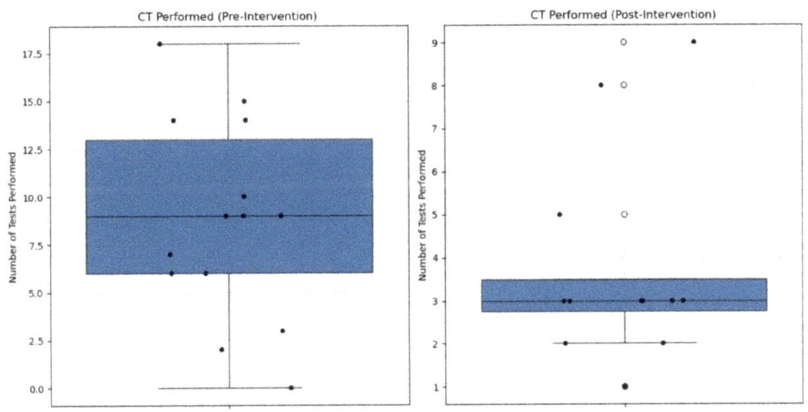

Figure 4. Boxplot of CT Scan utilization before and after the intervention. CT scan usage declined modestly in the post-intervention period.

3.3. *ITS Modeling Results*

Interrupted Time Series (ITS) analysis was used to estimate baseline trends (β_1), immediate post-intervention level changes (β_2), and changes in slope following the intervention (β_3) for each outcome.

3.3.1. Dix–Hallpike Performed

As shown in Table 1, a significant negative baseline trend was observed for Dix–Hallpike maneuvers ($\beta_1 = -4.34$, $p < 0.001$), followed by a significant immediate increase in test frequency post-intervention ($\beta_2 = 14.35$, $p = 0.001$), and a positive change in slope ($\beta_3 = 3.94$, $p < 0.001$). Figure 5 presents the corresponding interrupted time series plot.

Table 1. Segmented regression results for Dix–Hallpike performed.

Coefficient	Estimate	Std. Error	t	*p*-Value	95% CI (Lower)	95% CI (Upper)
Intercept	51.45	2.56	20.13	<0.001	46.39	56.71
Time	−4.34	0.39	−11.03	<0.001	−5.15	−3.53
Post-Intervention	14.35	3.63	3.95	0.001	6.87	21.82
Time After Intervention	3.94	0.46	8.62	<0.001	3.00	4.88

Model Statistics: $R^2 = 0.897$, Adjusted $R^2 = 0.884$; $F(3, 25) = 72.31$, $p < 0.001$; Durbin–Watson = 1.99 (no autocorrelation); AIC = 175.8; BIC = 181.3; Omnibus normality test: $p = 0.286$.

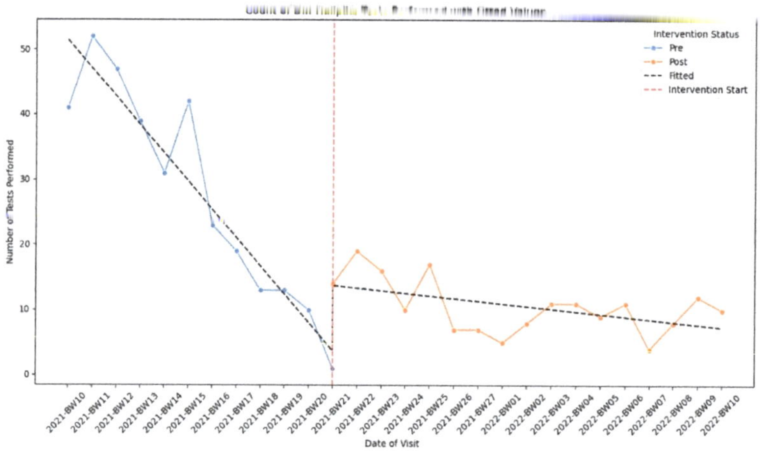

Figure 5. Interrupted time series plot showing the count of Dix–Hallpike maneuvers performed before and after the intervention.

3.3.2. Supine Roll Performed

The baseline trend was significantly negative ($\beta_1 = -4.58$, $p < 0.001$), followed by a significant level increase ($\beta_2 = 13.90$, $p = 0.003$) and a positive slope post-intervention ($\beta_3 = 4.37$, $p < 0.001$). Figure 6 illustrates these changes.

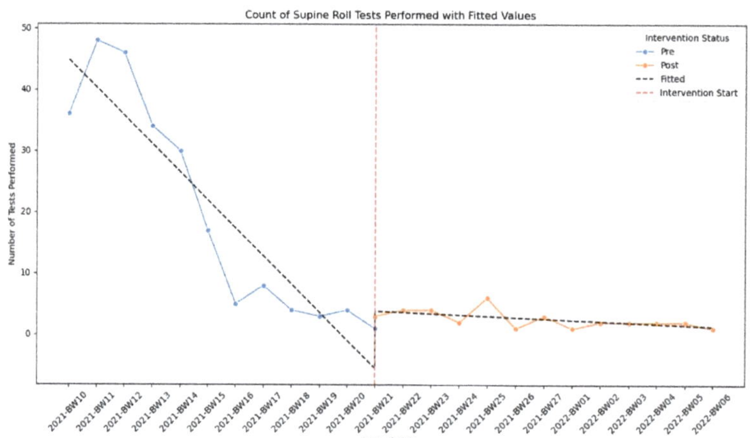

Figure 6. Interrupted time series plot showing the count of Supine Roll test performed before and after the intervention.

3.3.3. CRM Performed

CRM use declined slightly before the intervention ($\beta_1 = -1.30$, $p < 0.001$) but showed a significant immediate increase ($\beta_2 = 4.58$, $p = 0.012$) and a rising post-intervention trend ($\beta_3 = 1.23$, $p < 0.001$). Figure 7 presents the corresponding time series plot.

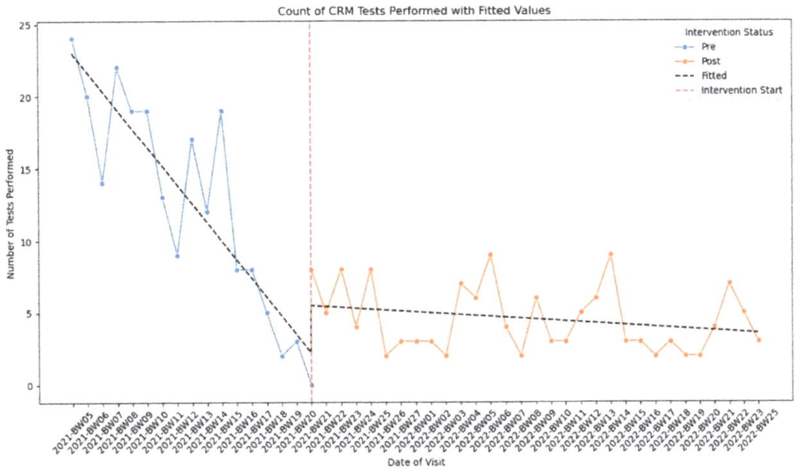

Figure 7. Interrupted time series plot showing the count of Canalith Repositioning Maneuvers (CRM) performed before and after the intervention.

3.3.4. CT Scan Performed

CT usage decreased pre-intervention ($\beta_1 = -1.02$, $p < 0.001$), but the immediate change post-intervention was not statistically significant ($\beta_2 = 3.48$, $p = 0.136$). However, a small upward trend was observed post-intervention ($\beta_3 = 0.87$, $p = 0.001$). Figure 8 illustrates the time series pattern.

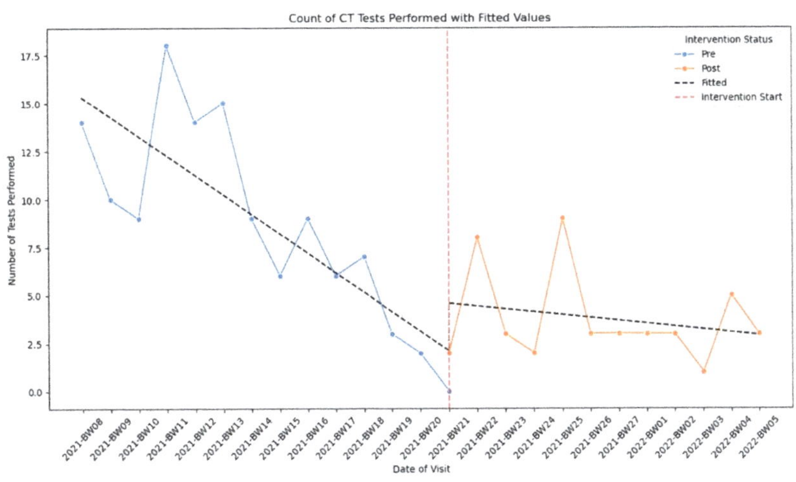

Figure 8. Interrupted time series plot showing the count of CT scans performed before and after the intervention.

3.4. Confounder Analysis

Potential confounding factors—including history of BPPV, dizziness, vomiting, and unsteadiness—were evaluated using multivariable regression models. The key findings are summarized below:

- Dix–Hallpike Performed: Adjustment rendered the immediate effect non-significant (β_2 adj. $p = 0.215$), although the post-intervention trend remained significant (β_3 adj. = 1.75, $p < 0.001$).
- Supine Roll Performed: All adjusted coefficients remained statistically significant (β_2 adj. = 19.81, $p < 0.001$; β_3 adj. = 5.11, $p < 0.001$).
- CRM Performed: Significance persisted after adjusting for vertigo (β_2 adj. = 4.67, $p = 0.006$; β_3 adj. = 0.77, $p = 0.004$).
- CT Scan Performed: After adjusting for dizziness and BPPV history, all effects became non-significant.

Table 2 presents a comparison of unadjusted and adjusted segmented regression coefficients and p-values for each outcome.

Table 2. Comparison of unadjusted and adjusted coefficients (β) and p-values for each outcome.

Outcome	Unadjusted β_1	Adjusted β_1	Unadjusted β_2	Adjusted β_2	Unadjusted β_3	Adjusted β_3
Dix–Hallpike Performed	−4.34 ($p < 0.001$)	−1.81 ($p < 0.001$)	14.35 ($p = 0.001$)	NS [1]	3.94 ($p = 0.001$)	1.75 ($p < 0.001$)
Supine Roll Performed	−4.58 ($p < 0.001$)	−5.57 ($p < 0.001$)	13.90 ($p = 0.003$)	19.81 ($p = 0.004$)	4.37 ($p = 0.001$)	5.11 ($p < 0.001$)
CRM Performed	−1.30 ($p < 0.001$)	−0.84 ($p < 0.001$)	4.58 ($p = 0.012$)	4.67 ($p = 0.006$)	1.23 ($p = 0.002$)	0.77 ($p = 0.004$)
CT Performed	−1.02 ($p < 0.001$)	NS	3.48 ($p = 0.033$)	NS	0.87 ($p = 0.010$)	NS

NS = Not significant ($p > 0.05$).

3.5. Model Diagnostics

Key regression assumptions—including autocorrelation, stationarity, seasonality, heteroscedasticity, linearity, normality of residuals, influential observations, and model specification—were evaluated using standard diagnostic tests. All models met these assumptions, with the exception of the CRM model, where heteroscedasticity was detected and addressed using Newey–West standard errors. Table 3 summarizes the diagnostic tests applied for each assumption.

Table 3. Diagnostic tests used to assess segmented regression model assumptions.

Model Assumption	Diagnostic Test(s) Applied
Autocorrelation	Durbin–Watson statistic Breusch–Godfrey test
Stationarity	Augmented Dickey–Fuller (ADF) test
Seasonality	STL Decomposition
Heteroscedasticity	Breusch–Pagan test White test

Table 3. *Cont.*

Model Assumption	Diagnostic Test(s) Applied
Linearity	Residuals vs. predictor variables plots
Normality of Residuals	Histogram Q-Q plot Shapiro–Wilk test
Influential Observations	Cook's Distance
Specification Errors	Ramsey's RESET test

4. Discussion

This study assessed the impact of an educational intervention on the diagnosis and treatment of BPPV using Interrupted Time Series (ITS) analysis. The findings offer important insights into the effectiveness of the intervention in improving adherence to key diagnostic maneuvers, including the Dix–Hallpike, Supine Roll, and Canalith Repositioning Maneuver (CRM). The ITS results demonstrated both immediate and sustained changes in practice patterns, indicating that the intervention was successful in promoting better alignment with clinical guidelines for BPPV management.

In interpreting these findings, it is also important to recognize that positional nystagmus (PN) can occur in healthy individuals without representing a pathological process. Studies have shown that PN is highly prevalent among asymptomatic adults, with reported rates of approximately 70% [18] and 88% [19]. Nelson et al. [20] proposed that nystagmus with a slow-phase velocity (SPV) $\leq 4°/s$ observed in $\leq$4 head positions is likely physiologic, particularly in the absence of vertigo. Domínguez-Durán et al. [21] further demonstrated that about 65% of healthy participants exhibit endpoint nystagmus during eccentric gaze without symptoms. Bisdorff et al. [22] also described upbeat PN in healthy subjects under dark conditions. These findings underscore the importance of not relying on nystagmus alone to diagnose BPPV. Instead, clinicians should consider the presence of vertigo during maneuvers, torsional eye movement components, fatigability of the response, and whether the SPV exceeds normative thresholds (e.g., >5°/s for horizontal, >6.5°/s for vertical PN). Over-diagnosis based solely on PN without accompanying clinical features should be avoided to prevent inappropriate treatment.

Although the intervention led to improvements in the use of diagnostic and treatment maneuvers, it did not result in a meaningful reduction in the use of CT scans. Even after adjusting for relevant confounders such as a history of BPPV and dizziness, no statistically significant decline in CT usage was observed. This suggests that while educational efforts can positively influence provider behavior for bedside practices, they may not be sufficient to alter decisions involving imaging, which are likely shaped by additional clinical, institutional, or medicolegal factors.

These findings underscore the complexity of changing imaging behaviors in clinical settings. Addressing the overuse of neuroimaging may require a combination of strategies, including decision support tools, institutional policies, audit and feedback mechanisms, or system-level changes in diagnostic pathways.

4.1. Interpretation of Key Findings

The analysis revealed that the Supine Roll test showed the most pronounced and sustained improvement following the intervention, with both immediate and long-term increases in usage.

In contrast, although the Dix–Hallpike maneuver showed a significant immediate increase in the unadjusted model, this effect became statistically non-significant after adjusting for patient-level confounders (β_2 adj. $p = 0.215$). This suggests that the initial post-intervention increase may have been influenced by shifts in patient characteristics—such as symptom presentation or prior BPPV history—rather than by the intervention alone. However, a statistically significant and positive long-term trend (β_3 adj. = 1.75, $p <$ 0.001) remained, indicating a gradual improvement in adherence over time.

These findings emphasize the importance of confounder adjustment in real-world evaluations and suggest that while the intervention did not produce an immediate effect on Dix–Hallpike usage, it may have facilitated sustained behavior change.

Similarly, the use of the CRM treatment maneuver showed both an immediate increase and a sustained upward trend, reflecting improved treatment delivery in line with best practice guidelines. In contrast, CT scan utilization did not exhibit meaningful change after the intervention. Although a slight increase was noted in the unadjusted model, this effect disappeared after adjusting for clinical history variables. This suggests that factors beyond provider education—such as diagnostic uncertainty in atypical or complex cases, institutional norms favoring imaging for liability protection, and medicolegal concerns regarding missed diagnoses—may continue to drive CT use. Additionally, the lack of integrated clinical decision support tools or system-level feedback may limit providers' ability to change imaging behavior based on education alone.

4.2. Comparison with Existing Literature

Our findings are consistent with prior studies that report educational interventions can lead to improvements in diagnostic accuracy and clinical practice adherence. For example, Neely et al. [6] used ITS analysis to evaluate interventions in emergency settings and found similar improvements in diagnostic behaviors. However, unlike their study, we did not observe a significant decrease in neuroimaging use, suggesting that imaging practices may be more resistant to change and influenced by local factors, such as institutional policies or clinician habits.

This difference highlights the importance of context when interpreting the impact of educational interventions. It also raises the need for further investigation into complementary strategies that might be more effective at curbing unnecessary imaging.

4.3. Strengths and Limitations

A major strength of this study is the use of ITS analysis, which offers a robust method for evaluating intervention effects over time. The application of Newey-West standard errors further strengthened the analysis by addressing heteroscedasticity where detected. Adjusting for relevant clinical confounders enhanced the internal validity of the findings.

Nonetheless, several limitations should be acknowledged. The study was limited to three healthcare institutions within Ontario, potentially affecting generalizability. The use of retrospective data may have introduced unmeasured confounding. Additionally, while bi-weekly aggregation was chosen to balance temporal resolution and statistical stability, different interval choices could yield slightly different estimates and should be considered in future studies.

5. Conclusions

This study applied Interrupted Time Series analysis to evaluate the effect of an educational intervention on the management of benign paroxysmal positional vertigo. The intervention was associated with increased use of diagnostic maneuvers, including Dix–Hallpike and Supine Roll, and with improved use of the CRM treatment technique. These findings support the value of educational programs in enhancing guideline-adherent care for BPPV.

However, the intervention did not lead to a significant reduction in CT scan usage, even after adjusting for relevant clinical confounders. This outcome highlights the challenges in altering imaging practices and suggests that education alone may be insufficient to drive such changes. Future efforts to reduce unnecessary imaging may require the integration of decision support systems, institutional policies, or provider feedback mechanisms.

Further research is needed to identify and evaluate multifaceted interventions that can address both clinical behavior and systemic factors influencing diagnostic decision-making.

Author Contributions: Conceptualization, E.A. and K.P.; methodology, E.A. and K.P.; software, E.A.; validation, E.A. and K.P.; formal analysis, E.A.; investigation, E.A.; resources, E.A. and R.O.; data curation, E.A. and R.O.; writing—original draft preparation, E.A. and K.P.; writing—review and editing, E.A.; visualization, E.A.; supervision, K.P. and R.O.; project administration, K.P. and R.O. All authors have read and agreed to the published version of the manuscript.

Funding: This research received no external funding.

Data Availability Statement: The datasets presented in this article are not readily available because the data has been acquired from the hospital in Sudbury, ON, Canada. Requests to access the datasets should be directed to the authors.

Conflicts of Interest: The authors declare no conflict of interest.

References

1. Von Brevern, M.; Radtke, A.; Lezius, F.; Feldmann, M.; Ziese, T.; Lempert, T.; Neuhauser, H. Epidemiology of benign paroxysmal positional vertigo: A population based study. *J. Neurol. Neurosurg. Psychiatry* **2006**, *78*, 710–715. [CrossRef] [PubMed]
2. Hu, Y.; Lu, Y.; Wang, S.; Quan, X.; Ren, Y.; Rong, K.; Pan, S.; Lu, X.; Chen, L.; Tian, C.; et al. Global research trends in benign paroxysmal positional vertigo: A bibliometric analysis. *Front. Neurol.* **2023**, *14*, 1204038. [CrossRef] [PubMed]
3. Hornibrook, J. Benign Paroxysmal Positional Vertigo (BPPV): History, pathophysiology, office treatment and future directions. *Int. J. Otolaryngol.* **2011**, *2011*, 835671. [CrossRef] [PubMed]
4. Cole, S.R.; Honaker, J.A. Benign paroxysmal positional vertigo: Effective diagnosis and treatment. *Clevel. Clin. J. Med.* **2022**, *89*, 653–662.
5. Lee, S.-H.; Kim, J.S. Benign paroxysmal positional vertigo. *J. Clin. Neurol.* **2010**, *6*, 51. [CrossRef] [PubMed]
6. Neely, P.; Patel, H.; McTaggart, J.; Bright, S.; Wellings, T. EVESTA: Emergency VESTIBULAR Algorithm and its impact on the acute management of benign paroxysmal positional vertigo. *Emerg. Med. Australas.* **2023**, *35*, 312–318. [CrossRef] [PubMed]
7. Self, W.H.; Speroff, T.; Grijalva, C.G.; McNaughton, C.D.; Ashburn, J.; Liu, D.; Arbogast, P.G.; Russ, S.; Storrow, A.B.; Talbot, T.R. Reducing blood culture contamination in the emergency department: An interrupted time series quality improvement study. *Acad. Emerg. Med.* **2013**, *20*, 89–97. [CrossRef] [PubMed]
8. Hudson, J.; Fielding, S.; Ramsay, C.R. Methodology and reporting characteristics of studies using interrupted time series design in healthcare. *BMC Med. Res. Methodol.* **2019**, *19*, 137. [CrossRef] [PubMed]
9. Turner, S.L.; Karahalios, A.; Forbes, A.B.; Taljaard, M.; Grimshaw, J.M.; Cheng, A.C.; Bero, L.; McKenzie, J.E. Design characteristics and statistical methods used in interrupted time series studies evaluating public health interventions: A review. *J. Clin. Epidemiol.* **2020**, *122*, 1–11. [CrossRef] [PubMed]
10. Wagner, A.K.; Soumerai, S.B.; Zhang, F.; Ross-Degnan, D. Segmented regression analysis of interrupted time series studies in medication use research. *J. Clin. Pharm. Ther.* **2002**, *27*, 299–309. [CrossRef] [PubMed]
11. Lopez Bernal, J.; Cummins, S.; Gasparrini, A. Interrupted time series regression for the evaluation of public health interventions: A tutorial. *Int. J. Epidemiol.* **2016**, *45*, dyw098. [CrossRef] [PubMed]
12. Turner, S.L.; Karahalios, A.; Forbes, A.B.; Taljaard, M.; Grimshaw, J.M.; McKenzie, J.E. Comparison of six statistical methods for interrupted time series studies: Empirical evaluation of 190 published series. *BMC Med. Res. Methodol.* **2021**, *21*, 134. [CrossRef] [PubMed]
13. Ewusie, J.E.; Soobiah, C.; Blondal, E.; Beyene, J.; Thabane, L.; Hamid, J.S. Methods, applications and challenges in the analysis of interrupted time series data: A scoping review. *J. Multidiscip. Healthc.* **2020**, *13*, 411–423. [CrossRef] [PubMed]
14. Wooldridge, J.M. *Introductory Econometrics: A Modern Approach*, 5th ed.; South-Western Cengage Learning: Mason, OH, USA, 2013.
15. Box, G.E.P.; Jenkins, G.M.; Reinsel, G.C.; Ljung, G.M. *Time Series Analysis: Forecasting and Control*, 5th ed.; Wiley Series in Probability and Statistics; John Wiley & Sons, Inc.: Hoboken, NJ, USA, 2016.

16. Montgomery, D.C.; Peck, E.A.; Vining, G.G. *Introduction to Linear Regression Analysis*, 5th ed.; Wiley Series in Probability and Statistics; John Wiley & Sons, Inc.: Hoboken, NJ, USA, 2012.
17. Lilja, D.J. *Linear Regression Using R: An Introduction to Data Modeling*, 1st ed.; University of Minnesota Libraries Publishing: Minneapolis, MN, USA, 2016. [CrossRef]
18. Rasmussen, M.B.; Sørensen, R.; Hougaard, D.D. Positional nystagmus is observed in the vast majority of healthy individuals. *Eur. Arch. Otorhinolaryngol.* **2024**, *281*, 3499–3507. [CrossRef] [PubMed]
19. Martens, C.; Goplen, F.K.; Nordfalk, K.F.; Aasen, T.; Nordahl, S.H.G. Prevalence and characteristics of positional nystagmus in normal subjects. *Otolaryngol. Head Neck Surg.* **2016**, *154*, 861–867. [CrossRef] [PubMed]
20. Nelson, M.D.; Mann, L.; Nicholson, C.; Lehman, M. Static positional nystagmus in the healthy vestibular system. *J. Am. Acad. Audiol.* **2019**, *30*, 883–895. [CrossRef] [PubMed]
21. Domínguez-Durán, E.; Prieto-Sanchez-de-Puerta, L.; Martín-Jiménez, D.I.; Sanchez-Gomez, S. Positional end-point nystagmus during positional testing: Prevalence, characteristics and differences with benign paroxysmal positional vertigo. *J. Clin. Med.* **2023**, *12*, 393. [CrossRef] [PubMed]
22. Bisdorff, A.R.; Sancovic, S.; Debatisse, D.; Bentley, C.; Gresty, M.A.; Bronstein, A.M. Positional nystagmus in the dark in normal subjects. *Neuro-Ophthalmology* **2000**, *24*, 283–290. [CrossRef]

algorithms

MDPI

Article

Understanding Physiological Responses for Intelligent Posture and Autonomic Response Detection Using Wearable Technology

Chaitanya Vardhini Anumula [1], Tanvi Banerjee [1] and William Lee Romine [2,*]

[1] Department of Computer Science and Engineering, College of Engineering and Computer Science, Wright State University, Fairborn, OH 45435, USA; anumula.12@wright.edu (C.V.A.); tanvi.banerjee@wright.edu (T.B.)
[2] Department of Biological Sciences, College of Science and Mathematics, Wright State University, Fairborn, OH 45435, USA
* Correspondence: william.romine@wright.edu

Abstract: This study investigates how Iyengar yoga postures influence autonomic nervous system (ANS) activity by analyzing multimodal physiological signals collected via wearable sensors. The goal was to explore whether subtle postural variations elicit measurable autonomic responses and to identify which sensor features most effectively capture these changes. Participants performed a sequence of yoga poses while wearing synchronized sensors measuring electrodermal activity (EDA), heart rate variability, skin temperature, and motion. Interpretable machine learning models, including linear classifiers, were trained to distinguish physiological states and rank feature relevance. The results revealed that even minor postural adjustments led to significant shifts in ANS markers, with phasic EDA and RR interval features showing heightened sensitivity. Surprisingly, micro-movements captured via accelerometry and transient electrodermal reactivity, specifically EDA peak-to-RMS ratios, emerged as dominant contributors to classification performance. These findings suggest that small-scale kinematic and autonomic shifts, which are often overlooked, play a central role in the physiological effects of yoga. The study demonstrates that wearable sensor analytics can decode a more nuanced and granular physiological profile of mind–body practices than traditionally appreciated, offering a foundation for precision-tailored biofeedback systems and advancing objective approaches to yoga-based interventions.

Keywords: autonomic nervous system; sympathetic and parasympathetic autonomic responses; Iyengar yoga; wearable; machine learning

1. Introduction

The autonomic nervous system (ANS) governs involuntary physiological processes through its sympathetic and parasympathetic branches, which respectively mediate arousal ("fight or flight") and recovery ("rest and digest") responses to maintain homeostatic balance [1]. Increasing parasympathetic autonomic activity is associated with numerous health benefits, including improved cardiovascular health [2] and anti-inflammatory effects [3], which are particularly valuable for managing chronic conditions. Chronic stress, cardiovascular risks, hypertension, and other ill health conditions are associated with sympathetic activity dominance or dysregulation [4,5]. Among the various yoga styles, Iyengar yoga [6] is uniquely suited for improving parasympathetic activity of the autonomic nervous system (ANS) due to its focus on precise body alignment while performing the posture (asana), targeted engagement of muscle groups, and sustained postural engagement. In Iyengar yoga, props like blocks, blankets, and straps are used to assist with alignment, deepen poses, allowing participants to spend more time in the asana, which often leads to the yoga only being performed under the guidance of certified instructors. This limits the extensive use of such therapeutic yoga for individuals on their own, which, in turn, decreases the possibility of gathering data in such settings. This study is one such setting where data was collected with the agreement of both the yoga practitioner and participants. The analysis of physiological mechanisms of Iyengar yoga, a relatively data-scarce area, was carried out in this study using robust and interpretable machine learning models. To that end, the study was guided by the following research questions:

1. Can machine learning models distinguish between different physiological states (relaxed vs. parasympathetic-inducing/sympathetic poses) based on features derived from physiological signals captured by the wearable device?
2. Can the models differentiate between sympathetic and parasympathetic autonomic responses based on pose-induced physiological changes?
3. What features contribute strongly to this distinction? Are there any physiological patterns specific to each autonomic response?

2. Related Work

Yoga therapy is known to improve cardiac autonomic tone and vagal modulation [7], and the practice of yoga therapy and breath work (pranayama) influences autonomic nervous system (ANS) function by enhancing parasympathetic activity and reducing sympathetic activation [8]. Preliminary studies, such as [9], have reported improvements in ambulation, mental health, and pain management, while others, such as [10,11], have highlighted its potential in addressing clinical depression and stress-related symptoms. Iyengar yoga's practice of holding poses for extended durations (5–10 min), as recommended by [12], facilitates the release of the myotatic reflex, increasing muscular range of motion and potentially eliciting distinct physiological responses.

However, these studies are limited to specific populations or conditions, and there is a need for more rigorous longitudinal research to better understand the physiological mechanisms underlying these benefits. To address this gap, a multi-case longitudinal study design is proposed through this study to investigate the physiological effects of Iyengar yoga at the pose level. Building on prior research, such as [13], which demonstrated improvements in acute physiological measures like arterial blood pressure and heart rate during 90 min yoga sessions, these measures were analyzed in this study at the *pose-level*. While the previous studies employed survey-based [9,11] and Holter ECG monitoring-based [7] data collection, EmbracePlus, a wearable smart watch, was employed in this study to record physiological data and ANS activity was measured using skin temperature, electrodermal activity (EDA), heart-rate variability, and other vitals, to assess sympathetic and parasympathetic responses. Prior studies [7] used statistical analyses and report-based methods, where as, machine learning models were implemented in this study to advance the understanding of differences in physiological responses at pose-level, lasting an average of 5–10 min, as opposed to entire 90 min sessions in previous studies [13].

3. Materials and Methods

3.1. Experimental Design

The EmbracePlus smartwatch (Empatica, Oakland, CA, USA), a wearable device equipped with multisensor capabilities, was used to continuously capture high-frequency physiological data from participants before and during the yoga sessions. The EmbracePlus device was configured to record raw data from a range of biosensors, including body-movement signals, blood volume pulse (BVP), electrodermal activity (EDA), skin temperature, and heart rate variability signals. Data were recorded under two primary conditions: a *baseline* phase, during which participants remained at their normal and restful state for approximately 5 minutes prior to the yoga session, and a *postural* phase, in which participants engaged in 1–2 specific Iyengar yoga poses altogether for an average duration of 11.75 min. The choice of yoga poses for each participant was made at the discretion of a certified yoga practitioner, Dr. Anuradha Oak, based on the participant's physical condition and needs, with the goal of eliciting either sympathetic or parasympathetic autonomic responses. Poses aimed at eliciting sympathetic activation, as shown in Figure 1a, involved greater muscular engagement or sustained effort, such as holding challenging positions for extended periods, thus promoting alertness and physiological arousal. In contrast, poses designed to elicit parasympathetic activation were generally passive and restorative, as shown in Figure 1b, requiring minimal muscular effort and allowing the participant to settle into the posture over time. Example poses/asanas are as in Table 1. Each pose was annotated with its intended autonomic effect (see Table 2) according to the expert assessment of the certified practitioner, rather than being grounded in direct physiological measurement. While this approach carries inherent subjectivity, it is consistent with other biomedical studies, such as [14], where expert interpretation serves as a reference standard in the absence of direct ground-truth measures. In addition to that, a subjective score of the perceived difficulty level by the participant, on a scale out of 5 was recorded using a post yoga session survey, with 50% of the participants reporting a difficulty level of 4 and 5. A chi-square test of independence was conducted to examine the association between autonomic response (sympathetic vs. parasympathetic) and participant's perceived difficulty level (rated 1 to 5) during postural engagement. The association was statistically significant, $\chi^2(4, N = [202]) = 45.49, p < 0.001$, (N = 202, accounting for the postural samples only), indicating that the difficulty level varied depending on the physiological state. The effect size, measured by Cramér's V, was 0.475, suggesting a moderate to strong association between autonomic state and perceived difficulty, implying that participants' autonomic responses are meaningfully related to their reported difficulty during yoga postures.

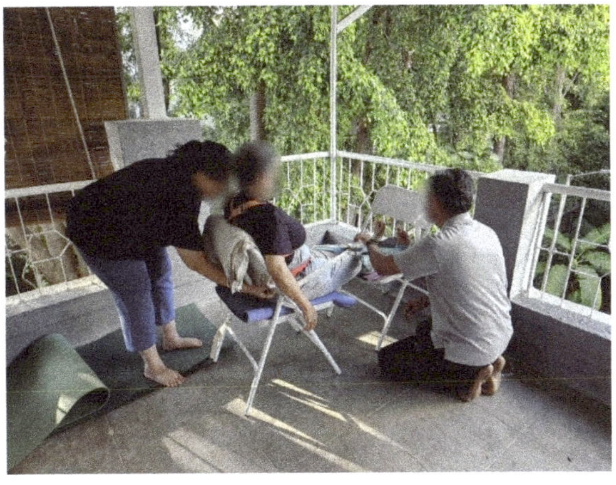

(**a**) Dandasana

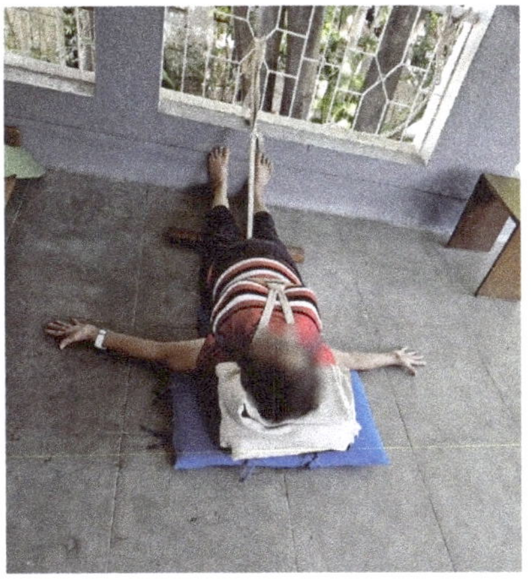

(**b**) Suptavirasana

Figure 1. Example poses for eliciting (**a**) sympathetic and (**b**) parasympathetic autonomic responses.

Overall, eleven wearable sensor signals were collected using the sensors of EmbracePlus, as shown in Table 3, to analyze physiological responses. Sessions were tagged in EmbracePlus at respective intervals for further analysis, i.e, the start and end of baseline and postural phases, respectively. The tagged activities were also cross-verified using the manual entry of timestamps recorded during the sessions. Each session lasted for approximately 20 min combining the baseline and postural phases. The baseline phase ranged from 2 to 10 min with an average of 3 min, while postural phase ranged from 10 to 20 min with an average of 11.75 min. An imbalance in the distribution of the sampled data was observed due to the unequal durations of the baseline and postural phases and our one-minute sampling interval, as seen in Figure 2, to predict the physiological states. An analysis of these physiological states based on differences in physiological features between the baseline and postural phases was performed using machine learning models such as logistic regression, Gaussian Naive Bayes, Decision Tree, Random Forest, and Support Vector Machines.

Table 1. Asanas (poses) selected by the certified practitioner for the subjects.

Asana	Description
Suptavirasana (Figure 1b)	Reclining Hero Pose
Suptabadhakonasana	Reclining Bound Angle Pose
Baddhakonasana	Bound Angle Pose (also known as Cobbler's Pose)
Setubandha	Bridge Pose (specifically, Supported Bridge Pose in the Iyengar tradition)
Viprit Dandasana	Inverted Staff Pose
Padangushtasana	Big Toe Pose
Dandasana (Figure 1a)	Staff Pose
Viprit karani	Legs-Up-the-Wall Pose
Trikonasana	Triangle Pose

Table 2. Definitions of baseline, parasympathetic, and sympathetic conditions used in the study.

Label	Description
Baseline	At Rest/Ease—When the participant is just not actively doing anything
Parasympathetic	In Pose—Engaged in a yoga pose eliciting parasympathetic ANS response
Sympathetic	In Pose—Engaged in a yoga pose eliciting sympathetic ANS response

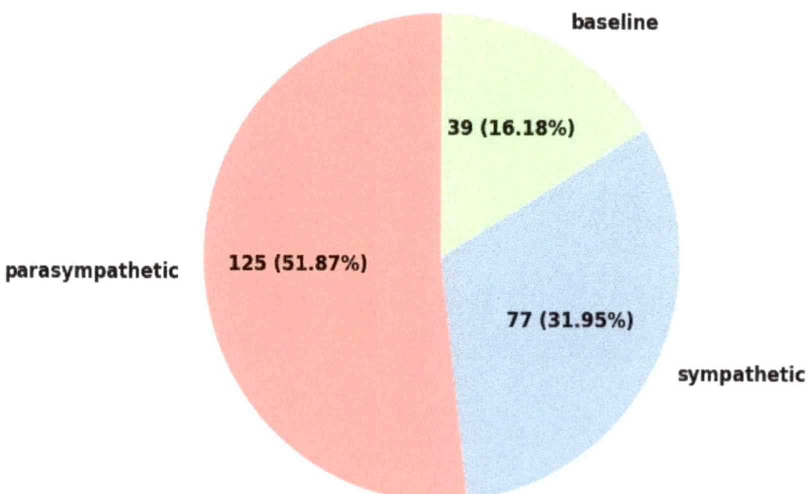

Figure 2. Distribution of subjects across baseline, sympathetic, and parasympathetic groups.

Using a convenience sampling approach, based on the availability, different subjects were recruited for the study. The risk of complications included subjects with a low risk (general fitness), moderate risk (musculoskeletal disorders), and high risk (chronic cardio-endocrine-musculoskeletal disorders). A total of 16 subjects were studied, with 10 female and 6 male subjects, aged between 30 and 65 years. The majority, 75%, reported having 0–1 years of experience with yoga, with a notable proportion (62.5%) falling within the 50–60-year age group. Targeted yoga poses were recommended to subjects based on their profiles. For example, subjects who lacked strength and tone of muscles to even hold the poses were recommended poses that elicit sympathetic response to build and improve the tone of muscles. An assessment of their engagement and postural alignment in a particular yoga pose was conducted using the judgment of the certified yoga practitioner. In total, 93.75% of subjects were observed to be *engaged* as required during the yoga poses, as per the therapist's assessment.

Table 3. Summary of sensor types and the physiological metrics recorded.

Sensor	Description
Acceleration (Acc-X, Acc-Y, Acc-Z)	The rate of change of velocity of an object with respect to time in three axes.
Blood Volume Pulse (BVP)	A measure of blood flow changes in the microvascular system, often used to assess heart rate and autonomic nervous system activity.
Electrodermal Activity (EDA)	The measure of continuous variation in the electrical characteristics of the skin, also known as skin conductance response (SCR) or electrodermal activity (EDA).
Skin Temperature (SkinTemp)	The temperature of the surface of the skin.
Systolic Peak Timestamp	The highest blood pressure value in arteries during a heartbeat, representing the peak pressure when the heart contracts.
Angular velocity (Gyro-X, Gyro-Y, Gyro-Z)	The velocity of an object rotating or revolving in three axes.
Steps (Steps)	The number of accumulated steps.

Note: The two sensor measurements (Angular velocity and Steps) were not used in the current analysis scope.

Data were collected using EmbracePlus at a frequency of 64 Hz, leaving us with *sixty-four* data points per *second*. Especially in a therapeutic yoga setting like Iyengar yoga, unlike strenuous activities such as running or any vinyasa practice, the physiological response does not vary drastically in a short period of time; therefore, the data were downsampled to *one* data point per *minute*. For example, the continuous data from the 5 min baseline phase, with data being recorded 3840 times a minute, was reduced to 1 time per minute, thus giving five data points for the baseline phase. This was carried out by averaging the 64 data points per sec to 1 data point per sec and 60 such data points (or less for few samples) per minute were averaged down to 1 data point per minute. With this approach, for the baseline and postural phases of 16 participants, a total of 247 min of data were obtained, i.e., 247 data points. Given this experimental design, wherein each participant contributed data from only two distinct sessions (baseline and postural) across 16 individuals, yielding 32 sessions in total, there was no complex nested repeated measures structure in the dataset. Therefore, traditional ANOVA and MANOVA approaches, with appropriate corrections such as Tukey's Honest Significant Difference (HSD) test [15] for multiple comparisons, were considered valid for the current scope of the study.

3.2. Feature Extraction

To transform the raw sensor signals listed in Table 3 to a more suitable data representation format, feature extraction was applied on the raw signals. Within the current Iyengar style of yoga therapy, the poses focus mainly on the alignment of the musculoskeletal system in a particular pose and holding that pose for a certain period. Consequently, the steps count and three-axis gyroscope signals were not considered for further analysis in this study. From the three-axis accelerometer signals, the accelerometer magnitude feature was extracted and the RR interval was extracted from systolic peaks. For the five signals, (extracted accelerometer magnitude, *blood volume pulse*, *electrodermal activity*, *skin temperature*, *extracted RR interval*), eight features for each of the signals were extracted. Table 4 provides a detailed description of all the features. The feature extraction yielded up to a total of 40 (5 × 8) features. These extracted features represented the properties of the original raw signals while reducing the volume of data. To reduce the redundant information, all features that correlated positively or negatively with other features at a level of at least 0.8 were eliminated, and 26 features were left in the feature set.

Table 4. Summary of computed features and their mathematical descriptions.

Feature	Description
Mean	Average value of the signal
Standard Deviation	Amount of variation of the signal
Mean of Derivative	Average rate of change of the signal
Root Mean Square (RMS)	Square root of the mean of the squares of a set of values
Peak to Peak	Difference between the maximum and minimum peak
Peak to RMS	The ratio of the largest absolute value to the RMS value
Number of Peaks	Number of local maximums (peaks)
Sample Entropy	Sample Entropy (*SampEn*) is a measure of complexity that quantifies the unpredictability of fluctuations in a time series. It is computed as: $$SampEn(m,r,N) = -\ln\left(\frac{A}{B}\right)$$ where A is the number of matched template vectors of length $m+1$, and B is the number of matched template vectors of length m

Embedded feature selection methods that perform feature selection in the process of training, such as L1-Regularized Logistic Regression (LASSO), Random Forest (RF) feature importance, Decision Tree (DT) feature importance, Gaussian Naive Bayes individual feature probabilities, Support Vector Machine (SVM) coefficient magnitudes, were used. LASSO applies an L1 penalty, which enforces sparsity by shrinking some coefficients to zero, effectively eliminating less relevant features. RF feature importance was computed based on the mean decrease in impurity (Gini index), aggregating information across multiple decision trees to provide a stable ranking of feature relevance. Additionally, DT feature importance, derived from a single decision tree, measures the contribution of each feature to reducing node impurity. While DT feature importance may be more sensitive to data variations compared to RF, it provides an interpretable, tree-structured assessment of feature relevance. Gaussian Naive Bayes (GNB) evaluates feature importance based on the probability distributions of each feature given the class label. Since GNB assumes conditional independence among features, it assigns importance by analyzing how strongly individual features contribute to class separation based on their likelihood estimates. This method is particularly useful for identifying features with distinct distributions across different classes, although it may not fully capture complex feature interactions. Linear Support Vector Machine (SVM) models assess feature relevance based on the absolute magnitude of learned weights, with larger weight magnitudes indicating greater influence on the classification decision boundary.

To systematically identify the most informative features while mitigating redundancy and overfitting, all embedded feature selection methods were evaluated under a stratified

10-fold cross-validation framework. This approach preserves class balance within each fold and provides a population-level assessment of physiological state separability, highlighting differences across the baseline, sympathetic, and parasympathetic phases irrespective of individual variation. To complement this holistic view, Leave-One-Subject-Out Cross-Validation (LOGO-CV) [16] was additionally employed, which offers a stricter estimate of subject-independent generalization by ensuring that no individual's data appear simultaneously in training and testing. In this approach, data from a single participant were held out as the test set, while the remaining participants' data were used to train the model. This process was repeated iteratively until every subject had served once as the test set, ensuring that no data from the same individual appeared simultaneously in training and testing, i.e, 16-fold CV. Unlike the stratified 10-fold cross-validation that was implemented, LOGO-CV provides a stricter and more realistic estimate of performance in scenarios where models must generalize to entirely new individuals. Performance metrics were computed for each held-out subject, and both the area under the receiver operating characteristic curve (AUC) and the F1-score were reported to capture the overall discriminative ability and class-balanced predictive accuracy, respectively. Final results are presented as mean $\pm$ standard deviation across all subjects, and per-subject performance distributions were analyzed to highlight inter-individual variability.

4. Results and Discussion

A multivariate analysis of variance (MANOVA) was conducted to evaluate the overall effect of the physiological state on a set of 40 physiological features. The multivariate test revealed a highly significant effect of the state on the combined physiological profile (Wilks' Lambda = 0.111, F(80, 398) = 9.98, $p < 0.001$), with a large effect size (η_p^2 = 0.889), indicating that approximately 89% of the variance in physiological responses is attributable to the underlying state. To further investigate which specific features contributed to this effect, follow-up univariate analyses were conducted on each feature. Thirty-two features were found to be significantly different across states at a stringent threshold of $p < 0.01$ and power > 0.8. For each of these features, the group means and standard deviations for baseline, parasympathetic, and sympathetic states are reported in Table 5. To identify which physiological states differed significantly on each feature, post hoc comparisons using Tukey's Honest Significant Difference (HSD) test were performed, which was also leveraged in other studies [15].

These comparisons revealed consistent patterns of autonomic modulation across sensor modalities. Notably, sympathetic states were associated with significantly elevated skin conductance variability (e.g., EDA std dev, EDA peak to peak), increased cardiovascular reactivity (e.g., BVP std dev, RR interval peak to peak), and greater temperature fluctuations (temperature std dev, peak to peak), relative to both baseline and parasympathetic conditions. In contrast, parasympathetic states exhibited increased mean RR intervals and lower accelerometer-derived motion features, consistent with reduced physiological arousal and physical movement. Baseline states typically showed intermediate values but were statistically distinct from the other two states for several features. These univariate results, supported by robust post hoc evidence, provide strong validation that specific physiological features reliably differentiate between autonomic states. The consistent group-wise differences across modalities affirm the potential of multimodal sensor fusion for state classification and underscore the biological plausibility of the derived features in capturing autonomic state dynamics. Based on this, subsequent analyses focused on feature-level importance using supervised machine learning models, aiming to identify core physiological features that are predictive of each physiological state.

Table 5. Univariate ANOVA results with effect sizes and descriptive statistics across physiological states.

Feature	F-Value	η_p^2	Baseline_m	Baseline_{SD}	Parasym_m	Parasym_{SD}	Sym_m	Sym_{SD}
Accelerometer Peak to Peak	64.55	0.35	−0.40	1.12	0.20	0.88	−0.05	1.09
Accelerometer Standard Deviation	62.56	0.34	1.18	1.64	−0.37	0.15	−0.06	0.64
Accelerometer Peak to RMS	59.75	0.33	1.18	1.70	−0.35	0.18	−0.10	0.57
RR Peak to Peak	57.78	0.33	1.28	1.43	−0.34	0.51	−0.11	0.84
RR Standard Deviation	52.69	0.31	1.25	1.54	−0.33	0.49	−0.10	0.82
EDA Peak to RMS	52.02	0.30	0.96	1.52	−0.46	0.26	0.18	0.84
RR Peak to RMS	46.38	0.28	1.12	1.40	−0.36	0.35	−0.01	1.01
Temperature Standard Deviation	44.45	0.27	1.09	1.79	−0.21	0.46	−0.29	0.33
BVP RMS	44.40	0.27	1.15	1.45	−0.38	0.67	0.00	0.81
BVP Mean	44.06	0.27	1.14	1.45	−0.38	0.68	0.01	0.81
Temperature Peak to Peak	39.25	0.25	1.03	1.82	−0.20	0.46	−0.28	0.31
BVP Standard Deviation	28.38	0.19	0.85	1.93	−0.19	0.34	−0.26	0.16
BVP Peak to Peak	27.90	0.19	0.85	1.94	−0.19	0.33	−0.25	0.18
Temperature Peak to RMS	24.53	0.17	0.83	1.96	−0.16	0.37	−0.23	0.26
Temperature Number of Peaks	19.77	0.14	−0.89	0.88	0.20	0.95	−0.14	0.98
EDA Peak to Peak	17.30	0.13	0.67	1.60	−0.25	0.36	−0.00	0.91
EDA Mean Derivative	16.93	0.12	0.72	1.53	−0.24	0.35	0.04	1.09
EDA Standard Deviation	15.64	0.12	0.64	1.59	−0.25	0.36	0.01	0.94
RR Number of Peaks	13.74	0.10	−0.51	0.87	0.25	1.07	−0.40	0.98
Accelerometer Sample Entropy	11.07	0.09	−0.53	0.98	0.20	0.92	−0.36	1.20
RR RMS	8.69	0.07	0.16	0.62	0.19	1.07	−0.36	0.86
RR Mean	8.63	0.07	0.11	0.63	0.20	1.06	−0.36	0.86
Accelerometer Number of Peaks	8.32	0.07	−0.42	0.88	0.23	1.08	−0.27	1.12
Temperature Mean Derivative	7.16	0.06	0.51	1.99	−0.10	0.49	−0.08	0.47
EDA Mean	6.44	0.05	0.00	1.05	0.25	1.04	−0.27	0.89
EDA RMS	6.37	0.05	0.01	1.06	0.24	1.04	−0.27	0.89
Accelerometer Mean	5.70	0.05	−0.40	1.12	0.20	0.00	0.05	1.09
Temperature Sample Entropy	5.66	0.05	−0.52	1.01	0.10	1.01	−0.04	1.00
Temperature Mean	5.59	0.04	−0.33	1.03	−0.05	0.92	0.31	1.18
Temperature RMS	5.59	0.04	−0.33	1.03	−0.05	0.92	0.31	1.18
Accelerometer RMS	5.57	0.04	−0.40	1.11	0.19	0.88	−0.05	1.09
Accelerometer Mean Derivative	5.38	0.04	−0.46	1.92	0.03	0.24	0.13	0.89

Note: Only features with p-value < 0.001 and statistical-power > 0.8 are included. Means and SDs are group statistics of respective physiological states and are represented as $\text{State}_{m\ or\ SD}$.

In this study, the feasibility and performance of various machine learning models were explored for distinguishing three physiological states: baseline, parasympathetic-dominant, and sympathetic-dominant poses from wearable sensor data in the context of Iyengar yoga. Given that this is the first known study exploring physiological signal classification within the specific practice of Iyengar yoga using machine learning techniques, we prioritized generalizability, interpretability, and robustness in our model selection process. Simpler and computationally efficient models were deliberately chosen to reduce the risk of overfitting in a low-data regime, a common concern when initiating modeling in novel application domains with no prior machine learning baselines. All models were evaluated using *10-fold stratified cross-validation* to ensure performance estimates were robust and class proportions preserved across folds. This approach enhanced the reliability of our findings despite limited data availability. Table 6 with comparative model performances reveals that ensemble learning and margin-based approaches are more suited to distinguish physiological states than probabilistic or linear models. The Random Forest model achieved the highest performance across all evaluation metrics, with an accuracy, precision, recall, and F1-score of 0.94 and an AUC of 0.99, which can be attributed to its ability to capture complex, nonlinear relationships and reduce variance through ensembling. In physiological signals, such nonlinearities are common due to individual variability, sensor noise, and the interaction of autonomic responses (e.g., heart rate, respiration, and electrodermal activity often covary under stress).

Table 6. Stratified 10-fold cross-validation model performances for physiological state prediction.

Metric	Logistic Regression	Naive Bayes	Decision Tree	SVM	Random Forest
Accuracy	0.78	0.69	0.85	0.84	0.94
F1-score	0.78	0.67	0.85	0.83	0.93
Precision	0.79	0.70	0.86	0.85	0.94
Recall	0.78	0.69	0.85	0.84	0.94
AUC	0.91	0.83	0.87	0.93	0.99

The SVM model also performed well, with an F1-score of 0.86 and AUC of 0.95, demonstrating strong performance particularly with the use of a linear kernel indicating a strong discrimination capability and balanced precision–recall tradeoff. The Decision Tree, outperforming logistic regression (F1-score = 0.70) and Naive Bayes (F1-score = 0.65), provided decent results (F1-score = 0.80) but was still susceptible to overfitting. These differences highlight the varying capacity of models to handle nonlinear patterns and interdependent physiological features. In contrast, logistic regression's performance indicated that linear models lack the flexibility to capture interdependencies in physiological signals, despite L1 regularization aiding in sparsity and interpretability. Naive Bayes exhibited the weakest performance, reflecting the impracticality of its core assumption of feature independence. Given the biological correlations among physiological channels (e.g., respiration affecting both BVP and temperature), this assumption is violated, leading to degraded model fidelity. Despite their reduced flexibility, both models showed reasonable performance. Failing to detect a sympathetic state (false negative) may result in missed intervention opportunities, whereas false positives can lead to unnecessary feedback or false alarms. Hence, maximizing both recall and precision is essential, making F1-score a central metric for model selection. These findings suggest that, for real-world deployment in biofeedback systems, models like Random Forest and SVM offer a favorable balance of accuracy, reliability, and interpretability.

4.1. *Leave-One-Group-Out (LOGO) Cross-Validation*

Leave-One-Subject-Out Cross-Validation (LOGO-CV) revealed substantial heterogeneity in classification performance across participants and models as seen in Table 7. On average, SVM achieved the highest discriminative power with an AUC of 0.89 ± 0.13, closely followed by logistic regression (LR, 0.88 ± 0.15) and Random Forest (RF, 0.82 ± 0.19), while Decision Tree (DT)'s performance was markedly less stable (0.66 ± 0.24). In terms of F1-scores, which better reflect balanced precision and recall, LR (0.62 ± 0.38) and RF (0.60 ± 0.37) provided the strongest results, with SVM (0.57 ± 0.36), DT (0.51 ± 0.37), and Naive Bayes (NB, 0.50 ± 0.36) performing less consistently. Importantly, the large standard deviations across all models highlight pronounced subject-level variability: while some participants (e.g., Subject 4, Subject 6, Subject 9) as in Figure 3, were classified with near-perfect accuracy across models (AUC and F1 ≈ 1.0), others (e.g., Subject 1, Subject 13, Subject 15) consistently approached chance-level outcomes (AUC ≈ 0.5, F1 ≤ 0.1). In several cases, models achieved high AUC but low F1 (e.g., Subject 3, Subject 8, Subject 14), suggesting that class probabilities were ranked correctly but hard decision thresholds failed, likely due to class imbalance or weak physiological separability. These patterns reinforce that model success is not uniform—for some individuals, physiological signals aligned well with the intended sympathetic/parasympathetic labels, while for others, either signal noise, atypical autonomic responses, or limited generalizability. Overall, while population-level metrics suggested strong average discriminative ability, the LOGO-CV analysis underscores the importance of inter-individual variability and points toward the need for personalized calibration or subgroup-specific modeling approaches in future work.

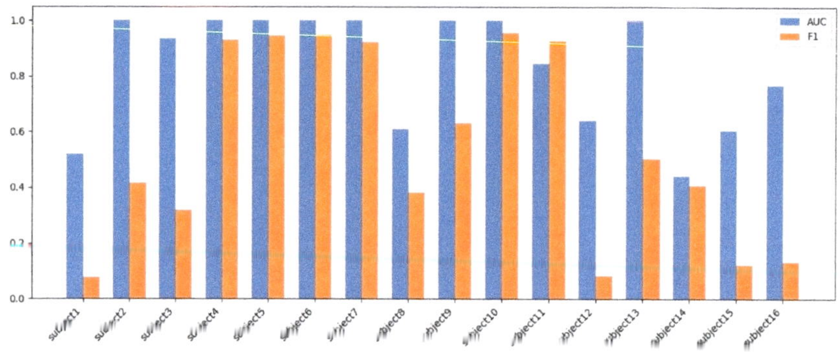

Figure 3. Random Forest (RF) model's per-subject AUC vs. F1.

Table 7. Per-subject model performance: AUC and F1-score.

Participant	DT		LR		NB		RF		SVM	
	AUC	F1	AUC	F1	AUC	F1	AUC	F1	AUC	F1
subject1	0.25	0.00	0.87	0.07	0.68	0.24	0.52	0.07	0.50	0.12
subject2	0.75	0.22	1.00	0.94	0.96	0.78	1.00	0.41	0.96	0.87
subject3	0.55	0.15	0.72	0.07	0.92	0.09	0.93	0.32	0.88	0.35
subject4	0.94	0.92	1.00	1.00	1.00	0.70	1.00	0.93	1.00	1.00
subject5	0.75	0.90	1.00	0.94	1.00	1.00	1.00	0.94	1.00	0.83
subject6	0.86	0.71	1.00	0.91	1.00	0.94	1.00	0.94	1.00	0.83
subject7	1.00	1.00	1.00	1.00	1.00	0.78	1.00	0.92	1.00	1.00
subject8	0.50	0.58	0.52	0.21	0.58	0.09	0.61	0.38	0.57	0.30
subject9	0.70	0.77	1.00	0.00	1.00	0.09	1.00	0.63	0.75	0.34
subject10	0.25	0.00	0.68	0.45	0.18	0.36	1.00	0.95	0.45	0.83
subject11	0.67	0.85	0.73	0.92	1.00	0.96	0.84	0.92	0.57	0.92
subject12	0.60	0.04	0.64	0.47	1.00	0.81	0.64	0.08	0.71	0.45
subject13	0.25	0.12	1.00	0.03	1.00	0.94	1.00	0.50	0.98	0.03
subject14	0.64	0.61	0.56	0.50	0.56	0.34	0.44	0.40	0.83	0.44
subject15	0.39	0.12	0.53	0.00	0.64	0.32	0.60	0.12	0.50	0.56
subject16	0.43	0.30	1.00	0.25	0.88	0.45	0.76	0.13	0.86	0.21

4.2. Building Sparse Models

Given the variability in model performance and inherent differences in learning paradigms, model-specific feature selection and interpretation were performed. Importantly, for building sparse models, we analyzed the feature importances, coefficients, and probabilities from the 10-fold cross-validation metrics and chose top-k, where *k* was the minimal number of features per model, as shown in Figure 4; thus, when used on a hold-out test set, it gave the best performance when compared with the base models using full feature set on a single train-test split setting, shown in Table 8. This individual top-k features per model approach avoids the risk of overinterpreting features from underperforming models and provides a more grounded understanding of physiological drivers for each classifier. Furthermore, any convergent features across models were noted as candidates for robust domain-level significance, for future investigation.

Several features appeared repeatedly in the top-k sets across models, indicating their robust relevance across different models and that they likely encode the most physiologically salient information for differentiating between relaxed, sympathetic-inducing, and parasympathetic-inducing physiological states. For instance, *accelerometer*-related features may reflect postural transitions, while *BVP*-related features relate to cardiovascular activity, which can vary under sympathetic arousal. *EDA*-related features capture phasic electrodermal responses and *temperature*-related features may reflect thermoregulatory shifts associated with relaxation or physical effort.

Random Forest emphasized both EDA dynamics (peak_rms, mean_derivative) and cardiorespiratory indicators like rr_std_dev, with its top features balancing well across modalities: EDA, BVP, temperature, RR interval, and accelerometry, indicating an ensemble's ability to capture inter-modality patterns. Logistic regression's top weights were assigned to features like eda_mean, peak_rms, and bvp_mean, aligning with known markers of autonomic state. Its reliance on a smaller but informative set of linearly separable features helped construct a compact and effective model. Naive Bayes highlighted more basic statistical descriptors (means, std devs), avoiding derivatives or entropy measures, making sense given NB's independence assumptions, and confirming it can serve as a lightweight, reasonably performant baseline.

Table 8. Comparison of full vs. sparse (top-k) feature models across classifiers.

Metric	LR ($k = 6$)		NB ($k = 8$)		DT ($k = 6$)		SVM ($k = 15$)		RF ($k = 9$)	
	Full	Sparse	Full	Sparse	Full	Sparse	Full	Sparse	Full	Sparse
Accuracy	0.78	0.82	0.69	0.71	0.85	0.87	0.84	0.87	0.94	0.97
F1-score	0.78	0.81	0.67	0.68	0.85	0.87	0.83	0.87	0.93	0.97
Precision	0.79	0.82	0.70	0.67	0.86	0.88	0.85	0.88	0.94	0.98
Recall	0.78	0.82	0.69	0.67	0.85	0.87	0.84	0.87	0.94	0.97
AUC	0.91	0.92	0.83	0.82	0.87	0.88	0.93	0.93	0.99	0.99

k indicates the number of top features selected for the sparse model.

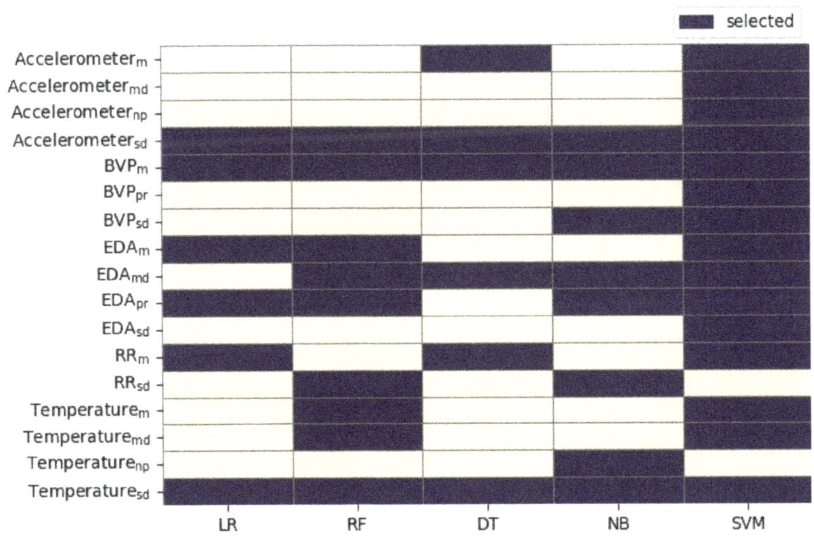

Figure 4. Top K optimal number of features per model based on the best performance. *Feature abbreviations*: Feature$_{sd}$ = Signal Standard Deviation; Feature$_m$ = Signal Mean; Feature$_{md}$ = Signal Mean Derivative; Feature$_{np}$ = Signal Number of Peaks; Feature$_{pr}$ = Signal Peak to RMS.

Consistent top features across the five models include *acc_std_dev*: a strong proxy for physical stillness vs. movement; *bvp_mean*: reflecting average blood flow changes tied to autonomic tone; *eda_peak_rms*: capturing phasic EDA response directly correlating sympathetic arousal; *temp_std_dev*: fluctuating skin temperature demonstrating transient autonomic reactions across conditions; and *rr_std_dev*: indicating variability in heart rate (HRV), a widely used marker of autonomic balance. Movement (accelerometer) and Cardiac

Signals (RR interval, BVP) were consistent top contributors, reflecting the interplay between posture, movement, and cardiac autonomic regulation during Iyengar yoga. Electrodermal and Temperature Signals underline the importance of arousal and peripheral circulation as non-invasive autonomic markers. Derivative and standard deviation signals were frequently selected over simple means, reinforcing the strength of dynamic features over static values in distinguishing subtle physiological states. A small number of features (especially those related to EDA, BVP, and HRV) consistently drove the classifiers' performance. These overlaps point to robust candidate features for autonomic state differentiation, offering stable physiological markers across multiple algorithmic viewpoints, despite their inherent modeling differences.

To assess the potential confounding impact of movement-related (accelerometer) features, we conducted an ablation experiment excluding all accelerometer-derived features and re-trained each classifier. As summarized in Table 9, the stratified cross-validation performance remained high across models (e.g., Random Forest: accuracy 0.94, F1 0.94, AUC 0.99 without the accelerometer), closely matching the results obtained with the full feature set that included movement metrics. These observations confirm that the models are not exclusively leveraging pose-related movement differences, but also capture meaningful autonomic signal modulation reflected in the heart rate variability, EDA, temperature, and BVP.

Table 9. Model performances with all features vs. without accelerometer features (stratified 10-fold CV).

Model	Feature Set	Accuracy	F1-Score	Precision	Recall	AUC
LR	All Feat.	0.78	0.78	0.79	0.78	0.91
LR	No Acc.	0.76	0.75	0.77	0.76	0.90
RF	All Feat.	0.94	0.93	0.94	0.94	0.99
RF	No Acc.	0.94	0.94	0.94	0.94	0.99
DT	All Feat.	0.85	0.85	0.86	0.85	0.87
DT	No Acc.	0.84	0.83	0.84	0.84	0.87
NB	All Feat.	0.69	0.67	0.70	0.69	0.83
NB	No Acc.	0.70	0.69	0.69	0.70	0.86
SVM	All Feat.	0.84	0.84	0.86	0.84	0.93
SVM	No Acc.	0.80	0.79	0.82	0.80	0.91

4.3. Feature Explanation

There is notable convergence between the insights gained from the SHapely Additive exPlanations (SHAP) analysis [17] of the top-performing Random Forest model and feature weights from classical models (logistic regression, SVM, Naive Bayes). This intersection highlights a set of physiological features that robustly predict autonomic states—sympathetic, parasympathetic, and baseline (relaxed)—within the Iyengar yoga dataset. These features are not model-specific artifacts; they encode stable, physiologically meaningful information evidenced across fundamentally different analytical approaches. From the best performing Random Forest model, the highly discriminative features were *rr_std_dev* (0.098), *acc_std_dev* (0.097), *bvp_mean* (0.094), *eda_peak_rms* (0.074), and *temp_mean* (0.066). SHAP analysis on this best performing RF model formed the basis for further analysis of how each of these features contributed to each physiological states. Feature importances from other classical models such as LR, GNB and SVM were used in complement to support the physiological robustness.

4.3.1. Heart Rate Variability (*RR Interval Mean and Standard Deviation*)

RR Interval Mean and standard deviation are markers of heart rate variability and cardiac autonomic balance. Long RR intervals (i.e., low heart rate) and high variability (std_dev) consistently increased parasympathetic predictions. The SHAP values in Figure 5 show strong positive effects; LR (+1.11; OR: 3.04) and SVM (+0.49; OR: 1.64) agree. This aligns well with the established physiology where parasympathetic dominance increases HRV and is strongly indicative of vagal dominance. Shorter RR intervals (lower HRV) drove sympathetic predictions in SHAP Figure 5 and LR (−0.88; OR: 0.42), matching known associations between sympathetic arousal and cardiac acceleration. RR interval values near the mean were associated with relaxed state in SHAP Figure 5, suggesting moderate HRV distinct from the extremes defining parasympathetic or sympathetic states. This reflects the relaxed state's position as a physiological middle ground. Parasympathetic activity promotes HRV and slower HR; sympathetic arousal suppresses HRV and raises heart rate.

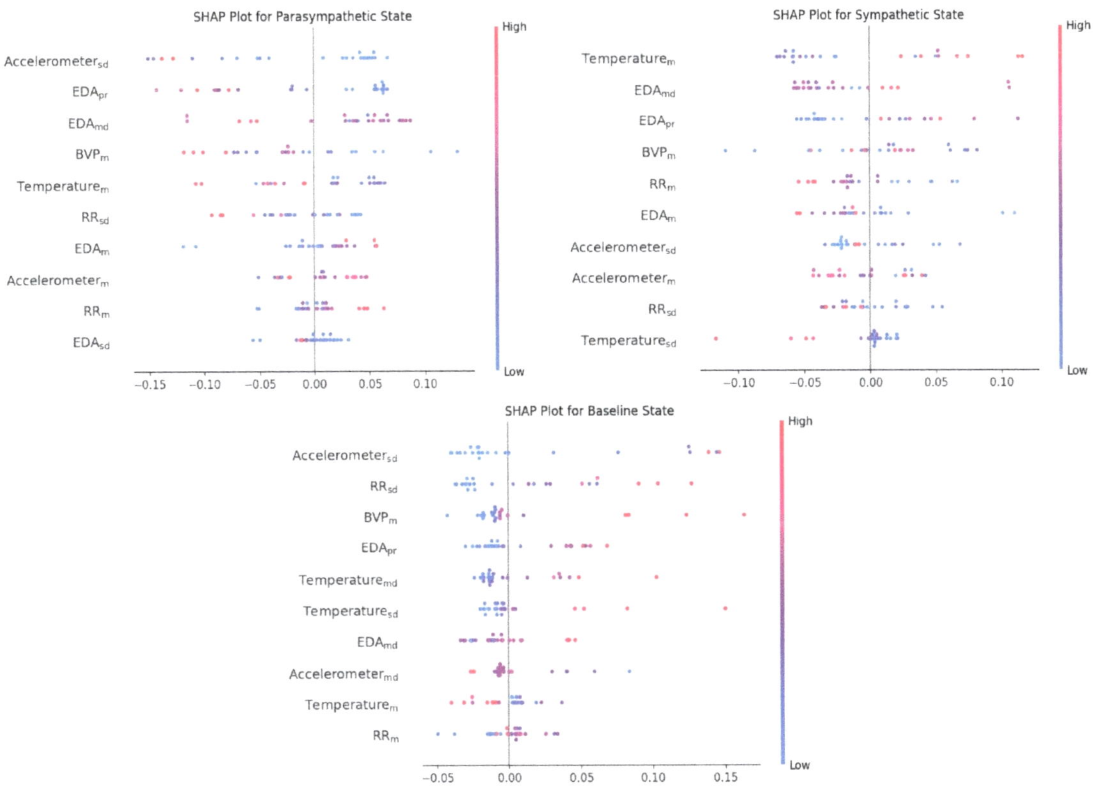

Figure 5. SHAP values illustrating the impact of each feature on the model's output across the three physiological states: parasympathetic, sympathetic, and baseline. (feature notation is same as in Figure 4).

4.3.2. Movement Variability (Accelerometer Standard Deviation)

Accelerometer standard deviation reflects movement variability/postural change. Unsurprisingly, low accelerometer standard deviation was strongly predictive of parasympathetic state, reflecting restorative poses. The SHAP values in Figure 5 were sharply negative for higher values, pushing the model away from parasympathetic classification. This was corroborated by LR (−1.99; OR: 0.14) and SVM (−1.27; OR: 0.28). Stillness aligns with the restorative, restful parasympathetic state. While high accelerometer variability increased sympathetic prediction in SHAP values in Figure 5 and SVM (coef: +1.00; OR: 2.72), suggesting movement during challenging or arousing postures. Interestingly, high accelerometer variability also contributed to relaxed class predictions in the SHAP values in Figure 5 and LR (coef: +2.06; OR: 7.82). This may reflect postural transitions or free movement within a calm, baseline context. Parasympathetic activation is associated with stillness, while sympathetic tone increases during exertion or challenging postures manifesting as more movement.

4.3.3. Blood Volume Pulse Amplitude (*BVP Mean*)

Blood volume pulse, a proxy for peripheral circulation, is a measure of cardiac and vascular activity often modulated by sympathetic tone. Low BVP amplitude was associated with parasympathetic predictions in SHAP Figure 5, suggesting reduced cardiac output and vasoconstriction typical of a resting state. High BVP amplitude pushed predictions toward a sympathetic state. This aligns with elevated cardiac activity and pulse wave amplitude under stress or arousal. Intermediate BVP levels were associated with relaxed predictions in SHAP Figure 5, again emphasizing the mid-range nature of this class.

4.3.4. Phasic Electrodermal Activity (*EDA Peak to RMS*)

EDA Peak to RMS represents the phasic, rapid component of skin conductance changes. Low peak-to-RMS values strongly promoted parasympathetic predictions in the SHAP values in Figure 5 and LR (−2.82; OR: 0.06), reflecting the dampening of sympathetic arousal typical of restful states. High values robustly indicated sympathetic activation, the SHAP values in Figure 5 showed a large positive push; LR (+0.77; OR: 2.17) and SVM (+0.14; OR: 1.15) supported this, reflecting a gold-standard biomarker for SNS activity. Mid-range values were weakly associated with relaxed state predictions, with the SHAP values contributions in Figure 5 being notably smaller, suggesting that neither extreme phasic arousal nor complete flatness defines this class. Electrodermal activity is governed by the sympathetic branch; phasic EDA increases during stress or effort, not during rest-and-digest periods.

4.3.5. Skin Temperature (*Temperature Mean*)

The temperature mean reflects the peripheral skin temperature responding to vascular changes and showed class-distinct but partially inconsistent behavior across models. The SHAP values in Figure 5 indicated slightly positive association, with higher skin temperature increasing parasympathetic prediction. However, LR (−0.67; OR: 0.51) and SVM (−0.18; OR: 0.83) suggested the opposite. While parasympathetic activity is classically linked to increased peripheral temperature due to vasodilation, because the parasympathetic data here is labeled in accordance with passive poses (e.g., lying down, resting), the body core temperature might drop due to less muscular activity. The data were collected through the wrist, as this region is very sensitive to peripheral vasoconstriction/vasodilation; thus, there may have been delayed or inverse changes compared to the core parasympathetic activity. The SHAP values in Figure 5 showed a positive influence, higher temperatures pushed predictions toward the sympathetic class, and LR (+0.68; OR: 1.97) agreed. However, SVM showed the reverse (−1.12; OR: 0.33). These mixed results suggest skin temperature may reflect non-autonomic processes. The SHAP values in Figure 5 associated mid-to-high temperatures with a relaxed state prediction. This aligns with a *comfort zone* interpretation of neither cold-stressed nor vasodilated extremes.

Among these best predictors, features such as *temp_mean*, *eda_mean*, *eda_std_dev*, *eda_peak_rms*, *eda_mean_deriv*, *rr_mean*, *rr_std_dev*, *acc_mean*, *acc_std_dev*, and *bvp_mean* appear to be the key discriminators for parasympathetic and sympathetic autonomic response-eliciting poses. This feature-centric analysis reveals that EDA peak to RMS, HRV, movement variability, and, to a lesser extent, skin temperature and BVP amplitude are consistent and interpretable predictors of autonomic state classification. Parasympathetic states are defined by stillness, high HRV, and low phasic arousal. Sympathetic states arise from dynamic movement, short RR intervals, and phasic EDA surges. Relaxed states are distinguished by moderate movement and balanced physiological values across modalities.

For instance, an increase in the magnitude of the RR interval from baseline to the postural phase is indicative of parasympathetic activity, aligning with previous findings that associate elevated RR intervals with higher vagal tone [7], can be observed in Figure 6. Skin temperature tends to rise under parasympathetic dominance due to a reduction in sympathetic vasoconstriction, reflecting increased peripheral blood flow. In contrast, EDA typically decreases as parasympathetic activity prevails. However, it is important to note that during the initial phase of posture execution, a brief surge in EDA may occur triggered by transient sympathetic arousal in response to physical effort before it subsides as the parasympathetic state establishes itself. BVP, reflecting peripheral vascular tone, also increases under parasympathetic influence, signifying vasodilation.

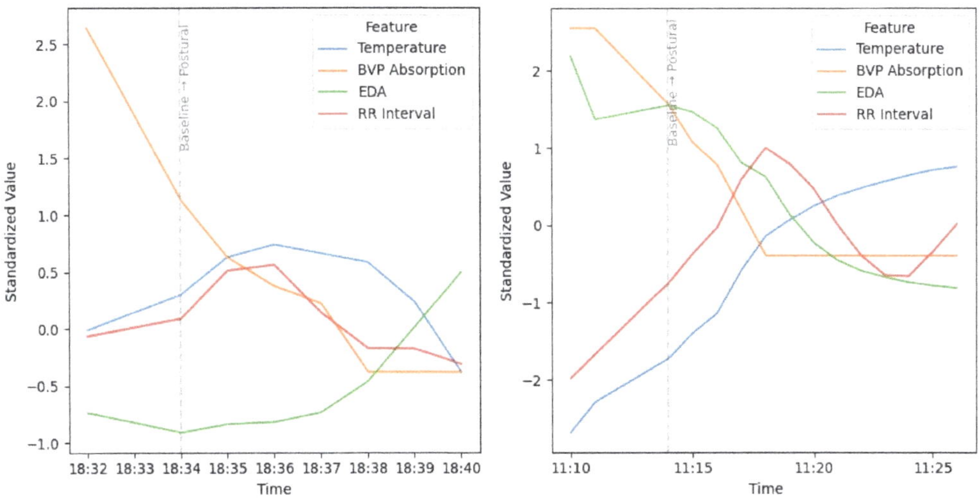

(**a**) Sympathetic Autonomic Response (**b**) Parasympathetic Autonomic Response

Figure 6. Comparison of physiological signals over time from baseline to postural phases for (**a**) sympathetic and (**b**) parasympathetic autonomic responses.

The parasympathetic response differs markedly from the sympathetic response across these modalities. While parasympathetic activation is associated with relaxation and recovery manifesting as increased RR interval (slower heart rate), elevated skin temperature (due to vasodilation), decreased EDA, and increased BVP absorption, the sympathetic response produces the opposite pattern. During sympathetic activation, such as in stress or challenge, the RR interval decreases (faster heart rate), skin temperature typically drops (stemming from vasoconstriction), EDA rises sharply (from sweat gland activation), and BVP absorption decreases (indicating vasoconstriction). These physiology-driven contrasts underscore the fundamental opposition between calming (parasympathetic) and arousing (sympathetic) branches of the ANS, and highlight the nuanced, sometimes overlapping, shifts detected by multimodal physiological monitoring.

5. Limitations

1. In this study, the autonomic states were labeled based on a certified yoga practitioner's expertise. This practitioner served as a clinical expert to validate the physiological annotations. This approach aligns with established practices in physiological and

clinical research where clinician-driven labeling is widely accepted as a valid and robust method, especially when purely data-driven ground truths are unavailable or limited [14]. Nonetheless, we recognize this as a limitation and plan to incorporate objective physiological validation (e.g., validating data against a rule-based algorithm with known biology of ANS) to strengthen construct validity in future work.

2. Our work provides valuable information and insights into the physiological effects of yoga as a therapeutic tool, focusing on elderly Indian adults with limited to moderate yoga experience. While these findings are most applicable to the population studied, caution should be exercised when extrapolating to other groups. This contribution serves as a foundational resource and may inform future studies seeking to broaden the evidence base for Iyengar yoga's effects across diverse demographic settings.
3. Our evaluation employed two complementary cross-validation strategies: stratified 10-fold CV to capture population-level separability of physiological states and Leave-One-Subject-Out CV (LOGO-CV) to assess subject-independent generalization. While stratified CV provides a holistic view of state differences across the dataset, it may overestimate performance due to potential subject-specific artifacts leaking across folds. We, therefore, emphasize LOGO-CV as the more realistic estimate of model generalizability to new individuals. Nevertheless, the relatively small sample size (N = 16) means that LOGO-CV estimates can still be unstable, and results should be interpreted as exploratory until validated in larger, more diverse cohorts.

6. Conclusions

This study establishes a robust methodological framework using wearable sensor data and machine learning models to discriminate different autonomic physiological states (baseline/relaxed, parasympathetic/restorative poses, and sympathetic/stimulating poses) during Iyengar yoga practice. Differentiating between phases (baseline and postural) and ANS response (parasympathetic and sympathetic) helps in providing the user with feedback for their engagement which is an essential step towards automated and personalized practice of such therapeutic yoga, which is currently limited to being performed under the guidance of certified instructors only. While the feedback about phases (relaxed or in-pose) provides information about getting into the pose, feedback about the type of autonomic response provides information on whether the required physiological response is elicited or not after holding the poses for sometime. As poses elicit a physiological response, this provides a chance to course-correct along the way, which makes it more feasible, reliable, and personalized. This work emphasizes that not only intense bodily movements but even slow, static yoga postures can induce rapid, multidimensional changes detectable via wearable sensors. While many studies documented ANS modulation using biomarkers such as HRV, EDA, or respiratory markers, the mechanisms are often attributed to breathing, meditation, or relaxation aspects rather than the pose mechanics themselves, which is the key aspect of this study, especially in Iyengar yoga. By mitigating overfitting and improving generalization, the developed sparse models create a strong foundation for future wearable-based health monitoring systems. Interpretable feature selection and model interpretation consistently highlighted acceleration and cardiac variability features, phasic EDA measures, and vascular/thermal dynamics as core predictors of the autonomic state. These results elucidate the complex interplay among movement, cardiovascular activity, electrodermal fluctuations, and thermoregulation during yoga, providing a physiologically sound and computationally validated pathway for future real-time, adaptive biofeedback and posture-aware health interventions. The findings from this study herein offer a scalable solution for objective autonomic assessment, enabling precision yoga therapy, self-monitoring, and broader applications in digital health and behavior medicine.

Author Contributions: Conceptualization, C.V.A. and T.B.; methodology, W.L.R., C.V.A. and T.B.; literature review, C.V.A.; validation, W.L.R. and C.V.A.; formal analysis, W.L.R. and C.V.A.; investigation, T.B. and C.V.A.; resources, W.L.R. and T.B.; data curation, T.B. and C.V.A.; writing-original draft preparation, C.V.A., T.B. and W.L.R.; writing-review and editing, W.L.R., C.V.A. and T.B.; visualization, C.V.A.; supervision, T.B. and W.L.R.; project administration, T.B. All authors have read and agreed to the published version of the manuscript.

Funding: This research received no external funding.

Institutional Review Board Statement: The study was conducted in accordance with the Declaration of Helsinki, and the protocol was approved by the Ethics Committee of Wright State University Institutional Review Board (FWA00002427; Study ID: IRB-2024-651) on 4 December 2024.

Informed Consent Statement: Informed consent was obtained from all subjects involved in the study.

Data Availability Statement: The datasets presented in this article are not readily available because the data are part of an ongoing study. Please reach out to the authors with questions regarding data access.

Acknowledgments: The authors wish to thank Anuradha Oak for her expert guidance in designing individualized Iyengar yoga sessions for each participant at the Atmaja Wellness Awareness Organization. Based on her assessment of each participant's condition, Oak selected and adapted the yoga poses, determined their duration, and provided in-person instruction to ensure correct form and technique throughout the sessions.

Conflicts of Interest: The authors report no conflicts of interest.

Abbreviations

The following abbreviations are used in this manuscript:

ANS	Autonomic Nervous System
EDA	Electrodermal Activity
BVP	Blood Volume Pulse
RF	Random Forest
LR	Logistic Regression
DT	Decision Tree
GNB	Gaussian Naive Bayes
NB	Naive Bayes
SVM	Support Vector Machine
AUC	Area Under the Curve
SHAP	SHapely Additive exPlanations
OR	Odds Ratio
RMS	Root Mean Square
HRV	Heart Rate Variability
HSD	Tukey's Honest Significant Difference

References

1. Hall, J.E. *Guyton and Hall Textbook of Medical Physiology*, 13th ed.; Elsevier: Amsterdam, The Netherlands, 2020.
2. Kay, M.W.; Jain, V.; Panjrath, G.; Mendelowitz, D. Targeting Parasympathetic Activity to Improve Autonomic Tone and Clinical Outcomes. *Physiology* **2022**, *37*, 39–45. [CrossRef] [PubMed]
3. Lujan, H.L.; DiCarlo, S.E. Physical activity, by enhancing parasympathetic tone and activating the cholinergic anti-inflammatory pathway, is a therapeutic strategy to restrain chronic inflammation and prevent many chronic diseases. *Med. Hypotheses* **2013**, *80*, 548–552. [CrossRef] [PubMed]
4. Esler, M.; Lambert, E.; Schlaich, M. Point: Chronic Activation of the Sympathetic Nervous System Is the Dominant Contributor to Systemic Hypertension. *J. Appl. Physiol.* **2010**, *109*, 1996–1998. [CrossRef] [PubMed]
5. Goldstein, D.S. Adrenal Responses to Stress. *Cell. Mol. Neurobiol.* **2010**, *30*, 1433–1440. [CrossRef] [PubMed]
6. Iyengar, B.K.S. *Yoga The Path To Holistic Health*, 2014th ed.; DK: London, UK, 2014.

7. Khattab, K.; Khattab, A.A.; Ortak, J.; Richardt, G.; Bonnemeier, H. Iyengar Yoga Increases Cardiac Parasympathetic Nervous Modulation among Healthy Yoga Practitioners. *Evid.-Based Complement. Altern. Med.* **2007**, *4*, 511–517. [CrossRef] [PubMed]
8. Bandi, H.K.; Pal, P.; Pal, G.K.; Balachander, J.; Jayasettiaseelon, E.; Sreekanth, Y.; Sridhar, M.G.; Gaur, G.S. Effect of Yoga Therapy on Heart Rate, Blood Pressure and Cardiac Autonomic Function in Heart Failure. *J. Clin. Diagn. Res.* **2014**, *8*, 14–16. [CrossRef] [PubMed]
9. Santana, M.J.; S-Parrilla, J.; Mirus, J.; Loadman, M.A.; Lien, D.C.; Feeny, D. An Assessment of the Effects of Iyengar Yoga Practice on the Health-Related Quality of Life of Patients with Chronic Respiratory Diseases: A Pilot Study. *Can. Respir. J.* **2013**, *20*, e17–e23. [CrossRef] [PubMed]
10. Scott, T.M.; Gerbarg, P.L.; Silveri, M.M.; Nielsen, G.H.; Owen, L.; Nyer, M.; Brown, R.P.; Streeter, C.C. Psychological Function, Iyengar Yoga, and Coherent Breathing. *J. Psychiatr. Pract.* **2019**, *25*, 437–450. [CrossRef]
11. Michalsen, A.; Jeitler, M.; Brunnhuber, S.; Lüdtke, R.; Büssing, A.; Musial, F.; Dobos, G.; Kessler, C. Iyengar Yoga for Distressed Women: A 3-Armed Randomized Controlled Trial. *Evid.-Based Complement. Altern. Med.* **2012**, *2012*, 408727. [CrossRef]
12. Bhattacharyya, K.B. The stretch reflex and the contributions of C David Marsden. *Ann. Indian Acad. Neurol.* **2017**, *20*, 1–4. [CrossRef]
13. Blank, S. Physiological Responses to Iyengar Yoga Performed by Trained Practitioners. *J. Exerc. Physiol. (JEPonline)* **2006**, *9*, 7–23.
14. Wieser, M.; Buetler, L.; Vallery, H.; Schaller, J.; Mayr, A.; Kofler, M.; Saltuari, L.; Zutter, D.; Riener, R. Quantification of Clinical Scores through Physiological Recordings in low-responsive patients: A Feasibility Study. *J. Neuroeng. Rehabil.* **2012**, *9*, 30. [CrossRef] [PubMed]
15. Kim, H.Y. Statistical Notes for Clinical researchers:post-hocmultiple Comparisons. *Restor. Dent. Endod.* **2015**, *40*, 176. [CrossRef] [PubMed]
16. Pedregosa, F.; Varoquaux, G.; Gramfort, A.; Michel, V.; Thirion, B.; Grisel, O.; Blondel, M.; Prettenhofer, P.; Weiss, R.; Dubourg, V.; et al. Scikit-learn: Machine Learning in Python. *J. Mach. Learn. Res.* **2011**, *12*, 2825–2830.
17. Lundberg, S.; Allen, P.; Lee, S.I. A Unified Approach to Interpreting Model Predictions. *arXiv* **2017**, arXiv:1705.07874. [CrossRef]

algorithms

MDPI

Article

SPADE: Superpixel Adjacency Driven Embedding for Three-Class Melanoma Segmentation

Pablo Ordóñez, Ying Xie *, Xinyue Zhang, Chloe Yixin Xie, Santiago Acosta and Issac Guitierrez

College of Computer Science and Software Engineering, Kennesaw State University, Marietta, GA 30060, USA; pordonez@kennesaw.edu (P.O.)
* Correspondence: yxie2@kennesaw.edu

Abstract: The accurate segmentation of pigmented skin lesions is a critical prerequisite for reliable melanoma detection, yet approximately 30% of lesions exhibit fuzzy or poorly defined borders. This ambiguity makes the definition of a single contour unreliable and limits the effectiveness of computer-assisted diagnosis (CAD) systems. While clinical assessment based on the ABCDE criteria (asymmetry, border, color, diameter, and evolution), dermoscopic imaging, and scoring systems remains the standard, these methods are inherently subjective and vary with clinician experience. We address this challenge by reframing segmentation into three distinct regions: background, border, and lesion core. These regions are delineated using superpixels generated via the Simple Linear Iterative Clustering (SLIC) algorithm, which provides meaningful structural units for analysis. Our contributions are fourfold: (1) redefining lesion borders as regions, rather than sharp lines; (2) generating superpixel-level embeddings with a transformer-based autoencoder; (3) incorporating these embeddings as features for superpixel classification; and (4) integrating neighborhood information to construct enhanced feature vectors. Unlike pixel-level algorithms that often overlook boundary context, our pipeline fuses global class information with local spatial relationships, significantly improving precision and recall in challenging border regions. An evaluation on the HAM10000 melanoma dataset demonstrates that our superpixel–RAG–transformer (region adjacency graph) pipeline achieves exceptional performance (100% F1 score, accuracy, and precision) in classifying background, border, and lesion core superpixels. By transforming raw dermoscopic images into region-based structured representations, the proposed method generates more informative inputs for downstream deep learning models. This strategy not only advances melanoma analysis but also provides a generalizable framework for other medical image segmentation and classification tasks.

Keywords: melanoma; deep learning; SLIC; border; embeddings; decoder; encoder; attention

1. Introduction

Melanoma is an aggressive malignant tumor that originates from melanocytic cells, which are primarily located in the skin. The development of melanoma is influenced by several key risk factors, including a history of excessive sun exposure and sunburns, Fitzpatrick skin types I and II, and the presence of atypical nevi.

According to epidemiological data, the incidence rate of melanoma in the United States was reported at 21.2 cases per 100,000 individuals in 2022 [1]. Projections from the American Cancer Society estimate that 104,960 new cases will be diagnosed in 2025 [2]. Despite significant advancements in therapeutic approaches, melanoma continues to exhibit a mortality rate of approximately 8% [3,4].

The determination of whether a pigmented lesion is benign or malignant has been approached from multiple perspectives. Clinically, physicians rely on visual inspection guided by the ABCDE criteria and dermoscopic patterns, often supported by scoring systems, though these remain highly dependent on expertise and prone to subjectivity. To reduce variability, computer-assisted diagnosis (CAD) systems have emerged, initially using handcrafted, feature-based methods to quantify asymmetry, border irregularity, color, and diameter and more recently advancing toward deep learning models, including convolutional neural networks and transformer-based architectures. While these approaches have improved diagnostic accuracy, both clinical assessment and CAD systems face limitations related to subjectivity in lesion boundaries and variability across datasets. A more detailed discussion of these methodologies is provided in Section 2.

A comprehensive meta-analysis conducted within the medical community evaluated the effectiveness of AI models in skin cancer detection. Following the PRISMA methodology, the review included 272 publications from an initial pool of 14,224 studies, spanning the years 2000 to 2021. The analysis reported a mean F1 score of 0.807 for melanoma detection, with scores ranging from 0.732 to 0.882 [5].

Despite significant advancements in deep learning-based melanoma detection, current AI methods remain insufficient for widespread clinical adoption, largely due to limitations in data quality, particularly regarding melanoma subtypes, patient demographics, image quality, dataset provenance, and the tendency for DL systems to use such data without sufficient contextual consideration. This study bridges computer science and medical perspectives to address these shortcomings by investigating biases arising from annotated lesion borders, especially in irregular or ambiguous cases, and introducing a region-based analysis using superpixels, rather than the traditional pixel-by-pixel approach employed in CAD systems.

Contributions

Although AI models have significantly advanced in recent years, delineating lesions remains a subjective task even for specialists. We propose that the lesion border should not be treated as a single, well-defined line but, rather, as a transitional region that separates the background from the core of the lesion. Figure 4b presents a blended image composed of the ground truth mask overlaid on the original lesion. In our work, the border region is defined as the area between the outer edge of the mask and the visible boundary of the lesion. This region can be more precisely delineated using superpixels, which provide a spatially coherent segmentation aligned with local image features. Our objective is to develop a model capable of accurately identifying all three regions. In this paper, we propose a new method called SPADE (Superpixel Adjacency Driven Embedding) for three-class melanoma segmentation. The main contributions of SPADE are as follows.

- Definition of three anatomical zones: we define three distinct zones in dermoscopy images, the background, the border, and the core of the lesion.
- Transformer-based superpixel embedding: we train a transformer autoencoder to generate embeddings for each superpixel, enabling the model to capture contextual relationships between spatially distant regions belonging to the same class.
- Context-Aware Region Adjacency Graph (RAG): we construct a region adjacency graph using superpixels obtained via the SLIC algorithm to model spatial relationships.
- Input definition based on the region adjacency graph: each input vector consists of the embedding of a given superpixel, along with the embeddings of its immediate neighbors, effectively capturing the local spatial context.
- Semantic representation of dermoscopy images: the system effectively captures the semantic content of dermoscopy images, supporting improved lesion characterization.

2. Assessing the Malignancy of Pigmented Lesions

The determination of whether a pigmented skin lesion is benign or malignant is a critical step in melanoma detection. Several approaches exist, spanning traditional clinical examination, computer-assisted diagnostic (CAD) tools, and modern machine learning–based systems. While clinical methods remain the standard in practice, CAD systems have evolved from handcrafted feature extraction to advanced deep learning models, each offering distinct advantages and limitations. This section outlines these approaches in detail.

2.1. Clinical Assessment Methods

Clinical examination of melanoma relies on the assessment of lesion characteristics based on the ABCDE criteria, as depicted in Figure 1, which evaluate asymmetry, border irregularity, color variation, diameter greater than 6 mm, and evolution over time [6]. Other than the diameter, the ABC criteria are subject to subjective interpretation. Furthermore, physicians with more clinical experience tend to demonstrate higher diagnostic accuracy [7].

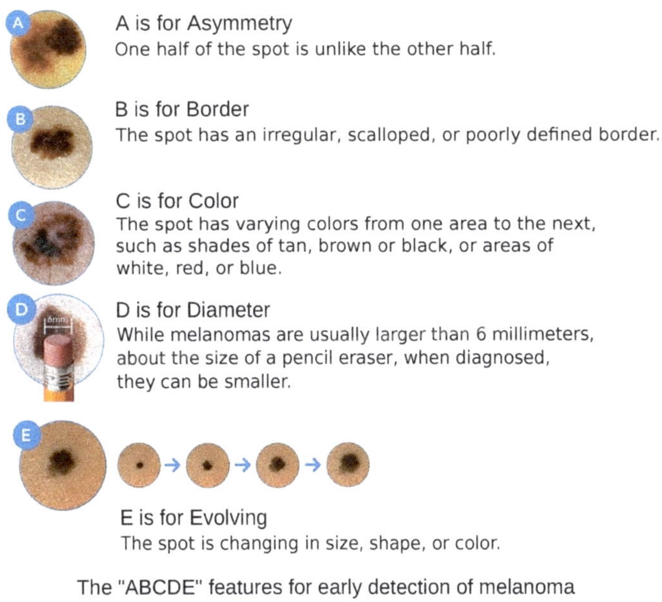

Figure 1. ABCD Features. Courtesy of American Academy of Dermatology Association.

Dermoscopy is a non-invasive diagnostic technique widely used by general practitioners (GPs) and dermatologists to improve the detection of skin lesions suspected of malignancy. A dermatoscope, in simple terms, is a magnifying lens equipped with illumination and, in many cases, digital imaging capabilities. It facilitates the visualization of subsurface skin structures that are not visible to the unaided eye, as shown in Figure 2a. Studies have demonstrated that the incorporation of dermoscopy into the diagnostic workflow enhances accuracy; it increases accuracy from 54% to between 76% and 79%, compared to visual inspection alone [8]. Dermoscopy captures unique and mixed basic structural patterns such as reticular, streaked, globular, and homogeneous, as illustrated in Figure 2b.

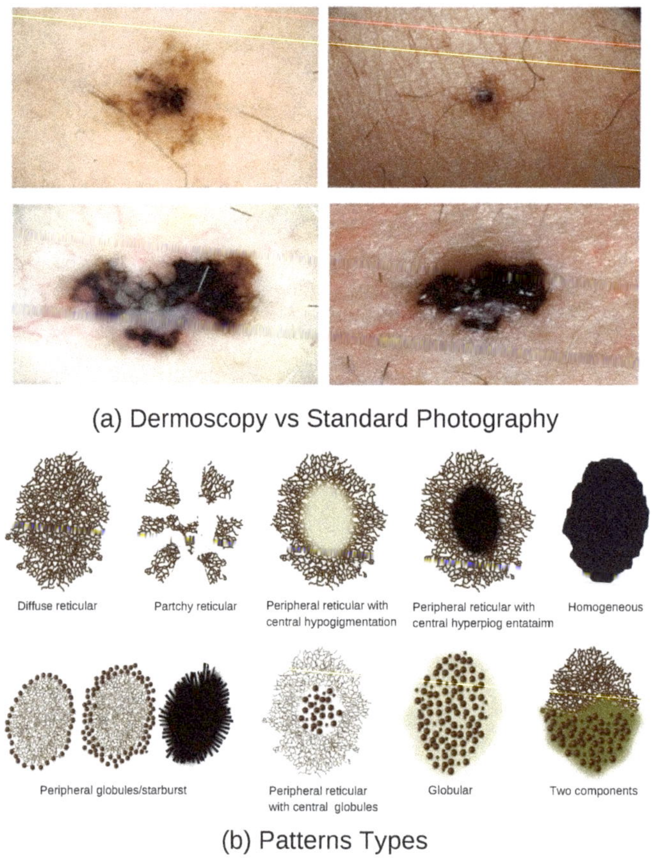

Figure 2. Dermoscopy Patterns. Courtesy American Family Physician.

For GPs, the initial step involves distinguishing melanocytic lesions from non-melanocytic ones through clinical evaluation to ensure accurate preliminary classification. The second step focuses on differentiating nevi from melanoma by applying clinical criteria such as the ABCDE rules, interpreting dermoscopic findings, and utilizing scoring systems. Suspicious lesions are typically referred to a specialist (dermatologist) for further assessment. We have described how human intelligence, through visual inspection, dermoscopic tools, and scoring systems, is used to determine whether a lesion is benign or malignant. Nonetheless, these evaluation methods rely heavily on human judgment, whether through clinical assessment, the use of tools such as dermoscopy, or the application of clinician-derived scoring systems, making them inherently prone to subjectivity.

2.2. CAD Systems

The diagnostic subjectivity and inter-observer variability associated with melanoma underscore the need for automated and objective computer-assisted diagnosis (CAD) systems.

2.2.1. Classification Based on the ABCD Rule

Two primary approaches have been developed for melanoma classification using CAD. The first approach aligns with the clinical methodology and employs scoring systems based on the ABCD rule. To ensure objectivity, automated methods have been proposed for detecting shape asymmetry, color variegation, and lesion diameter. Among these,

Fourier descriptors are considered the most robust techniques for quantifying asymmetry due to their mathematically rigorous formulation and demonstrated alignment with expert dermatological assessments, achieving up to 92% concordance with dermatologist evaluations [9,10]. For border irregularity, combined shape descriptors including fractal dimension, Zernike moments, and convexity coupled with convolutional neural network (CNN) classifiers have achieved state-of-the-art results, with reported classification accuracies reaching 93.6% [11]. In assessing color variegation, the CIELAB color space combined with the Minkowski distance metric has proven the most effective, offering perceptual uniformity that closely matches human color vision and handling wide color variations reliably [12]. Regarding lesion diameter, Feret's diameter has been identified as the most accurate and consistent measure, particularly for lesions with irregular boundaries [12].

2.2.2. Classification Based on Direct Feature Extraction

The second approach focuses on direct skin lesion classification, which can be performed using either full images or segmented lesion regions. Studies have shown that classifiers trained on segmented images generally outperform those trained on whole images [13]. In classical CAD systems, lesion segmentation is typically performed using three main approaches: edge-based, region-based, and threshold-based methods [14]. For classification, methods such as score averaging (AVGSC), linear SVM, and non-linear SVM using a histogram intersection kernel have demonstrated acceptable performance levels [15].

The advent of deep learning has significantly enhanced both segmentation and classification accuracy by leveraging CNNs and transformer-based architectures [16]. Deep supervised learning has led to the development of increasingly sophisticated architectures beyond traditional CNNs.

Popular CNN-based models for melanoma classification include ResNet [17], VGG16 [18], MobileNet [19], DenseNet [19], and Inception [20]. Transformer-based architectures have also demonstrated strong performance [21–23]. Reported classification performance across these models varies, with accuracy ranging from 80% to 98%, sensitivity from 60% to 90%, and specificity from 86% to 98%. Among these, EfficientNet-B7 [24] and transformer-based models [21–23] exhibit the highest diagnostic accuracy.

Models based solely on CNNs have been increasingly outperformed by architectures incorporating encoder–decoder frameworks, reflecting a shift towards more effective hierarchical feature representations. CNN-based segmentation models fall into two primary categories: pixel-wise upsampling techniques, such as fully convolutional networks (FCNs), and spatial and pyramidal upsampling approaches, such as the DeepLab family of models [25]. Notably, DeepLabV3+ introduces a decoder module designed to enhance segmentation accuracy and refine feature extraction, particularly at object boundaries [26]. An encoder–decoder architecture like U-Net and V-Net utilize symmetric upsampling at each layer to preserve spatial resolution during reconstruction. This improves the fidelity of the segmented output [27–29]. Further advancements have been realized through attention-based models, which improve both feature selection and contextual awareness. Prominent architectures in this category include the vision transformer (ViT) [30,31] and visual attention networks [32], which leverage self-attention mechanisms to capture long-range dependencies within an image. The segmentation accuracy of deep learning models for skin lesion analysis ranges from 80% to 98%, with recent architectures consistently surpassing their predecessors in both precision and generalization capacity.

Accurate lesion segmentation is essential for the reliable extraction of ABCD features and for effective classification. In most publicly available datasets, lesion boundaries are manually annotated by dermatologists, residents, medical students, or trained personnel. This process is not only time-consuming but also inherently subjective. For lesions with fuzzy or ambiguous boundaries, substantial inter-annotator variability exists. A study by Kittler et al. reported discrepancies of up to 20–30% due to ambiguous lesion edges and variations in annotator expertise [33–35]. To address this, some organizations provide standardized segmentation protocols. For instance, the ISIC archive employs multi-rater consensus in cases with ambiguous lesion boundaries [15]. These practices underscore the degree of subjectivity that remains embedded in CAD systems dependent on manual segmentation for classification or ABCD rule application.

3. Related Work

Fine-tuning AI models for accurate border delineation in blurry or low contrast dermoscopic images has been addressed through methods that identify and label regions adjacent to lesions. Adegun et al. employ probabilistic models in which each pixel is assigned a value between 0 and 1, representing the likelihood of belonging to the lesion [36]. The algorithm ultimately produces a lesion boundary represented as a line. Halil et al. utilize region of interest (ROI) bounding, where an initial bounding box or elliptical region is drawn around the lesion, followed by consensus among multiple annotators [37]. Although the initial stage localizes the lesion broadly, the final boundary is refined using the GrabCut algorithm, resulting in a sharply delimited line. Zahra et al. propose an approach based on multiple expert-generated masks, from which a consensus mask is derived through fusion [38]. The final output is again a single mask outlined by a distinct boundary line. Li et al. [39,40] introduce a method that explicitly marks regions of uncertainty, rather than enforcing a hard boundary. They use class activation maps to generate pseudo-labels and apply binary thresholding to create segmentation masks. This approach allows the model to learn from ambiguous regions, thereby improving robustness in uncertain contexts. In contrast to these methods, which ultimately produce a line-based lesion boundary, our approach focuses on defining lesion regions, providing a more granular and context-aware representation.

Graph-based methods also commonly leverage superpixels by constructing an RAG, where each node represents a superpixel and edges encode similarity metrics between neighboring regions such as color, texture, or boundary strength. Once the graph is constructed, segmentation is performed using algorithms such as spectral clustering, normalized cuts, or min-cut/max-flow, and neural networks, which partition the graph into semantically meaningful regions [41]. RAGs naturally integrate with graph neural networks (GNNs) and have been employed for image classification tasks. Nazir et al. applied graph convolutional neural networks (GCNNs) using both spatial and spectral convolution techniques, demonstrating that spectral-based models outperform spatial-based models and classical CNNs while requiring less computational cost [42]. Avelar et al. explored attention-based GNNs for classification and showed that the feature space can be enhanced by weighting the edges of a superpixel graph using a learned function based solely on geometric information [41]. Nowosad et al. apply graph-based segmentation to non-imagery geospatial data by grouping superpixels based on dissimilarity measures and pruning the resulting graph to a minimum spanning tree (MST) [43]. Additionally, Qin et al. propose a superpixel-based and boundary-sensitive CNN model specifically designed for liver segmentation, demonstrating the effectiveness of combining region-based pre-processing with deep learning techniques [44]. Similar to our work, these studies employed superpixels and RAG to construct graph representations. However, unlike prior work, the current phase of our study does not incorporate graph neural networks or edge attributes for classification.

4. Methods and Algorithm Design

The SPADE pipeline proceeds as follows: the images are first resized; superpixels are then generated using the Simple Linear Iterative Clustering (SLIC) algorithm; a region adjacency graph is constructed; each superpixel is labeled by class (background, border, and lesion); class-specific embeddings are generated using a transformer; and finally, a transformer is trained to predict the three classes.

4.1. Resizing Images

All images were initially adjusted to a landscape orientation and resized to a width of 1024 pixels and a height of 768 pixels using a bilinear interpolation algorithm from the OpenCV framework.

4.2. Superpixel Generation Strategy

Superpixel segmentation partitions an image into regions composed of similar and spatially connected pixels, providing perceptually meaningful atomic regions.

SLIC is classified as a neighborhood-based clustering algorithm. SLIC is an adaptation of the k-means clustering algorithm, specifically designed for efficient superpixel generation. It introduces two key parameters: a search radius that limits the number of distance computations, and a weighted distance metric that balances color similarity and spatial proximity, S. The distance function is defined as follows:

$$D_s = d_{\text{rgb}} + \frac{m}{S} d_{xy}$$

where d_{rgb} is the Euclidean distance in the RGB color space, d_{xy} is the geometric distance between pixels, and m is a compactness parameter that controls the trade-off between color and spatial proximity. These parameters enable control over the size and compactness of the resulting superpixels. Furthermore, SLIC's linear computational complexity contributes to its widespread adoption in superpixel generation tasks [45].

Each pixel in SLIC is represented by a five-dimensional feature vector consisting of three components for color and two for spatial coordinates $C_x = [R_k, G_k, B_k, x_k, y_k]$. The algorithm employs the CIELAB color space, which offers a perceptually uniform representation of color, ensuring a more meaningful similarity measure. The segmentation process in SLIC involves three main steps. First, clusters are initialized based on the desired number of superpixels. Second, an iterative clustering process assigns pixels to the nearest cluster using a distance function that incorporates both color and spatial information. Finally, a post-processing step enforces spatial connectivity to ensure that each superpixel forms a contiguous region [45,46].

SLIC superpixels effectively capture low-level image features like color, position, and depth while preserving fine-grained boundary details. This is essential for detecting subtle background transitions around lesions, which clinicians often rely on. Moreover, superpixels reduce noise by averaging local pixel variations within each region and help focus computational resources on meaningful structures since larger segments often carry more semantic information than individual pixels.

The SLIC algorithm was applied to each image to obtain its segmented regions. Specifically, we employed the SuperpixelSLIC algorithm from OpenCV with the following parameters: a desired number of superpixels k set to 600, an area size of 1320, $S = 34$, and a ruler value (m) of 19220, producing the segmentations shown in Figure 3. The software suite provides three different algorithms, SLIC, SLICO, and MSLIC, among which SLIC was chosen due to its balance between algorithmic compactness, boundary recall, and computational efficiency. Each superpixel was assigned a unique identifier, which was used to track and analyze the segmented regions [47]. At the beginning of the algorithm, each superpixel is assigned a unique identifier (ID) when the initial centroids are defined. This ID is stored as an integer value in the database and remains constant throughout the duration of the experiment.

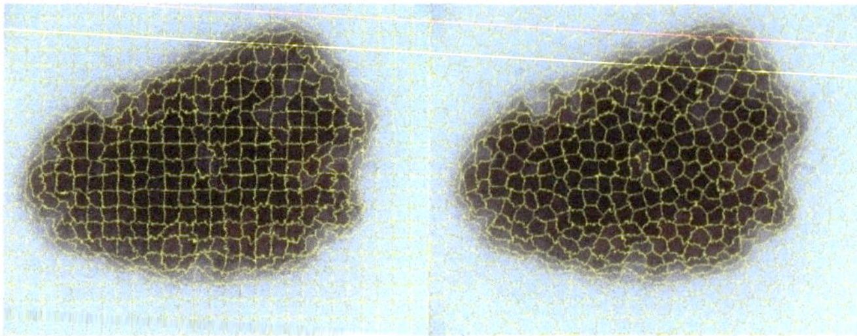

Figure 3. SLIC Superpixels Image Sequences.

4.3. Constructing the Region Adjacency Graph (RAG)

The RAG was constructed by traversing the labeled superpixel matrix and establishing undirected edges between adjacent superpixels with differing labels based on 4-and 8-connected neighborhood criteria, capturing spatial connectivity through horizontal, vertical, and diagonal adjacency, as depicted in Figure 4a [48].

We hypothesize that, similar to how transformers leverage the sequential ordering of words to learn language structure, our region adjacency graph (RAG) explicitly defines "neighbor" relationships among superpixels. Unlike vision transformers, where all patches are included as input tokens, our RAG-based approach provides meaningful context to the transformer. In this framework, the transformer's self-attention mechanism operates over graph nodes, attending preferentially to adjacent regions that share meaningful boundaries or semantic relationships. In contrast to vision transformers, which may waste computational resources attending to regions lacking relevant context, our RAG-based model focuses attention on superpixels containing semantically relevant information.

For instance, consider an image with a size of 224 × 224 pixels, with patch sizes of 16 × 16; this results in a total of 196 patches. In a vision transformer, each transformer layer computes self-attention with a complexity of $\mathcal{O}(N^2\dot{D})$, where N is the number of patches and D is the embedding dimension. In our superpixel-based approach, we observe that each superpixel has, on average, 7 neighbors (ranging from (2–19)), leading to a significantly reduced complexity of $\mathcal{O}(7^2\dot{D})$.

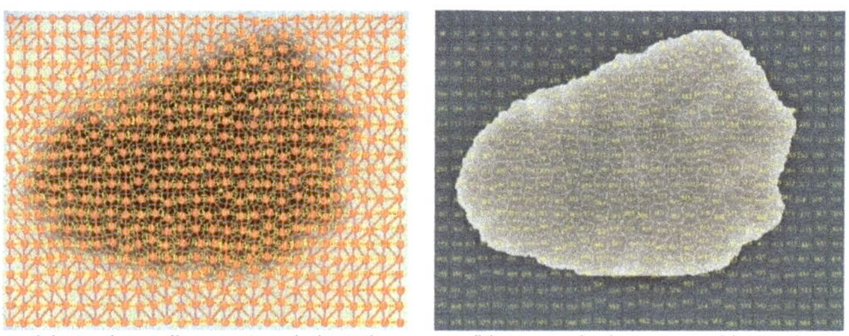

Figure 4. Dermoscopy Image, Superpixels, RAG, and Mask.

4.4. Creating Features

For each image, we extracted metadata including the filename, height, and width. We also computed the mean and standard deviation for each RGB channel. For each superpixel, we computed the mean, standard deviation, kurtosis, and skewness per RGB channel. Using the segmented region as a binary mask in a 2D image, where pixels belonging to the superpixel were set to 1 and all others to 0, we calculated the area $(m00)$, centroid $X = (m10/m00)$, centroid $Y = (m01/m00)$, and second central moments using the OpenCV moments function. Additionally, neighboring superpixels were identified and included as part of the superpixel-level information.

To facilitate further analysis, the superpixels were categorized into three classes (background, border, and core lesion) for a subset of 2000 images from the HAM10000 dataset ("Human Against Machine with 10,000 training images") [49]. A custom annotation tool was developed to allow manual labeling of superpixels. The supplementary video (Video S1) provides a visual demonstration of how the annotator selects the "border in" and "border out" regions on dermoscopic images. The "border out" class includes superpixels marking the transition between the lesion and the surrounding skin, whereas the "border in" class contains superpixels located just inside the lesion boundary.

To delineate the lesion interior, a concave hull algorithm was applied to enclose all superpixels within the "border in" region. Unlike the convex hull, which may encompass unrelated background superpixels, the concave hull prevents the inclusion of superpixels that do not belong to the lesion, as illustrated in Figure 5b.

Based on the proposed classification scheme, we define the core lesion as the union of superpixels labeled as "border in" and those enclosed by them. The border class corresponds to the "border out" superpixels, and all the remaining superpixels are assigned to the background class, as shown in Figure 5c.

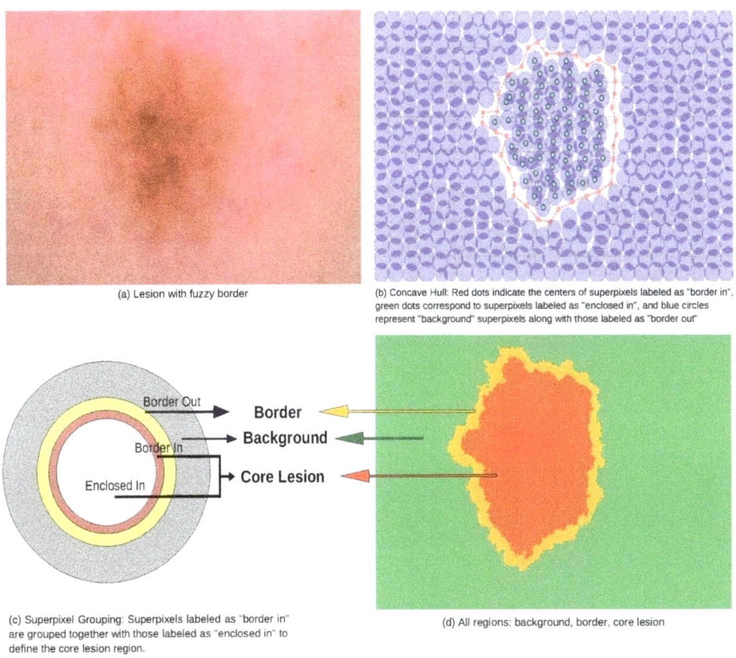

(a) Lesion with fuzzy border

(b) Concave Hull: Red dots indicate the centers of superpixels labeled as "border in", green dots correspond to superpixels labeled as "enclosed in", and blue circles represent "background" superpixels along with those labeled as "border out"

(c) Superpixel Grouping: Superpixels labeled as "border in" are grouped together with those labeled as "enclosed in" to define the core lesion region.

(d) All regions: background, border, core lesion

Figure 5. Grouping superpixels on classes.

Table 1 presents the total number of superpixels per category, where class labels 0, 1, and 2 correspond to background, core lesion, and border, respectively. We use these regions because they encode clinically meaningful cues: the background region supports estimation of the Fitzpatrick skin type, while the lesion border and core inform assessment of the ABCD features, enabling dermatologists to form a coherent mental map of the lesion.

Table 1. Superpixel class statistics.

Class	Label	Superpixels	%
0	Background	809,891	68.9
1	Lesion	284,116	24.1
2	Border	80,229	6.8

4.5. Transformer Autoencoders for Generating Embeddings

To generate embeddings for each superpixel, we train a transformer autoencoder independently for each semantic class (background, border, or core). Each superpixel is resized to contain 700 pixels per channel, and the latent space dimensionality is set to 256. The model architecture is illustrated in Figure 6. The encoder consists of four multi-head self-attention layers (with four heads each), interleaved with four feed-forward linear layers. This encoder maps the input patch tokens to a 256-dimensional latent vector. The decoder is symmetric, consisting of four self-attention layers and four linear layers, and it reconstructs the original input from the latent representation. Each attention and feed-forward sub-layer is followed by residual connections and layer normalization to stabilize training and improve gradient flow.

We train a separate autoencoder for each class using only superpixels labeled accordingly. The reconstruction loss is measured using the mean squared error (MSE) between the original input and the decoder's output. Optimization is performed using the Adam optimizer with early stopping, based on an 80/20 training-validation split (random seed = 40).

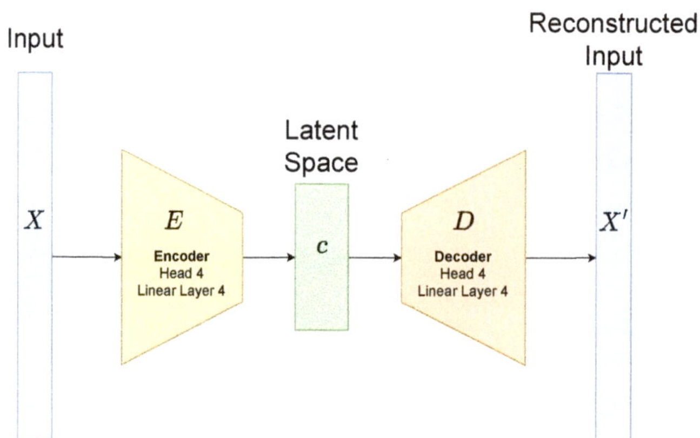

Figure 6. Transformer autoencoder.

By leveraging the transformer's self-attention mechanism, these autoencoders effectively learn to encode irregular, shape-conforming superpixels. This allows them to capture not only intra-region content but also inter-region semantic patterns—capabilities that fixed grid patches or traditional CNN encoders cannot achieve as efficiently. We hypothesize that combining these learned embeddings with our region adjacency graph (RAG) structure (Section 4.3) enables a context-aware segmentation framework built upon semantically meaningful, spatially grounded building blocks.

We also trained a vanilla autoencoder to obtain embeddings; however, it yielded a higher training loss and required longer training time than the transformer autoencoder.

The extracted information was stored in a Neo4j graph database [50], where the data was structured into three main entities, images, superpixels, and centroids, as shown in Figure 7a,b. The image entity contained all image-related properties, while the superpixel entity stored superpixel-specific characteristics, including the embeddings generated via the latent space. The centroid entity recorded the centroid's x and y coordinates. Within the database, IN_IMAGE relationships linked each image entity to its corresponding superpixel entities. NEIGHBOR_OF relationships connected superpixel entities with their neighboring superpixels, such that edge weights represented the Euclidean distance between RGB mean values. Finally, CENTER_AT relationships associated each Superpixel entity with its respective Centroid.

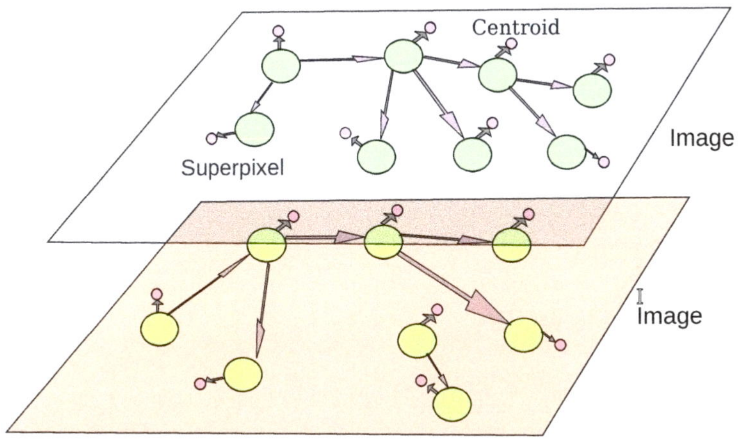

(a) Centroid → Superpixel → Image

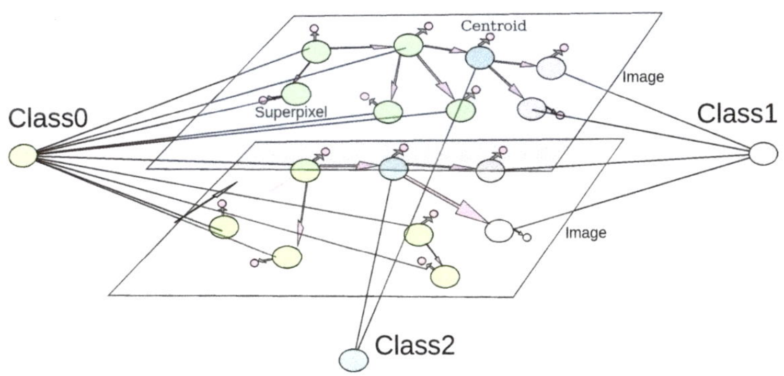

(b) Superpixel → Class

Figure 7. Graph representation of RAG.

PyTorch version 2.2.2 and CUDA 12 were used to create and run the deep learning models for training and inference. The data was normalized and split amongst training and validation sets, 80% and 20%, respectively. We set the random seed to 40 for all experiments.

The described steps to obtain the embeddings are clearly depicted on the Algorithm 1.

Algorithm 1: Obtain embeddings from superpixels and neighbors.

```
Input: RGB image I
Output: Embedding vectors for each superpixel and its neighbors
Function ResizeImage(I)
    Apply bilinear interpolation to standardize input size;
    return resized image I';
Function GenerateSuperpixels(I')
    Apply SLIC algorithm to RGB image;
    return set of superpixels S;
Function ConstructRAG(S)
    Build Region Adjacency Graph G using 8-connected neighbors;
    return graph G;
Function LabelSuperpixels(S)
    Manually annotate each superpixel as background, border, or core;
    return labeled set L;
Function TrainAutoencoderPerClass(S, L)
    foreach class c ∈ {background, border, core} do
        Resize each superpixel to 700 pixels per channel;
        Set latent space to 256 dimensions;
        Train transformer autoencoder for class c;
    return trained autoencoders A_c;
Function InferEmbeddings(S, A_c)
    foreach superpixel s ∈ S do
        Use corresponding class autoencoder A_c to infer embedding;
        Store embedding vector e_s;
        Store statistical features from superpixels s_f
    return {e_s, s_f}_{s∈S};
Function CombineWithNeighbors(G, {e_s})
    foreach superpixel s do
        Retrieve 8-connected neighbors N_s from G;
        Concatenate embedding e_s, and s_f features, and those of N_s;
    return final embedding set {E_s}_{s∈S};
I' ← ResizeImage(I);
S ← GenerateSuperpixels(I');
G ← ConstructRAG(S);
L ← LabelSuperpixels(S);
A_c ← TrainAutoencoderPerClass(S, L);
{e_s} ← InferEmbeddings(S, A_c);
{E_s} ← CombineWithNeighbors(G, {e_s});
return {E_s}
```

5. Results

5.1. Experiments Phase One

HAM10000 dataset contains dermatoscopic images of both malignant and benign pigmented lesions, with diagnoses confirmed through histopathology, dermatologist consensus, and clinical evolution.

The features can be originated solely from basic statistics extracted from each superpixel, or from a combination of basic statistics and learned embeddings, as illustrated in Figure 8a. Additionally, feature vectors were constructed using information either from a single superpixel or from its neighboring superpixels, as shown in Figure 8b. In the latter case, the order of concatenation was determined by sorting the superpixels according to their ID numbers in ascending order. The combination of these features and their spatial origin forms the basis for constructing our input vectors.

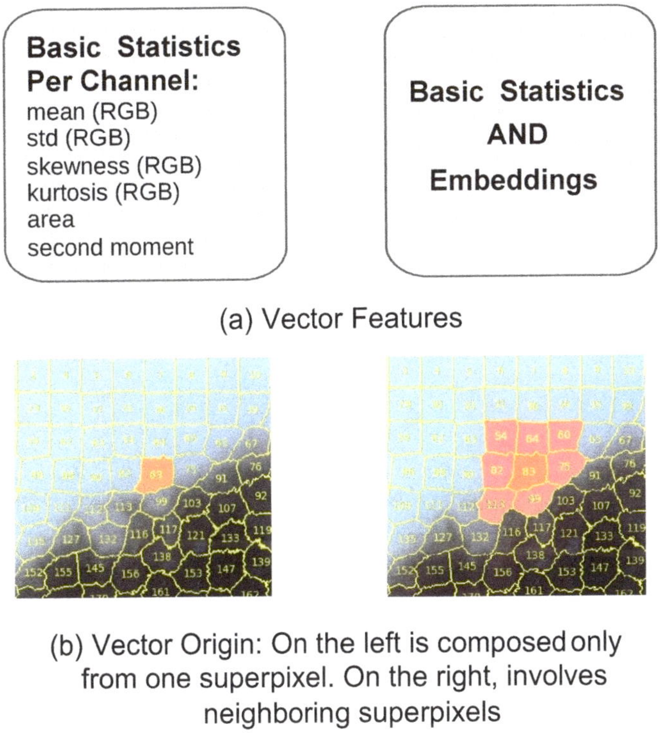

Figure 8. Building vectors.

In the first phase of our experiments, we constructed four distinct types of input–output feature vectors to support different modes of training and inference:

- Type I: The input vector consists of basic region descriptors mean, standard deviation, skewness, and kurtosis of the RGB channels, area, centroid, and shape moments extracted from the target superpixel. The output is the class label associated with the target superpixel.
- Type II: The input vector includes the basic descriptors of the target superpixel, as well as those of its neighboring superpixels. The output remains the class label of the target superpixel.
- Type III: Similar to Type II, the input concatenates descriptors of both the target and neighboring superpixels. However, the output vector extends to predict the class label for every superpixel included in the input group, encompassing both the target and its neighbors.
- Type IV: This configuration consists of two sets of input–output vectors. The first input vector encodes the statistical descriptors of the neighboring superpixels, with the corresponding output vector specifying their class labels. The second input vector

captures the descriptors of the target superpixel alone, with a dedicated output vector indicating its class.

The following neural architectures were used to model these input–output relationships:

- Linear neural network: a fully connected feed-forward network with three hidden layers of sizes 128, 64, and 32 applied to the Type I and Type II feature vectors.
- GRU RNN (many-to-one): A recurrent neural network utilizing four gated recurrent units (GRUs), applied to the sequential embedding of neighbor features (Type II). The final hidden state is passed to a softmax classifier for target class prediction.
- Transformer encoder–decoder (many-to-one): The encoder, composed of four self-attention heads, processes the sequence of target and neighbor superpixels (Type IV). A decoder with four attention heads attends to the encoded context and predicts the target superpixel's class.
- Transformer encoder (many-to-many): A transformer encoder block (with four self-attention heads) jointly processes the concatenated feature set from multiple superpixels (Type III). It outputs class predictions for each region simultaneously.

In our first experiment, we trained a linear neural network on the first vector type to predict the class of each superpixel. As shown in Table 2, the linear neural network performs adequately, given the limited feature set, particularly for Classes 0 and 1 with F1 scores of 0.8333 and 0.8077, respectively. Class 1 exhibits better differentiation from other classes, with the highest accuracy (0.9091) and competitive recall (0.7915). The model performs poorly on class 2 with an F1 score of 0.2937.

Table 2. Model performance.

		Class 0				Class 1				Class 2			
		F1 Score	**Accuracy**	**Precision**	**Recall**	**F1 Score**	**Accuracy**	**Precision**	**Recall**	**F1 Score**	**Accuracy**	**Precision**	**Recall**
Linear Neural Network	Single Superpixel	0.8333	0.794	0.944	0.7458	0.8077	0.9091	0.8246	0.7915	0.2937	0.794	0.1919	0.6251
	Neighbors Superpixels	0.8446	0.8087	0.9596	0.7542	0.8279	0.9185	0.8495	0.8074	0.3257	0.8011	0.2114	0.7097
RNN many(S) to one(S)	GRU	0.7985	0.7589	0.9383	0.695	0.7905	0.8941	0.763	0.8201	0.2397	0.7738	0.1559	0.5188
	Transformer Encoder–Decoder	0.9377	0.9126	0.9229	0.9529	0.8828	0.9432	0.8823	0.8833	0.3572	0.9271	0.4468	0.2976
RNN many(S) to many(S)	Transformer Encoder	0.9816	0.9685	0.9753	0.988	0.9196	0.9812	0.9199	0.9193	0.4816	0.9718	0.6026	0.4011
	Transformer Encoder with Embeddings	1	1	1	1	1	1	1	1	1	1	1	1

In the second experiment, we trained a linear neural network on the second vector type to predict the class of the target superpixel. As depicted in Table 2, compared to the previous model, the values are higher; however, the behavior is similar. The model is good enough for classes 0 and 1, but it underperforms for class 2. Class 1 is better differentiated than the other classes. These results suggest that incorporating neighboring superpixel properties enhances classification, especially for classes 0 and 1.

In the third experiment, we modeled the data as a sequential input of superpixels in ascending order, and we trained an RNN, specifically a GRU, on the second vector type to predict the class of the target superpixel. As illustrated in Table 2, this model, compared to the previous linear neural network experiments, performs marginally lower for classes 0 and 1, implying that sequential modeling may not fully exploit the contextual dependencies in the third vector type.

In the fourth experiment, we implemented a many-to-one RNN architecture using a transformer model with encoder–decoder components, trained on the fourth vector type to predict the class of the target superpixel. The encoder processes multiple superpixels (including their class information), while the decoder focuses on the target superpixel to generate its predicted class. As portrayed in Table 2, Class 0 achieves exceptional performance, with an F1 score of 0.9377, precision of 0.9229, and recall of 0.9529, indicating highly reliable predictions. Class 1 demonstrates strong results (F1: 0.8828; precision: 0.8823) and the highest accuracy (0.9432), suggesting the effective utilization of contextual information from neighboring superpixels. Class 2, however, continues to underperform, with an F1 score of 0.3572 and remarkably low recall (0.2976), despite moderate precision (0.4468).

In the fifth experiment, we employed a many-to-many RNN architecture, specifically a transformer model, trained on the third vector type to predict the classes of all superpixels simultaneously. As detailed in Table 2, Class 0 achieves near-perfect performance, with an F1 score of 0.9816, precision of 0.9753, and recall of 0.9880, demonstrating robust alignment between predictions and ground truth. Class 1 also exhibits strong performance (F1: 0.9196; precision: 0.9199; recall: 0.9193), with accuracy peaking at 0.9812. However, Class 2 remains a challenge, with an F1 score of 0.4816 and a low recall (0.4011), despite moderate precision (0.6026). These results underscore the efficacy of many-to-many transformers in leveraging global dependencies for multi-superpixel classification tasks, though Class 2 may require targeted architectural or data-centric interventions.

5.2. Experiment Phase Two

In the second phase of our experiments, we selected the best-performing model from the initial evaluation, the transformer encoder model, as the basis for further analysis. To enhance the feature representation, we expanded the Type III input vectors by incorporating additional embeddings generated via the transformer autoencoders. This augmentation resulted in a total of 270 features per input instance.

The updated feature vectors were trained using a many-to-many transformer encoder architecture, consisting of a single encoder block with four self-attention heads. The model demonstrated perfect classification performance, achieving an accuracy and F1 score of 1.0 across all semantic classes.

To assess the robustness and generalizability of this performance, we conducted a five-fold cross-validation. The model consistently produced the same results across all folds, confirming the stability and reliability of the learned representations.

As observed in the transformer many-to-many encoder model, using input vectors without embeddings yields strong classification performance for class 0 and class 1, with F1 scores of 0.98 and 0.91, and accuracies of 0.96 and 0.97, respectively. These results suggest that simple statistical features are sufficient for accurately identifying superpixels corresponding to the background and core of the lesion. In other words, distinguishing these two classes is not particularly challenging for the model. Therefore, incorporating embeddings naturally aligns with the goal of maintaining or improving performance.

In contrast, the classification of class 2 (the lesion border) proves significantly more difficult, with an F1 score of 0.48 despite a high accuracy of 0.97, showing the class imbalance and mis-classification When embeddings are added and the input is expanded to include information from neighboring superpixels, performance improves substantially.

These findings strongly suggest that the border superpixels carry the most significant information in the entire image. Moreover, the border regions may be crucial for distinguishing between benign and malignant lesions.

We acknowledge that our dataset consists of 2000 images, and it is likely that the variation in lesion morphology across diverse skin types and racial backgrounds is limited, an inherent limitation of the dataset.

6. Discussion

At this stage of our research, achieving high performance in either lesion classification (benign vs. malignant), or segmentation is not our primary objective. For the medical community to adopt AI in clinical settings, it is essential to address several challenges related to data quality, methodological rigor, and, most importantly, interpretability [5].

In our study, unlike previous approaches that focus on segmentation or disease classification, the primary role of superpixels is to capture the semantics of the superpixels. Each superpixel is labeled as a background, border, or lesion, corresponding to the classes identified in the image. Superpixels from each class are used to train transformer-based autoencoders in order to produce meaningful embeddings that capture the context of all superpixels of each class, regardless of distance between them. We proved that these embeddings capture the semantic content of the classes more effectively than relying solely on the statistical properties of the superpixels.

To enhance classification performance, we not only utilize the embedding of the target superpixel but also incorporate embeddings from its neighboring superpixels as an input to the classifier. The transformer captures the context of the near superpixels (spatial locality). We consider our approach to be novel, with the main contribution being a model that learns to interpret the semantic structure of an image through superpixel-based embeddings.

We hypothesize that superpixels provide more natural and semantically meaningful context for the classification transformer compared to the fixed 16×16 square patches used in the vision transformer (ViT) while maintaining the same number of features [51].

We establish the originality of our methodology in several key aspects:

- Defining the border as a region instead of a well-defined line.
- Generating embeddings for every superpixel using a transformer autoencoder.
- Incorporating those embeddings as features for further training.
- Taking into account the neighborhood to create the input vectors.

However, our study involved several limitations. These include the dependency on SLIC segmentation quality, the need for manual annotations, and the requirement of training the transformer autoencoder as a separate task for embedding generation. The algorithm is not simple and requires several steps for inference; however, it offers the advantage of requiring minimal computational power on both CPU and GPU. The dataset also presents limitations, including demographic imbalances, uneven diagnostic representation, and variable image quality.

The proposed approach converts raw dermoscopic images into structured, region-based representations, thereby producing enhanced input data for subsequent deep learning architectures. This methodology not only contributes to improved melanoma diagnostic capabilities but also establishes a transferable framework applicable to broader medical image segmentation and classification challenges. Future research could extend this approach by exploring its integration with multimodal data, such as clinical metadata or genomic profiles, to improve diagnostic accuracy across diverse patient populations.

7. Conclusions

The objective of our work is to classify superpixels extracted from natural skin images to identify background, border, and core lesion regions. An RAG is constructed from the superpixels to determine neighboring relationships for each individual superpixel. We first constructed input vectors based on the image statistics of each superpixel and used them to train linear neural networks. In our second approach, we expanded the input vectors to include features from both the superpixel and its neighbors, and trained RNNs, specifically GRUs and transformers. Finally, we generated embeddings for each superpixel using transformer-based autoencoders, and we used these embeddings as inputs to train transformer-based RNNs. The best results were achieved using the autoencoder-generated embeddings. We proved that these embeddings capture the semantic characteristics of each class more effectively than raw statistical features.

Supplementary Materials: The following supporting information can be downloaded at: https://www.mdpi.com/article/10.3390/a18090551/s1, Video S1: Labeling Superpixels.

Author Contributions: P.O. was responsible for the study design, data collection and analysis, software tool development, experiment execution, manuscript drafting, and revisions. S.A. contributed to software development, image annotation, and manuscript revisions. I.G. participated in software tool development and image annotation. Y.X. contributed to the study design and provided critical revisions of the manuscript. C.Y.X. and X.Z. both contributed to the critical revision of the manuscript. All authors have read and agreed to the published version of the manuscript.

Funding: This research received no external funding.

Data Availability Statement: We use ISIC (HAM) dataset: https://dataverse.harvard.edu/dataset.xhtml?persistentId=doi:10.7910/DVN/DBW86T (accessed on 20 August 2025).

Conflicts of Interest: The authors declare that the research was conducted in the absence of any commercial or financial relationships that could be construed as a potential conflict of interest.

References

1. SEER. Melanoma of the Skin–Cancer Stat Facts. 2025. Available online: https://seer.cancer.gov/statfacts/html/melan.html (accessed on 19 January 2025).
2. ACS (American Cancer Society). Melanoma Skin Cancer Statistics. 2025. Available online: https://www.cancer.org/cancer/types/melanoma-skin-cancer/about/key-statistics.html (accessed on 19 January 2025).
3. Siegel, R.L.; Miller, K.D.; Fuchs, H.E.; Jemal, A. Cancer statistics, 2022. *CA Cancer J. Clin.* **2022**, *72*, 7–33. [CrossRef]
4. Society, A.C. Cancer Facts and Figures 2022. 2025. Available online: https://www.cancer.org/research/cancer-facts-statistics/all-cancer-facts-figures/cancer-facts-figures-2022.html (accessed on 19 January 2025).
5. Jones, O.T.; Matin, R.N.; van der Schaar, M.; Prathivadi Bhayankaram, K.; Ranmuthu, C.K.I.; Islam, M.S.; Behiyat, D.; Boscott, R.; Calanzani, N.; Emery, J.; et al. Artificial intelligence and machine learning algorithms for early detection of skin cancer in community and primary care settings: A systematic review. *Lancet Digit. Health* **2022**, *4*, e466–e476. [CrossRef] [PubMed]
6. Hassel, J.C.; Enk, A.H. *Fitzpatrick's Dermatology, 9e*; Kang, S., Amagai, M., Bruckner, A.L., Enk, A.H., Margolis, D.J., McMichael, A.J., Orringer, J.S., Eds.; McGraw-Hill Education: New York, NY, USA 2019; Chapter 116.
7. Boiko, P.E.; Koepsell, T.D.; Larson, E.B.; Wagner, E.H. Skin cancer diagnosis in a primary care setting. *J. Am. Acad. Dermatol.* **1996**, *34*, 608–611. [CrossRef]
8. Soyer, H.P.; Smolle, J.; Kerl, H.; Stettner, H. Early diagnosis of malignant melanoma by surface microscopy. *Lancet* **1987**, *330*, 803. [CrossRef]
9. Zahn, C.T.; Roskies, R.Z. Fourier descriptors for plane closed curves. *IEEE Trans. Comput.* **1972**, *C-21*, 269–281. [CrossRef]
10. Toureau, V.; Bibiloni, P.; Talavera-Martínez, L.; González-Hidalgo, M. Automatic Detection of Symmetry in Dermoscopic Images Based on Shape and Texture. In Proceedings of the Information Processing and Management of Uncertainty in Knowledge-Based Systems (IPMU 2020), Lisbon, Portugal, 15–19 June 2020; Springer: Berlin/Heidelberg, Germany, 2020; pp. 591–603. [CrossRef]
11. Ali, A.M.; Li, J.; Yang, G.; O'Shea, S. A Novel Fuzzy Multilayer Perceptron (F-MLP) for the Detection of Border Irregularity in Skin Lesions. *Front. Med.* **2020**, *7*, 297. [CrossRef] [PubMed]
12. Ali, A.R.; Li, J.; O'Shea, S.J. Towards the automatic detection of skin lesion shape asymmetry, color variegation and diameter in dermoscopic images. *PLoS ONE* **2020**, *15*, e0234352. [CrossRef]
13. Samuel, N.E.; Anitha, J. Melanoma Detection and Classification based on Dermoscopic Images using Deep Learning Architectures-A Study. In Proceedings of the 2022 4th International Conference on Inventive Research in Computing Applications (ICIRCA), Coimbatore, India, 21–23 September 2022; pp. 993–1000. [CrossRef]
14. Alsahafi, Y.S.; Elshora, D.S.; Mohamed, E.R.; Hosny, K.M. Multilevel threshold segmentation of skin lesions in color images using Coronavirus Optimization Algorithm. *Diagnostics* **2023**, *13*, 2958. [CrossRef]
15. Codella, N.C.F.; Gutman, D.; Celebi, M.E.; Helba, B.; Marchetti, M.A.; Dusza, S.W.; Kalloo, A.; Liopyris, K.; Mishra, N.; Kittler, H.; et al. Skin Lesion Analysis Toward Melanoma Detection: A Challenge at the 2017 International Symposium on Biomedical Imaging (ISBI), Hosted by the International Skin Imaging Collaboration (ISIC). *arXiv* **2018**, arXiv:1710.05006 [CrossRef]
16. Patel, R.H.; Foltz, E.A.; Witkowski, A.; Ludzik, J. Analysis of Artificial Intelligence-Based Approaches Applied to Non-Invasive Imaging for Early Detection of Melanoma: A Systematic Review. *Cancers* **2023**, *15*, 4694. [CrossRef]
17. Rosas-Lara, M.; Mendoza-Tello, J.C.; Flores, A.; Zumba-Acosta, G. A Convolutional Neural Network-Based Web Prototype to Support Melanoma Skin Cancer Detection. In Proceedings of the 2022 Third International Conference on Information Systems and Software Technologies (ICI2ST), Quito, Ecuador, 8–10 November 2022; pp. 1–7. [CrossRef]

18. Subramanian, B.; Muthusamy, S.; Thangaraj, K.; Panchal, H.; Kasirajan, E.; Marimuthu, A.; Ravi, A. A new method for detection and classification of melanoma skin cancer using deep learning based transfer learning architecture models. *Res. Sq.* **2022**. [CrossRef]
19. Sagar, A.; Jacob, D. Convolutional Neural Networks for Classifying Melanoma Images. *bioRXiv* **2020**. [CrossRef]
20. Gangwani, D.; Liang, Q.; Wang, S.; Zhu, X. An Empirical Study of Deep Learning Frameworks for Melanoma Cancer Detection using Transfer Learning and Data Augmentation. In Proceedings of the 2021 IEEE International Conference on Big Knowledge (ICBK), Auckland, New Zealand, 7–8 December 2021; pp. 38–45. [CrossRef]
21. Cirrincione, G.; Cannata, S.; Cicceri, G.; Prinzi, F.; Currieri, T.; Lovino, M.; Militello, C.; Pasero, E.; Vitabile, S. Transformer-Based Approach to Melanoma Detection. *Sensors* **2023**, *23*, 5677. [CrossRef]
22. Khan, S.; Khan, A. SkinViT: A transformer based method for Melanoma and Nonmelanoma classification. *PLoS ONE* **2023**, *18*, e0295151. [CrossRef]
23. Xie, J.; Wu, Z.; Zhu, R.; Zhu, H. Melanoma Detection based on Swin Transformer and SimAM. In Proceedings of the 2021 IEEE 5th Information Technology, Networking, Electronic and Automation Control Conference (ITNEC), Xi'an, China, 15–17 October 2021; Volume 5, pp. 1517–1521. [CrossRef]
24. Tan, M.; Le, Q.V. EfficientNet: Rethinking Model Scaling for Convolutional Neural Networks. *arXiv* **2020**, arXiv:1905.11946. [CrossRef]
25. Hosny, K.M.; Elshoura, D.; Mohamed, E.R.; Vrochidou, E.; Papakostas, G.A. Deep Learning and Optimization-Based Methods for Skin Lesions Segmentation: A Review. *IEEE Access* **2023**, *11*, 85467–85488. [CrossRef]
26. Zafar, M.; Amin, J.; Sharif, M.; Anjum, M.A.; Mallah, G.A.; Kadry, S. DeepLabv3+-Based Segmentation and Best Features Selection Using Slime Mould Algorithm for Multi-Class Skin Lesion Classification. *Mathematics* **2023**, *11*, 364. [CrossRef]
27. Chen, B.; Liu, Y.; Zhang, Z.; Lu, G.; Kong, A.W.K. TransAttUnet: Multi-Level Attention-Guided U-Net With Transformer for Medical Image Segmentation. *IEEE Trans. Emerg. Top. Comput. Intell.* **2024**, *8*, 55–68. [CrossRef]
28. Akyel, C.; Arıcı, N. LinkNet-B7: Noise Removal and Lesion Segmentation in Images of Skin Cancer. *Mathematics* **2022**, *10*, 736. [CrossRef]
29. Shreshth, S.; Divij, G.; Anil, K.T. Detector-SegMentor Network for Skin Lesion Localization and Segmentation. *arXiv* **2020**, arXiv:2005.06550.
30. Zhang, L. FITrans: Skin Lesion Segmentation Based on Feature Integration and Transformer. In Proceedings of the 2023 3rd International Conference on Neural Networks, Information and Communication Engineering (NNICE), Guangzhou, China, 24–26 February 2023; pp. 324–329. [CrossRef]
31. Dong, Y.; Wang, L.; Li, Y. TC-Net: Dual coding network of Transformer and CNN for skin lesion segmentation. *PLoS ONE* **2022**, *17*, e0277578. [CrossRef]
32. Liu, S.; Zhuang, Z.; Zheng, Y.; Kolmanič, S. A VAN-Based Multi-Scale Cross-Attention Mechanism for Skin Lesion Segmentation Network. *IEEE Access* **2023**, *11*, 81953–81964. [CrossRef]
33. Kittler, H.; Pehamberger, H.; Wolff, K.; Binder, M. Diagnostic accuracy of dermoscopy. *Lancet Oncol.* **2002**, *3*, 159–165. [CrossRef]
34. Wighton, P.; Lee, T.K.; Lui, H.; McLean, D.I.; Atkins, M.S. Generalizing Common Tasks in Automated Skin Lesion Diagnosis. *IEEE Trans. Inf. Technol. Biomed.* **2011**, *15*, 622–629. [CrossRef]
35. Chen, L.C.; Zhu, Y.; Papandreou, G.; Schroff, F.; Adam, H. Encoder-Decoder with Atrous Separable Convolution for Semantic Image Segmentation. *arXiv* **2018**, arXiv:1802.02611. [CrossRef]
36. Adegun, A.A.; Viriri, S.; Yousaf, M.H. A Probabilistic-Based Deep Learning Model for Skin Lesion Segmentation. *Appl. Sci.* **2021**, *11*, 3025. [CrossRef]
37. Ünver, H.M.; Ayan, E. Skin Lesion Segmentation in Dermoscopic Images with Combination of YOLO and GrabCut Algorithm. *Diagnostics* **2019**, *9*, 72. [CrossRef] [PubMed]
38. Mirikharaji, Z.; Abhishek, K.; Izadi, S.; Hamarneh, G. D-LEMA: Deep Learning Ensembles from Multiple Annotations—Application to Skin Lesion Segmentation. *arXiv* **2021**, arXiv:2012.07206.
39. Li, X.; Peng, B.; Hu, J.; Ma, C.; Yang, D.; Xie, Z. USL-Net: Uncertainty Self-Learning Network for Unsupervised Skin Lesion Segmentation. *arXiv* **2024**, arXiv:2309.13289. [CrossRef]
40. Lu, W.; Gong, D.; Fu, K.; Sun, X.; Diao, W.; Liu, L. Boundarymix: Generating pseudo-training images for improving segmentation with scribble annotations. *Pattern Recognit.* **2021**, *117*, 107924. [CrossRef]
41. Avelar, P.H.C.; Tavares, A.R.; da Silveira, T.L.T.; Jung, C.R.; Lamb, L.C. Superpixel Image Classification with Graph Attention Networks. In Proceedings of the 2020 33rd SIBGRAPI Conference on Graphics, Patterns and Images (SIBGRAPI), Ipojuca, Brazil, 7–10 November 2020; pp. 203–209. [CrossRef]
42. Nazir, U.; Wang, H.; Taj, M. Survey of Image Based Graph Neural Networks. *arXiv* **2021**, arXiv:2106.06307. [CrossRef]
43. Nowosad, J.; Stepinski, T.F. Extended SLIC superpixels algorithm for applications to non-imagery geospatial rasters. *Int. J. Appl. Earth Obs. Geoinf.* **2022**, *112*, 102935. [CrossRef]

44. Qin, W.; Wu, J.; Han, F.; Yuan, Y.; Zhao, W.; Ibragimov, B.; Gu, J.; Xing, L. Superpixel-based and boundary-sensitive convolutional neural network for automated liver segmentation. *Phys. Med. Biol.* **2018**, *63*, 095017. [CrossRef]
45. Achanta, R.; Shaji, A.; Smith, K.; Lucchi, A.; Fua, P.; Süsstrunk, S. SLIC Superpixels Compared to State-of-the-Art Superpixel Methods. *IEEE Trans. Pattern Anal. Mach. Intell.* **2010**, *34*, 2274–2282. [CrossRef]
46. Gaur, U.; Manjunath, B.S. Superpixel Embedding Network. *IEEE Trans. Image Process.* **2020**, *29*, 3199–3212. [CrossRef]
47. OpenCV Team. OpenCV (Open Source Computer Vision Library). Version 4.9.0.2023. Available online: https://opencv.org/ (accessed on 19 January 2025).
48. Jaworek-Korjakowska, J.; Kleczek, P. Region Adjacency Graph Approach for Acral Melanocytic Lesion Segmentation. *Appl. Sci.* **2018**, *8*, 1430. [CrossRef]
49. Tschandl, P.; Rosendahl, C.; Kittler, H. The HAM10000 dataset, a large collection of multi-source dermatoscopic images of common pigmented skin lesions. *Sci. Data* **2018**, *5*, 180161. [CrossRef]
50. Neo4j, Inc. Neo4j: Graph Data Platform. 2023. Available online: https://neo4j.com/ (accessed on 19 January 2025).
51. Dosovitskiy, A.; Beyer, L.; Kolesnikov, A.; Weissenborn, D.; Zhai, X.; Unterthiner, T.; Dehghani, M.; Minderer, M.; Heigold, G.; Gelly, S.; et al. An Image is Worth 16x16 Words: Transformers for Image Recognition at Scale. *arXiv* **2020**, arXiv:2010.11929.

algorithms

MDPI

Article

Automated Subregional Hippocampus Segmentation Using 3D CNNs: A Computational Framework for Brain Aging Biomarker Analysis

Eshaa Gogia [1], Arash Dehzangi [2] and Iman Dehzangi [1,3,4,*]

[1] Department of Computer Science, Rutgers University, Camden, NJ 08102, USA; eg760@scarletmail.rutgers.edu
[2] Department of Electrical and Computer Engineering, University of Texas at Dallas, Richardson, TX 75080, USA; arash.dehzangi@utdallas.edu
[3] Center of Computational and Integrative Biology, Rutgers University, Camden, NJ 08102, USA
[4] Rutgers Cancer Institute, Rutgers University, New Brunswick, NJ 08901, USA
* Correspondence: i.dehzangi@rutgers.edu

Abstract: The hippocampus is a critical brain structure involved in episodic memory, spatial orientation, and stress regulation. Its volumetric shrinkage is among the earliest and most reliable indicators of both physiological brain aging and pathological neurodegeneration. Accurate segmentation and measurement of the hippocampal subregions from magnetic resonance imaging (MRI) is therefore essential for neurobiological age estimation and the early identification of at-risk individuals. In this study, we present a fully automated pipeline that leverages nnU-Net, a self-configuring deep learning framework, to segment the hippocampus from high-resolution 3D T1-weighted brain MRI scans. The primary objective of this work is to enable accurate estimation of brain age through quantitative analysis of hippocampal volume. By fusing domain knowledge in neuroanatomy with data-driven learning through a highly expressive and self-optimizing model, this work advances the methodological frontier for neuroimaging-based brain-age estimation. The proposed approach demonstrates that deep learning can serve as a reliable segmentation tool as well as a foundational layer in predictive neuroscience, supporting early detection of accelerated aging and subclinical neurodegenerative processes.

Keywords: hippocampus segmentation; neurodegeneration biomarkers; nn-Unet; 3D imaging; deep learning; brain-age estimation

1. Introduction

Aging is a complex, multidimensional biological process marked by gradual physiological decline and increased disease susceptibility. Within the brain, aging manifests structurally as regional atrophy, white matter degradation, and diminished functional connectivity. Among the regions most consistently affected is the hippocampus—a bilateral structure located within the medial temporal lobes, critical for memory consolidation, spatial navigation, and stress regulation [1]. Longitudinal neuroimaging studies have consistently shown that hippocampal volume decreases with age. Moreover, the rate and pattern of this decline serve as quantifiable proxies for biological brain age, which may diverge from chronological age due to genetic, environmental, or pathological influences [1]. Hippocampal atrophy is a hallmark of various neurodegenerative disorders, including Alzheimer's disease, frontotemporal dementia, and mild cognitive impairment (MCI), as well as psychiatric conditions such as major depressive disorder and post-traumatic stress disorder (PTSD) [2].

In many of these conditions, hippocampal shrinkage precedes clinical symptom onset by several years, positioning it as a compelling target for early detection, disease monitoring, and risk stratification. Traditional methods for assessing hippocampal volume via structural magnetic resonance imaging (MRI) typically rely on manual delineation by experts or atlas-based registration techniques [3]. Although these approaches provide anatomical interpretability, they are labor-intensive, subject to inter-rater variability, and poorly suited for large-scale applications. Furthermore, atlas-based methods often fail to capture individual variations in hippocampal morphology, particularly in elderly individuals or those with marked atrophy [3]. These limitations highlight the need for automated, high-precision segmentation tools that are both scalable and robust across diverse populations.

Recent advances in deep learning, particularly convolutional neural networks (CNNs), have significantly advanced medical image segmentation tasks [4]. Among these, nnU-Net ("no-new-Net") has emerged as a self-configuring framework that autonomously adapts to various biomedical segmentation tasks, eliminating the need for manual hyperparameter tuning or architectural design. The nnU-Net framework automatically selects from three architectural variants, namely 2D U-Net, 3D full-resolution U-Net, and 3D low-resolution cascade, based on data fingerprinting. In our case, the dataset exhibited isotropic resolution and moderate spatial dimensions, prompting the use of the 3D full-resolution variant. This variant is optimal for volumetric segmentation when inter-slice and in-plane resolution are comparable, allowing the network to leverage full 3D spatial context while preserving anatomical boundaries of curved structures like the hippocampus [5].

In this study, we employ nnU-Net for hippocampal segmentation on high-resolution T1-weighted MRI scans, aiming to estimate brain age through volumetric analysis. The study emphasizes data-centric optimization and clinical integration of an adaptive segmentation pipeline, enabling accurate hippocampal delineation in structurally variable MRI datasets. Specifically, we segment the anterior and posterior hippocampal subregions, which follow distinct aging trajectories and serve different cognitive functions. The anterior hippocampus is primarily associated with affective and stress-related processes, while the posterior region supports spatial memory and navigation [6]. This subregional differentiation enhances the specificity of brain-age estimation and may improve the detection of stress-related neurocognitive decline. Furthermore, the segmentation outcomes are not treated as end goals but are integrated into downstream volumetric estimation and brain aging analysis, thereby advancing clinically interpretable neuroimaging solutions. Our approach combines anatomical precision with computational scalability, offering a clinically relevant pipeline for using hippocampal volume as a non-invasive biomarker of accelerated brain aging. Our proposed pipeline is publicly available at https://github.com/Eshaa2001/BrainAge (Access date: 10 August 2025).

2. Literature Review

The structural and functional integrity of the hippocampus has remained central to aging and neurodegeneration research for over two decades [6]. With advancements in MRI and neuroinformatics, it is now one of the most thoroughly characterized regions in neuroimaging, noted both for its vulnerability to pathological processes and its utility as a biomarker of cognitive health. This section reviews the key literature across hippocampal segmentation, lifespan volumetric decline, and the evolution from classical approaches to deep learning frameworks like nnU-Net.

2.1. Hippocampal Atrophy in Stress, Depression, and Aging

Early foundational work highlighted the hippocampus's susceptibility to stress-induced neurotoxicity, driven primarily by HPA axis dysregulation and glucocorticoid exposure. These mechanisms trigger dendritic retraction, inhibit neurogenesis, and impair synaptic plasticity, ultimately leading to hippocampal volume loss and memory deficits [7]. Human neuroimaging studies have corroborated these findings, showing significantly reduced hippocampal volume in individuals with major depressive disorder (MDD) relative to healthy controls [7].

Atrophy in the hippocampus is also recognized as an early biomarker in Alzheimer's disease (AD) and mild cognitive impairment (MCI), detectable prior to clinical symptom onset. Furthermore, volumetric reductions have been consistently reported in psychiatric conditions such as MDD, PTSD, and chronic stress exposure, highlighting the region's dual vulnerability to neurodegenerative and environmental stressors [8]. The degree of volume loss correlates with both the number and duration of depressive episodes, indicating a cumulative neurotoxic effect. PTSD studies further support this, revealing pronounced hippocampal shrinkage linked to trauma-related psychopathology [9].

Subregional analyses suggest that the anterior hippocampus, implicated in emotion regulation, may be disproportionately affected in mood disorders compared to the posterior region [10]. In healthy populations, longitudinal imaging has revealed a nonlinear trajectory of hippocampal atrophy, with acceleration after the sixth decade of life, reinforcing its role as a marker of deviation from normative aging.

2.2. Hippocampal Volume as a Neurodegenerative Biomarker

Hippocampal atrophy remains a defining structural hallmark in early AD and MCI. MRI-based volumetry has proven effective in distinguishing AD patients from age-matched controls with high sensitivity [11]. Moreover, the rate of hippocampal volume loss is predictive of MCI-to-AD conversion, cementing its value as a diagnostic and prognostic marker.

While normative aging involves hippocampal shrinkage of ~0.8–2% annually, pathological aging often exceeds this rate [12]. Anatomical heterogeneity underlies this degeneration, with the anterior and posterior subregions showing distinct vulnerability profiles. Left-sided atrophy and subfield-specific loss, particularly in CA1 and the dentate gyrus, have also been reported. These localized patterns offer earlier indicators of neurodegeneration and support the utility of high-resolution, subfield-sensitive analysis [12]. Subsequent work emphasized that posterior hippocampal atrophy is more predictive of memory decline and tau pathology, further validating its role in longitudinal risk modeling [13].

2.3. Traditional Approaches to Hippocampal Segmentation

Manual segmentation using anatomical landmarks has long been considered the gold standard for hippocampal volumetry. However, it is labor-intensive, subjective, and unsuitable for high-throughput studies [14]. To address these limitations, probabilistic atlas-based methods emerged, including the Hammers atlas for medial temporal structures [15]. While these improved throughput, they underperformed in individuals with severe atrophy.

Automated tools such as FreeSurfer and FSL-FIRST offered rapid segmentation [16] but often failed to capture fine anatomical boundaries, particularly in aged or diseased brains. These limitations highlight the persistent trade-off between automation and anatomical precision in conventional pipelines.

2.4. Emergence of Deep Learning in Neuroanatomical Segmentation

Deep learning has significantly advanced neuroanatomical segmentation over the past decade. Encoder–decoder CNNs, particularly U-Net, became the foundation for volumetric segmentation tasks, leveraging skip connections and hierarchical representations to handle limited datasets effectively [17]. In hippocampal segmentation, CNNs have surpassed atlas-based and manual methods in both accuracy and generalizability [18]. Moreover, CNNs demonstrated resilience to anatomical variability and imaging artifacts. Targeted studies identified the benefits of task-specific augmentation, patch-based learning, and structure-sensitive loss functions for segmenting small subcortical regions such as the hippocampus [18]. These strategies contribute to model robustness and finer anatomical delineation.

2.5. Toward Brain-Age Modeling via Hippocampal Volume

Brain-age estimation leverages imaging-derived biomarkers to quantify biological aging. A brain age greater than chronological age is associated with elevated risk for cognitive decline, psychiatric conditions, and increased mortality [19]. Although whole-brain metrics are widely used, hippocampal volume offers distinct advantages due to its early and sensitive response to neurodegenerative processes. Deep learning-based segmentation methods, particularly nnU-Net, enable anatomically precise, reproducible extraction of hippocampal volumes. This precision facilitates integration into brain-age models. Furthermore, anterior and posterior subregional volumes allow refined analysis of stress-related and disease-specific aging signatures [20], underscoring the role of hippocampal morphometry in predictive neuroscience.

3. Dataset and Preprocessing

In this section, we introduce the dataset that is used in this study. We also present the preprocessing steps to prepare this dataset for experimentation.

3.1. Dataset Description

The dataset used in this study is publicly available through the Neuroimaging Informatics Tools and Resources Clearinghouse (NITRC) under group ID 377 [21]. It comprises high-resolution T1-weighted structural brain MRI volumes acquired specifically for temporal lobe analysis. The dataset is curated to support research in neurodegeneration and psychiatric disorders where hippocampal volume is a key variable.

Each MRI volume includes manually segmented hippocampal masks annotated by trained experts using standardized neuroanatomical landmarks. The segmentations differentiate the entire hippocampal structure from surrounding tissues, enabling precise volumetric analysis. All scans were acquired using a 3 Tesla (3T) MRI scanner to ensure high tissue contrast and consistent anatomical detail across the cerebral and subcortical structures. The voxel dimensions for all subjects were standardized at $1.0 \times 1.0 \times 1.0$ mm^3, yielding isotropic resolution suitable for volumetric segmentation. Images were stored in Neuroimaging Informatics Technology Initiative (NIfTI) format (.nii.gz), which preserves spatial orientation and supports downstream compatibility with common neuroimaging toolkits.

The MRI acquisition protocol included full-brain coverage in the axial plane, subsequently reoriented into RAS (Right–Anterior–Superior) alignment for standardized preprocessing [22]. Each image volume was subjected to quality control to confirm the absence of motion artifacts or acquisition abnormalities. Metadata accompanying each scan included anonymized subject identifiers, acquisition timestamps, imaging modality descriptors, and basic diagnostic annotations where applicable. These parameters provided a uniform and high-quality imaging foundation for subsequent segmentation and analysis of hippocampal morphology.

The dataset used in this study comprises high-resolution T1-weighted MRI scans from adolescents aged 7.7 to 15.6 years. This developmental window represents a critical period of hippocampal maturation, synaptic pruning, and neuroplastic adaptation. Unlike older cohorts, where hippocampal atrophy may indicate neurodegeneration, deviations from normative volume trajectories in adolescents may serve as early markers of atypical neurodevelopment. The dataset presents an opportunity to investigate structural vulnerability during early life, with potential implications for identifying stress-related or environmental influences on brain morphology prior to the onset of clinical symptoms.

Gender distribution in the cohort is relatively balanced, with near-equal representation of male and female participants. Handedness data indicate a majority of right-handed individuals, with a subset identified as mixed-handed, allowing for potential exploration of hemispheric dominance effects in future analyses. Pubertal development is recorded using the Tanner staging system, with subjects categorized from Stage 1 (prepubescent) to Stage 5 (fully mature), thereby enabling the integration of neuroendocrine status into volumetric interpretations. In addition to developmental indices, biometric measures such as height (ranging from approximately 51 to 62 inches), weight (68 to 188 lbs), and head circumference (52.2 to 57 cm) are also included. These anthropometric data are valuable for covariate adjustment in volumetric analysis and for investigating brain–body size relationships [ID2]. Together, the demographic and biometric richness of the dataset provides a multidimensional context for interpreting hippocampal segmentation results and supports stratified or normalized analyses critical for accurate modeling of brain age across individual developmental trajectories.

3.2. Motivation and Rationale for MSD Conversion

The raw NITRC dataset, although well-annotated, does not conform to the structure required by nnU-Net's self-configuring framework [23]. To enable automatic architecture and pipeline selection, the dataset was manually converted into the **Medical Segmentation Decathlon (MSD)** format, which is the expected standard for training with **nnU-Net**.

The conversion process serves several key purposes:

- **Standardization**: Harmonizes directory structure and naming conventions across all subject volumes and masks.
- **Pipeline Automation**: Enables nnU-Net to auto-detect modalities, voxel spacing, and channel configurations.
- **Reproducibility**: Aligns with best practices in open medical image science by adopting an interoperable, benchmarked dataset format.

3.3. Preprocessing Workflow

Medical image datasets vary widely in dimensionality, modality, and spatial resolution [24]. Differences in voxel spacing, target structure properties, and class imbalance further complicate standardized model development. For such scattered and unorganized spaces, nnU-Net model is tailored to analyze training data and automatically configure a corresponding U-Net pipeline for segmentation. It includes multiple phases to ensure high-quality data for model training and inference.

3.3.1. Image Normalization and Resampling

All scans were resampled to an isotropic voxel spacing of $1.0 \times 1.0 \times 1.0$ mm^3. This standardization reduces inter-scanner resolution bias, which is a known source of variability in multicenter neuroimaging datasets. Uniform spacing enables consistent convolutional kernel application across samples and improves spatial compatibility. Per-volume z-score normalization was subsequently applied to the intensity values, centering each image to zero mean and unit variance. This preprocessing step mitigates differences in scanner calibration, contrast dynamics, and tissue intensity distributions, which otherwise degrade model generalization and increase domain shift. Prior studies have shown that even subtle variations in voxel intensity or resolution can lead to a significant drop in segmentation accuracy when left uncorrected [25].

3.3.2. Spatial Cropping and ROI Localization

To minimize computational complexity and enhance anatomical specificity, hippocampus-focused sub-volumes were extracted using bounding boxes derived from ground truth segmentations [26]. This preprocessing step eliminated irrelevant background regions, reducing interference from surrounding brain structures such as the cerebellum, ventricles, and cortex. For unseen test scans, nnU-Net employed its built-in region proposal mechanism to autonomously identify the hippocampal region during inference, ensuring consistent localization.

3.3.3. Denoising and Artifact Reduction

Despite the overall quality of the NITRC dataset, certain volumes exhibited motion-induced artifacts and scanner-related signal fluctuations. To address these inconsistencies, spatial smoothing was applied to suppress isolated voxel-level noise, while a probabilistic outlier detection framework mitigated intensity spikes arising from acquisition instability [27]. Care was taken to preserve hippocampal boundary integrity and avoid excessive regularization.

4. Materials and Methods

In this section, we present our employed method, proposed pipeline, and employed evaluation measurements.

4.1. Setting up the Internal Pipeline

After conversion to the Medical Segmentation Decathlon (MSD) format, the dataset is processed by nnU-Net's modular framework. This triggers a multi-stage analysis called dataset fingerprinting. The framework extracts core characteristics of the input data. These include image resolution, voxel spacing, intensity distribution, and class balance. This information guides the automatic configuration of the segmentation architecture and training schedule.

Key parameters computed during this stage include the following:

- Spatial dimensions of each image volume, voxel spacing across all three anatomical axes, and the presence or absence of anisotropy;
- The ratio of foreground to background voxels, assessing class distribution balance across the segmentation labels;
- Statistical properties of intensity values—mean, variance, and intensity range—to inform the choice of normalization and augmentation strategies.

Based on a detailed analysis of dataset characteristics, nnU-Net employs heuristic-based rules to select the optimal architecture from three predefined U-Net variants. The 2D U-Net is designated for planar imaging or highly anisotropic volumes where inter-slice resolution is significantly lower than in-plane resolution [28]. The 3D full-resolution U-Net is best suited for isotropic or near-isotropic datasets, enabling the model to fully exploit volumetric spatial continuity without compromising resolution [29]. Lastly, the 3D low-resolution cascade is tailored for very large 3D volumes, where a coarse-resolution model provides initial localization, refined subsequently by a high-resolution network in a cascaded scheme.

We employed nnU-Net v2, which dynamically configures its architecture, preprocessing, and training parameters based on the dataset fingerprint. For our isotropic and moderately sized T1-weighted MRI volumes, nnU-Net selected the 3D full-resolution U-Net. This decision enables end-to-end volumetric segmentation without resampling compromises [29].

4.2. Mask Overlay and Region Localization

Before training, segmentation masks are visually overlaid on the corresponding MRI volumes. This overlay process serves two purposes:

- Validation of Ground Truth: Ensures alignment between anatomical landmarks and annotated hippocampal structures.
- Quality Assurance: Detects misregistrations, label inconsistencies, and outliers before model training.

Overlay visualizations are performed using *nibabel (Version 5.4.0)* for NIfTI parsing and *matplotlib* (Version 3.10.5) for slice-by-slice rendering as shown in Figure 1.

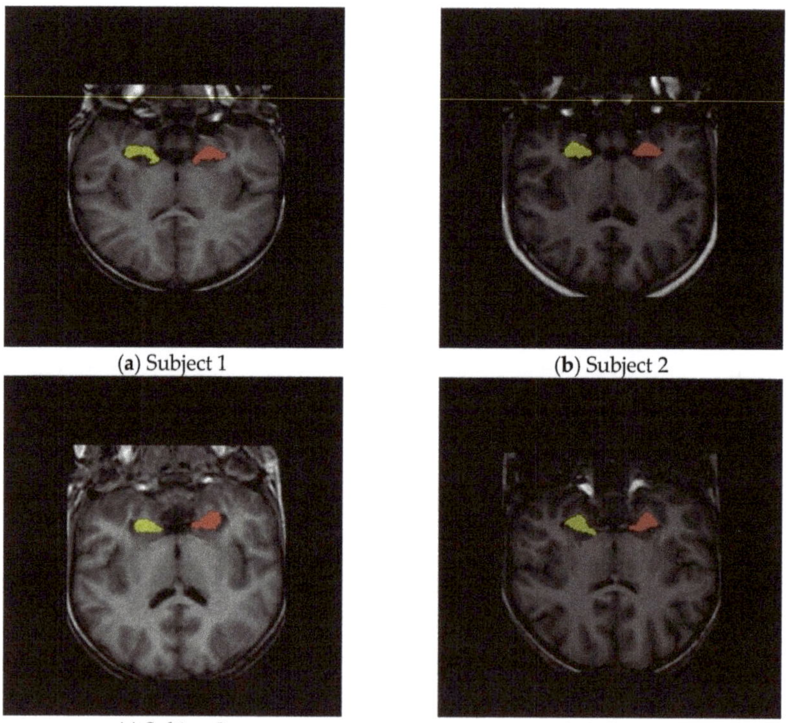

(**a**) Subject 1 (**b**) Subject 2 (**c**) Subject 3 (**d**) Subject 4

Figure 1. Hippocampus overlay masks on four subject samples.

4.3. NnU-Net Model

The nnU-Net framework represents a significant advancement in biomedical image segmentation, setting a new benchmark through its automation and adaptability [30]. Unlike conventional models that rely on manual tuning, nnU-Net configures the entire pipeline based on intrinsic dataset characteristics. This self-adaptation begins with a comprehensive fingerprinting process that evaluates voxel spacing, resolution, class distribution, and intensity histograms [31]. Based on this analysis, nnU-Net dynamically defines the network topology. The model selects appropriate encoder–decoder depth, kernel sizes, and filter counts. These parameters are scaled according to image shape and GPU memory constraints. Spatial resampling and intensity normalization are configured automatically for modality-specific preprocessing.

The framework generates its training schedule, including optimizer type, learning rate, and stopping criteria. Data augmentation strategies are selected heuristically and include elastic deformation, affine transformations, and gamma correction to promote robustness and generalization. Upon release, nnU-Net was benchmarked on **23** biomedical datasets from leading segmentation challenges. It consistently matched or outperformed state-of-the-art methods without any dataset-specific tuning. The architecture generalizes well across imaging modalities and anatomical structures, including anisotropic volumes and class-imbalanced problems. Its performance in hippocampal segmentation highlights the framework's precision in modeling small, structurally complex regions [31]. nnU-Net's reproducibility and data-centric design have made it the gold standard for automated medical image segmentation [31]. The General architecture of our proposed model is shown in Figure 2.

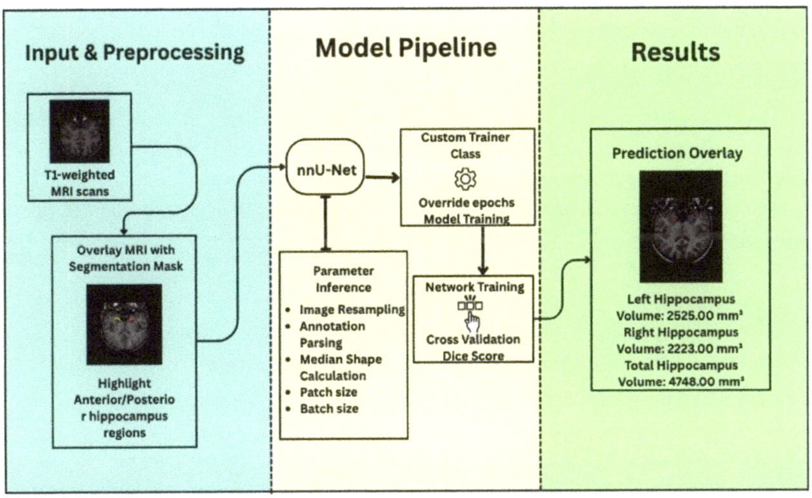

Figure 2. nnU-Net framework for hippocampus segmentation.

4.4. *Customization of the Training Pipeline*

While nnU-Net provides a fully functional baseline trainer, we implemented additional customization to suit hippocampus segmentation:

- The training duration was set to 100 epochs based on preliminary experiments and convergence patterns observed during model development.
- Empirical monitoring of the validation loss and Dice coefficient across training iterations revealed performance stabilization before the 100-epoch mark.
- We activated 5-fold cross-validation, ensuring robustness across variable anatomical morphologies.

Loss convergence and generalization were evaluated at each fold using Dice similarity coefficient and precision.

4.5. Prediction Phase and Postprocessing

During inference, nnU-Net processes each subject's MRI volume in overlapping patches. The default nnU-Net trainer was extended to allow logging of anterior and posterior subregion volumes separately by interpreting class labels 1 and 2. Postprocessing included threshold-based outlier detection and overlay visualization using matplotlib and nibabel libraries. The predicted segmentation masks are directly generated in the form of discrete label maps without voxel-level probability outputs. These predictions are automatically resampled back to the original image space and exported in NIfTI format. This preserves affine transformations and spatial orientation, enabling seamless integration with neuroimaging workflows.

Post-processing involves connected component analysis, which eliminates small, disconnected regions that deviate from the expected hippocampal morphology [32]. This step enhances anatomical precision and minimizes false positives. The refined binary masks are overlaid on the original structural scans to allow qualitative visual assessment. Hippocampal volumes are then computed in cubic millimeters (mm^3) from the segmented masks. These measurements are benchmarked against normative volumetric distributions, stratified by demographic variables such as age and sex. Subjects falling below established thresholds—such as the fifth percentile—are flagged for potential hippocampal atrophy. These cases warrant further investigation, particularly in the context of stress-related brain aging or neurodegenerative risk.

4.6. Evaluation Measurement

The Dice coefficient is the primary evaluation metric in this task. Medical images often contain small structures (e.g., tumors, hippocampus) surrounded by large background areas. Dice is robust to this imbalance, unlike accuracy, which can be misleading [33]. Given the relatively small size of the hippocampus, even minor segmentation errors can cause substantial clinical misinterpretations. Dice is preferred because of the following reasons:

- It balances false positives and false negatives.
- It emphasizes spatial overlap between predicted and ground truth masks.
- It is more stable than accuracy in class-imbalanced tasks.

We can compute the Dice score using the following mathematical equation:

$$\mathcal{L}Dice = 1 - (2 \times \sum(pi \times gi) + \epsilon) / \left(\sum\left(pi^2\right) \times \sum\left(gi^2\right) + \epsilon\right) \quad (1)$$

where $\mathcal{L}Dice$ is a Dice loss (a similarity-based loss function used in segmentation tasks), pi is predicted binary labels per voxel, gi is ground truth binary labels per voxel, and ϵ is a smoothing constant for numerical stability. The total loss function combines Dice and Cross-Entropy losses as follows:

$$Total = \lambda_1 \times Dice + \lambda_2 \times \mathcal{L}CE \quad (2)$$

where $\mathcal{L}total$ is the final loss function used for model optimization, λ_1 is the weighting coefficient for Dice Loss, λ_2 is the weighting coefficient for categorical cross entropy loss, and $\mathcal{L}CE$ is categorical cross-entropy loss. The Dice score quantifies spatial overlap between predicted and ground truth segmentations. A score of 1.0 denotes perfect agreement, while 0.0 indicates no overlap. In medical imaging, values above 0.7 are generally considered acceptable, depending on the anatomical region and modality.

5. Results and Discussion

In this section, we present our achieved results, compare them with the state-of-the-art deep learning models, and discuss them in detail.

5.1. Quantitative Evaluation Metrics

The quantitative performance of our hippocampus segmentation model was rigorously evaluated using 5-fold cross-validation on the curated MRI dataset. For each fold, the nnU-Net framework was trained on approximately 65 subjects and validated on 17, ensuring representative sampling and minimizing bias due to data partitioning. The primary metric used for performance evaluation was the Dice similarity coefficient (DSC), which quantifies spatial overlap between the predicted and ground-truth segmentation masks. The final model achieved a mean validation Dice score of 0.733, reflecting strong anatomical fidelity in a challenging task involving small, irregularly shaped brain structures.

This performance demonstrates the model's ability to generalize across varied anatomical presentations and scan dimensions, as reflected in the diverse tensor shapes observed during inference. While the Dice score does not exceed the threshold typically associated with large, easily segmented structures (e.g., liver or lung), it is well within the acceptable range for complex, low-volume regions such as the hippocampus—particularly when subregion differentiation (anterior/posterior) is factored in. This robust and consistent segmentation performance across folds underscores the reliability of nnU-Net's self-configuring architecture for hippocampal volumetry and lays the foundation for accurate downstream volume analysis and neurodegenerative risk flagging.

5.2. Visual Assessment and Mask Overlay Analysis

While quantitative metrics such as the Dice similarity coefficient provide essential numerical validation, the anatomical plausibility and spatial coherence of segmentation outputs must also be verified visually. To this end, overlay visualizations were generated by superimposing the predicted hippocampus masks onto the original T1-weighted MRI scans across axial, sagittal, and coronal planes. Figure 3 presents visual inspection confirmation that the model reliably captured the hippocampal contour, preserving the medial temporal morphology without significant over-segmentation or leakage into adjacent structures such as the amygdala or lateral ventricles [34]. These overlays also helped identify edge cases with partial coverage or morphological anomalies, enabling refined interpretation of volumetric outputs.

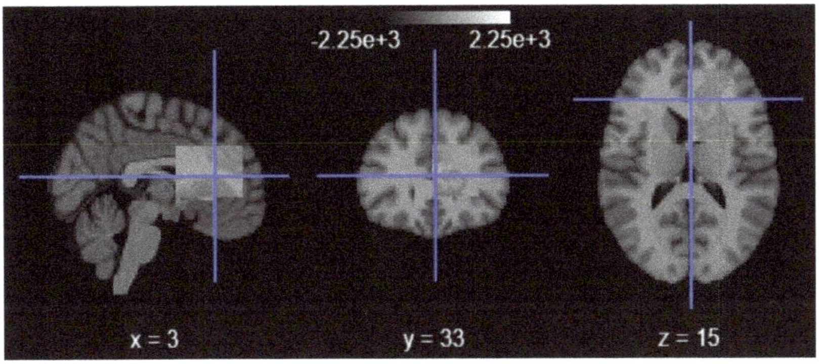

Figure 3. Overlay visualization on axial, sagittal, and coronal planes.

Following segmentation, we conducted extensive post hoc analyses to identify individuals at risk of early neurodegeneration or accelerated brain aging. Using the derived hippocampal volumes, we flagged cases where the total volume fell below a conservative threshold of 5000 mm^3 in subjects under the age of 16—an early atrophy marker. Additionally, the brain-age gap was computed as the difference between predicted biological brain age (derived from a regression model trained on hippocampal volume) and chronological age. A gap greater than 5 years was used to define accelerated aging. Subjects who met both criteria (low volume for age and high brain-age gap) were designated as high-risk. This criterion is supported by prior brain-age literature, where such deviations have been shown to correlate with cognitive decline and elevated risk of neurodegenerative progression [35]. While this threshold was originally validated in adult populations, its use here reflects a conservative and translational approach for detecting atypical neurodevelopment in younger cohorts as shown in Figure 4.

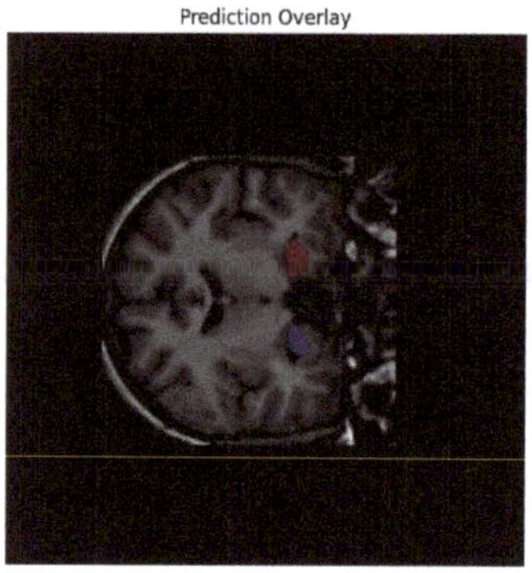

Figure 4. Model's predicted overlay results.

To further quantify and spatially contextualize hippocampal atrophy, we employed a second-level group-level statistical analysis using the nilearn neuroimaging library. T1-weighted scans were resampled, aligned, and modeled using a second-level GLM design matrix, contrasting low-volume subjects against those within normative ranges [35]. The resulting Z-statistical map revealed clusters of altered voxel intensities in hippocampal and adjacent limbic regions, offering group-level neuroanatomical evidence of structural deviation.

The illustration in Figure 5 visualizes the relationship between age and hippocampal volume using a bivariate scatterplot. Risk-coded subjects (based on a neurodegeneration threshold of 4700 mm^3) were highlighted using a color-coded hue and gender-based markers. This analysis revealed a distinct subset of individuals falling significantly below the expected volume for their age, consistent with early degenerative or stress-associated hippocampal shrinkage.

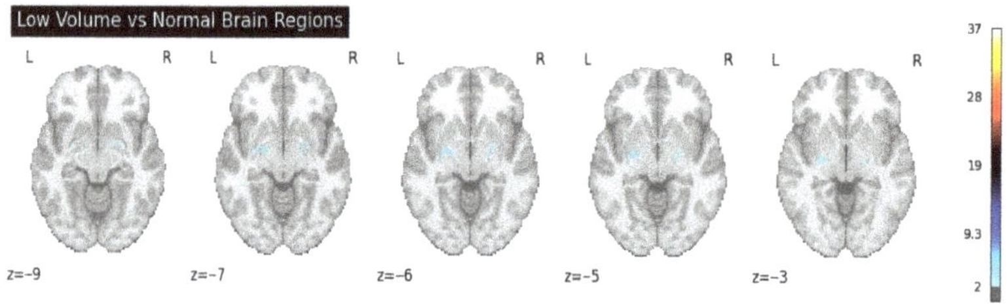

Figure 5. Second-level group-level statistical analysis.

The visualizations in Figure 6 not only provide qualitative validation of model outputs but also underscore the clinical and research value of integrating segmentation-driven volumetric biomarkers with demographic and neurodevelopmental metadata. By coupling deep learning outputs with structured risk inference, the pipeline transitions from mere anatomical segmentation to actionable neurobiological stratification.

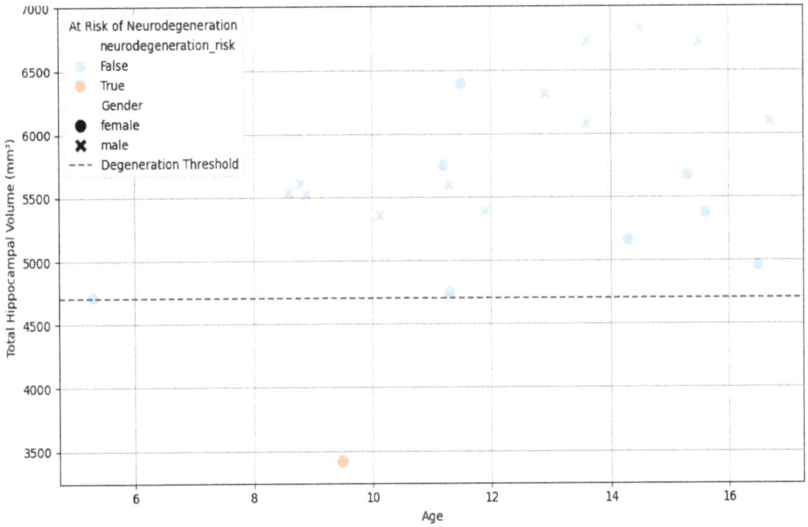

Figure 6. Scatter plot—age vs. total hippocampal volume, colored by neurodegeneration risk.

5.3. Volumetric Analysis

Quantifying hippocampal volume from the segmentation masks enables an important transition from raw anatomical delineation to biologically interpretable biomarkers [36]. Once the binary segmentation masks were generated by the nnU-Net model, volumetric calculations were performed by summing the number of foreground voxels within each mask and converting this count into cubic millimeters using the known voxel spacing (1 mm^3 for isotropic scans in our dataset).

Segmented volumes were converted to mm^3 by counting labeled voxels as follows:

$$V = N \times v, \text{ where } v = \text{voxel volume } (mm^3)$$

where N is the number of voxels labeled as hippocampus.

This calculation was conducted for each subject, with separate tracking of anterior and posterior hippocampal regions where label differentiation was available. Across the study cohort, volumetric analysis revealed considerable inter-individual variability, even among subjects within similar age groups. The total hippocampal volume for healthy children and adolescents in the dataset ranged from approximately 4800 mm^3 to 7600 mm^3, with volume generally increasing with age up to early adolescence, followed by stabilization or mild reduction in older teens. The posterior hippocampus consistently represented a larger fraction of total volume compared to the anterior subregion, aligning with the established anatomical literature on hippocampal longitudinal asymmetry. These regional volumes were not only biologically plausible but were also consistent across folds, underscoring the segmentation model's stability.

To enable risk stratification and developmental benchmarking, we calculated age-adjusted percentiles for total hippocampal volume. Subjects with volumes below the 5th percentile relative to age- and sex-matched peers were flagged for potential early atrophy. These flags were further cross-referenced with brain-age gap metrics and clinical metadata to identify individuals with disproportionately low volume for their chronological age. We also evaluated the inter-subject distribution of hippocampal volume using histograms and kernel density plots. These plots revealed a moderately left-skewed distribution, suggesting a small subset of subjects with abnormally low hippocampal volumes, some of whom were already flagged as "high-risk" based on combined atrophy and accelerated aging indicators [37]. These subjects were further analyzed in downstream volumetric-residual models, allowing for fine-grained assessment of their deviation from normative neurodevelopmental trajectories.

By anchoring the model's predictions to measurable and biologically grounded outcomes, this volumetric analysis validates the segmentation framework and enables clinically meaningful interpretations [38]. In doing so, it advances the hippocampus from a mere region of interest (ROI) to a fully quantitative marker of individual neurobiological status.

5.4. Analysis of Brain-Age Discrepancy Through Hippocampal Biomarkers

Brain age, defined as the predicted biological age of the brain based on structural markers, serves as a sensitive biomarker for subclinical neurodegeneration. Hippocampal volume was analyzed against age-related reference distributions to infer potential deviation from normative aging patterns, aligning with frameworks established in prior neuroimaging studies [39]. The predicted age was subtracted from the actual chronological age to derive the brain-age gap. Instead of a black-box regression, we adopted a clinically interpretable rule-based binning approach for brain-age estimation, guided by percentile analysis of predicted volumes. This approach enabled interpretability and aligned with prior clinical volumetry standards. A gap greater than +5 years flagged cases with potential accelerated aging. Additionally, individuals under 16 years of age with hippocampal volumes below 5000 mm^3 were identified as high-risk cases, indicating possible early atrophy. This hybrid analysis of anatomical volume and age deviation enabled stratification of at-risk cohorts without the need for opaque regression modeling.

5.5. Comparison with Other State-of-the-Art Segmentation Methods

To assess the effectiveness of our model, we conducted a comparative evaluation against several state-of-the-art segmentation approaches, including Atlas-Based Segmentation, 2D and 3D U-Net architectures, and UGCapsNet. A brief overview of the employed methods as well as their obtained results is provided below. Note that to the best of our knowledge, our employed dataset has never been used in previous studies.

5.5.1. Atlas-Based Segmentation

The atlas-based approach utilized probabilistic hippocampal maps from the Harvard-Oxford Subcortical Atlas [40], which were initially aligned to MNI standard space. When transformed into subject-specific native space, the templates exhibited substantial spatial misalignments. Multiple resampling and interpolation strategies failed to yield meaningful overlap with anatomical ground truth. The resulting segmentation masks contained only background voxels ([0]), precluding the calculation of a Dice coefficient. These findings underscore the inherent limitations of static, non-personalized atlases in pediatric neuroimaging, where anatomical variability necessitates adaptive alignment strategies.

5.5.2. 2D and 3D U-Net

Both 2D and 3D variants of the U-Net architecture were tested using volumetric MRI input. The 2D U-Net processed resized 256×256 slices, while the 3D U-Net handled full volumes at approximately $128 \times 128 \times 128$ resolution. In both cases, ReLU activations were followed by sigmoid outputs, and training used binary cross-entropy and Dice-based loss functions [41]. The implemented 3D U-Net architecture followed a classic encoder–

decoder structure with symmetric skip connections and was designed to capture volumetric context in high-resolution MRI [42]. Each encoding block used two successive $3 \times 3 \times 3$ convolutions, batch normalization, and ReLU activation, followed by $2 \times 2 \times 2$ max pooling. The decoder path mirrored this structure using transposed convolutions for upsampling and concatenation for spatial detail restoration.

Let x denote the input volume, and f_i be the output of each encoder layer i. The general encoder operation can be written as follows:

$$f_i = ReLU\ (BN\ (Conv3D\ (f_{i-1}))) \tag{3}$$

where f_i is the transformed feature map at encoder level i, f_{i-1} is the input feature map from the previous layer, $Conv3D$ is the 3D convolutional layer, BN is batch normalization, and $ReLU$ is the rectified linear unit activation function. Consequently, the decoder performs as follows:

$$d_i = ReLU\ \left(BN\ \left(Conv3D\ \left(\left[\text{UpConv}\left(d_{j+1}\right), f_j\right]\right)\right)\right) \tag{4}$$

where d_j is the decoded feature map at level j, d_{j+1} is the output from the next decoder level, f_j is the corresponding encoder feature map, UpConv is 3D up-convolutional or transposed convolution, and the square bracket ([ ]) is channel-wise concatenation. Final output logits are computed via a $1 \times 1 \times 1$ convolution:

$$Y = Conv3D_{out}(d_1) \tag{5}$$

where Y is the logits for each voxel, $Conv3D_{out}$ = $1 \times 1 \times 1$ convolutional layer producing the final output, and d_1 is the decoder feature map from the first decoder stage. For UGCapsNet, the formula is as follows:

$$\mathcal{L}\text{CE} = -\sum_{i=1}^{n} \sum_{c=1}^{C} y_{i,c} \times \log \hat{y}_{i,c} \tag{6}$$

where $\mathcal{L}$CE is a scalar value representing the total classification loss, n is the number of training samples, C is the number of classes, $y_{i,c}$ is the ground truth (1 if sample class belongs to class "c", else 0), and $\hat{y}_{i,c}$ is the predicted probability that sample i belongs to class "c". Upon initial experimentation, standard U-Net architectures (2D and 3D) demonstrated suboptimal performance, with output segmentations occasionally defaulting to background-only labels (i.e., Dice score = 0). However, subsequent debugging revealed that the U-Net models were not entirely non-functional. They produced non-zero label classes ([0–2]), yet the predictions lacked spatial precision and anatomical plausibility. Volumetric estimations derived from these masks were substantially inflated or deflated relative to ground truth, indicating instability in learning spatial boundaries of hippocampal structures [42].

5.5.3. UGCapsNet

The UGCapsNet architecture incorporated capsule layers to model hierarchical spatial relationships in 3D [43]. Input volumes were preprocessed and normalized to $64 \times 64 \times 64$ dimensions. Training used a cross-entropy loss and softmax activation. The model was able to distinguish multiple hippocampal subregions, producing labels [0–2] for background, anterior, and posterior, respectively. However, training was computationally intensive. Although segmentations were anatomically valid, no quantified Dice score was extracted, and performance metrics lagged behind fully automated solutions.

Multi-class entropy loss was calculated as follows:

$$LCE = -\ \sum\_\{i = 1\}\hat{}\{N\} \sum\{c = 1\}\hat{}\{C\}\ y_i{,}c \cdot log(\hat{y}_i{,}c)$$

where y_i,c is a binary indicator (1 if class label c is correct for voxel i, else 0) and $\hat{y}_i,c$ is the predicted probability for voxel i to belong to class c.

5.5.4. nnU-Net

In its adaptive design, nnU-Net considers three canonical U-Net variants based on dataset properties derived from a "dataset fingerprint". The first uses 2D U-Net, which is optimal for datasets with high anisotropy (i.e., large inter-slice gaps relative to in-plane resolution). The second uses 3D full-resolution U-Net, which is designed for isotropic or near-isotropic volumetric data and leverages complete spatial context. The final variat uses 3D low-resolution cascade, a two-stage configuration suitable for extremely large volumes, where an initial coarse segmentation guides a subsequent high-resolution refinement. Our dataset exhibited consistent isotropic resolution with manageable volume size, leading the nnU-Net framework to automatically select the 3D full-resolution U-Net. This variant utilizes full volumetric input while preserving fine-grained hippocampal boundaries, particularly across the curved anterior and posterior regions. Additionally, it fits within GPU memory constraints and benefits from extensive built-in data augmentation, automatic patch size determination, and deep supervision, making it the most effective topology for this task. These adaptive topological decisions are key to the superior performance demonstrated by nnU-Net over traditional 2D/3D U-Nets and atlas-based methods in our experiments, as summarized in Table 1.

Table 1. Comparative study of different models.

Model/Method	Preprocessing	Challenges	Performance
Atlas-Based Segmentation (Harvard-Oxford)	MNI registration, affine alignment	Dimensional mismatch; image–mask misalignment	Produced only background masks; not suitable for patient-specific precision
2D/3D U-Net (Manual)	Normalization, resizing, mask standardization	Poor convergence; sensitive to class imbalance and intensity variation	Revealed noisy [0–2] outputs, still anatomically inaccurate
UGCapsNet	Fully standardized inputs, label encoding	Memory intensive; slow convergence	Detected anterior/posterior; moderate Dice proxy (~0.03); viable but suboptimal
nnU-Net (AutoML)	Raw MSD-compliant input	Automatically resolves all preprocessing and architectural tuning	**High Dice (~0.772 anterior, ~0.711 posterior)**; robust, reproducible, ready for clinical use

To contextualize the reported Dice score of 0.733, we compared our model's performance with recent hippocampal segmentation studies using deep learning-based approaches. It is consistent with results reported in recent neuroimaging studies involving anatomically small or morphologically complex brain regions. Recent deep learning studies on neuroanatomical segmentation report Dice scores in the range of 0.66–0.71 when applied to structurally complex, small-volume brain regions. For instance, nnU-Net achieved a mean Dice score of 0.678 ± 0.050 for hippocampal-adjacent perivascular spaces in multi-site adult datasets [44], while a pediatric brain tumor study reported a Dice of 0.71 ± 0.33 for cystic subregion structures similar in size and variability to the hippocampus [45]. These results underscore the segmentation challenges inherent to such regions and place our model's performance (Dice $\approx$ 0.733) well within the upper bounds of current benchmarks. Looking forward, this pipeline can be extended into longitudinal studies to capture the dynamics of hippocampal volume change over time. Moreover, incorporating multimodal imaging and behavioral phenotyping may further refine brain-age models and enhance the predictive validity of imaging biomarkers. This study integrates deep learning with neuroanatomical expertise. It presents a scalable and clinically relevant method for the early detection of brain aging and neurodegeneration. The approach focuses on precise hippocampal segmentation.

6. Limitations

The current study is limited to an adolescent cohort aged 7.7–15.6 years, and we acknowledge that hippocampal volumetric patterns and their biological implications differ significantly across the lifespan. The biological meaning of volume reduction in adolescents is distinct from that in older adults. In younger cohorts, shrinkage may reflect neurodevelopmental disruption rather than aging per se. While this work establishes a pipeline for robust segmentation and volume quantification in younger populations, the findings cannot be directly extrapolated to older adults, where age-related atrophy follows different morphological trajectories and clinical correlates. Future work will expand the analysis to include adult and geriatric populations to validate the generalizability of the model across age groups and to better delineate the impact of pathological versus normative aging processes.

Another limitation of this study is that we have limited quantitative evaluation of our model compared to similar studies. The main reason is that there are just a limited number of studies that used the same dataset to solve this problem. However, we aim to extend this study and utilize other benchmarks as well as other models in the future.

7. Conclusions

This work presents a comprehensive, fully automated hippocampal segmentation pipeline leveraging the nnU-Net framework, applied to a meticulously curated dataset of structural brain MRIs. Unlike earlier approaches, which suffered from limitations such as misalignment in atlas-based techniques, inadequate convergence in shallow U-Net architectures, or interpretability challenges in correlation-driven methods, nnU-Net demonstrated unparalleled adaptability, robustness, and precision. Its dynamic configuration capabilities—ranging from patch size selection to architectural tuning—enabled it to outperform traditional models in delineating anterior and posterior hippocampal subregions with high anatomical fidelity and segmentation accuracy.

Through the use of volumetric analysis derived from the predicted segmentation masks, we uncovered meaningful patterns that associate hippocampal shrinkage with early signs of neurodegeneration. These volume reductions were significantly correlated with demographic risk factors such as younger age, female sex, and elevated predicted brain-age gaps. By identifying individuals whose hippocampal volumes fall below the normative thresholds for their age, the pipeline not only enables high-throughput anatomical annotation but also serves as a diagnostic tool capable of flagging potential cases of accelerated brain aging.

The implications of such findings are profound: hippocampal atrophy is a well-documented precursor in a variety of neuropsychiatric conditions, including Alzheimer's disease, major depressive disorder, and stress-related cognitive decline. A system capable of accurate, reproducible segmentation and volume quantification thus holds clinical utility in screening, monitoring, and potentially intervening in the neurodegenerative trajectory before irreversible damage occurs.

Author Contributions: E.G. and I.D. developed the original concept. E.G. conducted experiments and generated the figures. E.G., A.D. and I.D. wrote the article. E.G. prepared the computational pipeline. I.D. and A.D. supervised the project. All authors have read and agreed to the published version of the manuscript.

Funding: This research received no external funding.

Data Availability Statement: The data presented in this study are openly available in [NITRC] at [https://www.nitrc.org/rating/show_results.php?group_id=377], reference number [21].

Conflicts of Interest: The Authors declare no conflict of interest.

References

1. McEwen, B.S. Possible mechanisms for atrophy of the human hippocampus. *Mol. Psychiatry* **1997**, *2*, 255–262. [CrossRef] [PubMed]
2. Sapolsky, R.M. Why stress is bad for your brain. *Science* **1996**, *273*, 749–750. [CrossRef] [PubMed]
3. Carmichael, O.T.; Aizenstein, H.A.; Davis, S.W.; Becker, J.T.; Thompson, P.M.; Meltzer, C.C.; Liu, Y. Atlas-based hippocampus segmentation in Alzheimer's disease and mild cognitive impairment. *NeuroImage* **2005**, *27*, 979–990. [CrossRef]
4. Vieira, S.; Pinaya, W.H.L.; Mechelli, A. Using deep learning to investigate the neuroimaging correlates of psychiatric and neurological disorders: Methods and applications. *Neurosci. Biobehav. Rev.* **2017**, *74*, 58–75. [CrossRef] [PubMed]
5. McConnell, N.; Ndipenoch, N.; Cao, Y.; Miron, A.; Li, Y. Exploring advanced architectural variations of nnUNet. *Neurocomputing* **2023**, *560*, 126837. [CrossRef]
6. Mattson, M.P.; Rydel, R.E. Development and selective neurodegeneration in cell cultures from different brain regions. *Brain Res.* **1989**, *490*, 110–125. [CrossRef]
7. McEwen, B.S. Plasticity of the hippocampus: Adaptation to chronic stress and allostatic load. *Ann. N. Y. Acad. Sci.* **2001**, *933*, 265–277. [CrossRef]
8. Frodl, T.; Meisenzahl, E.M.; Zetzsche, T.; Born, C.; Groll, C.; Jäger, M.; Leinsinger, G.; Bottlender, R.; Hahn, K.; Möller, H.-J. Hippocampal changes in patients with a first episode of major depression. *Am. J. Psychiatry* **2002**, *159*, 1112–1118. [CrossRef]
9. Salunkhe, S.; Bachute, M.; Gite, S.; Vyas, N.; Khanna, S.; Modi, K.; Katpatal, C.; Kotecha, K. Classification of Alzheimer's Disease Patients Using Texture Analysis and Machine Learning. *Appl. Syst. Innov.* **2021**, *4*, 49. [CrossRef]
10. Raz, N.; Lindenberger, U.; Rodrigue, K.M.; Kennedy, K.M.; Head, D.; Williamson, A.; Dahle, C.; Gerstorf, D.; Acker, J.D. Regional brain changes in aging healthy adults: General trends, individual differences and modifiers. *Cereb. Cortex* **2005**, *15*, 1676–1689. [CrossRef]
11. Czéh, B.; Lucassen, P.J. What causes the hippocampal volume decrease in depression? Are neurogenesis, glial changes and apoptosis implicated? *Eur. Arch. Psychiatry Clin. Neurosci.* **2007**, *257*, 250–260. [CrossRef] [PubMed]
12. Hassouneh, A. Multimodal Feature Fusion and AI-Driven Framework for Early Detection of Alzheimer's Disease. Ph.D. Thesis, Western Michigan University, Kalamazoo, MI, USA, 2025.
13. Moreno-Jiménez, E.P.; Flor-García, M.; Terreros-Roncal, J.; Rábano, A.; Cafini, F.; Pallas-Bazarra, N.; Ávila, J.; Llorens-Martín, M. Adult hippocampal neurogenesis is abundant in neurologically healthy subjects and drops sharply in patients with Alzheimer's disease. *Nat. Med.* **2019**, *25*, 554–560. [CrossRef] [PubMed]
14. Hammers, A.; Heckemann, R.A.; Koepp, M.J.; Duncan, J.S.; Hajnal, J.V.; Rueckert, D.; Aljabar, P. Automatic detection and quantification of hippocampal atrophy on MRI in temporal lobe epilepsy: A proof-of-principle study. *NeuroImage* **2007**, *36*, 38–47. [CrossRef] [PubMed]
15. Sämann, P.G.; Iglesias, J.E.; Gutman, B.; Grotegerd, D.; Leenings, R.; Flint, C.; Dannlowski, U.; Clarke-Rubright, E.K.; Morey, R.A.; van Erp, T.G.M.; et al. FreeSurfer-based segmentation of hippocampal subfields: A review of methods and applications, with a novel quality control procedure for ENIGMA studies and other collaborative efforts. *Hum. Brain Mapp.* **2020**, *42*, 1027–1043. [CrossRef]
16. Du, G.; Cao, X.; Liang, J.; Chen, X.; Zhan, Y. Medical image segmentation based on U-Net: A review. *J. Imaging Sci. Technol.* **2020**, *64*, 1–12. [CrossRef]
17. Zhang, T.R.; Larosa, A.; Di Raddo, M.-E.; Wong, V.; Wong, A.S.; Wong, T.P. Negative memory engrams in the hippocampus enhance the susceptibility to chronic social defeat stress. *J. Neurosci.* **2019**, *39*, 7576–7590. [CrossRef]
18. Aghili, M.; Shojae, M.; Cabrerizo, M.; Rishe, N.; Wang, Y. Automated hippocampus segmentation and volume estimation using a transformer-based deep learning architecture. *Res. Sq.* **2024**. [CrossRef]
19. Raz, N.; Rodrigue, K.M.; Head, D.; Kennedy, K.M.; Acker, J.D. Differential aging of the medial temporal lobe: A study of a five-year change. *Neurology* **2004**, *62*, 433–438. [CrossRef]
20. Huang, L.; Miron, A.; Hone, K.; Li, Y. Segmenting Medical Images: From UNet to Res-UNet and nnUNet. In Proceedings of the 2024 IEEE 37th International Symposium on Computer-Based Medical Systems (CBMS), Guadalajara, Mexico, 26–28 June 2024; pp. 483–489.
21. Hippocampus Segmentation Dataset. Neuroimaging Informatics Tools and Resources Clearinghouse (NITRC). Available online: https://www.nitrc.org/frs/?group_id=377 (accessed on 13 March 2025).
22. Kalaiselvi, T.; Anitha, T.; Sriramakrishnan, P. Data preprocessing techniques for MRI brain scans using deep learning models. In *Brain Tumor MRI Image Segmentation Using Deep Learning Techniques*; Syed, I.S., Khan, M.A., Eds.; Academic Press: Cambridge, MA, USA, 2022; pp. 13–25.

23. Dolz, J.; Desrosiers, C.; Ben Ayed, I. 3D fully convolutional networks for subcortical segmentation in MRI: A large-scale study. *arXiv* **2017**, arXiv:1612.03925. [CrossRef]
24. Li, Y.; Ammari, S.; Balleyguier, C.; Lassau, N.; Chouzenoux, E. Impact of preprocessing and harmonization methods on the removal of scanner effects in brain MRI radiomic features. *Cancers* **2021**, *13*, 3000. [CrossRef]
25. De Raad, K.B.; Van Garderen, K.A.; Smits, M.; Van der Voort, S.R.; Incekara, F.; Oei, E.H.G.; Hirvasniemi, J.; Klein, S.; Starmans, M.P.A. The effect of preprocessing on convolutional neural networks for medical image segmentation. In Proceedings of the 2021 IEEE 18th International Symposium on Biomedical Imaging (ISBI), Nice, France, 13–16 April 2021; pp. 655–658.
26. Viswan, V.; Shaffi, N.; Subramanian, K.; Hajamohideen, F. Optimizing Medical Imaging Quality: An In-Depth Examination of Preprocessing Methods for Brain MRIs. In *Applied Intelligence and Informatics*; Mahmud, M., Ben-Abdallah, H., Kaiser, M.S., Ahmed, M.R., Zhong, N., Eds.; Communications in Computer and Information Science; AII 2023; Springer: Cham, Switzerland, 2024; Volume 2065.
27. SSuhas, C.R. Venugopal, MRI image preprocessing and noise removal technique using linear and nonlinear filters. In Proceedings of the 2017 International Conference on Electrical, Electronics, Communication, Computer, and Optimization Techniques (ICEECCOT), Mysuru, India, 15–16 December 2017; pp. 1–4.
28. Hazarika, R.A.; Maji, A.K.; Syiem, R.; Samarendra, N.S.; Debdatta, K. Hippocampus Segmentation Using U-Net Convolutional Network from Brain Magnetic Resonance Imaging (MRI). *J. Digit. Imaging* **2022**, *35*, 893–909. [PubMed]
29. Isensee, F.; Wald, T.; Ulrich, C.; Baumgartner, M.; Roy, S.; Maier-Hein, K.H.; Jäger, P.F. nnU-Net revisited: A call for rigorous validation in 3D medical image segmentation. In *Medical Image Computing and Computer Assisted Intervention—MICCAI 2024*; Springer: Berlin/Heidelberg, Germany, 2024; pp. 488–498.
30. Isensee, F.; Petersen, J.; Klein, A.; Zimmerer, D.; Jaeger, P.F.; Kohl, S.; Maier-Hein, K.H. nnU-Net: Self-adapting framework for U-Net-based medical image segmentation. *arXiv* **2018**, arXiv:1809.10486.
31. Choi, Y.; Bang, J.; Kim, S.-Y.; Seo, M.; Jang, J. Deep learning–based multimodal segmentation of oropharyngeal squamous cell carcinoma on CT and MRI using self-configuring nnU-Net. *Eur. Radiol.* **2024**, *34*, 5389–5400. [CrossRef] [PubMed]
32. Krause, F.; Heindl, D.; Jebril, H.; Karner, M.; Unterdechler, M. nnU-Net Pre- and Postprocessing Strategies for UW-OCTA Segmentation Tasks in Diabetic Retinopathy Analysis. In *Mitosis Domain Generalization and Diabetic Retinopathy Analysis*; Sheng, B., Aubreville, M., Eds.; MIDOG DRAC 2022 2022; Lecture Notes in Computer Science; Springer: Cham, Switzerland, 2023; Volume 13597.
33. Eelbode, T.; Jeroen, B.; Maxim, B.; Dirk, V.; Frederik, M.; Raf, B.; Matthew, B.B. Optimization for Medical Image Segmentation: Theory and Practice When Evaluating with Dice Score or Jaccard Index. In *IEEE Transactions on Medical Imaging*; IEEE: Troy, NY, USA, 2020; Volume 39, pp. 3679–3690. [CrossRef]
34. Franke, K.; Gaser, C. Ten Years of BrainAGE as a Neuroimaging Biomarker of Brain Aging: What Insights Have We Gained? *Front. Neurol.* **2019**, *10*, 789. [CrossRef]
35. Hassouneh, A.; Bazuin, B.; Kaku, H.; Abdel-Qader, I. A data fusion framework for mild cognitive impairment classification: Hippocampal volume and GLCM features using machine learning. In Proceedings of the International Conference on Information Technology and Applications, Sydney, Australia, 17–19 October 2024; pp. 435–445.
36. Ahmad, A.L.; Sanchez-Bornot, J.; Sotero, R.C.; Coyle, D.; Idris, Z.; Faye, I. A machine learning approach for identifying anatomical biomarkers of early mild cognitive impairment. *arXiv* **2024**, arXiv:2407.00040. [CrossRef]
37. Feng, Q.; Wang, L.; Tang, X.; Ge, X.; Hu, H.; Liao, Z.; Ding, Z. Machine learning classifiers and associations of cognitive performance with hippocampal subfields in amnestic mild cognitive impairment. *Front. Aging Neurosci.* **2023**, *15*, 1273658. [CrossRef]
38. Erickson, K.I.; Prakash, R.S.; Voss, M.W.; Chaddock, L.; Heo, S.; McLaren, M.; Martin, S.A.; Vieira, V.J.; Woods, J.A.; McAuley, E.; et al. Brain-derived neurotrophic factor is associated with age-related decline in hippocampal volume. *J. Neurosci.* **2010**, *30*, 5368–5375. [CrossRef]
39. Lener, M.S.; Iosifescu, D.V. In pursuit of neuroimaging biomarkers to guide treatment selection in major depressive disorder: A review of recent literature. *Ann. N. Y. Acad. Sci.* **2015**, *1344*, 50–65. [CrossRef]
40. Cabezas, M.; Oliver, A.; Lladó, X.; Freixenet, J.; Bach Cuadra, M. A review of atlas-based segmentation for magnetic resonance brain images. *Comput. Methods Programs Biomed.* **2011**, *104*, e158–e177. [CrossRef]
41. Huang, C.; Han, H.; Yao, Q.; Zhu, S.; Zhou, S.K. 3D U^2-Net: A 3D Universal U-Net for Multi-domain Medical Image Segmentation. In *Medical Image Computing and Computer Assisted Intervention—MICCAI 2019*; Shen, D., Liu, T., Peters, T.M., Staib, L.H., Essert, C., Zhou, S., Yap, P.-T., Khan, A., Eds.; Lecture Notes in Computer Science; Springer: Cham, Switzerland, 2019; Volume 11765.
42. Su, R.; Zhang, D.; Liu, J.; Cheng, C. MSU-Net: Multi-Scale U-Net for 2D Medical Image Segmentation. *Front. Genet.* **2021**, *12*, 639930. [CrossRef]
43. Tran, M.; Vo-Ho, V.-K.; Quinn, K.; Nguyen, H.; Luu, K.; Le, N. Chapter 3—CapsNet for medical image segmentation. In *Artificial Intelligence in Medicine*; Suzuki, A., Ed.; Academic Press: Cambridge, MA, USA, 2024; pp. 45–66.

44. Pham, W.; Jarema, A.; Rim, D.; Chen, Z.; Khlif, M.S.H.; Macefield, V.G.; Henderson, L.A.; Brodtmann, A. A Comprehensive Framework for Automated Segmentation of Perivascular Spaces in Brain MRI with the nnU-Net. *arXiv* **2024**, arXiv:2411.19564. [CrossRef]
45. Vossough, A.; Khalili, N.; Familiar, A.M.; Gandhi, D.; Viswanathan, K.; Tu, W.; Haldar, D.; Bagheri, S.; Anderson, H.; Haldar, S.; et al. Automatic segmentation of pediatric brain tumors in MRI with nnU-Net ensemble and post-processing techniques. *arXiv* **2024**, arXiv:2401.08404.

algorithms

MDPI

Article

Using Shapley Values to Explain the Decisions of Convolutional Neural Networks in Glaucoma Diagnosis

Jose Sigut [1,*], Francisco Fumero [1] and Tinguaro Díaz-Alemán [2]

1 Department of Computer Science and Systems Engineering, Universidad de La Laguna, Camino San Francisco de Paula, 19, La Laguna, 38203 Santa Cruz de Tenerife, Spain; ffumerob@ull.edu.es
2 Department of Ophthalmology, Hospital Universitario de Canarias, Carretera Ofra S/N, La Laguna, 38320 Santa Cruz de Tenerife, Spain; vtdac@hotmail.com
* Correspondence: jfsigut@ull.edu.es

Abstract: This work aims to leverage Shapley values to explain the decisions of convolutional neural networks trained to predict glaucoma. Although Shapley values offer a mathematically sound approach rooted in game theory, they require evaluating all possible combinations of features, which can be computationally intensive. To address this challenge, we introduce a novel strategy that discretizes the input by dividing the image into standard regions or sectors of interest, significantly reducing the number of features while maintaining clinical relevance. Moreover, applying Shapley values in a machine learning context necessitates the ability to selectively exclude features to evaluate their combinations. To achieve this, we propose a method involving the occlusion of specific sectors and re-training only the non-convolutional portion of the models. Despite achieving strong predictive performance, our findings reveal limited alignment with medical expectations, particularly the unexpected dominance of the background sector in the model's decision-making process. This highlights potential concerns regarding the interpretability of convolutional neural network-based glaucoma diagnostics.

Keywords: Shapley values; interpretability; explainability; glaucoma diagnosis; convolutional neural networks

1. Introduction

In domains where the decisions made by a machine learning model are critical, the interpretability of the model becomes a fundamental requirement, since in general, we will want to ensure that the abstraction learned by the model is free of errors [1]. From the medical point of view, the interpretability of machine learning models is especially relevant for regulatory aspects and also to gain confidence in the system by the medical specialist, as it allows us to know on what criteria the model has been based to arrive at a certain prediction. In some cases, it can even allow the medical specialist to find relationships in the data that were previously hidden from the naked eye or not given enough attention or importance [2]. In this context, Shapley values have achieved a high preponderance among the methods for explaining the decisions of a machine learning system. In the review carried out by Loh et al. [3] on the application of explainability techniques in artificial intelligence in the healthcare sector during the last decade, it is worth noting that almost half of the works reviewed used them for this purpose.

The Shapley values refer to a method that comes from the theory of cooperative games [4]. This method provides us with a way to distribute the benefits obtained in a cooperative game between the players of that game [5]. Moving this method to the field of machine learning, a prediction from a model could be explained assuming that each feature for a given instance is a "player" in a game in which the prediction is the payoff that we can obtain. The Shapley values tell us how to "fairly" distribute that payoff among the features, depending on the contribution of each one [1].

In a previous work [6], we explored the use of saliency maps to interpret convolutional neural networks for glaucoma diagnosis, highlighting both their potential and their limitations. In contrast, Shapley values offer a fundamentally different approach to assigning a degree of importance to each feature in a decision. They have the advantage of being based on a solid mathematical foundation derived from game theory, ensuring a series of desirable properties: efficiency, symmetry, null (or dummy) player, and linearity (or additivity) [5,7]. However, their main disadvantage is that they require evaluating all possible combinations of features in order to calculate these values accurately. When applied in a machine learning context where the number of features is high, this would produce a combinatorial explosion that could be unfeasible in many cases since it would require performing on the order of 2^n predictions of our model, being n the total number of features. In addition, in general, a machine learning model is not prepared to make predictions for any combination of input features, such as a smaller subset of them, so re-training may be required. For this reason, some methods arise that calculate the Shapley values in an approximate way, such as the sampling method of [8], the different methods based on SHAP proposed by [9] or Deep SHAP, specifically intended for Deep Learning systems [9,10].

The main objective of this work is the use of Shapley values to explain the decisions of convolutional neural networks trained to predict glaucoma. Glaucoma is one of the leading causes of irreversible blindness in the world [11], and it is a pathology that is difficult to address because of the lack of clear and unequivocal biomarkers that warn of its existence, especially in the most incipient stages [12]. Thus, only highly specialized experts can deal with this issue, usually following a holistic approach to diagnosis, using both functional and structural techniques. In this category of structural techniques are those based on images, and more specifically retinal or fundus images, which are the ones used in this research. Figure 1 shows an example of this type of image with the most relevant anatomical structures.

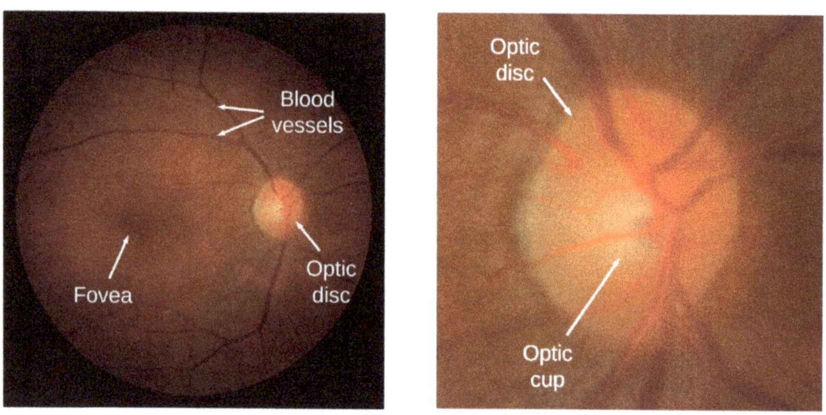

(a) (b)

Figure 1. Sample color fundus image illustrating the key anatomical structures: the optic disc, optic cup, fovea, and blood vessels. This image was obtained from a right eye. (**a**) Full fundus image with its main structures: optic disc, fovea, blood vessels. (**b**) A magnification of the image showing the optic disc and cup.

For the reasons mentioned above, the application of Shapley values to a machine learning problem can be difficult in practice. For this particular problem, we propose to follow a discretization procedure consisting of dividing the input images into standard sectors. This allows us to refer the results to regions of interest to the ophthalmic specialist while drastically reducing the number of features that will be used to form the various combinations of players required for the calculation of the Shapley values, moving from the pixel level to a much higher one. It remains to be resolved how players are removed from the game. The strategy adopted to simulate this in a given image is the occlusion of the corresponding sector, which facilitates the calculation of the Shapley values, thus obtaining the contributions of each sector to the prediction made by a given model. In Section 3.3 we will describe in more detail the discretization and occlusion performed.

Although there are a few papers that have used Shapley values to explain the decisions of conventional machine learning systems with handcrafted features for glaucoma diagnosis, to our knowledge, this is the first to approach the problem from the perspective of Deep Learning and referring to parts of the input image instead. This is possible thanks to the aforementioned discretization and occlusion strategies and therefore we consider them our main contribution.

The rest of the article is structured as follows. In Section 2 we review the related work. In Section 3 we describe the datasets and models used, how to discretize the problem to compute the Shapley values, how to occlude the different sectors, and the evaluation methodology adopted. The results of all experiments are presented and discussed in Section 4. Finally, Section 5 is devoted to the conclusions we have reached.

2. Related Work

There has been some work related to ophthalmology in which Shapley values have been used. One of these works is [13], where a study was conducted to determine the degree of agreement of 14 medical specialists with the results of 13 attribution methods applied to a neural network based on InceptionV3 to diagnose choroidal neovascularization, diabetic macular edema and drusen from retinal images captured with an OCT. The results show that the three methods most highly rated by clinicians were Deep Taylor, Guided backpropagation and Deep SHAP.

Another publication, also related to this field, is that of [14]. In this work, the authors train a convolutional neural network model based on DensetNet121 to detect different degrees of diabetic retinopathy in fundus images. In order to explain the results, they choose to use Grad-CAM and Deep SHAP.

As noted in the introduction, Deep SHAP is an approximate way to calculate Shapley values in Deep Learning systems, making the calculation feasible from a computational standpoint but with some disadvantages:

- It's approximate: Built on DeepLIFT [15], it estimates rather than computes exact Shapley values, which can cause inaccuracies, especially in complex models.
- Feature independence is assumed: It doesn't handle feature correlations well, which may lead to misleading explanations.
- Sensitive to background data: The quality of explanations hinges heavily on the choice of representative background samples.
- Model limitations: Only works with differentiable models that support backpropagation, so it is a no-go for many non-standard architectures.
- Harder to generalize: Local explanations don't always aggregate neatly into global insights, making interpretation tricky.
- Can still be resource-hungry: While faster than some alternatives, it can still be taxing on large-scale models.

The proposed method is much more straightforward, as it is based solely on discretizing the problem using image sectors and devising a strategy to hide those sectors in order to retrain the model.

Focusing now on glaucoma diagnosis, in [16] several models were developed, some based on clinical features to establish a baseline from which to start, and another deep learning model that combines information from macular OCT and color eye fundus images with the demographic, systemic, and ocular data that were used in the baseline models. For the interpretability of models using images, they used Integrated gradients and SmoothGrad, while for tree-based models developed with XGBoost they calculated SHAP values to assess the importance and interaction between features. A similar approach is followed in [17] using also OCT and SHAP values to develop a valuable user-friendly XAI software tool which provides transparent and interpretable insights to improve decision-making.

In the work carried out by [18], they collected 23 features, such as intraocular pressure, a visual field test, a retinal nerve fiber layer (RNFL) test performed with OCT and a fundus photograph, and carried out a feature selection process to finally keep only five of them. With the selected features, they tested several algorithms, such as support vector machines (SVM), C5.0, random forests, or XGBoost, and evaluated the importance of these features in the final decision using different graphs, including those derived from SHAP.

Also related to glaucoma, but using only structured data extracted from the electronic health record (EHR), we find the work of [19], where they train different models based on regression, decision trees or deep learning to predict whether a glaucoma patient would need surgery, based on progression data extracted from the follow-up of 4512 patients. They extracted 361 features from their medical records, including demographic, eye exam, diagnostic and prescription data. Then, using SHAP, they studied which of these features were the most important for the different models, finding that intraocular pressure, visual acuity or the use of medications commonly prescribed for glaucoma were among the most important. A very similar approach for the same problem is followed in [20–23]. Ref. [24] also focus on glaucoma progression, although, in their case, to predict long-term, rapid thinning of the retinal nerve fiber layer over a 5-year period in 505 patients with primary open-angle glaucoma in a South Korean population. They developed models based on decision trees using systemic and ophthalmologic data, applying SHAP to analyze the importance of the different features.

As mentioned earlier in Section 1, the main limitation of these studies on glaucoma diagnosis is that they are based on hand-crafted features, rather than addressing the problem from a Deep Learning perspective, as we do, using the entire image as input and regions of the images as features.

3. Materials and Methods

3.1. Datasets

The main color image datasets used in this work are RIM-ONE DL and HUC RGB. The publicly available image set RIM-ONE DL [25] resulted from the combination of the three previous versions of the well-known RIM-ONE dataset [26]. This new version consists of 313 images from healthy subjects and 172 images from patients with glaucoma acquired at three different hospitals. On the other hand, the HUC RGB dataset is a privately accessible set of retinal images collected by the medical specialists of our research team at the Hospital Universitario de Canarias. This set is composed of 191 images of patients with glaucoma and 63 images of healthy patients, and has been acquired with the Topcon TRC-NW8 multifunctional non-mydriatic retinograph (Topcon Healthcare, Spain). Considering the two sets, a total of 739 images have been used: 363 of glaucomatous eyes and 376 of healthy eyes. All these images have been annotated by two experts and include manual disc and cup segmentation.

Two other publicly available datasets have been used for further validation of the experiments carried out, namely REFUGE and DRISHTI-GS1. The REFUGE challenge dataset [27] is composed of 1200 retinal images, of which 10% (120 samples) correspond to glaucomatous subjects, including primary open-angle glaucoma and normal tension glaucoma. The dataset also contains the ground truth segmentation of the disc and cup. The DRISHTI-GS1 dataset [28] contains 101 fundus images, 31 belonging to healthy subjects and 70 to glaucomatous ones, with different resolutions and ground truth labels for the optic disc and cup.

Since the area of interest for glaucoma diagnosis is concentrated around the optic nerve head, all images used in this study were cropped squarely around it using the same proportionality criteria as shown in Figure 1b. Table 1 contains a summary of the aforementioned datasets, with the number of healthy and glaucomatous images per dataset and their resolution after cropping them around the optic disc.

Table 1. Summary of the datasets used in this work, indicating the number (No.) of healthy images, the number of glaucoma images, and the minimum (Min.) and maximum (Max.) resolution of the cropped images per dataset.

Dataset	No. of Healthy Images	No. of Glaucoma Images	Min. Resolution	Max. Resolution
RIM-ONE DL	313	172	274 × 274	793 × 793
HUC RGB	63	191	520 × 520	1035 × 1035
REFUGE	1080	120	268 × 268	562 × 562
DRISHTI-GS1	31	70	450 × 450	722 × 722

3.2. Deep Learning Models

In this section, we explain how the CNN models used in this work were trained. To do so, we describe how the training and test sets were obtained from the available data, the training strategy, and the parameters selected for each CNN.

In training the CNNs for this study, the initial set of 739 images underwent a random division into training and test sets, maintaining an 80/20 proportion, respectively. The training set comprised 290 retinographies of glaucoma and 301 of healthy eyes, while the test set included 73 retinographies of glaucoma and 75 of healthy eyes. Additionally, the training set was further partitioned into five distinct training and validation subsets, employing a 5-fold approach.

We selected four prominent convolutional neural network architectures, namely VGG19 [29], ResNet50 [30], InceptionV3 [31], and Xception [32]. The selection of architectures was guided by specific algorithmic features: ResNet50 employs residual connections to facilitate the training of deeper networks; Xception utilizes depthwise separable convolutions to optimize computational efficiency; InceptionV3 benefits from multi-scale feature extraction via parallel convolutions; and VGG19 offers a simpler sequential design known for its performance consistency. These complementary design principles offer diverse algorithmic trade-offs, enriching our analysis pipeline and enabling comparative evaluation across design paradigms. These architectures are widely adopted and have been extensively utilized in the domain of glaucoma diagnosis and other medical fields. They have also been evaluated in similar studies, such as the works analyzed in Section 2.

All specified neural network architectures are accessible in the Keras module of the Tensorflow v2 package [33]. To tailor these models to our specific problem, we modified the top layer of each network. The adaptation involved introducing a DropOut layer, succeeded by a Flatten layer, and then a Dense layer featuring 128 neurons with ReLU activation. Subsequently, another DropOut layer was added, followed by a final Dense layer with two outputs utilizing the SoftMax activation function.

The hyperparameters for each model were empirically selected based on the accuracy values obtained for the corresponding validation subset during training. For VGG19, the DropOut rate was set to 0.5, while for InceptionV3, ResNet50, and Xception, it was set to 0.2. Additionally, in these three networks, the BatchNormalization layers were maintained in inference mode to prevent the non-trainable weights from being updated during the training phase.

Concerning the size of the Input layer, it was configured as $224 \times 224 \times 3$ for ResNet50 and VGG19, and $299 \times 299 \times 3$ for InceptionV3 and Xception.

Our training strategy is the same for all the models. First, starting with the pre-trained weights from ImageNet, the base model was frozen and we trained the new top layer for 200 epochs using an Adam optimizer, with a learning rate of 1×10^{-6}, and categorical cross-entropy as the loss function. Second, we unfroze the base model, except for the BatchNormalization layers, and trained the entire model end-to-end for 250 epochs, using the same optimizer, with a learning rate of 1×10^{-5}, and the same loss function as before. In all cases, a batch size of 8 was used.

In the pre-processing stage, we utilized the built-in Keras pre-processing functions tailored for each network. To address overfitting, in addition to the DropOut rates described earlier, we applied on-the-fly data augmentation exclusively to the training subset of each fold in the 5-fold cross-validation setup (approximately 473 images per fold). The augmentation included random adjustments to contrast (± 0.3) and brightness (± 0.3), horizontal flipping, rotations up to $\pm 45°$, translations up to ± 0.05 along both axes, and zooming (± 0.2), all using the nearest neighbor fill mode and preserving the original aspect ratio. These transformations were applied dynamically at each epoch, so no new images were permanently added, and the total dataset size remained unchanged. Overfitting was monitored throughout training, and no significant divergence between training and validation metrics was observed, suggesting the combined augmentation and regularization strategy was effective.

The final weights for each model were chosen from the epoch that maximized the validation accuracy on average among the 5 folds. This resulted in 5 different models per network architecture, totaling 20 models.

3.3. Shapley Values Implementation

As discussed in the introduction, Shapley values are framed in cooperative game theory, and provide us with a way of assigning a payoff to each player: the average of all the marginal contributions of that player to each coalition of which he or she is a member. That is, those players who contribute more to the groups that include them should receive a higher payoff.

Formally, one of the most common representations of a cooperative game is through the characteristic function. Let $N = \{1, \ldots, n\}$ be a finite, non-empty set of players, and $S \subseteq N$ be a subset of players of N which we will call a coalition. A characteristic function set is given by the pair (N, v), where $v : 2^N \to \mathbb{R}$ is a characteristic function that assigns to each coalition S a real number $v(S)$. This number $v(S)$ is often referred to as the "value" or contribution of the coalition S [5,34]. Thus, the payoff assigned to player j is given by the corresponding Shapley value $\phi_j(v)$ and is defined as follows [5]:

$$\phi_j(v) = \phi_j = \sum_{S \subseteq N \setminus \{j\}} \frac{|S|!(n - |S| - 1)!}{n!} [v(S \cup \{j\}) - v(S)] \ , \ \forall j \in N \quad (1)$$

That is, a weighted average is made, for all coalitions S that do not contain player j, of the differences between the contribution when player j is included in the coalition and when is not included.

Note that the empty set $S = \emptyset$ is also part of the summation in the Equation (1). Therefore, the undistributed gain is also defined as follows $\phi_0 = v(\emptyset)$, which would be the fixed payoff that is not associated with any of the players.

In order to apply this method to a machine learning model, it would, in general, be necessary to re-train the model for all feature subsets $S \subseteq F$, where F is the set of all features [9,35–37]. Therefore, to use the Equation (1) in this case, one would train a model $f_{S\cup\{j\}}$ that includes feature j in its training set, and another model f_S that does not include that feature. With this in mind, making use of the notation of [9], we can adapt the Equation (1) as follows:

$$\phi_j(f) = \phi_j = \sum_{S\subseteq F\setminus\{j\}} \frac{|S|!(|F|-|S|-1)!}{|F|!}\left[f_{S\cup\{j\}}(x_{S\cup\{j\}}) - f_S(x_S)\right] \quad (2)$$

where x_S and $x_{S\cup\{j\}}$ represent, respectively, the values of the input features of the subsets S and $S\cup\{j\}$ for instance x. In this approach, the undistributed gain would be $\phi_0 = f_\emptyset(\emptyset)$, i.e., the model prediction that is not associated with any of the features.

In our particular case, dealing with images as input data, applying this equation at the pixel level would be impractical, since we would have to form a total of 2^n coalitions, where n is the number of pixels. However, if we divide the input images into standard sectors [38], as shown in Figure 2, and treat each sector as if it were a feature, the number of combinations is dramatically reduced, making the problem of computing Shapley values computationally tractable in a reasonable amount of time, even if we have to re-train the models for each possible coalition. This decision constitutes a key design trade-off in algorithm implementation: by treating sectors as features, we reduce the computational complexity of the Shapley value calculation from exponential in the number of pixels to exponential in the number of sectors (i.e., from 2^n to 2^7), making the algorithm feasible for execution while preserving anatomical relevance. This approach is similar to that adopted by [39], where a discretization of the problem is also proposed but through an arbitrary regular grid without medical significance.

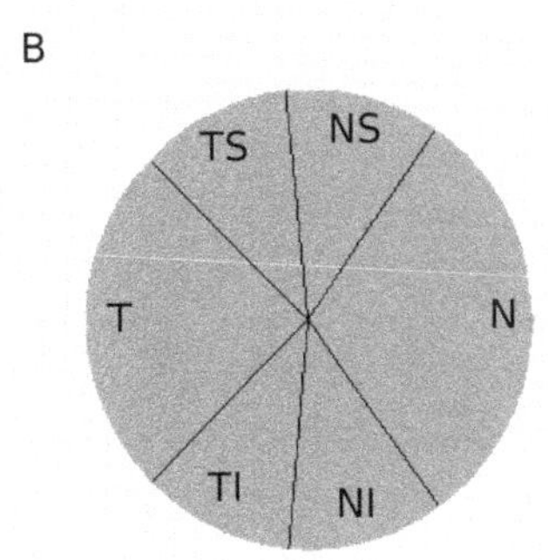

Figure 2. Diagram illustrating the division of the optic disc into six sectors: Nasal Superior (NS), Nasal (N), Nasal Inferior (NI), Temporal Inferior (TI), Temporal (T), and Temporal Superior (TS). Additionally, the Background (B) is treated as an additional sector. The image depicts the configuration for a right eye; for a left eye, the sectors are mirrored horizontally.

For practical purposes, another important problem to solve is how to obtain an image in which only a subset $S \subset N$ of sectors is present, i.e., how to simulate the absence of one or more sectors to form the coalitions required for the calculation of the Shapley values. In our case, we have solved this by occlusion. When we talk about occlusion in this context, we mean it in the same sense as the occlusion method in [40], i.e., hiding or covering parts of the image so that the neural network model does not have access to that information. Specifically, we have chosen to occlude the sectors with black, i.e., setting all their pixels to 0 in the three RGB channels, which gives us a total of 128 coalitions (2^7), including the occlusion of the image background. Figure 3 shows an example of occluded sectors in an image.

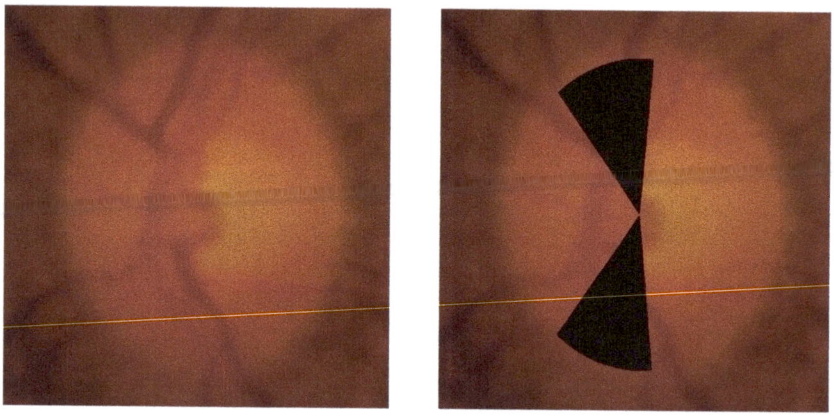

(**a**) (**b**)

Figure 3. Example of occluded sectors in an image of the left eye of a normal subject extracted from RIM-ONE DL. The nasal inferior (NI) and nasal superior (NS) sectors have been occluded. (**a**) Original color image. (**b**) Example of occlusion of the NI and NS sectors.

Note that we are alternatively using "coalition" and "combination of occluded sectors", although formally a coalition $C \subseteq N$ would represent the sectors that enter the game, while the corresponding combination O of occluded sectors would be the sectors that are not present in that coalition, $O = N \setminus C$. Note also that the calculation of the Shapley value also includes in particular $C = \emptyset$ and $C = N$, i.e., respectively, an image in which all sectors are occluded or an image in which none are occluded (the original image).

The Shapley values, as previously mentioned, are the contribution of each sector to the difference between the model prediction for the original image and the prediction for the empty set. In our case, since our models return two output probabilities (normal and glaucoma classes), where the sum of both will be 1 by the application of the softmax activation function, we are only considering the probability that the image corresponds to a glaucoma case. Therefore, to calculate the Shapley value for each sector $j \in F$ we have proceeded as follows:

1. For each input image I, generate all possible combinations of occluded sectors for I, taking into account whether the image belongs to a left or right eye to properly locate the sectors.
2. For each sector j of I, calculate the probability of the glaucoma class of the model f_S and $f_{S \cup \{j\}}$ for each possible coalition $S \subseteq F \setminus \{j\}$ of sectors, using as input I_S and $I_{S \cup \{j\}}$, the images generated from I with that coalition of sectors present in the image.
3. With the above probabilities, calculate the Shapley value ϕ_j for sector j following Equation (2).

The most straightforward way to calculate the output probabilities for all possible coalitions of sectors would be to use the original trained models, as they stand. However, as discussed in [41], one of the basic assumptions in machine learning is that training and testing data come from the same distribution, so if we occlude a portion of the sectors in the image when evaluating our models, we could be changing the distribution from which the testing data comes. In this scenario, it would be unclear whether the prediction of a model is affected because the removed features were important or because of the change in the distribution of the data. Therefore, it seems appropriate to re-train the models to accommodate these new images with occluded sectors. From an algorithm design perspective, we considered two alternative retraining strategies that reflect a trade-off between model-centric and data-centric fidelity:

1. Re-train only the last layer, i.e., the classification layer of the original models, keeping the convolutional base frozen, using as training data the different possible combinations of sectors, resulting in a model adapted to each combination, but without modifying the original feature extraction.
2. Re-train all layers of the original models, from start to finish, also using the same data as in the previous scenario, resulting in new models adapted to each combination.

The second assumption, according to the approach taken by [42], would be more "true to the data", as by re-training all layers one could start using different features that are correlated with the original ones, for example, redundant information contained in the images that was not used before, which could move us further away from the original model [43]. This, however, could also be interesting, because it allows us to better understand what information is contained in the data that can be exploited for predictions.

The first assumption according to [42], would be more "true to the model", as only the classification part would be re-trained so that it can adjust to possible outliers from the convolutional layers that the classifier had not seen before, but the features that the model extracts from the images are not modified. This would allow the classifiers to adapt to possible changes in the distribution, as previously discussed, while obtaining a prediction closer to the original model, since the same convolutional layers of the original model are used. We believe that this approach is more what is desired to better understand the decisions made by convolutional neural network models, and for this reason, the experiments have been carried out under this assumption.

Therefore, in order to re-train our original models and obtain new models for each combination of occluded sectors, we have generally followed the following steps:

1. Given a set of images with a combination O of occluded sectors, the training and test sets were divided using exactly the same division as in the corresponding original set. That is, if an image was originally in the training set, the same image with the combination O of occluded sectors will still be in the training set.
2. Similarly, the training set was subdivided into the same 5 training and validation partitions as the respective unoccluded set.
3. For each of the 5 partitions we built a new model, initializing it with the weights of the original model corresponding to that partition, and we re-trained it following the methodology described in Section 3.2, but only for 50 epochs, as we empirically observed that this was sufficient.
4. Finally, we selected the models for the epoch that achieved the highest average validation accuracy among the 5 partitions. This results in 5 models per network architecture for each combination O of occluded sectors.

The above procedure was repeated for each possible combination of occluded sectors and for each network architecture.

3.4. Evaluation Methodology

The degree of agreement between the Shapley values calculated in different situations was assessed:

- Agreement between Shapley values for re-trained models and randomly initialized models.
- Agreement between models with the same architecture.
- Agreement between models with different architectures.

In order to calculate the degree of agreement, Spearman's correlation coefficient [44] was used. The degree of correlation between the Shapley values for the re-trained and randomly initialized models will allow us to have a baseline from which a correlation can be considered reasonable in the following experiments. It will also serve us as an initial control, in the same way as suggested by [45] for the attribution/saliency methods, since it would be desirable to obtain a low correlation.

Additionally, the global relevance for each sector, calculated as the probability that the largest contribution provided by the Shapley values for a given image is located in that sector, has also been studied. It is important to consider that the resulting contributions of the Shapley values can be both positive and negative. We need to take this into account when determining which sector has contributed most to the prediction. If the network predicts that the image corresponds to a glaucoma (probability greater than 0.5), the sector that contributed the most will be the one with the maximum Shapley value. If the network predicts that the image corresponds to a healthy eye, the sector that contributed the most will be the one with the minimum Shapley value.

4. Experimental Results and Discussion

Different experiments have been carried out following the methodology described in Section 3. Details of these experiments can be found in the following subsections.

4.1. Performance Evaluation of the Deep Learning Models

The trained CNN models were tested with the previously mentioned independent set, which consists of 75 samples from healthy subjects and 73 from glaucoma subjects. The results achieved per network architecture and fold have been included in Table 2, highlighting those corresponding to the best performance per architecture in terms of balanced accuracy, which is the arithmetic mean of sensitivity and specificity [46]. Analogously, Tables 3 and 4 show the performance obtained by evaluating the trained models on the REFUGE and DRISHTI-GS1 datasets. It is important to remark that these additional image sets have only been used for testing.

Furthermore, as a representative example, we present in Figure 4 the validation accuracy and loss curves for the ResNet50 model, which achieved the highest test accuracy in one of the folds. These plots offer additional insights into the model's behavior during training, complementing the test performance metrics.

While a comprehensive evaluation of the trained CNN models' performance is beyond the scope of this article, it can be seen that the models classify the images across all considered datasets with reasonable accuracy.

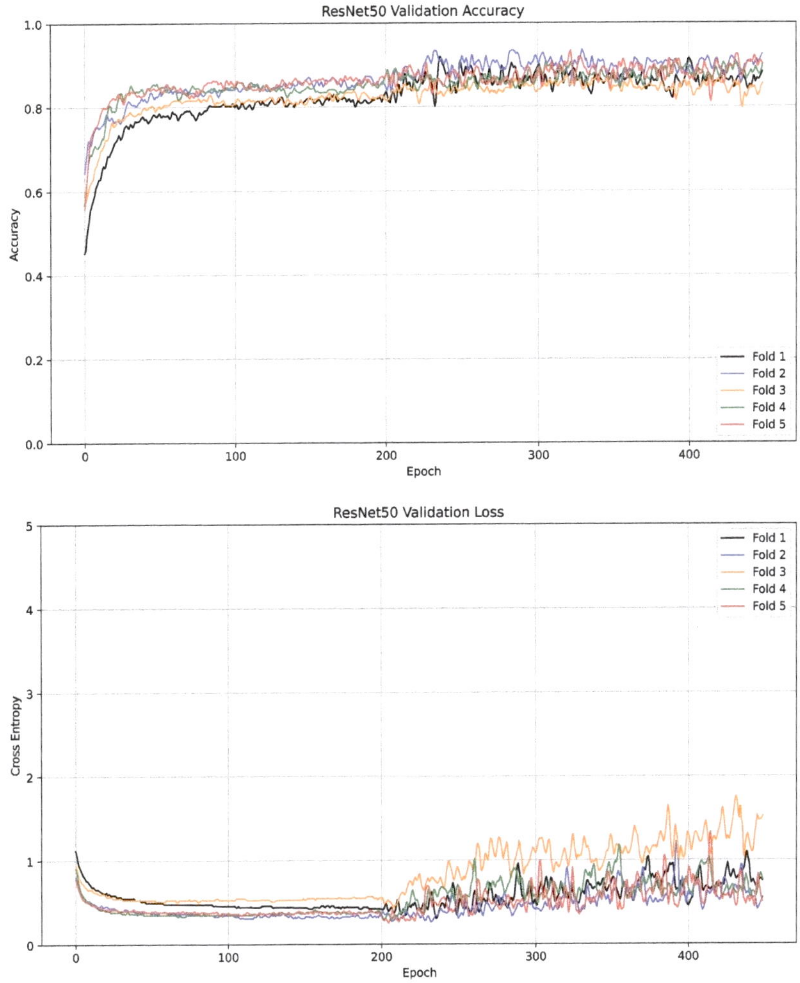

Figure 4. Validation accuracy and loss per epoch for each of the five cross-validation folds using the ResNet50 model. Each line and color represents a different fold. The plots illustrate the model's convergence behavior and consistency across folds, providing insight into the training dynamics and generalization performance.

Table 2. Results obtained by training and testing with our dataset, according to different metrics. Results corresponding to the maximum balanced accuracy (B. Accuracy) are highlighted in bold. The last row of each architecture shows the mean (M) ± the standard deviation (SD) for every metric.

Network	Fold	Sensitivity	Specificity	Accuracy	B. Accuracy	F1 Score
VGG19	1	0.8767	0.9467	0.9122	0.9117	0.9078
VGG19	2	0.9726	0.9467	0.9595	0.9596	0.9595
VGG19	3	0.9041	0.9733	0.9392	0.9387	0.9362
VGG19	**4**	**0.9863**	**0.9467**	**0.9662**	**0.9665**	**0.9664**
VGG19	5	1.0000	0.9200	0.9595	0.9600	0.9605
VGG19	M ± SD	0.9479 ± 0.0543	0.9467 ± 0.0189	0.9473 ± 0.0221	0.9473 ± 0.0225	0.9461 ± 0.0243

Table 2. *Cont.*

Network	Fold	Sensitivity	Specificity	Accuracy	B. Accuracy	F1 Score
ResNet50	1	0.9315	0.9067	0.9189	0.9191	0.9189
ResNet50	2	0.9589	0.9867	0.9730	0.9728	0.9722
ResNet50	**3**	**0.9863**	**0.9600**	**0.9730**	**0.9732**	**0.9730**
ResNet50	4	0.9178	0.9467	0.9324	0.9322	0.9306
ResNet50	5	0.8904	0.9200	0.9054	0.9052	0.9028
ResNet50	M ± SD	0.9370 ± 0.0370	0.9440 ± 0.0318	0.9405 ± 0.0311	0.9405 ± 0.0311	0.9395 ± 0.0318
InceptionV3	1	0.9589	0.8800	0.9189	0.9195	0.9211
InceptionV3	2	0.9452	0.8667	0.9054	0.9059	0.9079
InceptionV3	**3**	**0.9726**	**0.9067**	**0.9392**	**0.9396**	**0.9404**
InceptionV3	4	0.9178	0.9333	0.9257	0.9256	0.9241
InceptionV3	5	0.9178	0.9200	0.9189	0.9189	0.9178
InceptionV3	M ± SD	0.9425 ± 0.0245	0.9013 ± 0.0276	0.9216 ± 0.0123	0.9219 ± 0.0122	0.9223 ± 0.0118
Xception	**1**	**0.9452**	**0.9067**	**0.9257**	**0.9259**	**0.9262**
Xception	2	0.9315	0.8933	0.9122	0.9124	0.9128
Xception	3	0.9452	0.8267	0.8851	0.8859	0.8903
Xception	4	0.9178	0.9067	0.9122	0.9122	0.9116
Xception	5	0.9315	0.8133	0.8716	0.8724	0.8774
Xception	M ± SD	0.9342 ± 0.0115	0.8693 ± 0.0456	0.9014 ± 0.0222	0.9018 ± 0.0219	0.9036 ± 0.0195

Table 3. Results obtained by evaluating the models with the REFUGE dataset, according to different metrics. Results corresponding to the maximum balanced accuracy (B. Accuracy) are highlighted in bold. The last row of each architecture shows the mean (M) ± the standard deviation (SD) for every metric.

Network	Fold	Sensitivity	Specificity	Accuracy	B. Accuracy	F1 Score
VGG19	1	0.8000	0.8769	0.8692	0.8384	0.5501
VGG19	2	0.8167	0.8472	0.8442	0.8319	0.5117
VGG19	3	0.7333	0.9269	0.9075	0.8301	0.6132
VGG19	4	0.7833	0.8537	0.8467	0.8185	0.5054
VGG19	**5**	**0.8833**	**0.8898**	**0.8892**	**0.8866**	**0.6145**
VGG19	M ± SD	0.8033 ± 0.0545	0.8789 ± 0.0319	0.8713 ± 0.0273	0.8411 ± 0.0264	0.5590 ± 0.0529
ResNet50	1	0.7250	0.9620	0.9383	0.8435	0.7016
ResNet50	**2**	**0.8417**	**0.9009**	**0.8950**	**0.8713**	**0.6159**
ResNet50	3	0.8000	0.8981	0.8883	0.8491	0.5890
ResNet50	4	0.7833	0.9296	0.9150	0.8565	0.6483
ResNet50	5	0.8083	0.8065	0.8067	0.8074	0.4554
ResNet50	M ± SD	0.7917 ± 0.0429	0.8994 ± 0.0580	0.8887 ± 0.0498	0.8456 ± 0.0237	0.6020 ± 0.0921
InceptionV3	1	0.7500	0.9435	0.9242	0.8468	0.6642
InceptionV3	2	0.8333	0.9065	0.8992	0.8699	0.6231
InceptionV3	**3**	**0.8500**	**0.9389**	**0.9300**	**0.8944**	**0.7083**
InceptionV3	4	0.6750	0.9843	0.9533	0.8296	0.7431
InceptionV3	5	0.7750	0.9426	0.9258	0.8588	0.6764
InceptionV3	M ± SD	0.7767 ± 0.0701	0.9431 ± 0.0276	0.9265 ± 0.0193	0.8599 ± 0.0244	0.6830 ± 0.0454
Xception	1	0.7500	0.9083	0.8925	0.8292	0.5825
Xception	**2**	**0.8083**	**0.8963**	**0.8875**	**0.8523**	**0.5897**
Xception	3	0.7000	0.9241	0.9017	0.8120	0.5874
Xception	4	0.7333	0.9148	0.8967	0.8241	0.5867
Xception	5	0.9250	0.6898	0.7133	0.8074	0.3922
Xception	M ± SD	0.7833 ± 0.0884	0.8667 ± 0.0994	0.8583 ± 0.0812	0.8250 ± 0.0176	0.5477 ± 0.0870

Table 4. Results obtained by evaluating the models with the DRISHTI-GS1 dataset, according to different metrics. Results corresponding to the maximum balanced accuracy (B. Accuracy) are highlighted in bold. The last row of each architecture shows the mean (M) ± the standard deviation (SD) for every metric.

Network	Fold	Sensitivity	Specificity	Accuracy	B. Accuracy	F1 Score
VGG19	1	0.8429	0.7742	0.8218	0.8085	0.8676
VGG19	2	0.8857	0.7419	0.8416	0.8138	0.8857
VGG19	**3**	**0.8429**	**0.8065**	**0.8317**	**0.8247**	**0.8741**
VGG19	4	0.8857	0.7419	0.8416	0.8138	0.8857
VGG19	5	0.9571	0.6452	0.8614	0.8012	0.9054
VGG19	M ± SD	0.8829 ± 0.0467	0.7419 ± 0.0603	0.8396 ± 0.0147	0.8124 ± 0.0086	0.8837 ± 0.0144
ResNet50	**1**	**0.9286**	**0.7742**	**0.8812**	**0.8514**	**0.9155**
ResNet50	2	0.8571	0.7419	0.8218	0.7995	0.8696
ResNet50	3	0.8143	0.7419	0.7921	0.7781	0.8444
ResNet50	4	0.9143	0.7419	0.8614	0.8281	0.9014
ResNet50	5	0.9429	0.6774	0.8614	0.8101	0.9041
ResNet50	M ± SD	0.8914 ± 0.0540	0.7355 ± 0.0353	0.8436 ± 0.0360	0.8135 ± 0.0279	0.8870 ± 0.0293
InceptionV3	1	0.8429	0.8065	0.8317	0.8247	0.8741
InceptionV3	2	0.8571	0.7419	0.8218	0.7995	0.8696
InceptionV3	3	0.9000	0.7097	0.8416	0.8048	0.8873
InceptionV3	4	0.8571	0.7742	0.8317	0.8157	0.8759
InceptionV3	**5**	**0.8857**	**0.7742**	**0.8515**	**0.8300**	**0.8921**
InceptionV3	M ± SD	0.8686 ± 0.0235	0.7613 ± 0.0368	0.8356 ± 0.0113	0.8149 ± 0.0128	0.8798 ± 0.0095
Xception	1	0.8429	0.7097	0.8020	0.7763	0.8551
Xception	2	0.8714	0.6774	0.8119	0.7744	0.8652
Xception	**3**	**0.8286**	**0.7419**	**0.8020**	**0.7853**	**0.8529**
Xception	4	0.9143	0.6452	0.8317	0.7797	0.8828
Xception	5	0.8857	0.6774	0.8218	0.7816	0.8732
Xception	M ± SD	0.8686 ± 0.0341	0.6903 ± 0.0368	0.8139 ± 0.0129	0.7794 ± 0.0043	0.8659 ± 0.0125

4.2. Randomization of Model Weights

In this experiment, using the same architectures as for the re-trained models described in Section 3.3, different network models have been generated by initializing their weights randomly using the initialization proposed by [47], while the bias vectors have been initialized to zero.

Given that our test set contains 148 images, we constructed two vectors of Shapley values, each with 1036 elements (7 sectors $\times$ 148 images), to compute the correlation. One vector corresponds to the randomized model and the other to the re-trained model. By doing so, we have a correlation value for each partition per architecture. These 5 values are the ones we have used to calculate each box-and-whiskers diagram in Figure 5, where we present the correlations for each architecture between the randomized and the re-trained models.

It can be observed that both the medians of the correlations and their extreme values for each architecture present absolute values, in general, lower than 0.1, except for the maximum value of Xception which reached 0.25. These values are therefore within the expected range.

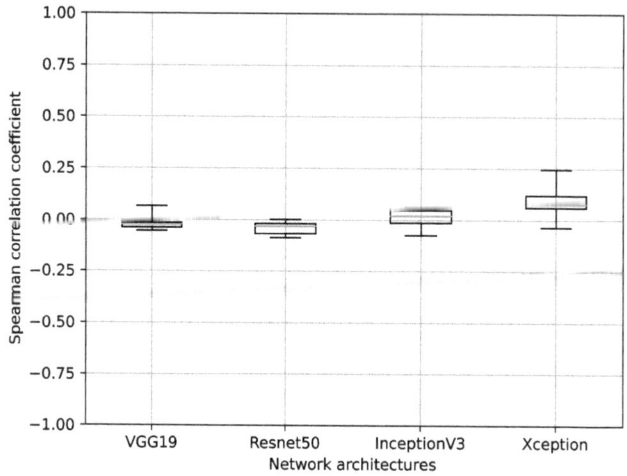

Figure 5. Boxplots of the correlation coefficients between the Shapley values of the random and re-trained models. There is one diagram per network architecture. Each diagram has been obtained from the 5 correlation values corresponding to each partition by architecture.

4.3. Correlation Between Shapley Values for Models with the Same Architecture

In this experiment, we calculate the correlation between Shapley values when the partition from which the models are re-trained changes but the neural network architecture remains the same.

In this case, the correlation was calculated between the results of each possible pair of partitions, per architecture. For each pair of partitions, a correlation value was obtained between two vectors of as many elements as test images and Shapley values per image. We therefore have $\binom{5}{2} = 10$ correlation values per architecture.

The results obtained are shown in Figure 6, where each box-and-whiskers plot has been calculated from the correlation values between the results for each pair of partitions per network architecture.

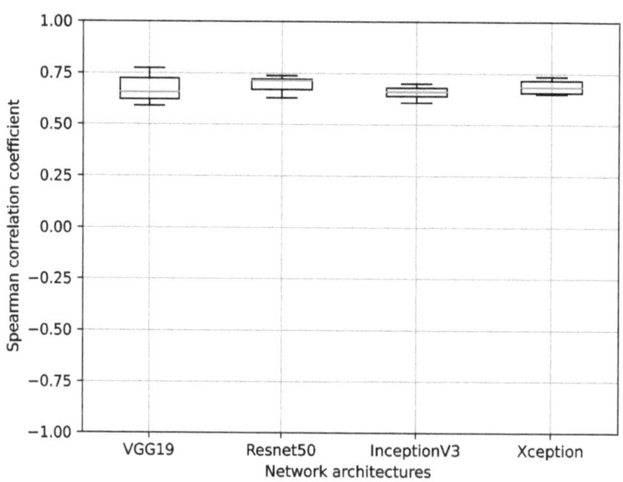

Figure 6. Boxplots of the correlation coefficients between the different pairs of partitions by architecture for the Shapley values.

All medians are above 0.65, which seems to indicate that, regardless of the architecture considered, the models are not very sensitive to the change of the training and validation partitions.

4.4. Correlation Between Shapley Values for Models with Different Architectures

These tests aim to assess the degree of agreement between Shapley values corresponding to re-trained models with different architectures but with the same data.

Correlation was calculated for all possible pairs of architectures, considering separately the results of each partition per architecture. In other words, to calculate each correlation value, a vector is constructed for each architecture with the Shapley values of each image of the test set for the models of each partition. We will therefore have 5 correlation values for each pair of architectures (one per partition).

The results obtained are shown in Figure 7 where each boxplot has been calculated from the Shapley values between each pair of architectures for the same partitions. It can be observed, as expected, that the change of architecture has a greater impact on the calculation of the Shapley values than the change of training and validation partitions.

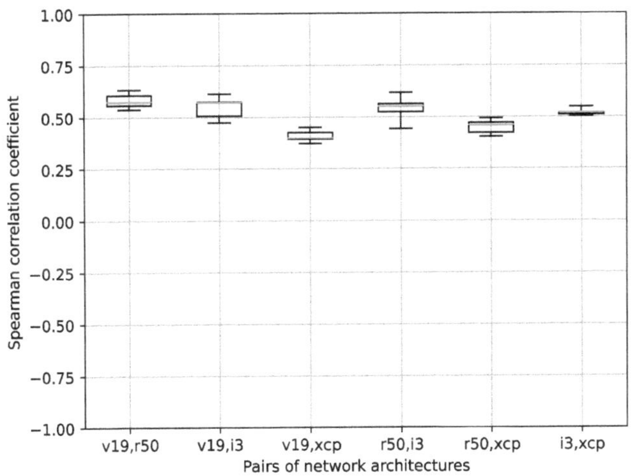

Figure 7. Boxplots showing the correlation coefficients between Shapley values for each pair of architectures: VGG19 (v19), ResNet50 (r50), InceptionV3 (i3), and Xception (xcp).

4.5. Relevance of Sectors According to Shapley Values

Glaucoma is characterized by a progressive enlargement of the optic cup area, leading to a narrowing of the neuroretinal rim [12]. Although this enlargement can occur in all directions, certain regions tend to be affected earlier than others. In eyes with mild glaucomatous damage, rim loss predominantly appears in the temporal inferior and temporal superior regions. As the disease advances to a moderate stage, the temporal region typically shows the most significant rim loss. In cases of severe glaucoma, the nasal disc area generally experiences the least rim loss, while the nasal inferior region tends to be more affected than the nasal superior region.

With this in mind, Shapley values have been calculated for the different sectors in order to assess in this section the degree of coincidence with the expected values from a medical point of view. For this purpose, a global relevance measure has been obtained for each sector, which indicates the probability that the maximum of the contributions provided by the Shapley values for a given image is found in that sector. More specifically, given the models trained for a specific network architecture (all the partitions have been considered as a whole) and a given test set, each sector has a global probability of $N\%$ of being the most relevant, i.e., the one that contributes the most for an input image, according to the Shapley values obtained for a normal or glaucoma prediction. In this sense, in the case of a normal prediction, the signs of the Shapley values were inverted to study the distribution of these values and their averages. The results obtained are shown in Figure 8.

What stands out the most in this figure is the predominance of the background (B) sector, being the most probable sector in most cases, although with some differences between classes. For the VGG19 and ResNet50 architectures, the probabilities assigned to the B sector are the highest in the case of a normal prediction. However, in the case of a glaucoma prediction, the highest predictions assigned to the B sector are found for the InceptionV3 and Xception architectures. This extremely high relevance of the B sector may seem very surprising from a medical perspective but in this regard, it is worth recalling the study carried out by [2] where they showed that the information contained in the background may allow the detection of glaucoma in this type of models.

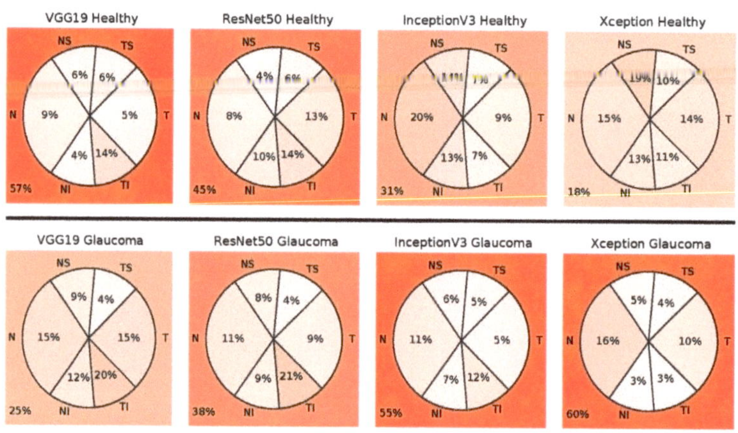

Figure 8. Global relevance by sector according to the Shapley values for the different network architectures, separating the data by the class predicted by the networks. Given an input image, the graph indicates each sector's probability of being the highest contributor according to the Shapley values for that class.

In Figures 9 and 10 we can see, respectively, the average Shapley values per class and their dispersion. We show only the results for the partitions that obtained the highest balanced accuracy per architecture for the re-trained models, as reported in Table 5. As we can see, for the selected partitions the average values generally reflect what we observed in Figure 8, with the background sector being one of the largest contributors in many cases. In some cases, negative averages appear which indicates that those sectors contribute negatively, on average, towards the class in question.

Table 5. Balanced accuracy of the re-trained models without occluding any sector. Results are shown by architecture and fold, with those with the highest balanced accuracy highlighted in bold. The last column displays the mean (M) ± the standard deviation (SD) per architecture.

Architecture	Fold 1	Fold 2	Fold 3	Fold 4	Fold 5	M ± SD
VGG19	0.9254	0.9322	0.9387	0.9459	**0.9663**	0.9417 ± 0.0157
ResNet50	0.9052	**0.9728**	0.9528	0.9391	0.8985	0.9337 ± 0.0315
InceptionV3	0.9391	0.9256	0.9185	0.9256	**0.9393**	0.9296 ± 0.0092
Xception	0.8995	0.9187	0.8789	**0.9393**	0.8791	0.9031 ± 0.0261

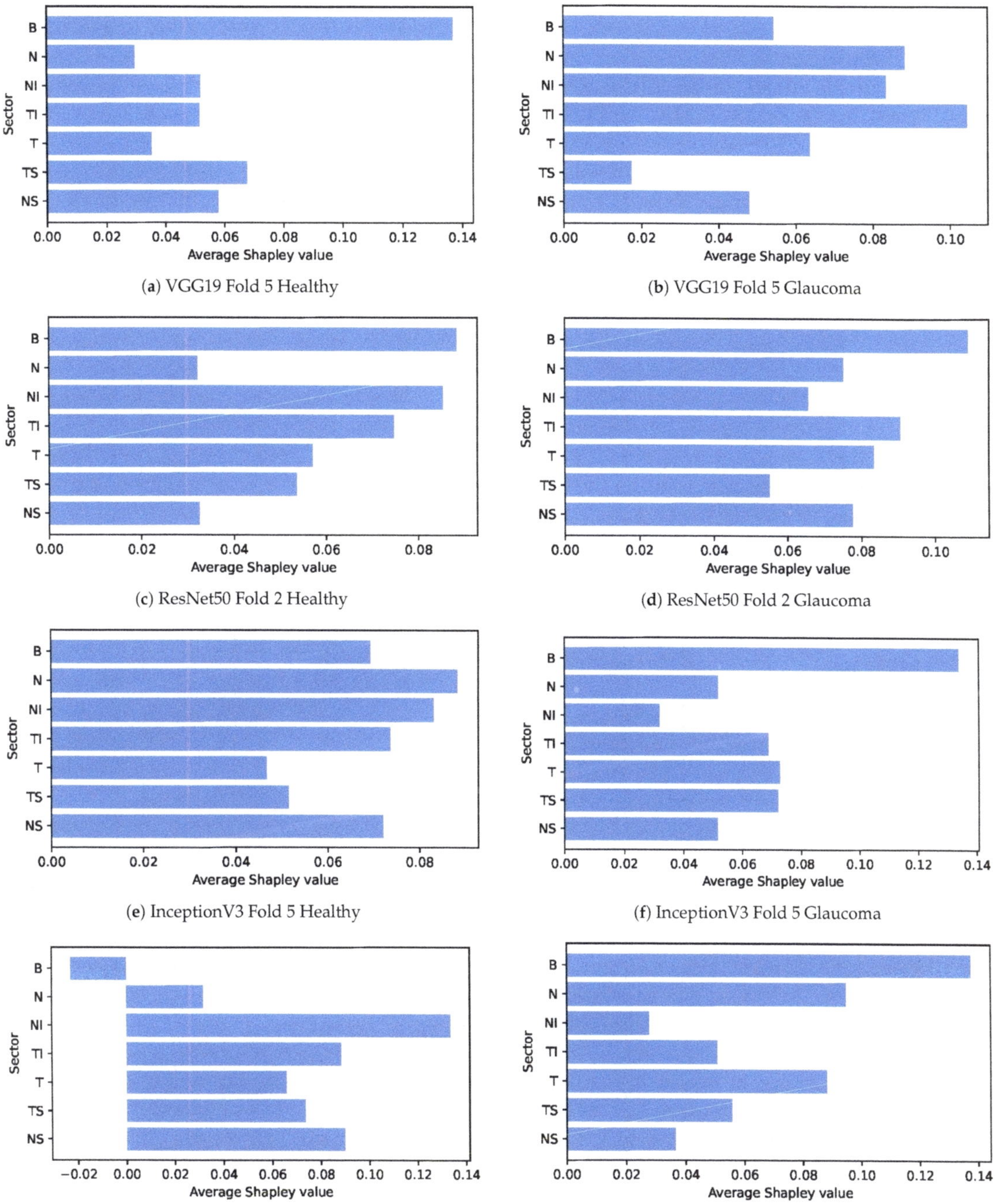

(a) VGG19 Fold 5 Healthy (b) VGG19 Fold 5 Glaucoma

(c) ResNet50 Fold 2 Healthy (d) ResNet50 Fold 2 Glaucoma

(e) InceptionV3 Fold 5 Healthy (f) InceptionV3 Fold 5 Glaucoma

(g) Xception Fold 4 Healthy (h) Xception Fold 4 Glaucoma

Figure 9. Average Shapley values per architecture, for each sector, for the folds with the highest balanced accuracy. The results are separated according to the class predicted by the network.

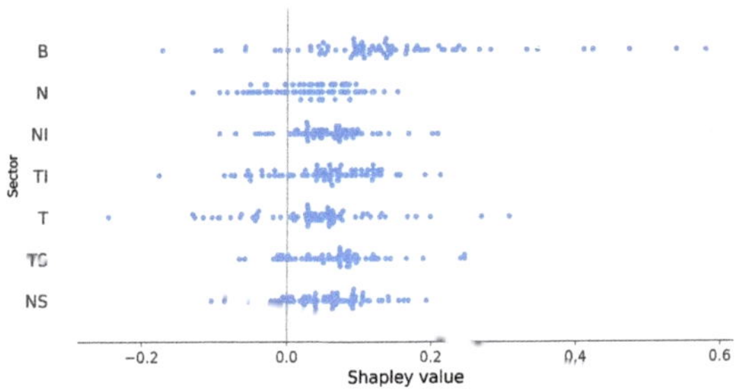

(a) VGG19 Fold 5 Healthy

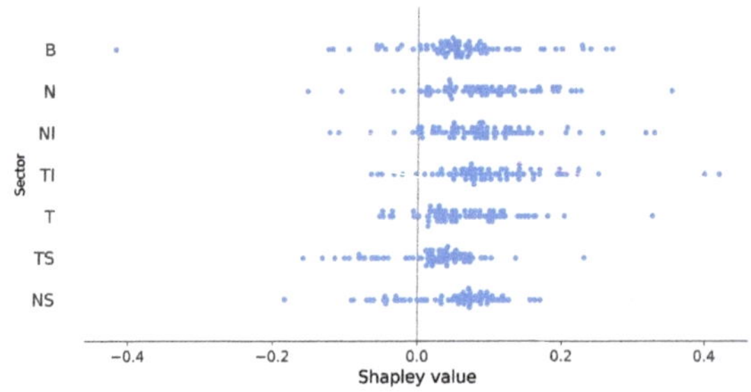

(b) VGG19 Fold 5 Glaucoma

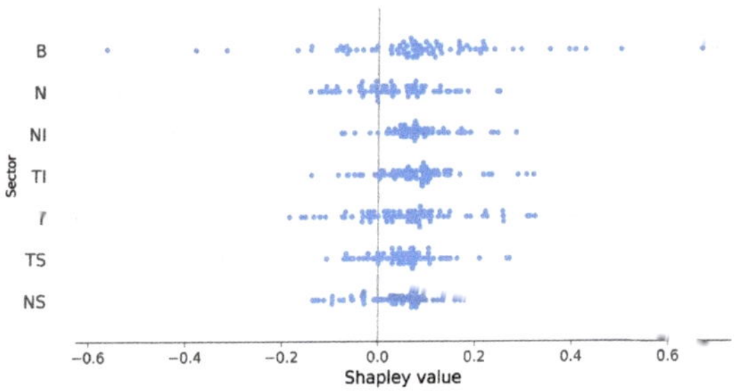

(c) ResNet50 Fold 2 Healthy

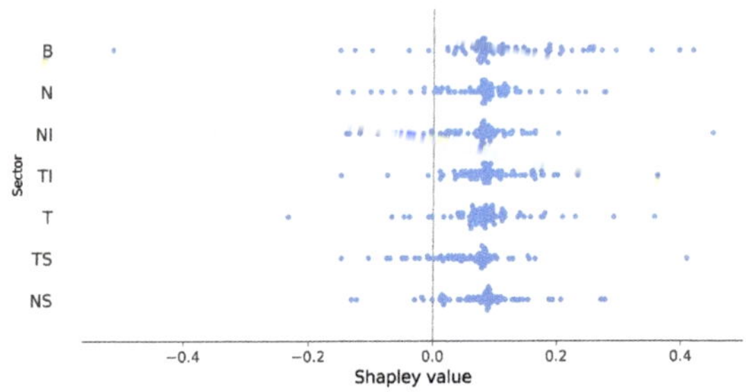

(d) ResNet50 Fold 2 Glaucoma

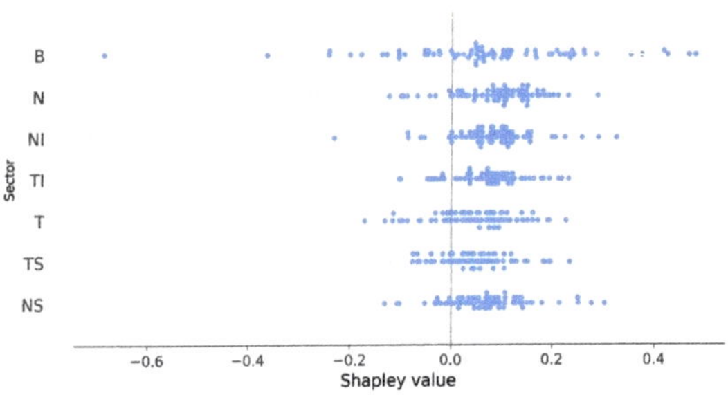

(e) InceptionV3 Fold 5 Healthy

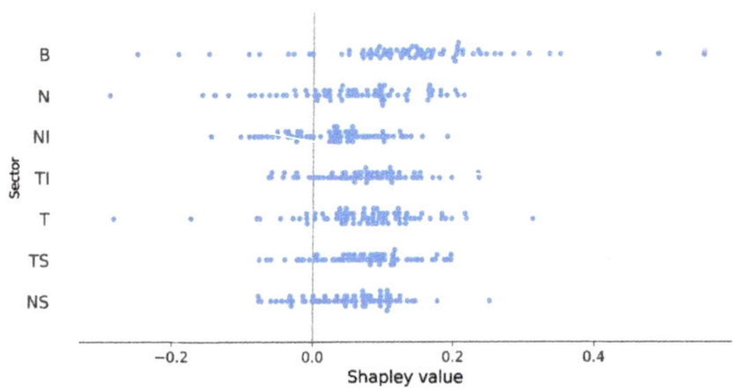

(f) InceptionV3 Fold 5 Glaucoma

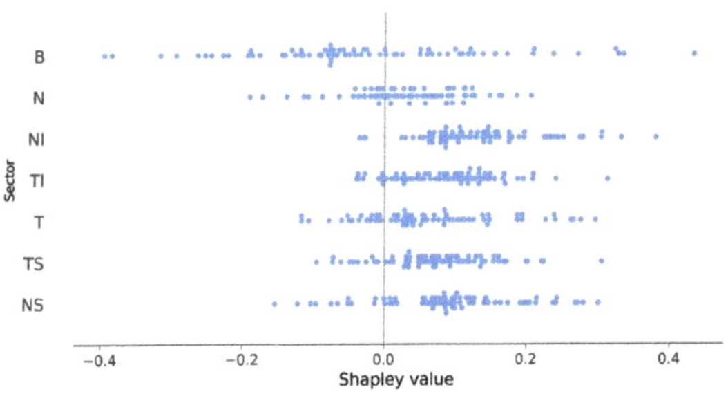

(g) Xception Fold 4 Healthy

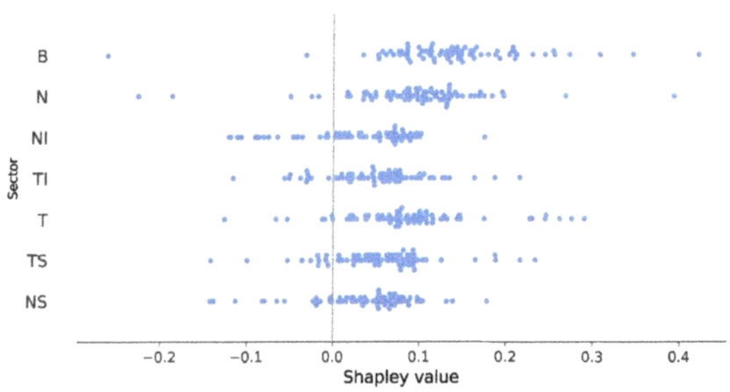

(h) Xception Fold 4 Glaucoma

Figure 10. Dispersion of Shapley values per architecture, for each sector, for the folds with the highest balanced accuracy. The results are separated according to the class predicted by the network. For each image in the test set, a dot is shown on the graph indicating the Shapley value for each sector. If any point overlaps with a point in another image in the same sector, it is shifted slightly on the y-axis.

4.6. Comparison Between Shapley Values for Different Datasets

The global relevance by sectors has also been evaluated for the other datasets considered, DRISHTI-GS1 and REFUGE. Figure 11 shows the results obtained.

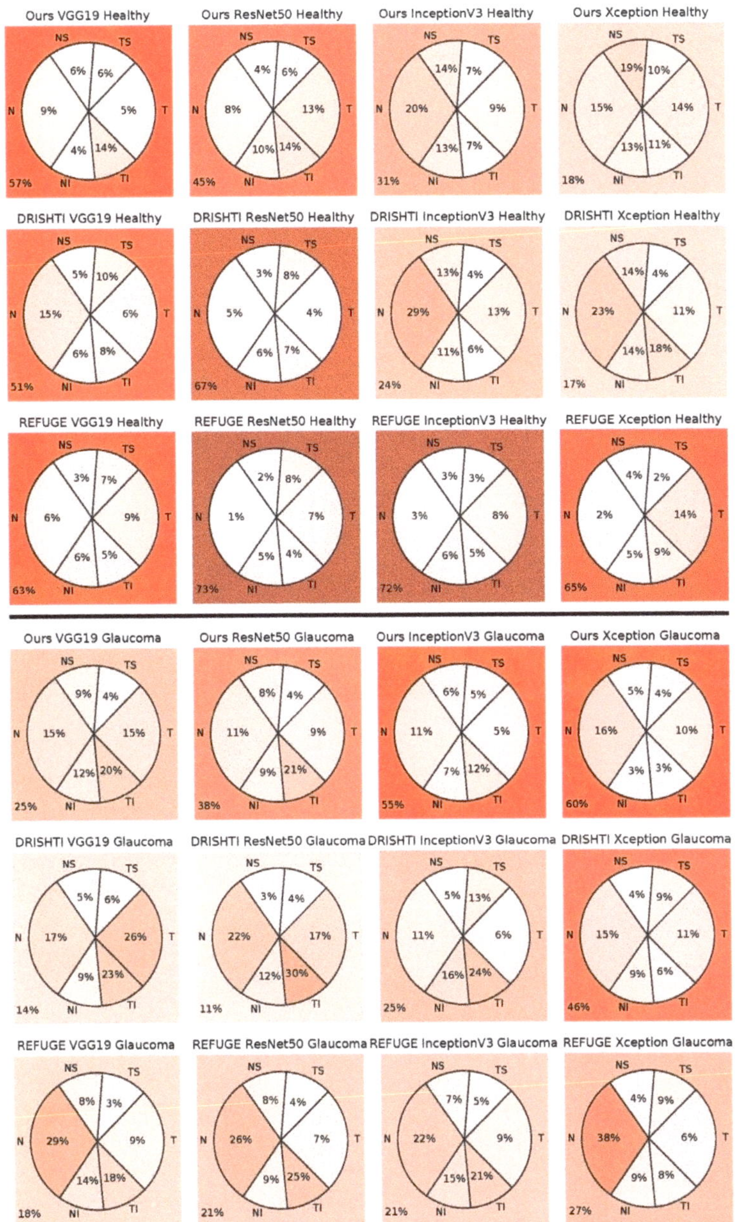

Figure 11. Global relevance by sectors according to the Shapley values for the different network architectures and the different data sets considered, separating the data by the class predicted by the networks. Given an input image, the graph indicates each sector's probability of being the highest contributor according to the Shapley values for that class. The relevance by sector is shown for our own set (1st and 4th rows), for DRISHTI-GS1 (2nd and 5th rows), and REFUGE (3rd and 6th rows).

It can be seen that the greatest similarity in terms of the distribution of probability values by sector is between our set and that of DRISHTI-GS1. The correlation in this case was 0.80679 (p-value < 0.001). Among some differences that we can appreciate, it stands out the rise of the background probability in ResNet50 for the normal class and its decrease for the glaucoma class. Additionally, the probability decreases in the T, TI, and N sectors in the normal class, but increases in the glaucoma class, whose TI sector is now the most probable. A decrease in the probability of the background sector in InceptionV3 is also noticeable for the glaucoma class, while the probability of the TI, NI, and TS sectors increases. In the normal class for this network architecture, there is an exchange of importance between the background and the nasal sector, which now appears as the major contributor in 29% of the cases. In VGG19 the probability of B also decreases in both classes. For the glaucoma class, the probability of the T sector increases, and for the normal class, the probability of the N sector increases, and that of TI decreases. In Xception, the probability of the N sector also increases for the normal class, which would now be the most probable, followed by TI, which also increases. For glaucomas, as with InceptionV3, there is a reduction in the percentage of the B sector and an increase in the TI, NI, and TS sectors.

The changes in probabilities are most notable between our set and REFUGE, where the background stands out mainly for the normal class in all architectures. However, for the glaucoma class, the N and TI sectors are the most relevant except for the Xception architecture where N and B are the most important contributors overall. The correlation between the Shapley values for our set and REFUGE was 0.53530 (p-value = 0.003).

5. Conclusions

The use of Shapley values has enabled us to assign a relevance score to each of the standard optic disc sectors typically considered by specialists in glaucoma diagnosis, reflecting the contribution of each sector to the network model's decision-making process. This sector-based discretization has proven essential in making the problem computationally manageable in practice.

To address the challenge of discarding features to evaluate different combinations for classification, we employed an approach based on occlusion and re-training the non-convolutional portion of the model. While we acknowledge that this method introduces some limitations, we believe it remains a reasonable compromise. This strategy allows us to stay close to the original model by re-training only the classification layer to adapt to occluded images, thus reducing the impact of outliers.

Regarding the relevance scores obtained for each sector, there appears to be limited alignment with what would typically be expected from a clinical perspective. The networks generally seem to extract useful information across all sectors, without any single sector consistently holding the majority of discriminative information.

Additionally, the frequent prominence of the background sector is unexpected and suggests that, despite achieving high accuracy, the model's decisions may not align with established medical criteria. This discrepancy raises concerns about the model's interpretability and its potential application in clinical practice.

As future work, as mentioned in Section 3.3, we plan to explore the possibility of retraining all layers of the original models following a more "true to the data" approach to see the difference with the "true to the model" approach adopted in this work. This will require more computing time, but we think it will be interesting to compare both approaches to the problem. We are also considering including new deep learning models in our study, such as newer CNN architectures and Vision Transformers.

Author Contributions: Methodology, J.S. and F.F.; software, J.S. and F.F.; validation, J.S. and F.F.; formal analysis, J.S. and F.F.; investigation, J.S., F.F. and T.D.-A.; resources, T.D.-A.; data curation, J.S., F.F. and T.D.-A.; writing—original draft preparation, J.S. and F.F.; writing—review and editing, J.S., F.F. and T.D.-A.; visualization, J.S. and F.F.; supervision, J.S. All authors have read and agreed to the published version of the manuscript.

Funding: Project (PROID2024010027) financed by the Canary Islands Agency for Research, Innovation and the Information Society (ACIISI) and by the European Regional Development Fund within the framework of the FEDER programme Canarias 2021–2027.

Informed Consent Statement: Patient consent was waived by the Ethics Committee of Hospital Universitario de Canarias due to the nature of the study and because the confidentiality of personal data was ensured.

Data Availability Statement: This study utilized four datasets for analysis. The HUC RGB dataset is not publicly available due to privacy restrictions. However, the remaining datasets—RIM-ONE DL, REFUGE, and DRISHTI-GS1—are publicly accessible and can be obtained online via their respective repositories or official websites. Specific access details for the publicly available datasets can be provided upon request.

Conflicts of Interest: The authors declare no conflicts of interest.

References

1. Molnar, C. *Interpretable Machine Learning*, 2nd ed.; Lulu Press, Inc.: Morrisville, NC, USA, 2022.
2. Hemelings, R.; Elen, B.; Barbosa-Breda, J.; Blaschko, M.B.; De Boever, P.; Stalmans, I. Deep learning on fundus images detects glaucoma beyond the optic disc. *Sci. Rep.* **2021**, *11*, 20313. [CrossRef] [PubMed]
3. Loh, H.W.; Ooi, C.P.; Seoni, S.; Barua, P.D.; Molinari, F.; Acharya, U.R. Application of explainable artificial intelligence for healthcare: A systematic review of the last decade (2011–2022). *Comput. Methods Programs Biomed.* **2022**, *226*, 107161. [CrossRef] [PubMed]
4. Shapley, L.S. *A Value for N-Person Games*; RAND Corporation: Santa Monica, CA, USA, 1952. [CrossRef]
5. Aas, K.; Jullum, M.; Løland, A. Explaining individual predictions when features are dependent: More accurate approximations to Shapley values. *Artif. Intell.* **2021**, *298*, 103502. [CrossRef]
6. Sigut, J.; Fumero, F.; Estévez, J.; Alayón, S.; Díaz-Alemán, T. In-Depth Evaluation of Saliency Maps for Interpreting Convolutional Neural Network Decisions in the Diagnosis of Glaucoma Based on Fundus Imaging. *Sensors* **2024**, *24*, 239. [CrossRef] [PubMed]
7. Roth, A.E. *The Shapley Value: Essays in Honor of Lloyd S. Shapley*; Cambridge University Press: Cambridge, UK, 1988.
8. Štrumbelj, E.; Kononenko, I. Explaining prediction models and individual predictions with feature contributions. *Knowl. Inf. Syst.* **2014**, *41*, 647–665. [CrossRef]
9. Lundberg, S.M.; Lee, S.I. A Unified Approach to Interpreting Model Predictions. In *Proceedings of the Advances in Neural Information Processing Systems*; Guyon, I., Luxburg, U.V., Bengio, S., Wallach, H., Fergus, R., Vishwanathan, S., Garnett, R., Eds.; Curran Associates, Inc.: Sydney, Australia, 2017; Volume 30.
10. Chen, H.; Lundberg, S.; Lee, S.I. Explaining Models by Propagating Shapley Values of Local Components. *arXiv* **2019**, arXiv:1911.11888. [CrossRef]
11. Tham, Y.C.; Li, X.; Wong, T.Y.; Quigley, H.A.; Aung, T.; Cheng, C.Y. Global Prevalence of Glaucoma and Projections of Glaucoma Burden through 2040: A Systematic Review and Meta-Analysis. *Ophthalmology* **2014**, *121*, 2081–2090. [CrossRef] [PubMed]
12. European Glaucoma Society. European Glaucoma Society Terminology and Guidelines for Glaucoma, 5th Edition. *Br. J. Ophthalmol.* **2021**, *105*, 1–169. [CrossRef] [PubMed]
13. Singh, A.; Jothi Balaji, J.; Rasheed, M.A.; Jayakumar, V.; Raman, R.; Lakshminarayanan, V. Evaluation of explainable deep learning methods for ophthalmic diagnosis. *Clin. Ophthalmol.* **2021**, *15*, 2573–2581. [CrossRef] [PubMed]
14. Shorfuzzaman, M.; Hossain, M.S.; El Saddik, A. An Explainable Deep Learning Ensemble Model for Robust Diagnosis of Diabetic Retinopathy Grading. *ACM Trans. Multimed. Comput. Commun. Appl.* **2021**, *17*, 113:1–113:24. [CrossRef]
15. Shrikumar, A.; Greenside, P.; Kundaje, A. Learning important features through propagating activation differences. In Proceedings of the 34th International Conference on Machine Learning-Volume 70, ICML'17, Sydney, Australia, 6–11 August 2017; pp. 3145–3153.
16. Mehta, P.; Petersen, C.A.; Wen, J.C.; Banitt, M.R.; Chen, P.P.; Bojikian, K.D.; Egan, C.; Lee, S.I.; Balazinska, M.; Lee, A.Y.; et al. Automated Detection of Glaucoma with Interpretable Machine Learning Using Clinical Data and Multimodal Retinal Images. *Am. J. Ophthalmol.* **2021**, *231*, 154–169. [CrossRef] [PubMed]

17. Hasan, M.M.; Phu, J.; Wang, H.; Sowmya, A.; Kalloniatis, M.; Meijering, E. OCT-based diagnosis of glaucoma and glaucoma stages using explainable machine learning. *Sci. Rep.* **2025**, *15*, 3592. [CrossRef] [PubMed]
18. Oh, S.; Park, Y.; Cho, K.J.; Kim, S.J. Explainable Machine Learning Model for Glaucoma Diagnosis and Its Interpretation. *Diagnostics* **2021**, *11*, 510. [CrossRef] [PubMed]
19. Tao, S.; Ravindranath, R.; Wang, S.Y. Predicting Glaucoma Progression to Surgery with Artificial Intelligence Survival Models. *Ophthalmol. Sci.* **2023**, *3*, 100336. [CrossRef] [PubMed]
20. Ravindranath, R.; Naor, J.; Wang, S.Y. Artificial Intelligence Models to Identify Patients at High Risk for Glaucoma Using Self-reported Health Data in a United States National Cohort. *Ophthalmol. Sci.* **2025**, *5*, 100685. [CrossRef] [PubMed]
21. Christopher, M.; Gonzalez, R.; Huynh, J.; Walker, E.; Radha Saseendrakumar, B.; Bowd, C.; Belghith, A.; Goldbaum, M.H.; Fazio, M.A.; Girkin, C.A.; et al. Proactive Decision Support for Glaucoma Treatment: Predicting Surgical Interventions with Clinically Available Data. *Bioengineering* **2024**, *11*, 140. [CrossRef] [PubMed]
22. Wang, S.Y.; Ravindranath, R.; Stein, J.D.; Amin, S.; Edwards, P.A.; Srikumaran, D.; Woreta, F.; Schultz, J.S.; Shrivastava, A.; Ahmad, B.; et al. Prediction Models for Glaucoma in a Multicenter Electronic Health Records Consortium: The Sight Outcomes Research Collaborative. *Ophthalmol. Sci.* **2024**, *4*, 100445. [CrossRef] [PubMed]
23. Wang, R.; Bradley, C.; Herbert, P.; Hou, K.; Ramulu, P.; Breininger, K.; Unberath, M.; Yohannan, J. Deep learning-based identification of eyes at risk for glaucoma surgery. *Sci. Rep.* **2024**, *14*, 599. [CrossRef] [PubMed]
24. Yoon, J.S.; Kim, Y.e.; Lee, E.J.; Kim, H.; Kim, T.W. Systemic factors associated with 10-year glaucoma progression in South Korean population: A single center study based on electronic medical records. *Sci. Rep.* **2023**, *13*, 530. [CrossRef] [PubMed]
25. Fumero, F.; Diaz-Aleman, T.; Sigut, J.; Alayon, S.; Arnay, R.; Angel-Pereira, D. RIM-ONE DL: A Unified Retinal Image Database for Assessing Glaucoma Using Deep Learning. *Image Anal. Stereol.* **2020**, *39*, 161–167. [CrossRef]
26. Fumero, F.; Alayon, S.; Sanchez, J.L.; Sigut, J.; Gonzalez-Hernandez, M. RIM-ONE: An open retinal image database for optic nerve evaluation. In Proceedings of the 2011 24th International Symposium on Computer-Based Medical Systems (CBMS), Bristol, UK, 27–30 June 2011; pp. 1–6. [CrossRef]
27. Orlando, J.I.; Fu, H.; Barbosa Breda, J.; van Keer, K.; Bathula, D.R.; Diaz-Pinto, A.; Fang, R.; Heng, P.A.; Kim, J.; Lee, J.; et al. REFUGE Challenge: A unified framework for evaluating automated methods for glaucoma assessment from fundus photographs. *Med. Image Anal.* **2020**, *59*, 101570. [CrossRef] [PubMed]
28. Sivaswamy, J.; Chakravarty, A.; Joshi, G.D.; Ujjwal; Syed, T.A. A Comprehensive Retinal Image Dataset for the Assessment of Glaucoma from the Optic Nerve Head Analysis. *JSM Biomed. Imaging Data Pap.* **2015**, *2*, 1004.
29. Simonyan, K.; Zisserman, A. Very Deep Convolutional Networks for Large-Scale Image Recognition. *arXiv* **2015**, arXiv:1409.1556. [CrossRef]
30. He, K.; Zhang, X.; Ren, S.; Sun, J. Deep Residual Learning for Image Recognition. In Proceedings of the IEEE Conference on Computer Vision and Pattern Recognition (CVPR), Las Vegas, NV, USA, 27–30 June 2016; pp. 770–778.
31. Szegedy, C.; Vanhoucke, V.; Ioffe, S.; Shlens, J.; Wojna, Z. Rethinking the Inception Architecture for Computer Vision. In Proceedings of the IEEE Conference on Computer Vision and Pattern Recognition (CVPR), Las Vegas, NV, USA, 27–30 June 2016; pp. 2818–2826.
32. Chollet, F. Xception: Deep Learning with Depthwise Separable Convolutions. In Proceedings of the IEEE Conference on Computer Vision and Pattern Recognition (CVPR), Honolulu, HI, USA, 21–26 July 2017; pp. 1800–1807.
33. Abadi, M.; Agarwal, A.; Barham, P.; Brevdo, E.; Chen, Z.; Citro, C.; Corrado, G.S.; Davis, A.; Dean, J.; Devin, M.; et al. TensorFlow: Large-Scale Machine Learning on Heterogeneous Systems, 2015. Available online: www.tensorflow.org (accessed on 16 May 2025).
34. Chalkiadakis, G.; Elkind, E.; Wooldridge, M. Basic Concepts. In *Computational Aspects of Cooperative Game Theory*; Chalkiadakis, G., Elkind, E., Wooldridge, M., Eds.; Synthesis Lectures on Artificial Intelligence and Machine Learning; Springer International Publishing: Cham, Switzerland, 2012; pp. 11–35. [CrossRef]
35. Campbell, T.W.; Roder, H.; Georgantas, R.W., III; Roder, J. Exact Shapley values for local and model-true explanations of decision tree ensembles. *Mach. Learn. Appl.* **2022**, *9*, 100345. [CrossRef]
36. Campbell, T.W.; Wilson, M.P.; Roder, H.; MaWhinney, S.; Georgantas, R.W.; Maguire, L.K.; Roder, J.; Erlandson, K.M. Predicting prognosis in COVID-19 patients using machine learning and readily available clinical data. *Int. J. Med. Inform.* **2021**, *155*, 104594. [CrossRef] [PubMed]
37. Štrumbelj, E.; Kononenko, I.; Robnik Šikonja, M. Explaining instance classifications with interactions of subsets of feature values. *Data Knowl. Eng.* **2009**, *68*, 886–904. [CrossRef]
38. Garway-Heath, D.F.; Poinoosawmy, D.; Fitzke, F.W.; Hitchings, R.A. Mapping the visual field to the optic disc in normal tension glaucoma eyes11The authors have no proprietary interest in the development or marketing of any product or instrument mentioned in this article. *Ophthalmology* **2000**, *107*, 1809–1815. [CrossRef] [PubMed]
39. Van Craenendonck, T.; Elen, B.; Gerrits, N.; De Boever, P. Systematic Comparison of Heatmapping Techniques in Deep Learning in the Context of Diabetic Retinopathy Lesion Detection. *Transl. Vis. Sci. Technol.* **2020**, *9*, 64. [CrossRef] [PubMed]

40. Covert, I.; Lundberg, S.; Lee, S.I. Explaining by Removing: A Unified Framework for Model Explanation. *arXiv* **2022**, arXiv:2011.14878. [CrossRef]
41. Hooker, S.; Erhan, D.; Kindermans, P.J.; Kim, B. A Benchmark for Interpretability Methods in Deep Neural Networks. In *Proceedings of the Advances in Neural Information Processing Systems*; Wallach, H., Larochelle, H., Beygelzimer, A., d'Alché-Buc, F., Fox, E., Garnett, R., Eds.; Curran Associates, Inc.: Sydney, NSW, Australia, 2019; Volume 32.
42. Chen, H.; Janizek, J.D.; Lundberg, S.; Lee, S.I. True to the Model or True to the Data? *arXiv* **2020**, arXiv:2006.16234. [CrossRef]
43. Lundberg, S.M.; Erion, G.; Chen, H.; DeGrave, A.; Prutkin, J.M.; Nair, B.; Katz, R.; Himmelfarb, J.; Bansal, N.; Lee, S.I. From Local Explanations to Global Understanding with Explainable AI for Trees. *Nat. Mach. Intell.* **2020**, *2*, 56–67. [CrossRef] [PubMed]
44. Zar, J.H. Significance Testing of the Spearman Rank Correlation Coefficient. *J. Am. Stat. Assoc.* **1972**, *67*, 578–580. [CrossRef]
45. Adebayo, J.; Gilmer, J.; Muelly, M.; Goodfellow, I.; Hardt, M.; Kim, B. Sanity Checks for Saliency Maps. In *Proceedings of the Advances in Neural Information Processing Systems*; Bengio, S., Wallach, H., Larochelle, H., Grauman, K., Cesa-Bianchi, N., Garnett, R., Eds.; Curran Associates, Inc.: Sydney, NSW, Australia, 2018; Volume 31.
46. Brodersen, K.H.; Ong, C.S.; Stephan, K.E.; Buhmann, J.M. The Balanced Accuracy and Its Posterior Distribution. In Proceedings of the 2010 20th International Conference on Pattern Recognition, Istanbul, Turkey, 23–26 August 2010; pp. 3121–3124. [CrossRef]
47. Glorot, X.; Bengio, Y. Understanding the difficulty of training deep feedforward neural networks. In Proceedings of the Thirteenth International Conference on Artificial Intelligence and Statistics, Sardinia, Italy, 13–15 May 2010; Chia Laguna Resort; Volume 9, pp. 249–256.

algorithms

MDPI

Article

Detecting SARS-CoV-2 in CT Scans Using Vision Transformer and Graph Neural Network

Kamorudeen Amuda [1], Almustapha Wakili [1], Tomilade Amoo [2], Lukman Agbetu [1], Qianlong Wang [3,*] and Jinjuan Feng [1,*]

1 Department of Computer and Information Sciences, Towson University, Towson, MD 21252, USA; kamuda@towson.edu (K.A.); awakili@towson.edu (A.W.); lagbetu1@students.towson.edu (L.A.)
2 Department of Business Analytics and Technology Management, Towson University, Towson, MD 21252, USA; tadeye1@students.towson.edu
3 Department of Electrical and Computer Engineering, Old Dominion University, Norfolk, VA 23529, USA
* Correspondence: q1wang@odu.edu (Q.W.); jfeng@towson.edu (J.F.)

Abstract: The COVID-19 pandemic has presented significant challenges to global healthcare, bringing out the urgent need for reliable diagnostic tools. Computed Tomography (CT) scans have proven instrumental in detecting COVID-19-induced lung abnormalities. This study introduces Convolutional Neural Network, Graph Neural Network, and Vision Transformer (ViTGNN), an advanced hybrid model designed to enhance SARS-CoV-2 detection by combining Graph Neural Networks (GNNs) for feature extraction with Vision Transformers (ViTs) for classification. Using the strength of CNN and GNN to capture complex relational structures and the ViT capacity to classify global contexts, ViTGNN achieves a comprehensive representation of CT scan data. The model was evaluated on a SARS-CoV-2 CT scan dataset, demonstrating superior performance across all metrics compared to baseline models. The model achieved an accuracy of 95.98%, precision of 96.07%, recall of 96.01%, F1-score of 95.98%, and AUC of 98.69%, outperforming existing approaches. These results indicate that ViTGNN is an effective diagnostic tool that can be applied beyond COVID-19 detection to other medical imaging tasks.

Keywords: COVID-19; SARS-CoV-2; CT scans; convolutional neural network; vision transformers; graph neural networks; feature extraction

1. Introduction

The COVID-19 pandemic has had a profound impact on healthcare systems around the world and emphasizes the urgent need for effective, rapid, and reliable diagnostic tools. Traditionally, Real-Time Polymerase Chain Reaction (RT-PCR) has been the primary method for detecting SARS-CoV-2 infection. However, despite being the gold standard, RT-PCR has notable limitations: It is time-consuming, prone to false negatives, and highly dependent on the quality of the sample and the timing of collection. This has led to an increasing interest in alternative diagnostic methods that can offer faster and potentially more reliable results, especially in clinical settings of high demand [1,2].

Computed Tomography (CT) imaging has emerged as a promising complementary diagnostic tool for COVID-19, primarily due to its high sensitivity in detecting COVID-19 related lung abnormalities such as ground-glass opacities, septal thickening, and consolidations. Unlike RT-PCR, which directly detects viral genetic material, CT imaging provides a visual representation of disease progression, capturing structural changes in lung tissue. Studies have shown that CT scans can reveal abnormalities even in cases with low viral load where RT-PCR might yield a false negative, making CT a valuable tool for timely and accurate diagnosis [3–5].

The application of artificial intelligence (AI), particularly deep learning, has transformed medical imaging by enabling automated analysis and interpretation of complex visual data. Convolutional Neural Networks (CNNs) have been widely adopted for image analysis and have demonstrated considerable success in detecting lung abnormalities associated with COVID-19. However, CNNs have limitations when it comes to capturing complex spatial dependencies in an image, which are crucial for understanding nuanced patterns in medical imaging [6]. Vision Transformers (ViTs), which leverage self-attention mechanisms, offer a solution by modeling global dependencies across an image, allowing them to identify broader patterns that may indicate the presence of COVID-19. Despite their strengths, ViTs can sometimes overlook local structural relationships, which are essential to detect fine-grained features in medical images, such as small lesions or subtle tissue changes specific to COVID-19.

Several research studies have explored the application of Graph Neural Networks (GNNs) and Vision Transformers (ViTs) in medical imaging and classification tasks; however, no existing research has explicitly combined GNNs and ViTs for SARS detection. GNNs are effective in capturing spatial and topological relationships within the data, making them suitable for structural pattern recognition in images. For instance, ClusterViG combined CNNs with GNNs for improved feature representation [7]. On the other hand, ViTs have shown strong performance in medical imaging, especially in the classification of COVID-19 using chest CT scans [8], and researchers have also investigated the impact of different patch sizes in ViTs for the classification of lung diseases, highlighting their ability to model global dependencies in image analysis [9].

Existing SARS-CoV-2 detection frameworks predominantly rely on CNN-based deep learning models or ViTs independently without leveraging GNNs for spatial and relational inference. This suggests that a Vision Transformer and Graph Neural Network (ViTGNN) architecture could introduce a novel and effective method to improve the diagnostic accuracy of SARS-CoV-2 detection from CT scans. The rationale behind the combination of ViT and GNN (ViTGNN) is based on their complementary strengths. The GNN captures relationships and structural patterns in data [10], while the ViT excels at processing visual information [11,12]. This hybrid process allows ViTGNN to overcome the individual limitations of CNNs and ViTs [13], offering a more comprehensive approach to the diagnosis of COVID-19. The key contributions of this paper are as follows.

- We develop ViTGNN, a hybrid model that uses a GNN for feature extraction and a ViT for classification to improve the detection of SARS-CoV-2 in CT scans.
- We enhance image representation using advanced preprocessing techniques such as CLAHE, Gaussian blurring, and data augmentation on COVID-19 and non-COVID-19 CT scan images.
- We train and optimize ViTGNN on a dataset in order to ensure generalization across unseen data.
- We evaluate ViTGNN performance against multiple baseline models using accuracy, precision, recall, F1-score, and AUC.

This paper is organized as follows: Section 2 provides a review of related work. Section 3 describes the materials and methods employed in the study. Section 4 presents the experimental results along with a comprehensive discussion. Section 5 concludes the paper by summarizing the key findings. Finally, Section 6 discusses the study limitations and outlines potential directions for future research.

2. Related Works

In this section, we present the frameworks and algorithms pertinent to our study. This review of the literature focuses on the application of artificial intelligence, such as deep learning and machine learning, in the detection of COVID-19, with an emphasis on their roles in the processing and analysis of image datasets.

Recently, wavelet-based super-resolution methods have gained attention for their ability to enhance fine-grained image features, which can be crucial for improving downstream medical diagnostic tasks. For instance, Yu et al. [14] proposed a wavelet pyramid recursive neural network (WPRNN) constrained by wavelet energy entropy, which fuses both shallow and deep wavelet coefficient features across multiple resolutions to reconstruct high-quality medical images. This approach not only improves perceptual reconstruction quality but also preserves subtle structural details critical for accurate interpretation.

Parikh et al. [7] proposed ClusterViG, a vision GNN that improves efficiency with Dynamic Efficient Graph Convolution (DEGC) by partitioning images, parallelizing graph construction, and integrating local–global feature learning. Additionally, it optimizes k-NN graph construction and enhances context awareness using GATv2. The results demonstrate 87.2% top-1 accuracy in ImageNet-1K, improved object detection and segmentation in MS COCO 2017, and up to 5× faster inference, making ClusterViG highly efficient and scalable for vision tasks. A transformer-based COVID-19 diagnosis framework that uses UNet for lung segmentation and Swin Transformer for classification was introduced by Zhang et al. [15]. Evaluated on MIA-COV19D, Swin Transformer achieved an F1-score of 0.935 (validation) and 0.84 (test), outperforming BiT-M and EfficientNetV2, with the latter excelling in precision (93.7%).

TransGNN was proposed, a hybrid Transformer–GNN model for recommender systems that alternates Transformer and GNN layers to expand the receptive field while preserving structural information. Attention sampling, positional encoding, and efficient sample updates enhance efficiency and scalability. The model was evaluated on Yelp, Gowalla, Tmall, Amazon-Book, and MovieLens. TransGNN outperforms GNN and Transformer baselines, achieving up to 21.04% improvement in Recall@20 while reducing computational complexity, demonstrating its effectiveness and scalability in recommendation systems [16]. Shome et al. [17] presented COVID-Transformer, a ViT-based model for COVID-19 detection using a 30K-image dataset (COVID-19, normal, pneumonia). It was trained with the NovoGrad optimizer and achieved 98% accuracy (AUC 99%) for binary and 92% accuracy (AUC 98%) for multi-class classification, outperforming CNN models. That is, Grad-CAM visualizations enhance interpretability for diagnosis.

In the study in [9], Vision Transformers (ViTs) were evaluated for COVID-19 and diseased lung classification using Iran's COVID-19 CT dataset (377 patients) and Malaysia's dataset (81 diseased, 15 normal cases), where 32 × 32 patches achieved the highest accuracy (95.36%), while larger patches reduced performance. ViT outperformed CNN models (ResNet50, Xception) in efficiency, demonstrating its potential in medical imaging. Wang et al. [4] introduced Contrastive Cross-Site Learning with Redesigned COVID-Net for COVID-19 CT classification, addressing domain shifts in multi-site datasets. The datasets include SARS-CoV-2 (2482 CT images) and COVID-CT (349 CT images), which incorporated domain-specific batch normalization and contrastive learning for feature extraction. The model achieved 96.24% AUC, 92.1% accuracy, 91.3% sensitivity, and 93.2% precision on SARS-CoV-2, and 85.32% AUC, 84.5% accuracy, 83.7% sensitivity, and 85.9% precision on COVID-CT. It outperforms standard COVID-Net by 12.16% and 14.23% in AUC and surpasses state-of-the-art multisite learning methods.

Xiao et al. [18] presented TCGN, a Transformer-CNN-GNN model for gene expression prediction from histopathological images. It processes single-spot images, integrating a

CNN for local features, a Transformer for global learning, and a GNN for cell organization analysis, which enhances interpretability. The model was evaluated on HER2+ (32 sections, eight patients), cSCC (12 sections, four patients), and spatialLIBD (59,904 spots, 20 sections, 3 donors). TCGN achieves the highest median PCC (0.232), outperforming ST-Net, HisToGene, and Hist2ST with fewer parameters (86.24 M) and lower GPU memory.

Choi et al. [19] proposed ICEv2, an interpretable method that assigns class-relevance probabilities to individual patches using adversarial normalization, circumventing the limitations of traditional attention-based visualizations. ICEv2 identifies foreground (task-relevant) and background patches without modifying the model's architecture or retraining weights. The method produces fine-grained visual saliency by interpreting output logits at the patch level rather than relying on [CLS] token contributions. Applied to segmentation datasets, ICEv2 demonstrated strong performance in visual localization, offering a viable pathway for producing trustworthy visual explanations in healthcare settings.

Marchetti et al. [20] addressed ViT inefficiencies by introducing Token Reduction via an Attention-Based Multilayer Network (TRAM). TRAM constructs a graph from multilayer attention matrices and computes centrality scores to prune less informative tokens at each transformer layer. Unlike methods that rely on [CLS] tokens or retraining, TRAM performs static, architecture-agnostic pruning, which maintains classification performance while substantially reducing memory usage and inference time. These characteristics are highly desirable in real-time or embedded diagnostic systems, where latency and resource consumption are constrained.

Englebert et al. [21] developed Transformer Input Sampling (TIS), a saliency technique that avoids the artifact generation associated with conventional perturbation-based methods, such as RISE or Score-CAM. TIS leverages the inherent flexibility of ViTs to handle variable-length token sequences, enabling interpretability by selectively omitting tokens post-embedding and measuring their impact on class predictions. Sampling embedded token subsets and assessing prediction shifts, TIS constructs faithful, class-specific saliency maps without corrupting the input image. This strategy ensures the generation of clinically meaningful explanations, which is essential for radiological review in COVID-19 diagnosis.

Artificial intelligence (AI) and deep learning (DL) have transformed CT-based diagnostics, allowing automated analysis and interpretation of intricate visual data. Convolutional Neural Networks (CNNs), widely used in medical imaging, have effectively captured long-range dependencies and complex spatial relationships across an image in detecting localized lung abnormalities associated with COVID-19 [22]. However, CNNs have limits, and Vision Transformers (ViTs), which use self-attention mechanisms to identify global patterns, offer an alternative by modeling image-wide dependencies. This global perspective enables ViTs to detect broader image patterns but can sometimes overlook local structural details essential for clinical precision [23].

To address these limitations, hybrid models that combine CNNs, ViTs, and Graph Neural Networks (GNNs) have gained attention. GNNs focus on relational data within images, representing patches as nodes and spatial relationships as edges, which is crucial for capturing local details. Nguyen et al. showed that incorporating spatial information through a GNN could improve diagnostic accuracy, supporting the potential of hybrid models for the detection of COVID-19 in CT imaging [24].

As summarized in Table 1, a wide range of deep learning approaches have been proposed for COVID-19 detection using chest CT and X-ray images. These methods vary significantly in terms of datasets used, network architectures, and reported performance. For instance, some models, such as Deep CNN [25] and COVID-Net citepwang2020covidnet, focus on conventional CNN architectures. In contrast, others incorporate more advanced designs, such as 3D CNNs [27], residual attention mechanisms [28], or hybrid ensembles, like Xception with ResNet50V2 [29]. Moreover, studies also differ in the imaging modality used either CT scans or X-rays and in their learning strategies, including weakly supervised learning [30], GAN-based augmentation [31], and radiological descriptive analysis [32]. These variations lead to a wide range of performance metrics, with accuracy values spanning from approximately 85% to over 99%, depending on task complexity, class balance, and dataset scale.

Table 1. Comparative Summary of Related Deep Learning Models for COVID-19 Detection.

Ref.	Method	Dataset	Architecture	Accuracy
[25]	Deep CNN	46,096 CT images (106 patients)	CNN	95.24%
[30]	Weakly supervised DL	274 CT cases	CNN + FPN	AUC = 0.95, Sensitivity = 96%, Precision=79%
[27]	Weakly supervised DL	630 CT images	3D CNN	ROC AUC = 0.959, Accuracy = 90.1%
[28]	Prior-Attention Residual	3D CT scans	3D ResNet	High (unspecified numerically)
[33]	COVNet	4352 CT scans	3D CNN	AUC = 0.96, Sensitivity = 90%, Specificity = [illegible]
[26]	COVID-Net	13,975 CXR images	Tailored CNN	High performance
[34]	Weakly supervised DL	630 CT images	3D CNN (UNet)	Accuracy = 90.1%, ROC AUC = 0.959
[35]	DarkNet YOLO	Chest X-ray images	YOLO CNN	Accuracy = 98.08% (binary), 87.02% (multi-class)
[36]	CNN with preprocessing	8474 X-ray images	VGG16 CNN	Accuracy = 94.5%, Sensitivity = 98.4%, Specificity = 98%
[37]	CVDNet	2905 X-ray images	Residual CNN	High accuracy
[29]	Modified CNN (Concatenation)	11,482 X-ray images	Xception + ResNet50V2	99.50% (COVID-19), 91.40% (Overall)
[31]	CovidGAN (ACGAN)	Synthetic CXR images	ACGAN + CNN	95% (augmented), 85% (non-augmented)
[38]	CNN (MobileNet v2)	3905 X-ray images	MobileNet v2	99.18% (COVID-19), 87.66% (7-class)
[32]	Chest CT Analysis	CT scans (reviewed cases)	Radiological Descriptive	Qualitative (typical vs. atypical features)
[39]	AI-assisted CT Imaging	1136 CT cases	[illegible]	Sensitivity = 97.4%, Specificity = 92.2%
[40]	CXR pre-processing pipeline	Public CXR datasets	Pre-processing Pipeline	Improved accuracy by up to [illegible]

3. Materials and Methods

3.1. Data Preprocessing

The SARS-CoV-2 CT Scan dataset, Figure 1, is publicly available on Kaggle. It consists of 1252 CT scans from patients diagnosed with SARS-CoV-2 infection (COVID-19) and 1230 scans from non-infected individuals, resulting in 2482 CT scans. Data were collected from actual patients in hospitals in São Paulo, Brazil [22]. In the context of COVID-19 image analysis, pre-processing techniques are important to enhance image quality, improve feature extraction, and increase the accuracy of machine learning and deep learning models.

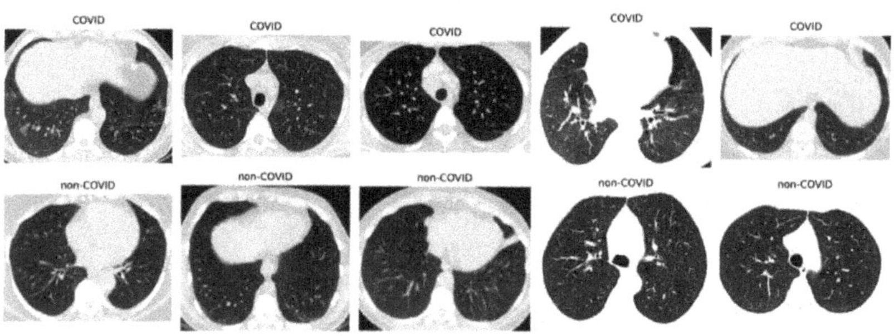

Figure 1. Sample images of SARS-CoV-2 in CT scans.

Here, we explain the specific image preprocessing methods used in this study to enhance the quality of the training data. A total of 1986 CT scans were used, comprising COVID-19 and non-COVID-19 cases, to train the model representing 80% of the complete dataset (2482 scans). The preprocessing steps included the following.

3.1.1. Contrast-Limited Adaptive Histogram Equalization (CLAHE)

CLAHE is an advanced local contrast enhancement technique that improves the visibility of features in low-contrast images [41]. In this study, CLAHE was applied using Python 3.11.7 library OpenCV (4.11.0 version) via the functions `cv2.createCLAHE()` and cv2.cvtColor(). The image was first converted from the BGR (Blue, Green, Red) color space to the YUV (Luminance, Chrominance) color space, allowing contrast enhancement to be applied specifically to the luminance (Y) channel. Previous research [42] demonstrated that applying CLAHE to fundus images significantly improved feature visibility and enhanced the classification performance of deep learning models such as VGG16 and EfficientNetB4.

3.1.2. Gaussian Blur

Gaussian blur is a widely used image processing technique to reduce noise and fine detail by convolving the input image with a Gaussian kernel. This method produces a smoothed version of the image in which each pixel value is replaced by a weighted average of its surrounding pixels, where the weights decrease with increasing distance from the center pixel [43]. In this work, we implemented Gaussian blur using the OpenCV function cv2.GaussianBlur(), which applied a 5 × 5 Gaussian kernel with an automatically computed standard deviation. The 5 × 5 kernel operates over a 25-pixel neighborhood, performing a weighted average in which the center pixel contributes most strongly. This effectively reduces noise while preserving the overall image structure.

3.1.3. Data Augmentation

To improve the generalization of the model in the unseen dataset and reduce the risk of overfitting, a set of data augmentation techniques was applied to the training dataset. These included random resized cropping, horizontal flipping, affine rotation, color jittering, and channel-wise normalization. Random resized cropping was used to simulate variations in object scale and spatial position, while horizontal flipping introduced invariance to image orientation. A random rotation of up to ±15 degrees addressed minor angular deviations commonly found in real-world scenarios. Photometric transformations were incorporated via brightness and contrast adjustments using color jittering, mimicking diverse lighting conditions. Finally, normalization was applied to standardize the pixel value distributions across image channels, facilitating stable and efficient model training. As highlighted in the work in [44], such geometric and photometric augmentation strategies are foundational to modern preprocessing pipelines, offering an efficient means of increasing both the diversity and realism of training data without compromising semantic integrity.

3.2. Evaluation Metrics

The performance of the ViTGNN model for detecting COVID-19 from CT scans is evaluated using key performance indicators, including accuracy, precision, recall, F1-score, and Area Under the Curve (AUC). These metrics provide a comprehensive evaluation of the ability of the model to accurately classify patients as COVID-positive or COVID-negative. The evaluation depends on components that include True Positives (TPs), True Negatives (TNs), False Positives (FPs), and False Negatives (FNs), which offer insight into the effectiveness of the model in distinguishing between COVID-19 and non-COVID-19 cases. These components ensure a thorough evaluation of ViTGNN diagnostic performance.

3.3. Experimental Setup

The experimental setup evaluated the performance of the ViTGNN framework for detecting SARS-CoV-2 from CT scan images. The dataset was divided into training, validation, and test sets (80:10:10). ViTGNN used Convolutional Neural Networks (CNNs) and Graph Neural Networks (GNNs) to extract graph-based features from CT scans, which were then processed by Vision Transformers (ViT) for high-level feature classification. This hybrid approach ensured that the model leveraged the strengths of both architectures for improved diagnostic accuracy. Training was carried out on a system with the following specifications:

128.0 GiB memory, an AMD Ryzen Threadripper 3960X 24-core processor × 48, NVIDIA Corporation GA102 [GeForce RTX 3090] graphics, 2.9 TB disk capacity, Ubuntu 22.04.5 LTS (64-bit) operating system, and GNOME version 42.9.

The training environment used the Adam optimizer with a learning rate of 0.0001. The model was trained for 50 epochs with a batch size of 32, incorporating early stopping to prevent overfitting. Image preprocessing techniques such as CLAHE, Gaussian blurring, and image augmentation enhance image quality and improve feature detection. The implementation was carried out using PyTorch v2.6.0 and PyTorch Lightning v2.3.1, with additional libraries such as NumPy v1.26.4, Pandas v2.2.1, and Matplotlib v3.8.3. ViTGNN performance was assessed using key metrics such as accuracy, precision, recall, F1-score, and AUC. The results demonstrate the ability of the model to effectively detect SARS-CoV-2 from CT scans, highlighting its potential for medical diagnostics and its broader applicability to other healthcare challenges involving complex imaging data.

3.4. Implementation

The ViTGNN architecture is a hybrid model that combines Convolutional Neural Networks (CNNs), Graph Neural Networks (GNNs), and Vision Transformers (ViTs) to make use of their strengths in image analysis. The architecture captures both local and global features as well as structured relational information within an image. CNNs are good at extracting low-level and mid-level visual features such as edges, textures, and shapes through localized reception, but CNNs struggle to model long-range dependencies and relationships [45,46]. GNNs introduce a graph-based representation that can model spatial relationships or other structured connections between image regions, addressing the limitation that CNN feature maps alone do not explicitly encode higher-level topological relations [10,46]. Although ViT, on the other hand, uses self-attention to capture global context and long-range interaction across an entire image, pure ViT models can miss local details without a large training dataset [11,12,45].

The integration of these three components, called ViTGNN, as shown in Figure 2, is specifically designed to improve the detection of SARS-CoV-2 in CT scans, which aims to explore CNNs for hierarchical local feature extraction, GNNs for spatially structured feature refinement, and ViTs for global feature interaction and classification. This synergy addresses the shortcomings of using each network type in isolation, and information passed through these stages can achieve a more effective representation and detection of COVID-19 and non-COVID-19 cases. The following sections detail each component and its integration with ViTGNN.

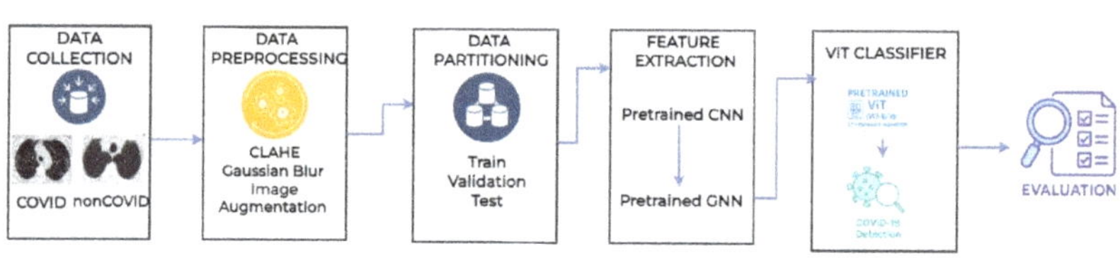

Figure 2. Architecture model of the proposed ViTGNN framework.

3.5. CNN Feature Extractor

The first component is the Convolutional Neural Network feature extractor, where the CNN model is trained to learn spatial features like edges and textures from the preprocessed images (128 * 128 images—each image has a width of 128 pixels and a height of 128 pixels). The CNN architecture is designed similarly to classic models such as VGG or ResNet, and comprises two convolutional layers comprising batch normalization, ReLU activation, dropout for regularization, and global average pooling to aggregate the extracted features.

That is, the first convolutional layer (conv1) applies a 3 × 3 filter with 32 filters, extracting basic features like edges, and the second layer (conv2) uses a 3 × 3 filter, but with 64 filters, to capture more complex patterns for better feature representation in the COVID-19 and non-COVID-19 cases. Batch normalization is used after convolutional layers to stabilize and speed training by normalizing the activation, while Dropout is used to regularize fully connected layers. However, in traditional CNN, it is common to use dropouts toward the end of the network rather than between convolutional layers. The final CNN layer (before the GNN module) outputs a feature map of size H×W with D feature channels; this can be thought of as a set of D-dimensional feature vectors arranged on a 2D grid corresponding to different image locations.

In summary, the CNN provides a rich, low-dimensional image representation that retains essential spatial information. Transforming raw pixels into feature vectors that encode local patterns, the CNN performs feature extraction and dimensionality reduction, making subsequent processing easier.

3.6. GNN-Based Spatial Representation Module

After the CNN, the output incorporates a Graph Neural Network module to take advantage of a graph-based representation of the features of the image. The motivation for this step is that treating the image as a graph of regions allows the model to explicitly reason about spatial relationships and context in a way that a regular CNN cannot [46]. In the CNN feature map, each cell (spatial location) is independent beyond the localized receptive field captured by convolution; by building a graph, we can connect distant regions or enforce longer-range interactions through message passing. This helps capture topological and relational information; for example, parts of an object can be connected on the graph to ensure that their features influence each other's representation.

3.6.1. Graph Construction

We construct a graph $G = (V, E)$, where each node $v \in V$ represents a spatial region in the CNN feature map. Each node is initialized with a feature vector extracted from the CNN at its corresponding location. Given a CNN-generated feature map of size $H \times W \times D$, the graph consists of $N = H \times W$ nodes, where each node is associated with a D-dimensional feature vector. The edge set E defines the connectivity between nodes according to spatial adjacency, and each node (i, j) is connected to its immediate neighbors in a four-connected grid structure, linking to adjacent nodes in the left, right, top, and bottom directions. This was implemented using relative coordinate offset neighbors = [(−1, 0), (1, 0), (0, −1), (0, 1)] that represent the top, bottom, left, and right neighbors, respectively. That is, only neighbors that fall within the valid spatial boundaries of the feature map are included in the graph. The grid-based graph structure preserves the spatial relationships in the CNN feature map, facilitating information propagation through the GCN. The 2D grid connectivity is computationally efficient and is well-suited for structured feature extraction from medical images. In addition, self-loops are included, which allow each node (i, j) to retain its feature information during the Graph Convolutional Network (GCN) aggregation process. This helps stabilize the model by preserving local feature representations. That is, the self-loop is an edge that connects a node to itself.

3.6.2. GCN Architecture

With the graph defined, we apply a Graph Convolutional Network (GCN) to refine the node features. The GCN propagates information across these connections through message passing, where each node updates its feature representation by aggregating information from its neighbors. The GCN in our implemented model consists of two graph convolutional layers, which sequentially update the node features. The first GCN layer transforms the initial node features, while the second layer further refines these representations. Mathematically, the update of the feature for a node i is defined as

$$\mathbf{h}_i^{(\text{new})} = \sigma\left(\sum_{j\in\mathcal{N}(i)\cup\{i\}} \frac{1}{c_{ij}}\mathbf{W}\mathbf{h}_j^{(\text{old})}\right) \tag{1}$$

where:

- $\mathcal{N}(i)$ represents the set of neighboring nodes connected to node i.
- c_{ij} is a normalization factor based on the degrees of the nodes to ensure numerical stability.
- $\mathbf{W}$ is a learnable weight matrix that applies a linear transformation to the features.
- σ is a non-linear activation function (ReLU).

Each GCN layer in our model follows three key steps.

1. Linear transformation, where we project the feature vectors of the nodes into a new feature space using $\mathbf{W}$.
2. Neighborhood aggregation, where we sum the transformed features of neighboring nodes using the adjacency matrix.
3. Nonlinearity, where we use a Rectified Linear Unit (ReLU) activation function to add complexity to the feature representations. To avoid overfitting, we add dropout regularization after each GCN layer.

3.6.3. Node Feature Updates and Message Passing

The two-layer GCN architecture allows information to propagate beyond immediate neighbors. Each node aggregates features from its direct one-hop neighbors in the first layer. In contrast, in the second layer, each node incorporates information from its two-hop neighborhood, allowing our model to learn more contextual representations while preserving local spatial relationships. The GCN output retains the graph structure but contains refined node embeddings that integrate information from the surrounding regions. After graph convolution, we reshape the output node features into a 2D feature map to ensure compatibility with the Vision Transformer (ViT) for final classification. Unlike more complex graph-based architectures, such as Graph Attention Networks (GATs), which assign different importance to neighbor nodes, the GCN in our model applies uniform neighborhood aggregation, making it computationally efficient while capturing local dependencies in the image. In structuring the graph with spatial adjacency, we maintain the hierarchical feature representation obtained from the CNN while allowing information to flow across spatially connected nodes. The refined features provide a better representation of the image data before being processed by ViT for classification.

The GNN module adds a relational inductive bias. That is, it forces feature propagation in ways that reflect image topology, which can improve the learned representation for the subsequent classifier. CNNs model local patterns well but fail to capture long-range or topological relations. In contrast, GCNs easily capture contextual relationships, combining them and incorporating local features and long-distance dependencies [46].

In summary, the proposed framework uses a staged pre-training approach for feature extraction (Figure 1). In Stage 1, a CNN is pre-trained on the whole training set to extract localized visual features from the CT scan. The CNN comprises convolutional blocks with ReLU activations, batch normalization, and max-pooling, followed by dense layers used only during pre-training. Once trained, the convolutional layers serve as a fixed feature extractor, and their output feature maps are retained for use in downstream applications. In Stage 2, these feature maps are converted into a grid-structured graph where each spatial region corresponds to a node and edges encode local spatial adjacency. A Graph

Convolutional Network is then applied to propagate contextual information across the graph. This integration allows the GCN to operate on rich, pre-trained local features, enabling the model to learn both local and global representations for robust downstream classification.

3.7. Vision Transformer (ViT) Classifier

The final stage of the model is a Vision Transformer (ViT) that serves as the classifier. The ViT takes the set of node features output by the GNN and processes them with a self-attention-based transformer encoder to produce a classification. In practice, the GNN output (the graph node features) is converted into a sequence of vectors suitable for transformer input. This involves flattening the graph node feature matrix into a sequence of length N (where N is the number of graph nodes, e.g., $H \times W$ if using a grid graph). Each of these N feature vectors acts as a token or patch embedding for the transformer [47,48]. Before data is fed into the transformer, a learned positional encoding is added to each token. Unlike the CNN feature map, which has an implicit positional structure by its index, and the graph, which has an inherent structure, the transformer self-attention mechanism lacks an inherent sense of position. If the graph is a regular grid, 2D positional encodings can be flattened to align with the sequence. For simplicity, one can also flatten in row-major order and use a 1D positional embedding of length N. This positional information helps the ViT distinguish spatial relationships, allowing it to differentiate. We adopt a Vision Transformer encoder for classification, which consists of multiple layers of multi-head self-attention and feedforward networks with skip connections. A special classification token (CLS token) is added to the sequence, a learned embedding vector that does not correspond to a specific image patch but serves as an aggregate representation. The sequence length entering the transformer becomes $N + 1$ (the N node features plus the CLS token). The self-attention mechanism of the transformer enables each token to attend to the content of the features of each other, allowing the model to focus on the relevant regions for classification.

For instance, if combinations of distant regions are important for a class, the self-attention layers capture these interactions, something neither the CNN nor the local GNN neighborhood fully captures. Multi-head attention enables the model to attend to multiple patterns or relationships in parallel, with each attention head learning a distinct attention map. The output of each attention layer is processed through a feedforward network and normalization, following the standard transformer architecture. During forward propagation, self-attention computes attention weights between every pair of tokens based on the products of their projected feature vectors. This results in a globally aware feature update, where each token receives a weighted sum of all other tokens' features. Consequently, the transformer output features encode global dependencies, with the representation of the CLS token at the final layer serving as an aggregated image descriptor that has attended to various important regions of the image, and CLS token output is then fed to a classification head.

3.8. Integration of CNN-GNN-ViT

Integrating CNN, GNN, and ViT into a unified model called ViTGNN involves structuring the data flow and potentially training in multiple stages. The process begins with the CNN extracting spatial features from the input image, producing a feature map where each spatial location corresponds to a feature vector. These feature vectors are then used as node features in a graph, with edges strictly defined based on four-connected spatial adjacency. The adjacency matrix is constructed by connecting each node to its immediate top, bottom, left, and right neighbors, ensuring that local spatial relationships are preserved. In addition, self-loops are included to retain individual node features during the message passage. The GNN processes these node features by applying graph convolution layers, updating each node's representation based on its neighbors. The refined node features are then flattened into a sequence, positional encodings are added, and a CLS token is prepended to prepare the data for the transformer. The ViT processes this sequence using self-attention layers, producing a final representation where the CLS token embedding serves as a global descriptor of the image. This representation is then passed through a fully connected layer to generate class scores, with a softmax function applied to obtain class probabilities. Training the entire model from scratch, especially the Vision Transformer (ViT), is computationally expensive. In order to mitigate this, we adopt a staged training approach where the ViT is initialized with pre-trained weights (ViT-B/16 model) from ImageNet and fine-tuned on our dataset with a freezing ratio of 0.5. That is, 50% of the ViT architecture layers are kept frozen so their weights do not change during training. Meanwhile, the CNN and GCN components are trained from scratch to extract local and relational features. This integration allows CNNs to capture local spatial patterns, GCNs to model relational structures, and ViTs to process global dependencies, creating a powerful framework for medical image analysis.

3.9. Model Training and Backpropagation

We train the ViTGNN model using supervised learning, where the pre-trained CNN and GNN are used as a feature extractor, and only the Vision Transformer is fine-tuned during the final training stage for classification. The CNN extracts spatial features from input images, which are then structured into a graph representation for processing by the GCN. The GCN aggregates information from immediate and second-order neighbors to refine spatial relationships before passing the processed features to the ViT classifier for final classification. The GCN is trained on the CNN output, where CNN-extracted feature maps serve as initial node attributes. The CNN and GCN are pre-trained in the feature extraction stage to ensure meaningful feature representations. The CNN extracts spatial features, while the GCN enhances them through neighborhood aggregation. The ViT, initialized with pre-trained weights, is fine-tuned during training to classify the refined feature representation. Unlike node-level supervision, where each graph node has a distinct label, ViTGNN employs image-level labels, assigning a single label to the entire image (COVID-19 or non-COVID-19). The cross-entropy loss is computed at the ViT output layer, providing global supervision that indirectly guides both the CNN and GCN. Since the GCN does not have explicit node-level labels, it learns representations based on the overall classification objective. Gradients are propagated backward, optimizing parameters at each stage, and trainable weight matrices W in the GCN layers are updated using gradient descent, with the AdamW optimizer improving convergence and weight decay regularization, preventing overfitting. Batch normalization and dropout regularization are applied across the CNN and GCN layers to maintain stability and avoid overfitting. Also, early stopping monitors validation loss and terminates training when no further improvement is observed.

In summary, the ViTGNN Algorithm 1 integrates CNN-GNN-based feature extraction with a ViT-based classifier, providing an effective approach for COVID-19 detection in CT scans. Image preprocessing involves CLAHE and Gaussian blur, followed by resizing and normalization. The dataset is divided into training, validation, and test sets, with a custom transformation pipeline. Initially, a CNN is used to extract low-level visual features, which are then passed to a GNN for spatial relationship modeling. Subsequently, these features are fused into a ViT for classification. The model is trained using cross-entropy loss, the Adam optimizer, and early stopping. After training, it is evaluated on test data using accuracy, precision, recall, F1-score, and AUC. This hybrid model captures detailed local features and broader image context, enhancing both accuracy and interpretability compared to traditional models.

Algorithm 1: ViTGNN Model for SARS-CoV-2 Detection

Input: Medical image dataset D (COVID, Non-COVID) ;
CNN-GNN feature extractor FE_θ ;
Transformer classifier ViT_ϕ
Output: Trained **ViTGNN** model

Step 1: Preprocessing ;
Apply CLAHE, Gaussian blur, normalization, and resizing on D;
Augment data (crop, flip, rotation, color jitter);

Step 2: Dataset Splitting ;
Split D into training (80%), validation (10%), and test (10%);
Initialize data loaders;

Step 3: CNN Pretraining ;
Train a baseline CNN classifier on D_{train};
Save trained CNN weights;

Step 4: GNN Pretraining ;
Freeze CNN weights;
Add GNN layers and train on CNN feature maps;
Save CNN-GNN combined weights;

Step 5: ViT Integration ;
Load pretrained CNN-GNN as FE_θ;
Adjust channel dimensions and upsample to 224×224;
Initialize ViT_ϕ with 50% trainable parameters;
Replace ViT classifier head;

Step 6: Model Training ;
Train ViTGNN model ($\mathrm{FE}_\theta \rightarrow ViT_\phi$) with AdamW;
Apply early stopping based on validation loss;

Step 7: Evaluation ;
Evaluate model on D_{test}; accuracy, precision, recall, F1-score, and AUC;

4. Results and Discussion

4.1. Baseline Models on SARS-CoV-2 Dataset

Wang et al. [4] conducted a comprehensive evaluation of multiple models on the SARS-CoV-2 CT dataset (Site A), which comprises 2482 CT images from 120 patients. In particular, this is the same dataset that we used to train and evaluate our proposed ViTGNN model. Their research provides benchmarks for assessing the effectiveness of different model designs in the diagnosis of COVID-19 in the cross-domain using CT imaging.

Initially designed for chest X-ray imaging, the **Single (COVID-Net)** model was applied directly to CT scans without architectural modifications. As a result, it showed limited performance, achieving the accuracy of 77.12%, precision of 80.04%, recall of 70.97%, F1-score of 76.03%, and an AUC of 84.08%. Recognizing these limitations, Wang et al proposed the **Single (Redesign)** model which introduced architectural and training enhancements, including selective batch normalization layers to stabilize feature distributions, global average pooling to reduce model parameters, and a cosine annealing learning rate strategy to facilitate smoother convergence. These improvements significantly improved model performance across all metrics. In an effort to address dataset variability, the **Joint (COVID-Net)** model was trained jointly on data combined from multiple clinical sites without considering domain shifts. However, this naive merging approach led to a performance degradation with the model attaining the accuracy of 68.72%, precision of 68.27%, recall of 69.41%, F1-score of 69.17%, and an AUC of 74.78%.

With an enhanced architecture in the **Joint (Redesign)** model, performance remained limited due to persistent challenges related to inter-site discrepancies. This resulted in an accuracy of 78.42%, precision of 80.82%, recall of 74.07%, F1-score of 77.86%, and an AUC of 85.72%. In order to mitigate domain heterogeneity, Wang et al introduced domain-adaptive architectures such as the **Series Adapter** model. This model sequentially inserted domain-specific adaptive layers after convolutional blocks, enabling limited site-specific adjustments while maintaining a shared backbone. As a result, it achieved improved performance with the accuracy of 85.73%, precision of 90.98%, recall of 81.91%, F1-score of 86.19%, and an AUC of 92.93%. Alternatively, the **Parallel Adapter** model placed domain-adaptive convolutional filters alongside the main convolution operations within residual blocks. This parallel structure allowed the network to learn domain-specific and shared features simultaneously, achieving an accuracy of 82.13%, precision of 83.51%, recall of 80.02%, F1-score of 82.39%, and an AUC of 89.99%.

Further advancing domain generalization, the **MS-Net** (Multi-Site Network) architecture was developed, which combined domain-specific auxiliary branches with a primary shared backbone and used an online knowledge transfer mechanism during training. This design further improved generalization across datasets, achieving an accuracy of 87.98%, precision of 93.78%, recall of 84.91%, F1-score of 88.73%, and an AUC of 94.37%, albeit at the expense of increased model complexity and computational overhead. Another notable contribution was the **SepNorm** (Separate Normalization) model, which addressed domain heterogeneity by replacing standard batch normalization with domain-specific batch normalization (DSBN) layers. In this setup, each clinical site maintained independent normalization statistics during training and inference, eliminating statistical mismatches between domains. This simple yet powerful modification resulted in an accuracy of 88.76%, precision of 95.46%, recall of 82.97%, F1-score of 87.88%, and an AUC of 94.57%.

Finally, the best performance was achieved with the **Contrastive** model. Building on the SepNorm framework, this model incorporated a contrastive learning objective that enforced samples from the same class across different domains to be closely clustered in the feature space while separating samples from different classes. By encouraging the learning of domain-invariant and class-discriminative representations, the Contrastive model achieved the highest metrics across all evaluated methods, recording an accuracy of 90.83%, precision of 95.75%, recall of 85.89%, F1-score of 90.87%, and an AUC of 96.24%.

4.2. Results

Table 2 presents a comparative analysis of the performance metrics of ViTGNN, the proposed model, against several established baseline models, evaluated using four key metrics: accuracy, precision, recall, and F1-score. These metrics collectively evaluate the model's ability to detect COVID-19 correctly, avoid false positives, and minimize false negatives while providing a harmonic balance between precision and recall. The baseline models include various configurations such as COVID-NET (Single and Joint), redesigned versions, Series and Parallel Adapters, MS-NET, and a Contrastive model. Each baseline represents different approaches to feature extraction and classification, showing varying performance levels.

The proposed ViTGNN demonstrates superior performance in all metrics, achieving an accuracy of 95.98%, with a precision of 96.07%, a recall of 96.01%, and an F1-score of 95.98%.

These results surpass all baseline models by significant margins. Among the baseline models, the best-performing approach, the Contrastive model, achieves an accuracy of 90.83%, with a precision of 95.75%, a recall of 85.89%, and an F1-score of 90.97%. Although the Contrastive model exhibits a strong balance between precision and recall, it still falls short of the performance of ViTGNN, especially in recall and the F1-score, highlighting the effectiveness of the proposed model in achieving a more comprehensive generalization.

Table 2. Performance metrics comparison of ViTGNN and baseline models.

Model	Accuracy (%)	Precision (%)	Recall (%)	F1-score (%)	AUC (%)
Single (COVID-NET [4])	77.12	80.04	70.97	76.03	84.08
Single (Redesign [4])	89.09	94.58	83.78	88.97	94.12
Joint (COVID-NET [4])	68.72	68.27	69.41	69.17	74.12
Joint (Redesign [4])	78.42	80.82	74.07	77.86	85.72
Series Adapter [4]	85.73	90.98	81.91	86.19	92.93
Parallel Adapter [4]	82.13	83.51	80.02	82.39	89.99
MS-NET [4]	87.98	93.78	84.91	88.73	94.37
SepNorm [4]	88.76	95.46	82.97	87.88	94.57
Contrastive [4]	90.83	95.75	85.89	90.97	96.24
ViTGNN (Proposed)	**95.98**	**96.07**	**96.01**	**95.98**	**98.69**

Interestingly, other baseline models such as MS-NET and the redesigned Single COVID-NET also perform well, with MS-NET achieving an accuracy of 87.98% and the redesigned Single COVID-NET achieving 89.09%. However, these models show limitations in precision and recall, indicating challenges in balancing the trade-offs between false positives and false negatives. In addition, joint models consistently underperform compared to their single counterparts, suggesting potential overfitting or noise amplification when combining features. Similarly, the Series Adapter outperforms the Parallel Adapter, which indicates structural differences in how the adapters handle feature hierarchies. The loss curve for training and validation, illustrated in Figure 3, further supports the effectiveness of the ViTGNN training process. The steady decline in training loss, accompanied by a consistent reduction in validation loss, indicates that the model effectively generalizes without overfitting. Furthermore, the training and validation accuracy curve in Figure 4 shows a convergence towards high accuracy, with a minimal divergence between training and validation accuracy, highlighting the robustness of the model during training.

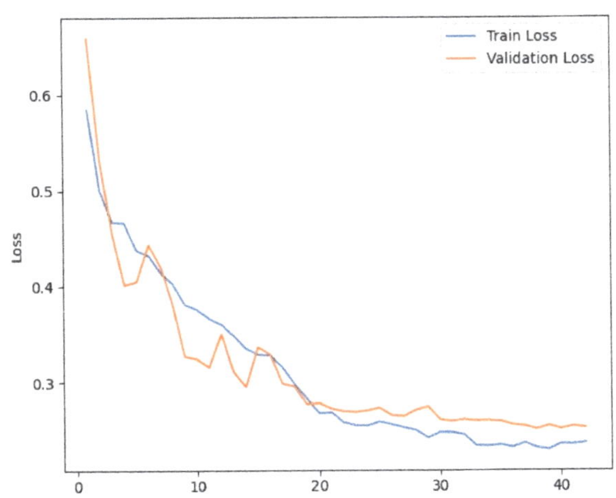

Figure 3. Training and Validation Loss for ViTGNN Model.

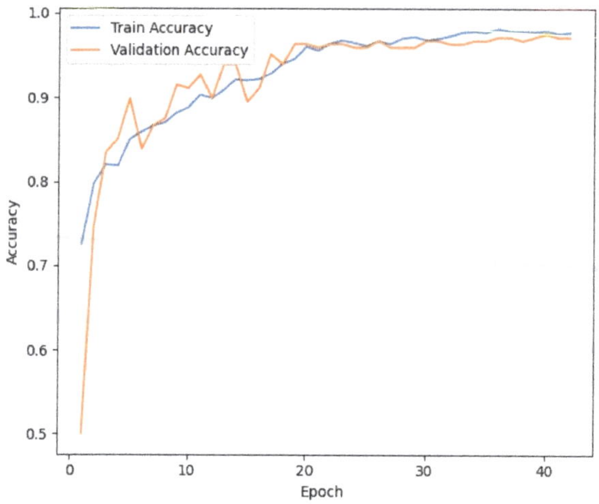

Figure 4. Training and Validation Accuracy for ViTGNN Model.

The ROC curve in Figure 5 provides further evidence of ViTGNN's superior classification capabilities. The model achieves an AUC score of 0.9869, indicating exceptional performance in distinguishing between classes. This high AUC score reflects the ability of ViTGNN to minimize false positives and false negatives, which is essential in high-stakes applications such as medical imaging. The superior performance of ViTGNN can be attributed to its advanced architectural design, which incorporates graph-based learning and visual transformers. This combination enables the model to leverage both spatial and contextual relationships in the data, leading to enhanced feature extraction and representation. The results indicate that ViTGNN not only excels in predictive accuracy but also maintains a consistent balance across all metrics, making it highly reliable for real-world applications.

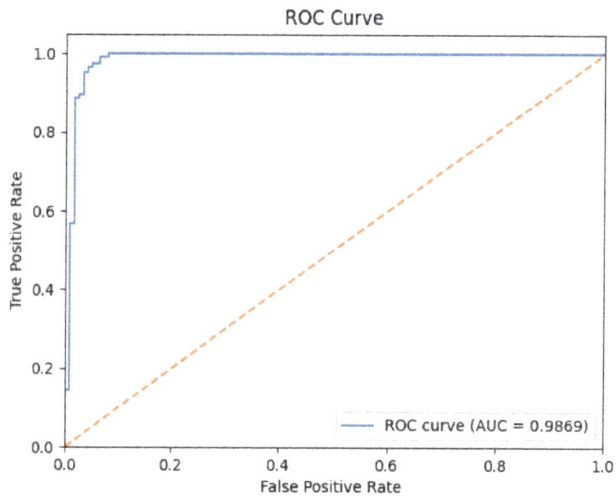

Figure 5. ROC curve for the ViTGNN model. **Note:** The yellow dotted diagonal line in the ROC curve represents the performance of a random classifier and serves as a baseline, where the True Positive Rate (TPR) equals the False Positive Rate (FPR). That is, any model performing above this line demonstrates predictive power better than random guessing. In this plot, the solid blue line (AUC = 0.9869) significantly exceeds the diagonal, indicating the excellent classification performance of our proposed ViTGNN model.

In general, the results highlight ViTGNN as a state-of-the-art solution that outperforms established methods and sets a new benchmark for classification tasks. Its consistent performance across metrics demonstrates its potential in critical applications, paving the way for further research and optimization in related fields.

4.3. Generalizability of the Proposed Model and Ablation Study

4.3.1. Generalizability of the Proposed Model:

In order evaluate the performance of the proposed model, we tested it on two external chest X-ray datasets that varied substantially in disease categories, imaging protocols, and patient populations (Table 3).

1. Tuberculosis (TB) Chest X-ray Dataset: This dataset, Figure 6, was compiled through a collaboration between Qatar University, the University of Dhaka, and medical institutions in Bangladesh and Malaysia. It consists of 700 publicly available TB-positive chest X-ray images and approximately 3500 normal cases [49]. These images were collected from various clinical settings and provide a valuable benchmark for testing cross-condition model generalization beyond COVID-19.

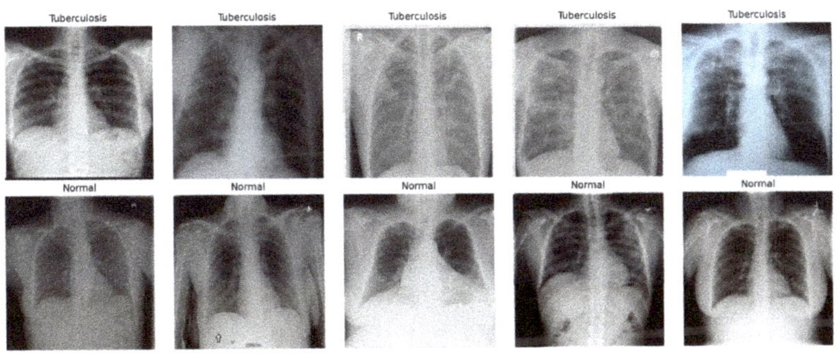

Figure 6. Sample images of Tuberculosis (TB) Chest X-ray Dataset.

2. Pneumonia Chest X-ray Dataset: Sourced from pediatric patients aged 1 to 5 years at Guangzhou Women and Children's Medical Center, this dataset, Figure 7, comprises 5863 anterior/posterior chest X-ray images labeled as pneumonia and normal [50].

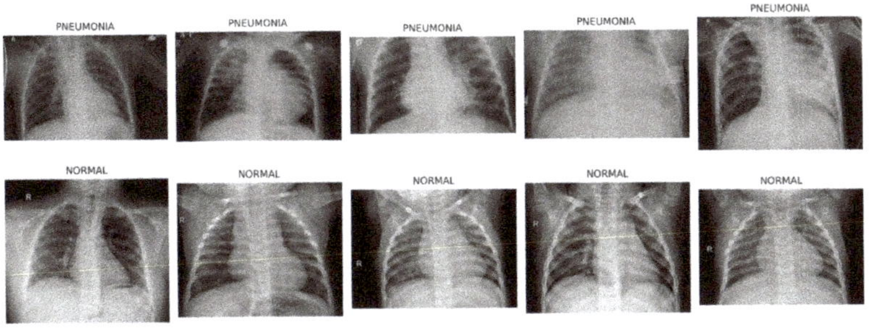

Figure 7. Sample images of Pneumonia Chest X-ray Dataset.

4.3.2. Ablation Study

We conducted an ablation study to evaluate the contribution of each component within the proposed hybrid CNN-GNN-ViT model. The effectiveness of each stage was systematically assessed and measured by its impact on classification performance using metrics such as accuracy, precision, recall, and F1-score.

CNN Only

In this stage, we evaluated a Convolutional Neural Network (CNN) composed of convolutional and pooling layers, batch normalization, dropout regularization, and fully connected layers. This model primarily captures local spatial features within chest X-ray images. In the Tuberculosis dataset, the CNN achieved an accuracy of 91.67%, a precision of 95.45%, a recall of 75.00%, and an F1-score of 80.95%. On the Pneumonia dataset, the same model yielded 86.02% accuracy, 82.14% precision, 80.33% recall, and an F1-score of 81.16%. While the CNN was capable of detecting prominent local features associated with pulmonary diseases, its limited receptive field hindered the ability to model long-range spatial dependencies across image regions.

CNN + GNN

To address the limitations of local feature modeling, we augmented the CNN with a Graph Neural Network (GNN) in Stage 2. This hybrid CNN-GNN architecture used a grid-based graph structure to model spatial relationships among regional features. In the Tuberculosis dataset, the CNN-GNN model achieved better performance, with an accuracy of 92.14%, a precision of 95.69%, a recall of 76.43%, and an F1-score of 82.28%. For the Pneumonia dataset, the model achieved 85.25% accuracy, 80.60% precision, 81.04% recall, and 80.81% F1-score. The improvement, especially in F1-score and recall, suggests that the GNN component improves global context understanding, allowing the model to detect subtle, spatially diffuse patterns commonly seen in respiratory infections.

Our proposed ViTGNN model, a novel hybrid architecture that combines a Vision Transformer (ViT) with a Convolutional Neural Network and a Graph Neural Network, demonstrated consistently superior performance on both the Tuberculosis and Pneumonia datasets (see Table 3). This architecture effectively uses the ViT's global self-attention mechanism along with the CNN's local feature extraction and the GNN's capacity to model spatial relationships among image regions. Specifically, on the Tuberculosis dataset, ViTGNN achieved an accuracy of 98.81%, a precision of 99.30%, a recall of 96.43%, and an F1-score of 97.79%. On the Pneumonia dataset, it recorded 95.59% accuracy, 92.68% precision, 97.04% recall, and a 94.52% F1-score. Remarkably, although ViTGNN was trained exclusively on datasets, it maintained high performance on both target datasets without requiring additional fine-tuning. This suggests a substantial degree of feature generalizability and robustness to domain shifts, emphasizing the model's potential for broader clinical applicability across diverse respiratory pathologies and imaging conditions.

Table 3. Proposed model on Tuberculosis and Pneumonia datasets.

		Tuberculosis Dataset		
Model	**Accuracy (%)**	**Precision (%)**	**Recall (%)**	**F1-score (%)**
ViTGNN	**98.81**	**99.30**	**96.43**	**97.79**
CNN	91.67	95.45	75.00	80.95
CNN-GNN	92.14	95.69	76.43	82.28
		Pneumonia Dataset		
ViTGNN	**95.59**	**92.68**	**97.04**	**94.52**
CNN	86.02	82.14	80.33	81.16
CNN-GNN	85.25	80.60	81.04	80.81
		SARS-CoV-2 Dataset		
ViTGNN	**95.98**	**96.07**	**96.01**	**95.98**
CNN	81.93	82.83	82.03	81.83
CNN-GNN	81.93	82.51	82.01	81.87

4.4. Computational Cost

We evaluate the trade-off between model performance and resource usage and consider the computational efficiency of all model variants across three medical imaging datasets: SARS-CoV-2, Tuberculosis, and Pneumonia. The comparison focused on two key metrics: total inference time and computational cost, both measured in seconds see Table 4.

Computational cost refers to the time required to complete the training of each model. This include forward and backward passes, weight updates and optimizer operations across all training epochs. It reflects the resource demands of the model in term of processor (CPU/GPU) usage, memory consumption and processing latency. Inference time, on the other hand, measures the duration required by a trained model to generate predictions on unseen test data. Specifically, it captures the average time taken for a single forward pass through the network per input sample during the testing phase [51,52].

Table 4. Comparison of inference time and computational cost (in seconds)

	SAR-CoV-2 Dataset	
Model	Inference Time (s)	Computational Cost
ViTGNN	**22.10**	**8902.39**
CNN	0.72	86.09
CNN-GNN	21.43	967.29
	Tuberculosis Dataset	
ViTGNN	**38.16**	**11,009.81**
CNN	2.16	224.33
CNN-GNN	37.43	1703.91
	Pneumonia Dataset	
ViTGNN	**47.60**	**11,836.54**
CNN	2.88	295.48
CNN-GNN	46.27	2100.16

Across all datasets, the **CNN model** consistently exhibited the lowest computational demands. Specifically, it completed inference in 0.72 s on the SARS-CoV-2 dataset with a computational cost of 86.09 s, followed by 2.16 s and 224.33 s for the Tuberculosis dataset and 2.88 s and 295.48 s for the Pneumonia dataset. This efficiency is attributed to its relatively lightweight and straightforward architecture, making it ideal for deployment in real-time or resource-constrained clinical environments.

In contrast, the **CNN-GNN model** introduced a substantial increase in both inference time and computational cost. On the SARS-CoV-2 dataset, inference required 21.43 s and incurred a computational cost of 967.29 s. Similar patterns were observed for the Tuberculosis (37.43 s, 1703.91 s) and Pneumonia (46.27 s, 2100.16 s) datasets. This increase is due to the added complexity of graph construction and the iterative message-passing operations inherent to Graph Neural Networks (GNNs).

The most computationally demanding model was the full hybrid **ViTGNN**, see Table 4 which integrates a Vision Transformer (ViT) with both CNN and GNN components. For the SARS-CoV-2 dataset, ViTGNN required 22.10 s for inference and a total computational cost of 8902.39 s. For the Tuberculosis and Pneumonia datasets, the respective values rose to 38.16 s and 11,009.81 s, and 47.60 s and 11,836.54 s. This overhead is attributed to the self-attention mechanisms and the model's deeper and more parameter-intensive architecture.

Overall, while ViTGNN incurs the highest computational burden, its superior diagnostic accuracy and robust generalization performance may justify its use in scenarios where processing time is less critical than predictive precision.

5. Conclusions

This research highlights the effectiveness of the ViTGNN framework in addressing the challenge of SARS-CoV-2 detection from CT scan images. Combining the strengths of Convolutional Neural Networks and Graph Neural Networks (GNNs) for detailed feature extraction and Vision Transformers (ViTs) for high-level feature classification, ViTGNN has demonstrated superior diagnostic accuracy. Through a comprehensive experimental setup, the framework consistently achieved exceptional performance metrics, including high accuracy, precision, recall, F1-score, and AUC, validating its utility in medical imaging applications. The use of advanced preprocessing techniques ensured that the input data was optimized for feature extraction, further enhancing the model's diagnostic capabilities. In addition, the efficient use of computational resources, coupled with techniques such as early stopping, demonstrated the model's ability to balance performance and computational efficiency effectively. The results confirm the potential of ViTGNN for SARS-CoV-2 detection and highlight its applicability to larger healthcare challenges that involve complex imaging data. Its ability to generalize across various scenarios and provide consistent performance makes it a promising tool for integration into clinical workflows.

6. Limitation

The proposed ViTGNN model demonstrates strong performance in COVID-19 detection from CT scan images; however, several limitations must be acknowledged. Due to the high computational cost and resource constraints associated with training the model, only a single evaluation run was performed. Although this run produced favorable performance metrics, the absence of repeated trials limits the ability to report variability measures such as standard deviations or to perform statistical significance tests. In addition, the current model lacks integrated explainability mechanisms, and the computational complexity introduced by the Vision Transformer component results in increased training and inference time.

Future Work

Future work will address the limitations mentioned earlier and further advance the ViTGNN to enhance its clinical viability and trustworthiness. We will conduct multiple experimental runs using different random seeds to enable statistical effectiveness through the computation of confidence intervals and the application of hypothesis testing methods such as paired t-tests. This will strengthen the reproducibility and generalizability of performance outcomes. In parallel, we will focus on improving the model's interpretability and transparency by integrating explainable AI (XAI) methods. In addition to graph-based and gradient-based approaches such as GNNExplainer, Layer-wise Relevance Propagation (LRP), and Grad-CAM, we plan to explore recent developments in Vision Transformer explainability. Specifically, we will investigate ICEv2 for patch-wise, class-discriminative visualization without modifying the core architecture (Choi et al. [19]), Transformer Input Sampling (TIS) for perturbation-free token-based saliency mapping (Englebert et al. [21]), and TRAM for efficient token pruning through attention-based centrality (Marchetti et al. [20]).

Moreover, wavelet-based super-resolution methods have demonstrated promise in enhancing fine-grained features crucial for accurate medical diagnosis. Yu et al. [14] introduced a WPRNN constrained by wavelet energy entropy, which fuses shallow and deep features across resolutions to improve perceptual quality and preserve subtle anatomical details. Although our current ViTGNN framework emphasizes end-to-end classification, integrating such low-level vision enhancements in future extensions could further improve feature extraction and classification performance.

Author Contributions: Conceptualization, K.A., A.W., T.A. and L.A.; Data curation, K.A.; Investigation, K.A., A.W., T.A. and L.A.; Methodology, K.A., Q.W. and J.F.; Project administration, K.A.; Resources, K.A., Q.W. and J.F.; Implementation, K.A.; Supervision, Q.W. and J.F.; Validation, K.A., Q.W. and J.F.; Visualization, K.A.; Writing—original draft preparation, K.A., A.W., T.A. and L.A.; Writing—review and editing, K.A., Q.W. and J.F. All authors have read and agreed to the published version of the manuscript.

Funding: This work was supported by the U.S. National Science Foundation (NSF) under Grant No. 2447364. Any opinions, findings, and conclusions or recommendations expressed in this material are those of the authors and do not necessarily reflect the views of the National Science Foundation.

Data Availability Statement: The datasets used in this study are publicly available at the following sources: SARS-CoV-2 CT Scan Dataset (https://www.kaggle.com/datasets/plameneduardo/sarscov2-ctscan-dataset, accessed on 10 December 2024); Chest X-ray Pneumonia Dataset (https://www.kaggle.com/datasets/paultimothymooney/chest-xray-pneumonia, accessed on 6 June 2025); and Tuberculosis Chest X-ray Dataset (https://www.kaggle.com/datasets/tawsifurrahman/tuberculosis-tb-chest-xray-dataset, accessed on 6 June 2025).

Acknowledgments: The authors acknowledge the Department of Computer and Information Sciences, Towson University, Maryland, USA, for providing the computational resources and academic environment that supported this study. Access to high-level computing resources such as the NVIDIA GeForce RTX 3090 GPU significantly facilitated experimental design, data analysis, and overall research quality. All content was thoroughly reviewed and revised by the authors, who take full responsibility for the final version of this publication.

Conflicts of Interest: The authors declare no conflicts of interest.

Abbreviations

The following abbreviations are used in this manuscript:

ReLU	Rectified Linear Unit
GCN	Graph Convolutional Network
CNN	Convolutional Neural Network
GNN	Graph Neural Network
ViT	Vision Transformer
ROC	Receiver Operating Characteristic
SARS-CoV-2	Severe Acute Respiratory Syndrome Coronavirus 2
AUC	Area Under Curve
CLAHE	Contrast-Limited Adaptive Histogram Equalization
CT	Computed Tomography
VITGNN	Vision Transformer, Graph Neural Network, and Convolutional Neural Network

References

1. Jaiswal, A.; Gianchandani, N.; Singh, D.; Kumar, V.; Kaur, M. Classification of the COVID-19 infected patients using DenseNet201 based deep transfer learning. *J. Biomol. Struct. Dyn.* **2021**, *39*, 5682–5689. [CrossRef] [PubMed]
2. Afshar, P.; Heidarian, S.; Enshaei, N.; Naderkhani, F.; Rafiee, M.J.; Oikonomou, A.; Fard, F.B.; Samimi, K.; Plataniotis, K.N.; Mohammadi, A. COVID-CT-MD, COVID-19 computed tomography scan dataset applicable in machine learning and deep learning. *Sci. Data* **2021**, *8*, 121. [CrossRef] [PubMed]
3. Sahoo, P.; Saha, S.; Mondal, S.; Chowdhury, S.; Gowda, S. Vision Transformer-Based Federated Learning for COVID-19 Detection Using Chest X-Ray. In Proceedings of the 29th International Conference on Neural Information Processing, Virtual Event, *22–26 November* **2022**; Part VII; Springer: Cham, Switzerland, 2023; Volume 1794, pp. 77–88. [CrossRef]

4. Wang, Z.; Liu, Q.; Dou, Q. Contrastive cross-site learning with redesigned net for COVID-19 CT classification. *IEEE J. Biomed. Health Inform.* **2020**, *24*, 2806–2813. [CrossRef]
5. Soares, E.; Angelov, P.; Biaso, S.; Cury, M.; Abe, D. A large multiclass dataset of CT scans for COVID-19 identification. *Evol. Syst.* **2024**, *15*, 635–640. [CrossRef]
6. Ibrahim, M.R.; Youssef, S.M.; Fathalla, K.M. Abnormality detection and intelligent severity assessment of human chest computed tomography scans using deep learning: a case study on SARS-COV-2 assessment. *J. Ambient. Intell. Humaniz. Comput.* **2023**, *14*, 5665–5688. [CrossRef]
7. Parikh, D.; Fein-Ashley, J.; Ye, T.; Kannan, R.; Prasanna, V. ClusterViG: Efficient Globally Aware Vision GNNs via Image Partitioning. *arXiv* **2025**, arXiv:2501.10640.
8. Sahoo, P.; Saha, S.; Mondal, S.; Gowda, S. Vision transformer based COVID-19 detection using chest ct-scan images. In Proceedings of the 2022 IEEE-EMBS International Conference on Biomedical and Health Informatics (BHI), Ioannina, Greece, 27–30 September 2022; pp. 1–4.
9. Than, J.C.; Thon, P.L.; Rijal, O.M.; Kassim, R.M.; Yunus, A.; Noor, N.M.; Then, P. Preliminary study on patch sizes in vision transformers (vit) for COVID-19 and diseased lungs classification. In Proceedings of the 2021 IEEE National Biomedical Engineering Conference (NBEC), Kuala Lumpur, Malaysia, 9–10 November 2021; pp. 146–150.
10. Xu, H.; Wu, Y. G2ViT: Graph neural network-guided vision transformer enhanced network for retinal vessel and coronary angiograph segmentation. *Neural Netw.* **2024**, *176*, 106356. [CrossRef]
11. Mondal, A.K.; Bhattacharjee, A.; Singla, P.; Prathosh, A. xViTCOS: Explainable vision transformer based COVID-19 screening using radiography. *IEEE J. Transl. Eng. Health Med.* **2021**, *10*, 1–10. [CrossRef]
12. Wang, Y.; Deng, Y.; Zheng, Y.; Chattopadhyay, P.; Wang, L. Vision Transformers for Image Classification: A Comparative Survey. *Technologies* **2025**, *13*, 32. [CrossRef]
13. Dosovitskiy, A.; Beyer, L.; Kolesnikov, A.; Weissenborn, D.; Zhai, X.; Unterthiner, T.; Dehghani, M.; Minderer, M.; Heigold, G.; Gelly, S.; et al. An image is worth 16x16 words: Transformers for image recognition at scale. *arXiv* **2020**, arXiv:2010.11929.
14. Yu, Y.; She, K.; Shi, K.; Cai, X.; Kwon, O.M.; Soh, Y. Analysis of medical images super-resolution via a wavelet pyramid recursive neural network constrained by wavelet energy entropy. *Neural Netw.* **2024**, *178*, 106460. [CrossRef]
15. Zhang, L.; Wen, Y. A transformer-based framework for automatic COVID19 diagnosis in chest CTs. In Proceedings of the Proceedings of the IEEE/CVF International Conference on Computer Vision, Montreal, BC, Canada, 11–17 October 2021; pp. 513–518.
16. Zhang, P.; Yan, Y.; Zhang, X.; Li, C.; Wang, S.; Huang, F.; Kim, S. TransGNN: Harnessing the collaborative power of transformers and graph neural networks for recommender systems. In Proceedings of the 47th International ACM SIGIR Conference on Research and Development in Information Retrieval, (SIGIR '24), Washington, DC, USA, 14–18 July 2024; pp.1285—1295.
17. Shome, D.; Kar, T.; Mohanty, S.N.; Tiwari, P.; Muhammad, K.; AlTameem, A.; Zhang, Y.; Saudagar, A.K.J. Covid-transformer: Interpretable covid-19 detection using vision transformer for healthcare. *Int. J. Environ. Res. Public Health* **2021**, *18*, 11086. [CrossRef]
18. Xiao, X.; Kong, Y.; Li, R.; Wang, Z.; Lu, H. Transformer with convolution and graph-node co-embedding: an accurate and interpretable vision backbone for predicting gene expressions from local histopathological image. *Med. Image Anal.* **2024**, *91*, 103040. [CrossRef]
19. Choi, H.; Jin, S.; Han, K. ICEv2: Interpretability, Comprehensiveness, and Explainability in Vision Transformer. *Int. J. Comput. Vis.* **2025**, *133*, 2487–2504;. [CrossRef]
20. Marchetti, M.; Traini, D.; Ursino, D.; Virgili, L. Efficient token pruning in Vision Transformers using an attention-based Multilayer Network. *Expert Syst. Appl.* **2025**, *279*, 127449. [CrossRef]
21. Englebert, A.; Stassin, S.; Nanfack, G.; Mahmoudi, S.A.; Siebert, X.; Cornu, O.; De Vleeschouwer, C. Explaining through Transformer Input Sampling. In Proceedings of the IEEE/CVF International Conference on Computer Vision Workshops (ICCVW), Paris, France, 2–6 October 2023; pp. 806–815. . [CrossRef]
22. Soares, E.; Angelov, P.; Biaso, S.; Froes, M.H.; Abe, D.K. SARS-CoV-2 CT-scan dataset: A large dataset of real patients CT scans for SARS-CoV-2 identification. *MedRxiv* **2020**. . [CrossRef]
23. Chetoui, M.; Akhloufi, M.A. Explainable Vision Transformers and Radiomics for COVID-19 Detection in Chest X-rays. *J. Clin. Med.* **2022**, *11*, 3013. [CrossRef]
24. Nguyen, V.B.; Hy, T.S.; Tran-Thanh, L.; Nghiem, N. Predicting COVID-19 pandemic by spatio-temporal graph neural networks: A New Zealand's study. *arXiv* **2023**, arXiv:2305.07731.
25. Chen, J.; Wu, L.; Zhang, J.; Zhang, L.; Gong, D.; Zhao, Y.; Chen, Q.; Huang, S.; Yang, M.; Yang, X.; et al. Deep learning-based model for detecting 2019 novel coronavirus pneumonia on high-resolution computed tomography. *Sci. Rep.* **2020**, *10*, 19196. [CrossRef]
26. Wang, L.; Lin, Z.Q.; Wong, A. COVID-Net: A tailored deep convolutional neural network design for detection of COVID-19 cases from chest X-ray images. *Sci. Rep.* **2020**, *10*, 1–12. [CrossRef]

27. Hu, S.; Gao, Y.; Niu, Z.; Jiang, Y.; Li, L.; Xiao, X.; Wang, M.; Fang, E.F.; Menpes-Smith, W.; Xia, J.; et al. Weakly supervised deep learning for COVID-19 infection detection and classification from CT images. *IEEE Access* **2020**, *8*, 118869–118883. [CrossRef]
28. Wang, J.; Bao, Y.; Wen, Y.; Lu, H.; Luo, H.; Xiang, Y.; Li, X.; Liu, C.; Qian, D. Prior-attention residual learning for more discriminative COVID-19 screening in CT images. *IEEE Trans. Med. Imaging* **2020**, *39*, 2572–2583. [CrossRef] [PubMed]
29. Shibly, K.; Dey, R.; Rahman, M.T.; Shah, F.; Rahman, T.; Sarker, M.H.; Islam, M.N.; Saba, T.; Arshad, H.; Rahman, M.M. COVID Faster R-CNN: A Novel Deep Learning Framework for COVID-19 Detection from Chest X-Ray Images. *Comput. Biol. Med.* **2021**, *132*, 104306. [CrossRef]
30. Song, Y.; Zheng, S.; Li, L.; Zhang, X.; Zhang, X.; Huang, Z.; Chen, J.; Wang, R.; Zhao, H.; Chong, Y.; et al. Deep learning enables accurate diagnosis of novel coronavirus (COVID-19) with CT images. *IEEE Trans. Med. Imaging* **2020**, *39*, 2625–2635. [CrossRef] [PubMed]
31. Loey, M.; Smarandache, F.; Khalifa, N. Within the Lack of Chest COVID-19 X-ray Dataset: A Novel Detection Model Based on GAN and Deep Transfer Learning. *Symmetry* **2020**, *12*, 651. [CrossRef]
32. Salehi, S.; Abedi, A.; Balakrishnan, S.; Gholamrezanezhad, A. Coronavirus Disease 2019 (COVID-19): A Systematic Review of Imaging Findings in 919 Patients. *AJR Am. J. Roentgenol.* **2020**, *215*, 87–93. [CrossRef]
33. Li, L.; Qin, L.; Xu, Z.; Lu, H.; Luo, H.; Xiang, Y.; Li, X.; Liu, C.; Qian, D. Using artificial intelligence to detect COVID-19 and community-acquired pneumonia based on pulmonary CT: Evaluation of the diagnostic accuracy. *Radiology* **2020**, *296*, E65–E71. [CrossRef]
34. Wang, X.; Deng, X.; Fu, Q.; Zhou, Q.; Feng, J.; Ma, H.; Liu, W.; Zheng, C. A weakly-supervised framework for COVID-19 classification and lesion localization from chest CT. *IEEE Trans. Med. Imaging* **2020**, *39*, 2615–2625. [CrossRef]
35. Ozturk, T.; Talo, M.; Yildirim, E.A.; Baloglu, U.B.; Yildirim, O.; Acharya, U.R. Automated detection of COVID-19 cases using deep neural networks with X-ray images. *Comput. Biol. Med.* **2020**, *121*, 103792. [CrossRef]
36. Heidari, M.; Mirniaharikandehei, S.; Khuzani, A.Z.; Danala, G.; Qiu, Y.; Zheng, B. Improving the performance of CNN to predict the likelihood of COVID-19 using chest X-ray images with preprocessing algorithms. *Int. J. Med. Inform.* **2020**, *144*, 104284. [CrossRef]
37. Ouchicha, C.; Ammor, O.; Meknassi, M. CVDNet: A novel deep learning architecture for detection of coronavirus (COVID-19) from chest X-ray images. *Chaos Solitons Fractals* **2020**, *140*, 110245. [CrossRef] [PubMed]
38. Chowdhury, M.E.; Rahman, T.; Khandakar, A.; Mazhar, R.; Kadir, M.A.; Mahbub, Z.; Islam, M.T.; Ayari, M.A.; Al-Emadi, N.; Reaz, M.B.I. Can AI Help in Screening Viral and COVID-19 Pneumonia? *IEEE Access* **2020**, *8*, 132665–132676. [CrossRef]
39. Zheng, C.; Deng, X.; Fu, Q.; Zhou, Q.; Feng, J.; Ma, H.; Liu, W.; Wang, X. Deep learning-based detection for COVID-19 from chest CT using weak label. *medRxiv* **2020**. [CrossRef]
40. Aslani, S.; Lilaonitkul, W.; Gnananthan, V.; Raj, D.; Rangelov, B.; Young, A.L.; Hu, Y.; Taylor, P.; Alexander, D.C.; Jacob, J. Optimising Chest X-Rays for Image Analysis by Identifying and Removing Confounding Factors. *arXiv* **2022**, arXiv:2208.10320.
41. Fu, Q.; Celenk, M.; Wu, A. An improved algorithm based on CLAHE for ultrasonic well logging image enhancement. *Clust. Comput.* **2019**, *22*, 12609–12618. [CrossRef]
42. Hayati, M.; Muchtar, K.; Roslidar; Maulina, N.; Syamsuddin, I.; Elwirehardja, G.N.; Pardamean, B. Impact of CLAHE-based image enhancement for diabetic retinopathy classification through deep learning. *Procedia Comput. Sci.* **2023**, *216*, 57–66. [CrossRef]
43. Flusser, J.; Farokhi, S.; Höschl, C.; Suk, T.; Zitova, B.; Pedone, M. Recognition of images degraded by Gaussian blur. *IEEE Trans. Image Process.* **2015**, *25*, 790–806. [CrossRef]
44. Khalifa, N.E.; Loey, M.; Mirjalili, S. A comprehensive survey of recent trends in deep learning for digital images augmentation. *Artif. Intell. Rev.* **2022**, *55*, 2351–2377. [CrossRef]
45. Kim, J.W.; Khan, A.U.; Banerjee, I. Systematic review of hybrid vision transformer architectures for radiological image analysis. *J. Imaging Inform. Med.* **2025**. [CrossRef]
46. Liu, Z.Q.; Tang, P.; Zhang, W.; Zhang, Z. CNN-enhanced heterogeneous graph convolutional network: inferring land use from land cover with a case study of park segmentation. *Remote Sens.* **2022**, *14*, 5027. [CrossRef]
47. Han, K.; Wang, Y.; Guo, J.; Tang, Y.; Wu, E. Vision gnn: An image is worth graph of nodes. *Adv. Neural Inf. Process. Syst.* **2022**, *35*, 8291–8303.
48. Chen, T.; Philippi, I.; Phan, Q.B.; Nguyen, L.; Bui, N.T.; Nguyen, T.T. A vision transformer machine learning model for COVID-19 diagnosis using chest X-ray images. *Healthc. Anal.* **2024**, *5*, 100332. [CrossRef]
49. Rahman, T.; Khandakar, A.; Kadir, M.A.; Islam, K.R.; Islam, K.F.; Mazhar, R.; Hamid, T.; Islam, M.T.; Kashem, S.; Mahbub, Z.B.; et al. Reliable Tuberculosis Detection Using Chest X-Ray With Deep Learning, Segmentation and Visualization. *IEEE Access* **2020**, *8*, 191586–191601. [CrossRef]
50. Kermany, D.S.; Goldbaum, M.; Cai, W.; Valentim, C.C.; Liang, H.; Baxter, S.L.; McKeown, A.; Yang, G.; Wu, X.; Yan, F.; et al. Identifying medical diagnoses and treatable diseases by image-based deep learning. *Cell* **2018**, *172*, 1122–1131. [CrossRef]

51. Justus, D.; Brennan, J.; Bonner, S.; McGough, A.S. Predicting the Computational Cost of Deep Learning Models. In Proceedings of the 2018 IEEE International Conference on Big Data (Big Data), Seattle, WA, USA, 10–13 December 2018; pp. 3873–3882; [CrossRef]
52. Zhang, H.; Huang, Y.; Wen, Y.; Yin, J.; Guan, K. InferBench: Understanding Deep Learning Inference Serving with an Automatic Benchmarking System. *arXiv* **2020**, arXiv:2011.02327. Available online: https://arxiv.org/abs/2011.02327 (accessed on 27 June 2025).

algorithms

MDPI

Review

A Review of Key Signal Processing Techniques for Structural Health Monitoring: Highlighting Non-Parametric Time-Frequency Analysis, Adaptive Decomposition, and Deconvolution

Yixin Zhou [1,2], Zepeng Ma [1,2] and Lei Fu [1,2,*]

[1] College of Mechanical Engineering, Zhejiang University of Technology, Hangzhou 310023, China; 302023503169@zjut.edu.cn (Y.Z.); zepeng.ma@zjut.edu.cn (Z.M.)

[2] Key Laboratory of Special Purpose Equipment and Advanced Manufacturing Technology, Zhejiang University of Technology, Ministry of Education & Zhejiang Province, Hangzhou 310023, China

* Correspondence: fulei@zjut.edu.cn; Tel.: +86-571-8795-3851

Abstract: This paper reviews key signal processing techniques in structural health monitoring (SHM), focusing on non-parametric time–frequency analysis, adaptive decomposition, and deconvolution methods. It examines the short-time Fourier transform (STFT), wavelet transform (WT), and Wigner–Ville distribution (WVD), highlighting their applications, advantages, and limitations in SHM. The review also explores adaptive techniques like empirical mode decomposition (EMD) and its variants (EEMD, MEEMD), as well as variational mode decomposition (VMD) and its improved versions (SVMD, AVMD), emphasizing their effectiveness in handling nonlinear and non-stationary signals. Additionally, deconvolution methods such as minimum entropy deconvolution (MED) and maximum correlated kurtosis deconvolution (MCKD) are discussed for mechanical fault diagnosis. The paper aims to provide a comprehensive overview of these techniques, offering insights for future research into SHM signal processing.

Keywords: signal processing techniques; structural health monitoring; non-parametric time–frequency analysis; adaptive decomposition; deconvolution

1. Introduction

When delving into modern and developed societies, one finds that strategically significant and intricately complete civil infrastructures and buildings constitute their core commonality. This commonality manifests broadly in widespread applications across transportation, industrial production, economic activities, and the protection of personnel and materials. Given the importance of these facilities, we cannot overlook their aging and degradation, nor can we afford the inestimable losses and harm that may result from failing to detect issues and take timely action. Furthermore, due to the large number and ubiquity of these structures, the majority of them are inevitably and frequently exposed to continuous environmental vibrations and severe disaster events, such as earthquakes, floods, tornadoes, and corrosion, as well as other uncertain factors like traffic loads, material aging, impacts, and environmental corrosion. Consequently, monitoring and assessing structural performance has become a fundamental requirement for enhancing structural integrity and safety.

Structural health monitoring (SHM) and structural damage detection methods are continuously evolving, with research gaining new life across various scientific fields such as aerospace, civil, and mechanical engineering [1]. To achieve SHM, researchers employ a variety of different sensor devices to collect signal data, including acoustic, pressure, temperature, force, and accelerometer sensors. This has given rise to the processing of multivariate signals.

The core objective of signal processing is to collect, analyze, and process multivariate signals such as vibrations, noise, temperature, and pressure generated during the operation of mechanical systems, extracting key features that reflect the system's state, thereby enabling early fault detection, precise diagnosis, and effective prevention. In recent years, SHM researchers have dedicated themselves to integrating and fusing various cutting-edge technologies—particularly those from different information technologies and engineering methodologies—to develop economical, accurate, and reliable monitoring methods. Additionally, various data mining techniques, visualization tools, and statistical computations frequently appear in monitoring and processing solutions. Beyond traditional vibration-based monitoring, detections methods related to sound, temperature, and motor current are now emerging, as mentioned by Wonho Jung [2]. Moreover, changes in structural properties, such as stiffness, are significantly observable in variations of multivariate signals, and internal structural components can also be accurately represented through these signals. Therefore, it is crucial that signal processing techniques for monitoring changes in structural vibration responses are robust during the process of damage localization, quantification, and detection.

The diversity of signals requires the adoption of correspondingly diverse processing techniques based on their specific characteristics, and for a particular signal, a so-called powerful signal technique is one that is appropriately adapted. For example, linear signals satisfy the superposition principle and can thus be analyzed using linear processing techniques such as linear filters and Fourier transforms. Nonlinear signals, however, do not satisfy the superposition principle, and they require nonlinear processing techniques such as nonlinear filters and Hilbert–Huang transforms to reveal their complex characteristics. Directly applying a highly powerful linear signal processing model cannot guarantee perfect representation of nonlinear signals. Therefore, in the process of studying nonlinear signal processing models, new and specific technologies are often required.

In mechanical systems and structures, due to the complexity of operating conditions, external environmental interference, and the gradual aging and damage of materials and components, the collected signals are often non-stationary and nonlinear. These non-stationary and nonlinear signals contain rich state information, such as vibrations, stresses, and strains, which can reflect the health status of mechanical systems and structures. Therefore, signal processing techniques in the field of structural health require the integration of time-domain, frequency-domain, and time–frequency-domain characteristics to provide a more comprehensive understanding of the nature of signals and improve the accuracy of diagnosis.

In recent years, researchers have made unremitting efforts to achieve precise processing of signals in the field of structural health monitoring (SHM), particularly for non-stationary and nonlinear signals. The emergence of non-parametric time–frequency analysis techniques, such as short-time Fourier transform (STFT), wavelet transform (WT), and Wigner–Ville distribution (WVD), has found widespread application in SHM. These techniques can simultaneously provide information about signals in both the time and frequency domains, aiding in the development of a more comprehensive understanding of signal characteristics. However, these techniques have their limitations, such as the trade-off between time resolution and frequency resolution in STFT, the sensitivity of WT to the choice of basis functions, and the cross-term and noise sensitivity issues in WVD.

To address these issues, adaptive signal processing techniques have emerged. Empirical mode decomposition (EMD) and its optimized models (e.g., ensemble EMD (EEMD) and multivariate EMD (MEEMD)) decompose signals into a series of intrinsic mode functions (IMFs) through an iterative process, with each IMF representing a natural oscillation mode in the signal. This method excels in processing nonlinear and non-stationary signals but also faces challenges in practical applications, such as endpoint effects and energy non-conservation.

Furthermore, variational mode decomposition (VMD) and its variants (e.g., sparse VMD (SVMD) and adaptive VMD (AVMD)) achieve signal decomposition by minimizing a variational problem, offering higher flexibility and stability. The optimized model, empirical wavelet transform, combines the adaptive decomposition concept of EMD with the compact support framework of wavelet transform theory. By decomposing the signal into multiple frequency bands and constructing wavelet functions compatible with a wavelet filter bank for each band, it achieves adaptive decomposition of the signal. This approach can capture local features of the signal and is particularly suitable for processing nonlinear and non-stationary signals.

The latest technology, deconvolution techniques such as minimum entropy deconvolution (MED) and maximum correlated kurtosis deconvolution (MCKD), enhance signal fault features through filtering processing, improving diagnostic accuracy. These techniques can be regarded as a method of adaptive signal processing. In the deconvolution process, it is often necessary to estimate the point spread function (PSF) or convolution kernel of the signal, a process that typically relies on adaptive algorithms like the expectation–maximization (EM) algorithm or blind deconvolution algorithms. These algorithms can automatically adjust parameters based on observed data and prior knowledge in order to optimize the deconvolution effect. The combination of deconvolution with the aforementioned adaptive and non-parametric time–frequency analyses elevates signal processing techniques to a new level.

This paper aims to review key signal processing techniques in SHM, particularly non-parametric time–frequency analysis, adaptive decomposition, and deconvolution techniques, as shown in Figure 1. The first section introduces non-parametric time–frequency analysis. It begins by presenting the concept, applications, advantages, and disadvantages of STFT and discussing its widespread use in SHM. It then elaborates on the basic principles of WT, application examples, and its advantages and disadvantages compared to STFT. Furthermore, this paper delves into the application of WVD in time–frequency analysis, including its definition, specific application cases in SHM, and the advantages of high time resolution and instantaneous frequency analysis, while also pointing out the limitations of cross-terms and noise sensitivity. The second section introduces adaptive time–frequency analysis, detailing the principles, applications, and advantages and disadvantages of EMD and its optimized models (e.g., EEMD, MEEMD), emphasizing EMD's unique advantages for processing nonlinear and non-stationary signals. Additionally, it explores the concepts and applications of VMD and its variants (e.g., SVMD, AVMD) and compares VMD with traditional methods, highlighting it's flexibility and stability in signal decomposition. The final section discusses deconvolution techniques, examining the applications of deconvolution techniques such as MED and MCKD in machinery fault diagnosis and analyzing their advantages and disadvantages. This paper aims to provide researchers in the SHM field with a comprehensive understanding of signal processing techniques and to serve as a reference for future research.

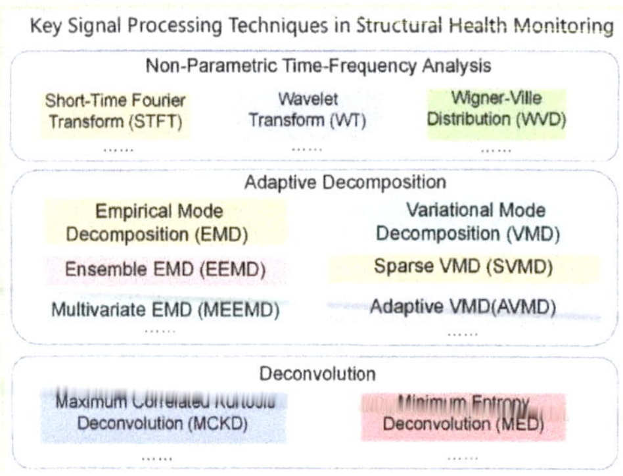

Figure 1. Key signal processing techniques in structural health monitoring.

2. Non-Parameterized Time–Frequency Analysis

This section introduces three representative examples of non-parameterized time–frequency analysis: the short-time Fourier transform, wavelet transform, and Wigner–Ville distribution. Each method will be systematically examined in terms of its definition, practical applications, and strengths and weaknesses to provide a comprehensive understanding of its role in signal processing.

2.1. Short-Time Fourier Transform

This subsection will introduce the definition, applications, as well as the advantages and disadvantages of short-time Fourier transform.

2.1.1. Definition

The short-time Fourier transform (STFT) provides a local time–frequency analysis by sliding a window function over the signal and performing Fourier transforms segment by segment. The definition is as follows:

1. Continuous-Time Signal: For a continuous signal $x(t)$, the STFT is defined as

$$X(\tau, f) = \int_{-\infty}^{\infty} x(t)\, w(t-\tau)\, e^{-j2\pi ft}\, dt \tag{1}$$

   where τ is the time position parameter, indicating the center of the window function; f is the frequency variable; and $w(t-\tau)$ is the window function (such as a rectangular window or Hamming window), used to extract a local segment of the signal around time τ [3].

2. Discrete-Time Signal: For a discrete signal $x[n]$, the discrete form of the STFT is

$$X[m,k] = \sum_{n=-\infty}^{\infty} x[n]\, w[n-m]\, e^{-j\frac{2\pi kn}{N}} \tag{2}$$

   where m is the discrete time frame index. k is the discrete frequency index. N is the length of the window function or the number of FFT points. $w[n-m]$ is the discrete window function, which slides with m.

Key Points

- Time–Frequency Analysis: The STFT divides the signal into short segments, and each segment is transformed into the frequency domain via Fourier transform to reveal how frequency components vary over time.

- Role of the Window Function: It restricts the signal to a local time segment, balancing time resolution and frequency resolution (the narrower the window, the higher the time resolution and the lower the frequency resolution).

2.1.2. Application

First, the integration with classical models elevates their performance to a higher level while better aligning with signal characteristics. For instance, a method that first processes the signal using STFT and further integrates it with Google-Net CNN [4] demonstrated in its experimental results that this innovation not only enhances the accuracy of signal processing but also effectively reduces the false alarm rate. Another study significantly improved diagnostic accuracy by combining STFT with CNN [5]. These achievements fully showcase the unique advantages of STFT in enhancing signal processing performance.

Furthermore, significant breakthroughs have been made in optimizing the time–frequency resolution of STFT. The introduction of the ASTFT–CMGW–FVVA method [6], which employs multi-window techniques and linear frequency modulation Gaussian windows, notably improves time–frequency resolution, enabling more refined signal analysis. Meanwhile, the integration of STFT into models has played a pivotal role in bearing health assessment and enhancing the time resolution of PET detectors. An autoencoder modeling approach based on STFT and ensemble strategies [7] effectively extracts deep vibration features of bearings. Another study combined STFT with residual neural networks [8], significantly improving time-of-flight estimation and coincidence time resolution for PET detectors.

STFT also plays a crucial role in sparse representation and synchrosqueezing transforms. By combining these techniques with STFT, researchers have achieved optimized signal processing and applications [9]. This innovation not only expands the application scope of STFT but also introduces new ideas and methods to the field of signal processing. Target localization algorithms represent another important area of STFT application. Researchers have proposed an improved target localization algorithm based on STFT [10], and it significantly enhances the accuracy of target instantaneous frequency estimation and localization by dynamically adjusting the window function and introducing a new distribution estimator.

Beyond the aforementioned applications, STFT also plays a vital role in signal processing decomposition, linear axis misalignment diagnosis, and train wheel anomaly detection. A decomposition method based on STFT [11] was shown to improve the time and frequency resolution of signal processing. Another study, based on servo motor current data and an STFT-based linear axis misalignment diagnosis method [12], had the aim of diagnosing faults without using sensors and external data collection systems but rather by capturing motor current data from the servo motor of the machine. Additionally, a train wheel anomaly detection method using STFT and unsupervised learning algorithms [13] was shown to effectively monitor wheel health. Furthermore, STFT has been applied to analyze multi-time scale variations [14], further expanding its application scope.

Notably, researchers have also conducted innovative studies by combining STFT with fractal theory and the uncertainty principle. They have investigated the fractal uncertainty principle of STFT and Gaussian windows [15] and explored its application in discrete Gaussian Gabor multipliers. This innovation not only provides new perspectives and methods for STFT research but also brings new insights to the study of fractal theory and the uncertainty principle.

Some researchers have introduced ST-QPFT and studied the fundamental properties and uncertainty inequalities of STFT, contributing to the field of short-time quadratic-phase Fourier transforms [16]. Another study proposed the FrFTSG method related to short-time fractional Fourier transforms [11], improving the time and frequency resolution of signal processing.

2.1.3. Strength and Weakness

- High-resolution and efficient computation
- Window effect and time–frequency trade-off

First, STFT provides excellent time–frequency resolution, allowing signals to be represented in detail in both the time and frequency domains. This is particularly crucial for structural health monitoring, as the response signals of structures often exhibit non-stationary characteristics when subjected to external excitations or internal damages. Traditional Fourier transform methods are ineffective in processing such non-stationary signals, whereas STFT can accurately capture the temporal variations in signals, providing a solid basis for structural health assessment.

Second, STFT is computationally efficient. Compared to other time–frequency analysis methods, STFT has relatively low complexity, enabling it to play a significant role in real-time applications. In structural health monitoring systems, real-time performance is a key indicator, as the timely and accurate detection of structural damages is vital for ensuring structural safety. The efficiency of STFT enables it to meet this requirement, providing strong support for real-time structural health monitoring.

However, the short-time Fourier transform also has some limitations in signal processing within the field of structural health monitoring:

One notable drawback is the window effect. The analysis results of STFT are highly dependent on the choice and length of the window function. In structural health monitoring, different window functions and lengths may lead to variations in time–frequency resolution, thereby affecting the accuracy of damage identification. Therefore, careful consideration is needed when selecting the window function and length to ensure consistent and accurate analysis results. Another key limitation is the inherent trade-off between time and frequency resolution. Due to the characteristics of the windowing process in STFT, it cannot achieve optimal resolution in both the time and frequency domains simultaneously. According to the Nyquist sampling theory, larger windows give higher frequency resolution but lower time resolution, and vice versa for shorter windows. In structural health monitoring, certain types of damage may exhibit rapidly changing characteristics, requiring time–frequency analysis methods to capture high-frequency components of signals within short periods. However, the performance of STFT in this aspect may be limited, leading to inaccurate identification of certain rapidly changing damage features.

Furthermore, STFT struggles to accurately capture the time–frequency features of highly non-stationary signals, especially those with abrupt or transient components. In structural health monitoring, certain types of damage may cause abrupt or transient changes in signals, requiring time–frequency analysis methods to sensitively capture these changes. However, STFT may have deficiencies in this regard, leading to inaccurate identification of certain damage features.

To address these limitations, STFT often needs to be combined with complementary methods, such as wavelet transforms or adaptive time–frequency techniques. These methods can compensate for the shortcomings of STFT in terms of time–frequency resolution and the capture of abrupt signals, improving its performance in complex signal analysis scenarios. Despite these challenges, STFT remains a fundamental and widely used time–frequency analysis tool. Owing to its advantages of simplicity, efficiency, and broad applicability, it plays a significant role in signal processing within the field of structural health monitoring.

2.2. *Wavelet Transform*

This subsection will introduce the definition, applications, as well as the advantages and disadvantages of wavelet transform.

2.2.1. Definition

Wavelet transform is a time–frequency analysis method used to analyze the local characteristics of non-stationary signals. Different from Fourier transform, wavelet transform represents the signal through a set of scalable and shiftable wavelet functions and is thereby able to provide simultaneous high-resolution analysis in time and frequency domains. Wavelet transform can be divided into continuous wavelet transform (CWT) and discrete wavelet transform (DWT). The former is mainly used for signal analysis, while the latter is often used in signal compression and feature extraction.

2.2.2. Application

The number of research papers on wavelet transform-related topics far exceeds that of similar signal processing models. Moreover, a large number of optimized models based on DWT have emerged. One such method is the identification of homologous acoustic emission signals based on synchrosqueezing wavelet transform coherence (SWTC). This method aims to improve the accuracy of identifying homologous acoustic emission signals in structural health monitoring, thereby enhancing the precision of damage localization [17]. Additionally, an unsupervised tunnel damage identification method based on convolutional variational autoencoder (CVAE) and wavelet packet analysis has been proposed, with experimental results validating its efficiency and accuracy [18].

The integration of wavelet analysis with deep learning models has led to a new breakthrough. SWT [19] represents an innovative approach for bearing fault diagnosis, which combines wavelet packet transform with convolutional neural networks and further optimizes network parameters through a simulated annealing algorithm. The Swin residual network (WSRN) based on multi-level discrete wavelet transform has been employed to reconstruct continuously missing data [20]. By replacing the traditional sampling layers with multi-level DWT, this approach significantly enhances the recovery of weak signals and the extraction of multi-scale features, thereby greatly improving the accuracy of data reconstruction.

In the field of structural health monitoring, DWT has proven to be a powerful tool. However, its accuracy heavily relies upon the selected wavelet basis function and the number of vanishing moments, posing significant challenges in practical applications. To address this issue, one method [21] cleverly combines statistical properties with DWT, markedly improving the accuracy of steel beam crack identification.

2.2.3. Strength and Weakness

- Time–frequency localization and flexible multi-scale analysis
- Challenges in selecting wavelet basis and parameters

The application of wavelet transform in the field of structural health monitoring (SHM) presents multiple advantages and disadvantages, with its strengths being particularly prominent: First, wavelets exhibit excellent time–frequency localization characteristics. This property enables wavelet transform to perform high-resolution analysis simultaneously in both the time and frequency domains, providing a unique advantage for processing non-stationary signals. In SHM, structural responses are often influenced by various factors, resulting in non-stationary signals. Wavelet transform can therefore more accurately capture the changing features of these signals, providing strong support for structural condition assessment. Second, wavelets facilitate multi-scale analysis. By adjusting the scale and position of the wavelet function, signals can be decomposed at different scales, thereby extracting hierarchical features. These features can reflect damage conditions and performance changes in the structure at different scales, providing rich information for SHM and damage identification. Furthermore, the flexibility of wavelets is another significant advantage. The diversity of wavelet basis functions allows for the selection of appropriate wavelet bases for transformation based on specific signal types and requirements. In the field of SHM, different structural types and damage forms may require different wavelet bases to better represent signal characteristics, and the flexibility of wavelets satisfies this need.

Notably, the discrete wavelet transform (DWT) possesses high computational efficiency. This characteristic gives wavelet transform significant potential for real-time SHM. Especially in signal compression and feature extraction, DWT can efficiently process large amounts of data, providing rapid and accurate analysis results for the online monitoring of structures and generation of damage warnings.

However, application of wavelet transform to the field of SHM also faces some challenges. First, the selection of wavelet basis functions is crucial. Different wavelet basis functions have significant impacts on analysis results, necessitating professional knowledge and insight to choose the appropriate ones. Regarding signal characteristics, it is necessary to fully take into account features such as the singularity, frequency components, and non-stationarity of the signal. Meanwhile, task requirements also play a decisive role. Different application scenarios, such as denoising, feature extraction, or fault location, impose diverse demands on wavelet bases. Additionally, the inherent properties of wavelet bases, including compact support, symmetry, vanishing moments, and regularity, are important factors that cannot be overlooked during the selection process. Common wavelet bases each have their own characteristics and applicable scopes. The Daubechies wavelet (dbN) exhibits compact support and high-order vanishing moments, enabling it to keenly capture the local singularities of signals. It performs remarkably well in the vibration signal analysis of mechanical faults in components like bearings and gears, and it has a distinct advantage in detecting transient signals (such as impact pulses). The Symlet wavelet (symN) is approximately symmetric, making it suitable for processing non-stationary signals. It plays a significant role in the early fault detection of rotor cracks and gears, and it can effectively preserve the phase information of signals during the signal decomposition process. As a continuous wavelet, the Morlet wavelet is widely applied in time–frequency analysis and is especially suitable for early fault detection, particularly the extraction of weak fault signals. It also offers high resolution for non-stationary signals. The Haar wavelet is characterized by simplicity and high computational efficiency. Although it has a low-order vanishing moment, it is applicable for rapid fault detection and the detection of signal mutation points. However, its resolution ability for complex fault signals is relatively weak. In practical applications, experts in the field of SHM need to make careful selections based on specific circumstances.

Second, the choice of parameters in wavelet transform (such as scale and position) has a substantial influence on the results. However, a rigorous methodology for this process is currently lacking. This may lead to instability and inaccuracy in analysis results, necessitating further research and exploration to refine this method. Finally, the sensitivity of wavelets to noise is also a concern for their application. In SHM, signals are often contaminated with noise due to environmental noise and measurement errors. Wavelet transform may face interference from noise when processing these noisy signals, leading to distorted analysis results. Therefore, complementary denoising techniques need to be integrated to mitigate the impact of noise on analysis results and improve the accuracy and reliability of wavelet transform in SHM.

2.3. Wigner–Ville Distribution

In this chapter, we will explore the definition of Wigner–Ville distribution and its applications in various scenarios, and we will analyze both its strengths and weaknesses.

2.3.1. Definition

The Wigner–Ville distribution (WVD) is a sophisticated time–frequency analysis technique employed to examine the time–frequency properties of non-stationary signals. It offers a means to simultaneously visualize both temporal and spectral information by transforming the signal into the time–frequency domain. The WVD is formally defined as follows:

$$\mathcal{W}_x(t,f) = \int_{-\infty}^{\infty} \mathbf{x}\left(t+\frac{\tau}{2}\right)\mathbf{x}^*\left(t-\frac{\tau}{2}\right)e^{-j2\pi f\tau}d\tau \tag{3}$$

where $x(t)$ is the input signal, $*$ is the complex conjugation, and t and f are the time and frequency variables, respectively.

2.3.2. Application

From traditional signal processing, to the enhancement of deep learning models, and further to integration with other advanced technologies such as dynamic mode decomposition (DMD), variational mode decomposition (VMD), and convolutional neural networks (CNNs), the applications of the WVD in the field of structural health continue to expand. These applications not only improve the accuracy and efficiency of signal processing but also provide more comprehensive and accurate data support for SHM. Ref. [22] employs the smoothed pseudo Wigner–Ville distribution (SPWVD) to enhance deep learning models. The DMD-WVD method [23] combines dynamic mode decomposition with the Wigner–Ville distribution to eliminate cross-terms.

The introduction of the quadratic chirp-scaled Wigner distribution (QSWD) [24] further enhances the advantages of signal detection. In combination with other deep learning models, time–frequency analysis methods for partial discharge signals based on VMD and WVD [25] have emerged, and the WVD has been integrated with CNNs for classification [26], specifically applied to composite material damage classification methods [27]. Additionally, there are methods based on the polynomial Wigner–Ville distribution [28], hybrid Wigner–Ville distributions defined in the octonion domain [29], and other innovative technical approaches that provide new ideas and methods for SHM.

The development of the WVD in the field of structural health is also reflected in the depth of theoretical research. Researchers have not only conducted in-depth studies on the WVD itself but have also combined it with other mathematical and physical theories to explore its application potential in SHM. For example, study of the uncertainty principle of the coupled fractional Wigner–Ville distribution (CFrWVD) [30] helps us to better understand the behavior of the WVD in complex signal analysis; combination of the WVD with theories such as the quaternion linear canonical transform (QOLCT) [31] also provides new perspectives and methods for signal processing. The emergence of the WVD in special mathematical domains, such as the study of the interaction between the two-dimensional hypercomplex WVD and the quadratic-phase Fourier transform [23], is also noteworthy.

2.3.3. Strength and Weakness

- High time–frequency resolution and energy concentration
- Precision in instantaneous frequency analysis
- Mathematical completeness and cross-term interference

The advantages of the Wigner–Ville distribution (WVD) in structural health signal processing are evident.

First, it possesses high time–frequency resolution and energy concentration [32]. The WVD directly reflects the distribution of signal energy in the time–frequency plane through the Fourier transform of the instantaneous correlation function, without the constraints of a window function, thereby breaking through the limitations of time–frequency resolution imposed by the short-time Fourier transform (STFT) and wavelet transform. For single-component linear frequency-modulated signals, such as the impulse response generated by structural damage, the time–frequency energy concentration of the WVD reaches theoretical optimality, enabling clear capture of high-frequency transient components, such as nonlinear vibrations resulting from crack propagation or bolt loosening [33].

Furthermore, it exhibits precision in instantaneous frequency analysis [1]. The quadratic nature of the WVD allows it to directly represent changes in the instantaneous frequency of a signal, such as the time-varying characteristics of structural modal frequencies or frequency modulation phenomena in nonlinear vibrations. Compared to linear time–frequency methods (e.g., STFT), the WVD offers higher accuracy in the analysis of frequency-hopping signals and rapid frequency changes.

Additionally, it is characterized by mathematical completeness and information richness. The WVD satisfies the marginal conditions (the integrals of time and frequency energy equal the total signal energy) and possesses phase shift invariance. The Fourier transform of its autocorrelation function can be directly used for modal parameter identification and damage localization. Moreover, the real-valued nature of the WVD simplifies the physical interpretation of the energy density distribution, making it suitable for energy decay analysis in structural health monitoring. Finally, it demonstrates adaptability as a non-parametric method. The WVD does not require pre-assuming a signal model, making it suitable for extracting unknown damage features under complex operating conditions. For example, in composite material delamination damage monitoring, the WVD can adaptively analyze the time–frequency characteristics of nonlinear acoustic emission signals without relying on a preset damage model [26,33].

Of course, the WVD has limitations and challenges. First, there is the interference of cross-terms [25]. The bilinear nature of the WVD leads to the generation of spurious cross-terms in the time–frequency distribution of multicomponent signals (such as multi-mode vibrations or environmental noise interference). These cross-terms can obscure real damage features, potentially leading to misjudgment, especially in the presence of multiple coexisting types of damage or highly noisy environments.

Second, there is the issue of non-positivity of energy and ambiguity in physical meaning. Although the WVD is a real-valued distribution, its energy density may exhibit negative values, conflicting with the concept of energy in a physical sense and limiting its application in quantitative energy analysis, such as damage severity assessment.

Finally, there are limitations in computational complexity and real-time performance. The high resolution of the WVD relies on instantaneous correlation calculations over the entire data length, leading to low processing efficiency for long time series signals (such as long-term structural monitoring data) and making it difficult to meet real-time monitoring requirements.

3. Adaptive Time–Frequency Analysis

This section introduces adaptive time–frequency analysis, including three key methodologies and their optimization models: empirical mode decomposition (EMD), variational mode decomposition (VMD), and empirical wavelet transform (EWT). Each method and its associated optimization framework will be systematically analyzed from three perspectives: definition, practical applications, and strengths and weaknesses. This comparative examination aims to clarify their theoretical foundations, implementation challenges, and suitability for diverse signal processing scenarios.

3.1. Empirical Mode Decomposition and Optimization Models

This subsection explores different variants of EMD, including Empirical Mode Decomposition, Ensemble Empirica, and Multivariate Ensemble Empirical Mode Decomposition, highlighting their unique features, applications, and the underlying theoretical foundations.

3.1.1. Empirical Mode Decomposition

Definition

Empirical mode decomposition (EMD), proposed by Huang et al. [34], is an adaptive signal processing method that decomposes a signal into a set of intrinsic mode functions (IMFs), each representing a natural oscillation mode in the signal. The EMD method extracts different frequency components from the signal through an iterative process based on the signal's local characteristic time scale.

An IMF, which is the basic function obtained during the EMD decomposition process, must satisfy the following two conditions: (1) Relationship between the number of extrema and the number of zero-crossings: They must be equal or differ by at most one. (2) Mean of the local envelope: At any point, the mean of the envelope defined by the local maxima and minima is zero [35]. It is worth noting that IMFs are determined by the signal itself rather than predefined kernel functions, making EMD an adaptive signal processing method.

The formula for the EMD method can be expressed as

$$x(t) = \sum_{i=1}^{N} C_i(t) + R(t) \quad (4)$$

where

- $x(t)$ is the original signal,
- $C_i(t)$ is the i-th IMF,
- $R(t)$ is the residual term, representing the part of the signal not decomposed into IMFs,
- N is the number of IMFs.

Application

In recent years, researchers have applied empirical mode decomposition (EMD) in conjunction with various network models.

A multitude of methods have emerged for sequence prediction by integrating EMD with neural networks. Typically, EMD is used to decompose signals into modal functions, which are then analyzed using classical networks. One approach combines EMD with long short-term memory neural networks to estimate the state of health (SOH) and predict the remaining useful life (RUL) of lithium-ion batteries. EMD is utilized to decompose the voltage signals of lithium-ion batteries and extract intrinsic mode functions (IMFs). These IMFs are then processed by an LSTM network to predict the battery's SOH and RUL [36]. Another method involves a model that combines EMD with gated recurrent unit (GRU) neural networks. EMD is used to decompose time series data and extract IMFs, which are subsequently processed by a GRU network to enhance prediction accuracy and robustness [37]. Additionally, there is a predictive model that combines EMD with least squares support vector regression (LSSVR). EMD is used to decompose time series data and extract IMFs and residuals, which are then individually predicted by LSSVR. The final prediction is obtained by aggregating these individual predictions [38]. Furthermore, a hybrid model that integrates three classical models—EMD, LSTM, and autoregressive incorporated moving average (ARIMA)—is used for wind speed prediction. EMD is used to decompose wind speed data and extract IMFs, LSTM processes the time series data, and ARIMA captures the linear trends in the data. The overall model improves prediction accuracy and stability [39].

Moreover, research on noise reduction methods is also making progress. One noise reduction method combines uniform-phase empirical mode decomposition (MUPEMD) with a genetic algorithm–dynamic zero-phase interval filtering algorithm (GA-DZPIF) to improve the processing efficiency of ship-radiated noise signals and mitigate modal aliasing issues. MUPEMD is used to decompose the signals, while GA-DZPIF is used to filter the single-mode components, with structural similarity (SSIM) being used as an evaluation metric [40]. Additionally, a method based on improved ensemble noise reconstruction empirical mode decomposition (IENEMD) and adaptive threshold denoising (ATD) has been proposed. This method combines IENEMD and ATD to extract weak fault features of rolling bearings. IENEMD is used to decompose the signals, while ATD is used for denoising. The effectiveness and robustness of this method have been verified through simulation experiments and practical cases [41].

Furthermore, Guo Junyu et al. have proposed a hybrid scheme for rolling bearing fault prediction based on empirical mode decomposition (EMD) and kernel principal component analysis (PCA). This hybrid scheme combines complete ensemble empirical mode decomposition with multiscale interpolation (CEEMD-MsI) and PCA to construct a nonlinear health indicator, and it uses a dual-channel transformer network and convolutional block attention module to extract multi-domain features for rolling bearing fault prediction [42].

Strength and Weakness

- No need to preset the number of modes or frequency ranges
- Capable of capturing complex patterns and transient features

Empirical mode decomposition (EMD) is the most classic adaptive time–frequency analysis technique. Compared to the aforementioned non-parametric dependent time–frequency analysis techniques, it can decompose signals based on their inherent characteristics without the need to preset the number of modes or frequency ranges. This method is particularly suitable for processing signals with complex nonlinear and multiscale characteristics. Furthermore, the decomposition process of EMD is driven by data iteration, based on the local maxima and minima of the signal. During this process, the signal is naturally decomposed into a series of intrinsic mode functions (IMFs) without the need for additional prior knowledge or model parameter adjustments.

Compared with traditional Fourier transform and wavelet transform, the mode-mixing phenomenon in EMD is reduced. Each IMF represents a local manifestation of the signal within a specific frequency range. Although they are not completely orthogonal, they ensure a certain degree of frequency–time resolution of the signal. In terms of handling boundary effects, EMD has also undergone certain optimizations. By specially processing the signal boundaries, the influence of boundary effects on the decomposition results is reduced. In contrast, the aforementioned time–frequency analysis methods may encounter issues such as reduced resolution or spectrum leakage at signal boundaries. Additionally, the IMFs obtained after EMD decomposition can be reconstructed through simple addition operations with high reconstruction accuracy. This characteristic gives EMD advantages in applications such as signal denoising, feature extraction, and pattern recognition. It is particularly noteworthy that EMD is especially suitable for processing nonlinear and non-stationary signals and is capable of capturing complex patterns and transient features in the signal. In contrast, Wavelet transform and short-time Fourier transform may require more complex multiscale analysis when processing nonlinear signals.

Finally, regarding the adaptability of EMD, it can process any type of signal, including process control [43,44], modeling [45,46], surface engineering, wind speed prediction [47], system identification [48], bearing diagnosis [49], etc. This excellent adaptability makes its application versatile.

Of course, as the most basic adaptive time–frequency analysis technique, EMD still has much room for improvement. Its disadvantages include endpoint effects and energy non-conservation, which are inherent to the EMD algorithm itself. Since IMFs are not strictly orthogonal, the total energy of the decomposed IMFs may not match the energy of the original signal, leading to energy non-conservation in some cases. For example, in the study by Yaguo Lei [35], simulations and analyses of IMFs revealed distortions at both ends of the IMFs, and the decomposition results also exhibited distortions at both ends. Mode mixing, although less severe than in traditional methods, remains an issue, with single IMFs containing oscillations of different scales, or oscillations of similar scales being distributed across different IMFs. This is caused by the intermittency of the signal. As stated by Huang et al. [34], intermittency can lead to severe mixing of time–frequency distributions, making the physical meaning of individual IMFs ambiguous.

3.1.2. Ensemble Empirical Mode Decomposition

Definition

Ensemble empirical mode decomposition (EEMD) is an improved method of empirical mode decomposition designed to address the mode mixing issue that may arise when EMD processes signals. EEMD adds white noise of a certain amplitude to the signal to be analyzed and performs multiple EMD decompositions, which are then averaged to obtain more stable and accurate intrinsic mode functions. EEMD retains the adaptive characteristics of EMD, enabling decomposition based on the local characteristic time scales of the signal itself.

Application

Researchers have adopted data-driven models such as EEMD-RF, EEMD-ANN, and EEMD-GBM for precise prediction and conducted sensitivity analyses to understand model behavior [50]. Another study employed a method that combined EEMD with SVM [51]. Similarly, the W-EEMD-ARIMA model achieved the same objective [52]. A method using the EEMD-ANN model for prediction has been proposed, aiming to address inherent challenges in prediction, such as difficulties in model construction, low prediction accuracy, and high computational intensity [53].

EEMD exhibits good denoising performance. The effectiveness of the EEMD-based denoising method proposed in [54] was compared with various wavelet transform-based threshold denoising methods, demonstrating the potential of EEMD in signal denoising applications. A study combined the EEMD–independent component analysis (ICA) method to effectively remove artifacts [55]. Furthermore, several innovative models and applications have emerged. For example, an ensemble empirical mode decomposition–temporal convolutional network (EEMD-TCN) machine learning method has been employed in relevant research [56].

Strength and Weakness

- Alleviates the mode mixing issue by adding Gaussian white noise
- Residual noise contamination and energy non-conservation

Ensemble empirical mode decomposition (EEMD), as an enhanced version of classical empirical mode decomposition (EMD), demonstrates unique application value in structural health signal processing while facing several limitations that require urgent resolution. Its core advantage lies in effectively alleviating the mode mixing issue caused by signal intermittency in traditional EMD through multiple additions of Gaussian white noise to the original signal and ensemble averaging. For instance, in the analysis of bridge vibration signals with multiple damage sources, EEMD can separate high-frequency transient components from crack propagation and low-frequency modulated signals from bolt loosening into distinct intrinsic mode functions (IMFs), significantly improving the accuracy of damage feature extraction. This noise-assisted mechanism not only enhances decomposition stability but also preserves EMD's adaptability, enabling it to process nonlinear, non-stationary signals, such as acoustic emission signals from composite material delamination or dynamic structural responses under seismic excitation, without predefined basis functions. Furthermore, the decomposed IMFs possess clear multi-scale physical meanings: high-frequency components typically correspond to transient features of localized structural damage (e.g., impact components in early-stage gearbox faults), while low-frequency components reflect global structural vibration modes, providing reliable references for the early detection of fatigue cracks in wind turbine blades [57].

However, the engineering application of EEMD still faces multiple challenges. First, its performance heavily depends on manually set noise intensity and decomposition iterations. Improper parameter selection may lead to signal features being obscured by noise or incomplete modal separation. For example, in rail crack monitoring, excessive noise amplitude settings could contaminate high-frequency IMFs related to damage, compromising diagnostic accuracy. Second, the algorithm's computational complexity increases significantly, with single decomposition time approximately a hundredfold that of EMD, limiting real-time processing capabilities for massive datasets in long-term monitoring scenarios such as bridges and dams. Although boundary distortion in IMFs caused by end effects can be partially mitigated through mirror extension or local mean prediction (e.g., the OFCEEMDAN algorithm), signal anomalies under extreme operating conditions may still interfere with envelope fitting precision. Additionally, residual noise contamination from repeated noise additions and energy non-conservation in IMFs might affect the reliability of quantitative damage assessment, necessitating post-processing optimization through wavelet threshold denoising or energy compensation algorithms.

To address these limitations, current research focuses on improvements from two dimensions: algorithm optimization and engineering implementation. Regarding noise-assisted strategies, complementary ensemble empirical mode decomposition (CEEMD) reduces residual noise while preserving modal separation advantages through symmetric positive–negative noise pair addition, significantly enhancing signal-to-noise ratio. Adaptive parameter adjustment methods dynamically optimize noise amplitude based on signal entropy or energy distribution, reducing manual intervention requirements. The introduction of hardware acceleration technologies provides new pathways for real-time breakthroughs—for instance, GPU-based parallel computing can improve long-sequence signal processing efficiency by 5–8 times, while the development of FPGA-embedded modules meets low-power demands for field monitoring equipment. Multi-sensor fusion strategies further expand EEMD's application boundaries. Multivariate EEMD achieves cross-scale feature extraction in composite damage diagnosis of wind turbine blades through joint analysis of multi-physical field data (vibration, acoustic emission, and fiber optic sensing), with false alarm rates reduced to below 3%.

3.1.3. Multivariate Ensemble Empirical Mode Decomposition

Definition

Multivariate ensemble empirical mode decomposition (MEEMD) is an improved method of empirical modal decomposition. It evenly distributes the extrema of the signal by adding pairs of positive and negative Gaussian white noise and reduces the number of spurious components through multiple trials. MEEMD not only inherits adaptability and the ability to address mode-mixing issues from ensemble empirical mode decomposition (EEMD), but it also further enhances the accuracy and stability of the decomposition by introducing a median operator.

The specific steps are as follows: (1) Adding Gaussian white noise: Pairs of positive and negative Gaussian white noise are added to the original signal, ensuring that the noise has a mean of zero and equal standard deviations. (2) Empirical modal decomposition: Multiple empirical modal decompositions are performed on the noise-added signal, with each decomposition yielding a series of intrinsic mode functions (IMFs) and a residual. (3) Median operation: A median operation is applied to the IMFs and residuals obtained from each decomposition to produce the final IMFs and residual.

Application

Multivariate ensemble empirical mode decomposition (MEEMD) effectively addresses the complexity and non-stationarity of signals by decomposing composite waves into distinct components, thereby facilitating the examination of their spatiotemporal heterogeneity and separation characteristics [58].

Research has also leveraged this attribute, employing MEEMD to manage the nonlinear and non-stationary nature of normalized difference vegetation index (NDVI) data, integrating MEEMD with the geographically and temporally weighted regression (GTWR) method [59].

Innovatively, MEEMD has been applied to non-destructive testing. By processing data obtained from pulsed thermography with MEEMD, signals of different frequency components can be separated. Due to the differences in thermal responses between defective and non-defective regions, the decomposition by MEEMD better highlights these discrepancies, thereby enabling non-destructive testing and enhancing the accuracy and reliability of detection [60]. A method combining MEEMD and Prony [61], wherein MEEMD decomposes the signal and introduces permutation entropy to detect randomness followed by the reconstruction of the remaining intrinsic mode function (IMF) components, has also made innovative progress.

Furthermore, MEEMD is extensively utilized for prediction [62]. A sequence prediction method based on the MEEMD–long short-term memory (LSTM) network model has been proposed. Another prediction approach employs a model based on MEEMD, LSTM, and multilayer perceptron (MLP) [63]. MEEMD initially decomposes the data, LSTM handles the dynamic changes in time series, and MLP models complex nonlinear relationships. The synergy of these three enhances prediction accuracy and stability under different conditions and data characteristics. A prediction model based on improved MEEMD and a quasi-affine transformation (QUATRE)-optimized bidirectional long short-term memory (BILSTM) network has also been developed. In this model, MEEMD processes photovoltaic output data to extract key features, QUATRE optimizes these features, and BILSTM captures forward and backward dependencies in time series data.

Simultaneously, MEEMD is applied to fault detection. A rotor fault detection method based on MEEMD energy entropy and an artificial neural network (ANN) has been developed. MEEMD decomposes the operational signals of the rotor and calculates energy entropy to construct a feature vector reflecting the energy distribution characteristics of the signal [64]. Another fault diagnosis method for reciprocating machinery based on improved MEEMD-SqueezeNet has also been proposed [65].

Researchers have further optimized MEEMD focusing on the crucial issue of noise in signal processing. To address the noise reduction problem in tunnel blasting vibration signals, a complete method based on MEEMD and least mean squares (LMS) has been developed. Additionally, a method combining MEEMD and singular value decomposition

(SVD) is used to remove noise from high slope deformation data. MEEMD is employed for the initial decomposition of high slope deformation data, and SVD further processes the decomposed matrix to effectively eliminate noise, fully preserving the intrinsic details of the deformation data and providing a more accurate basis for subsequent data analysis and processing [66].

Strength and Weakness

- Suppression of modal aliasing and fusion of multi-physical field signals
- Parameter sensitivity, residual noise, and endpoint effect
- Algorithm generalization and poor adaptability to extreme working conditions

On the one hand, MEEMD (multivariate ensemble empirical mode decomposition) possesses multiple advantages. First, it excels in mode mixing suppression and computational efficiency enhancement. By adopting a multivariate signal ensemble decomposition strategy and incorporating a median operator to integrate and average the decomposition results of multiple signal sets, MEEMD effectively reduces spurious components induced by the addition of random noise in EEMD (ensemble empirical mode decomposition).

Second, it enhances multi-physical field signal fusion and robustness. The multivariate signal ensemble nature of MEEMD enables it to process multi-channel sensor data simultaneously (such as vibration, acoustic emission, and fiber optic sensing). Through joint analysis of the time–frequency characteristics of signals from different physical fields, it strengthens its identification capability for complex damage patterns (such as the coexistence of composite delamination and metal fatigue). Experiments demonstrate that when applied to the diagnosis of composite damages in wind turbine blades, MEEMD can reduce the false alarm rate, significantly outperforming the single-channel EEMD method [67]. Furthermore, its adaptive noise bandwidth design dynamically adjusts to different signal characteristics (such as high-frequency transients or low-frequency slow variations), avoiding the masking of signal features by fixed-bandwidth noise. Additionally, computational cost optimization and real-time performance improvement are achieved. By optimizing the ensemble averaging strategy (for example, through stage-wise averaging instead of global averaging), MEEMD shortens the computation time while maintaining decomposition accuracy [68]. This improvement is particularly suitable for long-term health monitoring scenarios, such as dam deformation analysis or aerospace structural fatigue assessment.

The main technical challenges of MEEMD are as follows: First, parameter sensitivity and residual noise persistence. The performance of MEEMD still relies on a manually set noise bandwidth and number of ensemble trials. If the noise bandwidth is too wide, it may introduce high-frequency artifacts; if it is too narrow, then it may result in incomplete mode separation. For instance, in rail crack monitoring, improper noise parameter settings can contaminate damage-related high-frequency IMFs (intrinsic mode functions) with noise, reducing the signal-to-noise ratio [58]. Moreover, multiple overlays of limited-bandwidth noise may lead to the accumulation of low-frequency residual noise, necessitating post-processing with wavelet threshold denoising or energy compensation algorithms.

Second, endpoint effects can distort the decomposition results, and the method shows poor adaptability to extreme conditions, such as high-temperature or high-humidity environments where signals may be severely affected. Although MEEMD partially suppresses endpoint distortions through local mean prediction (such as the OFCEEMDAN algorithm), under extreme conditions of strong impact loads or abrupt signal amplitude changes (such as building responses during earthquakes), envelope fitting errors may still cause IMF boundary frequency shifts, affecting damage localization accuracy. Experiments indicate that modal energy leakage in such cases can reach a significant level, which may have a negative impact on the accuracy of signal decomposition. Third, hardware resource constraints and algorithm generalization limitations. The multi-channel data processing requirements of MEEMD significantly increase memory usage, posing challenges to the hardware resources of embedded devices (such as wireless sensor nodes). For example, when compared to standard FPGA-implemented modules implemented for single signal processing, FPGA-implemented MEEMD modules require an additional 20% of logic units for multi-signal synchronous processing, which limits their promotion in low-power scenarios [68]. Furthermore, the algorithm's generalization capability for non-stationary signals still needs verification; in particular, the decomposition stability under multi-physical field coupling (such as the combined effect of temperature and strain) has not been fully investigated.

3.2. Variational Mode Decomposition and Optimization Models

Variational mode decomposition (VMD) is a relatively new and powerful signal decomposition method. It formulates the decomposition problem as a variational optimization problem, enabling the extraction of multiple intrinsic mode components from a signal. In this subsection, we will discuss VMD in detail, including variational mode decomposition, successive variational mode decomposition, variational mode extraction, and adaptive variational mode decomposition. We will explore how these methods operate, their advantages in handling different types of signals, and their potential applications across various disciplines.

3.2.1. Variational Mode Decomposition

Definition

Variational mode decomposition (VMD) is a signal processing method proposed by Dragomiretskiy et al. in 2013 [65]. VMD decomposes a signal into several intrinsic mode functions (IMFs), each of which possesses a specific center frequency and bandwidth. The core idea of VMD is to achieve signal decomposition by minimizing the solution to a variational problem, ensuring that each IMF is as concentrated as possible within a certain frequency band [69].

Application

Variational mode decomposition (VMD) has demonstrated remarkable performance in machinery fault diagnosis, particularly in extracting fault features from rotating machinery such as bearings and gearboxes. By decomposing vibration signals, VMD effectively isolates fault characteristic frequencies and, when combined with methods like envelope spectrum analysis, achieves precise fault diagnosis. For instance, a method for estimating spalling size in rolling bearings based on signal processing techniques has been proposed [70]. Another example is a natural gas pipeline leak detection method based on optimized VMD and the ConvFormer model [71].

Furthermore, VMD has been applied to the prediction of structures such as bridges and buildings. For example, by decomposing the vibration response signals of structures, VMD can identify modal changes caused by damage, providing a basis for predictive assessment. To accommodate different prediction scenarios, researchers have also optimized the VMD model in various ways. One study introduced a thermal load time series decomposition and prediction model based on VMD and fast independent component analysis (FastICA) [72]. Another proposed a short-term offshore wind speed prediction method based on a hybrid VMD-PE-FCGRU model [73]. Additionally, a lithium-ion battery health state estimation method based on the MEWOA-VMD and Transformer architecture has been developed [74]. There is also a concrete dam displacement prediction model based on VMD, TSVR, and GRU [75]. In another approach, complex power load time series are decomposed into multiple relatively simple subsequences using VMD, and by integrating the ICSS algorithm, abrupt and irregular changes in the time series are identified and separated. Finally, neural networks in deep learning are used to predict these subsequences, and the final prediction results are obtained through ensemble learning, significantly improving the accuracy and stability of predictions [76].

VMD is also widely applied in signal denoising and feature extraction. Thanks to its inherent proficiency in handling noise, VMD excels in these applications. Moreover, researchers are dedicated to optimizing and upgrading VMD using innovative methods. One such method is a signal preprocessing approach based on VMD technology and sample entropy. This method decomposes milling robot response signals into multiple modal components using VMD and then calculates the sample entropy of each component to assess its complexity and irregularity. By setting appropriate thresholds, modal components containing amplitude and frequency modulation (AM-FM) harmonic components can be identified and eliminated, achieving the goals of denoising and signal optimization [77]. Another method combines VMD, empirical wavelet transform (EWT), and continuous wavelet transform (CWT) to improve the signal-to-noise ratio of acoustic signals and accurately detect pipeline leak locations. By analyzing and processing signals in different frequency domains, noise can be effectively suppressed, and useful information can be extracted, significantly enhancing the accuracy of leak detection [78].

A joint denoising method based on VMD parameter optimization has been proposed for removing noise from the acoustic signals of high-voltage shunt reactors [79]. This method integrates VMD, complete ensemble empirical mode decomposition with adaptive noise (CEEMDAN), and an improved continuous wavelet transform (ICWT) structure. The combination of these three methods allows for more effective noise removal from density logging data, improving data resolution and thin-layer identification accuracy [80]. An optimized VMD algorithm based on tunable diode laser absorption spectroscopy (TDLAS) has been developed for signal denoising [81]. A wavelet threshold function based on a combination of grey wolf optimization (GWO) and VMD has been proposed to address noise interference in ultrasonic echo signals [82]. An adaptive denoising and detrending method based on an improved seagull optimization algorithm (ISOA) and VMD has been developed for processing signals from nuclear circulating water pump impellers [83]. VMD can effectively remove trend components from signals, significantly improving the signal-to-noise ratio of nuclear circulating water pump impeller signals while preserving valuable information. Additionally, a photoacoustic spectroscopy second harmonic signal denoising method that utilizes the sparrow search algorithm (SSA) to optimize VMD combined with wavelet threshold denoising (WTD) technology has been proposed, and it improves the detection accuracy and real-time measurement stability of acetylene sensors [84].To enhance the performance of VMD, researchers have proposed various parameter optimization methods, such as adaptive parameter selection methods based on particle swarm optimization (PSO) and genetic algorithms. These methods automatically adjust VMD parameters, thereby improving decomposition accuracy and efficiency. A fault diagnosis method for electric valves in nuclear power plants based on a random forest model that integrates VMD, MDI, and ISSA has been proposed [85]. Another study introduced an ultrasonic machining vibration signal processing method based on SE, PSO, and VMD that improves signal processing efficiency by optimizing VMD parameters [86].

The pursuit of high anti-interference capability and precision in models is also a direction of model optimization. The complex variational mode decomposition (CVMD) algorithm has been proposed for analyzing complex-valued data [87]. VMD can also be used to decompose projectile signals [88], and by detecting the mathematical model of the skyscreen, the measurement accuracy of projectile muzzle velocity can be improved.

Compared to traditional methods, this algorithm has significant advantages in term of anti-interference capability and measurement accuracy.

Strength and Weakness

- Susceptible to the influences of noise and spurious components
- Stability and noise resistance
- Adaptability and parameter controllability
- Effective mitigation of mode mixing

First, VMD demonstrates a robust capacity to mitigate mode mixing. By integrating a regularization term within a variational optimization framework, VMD effectively curtails the occurrence of mode mixing, a pervasive challenge in signal decomposition, particularly when confronting nonlinear and non-stationary signals. Traditional approaches, exemplified by empirical mode decomposition (EMD), are prone to mode mixing due to the perturbations induced by local extrema points. In contrast, variational mode decomposition (VMD) dissects the signal into multiple narrowband mode components through the judicious application of frequency-domain constraints and bandwidth limitations, thereby significantly reducing the likelihood of mode mixing.

Second, VMD distinguishes itself through its adaptability and parameter controllability. It possesses the proficiency to adaptively determine the number of modes and frequency centers, obviating the necessity of relying on envelope calculations predicated at signal extrema points. This attribute endows VMD with heightened flexibility and precision in the processing of complex signals. For instance, within the context of structural health monitoring, VMD has the capability to dynamically adjust decomposition parameters in accordance with the idiosyncrasies of vibration signals, thereby facilitating the extraction of fault features with unparalleled accuracy. Moreover, while the parameters of VMD, such as the penalty factor and bandwidth constraint, necessitate manual calibration, their controllability opens up avenues for extensive optimization in signal processing.

Third, by formulating the signal decomposition as an optimization problem and achieving an optimal solution through iteration, VMD ensures algorithm stability and demonstrates strong noise resistance, effectively reducing noise-induced perturbations in decomposition results. For example, in the domain of bearing fault diagnosis, VMD adeptly isolates fault characteristic frequencies, preserving high decomposition accuracy even in noisy environments.

Conversely, VMD is not without its limitations in structural health signal processing. First, its efficacy is contingent upon the judicious selection of parameters. Despite its adaptive prowess, the performance of VMD is significantly influenced by the choice of parameters, including the penalty factor (α) and the number of modes (K). The determination of these parameters often necessitates empirical insight or refinement through optimization algorithms, thereby escalating the complexity and application challenge of the algorithm. For instance, in the analysis of acoustic emission signals emanating from centrifugal pump cavitation, inappropriate parameter configurations may engender inaccurate decomposition results, thereby impeding the extraction of fault features [89].

Second, VMD is encumbered by computational complexity and time costs. While its iterative optimization process ensures decomposition stability, it also imposes substantial computational demands. When confronted with prolonged signals or high-sampling-rate data, the computational onus of VMD escalates markedly, thereby constraining its applicability in real-time monitoring systems.

Finally, VMD is susceptible to the influences of noise and spurious components. Notwithstanding its noise resistance, decomposition results may still be corrupted in high-noise environments. Furthermore, the decomposition process of VMD may introduce spurious components, which not only exacerbate the complexity of signal processing but may also obscure genuine fault features.

3.2.2. Successive Variational Mode Decomposition

Definition

Successive variational mode decomposition (SVMD) is a signal decomposition method proposed by Nazari and Sakhaei [90] that does not require prior knowledge of the number of modes in the signal. Through an iterative optimization process, SVMD decomposes the signal into multiple intrinsic mode functions (IMFs), each representing a specific frequency component of the signal.

Application

Research on the underlying principles of self-adaptive variational mode decomposition (SVMD) has yielded comprehensive findings and in-depth insights [91]. One such method is the self-adjusting SVMD, which adaptively updates the mode number K and penalty parameter α based on the energy ratio and frequency-domain mode orthogonality, thereby addressing the issues of parameter selection and poor adaptability in the original variational mode decomposition (VMD). Ref. [90] introduces a novel signal decomposition approach termed continuous variational mode decomposition (also abbreviated as SVMD in this context) that obviates the need for prior knowledge of the number of signal modes and boasts lower computational complexity and higher robustness. In terms of lateral development, SVMD has been integrated with other network models. One example is a milling chatter detection method based on SVMD and a deep attention information fusion network, which extracts chatter features from multi-channel time-series signal data for detection [92]. It can also be combined with the instantaneous linear mixture model, resulting in the SMVMD method, which adaptively extracts joint or common modes from multi-channel signals. Furthermore, SVMD has been combined with other signal processing techniques. An improved Wigner–Ville distribution method based on SVMD [93] is used for the time–frequency analysis of multicomponent signals, reducing cross-terms and enhancing signal reconstruction accuracy. In [94], a new method called narrowband constraint-enhanced continuous variational mode decomposition (NCESVMD) is proposed which improves signal decomposition by introducing a minimum bandwidth constraint. Given the inherent characteristics of SVMD, parameter optimization is also a crucial aspect of optimizing the model. In [95], an ultra-weak fiber Bragg grating (UWFBG) hydrophone array-enhanced distributed acoustic sensing (DAS) system based on optimized SVMD and matched interference methods is proposed for noise resistance, with SVMD parameters optimized using the RIME algorithm. Ref. [96] demonstrates the combination of spatial dependency recursive sample entropy and improved wavelet thresholding for noise reduction.

In [97], researchers introduce a dual-end traveling wave fault location method based on SVMD and frequency-dependent propagation velocity. This method extracts the intrinsic mode functions of the signal through SVMD and uses the Teager energy operator to determine the arrival time of the traveling wave. Additionally, researchers have designed adaptive SVMD algorithms that dynamically adjust decomposition parameters based on signal characteristics to avoid falling into local optimal solutions.

Strength and Weakness

- Insensitive to initial values and successive extraction
- Prone to getting trapped in local optimal solutions
- Limited parallelism resulting in low real-time efficiency

Unlike the traditional variational mode decomposition method, SVMD (successive variational mode decomposition) extracts signals by successively implementing the variational mode decomposition technique. SVMD decomposes multicomponent signals into a series of band-limited intrinsic mode functions (IMFs) in a successive manner, whereas in the VMD method, modes are extracted concurrently. This successive approach eliminates the need for prior knowledge of the number of modes to be extracted, which is a significant advantage in practical applications where the mode count may be unknown or variable [90].

Moreover, compared to VMD, SVMD reduces the computational burden, especially when dealing with complex signals. In specific applications within the field of structural health signal processing, where certain modes are considered as interference or noise and are not of interest, the concurrent implementation of VMD may lead to a wastage of computational resources. On the other hand, SVMD can extract modes one by one, skipping unnecessary modes, which significantly improves convergence speed and reduces overall computation time [90].

Furthermore, SVMD overcomes the issue of VMD's sensitivity to initialization parameters. As SVMD is less sensitive to the initial values of the modal center frequencies, it can reduce the likelihood of converging to incorrect or duplicate modes, a problem that has been noted by Dragomiretskiy and Zosso in their work [65]. This robustness enhances the reliability of the decomposition results in structural health monitoring, where accurate mode identification is crucial.

However, SVMD is not without its drawbacks. In some cases, it may get trapped in local optimal solutions, particularly when dealing with signals that have highly similar modal components or when the signal-to-noise ratio is low. This can affect the decomposition effect and lead to inaccurate mode separation. Additionally, the sequential nature of SVMD may limit its parallelization potential, making it less efficient than VMD in applications requiring real-time processing. Despite these limitations, SVMD remains a promising method for structural health signal processing, offering a balance between accuracy, efficiency, and robustness.

3.2.3. Variational Mode Extraction

Definition

Variational Mode Extraction (VME) is a signal processing method based on variational Bayesian inference. In VME, the modal functions of the signal are treated as latent variables, while the observed signal data are used to estimate the distributions of these latent variables. By maximizing the likelihood function, VME can find the modal function parameters that best fit the signal data.

Application

This method converts time lags into phase period differences through a variational mode extraction algorithm, enhancing the accuracy and automation of frequency domain analysis. Its effectiveness has been verified in the actual SHM system of the Shanghai Tower [98].

In terms of innovations, first, deep learning networks have been integrated. For instance, an intelligent fault diagnosis method for rolling bearings based on VME and an improved one-dimensional convolutional neural network (I-1DCNN) has been proposed. By combining VME and I-1DCNN, useful features of bearing vibration signals are extracted from noisy environments, improving the accuracy and computational efficiency of fault diagnosis [99]. Another method [100] involves rolling bearing fault diagnosis based on power spectral density–variational mode extraction (PSD-VME), multiclass relevance vector machines (mRVM), and Dempster–Shafer evidence theory. Features are extracted through PSD-VME and classified using mRVM and DS evidence theory, verifying the method's high classification accuracy with a small amount of sample data.

Furthermore, innovations have been made by accurately grasping the advantages of VME. In the multi-fault diagnosis of rolling bearings, a variational mode extraction method based on the convergence trend of variational mode decomposition (VMD) has been applied [101]. The initial center frequency is adaptively determined through the VMD convergence trend graph, and kurtosis is used as an evaluation index to optimize the balance factor, enhancing the accuracy and computational efficiency of fault feature extraction.

Additionally, parameter optimization algorithms have been employed. A parameter-adaptive variational mode extraction method based on particle swarm optimization (PSO) has been proposed for bearing fault diagnosis [102]. Researchers have constructed a comprehensive index, L-KCIE, to optimize VME parameters, and they verified its effectiveness and superiority in fault feature extraction.

Strength and Weakness

- Extracts specific frequency components by setting the modal center frequencies.

First, the VME method has a clear objective, enabling it to extract signals targeting specific desired modal center frequencies, thereby successfully obtaining valuable intrinsic modal functions and accurate fault characteristic frequencies. This makes VME more targeted and effective in signal processing. Second, VME offers high flexibility, allowing users to extract specific frequency components in signals by setting the desired modal center frequencies. This flexibility enables VME to adapt to different signal characteristics and analysis requirements. Third, VME demonstrates strong robustness when processing signals containing noise. By setting parameters reasonably, it can effectively extract useful information from signals while suppressing noise interference. Finally, compared to some traditional signal processing methods, VME may have certain advantages in terms of computational efficiency thanks to the optimization of its algorithm design and the simplification of the iteration process.

However, VME also has some disadvantages. First, it cannot adaptively decompose multi-component signals and usually can only extract one component from a desired modal center frequency, which means that multiple processing steps or combining other methods may be required when dealing with complex signals. Second, the performance of VME can be significantly affected by initialization parameters. Improper parameter settings may lead to inaccurate extraction results or convergence to incorrect modes. Third, in some cases, the VME algorithm may fall into a local optimum without finding the global optimum, which can result in deviations between the extracted modes and the true signal characteristics. Finally, the VME method may not be suitable for all types of signal processing tasks. In certain specific scenarios, it may be necessary to combine other signal processing methods or adopt other algorithms to achieve better processing results.

3.2.4. Adaptive Variational Mode Decomposition

Definition

Adaptive variational mode decomposition (AVMD) is a signal decomposition method based on variational mode decomposition, but it possesses higher adaptability and applicability. AVMD adaptively selects the number of mode functions and the weighted average standard deviation through an online hyperparameter estimation method in order to minimize reconstruction error. Based on the selection results, adaptive basis functions and mode functions are computed, and signal separation is achieved.

Application

In the literature, researchers have focused on the fundamental research concerning AVMD. In robotic machining, chatter detection constitutes a complex task owing to the significant yet subtle variations in system stiffness. Consequently, an adaptive variational mode decomposition (AVMD) method grounded in kurtosis and instantaneous frequency has been proposed. This method aims to circumvent the issue of mode mixing inherent to the variational mode decomposition (VMD) process and facilitate the adaptive selection of decomposition parameters. The approach leverages a genetic algorithm to optimize decomposition parameters, significantly reducing optimization time by refining the discrete step size of these parameters. Approximate entropy, energy entropy, and a novel chatter feature based on entropy, termed the entropy drift coefficient, are extracted to differentiate between chatter and stable machining states [103]. Additionally, an adaptive noise reduction method based on automatic variational mode decomposition (AVMD) has been introduced for liquid pipeline leak detection [104]. This method enhances the VMD framework to effectively extract signal modes in environments with low signal-to-noise ratios.

Furthermore, numerous models employ intelligent algorithms and local optimization techniques. A differential evolution-based adaptive variational mode decomposition technique (DAVMD) has been proposed [105]. This technique continuously adjusts the number of decompositions and the penalty factor of VMD through the differential evolution (DE) algorithm, optimizing the decomposition results in terms of energy distribution, frequency characteristics, and other aspects. By optimizing the number of decompositions and the penalty factor, the performance of variational mode decomposition is enhanced. Moreover, an adaptive variational mode decomposition (VMD) denoising scheme based on the whale optimization algorithm (WOA) has been developed for denoising ground-penetrating radar (GPR) data [106]. This scheme optimizes the denoising parameters of VMD using WOA, significantly improving the signal-to-noise ratio (SNR).

Strength and Weakness

- Adapts mode count
- Has strong noise resistance

AVMD possesses unique advantages. First, AVMD has the merit of adaptive determination of the number of modes, making it a model of adaptive signal processing within the realm of signal processing. Traditional variational mode decomposition (VMD) is a fully non-recursive decomposition model, but it requires the predefinition of the number of modes, which limits the method's adaptability. Deviations in the predefined number of modes can lead to mode loss or mixing, affecting the accuracy of signal decomposition. In contrast, AVMD automatically determines the number of modes by analyzing signal characteristics (such as permutation entropy and kurtosis criteria), thereby avoiding the issues of mode loss or aliasing caused by inaccurate predefined mode numbers in VMD. For example, during the processing of electromechanical oscillation signals in power systems, AVMD can adaptively select the number of modes based on the spectral distribution, significantly improving decomposition accuracy [107].

Second, AVMD exhibits strong noise resistance and performs exceptionally well in noisy environments, effectively separating noise components from signals. For instance, in the analysis of hydropower station signals, AVMD demonstrates greater robustness compared to traditional methods (such as EMD and EWT), accurately extracting effective modes.

Furthermore, AVMD typically possesses efficient computational capabilities. By utilizing optimization algorithms (such as fast iterative operators and energy entropy), it shortens convergence time and enhances computational efficiency. For example, when performing fault diagnosis on wind turbine gearboxes, AVMD combined with the firefly algorithm optimizes the number of modes and penalty factors, significantly reducing computation time.

Previously mentioned methods, including empirical mode decomposition (EMD) and the subsequently discussed empirical wavelet transform (EWT), suffer from error accumulation due to recursive decomposition and sensitivity to noise and sampling frequency, respectively. In contrast, AVMD performs well when dealing with harmonic signals with similar frequencies. Ref. [107] verifies the effectiveness of AVMD through simulated signals and actual hydropower station measurement signals, highlighting its ability to accurately separate each harmonic component, a feat not achieved by EMD or EWT.

However, AVMD also has its disadvantages. Issues unresolved by classic models have been improved but not completely eliminated. First, parameter selection still poses a certain level of complexity. Although AVMD reduces the need for predefined parameters, the choice of its internal parameters (such as the penalty factor and convergence criteria) still significantly impacts the decomposition results. Improper parameter settings can lead to the over- or under-decomposition of modes, affecting signal reconstruction accuracy.

Similarly, the issue of local optimal solutions requires further research. In some complex signal processing scenarios, AVMD may fall into local optimal solutions, resulting in unsatisfactory decomposition effects. Additionally, AVMD may experience mode aliasing when processing modal components with similar frequencies. Finally, although AVMD improves computational efficiency compared to VMD, its computational complexity remains high when processing large-scale data or high-dimensional signals. In real-time structural health monitoring, AVMD may not meet the requirements for real-time processing. Therefore, it may be necessary to reduce the computational complexity of AVMD through GPU acceleration or distributed computing technologies to satisfy real-time processing demands.

3.3. *Empirical Wavelet Transform and Optimization Models*

empirical wavelet transform (EWT) combines the concepts of wavelet analysis with data-driven approaches. It provides an effective way to analyze signals with complex time–frequency structures. This section focuses on EWT and its ensemble-based counterparts like ensemble empirical wavelet transform and empirical Fourier decomposition. We will introduce the basic principles of these methods, their implementation details, and how they can be utilized to extract meaningful information from non-stationary signals.

3.3.1. Empirical Wavelet Transform

Definition

The empirical wavelet transform (EWT) is an adaptive signal decomposition method that constructs a wavelet filter bank by analyzing the spectral characteristics of the signal. The core formulas are as follows:

1. Fourier Transform: Perform Fourier transform on the signal $f(t)$ to obtain the spectrum $F(\omega)$:

$$F(\omega) = \int_{-\infty}^{\infty} f(t)e^{-i\omega t}dt \tag{5}$$

2. Frequency Band Division: Detect the local maxima of $|F(\omega)|$ to determine the frequency band boundaries $\{\omega_n\}_{n=0}^{N+1}$, where $\omega_0 = 0$ and $\omega_{N+1} = \pi$ (normalized frequency).
3. Construction of Empirical Wavelet Functions: For each frequency band $[\omega_n, \omega_{n+1}]$, construct the empirical wavelet function $\psi_n(\omega)$ and scaling function $\phi_1(\omega)$, satisfying the tight frame condition:

$$|\phi_1(\omega)|^2 + \sum_{n=1}^{N} |\psi_n(\omega)|^2 = 1, \quad \forall\omega \tag{6}$$

Scaling Function $\phi_1(\omega)$ (Low-Pass Filter):

$$\phi_1(\omega) = \begin{cases} 1, & |\omega| \leq \omega_1 - \tau_1, \\ \cos\left(\frac{\pi}{2}\beta\left(\frac{|\omega|-(\omega_1-\tau_1)}{2\tau_1}\right)\right), & \omega_1 - \tau_1 \leq |\omega| < \omega_1 + \tau_1, \\ 0, & \text{otherwise.} \end{cases} \tag{7}$$

Wavelet Function $\psi_n(\omega)$ (Band-Pass Filter):

$$\psi_n(\omega) = \begin{cases} \sin\left(\frac{\pi}{2}\beta\left(\frac{|\omega|-(\omega_n-\tau_n)}{2\tau_n}\right)\right), & \omega_n - \tau_n \leq |\omega| < \omega_n + \tau_n, \\ 1, & \omega_n + \tau_n \leq |\omega| < \omega_{n+1} - \tau_{n+1}, \\ \cos\left(\frac{\pi}{2}\beta\left(\frac{|\omega|-(\omega_{n+1}-\tau_{n+1})}{2\tau_{n+1}}\right)\right), & \omega_{n+1} - \tau_{n+1} \leq |\omega| < \omega_{n+1} + \tau_{n+1}, \\ 0, & \text{otherwise.} \end{cases} \tag{8}$$

Here, $\beta(x)$ is a smoothing function, for example

$$\beta(x) = x^4(35 - 84x + 70x^2 - 20x^3), \tag{9}$$

which satisfies $\beta(0) = 0$, $\beta(1) = 1$, and has zero derivatives at the endpoints. The transition band width τ_n is usually taken as a certain proportion of the adjacent boundary spacing, such as $\tau_n = \gamma(\omega_n - \omega_{n-1})$, (where $\gamma \in (0, 0.5)$).

4. Mode Decomposition: Extract the mode components via inverse Fourier transform: Residual (Low-Frequency Part):

$$W_f(0,t) = \mathcal{F}^{-1}[F(\omega)\phi_1(\omega)](t) \tag{10}$$

n-th Mode Component:

$$W_f(n,t) = \mathcal{F}^{-1}[F(\omega)\psi_n(\omega)](t), \quad n \geq 1 \tag{11}$$

5. Signal Reconstruction: The signal can be reconstructed exactly as follows:

$$f(t) = W_f(0,t) + \sum_{n=1}^{N} W_f(n,t) \tag{12}$$

Key Points

- Adaptivity: The frequency band division is based on the local maxima of the signal spectrum, without the need for predefined basis functions.
- Compact Support: The wavelet functions have compact support and smooth transitions in the frequency domain, reducing ringing effects in the time domain.
- Perfect Reconstruction: The filter bank satisfies the condition that the sum of squares is 1, ensuring lossless signal recovery.

By combining signal-driven wavelet design with traditional wavelet theory, EWT achieves effective analysis and processing of non-stationary signals.

Application

First, in combination with neural networks or high-order algorithms, researchers have proposed a novel damage detection method based on empirical wavelet transform

(EWT) and artificial neural network (ANN) for detecting and localizing damage in steel truss bridge models [108]. Additionally, there is a time series prediction method based on EWT and echo state network (ESN). This method decomposes the original time series into multivariate subsequences and employs ESN for modeling and prediction. Experimental results demonstrate that this method outperforms other benchmark models on multiple public datasets [109]. Another fault diagnosis method for rolling bearings combines an improved adaptive parameter-free empirical wavelet transform (IAPEWT) with an adaptive sparse coding shrinkage denoising (ASCSD) algorithm. IAPEWT automatically segments the spectrum and determines the boundaries of the filter bank, and when combined with the ASCSD algorithm, it enhances periodic impulse features, improving fault identification accuracy [110].

Furthermore, technologies that enhance the mathematical logic of EWT have also emerged. A new EWT method based on Fourier–Bessel series expansion (FBSE) has been used for the time–frequency representation of non-stationary signals. By improving EWT through FBSE, experimental results indicate that FBSE-EWT performs better than existing EWT and Hilbert–Huang transform (HHT) methods in terms of representing non-stationary signals with closely adjacent frequency components [111]. A new multichannel signal processing method called quaternion empirical wavelet transform (QEWT) has been used for fault diagnosis in rolling bearings. QEWT can synchronously process multiple sets of vibration signals, achieving spectrum segmentation, fusion, and modal decomposition, thereby improving the accuracy and efficiency of fault diagnosis [112]. Similarly, an EWT method based on Fourier–Bessel series expansion (FBSE-EWT) [113] has also been mentioned. Moreover, in the iterative process of various optimization models, an improved empirical wavelet transform (IEWT) has emerged, leading to subsequent optimizations based on it. A hybrid model based on IEWT and a long short-term memory network (LSTM) has been used to predict significant wave height. By decomposing buoy data using IEWT and combining them with LSTM for time series prediction, results show that the model exhibits higher prediction accuracy over longer prediction windows [114]. Additionally, a scheme based on IEWT, energy feature vector (EFV), and Bayesian optimized convolutional neural network (BOCNN) has been used to extract the hydrodynamic features of hydraulic turbines and intelligently identify their flow states. By decomposing signals using IEWT and combining EFV and BOCNN for feature extraction and classification, experimental results indicate that the average recognition accuracy of this scheme reaches 99.15% [115]. Furthermore, an approach combining IEWT and a sensitive component selection method has been used for bearing fault diagnosis. It enhances EWT performance through cyclic envelope spectrum segmentation and correlation-based component optimization, and it extracts fault information using the sensitive intrinsic mode function evaluation index (SIAI) [116]. Finally, an improved extended empirical wavelet transform (IEEWT) method has been used to detect and characterize multivariate oscillations in industrial control systems. Combined with a noise-reduced power spectrum and detrended fluctuation analysis (DFA) techniques, the IEEWT method demonstrates higher accuracy and robustness when processing multivariate signals with high noise levels [117].

In addition, researchers have professionally implemented EWT, leading to the emergence of innovative methods and studies. An improved demodulation analysis method based on cepstrum-assisted empirical wavelet transform (CEWT) has been used for fault diagnosis in planetary gearboxes. As demonstrated through numerical simulation and experimental validation, this method outperforms existing signal decomposition methods in terms of fault diagnosis [118]. Two other methods excel in noise reduction. A new variable spectrum segmentation empirical wavelet transform (VEWT) improves signal decomposition efficiency and noise resistance through selective spectrum segmentation and modal estimation based on multi-window power spectral density. Experimental results show that VEWT outperforms traditional EWT and extended EWT (EEWT) at processing noisy signals [119]. An EWT method enhanced by synchronous extraction transform (SET) has been used for the identification of time-varying systems. Results indicate that this method can effectively and accurately identify the instantaneous frequency of time-varying systems in noisy environments [120]. Furthermore, several emerging models have been proposed and applied to fault diagnosis. A new vibration model and EWT method have been used for compound fault diagnosis and analysis of wind turbine generator gearboxes. By decomposing signals using EWT and combining it with the vibration model for fault diagnosis, multiple faults can be effectively detected and diagnosed [121]. A weak feature enhancement method for mechanical fault diagnosis based on EWT and improved adaptive bistable stochastic resonance (IABSR) has been proposed. By combining EWT and IABSR for signal separation and fault feature enhancement, numerical simulations and case studies have verified the effectiveness and superiority of this method [122].

Strength and Weakness

- Adaptive frequency band partitioning and captures local features
- Sensitive to noise and may have endpoint effect
- May cause modal aliasing or modal loss issues

Its adaptive frequency band partitioning capability effectively captures local features based on the spectral characteristics of the signal, making it particularly suitable for processing nonlinear and non-stationary signals. Furthermore, through high-resolution time–frequency analysis, EWT can simultaneously provide both the temporal and frequency information of the signal, accurately capturing transient features in mechanical fault diagnosis. Additionally, EWT boasts high computational efficiency, enabling rapid processing of large-scale data, as exemplified by its integration with LSTM neural networks for efficient prediction in the processing of electromechanical oscillation signals in power systems, which was mentioned previously.

However, EWT also exhibits certain limitations. First, it is relatively sensitive to noise, which may lead to inaccurate frequency band partitioning in high-noise environments, though numerous studies have been conducted to optimize this limitation [109–113,118–122]. Second, parameter selection is complex, and improper settings can trigger modal aliasing or modal loss. Finally, the endpoint effect problem may cause decomposition distortion at the signal boundaries.

3.3.2. Ensemble Empirical Wavelet Transform

Definition

Ensemble empirical wavelet transform ïijĹEEWTïijĽ combines the advantages of EEMD and EWT, aiming to improve the stability and accuracy of signal decomposition. It performs empirical wavelet transform multiple times and averages the results to reduce noise and uncertainty during the decomposition process.

1. Signal and Noise Superposition: The signal and noise superposition is given by

$$x'(t) = x(t) + n_i(t) \tag{13}$$

   where $x(t)$ is the original signal, $n_i(t)$ is the i-th added Gaussian white noise, and $x'(t)$ is the signal after noise superposition.
2. EMD Decomposition: Perform EMD decomposition on $x'(t)$ to obtain a series of intrinsic mode functions (IMFs):

$$x'(t) = \sum_{j=1}^{N} \text{IMF}_{i,j}(t) + r_i(t) \tag{14}$$

where $\text{IMF}_{i,j}(t)$ is the j-th IMF obtained from the i-th decomposition, and $r_i(t)$ is the residual term.

3. Repetition and Averaging: Repeat the above process M times, adding different white noise each time, and average all the obtained IMFs:

$$\text{IMF}_j(t) = \frac{1}{M} \sum_{i=1}^{M} \text{IMF}_{i,j}(t) \tag{15}$$

The final $\text{IMF}_j(t)$ obtained is the result of the EEMD decomposition.

Strength and Weakness

- Strong noise resistance and high resolution time frequency analysis
- High computational complexity and endpoint effect

First, regarding adaptive frequency band partitioning and ensemble processing, EEWT dynamically adjusts the decomposition process based on the spectral characteristics of the signal through adaptive frequency band partitioning, thereby effectively capturing local features of the signal. Compared to the traditional EWT, EEWT introduces an ensemble processing mechanism, which significantly enhances the stability and robustness of the decomposition through multiple decompositions and averaging. For instance, during the analysis of bridge vibration signals, EEWT can effectively separate modal components of different frequencies, providing more accurate data support for structural damage identification [123].

Second, EEWT exhibits strong noise resistance. By utilizing the ensemble processing mechanism, EEWT can effectively suppress noise interference and improve the signal-to-noise ratio. In environments with high noise levels, the decomposition results of EEWT are more stable, allowing for the accurate extraction of effective modal components.

Third, EEWT offers high-resolution time–frequency analysis through the dilation and translation of wavelet basis functions. This enables EEWT to simultaneously provide both the temporal and frequency information of the signal, making it particularly suitable for analyzing transient signals and complex vibration patterns. For example, in mechanical fault diagnosis, EEWT can accurately capture the transient features of fault signals, thereby improving the accuracy of fault detection.

Next, the disadvantages of EEWT are discussed:

First, EEWT has a relatively high computational complexity. Although EEWT performs excellently in terms of decomposition accuracy and noise resistance, its computational complexity is relatively high, especially when processing large-scale or high-dimensional signals, leading to a significant increase in computation time. As a result, in real-time structural health monitoring, EEWT may not meet the requirements for real-time processing.

Second, parameter selection remains somewhat complex. The performance of EEWT depends on the choice of parameters, such as the thresholds for frequency band partitioning, the number of ensemble iterations, and the selection of wavelet basis functions. Inappropriate parameter settings may lead to modal aliasing or modal loss, affecting the decomposition results.

Like many signal decomposition methods, EEWT has an endpoint effect, distorting decomposition results at signal boundaries, which can cause error accumulation in real-time structural health monitoring, reducing the monitoring system's reliability.

3.3.3. Empirical Fourier Decomposition

Definition

Empirical Fourier decomposition (EFD) is a signal processing technique that analyzes the local frequency spectrum of a signal, identifies the main frequency components and their variation characteristics in the signal, and then decomposes the signal into several components based on this. It aims to decompose complex signals into a series of components with clear physical meaning, which are usually expressed in the form of amplitude modulation–frequency modulation (AM-FM).

Application

Many researchers have employed spectral analysis methods to optimize and implement empirical Fourier decomposition (EFD). A spectral envelope-based adaptive empirical Fourier decomposition (SEAEFD) method has been proposed and applied to fault diagnosis in rolling bearings. The core of this method lies in optimizing the EFD process through spectral envelope analysis, thereby enhancing the orthogonality, correlation coefficient, and overall decomposition accuracy. By adaptively adjusting the spectral envelope analysis strategy, SEAEFD can maintain high decomposition accuracy in highly noisy environments and effectively extract the fault features of rolling bearings [124]. Another automatic modal identification method based on free vibration response and enhanced empirical Fourier decomposition (EFD) technology has also been developed. By combining improved spectral segmentation techniques with zero-phase shift filters, this method can more accurately decompose non-stationary signals and closely spaced modal signals. Through the automatic adjustment of the number of spectral segmentations, it can adapt to different signal characteristics, thereby improving the accuracy and robustness of modal identification [125]. Furthermore, a power spectrum envelope adaptive empirical Fourier decomposition (PSEEFD) method has been proposed for processing signals with low signal-to-noise ratios. The PSEEFD method adaptively adjusts the EFD decomposition strategy based on signal characteristics, thereby automatically selecting appropriate decomposition parameters in order to achieve more accurate signal decomposition under low signal-to-noise ratio conditions. Experimental results have verified the effectiveness of this method in processing vibration signals from ship stabilizing platforms [126].

The integration of EFD with algorithms, neural networks, and other classic signal processing techniques is also one of its important applications. First, improved spectral segmentation techniques and the construction of zero-phase shift filters have been utilized to optimize EFD. The improved spectral segmentation techniques can more accurately identify abrupt changes in signals, thereby enhancing decomposition accuracy. The construction of zero-phase shift filters ensures that the decomposed components maintain the correct phase relationships, thus improving the reliability of the decomposition results. Numerical and experimental methods have verified the effectiveness of EFD in processing non-stationary signals and closely spaced modal signals, and comparisons have been made with other decomposition methods [127]. Additionally, a wind speed prediction model that combines empirical Fourier decomposition, a long short-term memory network (LSTM), and grey wolf optimizer (GWO) has been proposed. The literature provides a detailed description of the working principle and implementation steps of this model, and experimental results have verified its effectiveness in wind speed prediction [128]. Finally, due to its superiority, empirical Fourier decomposition has been applied to bridge health monitoring [129].

Strength and Weakness

- Components with clear physical meanings
- Excellent modal separation for multi-modal vibration identification

- Sensitive to noise and possible modal aliasing

Empirical Fourier decomposition (EFD), as a signal processing technique, demonstrates remarkable advantages in fields such as structural health monitoring. First, the components obtained through EFD decomposition typically possess clear physical meanings, reflecting the natural modes of vibration systems and the modulation characteristics of signals. This attribute renders EFD a powerful tool for understanding the essence of signals and accurately identifying structural damages or anomalous states. Second, EFD exhibits strong adaptability, being capable of processing nonlinear and non-stationary signals, which is particularly crucial in the analysis of vibration signals in practical engineering. By conducting local spectrum analysis, EFD can better capture the instantaneous features of signals, providing accurate information for the analysis of structural dynamic behavior. Furthermore, EFD possesses excellent modal separation capability, effectively separating different modal components in signals, which is greatly beneficial for identifying the multi-modal vibration characteristics of structures.

However, EFD also has some disadvantages that cannot be ignored. Its computational complexity is relatively high, necessitating detailed analysis of the local spectrum of signals and involving complex processes of modal identification and component extraction. This may lead to prolonged computation times, especially when dealing with large-scale data or conducting real-time monitoring, where computational efficiency may become a bottleneck. Additionally, EFD is relatively sensitive to noise, with environmental or measurement noise potentially interfering with local spectrum analysis and affecting the accuracy of decomposition results. Meanwhile, the performance of EFD depends on the selection of parameters, such as the window size for local spectrum analysis, and improper parameter selection may result in unsatisfactory decomposition results, increasing the difficulty of use. Finally, in some cases, EFD may exhibit modal aliasing, where components of different modes fail to be completely separated, further reducing the accuracy of decomposition results and adversely affecting subsequent analysis and diagnosis.

4. Deconvolution

In the realm of signal processing and related scientific research, deconvolution techniques play a pivotal role. They are employed to reverse the effects of convolution, aiding in tasks such as noise reduction, signal restoration, and feature extraction. This section delves into several key deconvolution-based approaches. It begins with minimum entropy deconvolution, exploring its definition, application scenarios, as well as its strengths and weaknesses. Subsequently, maximum correlated kurtosis deconvolution is examined in a similar vein. The section then moves on to feature model decomposition, covering its definition, methods, and performance aspects. Finally, other relevant models and applications are briefly introduced, aiming to provide a comprehensive overview of the deconvolution-related techniques for readers.

4.1. Minimum Entropy Deconvolution

Minimum entropy deconvolution (MED) has carved out a significant niche in the deconvolution landscape. Rooted in information theory concepts, MED seeks to find a deconvolution filter that minimizes the entropy of the output signal. This approach has proven invaluable in scenarios where extracting hidden or obscured features in signals is crucial. In the following subsections, we will delve into the definition of MED, explore its wide-ranging applications, and critically assess its strengths and weaknesses.

4.1.1. Definition

Minimum entropy deconvolution (MED) is a blind deconvolution method based on signal sparsity. The basic idea is that when mechanical failure occurs, the resulting shock vibration signal usually has sparsity, that is, the energy is mainly concentrated in a few shock pulses. Therefore, MED estimates the deconvolution filter by maximizing the negative entropy of the signal, thereby enhancing the sparsity of the output signal and better highlighting the impact features. Endo et al. [130] first applied MED to the field of fault detection successfully. The core formulas are as follows:

1. Signal Model

Assume that the observed signal $y[n]$ is the result of the original impulsive signal $x[n]$ convolved with the system response $h[n]$ and superimposed with noise $e[n]$:

$$y[n] = x[n] * h[n] + e[n], \tag{16}$$

where $*$ denotes the convolution operation.

2. Deconvolution Objective

Design a deconvolution filter $w[n]$ such that the output signal $s[n]$ approximates the original signal $x[n]$ while minimizing the entropy:

$$s[n] = w[n] * y[n]. \tag{17}$$

3. Definition of Entropy

In MED, "entropy" typically refers to a measure of signal sparsity, commonly in the following two forms:

(a) Kurtosis Maximization Kurtosis measures the impulsiveness of the signal and is defined as

$$\text{Kurtosis}(s) = \frac{E[s^4]}{(E[s^2])^2} - 3, \tag{18}$$

where $E[\cdot]$ denotes the expectation. MED enhances impulsive components by maximizing kurtosis.

$$w_{\text{opt}} = \arg\max_{w} \frac{E[s^4]}{(E[s^2])^2}. \tag{19}$$

(b) Shannon Entropy Minimization Normalize the signal energy to a probability distribution $p_n = \frac{|s[n]|^2}{\|s\|^2}$ and minimize its Shannon entropy:

$$H(s) = -\sum_{n} p_n \log p_n, \tag{20}$$

where the optimization problem is

$$w_{\text{opt}} = \arg\min_{w} H(s). \tag{21}$$

4. Optimization

Update the filter coefficients w using gradient descent or iterative methods. For example, with kurtosis maximization, the objective function is

$$J(w) = \frac{\frac{1}{N}\sum_{n=1}^{N} s[n]^4}{\left(\frac{1}{N}\sum_{n=1}^{N} s[n]^2\right)^2}, \tag{22}$$

where the derivative is computed, and w is iteratively updated until convergence.

5. Summary of Formulas

The core formula of MED can be summarized as

$$w_{\text{opt}} = \arg\max_{w} \frac{E[s^4]}{(E[s^2])^2}, \tag{23}$$

where $s = w * y$.

Key Points

- Adaptivity: No prior system model is required; the method is entirely data-driven.
- Sparse Enhancement: Impulsive components are highlighted by minimizing entropy (or maximizing kurtosis).

4.1.2. Application

A new target vector has been introduced to accommodate the random impulse characteristics of planetary bearing vibrations. By adopting the multipoint optimal minimum entropy deconvolution adjustment (MOMEDA) method, the influence of roller slippage on the vibration signal is considered, enabling the detection of outer race, inner race, and roller faults in planetary bearings [131].

To further enhance the accuracy of fault feature extraction, minimum entropy deconvolution (MED) can be utilized to improve resistance to noise. A model known as the MOMEDA method incorporates MED to enhance acoustic features in rolling bearing fault diagnosis. This method effectively extracts and enhances bearing fault features under complex background noise and unknown transmission paths [132]. Some researchers have also introduced an enhanced minimum entropy deconvolution method: minimum entropy deconvolution with adaptive filter parameters (EMED-AFP). By integrating nonlinear transformations and a sample entropy minimization strategy, this method adaptively determines optimal filter parameters and effectively extracts fault features [133]. In terms of parameter optimization, the whale optimization algorithm (WOA) has been used to optimize variational mode decomposition (VMD) parameters, combined with MOMEDA to enhance fault-related impulse signals [134]. The combination of other technologies has elevated the application of MED to new heights. Minimum entropy morphological deconvolution (MEMD) has been proposed for bearing fault diagnosis, integrating morphological filtering into minimum entropy deconvolution (MED) and determining optimal filtering results through the diagonal slice spectrum (DSS) of higher-order spectra [135]. By combining continuous vibration separation (CVS) with minimum entropy deconvolution (MED), the technical challenge of sun gear fault diagnosis in planetary gearboxes has been overcome, with the model particularly excelling at signal modulation effects and weak signal detection [136].

Furthermore, coarse-to-fine minimum entropy deconvolution (CFMED) has been introduced for rotating machinery fault detection. Through pre-iteration and discarding strategies, this method effectively extracts repetitive impulse signals related to faults and is robust to filter sizes [137]. A method to improve the accuracy of rotating machinery fault diagnosis, by combining kernel local outlier factor (KLOF) and phase editing (PE) with minimum entropy deconvolution (MED), has been shown to effectively extract repetitive impulse signals caused by faults [138]. An improved minimum entropy deconvolution method has been proposed to enhance the performance of rolling bearing fault diagnosis. Utilizing the standard particle swarm optimization algorithm and generalized spherical coordinate transformation, this method effectively detects and enhances periodic impulses in rolling bearing fault signals [139]. Additionally, combining minimum entropy deconvolution (MED) with the spectral centroid indicator (SCI) has been shown to help with the identification of bearing states with insufficient lubrication at different rotational speeds [140]. Combining time-delayed feedback stochastic resonance with minimum entropy deconvolution enhances the detection of weak fault features in rolling bearings. Through simulation and experimental validation, this method has been shown to outperform traditional minimum entropy deconvolution and the fast kurtosis Gram method at weak fault detection [141].

4.1.3. Strength and Weakness

- Enhances signal sparsity
- Sensitive to random pulses
- Sensitive to parameters

In the field of structural health signal processing, minimum entropy deconvolution (MED) stands out as a unique signal processing method, demonstrating distinct advantages and disadvantages.

Its advantages are mainly manifested in the following aspects: First, MED can effectively enhance the sparsity of signals, which is extremely beneficial for extracting fault features in structural health monitoring. This makes the impact components or fault pulses in the signal more prominent, facilitating the identification of structural damage or anomalies. Second, MED exhibits high sensitivity to random pulses in the signal, a characteristic that makes it excel at detecting non-periodic or random faults, aiding in the capture of sudden damage or transient events. By adjusting the filter to make the output signal sparse, MED effectively separates noise and recovers the original impulsive features. Furthermore, MED does not rely on the periodic characteristics of faults, thus offering greater flexibility in processing complex or irregular signals and being suitable for the processing of non-periodic fault signals. Finally, as a method based on signal processing theory, MED is not entirely data driven and can still effectively operate in the absence of large amounts of training data, demonstrating high practicality.

However, MED also has some notable disadvantages. First, it performs poorly in processing periodic fault pulses, tending to enhance the sparsity of random pulses instead. This may render it ineffective in extracting fault features for periodic faults, such as periodic impacts in bearing faults. Second, the performance of MED is relatively sensitive to parameter selection. Improper parameter settings can lead to unsatisfactory signal decomposition results or even introduce spurious components, requiring users to possess a certain level of experience and skill. Additionally, the computational process of MED involves iterative optimization, resulting in relatively high computational complexity, which may pose a challenge for real-time monitoring or large-scale data processing. Moreover, although MED can enhance the impact components in the signal, its robustness to noise is limited. In environments with strong noise, noise may be mistaken for fault pulses, potentially reducing the accuracy of diagnosis. Finally, the results of MED may be influenced by the initial conditions of the signal. Improper selection of initial conditions may lead to unstable or unreliable decomposition results.

4.2. Maximum Correlated Kurtosis Deconvolution

Maximum correlated kurtosis deconvolution (MCKD) takes advantage of the statistical property of kurtosis to enhance the detectability of periodic transients in signals. By maximizing the correlated kurtosis, MCKD is particularly effective in fault diagnosis in rotating machinery and other applications where identifying repetitive impulsive events is key. Here, we will define MCKD precisely, examine its practical applications across different industries, and analyze its performance pros and cons.

4.2.1. Definition

MED has the limitation of only deconvolving a single pulse or partial pulse, so McDonald et al. Maximum correlated kurtosis deconvolution (MCKD) is proposed, which considers the periodicity of the fault and aims to extract periodic pulse faults from machine vibration signals. It uses the correlation kurtosis as the objective function of deconvolution, and it maximizes the correlation kurtosis value by finding the optimal filter parameters. By deconvolving the continuous pulse buried in noise, the correlation kurtosis value of the original signal is enhanced, making it suitable for extracting weak fault signals from continuous transient shocks.

4.2.2. Application

In recent years, researchers have pursued the development of efficient and robust methods for signal acquisition and processing in conjunction with maximum correlated kurtosis deconvolution (MCKD) technology, aiming to enhance the signal-to-noise ratio and the accuracy of feature extraction. A study presented an improved maximum correlated kurtosis deconvolution adjustment (IMCKDA) method for fault detection in wind turbine gears [142]. By introducing the concept of convolution adjustment and utilizing the correlated Gini index (CG) to guide the selection of filter length, the method improved both the signal-to-noise ratio and robustness.

The combination of customized balanced multi-wavelets with adaptive maximum correlated kurtosis deconvolution (MCKD) has been demonstrated to be effective and feasible for the diagnosis of compound faults in rotating machinery [143]. Another approach, namely improved maximum correlated kurtosis deconvolution (IMCKD), enhances robustness and efficiency in rolling bearing fault diagnosis by automatically estimating the iteration period and selecting the filtered signal with the maximum kurtosis [144]. Furthermore, a maximum correlated kurtosis deconvolution based on deep networks (MCKD-DeNet) method has been proposed for bearing fault diagnosis, integrating deep learning to optimize the deconvolution filter coefficients. This method improves the accuracy and efficiency of fault feature extraction [145].

4.2.3. Strength and Weakness

- Good at extracting periodic fault pulses in rotating machinery
- Improves fault diagnosis accuracy for early -stage faults
- Preserves and enhances fault-related periodic components
- Sensitive to high noise levels and poor signal quality
- Heavily depends on accurate fault cycle estimation

Maximum correlated kurtosis deconvolution (MCKD) and minimum entropy deconvolution (MED) stand out as two prominent signal processing techniques in mechanical fault diagnosis, especially for rotating machinery like rolling bearings and gears. Although both aim to enhance fault characteristics in signals, they diverge in their optimization goals and application efficacy. This analysis delves into the merits and demerits of MCKD in the realm of structural health signal processing.

MCKD boasts several advantages. First, it excels at extracting periodic fault pulses, making it highly effective for identifying faults with repetitive patterns, which are typical in rotating machinery. By maximizing the correlation kurtosis of the output signal, MCKD amplifies weak periodic fault features often obscured by noise or other signal components. Second, its ability to highlight these periodic fault characteristics enhances fault diagnosis accuracy, particularly for subtle or early-stage faults, proving invaluable for predictive maintenance and early fault detection in industrial settings. Finally, unlike MED, which targets random pulse extraction and signal sparsity, MCKD's tailored approach to periodic signals ensures that fault-related periodic components are preserved and enhanced, facilitating better signal interpretability [146].

However, MCKD also presents certain disadvantages. It heavily relies upon accurate fault cycle estimation, which can be challenging to obtain in industrial applications due to varying operating conditions, noise, and complex signal interactions. This dependency limits MCKD's effectiveness when fault cycles are unknown or hard to estimate. Additionally, while adept at handling periodic faults, MCKD is less effective for non-periodic or random faults where MED might be more suitable. Furthermore, MCKD's iterative optimization process to maximize correlation kurtosis can be computationally intensive, hindering its use in time-sensitive or resource-constrained environments. Finally, its performance can suffer in the presence of high noise levels or poor signal quality, necessitating preprocessing steps like noise reduction for optimal results.

In comparison to MED, MCKD is more effective for periodic faults, while MED is better suited for random fault pulses. MED's versatility stems from its lesser reliance on fault cycle information, whereas MCKD's performance is closely tied to accurate fault cycle estimation. The two methods also differ in their optimization objectives: MED minimizes signal entropy for sparsity, while MCKD maximizes correlation kurtosis to emphasize periodic features.

In conclusion, MCKD offers significant benefits for structural health signal processing, particularly in diagnosing periodic faults in rotating machinery. Its ability to amplify weak periodic fault features makes it a potent tool for early fault detection and predictive maintenance. Nevertheless, its reliance on accurate fault cycle estimation, its computational complexity, and its limited applicability to non-periodic faults are notable drawbacks. When choosing between MCKD and MED, practitioners should consider the fault's nature and the availability of fault cycle information in order to determine the most suitable method. Ultimately, while MCKD is a valuable technique for periodic fault diagnosis, its effectiveness hinges on the specific application context and input signal quality. Future research could aim to reduce MCKD's dependency on fault cycle estimation and enhance its robustness to noise, broadening its industrial applicability.

4.3. Feature Model Decomposition

Feature model decomposition offers a distinct perspective on deconvolution by focusing on breaking down complex models into more interpretable and useful components. It provides a framework for extracting relevant features from data, which can then be leveraged for tasks such as classification, prediction, and anomaly detection. In this segment, we will start by defining feature model decomposition, detail the methods employed in the process, and evaluate its overall performance in terms of strengths and weaknesses.

4.3.1. Definition

Feature mode decomposition (FMD) is a relatively new signal decomposition method that aims to decompose different modes through the design of adaptive finite impulse response (FIR) filters. FMD utilizes the superiority of correlation kurtosis, taking into account the impulsivity and periodicity of signals, and is suitable for feature extraction in mechanical fault diagnosis and other fields.

4.3.2. Method

The specific workflow of FMD includes the following steps: (1) Initialize the filter bank: First, initialize a set of evenly distributed FIR filters that cover the entire frequency band to decompose the original signal. (2) Iterative updating of filters: Using correlated kurtosis (CK) as the objective function, iteratively update the filter bank. Estimate the fault cycle during each filtering process. (3) Screening mode: After comparing the correlation coefficients (CCs) between every two modes, discard the mode with a lower CK. (4) Termination conditions: When the termination conditions are met, the decomposition process is ended.

4.3.3. Strength and Weakness

- Uses adaptive FIR filters
- Can resist interference and noise
- Highly dependent on signal characteristics

The decomposition goal of FMD is to capture the characteristics of mechanical faults, taking into comprehensive consideration the impulsivity and periodicity of signals, while exhibiting robust resistance to other interference and noise. This method employs adaptive finite impulse response (FIR) filters for signal decomposition, unconstrained by filter shape, bandwidth, or center frequency, thereby achieving a more thorough decomposition effect.

Notably, FMD can accurately decompose mechanical fault information without prior knowledge of the fault period, especially for compound faults that dominate in different frequency bands. However, the introduction of adaptive FIR filters also means that the performance of FMD is influenced to some extent by the initial parameter selection of the filter bank. Improper initial parameter settings may lead to suboptimal signal decomposition results or even the inability to effectively extract fault features. Furthermore, the performance of FMD is highly dependent on the characteristics of the signal itself.

4.4. Other Models and Applications

Beyond the specific deconvolution methods explored above, there exists a rich tapestry of other models and applications within the realm of deconvolution. These include emerging techniques, hybrid approaches that combine multiple deconvolutional concepts, or applications in niche areas that have not been as widely explored. This section aims to provide a glimpse into these diverse aspects, highlighting their potential contributions to the broader field of deconvolution.

- Wiener Deconvolution
- Blind Deconvolution

Wiener deconvolution is a deconvolution method based on the criterion of minimum mean square error. It utilizes the statistical properties of signals (such as power spectrum) to design an optimal filter for recovering the convolved signal. Wiener deconvolution performs well at processing signals containing noise.

Blind deconvolution estimates the point spread function (PSF) and the original signal through iterative algorithms when the PSF is unknown. For instance, a blind deconvolution method based on generalized Gaussian cyclostationarity (CYCBD β) can be used to extract bearing fault features under non-Gaussian conditions. CYCBD β exhibits higher robustness in the presence of strong non-Gaussian noise and can extract fault features without knowing the fault frequency [147]. When combined with spectral kurtosis, it can be applied to gear fault diagnosis. Under both constant and actual operating speeds, this method outperforms existing blind deconvolution methods, effectively enhancing fault features and improving detection accuracy [148].

To enhance adaptive performance, a method based on maximum autocorrelation kurtosis deconvolution (MACKD) has been developed for detecting abnormal noise in vehicle axles. This method identifies abnormal noise by quantifying periodic impulse components in the signal. Experiments have shown that it outperforms the MCKD and MED methods in feature extraction [149]. Similarly, an improved adaptive multipoint optimal minimum entropy deconvolution adjustment (MOMEDA) fault diagnosis method has been proposed, which improves the effectiveness of signal processing through a grid search optimization algorithm. Combining EEMD and MOMEDA techniques, it can effectively extract feature signals of complex faults in environments with high noise [150].

There is also the periodic component pursuit kurtosis deconvolution (PCPKD) method for the compound fault diagnosis of rolling bearings. It excels at signal period enhancement and multi-frequency component separation, effectively extracting intrinsic periodic components [151].

In addition, optimizations in kurtosis have significantly impacted the performance of model-based methods. The combination of the maximum L-kurtosis deconvolution (MLKD) algorithm and the frequency domain filtering (FDF) algorithm has significant advantages in suppressing outliers and noise, effectively extracting fault features for bearing fault diagnosis [152]. Furthermore, maximum average kurtosis deconvolution (MAKD) is utilized to enhance impact fault features in rotating machinery. MAKD exhibits strong robustness to typical types of interference and is not affected by speed variations or estimation deviations of fault characteristic frequencies [153].

The primary objectives of these deconvolution techniques are to extract useful information from measured signals, recover convolved signals, and estimate unknown system parameters. Each technique is based on different mathematical principles and implementation methods, such as the criterion of minimum mean square error, iterative algorithms, spectral kurtosis, and periodic component pursuit. Although all can be applied in the field of signal processing and structural health monitoring, each technique has its specific application scenarios and advantages. For example, Wiener deconvolution is suitable for processing signals containing noise; blind deconvolution is very useful when the PSF is unknown; and MACKD is particularly suitable for detecting impact faults.

In practical applications, these techniques can complement each other and be used in combination to improve the effectiveness of signal processing and the accuracy of fault diagnosis. For instance, blind deconvolution can be used first to estimate the system's response function and the original excitation signal, and then other techniques can be employed for fault feature extraction and diagnosis.

5. Comprehensive Discussion

The application of non-parametric dependent signal processing, adaptive signal processing, and deconvolution techniques in the mechanical field exhibits unique characteristics and entails significant advantages as well as inherent limitations. Non-parametric signal processing methods, including short-time Fourier transform (STFT) and Wigner–Ville distribution (WVD), have found widespread usage in mechanical fault diagnosis due to their simplicity and intuitive properties. These techniques do not necessitate prior knowledge of the signal's statistical properties, enabling direct analysis in the time–frequency domain and effective extraction of fault characteristics. However, in complex and variable mechanical signal environments, non-parametric methods may face limitations in analysis accuracy due to insufficient prior knowledge, making it challenging to accurately capture subtle, dynamic changes within the signal.

Adaptive signal processing technology achieves a high degree of adaptability to changes in signal environments by incorporating optimal criteria, such as adaptive filtering and adaptive noise cancellation techniques. These technologies can track signal characteristics in real-time, effectively addressing non-stationarity and uncertainty factors in mechanical systems. Nonetheless, when dealing with highly nonlinear mechanical signals, adaptive signal processing may encounter issues related to slow convergence speeds, particularly when signal characteristics undergo rapid changes. The algorithm may struggle to adapt promptly to the new signal environment, potentially impacting the accuracy and real-time performance of diagnosis.

As a signal recovery technique, deconvolution technology has demonstrated notable advantages in fields like mechanical image processing and vibration signal analysis. By performing deconvolution operations, the blurring effects and convolution components within the signal can be effectively removed, restoring the characteristic information of the original signal. This is particularly crucial for extracting weak fault characteristics in mechanical systems. However, in practical applications, deconvolution techniques may be significantly impacted by noise and interference. Mechanical signals are frequently contaminated with substantial background noise and interference components, which can be amplified or introduce new error sources during the deconvolution process, thereby reducing the accuracy and reliability of signal recovery.

Given these considerations, in practical applications, it is imperative to meticulously select appropriate signal processing methods based on specific requirements or adopt a strategy that integrates multiple methods for processing. Taking mechanical fault diagnosis as an illustrative example, non-parametric dependent signal processing methods can be initially employed to conduct a preliminary time–frequency domain analysis of the signal, thereby extracting potential fault characteristics. Subsequently, adaptive signal processing technology can be utilized to further filter noise interference and enhance signal quality. Finally, deconvolution technology can be applied to recover clearer and more precise fault feature information. This strategy of integrating multiple signal processing techniques can fully exploit their respective technical advantages, significantly improving the accuracy and efficiency of mechanical fault diagnosis. Table 1 summarizes the application scenarios and optimization methods of the key signal decomposition techniques highlighted in this review. Table 2 Comparison of the signal processing techniques for structural health monitoring (SHM)

Table 1. Applicable scenarios and optimization methods for various signal decomposition techniques.

Method	Applicable Scenarios	Optimization Methods
STFT	Preliminary analysis and signal feature extraction	Multi-window techniques, linear frequency modulation, Gaussian windows
WT	Local signal feature analysis	Optimization of wavelet basis function selection
WVD	Single-component linear frequency-modulated signals	Cross-term suppression methods (e.g., DMD-WVD)
EMD	Complex signal analysis	Noise-assisted methods (e.g., EEMD), parameter optimization
EEMD	Complex signal analysis	Parameter optimization (e.g., adaptive noise bandwidth), hardware acceleration
MEEMD	Multi-physical field signal fusion	Parameter optimization, multi-signal synchronous processing
VMD	Complex signal analysis	Parameter optimization (e.g., particle swarm optimization), multi-variable signal processing
SVMD	Complex signal analysis	Parameter self-adaptive update, minimum bandwidth constraint
AVMD	Complex signal analysis	Parameter self-adaptive update, optimization algorithms (e.g., differential evolution)
EWT	Complex signal analysis	Optimization of filter design, multi-variable signal processing
EEWT	Complex signal analysis	Parameter optimization, multi-signal synchronous processing
EFD	Complex signal analysis	Optimization of spectral segmentation, noise suppression
MED	Random pulse signals	Noise suppression methods (e.g., wavelet threshold), parameter optimization

Table 1. *Cont.*

Method	Applicable Scenarios	Optimization Methods
MCKD	Periodic fault signals	Fault cycle estimation optimization, noise suppression
FMD	Complex signal analysis	Parameter optimization, multi-variable signal processing

Table 2. Comparison of signal processing techniques for structural health monitoring (SHM).

Method Abbr.	References	Key Feature	Advantage	Difficulty
STFT	[3–16]	TF Resolution	Good for Stationary	Window Sel.
WT	[17–21]	TF Localization	High Resolution	Basis Sel.
WVD	[1,22–30,32,33]	TF Analysis	High Resolution	Cross-term Issue
EMD	[34,36–42]	Adaptive Decomp.	Self-adaptability	Mode Mixing
EEMD	[44–49]	Noise Addition	Suppress Mixing	Noise Difficulty
VMD	[69–71,73–83,85–89]	Bandwidth Opt.	Flexibility	Parameter Sel.
MED	[131–141]	Signal Sparsity	Enhance Impact	Computational

6. Conclusions

Most algorithms are proposed for processing non-stationary signals in structural health monitoring, and significant progress has been observed in models' adaptability to non-stationary signals during the iterative process. However, some unresolved issues remain in current research. Below, the prospects for signal processing technology in the field of structural health are discussed. (1) As mentioned in Section 2, real-time data processing, such as dealing with rapidly changing damage characteristics, often requires sacrificing computational efficiency. However, improving computational efficiency often leads to increased computational complexity. For instance, STFT, when processing highly non-stationary signals, exhibits inadequate capture of time–frequency signal features. Although WT offers higher computational efficiency, it has low computational complexity, while WVD's high resolution relies on instantaneous calculations, resulting in low computational efficiency. Therefore, effectively balancing computational complexity, efficiency, and resolution is crucial for models to process real-time signals and achieve practical application. Further research in this area is recommended. (2) As stated in Section 3, adaptive time–frequency analysis effectively addresses the issue of basis function selection in non-parametric processing techniques. However, these models still face parameter selection issues. For example, the performance of MEEMD is sensitive to parameters like noise bandwidth, and VMD's performance is significantly affected by parameters such as the penalty factor and the number of modes. Some researchers have manually tuned these parameters using intelligent algorithms, but critical breakthroughs are still lacking, with efforts remaining at the stage of algorithmic iteration and approximation. Therefore, it incorporating clear physical meanings of signal processing into the development of parameter optimization algorithms, rather than relying on simple numerical comparisons, is suggested. (3) Researchers have made significant efforts at denoising, but there is limited research on periodic impulse signals, which are often treated as noise and removed. (4) Most current research on fault diagnosis in signal processing can identify fault locations, such as planetary gears, sun gears, or ring gears, but some can only identify fault states from normal states. However, determining fault types such as tooth root cracks and tooth surface pitting remains challenging. Therefore, it is recommended to focus more on more precise fault diagnosis, including establishing accurate dynamic models for different fault types, designing more targeted representative features, and developing more powerful classifiers. (5) Most of the studies reviewed above focus on detecting one type of fault in certain components (such as gears and bearings) or on a single signal type (such as vibration or acoustic signals). Therefore, it is important to focus on the operation of the entire machine and the processing of multi-sensor data. (6) As observed in the "Applications" section of this review, the combination of multiple signal processing models is becoming a trend. Existing technologies include the integration of wavelet transforms and adaptive time–frequency analysis models. Furthermore, the emergence of autoregressive deconvolution highlights the significance of model combination, bringing clarity to physical meanings. (7) Additionally, clarity in physical meaning is an important advancement in signal processing for structural health. Transitioning from data-driven approaches to optimization based on physical meanings not only improves computational accuracy but also provides a more scientific approach for handling large-scale data.

7. Comparison

Compared to the black-box models of machine learning that rely on data-driven feature extraction, the above traditional methods have significant advantages in terms of interpretability and scenarios with small sample sizes. The time–frequency diagrams, intrinsic mode function (IMF) components, and deconvolution results can be directly associated with the physical characteristics of the structure (such as resonance frequencies and damage impacts), and real-time processing of a single signal can be achieved without the need for training data. However, their performance is limited by manual parameter tuning (such as the window length of the short-time Fourier transform (STFT) and the number of modes in variational mode decomposition (VMD)), and their adaptability to complex working conditions like multi-source coupled vibrations is weaker than that of the end-to-end modeling of deep learning. Future directions may require the integration of the advantages of both. For example, wavelet transform (WT) or empirical mode decomposition (EMD) can be used for preprocessing to enhance the physical significance of features, and then a lightweight network (such as a 1D-convolutional neural network (1D-CNN)) can be applied to mine deep patterns. Alternatively, explainable artificial intelligence (XAI) tools can be utilized to establish explicit associations between traditional features and network decisions, so as to meet the stringent requirements for transparency in engineering scenarios while ensuring diagnostic accuracy.

Author Contributions: Each author contributed extensively to the preparation of this manuscript. Writing—original draft preparation, Y.Z.; investigation, Z.M.; writing—review and editing, L.F.; funding acquisition, L.F. All authors have read and agreed to the published version of the manuscript.

Funding: This work is supported by the National Natural Science Foundation of China under Contract No. 5247514 and No. 52005442 and the Zhejiang Provincial Natural Science Foundation of China under Contract No. LY22E050014.

Institutional Review Board Statement: Not applicable.

Data Availability Statement: No data were used for the research described in the article.

Conflicts of Interest: The authors declare no conflicts of interest.

Abbreviations

The following abbreviations are used in this manuscript:

SHM	Structural Health Monitoring
STFT	Short-Time Fourier Transform
WT	Wavelet Transform

WVD	Wigner–Ville Distribution
EMD	Empirical Mode Decomposition
VMD	Variational Mode Decomposition
MED	Minimum Entropy Deconvolution
MCKD	Maximum Correlated Kurtosis Deconvolution
MEEMD	Modified Ensemble Empirical Mode Decomposition
EEMD	Ensemble Empirical Mode Decomposition
SVMD	Successive Variational Mode Decomposition
IMFs	Intrinsic Mode Functions
SMVMD	Successive Multivariable Variational Mode Decomposition
NCESVMD	Narrowband Constrained Enhanced Continuous Variational Mode Decomposition
AVMD	Automatic Variational Mode Decomposition
D-VMD	De-aliasing Variational Mode Decomposition
D-MVMD	De-aliasing Multivariable Variational Mode Decomposition
I-1DCNN	Improved One-Dimensional Convolutional Neural Network
PSD-VME	Power Spectral Density-Variational Mode Extraction
mRVM	Multiclass Relevance Vector Machines
DAVMD	Differential Evolution-Based Adaptive Variational Mode Decomposition Technique
WOA	Whale Optimization Algorithm
GPR	Ground-Penetrating Radar
SNR	Signal-to-Noise Ratio
EWT	Empirical Wavelet Transform
IEWT	Improved Empirical Wavelet Transform
LSTM	Long Short-Term Memory Network
EFV	Energy Feature Vector
BOCNN	Bayesian Optimized Convolutional Neural Network
CEWT	Cepstrum-Assisted Empirical Wavelet Transform
SIAI	Sensitive IMFs Assessment Index
IEEWT	Improved Extended Empirical Wavelet Transform
DFA	Detrended Fluctuation Analysis
FBSE	Fourier-Bessel Series Expansion
HHT	Hilbert–Huang Transform
VEWT	Variable Spectrum Segmentation Empirical Wavelet Transform
QEWT	Quaternion Empirical Wavelet Transform
IAPEWT	Improved Adaptive Parameter-Free Empirical Wavelet Transform
ASCSD	Adaptive Sparse Coding Shrinkage Denoising
ESN	Echo State Network
IABSR	Improved Adaptive Bistable Stochastic Resonance
AM-FM	Amplitude Modulation–Frequency Modulation
MOMEDA	Minimum Entropy Deconvolution Adjustment
CVS	Continuous Vibration Separation
MEMD	Minimum Entropy Morphological Deconvolution
DSS	Diagonal Slice Spectrum
CFMED	Coarse-to-Fine Minimum Entropy Deconvolution
KLOF	Kernel Local Outlier Factor
PE	Phase Editing
SCI	Spectral Centroid Indicator
IMCKDA	Improved Maximum Correlated Kurtosis Deconvolution Adjustment
IMCKD	Improved Maximum Correlated Kurtosis Deconvolution
MCKD-DeNet	Maximum Correlated Kurtosis Deconvolution Method Based on Deep Networks
FMD	Feature Mode Decomposition
FIR	Finite Impulse Response
PSF	Point Spread Function
MACKD	Maximum Autocorrelation Kurtosis Deconvolution

MLKD	Maximum L-Kurtosis Deconvolution
FDF	Frequency Domain Filtering
MAKD	Maximum Average Kurtosis Deconvolution
UWFBG	Ultra-weak Fiber Bragg Grating
DAS	Distributed Acoustic Sensing
SEAEFD	Spectral Envelope-Based Adaptive Empirical Fourier Decomposition
PSEEFD	Power Spectrum Envelope Adaptive Empirical Fourier Decomposition
GWO	Grey Wolf Optimizer
EMED-AFP	Enhanced Minimum Entropy Deconvolution with Adaptive Filter Parameters
CYCBD β	Generalized Gaussian Cyclostationarity
MOMEDA	Multipoint Optimal Minimum Entropy Deconvolution Adjusted
PCPKD	Periodic Component Pursuit-Based Kurtosis Deconvolution
TF	Time–Frequency
NL	Non-linear Signal
NS	Non-stationary Signal
EFS	Early Fault Signal
CFS	Composite Fault Signal
Window Sel.	Window Selection
Basis Sel.	Basis Function Selection
Mode Mixing	Mode Mixing
Noise Difficulty	Noise Difficulty
Parameter Sel.	Parameter Selection
Computational	Computational Complexity
Parameter Sens.	Parameter Sensitivity

References

1. Amezquita-Sanchez, J.P.; Adeli, H. Signal Processing Techniques for Vibration-Based Health Monitoring of Smart Structures. *Arch. Comput. Methods Eng.* **2016**, *23*, 1–15. [CrossRef]
2. Jung, W.; Kim, S.H.; Yun, S.H.; Bae, J.; Park, Y.H. Vibration, acoustic, temperature, and motor current dataset of rotating machine under varying operating conditions for fault diagnosis. *Data Brief* **2023**, *48*, 109049. [CrossRef] [PubMed]
3. Lizhong, J.; Shaohui, L.; Wangbao, Z.; Jian, Y.; Kang, P.; Zhenbin, R. Evolutionary power spectral density study of the earthquake-induced dynamic irregularity based on short-time Fourier transform. *Eng. Struct.* **2023**, *296*, 116901. [CrossRef]
4. Shen, M.; Yang, F.; Wen, P.; Song, B.; Li, Y. A real-time epilepsy seizure detection approach based on EEG using short-time Fourier transform and Google-Net convolutional neural network. *Heliyon* **2024**, *10*, e31827. [CrossRef]
5. Qi, Y.; Yang, L.; Liu, B.; Liu, L.; Liu, Y.; Zheng, Q.; Liu, D.; Luo, J. Accurate diagnosis of lung tissues for 2D Raman spectrogram by deep learning based on short-time Fourier transform. *Anal. Chim. Acta* **2021**, *1179*, 338821. [CrossRef]
6. Li, B.; Zhang, Z.; Zhu, X. Multitaper adaptive short-time Fourier transform with chirp-modulated Gaussian window and multitaper extracting transform. *Digit. Signal Process.* **2022**, *126*, 103472. [CrossRef]
7. Hao, Y.; Zhang, C.; Lu, Y.; Zhang, L.; Lei, Z.; Li, Z. A novel autoencoder modeling method for intelligent assessment of bearing health based on Short-Time Fourier Transform and ensemble strategy. *Precis. Eng.* **2024**, *85*, 89–101. [CrossRef]
8. Muhashi, A.; Feng, X.; Onishi, Y.; Ota, R.; Liu, H. Enhancing Coincidence Time Resolution of PET detectors using short-time Fourier transform and residual neural network. *Nucl. Instru. Methods Phys. Res. Sect. Accel. Spectrometers Detect. Assoc. Equip.* **2024**, *1065*, 169540. [CrossRef]
9. Amiri, M.; Aghaeinia, H.; Amindavar, H.R. Automatic epileptic seizure detection in EEG signals using sparse common spatial pattern and adaptive short-time Fourier transform-based synchrosqueezing transform. *Biomed. Signal Process. Control* **2023**, *79*, 104022. [CrossRef]
10. Tang, B.; Ding, Y.; Peng, Y.; Cao, J. Target localization algorithm based on improved short-time Fourier transform. *Digit. Signal Process.* **2024**, *155*, 104734. [CrossRef]
11. Tian, L. Seismic spectral decomposition using short-time fractional Fourier transform spectrograms. *J. Appl. Geophys.* **2021**, *192*, 104400. [CrossRef]
12. Mustafa, D.; Yicheng, Z.; Minjie, G.; Jonas, H.; Jürgen, F. Motor Current Based Misalignment Diagnosis on Linear Axes with Short-Time Fourier Transform (STFT). *Procedia CIRP* **2022**, *106*, 239–243. [CrossRef]
13. Wan, T.H.; Tsang, C.W.; Hui, K.; Chung, E. Anomaly detection of train wheels utilizing short-time Fourier transform and unsupervised learning algorithms. *Eng. Appl. Artif. Intell.* **2023**, *122*, 106037. [CrossRef]

14. Zhang, L.; Luo, F.; Pan, G.; Zhang, W.; Ren, G.; Zheng, Z.; Yang, Y. Elucidating the Multi-Timescale Variability of a Canopy Urban Heat Island by Using the Short-Time Fourier Transform. *Geophys. Res. Lett.* **2024**, *51*, e2023GL106221. [CrossRef]
15. Knutsen, H. A fractal uncertainty principle for the short-time Fourier transform and Gabor multipliers. *Appl. Comput. Harmon. Anal.* **2023**, *62*, 365–389. [CrossRef]
16. Shah, F.A.; Lone, W.Z.; Tantary, A.Y. Short-time quadratic-phase Fourier transform. *Optik* **2021**, *245*, 167689. [CrossRef]
17. Wang, J.; Huo, L.; Liu, C.; Song, G. Theoretical and Experimental Study on Homologous Acoustic Emission Signal Recognition Based on Synchrosqueezed Wavelet Transform Coherence. *Struct. Control Health Monit.* **2023**, *2023*, 6968338. [CrossRef]
18. Zhang, Y.; Xie, X.; Li, H.; Zhou, B. An Unsupervised Tunnel Damage Identification Method Based on Convolutional Variational Auto-Encoder and Wavelet Packet Analysis. *Sensors* **2022**, *22*, 2412. [CrossRef]
19. He, F.; Ye, Q. A Bearing Fault Diagnosis Method Based on Wavelet Packet Transform and Convolutional Neural Network Optimized by Simulated Annealing Algorithm. *Sensors* **2022**, *22*, 1410. [CrossRef]
20. Liu, P.; Dong, A.; Wang, C.; Zhang, C.; Zhang, J. Consecutively Missing Seismic Data Reconstruction Via Wavelet-Based Swin Residual Network. *IEEE Geosci. Remote Sens. Lett.* **2023**, *20*, 7502405. [CrossRef]
21. Saadatmorad, M.; Talookolaei, R.A.J.; Pashaei, M.H.; Khatir, S.; Wahab, M.A. Pearson Correlation and Discrete Wavelet Transform for Crack Identification in Steel Beams. *Mathematics* **2022**, *10*, 2689. [CrossRef]
22. Çelebi, M.; Öztürk, S.; Kaplan, K. An enhanced deep learning model based on smoothed pseudo Wigner-Ville distribution technique for emotion recognition with channel selection. *Ain Shams Eng. J.* **2025**, *16*, 103264. [CrossRef]
23. Reddy, A.S.S.; Pachori, R.B. Dynamic mode decomposition-based technique for cross-term suppression in the Wigner-Ville distribution. *Digit. Signal Process.* **2025**, *156*, 104833. [CrossRef]
24. Bhat, M.Y.; Dar, A.H. Quadratic-phase scaled Wigner distribution: Convolution and correlation Quadratic-phase scaled Wigner distribution. *Signal Image Video Process.* **2023**, *17*, 2779–2788. [CrossRef]
25. Yafei, J.; Yongli, Z.; Liuwang, W. Time-frequency Analysis of Partial Discharge Signal Based on VMD and Wigner-Ville Distribution. *J. Syst. Simul.* **2018**, *30*, 569–578.
26. Marios, C.A.; van Eijndhoven, S.; Duin, P. "Seeing Sound": Audio Classification Using theWigner-Ville Distribution and Convolutional Neural Networks. In *Intelligent Systems and Applications, Proceedings of the 2023 Intelligent Systems Conference (IntelliSys), Amsterdam, The Netherlands, 7–8 September 2023*; Lecture Notes in Networks and Systems 822; Arai, K., Ed.; Springer: Berlin/Heidelberg, Germany, 2024; Volume 1, pp. 145–155. [CrossRef]
27. de Carvalho Monson, P.M.; de Oliveira Conceição Junior, P.; Lofrano Dotto, F.R.; de Aguiar, P.R.; Rodrigues, A.R.; David, G.A. Structural damage classification in composite materials using the Wigner-Ville distribution and convolutional neural networks. *Mater. Lett.* **2024**, *369*, 136734. [CrossRef]
28. Rajshekhar, G.; Gorthi, S.S.; Rastogi, P. Polynomial Wigner–Ville distribution-based method for direct phase derivative estimation from optical fringes. *J. Opt. Pure Appl. Opt.* **2009**, *11*, 125402. [CrossRef]
29. Bhat, Y.A.; Sheikh, N. Special Affine Wigner–Ville Distribution in Octonion Domains: Theory and Applications. *Optik* **2023**, *274*, 170531. [CrossRef]
30. Nur, A.T.A.; Bahri, M.; Bachtiar, N.; Rahim, A. Uncertainty principles for coupled fractional Wigner-Ville distribution. *R. Soc. Open Sci.* **2024**, *11*, 231579. [CrossRef]
31. Bhat, M.Y.; Almanjahie, I.M.; Dar, A.H.; Dar, J.G. Wigner-Ville distribution and ambiguity function associated with the quaternion offset linear canonical transform. *Demonstr. Math.* **2022**, *55*, 786–797. [CrossRef]
32. Bhat, M.Y.; Dar, A.H.; Nurhidayat, I.; Pinelas, S. An Interplay of Wigner-Ville Distribution and 2D Hyper-Complex Quadratic-Phase Fourier Transform. *Fractal Fract.* **2023**, *7*, 159. [CrossRef]
33. Neild, S.; McFadden, P.; Williams, M. A review of time-frequency methods for structural vibration analysis. *Eng. Struct.* **2003**, *25*, 713–728. [CrossRef]
34. Huang, N.E.; Shen, Z.; Long, S.R.; Wu, M.C.; Shih, H.H.; Zheng, Q.; Yen, N.C.; Chang, C.C.; Liu, H.H. The empirical mode decomposition and the Hilbert spectrum for nonlinear and non-stationary time series analysis. *Proc. R. Soc. Lond. Ser. Math. Phys. Eng. Sci.* **1998**, *454*, 903–995. [CrossRef]
35. Lei, Y.; Lin, J.; He, Z.; Zuo, M.J. A review on empirical mode decomposition in fault diagnosis of rotating machinery. *Mech. Syst. Signal Process.* **2013**, *35*, 108–126. [CrossRef]
36. Cheng, G.; Wang, X.; He, Y. Remaining useful life and state of health prediction for lithium batteries based on empirical mode decomposition and a long and short memory neural network. *Energy* **2021**, *232*, 121022. [CrossRef]
37. Huang, G.; Li, X.; Zhang, B.; Ren, J. PM2.5 concentration forecasting at surface monitoring sites using GRU neural network based on empirical mode decomposition. *Sci. Total. Environ.* **2021**, *768*, 144516. [CrossRef]
38. Zhu, B.; Han, D.; Wang, P.; Wu, Z.; Zhang, T.; Wei, Y.M. Forecasting carbon price using empirical mode decomposition and evolutionary least squares support vector regression. *Appl. Energy* **2017**, *191*, 521–530. [CrossRef]
39. Liu, M.D.; Ding, L.; Bai, Y.L. Application of hybrid model based on empirical mode decomposition, novel recurrent neural networks and the ARIMA to wind speed prediction. *Energy Convers. Manag.* **2021**, *233*, 113917. [CrossRef]

40. Li, G.; Bu, W.; Yang, H. Noise reduction method for ship radiated noise signal based on modified uniform phase empirical mode decomposition. *Measurement* **2024**, *227*, 114193. [CrossRef]
41. Yin, C.; Wang, Y.; Ma, G.; Wang, Y.; Sun, Y.; He, Y. Weak fault feature extraction of rolling bearings based on improved ensemble noise-reconstructed EMD and adaptive threshold denoising. *Mech. Syst. Signal Process.* **2022**, *171*, 108834. [CrossRef]
42. Guo, J.; Wang, Z.; Li, H.; Yang, Y.; Huang, C.G.; Yazdi, M.; Kang, H.S. A hybrid prognosis scheme for rolling bearings based on a novel health indicator and nonlinear Wiener process. *Reliab. Eng. Syst. Saf.* **2024**, *245*, 110014. [CrossRef]
43. Zheng, Q.; Tian, X.; Yu, Z.; Jin, B.; Jiang, N.; Ding, Y.; Yang, M.; Elhanashi, A.; Saponara, S.; Kpalma, K. Application of complete ensemble empirical mode decomposition based multi-stream informer (CEEMD-MsI) in PM2.5 concentration long-term prediction. *Expert Syst. Appl.* **2024**, *245*, 123008. [CrossRef]
44. Luo, L.; Yan, Y.; Xie, P.; Sun, J.; Xu, Y.; Yuan, J. Hilbert-Huang transform, Hurst and chaotic analysis based flow regime identification methods for an airlift reactor. *Chem. Eng. J.* **2012**, *181–182*, 570–580. [CrossRef]
45. Xu, G.; Tian, W.; Qian, L. EMD- and SVM-based temperature drift modeling and compensation for a dynamically tuned gyroscope (DTG). *Mech. Syst. Signal Process.* **2007**, *21*, 3182–3188. [CrossRef]
46. Tang, J.; Zhao, L.; Yue, H.; Yu, W.; Chai, T. Vibration Analysis Based on Empirical Mode Decomposition and Partial Least Square. *Procedia Eng.* **2011**, *16*, 646–652. [CrossRef]
47. Suo, L.; Peng, T.; Song, S.; Zhang, C.; Wang, Y.; Fu, Y.; Nazir, M.S. Wind speed prediction by a swarm intelligence based deep learning model via signal decomposition and parameter optimization using improved chimp optimization algorithm. *Energy* **2023**, *276*, 127526. [CrossRef]
48. Yang, Y.; Chang, K. Extraction of bridge frequencies from the dynamic response of a passing vehicle enhanced by the EMD technique. *J. Sound Vib.* **2009**, *322*, 718–739. [CrossRef]
49. Randall, R.B.; Antoni, J. Why EMD and similar decompositions are of little benefit for bearing diagnostics. *Mech. Syst. Signal Process.* **2023**, *192*, 110207. [CrossRef]
50. Sezen, C. Pan evaporation forecasting using empirical and ensemble empirical mode decomposition (EEMD) based data-driven models in the Euphrates sub-basin, Turkey. *Earth Sci. Inform.* **2023**, *16*, 3077–3095. [CrossRef]
51. Rezaiy, R.; Shabri, A. Improving Drought Prediction Accuracy: A Hybrid EEMD and Support Vector Machine Approach with Standardized Precipitation Index. *Water Resour. Manag.* **2024**, *38*, 5255–5277. [CrossRef]
52. Rezaiy, R.; Shabri, A. An innovative hybrid W-EEMD-ARIMA model for drought forecasting using the standardized precipitation index. *Nat. Hazards* **2024**, *120*, 13513–13542. [CrossRef]
53. Liao, S.; Wang, H.; Liu, B.; Ma, X.; Zhou, B.; Su, H. Runoff Forecast Model Based on an EEMD-ANN and Meteorological Factors Using a Multicore Parallel Algorithm. *Water Resour. Manag.* **2023**, *37*, 1539–1555. [CrossRef]
54. Li, J.; Tong, Y.; Guan, L.; Wu, S.; Li, D. A UV-visible absorption spectrum denoising method based on EEMD and an improved universal threshold filter. *RSC Adv.* **2018**, *8*, 8558–8568. [CrossRef]
55. Xu, J.; Jiang, W.; Wang, W.; Chen, J.; Shen, Y.; Qi, J. *Removal of EOG Artifact in Electroencephalography with EEMD-ICA: A Semi-Simulation Study on Identification of Artifactual Components*; Springer: Berlin/Heidelberg, Germany, 2023.
56. Sarkar, P.P.; Sen, M.K.; Kabir, G.; Ibne Hossain, N.U. Exploring evolutionary patterns in the teleconnections between Indian summer monsoon rainfall and Indian Ocean dipole over decades. *Clim. Dyn.* **2024**, *62*, 4041–4061. [CrossRef]
57. Zhong, X.Y.; Zeng, L.C.; Zhao, C.H.; Liu, X.M.; Chen, S.J. Fault Diagnosis for Wind Turbine Gearboxes Based on EMD and the Energy Operator. *Appl. Mech. Mater.* **2013**, *281*, 10–13. [CrossRef]
58. Sun, J.; Wu, Z. Isolating spatiotemporally local mixed Rossby-gravity waves using multi-dimensional ensemble empirical mode decomposition. *Clim. Dyn.* **2020**, *54*, 1383–1405. [CrossRef]
59. Yang, L.; Guan, Q.; Lin, J.; Tian, J.; Tan, Z.; Li, H. Evolution of NDVI secular trends and responses to climate change: A perspective from nonlinearity and nonstationarity characteristics. *Remote Sens. Environ.* **2021**, *254*, 112247. [CrossRef]
60. Chang, Y.S.; Yan, Z.; Wang, K.H.; Yao, Y. Non-destructive testing of CFRP using pulsed thermography and multi-dimensional ensemble empirical mode decomposition. *J. Taiwan Inst. Chem. Eng.* **2016**, *61*, 54–63. [CrossRef]
61. Ahmed, S.; Huang, Y.; Tayyab, Q.; Senjyu, T.; Elkholy, M. Identification of power grids low-frequency oscillations through a combined MEEMD-Prony method. *Energy Rep.* **2024**, *11*, 4245–4253. [CrossRef]
62. Min, Y.; Shuzhen, Z.; Wuwei, L. Carbon price prediction based on multi-factor MEEMD-LSTM model. *Heliyon* **2022**, *8*, e12562. [CrossRef]
63. Yang, Q.; Yu, Y.; Dai, D.; He, Q.; Lin, Y. Can hybrid model improve the forecasting performance of stock price index amid COVID-19? Contextual evidence from the MEEMD-LSTM-MLP approach. *N. Am. J. Econ. Financ.* **2024**, *74*, 102252. [CrossRef]
64. Yang, Z.; Kong, C.; Wang, Y.; Rong, X.; Wei, L. Fault diagnosis of mine asynchronous motor based on MEEMD energy entropy and ANN. *Comput. Electr. Eng.* **2021**, *92*, 107070. [CrossRef]
65. Dragomiretskiy, K.; Zosso, D. Variational Mode Decomposition. *IEEE Trans. Signal Process.* **2014**, *62*, 531–544. [CrossRef]

66. Duan, Q.; Xia, H.; Zhang, C. Noise reduction analysis of deformation data based on MEEMD-SVD modeling. In Proceedings of the International Conference on Remote Sensing Technology and Survey Mapping (RSTSM 2024), Changchun, China, 12–14 January 2024; SPIE: Bellingham, WA USA, 2024; Volume 13166.
67. de Oliveira, B.C.F.; Fröhlich, H.B.; Barrera, E.S.; Baldo, C.R.; Albertazzi G., A., Jr.; Schmitt, R. Impact Damage Characterization in CFRP Plates Using PCA and MEEMD Decomposition Methods in Optical Lock-in Thermography Phase Images. In Proceedings of the Optical Measurement Systems for Industrial Inspection XI, Munich, Germany, 24–27 June 2019; SPIE: Bellingham, WA USA, 2019; Volume 11056, p. 110562N. [CrossRef]
68. Zhang, J.; Yan, R.; Gao, R.X.; Feng, Z. Performance enhancement of ensemble empirical mode decomposition. *Mech. Syst. Signal Process.* **2010**, *24*, 2104–2123. [CrossRef]
69. Ravi.; Taran, S. A nonlinear feature extraction approach for speech emotion recognition using VMD and TKEO. *Appl. Acoust.* **2023**, *214*, 109667. [CrossRef]
70. Chen, A.; Kurfess, T.R. Signal processing techniques for rolling element bearing spall size estimation. *Mech. Syst. Signal Process.* **2019**, *117*, 16–32. [CrossRef]
71. Li, K.; Chen, W.; Zou, Y.; Wang, Z.; Zhou, X.; Shi, J. Optimized PSOMV-VMD combined with ConvFormer model: A novel gas pipeline leakage detection method based on low sensitivity acoustic signals. *Measurement* **2025**, *247*, 116804. [CrossRef]
72. Xue, G.; Zhang, Y.; Yu, S.A.; Song, J.; Bian, T.; Gao, Y.; Yan, W.; Guo, Y. Daily residential heat load prediction based on a hybrid model of signal processing, econometric model, and support vector regression. *Therm. Sci. Eng. Prog.* **2023**, *43*, 102005. [CrossRef]
73. Gong, Z.; Wan, A.; Ji, Y.; AL-Bukhaiti, K.; Yao, Z. Improving short-term offshore wind speed forecast accuracy using a VMD-PE-FCGRU hybrid model. *Energy* **2024**, *295*, 131016. [CrossRef]
74. Chen, Y.; Huang, X.; He, Y.; Zhang, S.; Cai, Y. Edge–cloud collaborative estimation lithium-ion battery SOH based on MEWOA-VMD and Transformer. *J. Energy Storage* **2024**, *99*, 113388. [CrossRef]
75. Yuan, D.; Gu, C.; Wei, B.; Qin, X.; Xu, W. A high-performance displacement prediction model of concrete dams integrating signal processing and multiple machine learning techniques. *Appl. Math. Model.* **2022**, *112*, 436–451. [CrossRef]
76. Ma, K.; Nie, X.; Yang, J.; Zha, L.; Li, G.; Li, H. A power load forecasting method in port based on VMD-ICSS-hybrid neural network. *Appl. Energy* **2025**, *377*, 124246. [CrossRef]
77. Ge, X.; Wang, G.; Liu, H.; Huang, T. Removal of AM-FM harmonics using VMD technology for operational modal analysis of milling robot. *Mech. Syst. Signal Process.* **2023**, *200*, 110475. [CrossRef]
78. Ali, A.; Xinhua, W.; Razzaq, I. Optimizing acoustic signal processing for localization of precise pipeline leakage using acoustic signal decomposition and wavelet analysis. *Digit. Signal Process.* **2025**, *157*, 104890. [CrossRef]
79. Lei, W.; Wang, G.; Wan, B.; Min, Y.; Wu, J.; Li, B. High voltage shunt reactor acoustic signal denoising based on the combination of VMD parameters optimized by coati optimization algorithm and wavelet threshold. *Measurement* **2024**, *224*, 113854. [CrossRef]
80. Zhang, H.; Wu, W.; Song, X.; Chen, Z. Improving density logging resolution by VMD-CEEMDAN-ICWT method and its application in thin layer identification. *Geoenergy Sci. Eng.* **2024**, *239*, 212993. [CrossRef]
81. Qi, G.; Zhao, Z.; Zhang, R.; Wang, J.; Li, M.; Shi, X.; Wang, H. Optimized VMD algorithm for signal noise reduction based on TDLAS. *J. Quant. Spectrosc. Radiat. Transf.* **2024**, *312*, 108807. [CrossRef]
82. Li, H.; Li, S.; Sun, J.; Huang, B.; Zhang, J.; Gao, M. Ultrasound signal processing based on joint GWO-VMD wavelet threshold functions. *Measurement* **2024**, *226*, 114143. [CrossRef]
83. Cheng, W.; Zhou, Q.; Wu, S.; Xing, J.; Chen, X.; Du, S.; Xu, Z.; Zhang, R. EI-ISOA-VMD: Adaptive denoising and detrending method for nuclear circulating water pump impeller. *Measurement* **2025**, *242*, 115890. [CrossRef]
84. Du, X.; Zhang, Q.; Wei, Y.; Zhang, T.; Zhang, Y.; Li, Y. Research on denoising of second harmonic signal in photoacoustic spectroscopy based on SSA-VMD-WTD method. *Infrared Phys. Technol.* **2024**, *138*, 105204. [CrossRef]
85. Gao, J.R.; Liu, Y.K.; Duan, C.J.; Ding, P.; Song, J.Q. Research on fault diagnosis of electric gate valve in nuclear power plant based on the VMD-MDI-ISSA-RF model. *Ann. Nucl. Energy* **2024**, *207*, 110701. [CrossRef]
86. Chen, H. A vibration signal processing method based on SE-PSO-VMD for ultrasonic machining. *Syst. Soft Comput.* **2024**, *6*, 200081. [CrossRef]
87. Wang, Y.; Liu, F.; Jiang, Z.; He, S.; Mo, Q. Complex variational mode decomposition for signal processing applications. *Mech. Syst. Signal Process.* **2017**, *86*, 75–85. [CrossRef]
88. Li, H.; Li, M.; Ma, Y.; Zheng, Y.; Li, S. A variational mode decomposition projectile signal processing algorithm of infrared sky screen velocity measurement system and detection mathematical model of detection screen. *Optik* **2023**, *287*, 171077. [CrossRef]
89. Fang, M.; Zhang, F.; Yang, Y.; Tao, R.; Xiao, R.; Zhu, D. The influence of optimization algorithm on the signal prediction accuracy of VMD-LSTM for the pumped storage hydropower unit. *J. Energy Storage* **2024**, *78*, 110187. [CrossRef]
90. Nazari, M.; Sakhaei, S.M. Successive variational mode decomposition. *Signal Process.* **2020**, *174*, 107610. [CrossRef]
91. Chen, Q.; Chen, J.; Lang, X.; Xie, L.; ur Rehman, N.; Su, H. Self-tuning variational mode decomposition. *J. Frankl. Inst.* **2021**, *358*, 7825–7862. [CrossRef]

92. Sun, L.; Huang, X.; Zhao, J.; Wang, X.; Ma, M. An intelligent chatter detection method for high-speed milling under variable tool-workpiece systems and cutting parameters. *Mech. Syst. Signal Process.* **2025**, *224*, 111960. [CrossRef]
93. Faisal, K.N.; Sharma, R.R. Successive variational mode decomposition-based enhanced Wigner-Ville distribution for seismo-volcanic events identification. *J. Volcanol. Geotherm. Res.* **2023**, *440*, 107847. [CrossRef]
94. Gao, W.; Liu, D.; Wang, Q.; Zhao, Y.; Sun, J. Narrowband constraint-enhanced successive variational mode decomposition. *Biomed. Signal Process. Control* **2025**, *104*, 107396. [CrossRef]
95. Wu, S.; Huang, J.; Liu, W.; Pang, Y.; Zhu, T. Anti-noise UWFBG hydrophone array enhanced DAS system using optimising SVMD based on matched interferometric. *Opt. Fiber Technol.* **2024**, *88*, 104051. [CrossRef]
96. Yang, H.; Cheng, Y.; Li, G. A denoising method for ship radiated noise based on Spearman variational mode decomposition, spatial-dependence recurrence sample entropy, improved wavelet threshold denoising, and Savitzky-Golay filter. *Alex. Eng. J.* **2021**, *60*, 3379–3400. [CrossRef]
97. Zeng, R.; Wu, Q.; Zhang, L. Two-terminal traveling wave fault location based on successive variational mode decomposition and frequency-dependent propagation velocity. *Electr. Power Syst. Res.* **2022**, *213*, 108768. [CrossRef]
98. Fu, S.; Wu, J.; Zhang, Q.; Xie, B. Robust and efficient synchronization for structural health monitoring data with arbitrary time lags. *Eng. Struct.* **2025**, *322*, 119183. [CrossRef]
99. Ye, M.; Yan, X.; Chen, N.; Jia, M. Intelligent fault diagnosis of rolling bearing using variational mode extraction and improved one-dimensional convolutional neural network. *Appl. Acoust.* **2023**, *202*, 109143. [CrossRef]
100. Feng, Z.; Zhang, Z. A small sample rolling bearing fault diagnosis based on PSD-VME and DS evidence theory enhanced mRVM. *Comput. Electr. Eng.* **2024**, *118*, 109458. [CrossRef]
101. Li, C.; Liu, Y.; Liao, Y.; Wang, J. A VME method based on the convergent tendency of VMD and its application in multi-fault diagnosis of rolling bearings. *Measurement* **2022**, *198*, 111360. [CrossRef]
102. Zhong, X.; Xia, T.; Mei, Q. A Parameter-Adaptive VME Method Based on Particle Swarm Optimization for Bearing Fault Diagnosis. *Exp. Tech.* **2023**, *47*, 435–448. [CrossRef]
103. Chen, Q.; Zhang, C.; Hu, T.; Zhou, Y.; Ni, H.; Wang, T. Online chatter detection in robotic machining based on adaptive variational mode decomposition. *Int. J. Adv. Manuf. Technol.* **2021**, *117*, 555–577. [CrossRef]
104. Lu, J.; Li, J.; Zhao, X.; Chen, Y.; Meng, L.; Yang, D.; Hou, N. Adaptive denoising method for leakage detection of liquid pipelines using automatic variational mode decomposition. *J. Frankl. Inst.* **2025**, *362*, 107475. [CrossRef]
105. Wang, Y. An Adaptive Variational Mode Decomposition Technique with Differential Evolution Algorithm and Its Application Analysis. *Shock Vib.* **2021**, *2021*, 2030128. [CrossRef]
106. Yang, D.; Persico, R.; Guo, C.; Liu, Y.; Yang, J.; Liu, H.; Bai, C.; Zhao, Q. Adaptive variational mode decomposition denoising scheme for ground penetrating radar data. *J. Phys. Conf. Ser.* **2024**, *2887*, 012031. [CrossRef]
107. Lian, J.; Liu, Z.; Wang, H.; Dong, X. Adaptive variational mode decomposition method for signal processing based on mode characteristic. *Mech. Syst. Signal Process.* **2018**, *107*, 53–77. [CrossRef]
108. Mousavi, A.A.; Zhang, C.; Masri, S.F.; Gholipour, G. Damage detection and localization of a steel truss bridge model subjected to impact and white noise excitations using empirical wavelet transform neural network approach. *Measurement* **2021**, *185*, 110060. [CrossRef]
109. Gao, R.; Du, L.; Duru, O.; Yuen, K.F. Time series forecasting based on echo state network and empirical wavelet transformation. *Appl. Soft Comput.* **2021**, *102*, 107111. [CrossRef]
110. Li, J.; Wang, H.; Wang, X.; Zhang, Y. Rolling bearing fault diagnosis based on improved adaptive parameterless empirical wavelet transform and sparse denoising. *Measurement* **2020**, *152*, 107392. [CrossRef]
111. Bhattacharyya, A.; Singh, L.; Pachori, R.B. Fourier–Bessel series expansion based empirical wavelet transform for analysis of non-stationary signals. *Digit. Signal Process.* **2018**, *78*, 185–196. [CrossRef]
112. Zhang, K.; Deng, Y.; Chen, P.; Ma, C.; Xu, Y. Quaternion empirical wavelet transform and its applications in rolling bearing fault diagnosis. *Measurement* **2022**, *195*, 111179. [CrossRef]
113. Anuragi, A.; Singh Sisodia, D.; Bilas Pachori, R. EEG-based cross-subject emotion recognition using Fourier-Bessel series expansion based empirical wavelet transform and NCA feature selection method. *Inf. Sci.* **2022**, *610*, 508–524. [CrossRef]
114. Wang, J.; Bethel, B.J.; Xie, W.; Dong, C. A hybrid model for significant wave height prediction based on an improved empirical wavelet transform decomposition and long-short term memory network. *Ocean Model.* **2024**, *189*, 102367. [CrossRef]
115. Zheng, X.; Li, H.; Zhang, S.; Zhang, Y.; Li, J.; Zhang, Y.; Zhao, W. Hydrodynamic feature extraction and intelligent identification of flow regimes in vaneless space of a pump turbine using improved empirical wavelet transform and Bayesian optimized convolutional neural network. *Energy* **2023**, *282*, 128705. [CrossRef]
116. Liu, Q.; Yang, J.; Zhang, K. An improved empirical wavelet transform and sensitive components selecting method for bearing fault. *Measurement* **2022**, *187*, 110348. [CrossRef]
117. Bounoua, W.; Aftab, M.F. Improved extended empirical wavelet transform for accurate multivariate oscillation detection and characterisation in plant-wide industrial control loops. *J. Process Control* **2024**, *138*, 103226. [CrossRef]

118. Kim, Y.; Ha, J.M.; Na, K.; Park, J.; Youn, B.D. Cepstrum-assisted empirical wavelet transform (CEWT)-based improved demodulation analysis for fault diagnostics of planetary gearboxes. *Measurement* **2021**, *183*, 109796. [CrossRef]
119. Zhang, K.; Shi, L.; Hu, Y.; Chen, P.; Xu, Y. Variable spectral segmentation empirical wavelet transform for noisy signal processing. *Digit. Signal Process.* **2021**, *117*, 103151. [CrossRef]
120. Xin, Y.; Hao, H.; Li, J. Time-varying system identification by enhanced Empirical Wavelet Transform based on Synchroextracting Transform. *Eng. Struct.* **2019**, *196*, 109313. [CrossRef]
121. Teng, W.; Ding, X.; Cheng, H.; Han, C.; Liu, Y.; Mu, H. Compound faults diagnosis and analysis for a wind turbine gearbox via a novel vibration model and empirical wavelet transform. *Renew. Energy* **2019**, *136*, 393–402. [CrossRef]
122. Zhang, X.; Wang, J.; Liu, Z.; Wang, J. Weak feature enhancement in machinery fault diagnosis using empirical wavelet transform and an improved adaptive bistable stochastic resonance. *ISA Trans.* **2019**, *84*, 283–295. [CrossRef]
123. Karimpour, A.; Rahmatalla, S. Extended Empirical Wavelet Transformation: Application to structural updating. *J. Sound Vib.* **2021**, *500*, 116026. [CrossRef]
124. Zheng, J.; Cao, S.; Pan, H.; Ni, Q. Spectral envelope-based adaptive empirical Fourier decomposition method and its application to rolling bearing fault diagnosis. *ISA Trans.* **2022**, *129*, 476–492. [CrossRef]
125. Wei, P.; Li, Q.; Sun, M.; Huang, J. Modal identification of high-rise buildings by combined scheme of improved empirical wavelet transform and Hilbert transform techniques. *J. Build. Eng.* **2023**, *63*, 105443. [CrossRef]
126. Gong, W.B.; Li, A.; Wu, Z.H.; Qin, F.J. Nonlinear vibration feature extraction based on power spectrum envelope adaptive empirical Fourier decomposition. *ISA Trans.* **2023**, *139*, 660–674. [CrossRef] [PubMed]
127. Zhou, W.; Feng, Z.; Xu, Y.; Wang, X.; Lv, H. Empirical Fourier decomposition: An accurate signal decomposition method for nonlinear and non-stationary time series analysis. *Mech. Syst. Signal Process.* **2022**, *163*, 108155. [CrossRef]
128. Kumar, B.; Yadav, N.; Sunil. A novel hybrid algorithm based on Empirical Fourier decomposition and deep learning for wind speed forecasting. *Energy Convers. Manag.* **2024**, *300*, 117891. [CrossRef]
129. Singh, P.; Bana, D.; Sadhu, A. Improved bridge modal identification from vibration measurements using a hybrid empirical Fourier decomposition. *J. Sound Vib.* **2024**, *590*, 118598. [CrossRef]
130. Endo, H.; Randall, R. Enhancement of autoregressive model based gear tooth fault detection technique by the use of minimum entropy deconvolution filter. *Mech. Syst. Signal Process.* **2007**, *21*, 906–919. [CrossRef]
131. Ma, H.; Feng, Z. Planet bearing fault diagnosis using multipoint Optimal Minimum Entropy Deconvolution Adjusted. *J. Sound Vib.* **2019**, *449*, 235–273. [CrossRef]
132. Hou, Y.; Zhou, C.; Tian, C.; Wang, D.; He, W.; Huang, W.; Wu, P.; Wu, D. Acoustic feature enhancement in rolling bearing fault diagnosis using sparsity-oriented multipoint optimal minimum entropy deconvolution adjusted method. *Appl. Acoust.* **2022**, *201*, 109105. [CrossRef]
133. Wu, L.; Zhang, X.; Wang, J.; Liu, Z.; Gong, Z. An enhanced minimum entropy deconvolution with adaptive filter parameters for gear fault diagnosis. *Measurement* **2023**, *206*, 112343. [CrossRef]
134. Zhou, X.; Li, Y.; Jiang, L.; Zhou, L. Fault feature extraction for rolling bearings based on parameter-adaptive variational mode decomposition and multi-point optimal minimum entropy deconvolution. *Measurement* **2021**, *173*, 108469. [CrossRef]
135. Duan, R.; Liao, Y.; Yang, L.; Xue, J.; Tang, M. Minimum entropy morphological deconvolution and its application in bearing fault diagnosis. *Measurement* **2021**, *182*, 109649. [CrossRef]
136. Zhang, L.; Hu, N. Fault diagnosis of sun gear based on continuous vibration separation and minimum entropy deconvolution. *Measurement* **2019**, *141*, 332–344. [CrossRef]
137. Miao, Y.; Li, C.; Zhang, B.; Lin, J. Application of a coarse-to-fine minimum entropy deconvolution method for rotating machines fault detection. *Mech. Syst. Signal Process.* **2023**, *198*, 110431. [CrossRef]
138. Shao, H.; Li, B.; Xu, X.; Shi, P.; Qiao, Z.; Li, R. Minimum entropy deconvolution enhanced by KLOF and phase editing for fault diagnosis of rotating machinery. *Appl. Acoust.* **2023**, *209*, 109423. [CrossRef]
139. Cheng, Y.; Zhou, N.; Zhang, W.; Wang, Z. Application of an improved minimum entropy deconvolution method for railway rolling element bearing fault diagnosis. *J. Sound Vib.* **2018**, *425*, 53–69. [CrossRef]
140. Xu, X.; Liao, X.; Zhou, T.; He, Z.; Hu, H. Vibration-based identification of lubrication starved bearing using spectral centroid indicator combined with minimum entropy deconvolution. *Measurement* **2024**, *226*, 114156. [CrossRef]
141. Yun, X.; Mei, X.; Jiang, G. Time-delayed feedback stochastic resonance enhanced minimum entropy deconvolution for weak fault detection of rolling element bearings. *Chin. J. Phys.* **2022**, *76*, 1–13. [CrossRef]
142. Miao, Y.; Zhao, M.; Liang, K.; Lin, J. Application of an improved MCKDA for fault detection of wind turbine gear based on encoder signal. *Renew. Energy* **2020**, *151*, 192–203. [CrossRef]
143. Hong, L.; Liu, X.; Zuo, H. Compound faults diagnosis based on customized balanced multiwavelets and adaptive maximum correlated kurtosis deconvolution. *Measurement* **2019**, *146*, 87–100. [CrossRef]
144. Miao, Y.; Zhao, M.; Lin, J.; Lei, Y. Application of an improved maximum correlated kurtosis deconvolution method for fault diagnosis of rolling element bearings. *Mech. Syst. Signal Process.* **2017**, *92*, 173–195. [CrossRef]

145. Miao, Y.; Li, C.; Shi, H.; Han, T. Deep network-based maximum correlated kurtosis deconvolution: A novel deep deconvolution for bearing fault diagnosis. *Mech. Syst. Signal Process.* **2023**, *189*, 110110. [CrossRef]
146. McDonald, G.L.; Zhao, Q.; Zuo, M.J. Maximum correlated Kurtosis deconvolution and application on gear tooth chip fault detection. *Mech. Syst. Signal Process.* **2012**, *33*, 237–255. [CrossRef]
147. Peng, D.; Zhu, X.; Teng, W.; Liu, Y. Use of generalized Gaussian cyclostationarity for blind deconvolution and its application to bearing fault diagnosis under non-Gaussian conditions. *Mech. Syst. Signal Process.* **2023**, *196*, 110351. [CrossRef]
148. Hashim, S.; Shakya, P. A spectral kurtosis based blind deconvolution approach for spur gear fault diagnosis. *ISA Trans.* **2023**, *142*, 492–500. [CrossRef]
149. Ni, Z.; He, D.; Wang, X.; Zhang, Y. Research on the detection of axle abnormal noise based on maximum autocorrelation kurtosis deconvolution. *Appl. Acoust.* **2023**, *203*, 109228. [CrossRef]
150. Wang, Z.; Du, W.; Wang, J.; Zhou, J.; Han, X.; Zhang, Z.; Huang, L. Research and application of improved adaptive MOMEDA fault diagnosis method. *Measurement* **2019**, *140*, 63–75. [CrossRef]
151. Pan, H.; Yin, X.; Cheng, J.; Zheng, J.; Tong, J.; Liu, T. Periodic component pursuit-based kurtosis deconvolution and its application in roller bearing compound fault diagnosis. *Mech. Mach. Theory* **2023**, *185*, 105337. [CrossRef]
152. Xu, H.; Zhou, S. Maximum L-Kurtosis deconvolution and frequency-domain filtering algorithm for bearing fault diagnosis. *Mech. Syst. Signal Process.* **2025**, *223*, 111916. [CrossRef]
153. Liang, K.; Zhao, M.; Lin, J.; Jiao, J.; Ding, C. Maximum average kurtosis deconvolution and its application for the impulsive fault feature enhancement of rotating machinery. *Mech. Syst. Signal Process.* **2021**, *149*, 107323. [CrossRef]

algorithms

MDPI

Article

Forecasting Cancer Incidence in Canada by Age, Sex, and Region Until 2026 Using Machine Learning Techniques

Ehsan Kaviani and Kalpdrum Passi *

School of Engineering and Computer Science, Laurentian University, Sudbury, ON P3E 2C6, Canada; ekaviani@laurentian.ca
* Correspondence: kpassi@laurentian.ca

Abstract: This study analyzes cancer trends in Canada using machine learning techniques to extract insights from extensive cancer data sourced from the Canadian Cancer Society and Statistics Canada. It aims to enhance the understanding of cancer epidemiology and inform better prevention, diagnosis, and treatment strategies. Data preprocessing addressed issues like missing values and normalization, ensuring reliability. The findings indicate a steady increase in new cancer cases, with estimates reaching 248,700 in 2026, up from 244,000 in 2022. Male incidence rates are projected to rise slightly to 602.3 per 100,000, while female rates may decline to 530.6. Regions such as Alberta, British Columbia, Ontario, and Quebec show rising incidence rates, contrasted by declines in Newfoundland and Labrador, Nunavut, and Yukon. Notably, this research reveals significant increases in cancer cases among individuals aged 60 and older, particularly those 70+. The hybrid ARIMA-LSTM model demonstrated superior forecasting accuracy compared with the other selected models. These findings offer valuable insights for health policymakers and highlight the potential of machine learning in public health forecasting, providing a framework for future research in other disease areas.

Keywords: machine learning; cancer incidence; data analysis; forecasting; Canada

1. Introduction

Cancer is a multifaceted and devastating disease with a significant impact on individuals, communities, and economies. Its complex nature is due to genetic, environmental, and behavioral factors [1]. Despite substantial advances in research, cancer remains a global challenge, hampered by economic, political, and legislative barriers [2]. Advances in technology, such as cancer informatics and molecular genetics, have paved the way for new tools and methods for prevention, diagnosis, and treatment. However, this development's ethical and social implications and the need for comprehensive global strategies to address the growing cancer burden require careful consideration [3].

Machine learning techniques have revolutionized computing by enabling the extraction of patterns and knowledge from large and complex datasets [4]. These techniques, which include supervised, unsupervised, semi-supervised, and reinforcement learning, are particularly effective in solving big data problems [5]. This field has made significant progress, especially in deep learning, which could analyze and learn from vast amounts of real data [6]. Therefore, ML is widely used in various industries to obtain relevant information for analysis [7].

Advanced technologies such as mitochondrial, epigenomic, and metabolic profiling offer significant potential in cancer epidemiology, especially in identifying at-risk populations and treatment responses [8]. However, using electronic health record data in oncology presents challenges, including missing or unstructured data elements [9]. AI techniques, including machine learning and deep learning, have shown promise in predicting and detecting cancer, sometimes better than doctors [10]. The use of big data in cancer treatment is promising. Still, it is hindered by incomplete and fragmented data, which can be solved by integrating health systems and using AI [11].

Recent studies have highlighted the potential of ML in cancer prediction and survival research [12,13]. These techniques transform healthcare by providing insights into patient care, operational efficiency, and cost reduction [14]. The application of ML in cancer research and care is particularly promising, with the potential to construct real-world data cohorts and improve predictive modeling [15]. However, concerns over patient data privacy and security, algorithmic bias, and needing trained individuals to interpret results remain important considerations [14].

In Canada, a country that is struggling with the ever-changing landscape of cancer diagnoses, it is critical to use state-of-the-art techniques to analyze incidence patterns. Canada's diverse population, regional differences, and changing medical practices provide an exceptional environment for a thorough cancer data analysis. For delivering insightful information, proactive healthcare management, and policy creation, this research aims to utilize ML skills to identify current trends and predict future ones.

This study's backdrop essentially stems from the realization that cancer is a complex, multifaceted phenomenon with implications for society and the economy in addition to being a medical problem. Despite significant advancements in oncology, the dynamic nature of cancer trends and disparities across populations demands more adaptive and predictive analytical tools. Given these challenges, leveraging machine learning—a powerful tool for analyzing large-scale, complex datasets—offers promising new avenues to more accurately understand and forecast cancer trends. By integrating machine learning's computational capabilities with the intricacies of cancer data, this research aims to uncover new insights that may lead to tailored treatment plans, more efficient interventions, and, ultimately, a significant decrease in cancer incidence in Canada and other countries. Additionally, the research emphasizes the need for collaborative efforts across disciplines, bringing together oncology, data science, and public health experts to address the intricate challenges cancer poses on a global scale.

2. Related Works

The Canadian population and healthcare systems are significantly affected by cancer. It is the leading cause of death in Canada, as stated by multiple sources [16–19]. Studies have estimated that 43% of all Canadians are expecting to receive a cancer diagnosis in their lifetime [16,20]. As the population increases and ages, the number of new cancer cases and deaths in Canada is also growing [16,21]. Additionally, cancer is a costly disease, with the economic burden of cancer care in Canada rising from CAD 2.9 billion in 2005 to CAD 7.5 billion in 2012 annually, as reported by various sources [16,22].

Because cancer significantly impacts Canadian health and the economy, accurate and comprehensive surveillance data are critical for determining progress and allocating resources accordingly. The Canadian Advisory Committee on Cancer Statistics collaborates with the Canadian Cancer Society, Statistics Canada, and the Public Health Agency of Canada to produce the latest statistics on cancer surveillance in Canada [16].

Cancer data can take several years to catch up to the present due to the lengthy process of collecting, verifying, and analyzing the information. However, statistical models can project short-term incidence and mortality rates by extrapolating past trends. This provides a more current understanding of the cancer landscape in Canada, which is crucial for resource planning, research, and informing cancer control programs. *Canadian Cancer*

Statistics 2021 offers detailed estimates of cancer incidence, mortality, and survival in Canada for 22 cancer types, broken down by age, sex, geographic region, and over time. Brenner et al. [16–18] also provided updated estimates for 2020, 2022, and 2024 for new cancer cases and deaths expected for all ages, broken down by sex, province, and territory.

To acquire the latest cancer incidence and mortality estimates, the study utilized the CANPROJ projection R package to project counts and rates until 2024. CANPROJ employs trends in factual data to determine the most suitable model for forthcoming years through a decision algorithm composed of a range of age-based, period-based, and cohort-based models [16–18,23].

According to Brenner [16], cancer case data from Quebec, starting from 2011, were unavailable as they had not yet been submitted to the Canadian Cancer Registry. Because only data up to 2010 were accessible for Quebec, estimates for cancer cases and incidence rates from 2011 to 2022 were generated by initially applying the cancer rates of Canada (excluding Quebec) to Quebec's population. Based on the average rate for the rest of the country, adjusted Quebec rates were then modified using the ratio of sex- and age-specific cancer estimates for Quebec relative to the rest of Canada from 2006 to 2010. Additional correction factors were incorporated, considering provisional 2011 counts for cancers that are typically underreported, such as prostate and melanoma. These projections provided estimates for 22 cancer types, categorized by sex assigned at birth and geographic region (provinces and territories). The national estimates for Canada were derived by summing the individual projections for each province and territory. All incidence and mortality rates were age-standardized to the 2011 Canadian standard population using the direct method.

Brenner's study [16] utilized historical cancer data from the National Cancer Reporting System (1984–1991) and the Canadian Cancer Registry (1992–2018), as well as mortality data from the Vital Statistics Canada Death Database (1984–2019). It applied the CANPROJ projection package, which uses trends in historical data to select the most appropriate model to predict future cancer incidence and mortality. This approach involved a decision algorithm from a series of six age-period-cohort (APC) models aimed to provide the most accurate projections up to 2022. For the province of Quebec, particular adjustments were made for incidence estimates due to missing data after 2010.

While Brenner's studies do not specify numerical values for the accuracy of its projections, the methodology implies a reliance on historical trends and demographic data to make informed predictions. The projections estimated that there were an estimated 225,800 new cancer cases and 83,300 cancer deaths in 2020. This increased to 233,900 new cases and 85,100 deaths in 2022. Projections for 2024 indicate a further rise, with 247,100 new cancer cases and 88,100 cancer deaths expected [16–18].

While Brenner's studies offered valuable cancer projections using the CANPROJ statistical framework, their approach primarily relies on historical trend extrapolation using age-period-cohort models. These models assume a consistent pattern in past data and select the best-fit trend-based model for projection. However, they do not incorporate modern performance evaluation metrics (e.g., MAE, RMSE, R^2) and are limited in handling incomplete, noisy, or complex datasets.

In contrast, our study applies machine learning models—such as LSTM, ARIMA, Prophet, and a hybrid ARIMA-LSTM—which not only provide greater flexibility in modeling both linear and nonlinear relationships but also allow for rigorous evaluation through quantitative performance metrics. ML models are also better suited for large-scale healthcare data where variability and missing values are common. This methodological distinction enables our research to offer more accurate and adaptable forecasts for cancer incidence in Canada.

3. Materials and Methods

3.1. Research Design

This research employs a combination of quantitative methodologies to analyze cancer incidence trends in Canada, utilizing advanced machine learning models. By applying LSTM, Prophet, ARIMA, and hybrid ARIMA-LSTM models, the research aims to predict future cancer incidence rates and the number of new cases. This comprehensive approach allows for a deep understanding of cancer trends, contributing to better healthcare planning and policymaking. The study employs a longitudinal design, analyzing time series data of cancer incidence rates in Canada over multiple years. This approach facilitates the identification of trends and patterns in cancer rates, allowing for accurate predictions. Using multiple predictive models ensures the robustness and reliability of the forecasts, catering to the nonlinear and complex nature of the data. The study's predictive nature addresses a significant gap in current knowledge, offering insights into potential future cancer rates and enabling proactive measures in public health strategies. Figure 1 shows the research process.

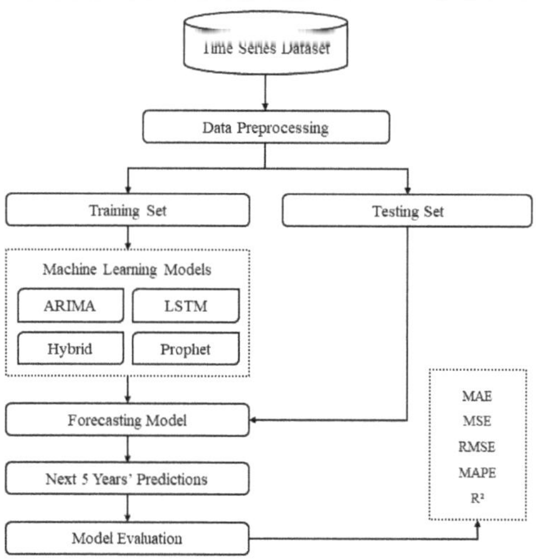

Figure 1. Research process.

The dataset was divided into training (80%) and testing (20%) subsets to ensure robust model evaluation. This partitioning strategy ensures that the models are trained on historical cancer incidence data while reserving a separate portion for performance evaluation.

The models were trained using historical data (1992–2016) and validated with a test set (2017–2021). Once validated and finalized, each model (ARIMA, LSTM, Prophet, hybrid ARIMA-LSTM) was then used to forecast the number of new cancer cases and incidence rates sequentially for future years (2022 to 2026).

The study implemented a validation procedure for forecasting models, including time series cross-validation. Due to the sequential nature of data, traditional random cross-validation methods are not used, and 10-fold cross-validation must be used to verify the time series. This process is repeated by moving the cutoff point through the time series to ensure that each model's performance is tested in different periods and conditions.

Evaluation metrics such as mean absolute error (MAE), mean squared error (MSE), root mean squared error (RMSE), and R-squared (R^2) were calculated on the test set to assess prediction accuracy.

3.2. Data Source

This study obtained data on cancer incidence from the Canadian Cancer Registry Tabulation Master File, which Statistics Canada released on 31 January 2024. The table includes cancer cases diagnosed from 1992 to 2021 and is available by cancer type, region, age group, and sex.

The Canadian Cancer Registry (CCR) is a population-based registry with data collected and reported to Statistics Canada by each provincial/territorial cancer registry. This person-based system aims to collect information about each new primary cancer diagnosed among Canadian residents since 1992 [24]. Cancer incidence refers to the number of new cancers in a population during a specific period (usually a year). It is generally expressed as the number of new cancer cases per 100,000 population. Data presented in [25] were age-adjusted using the 2011 Canadian standard population to ensure accuracy and consistency [24].

3.3. Data Preprocessing

Prior to model training and evaluation, several preprocessing steps were applied to ensure data quality and model compatibility:

3.3.1. Handling Missing Data

Quebec's cancer incidence data was unavailable after 2017 due to incomplete submissions to the Canadian Cancer Registry. To address this gap, Quebec's missing incidence data from 2018 to 2022 were imputed using a multiple imputation strategy based on available historical trends and region-specific cancer patterns. Other provinces with minor missing values, less than 3% of the data, were handled using multiple imputations again.

3.3.2. Normalization

To ensure consistency across features and models, all incidence rate and case count values were normalized using min-max scaling to a range between 0 and 1. This was especially important for neural network models (e.g., LSTM), which are sensitive to the scale of input features. Normalization helped stabilize the training process and improve model convergence.

3.3.3. Temporal Indexing

Dates were converted into a standardized time index to ensure uniform time series input formats across all models, especially for ARIMA and Prophet, which require a consistent datetime structure.

3.3.4. Stationarity Checks

For models like ARIMA and ARIMA-LSTM, stationarity was assessed using the Augmented Dickey–Fuller test. Non-stationary series were differenced as required to satisfy model assumptions.

These preprocessing steps were essential for maintaining data integrity and enabling fair comparison across diverse model architectures.

3.4. Model Selection

To investigate the trends in cancer incidence in this study, four popular machine learning algorithms and statistical techniques for time series prediction were selected based on their proven track record in time series forecasting: Prophet, long short-term memory (LSTM) networks, autoregressive integrated moving average (ARIMA), and the hybrid ARIMA-LSTM model.

3.4.1. Long Short-Term Memory (LSTM)

Introduced by Hochreiter and Schmidhuber in 1997 [26], LSTM networks are a variant of RNNs that overcome the shortcomings of standard RNNs. These disadvantages include poor performance in handling long-term dependencies and the vanishing or exploding gradient problem. In 1999, a forgotten gate was added to LSTM to restore cell memory, improve the original structure, and become the standard structure for LSTM networks. Unlike deep feedforward neural networks (DFNN), LSTMs contain feedback connections and can process data sequences, not just individual data points such as vectors or arrays [27].

In LSTM networks, the fundamental building block is called a memory block or LSTM unit. Composed of a cell that acts as the memory component and three gates (input, output, forget/keep), these units can retain information over arbitrary periods. The gates of the LSTM unit are responsible for regulating the flow of data through the cell. One of the most prominent features of the LSTM cell is the "constant error carousel" (CEC). An LSTM network is structured similarly to an RNN, except the hidden layers comprise memory blocks instead of neurons [27].

Input gate: The unit features a sigmoidal function that regulates the inflow of data into the cell. It obtains activation from the previous output $h^{(t-1)}$ and the current input $x^{(t)}$. By means of the sigmoid function, an input gate produces values ranging from zero to one. A value of zero acts as a complete blockage of information, while a value of one permits the passage of all information. Equation (1) shows this process [27].

$$i^t = \sigma\left(W^{(ix)}\, x^{(t)} + U^{(ih)}\, h^{(t-1)} + b^i\right) \tag{1}$$

Cell input layer: The input to the cell is like the input gate. It takes in the previously hidden state $h^{(t-1)}$ and the current input $x^{(t)}$. However, a "tanh" activation function is used to squash the input values to a range between -1 and 1, which is indicated by the symbol l^t in the Equation (2) [27].

$$l^t = tanh\,\left(W^{(lx)}\, x^{(t)} + U^{(lh)}\, h^{(t-1)} + b^l\right) \tag{2}$$

Forget gate: A unit using a sigmoidal function decides what information from previous steps of the cell should be remembered or discarded. The forget gate takes input from $h^{(t-1)}$ and $x^{(t)}$ and assumes values between zero and one. The next step involves a Hadamard product with the old cell state c^{t-1} to update to a new cell state c^t in the below equation. If the forget gate has a value of zero, it is closed and will completely forget the information of the old cell state c^{t-1}. On the other hand, the value of one will make all information memorable. Thus, the forget gate has the authority to reset the cell state if the old data are deemed irrelevant. Equation (3) summarizes the forget gate mechanism [27].

$$f^t = \sigma\left(W^{(fx)}\, x^{(t)} + U^{(fh)}\, h^{(t-1)} + b^f\right) \tag{3}$$

Cell state: The cell state is responsible for storing a cell's memory over an extended period. Each cell contains a self-connected linear unit known as a constant error carousel (CEC), which recurrently operates to prevent the vanishing or exploding gradient problem in an LSTM network. The CEC incorporates a forget gate that regulates and resets the gate as needed. At time t, the present cell state c^t is modified by the previous cell state c^{t-1}, controlled by the forget gate, and the current input and cell input product ($i^t \circ l^t$). Equation (4) summarizes the overall update of a cell state [27].

$$c^t = f^t \circ c^{t-1} + i^t \circ l^t \tag{4}$$

Output gate: A unit equipped with a sigmoidal function has the ability to regulate the passage of information from a cell. In contrast, an LSTM network utilizes the output gate values at a particular time (represented by o^t) to govern the present cell state c^t, which is then stimulated by a "tanh" function to produce the ultimate output vector $h^{(t)}$. Equations (5) and (6) show the mechanism of the output gate [27].

$$o^t = \sigma\left(W^{(ox)}\, x^{(t)} + U^{(oh)}\, h^{(t-1)} + b^o\right) \tag{5}$$

$$h^t = o^t \circ \tanh\left(c^t\right) \tag{6}$$

3.4.2. Facebook Prophet Forecasting Model

Facebook's Prophet network is a strong tool that can accurately predict time-series data using daily observations of patterns at different scales. Forecast time-series data are derived from additional models, where nonlinear trends account for seasonal, weekly, and daily periods, including holiday results. This tool works best during periods with stable seasonal results and a few seasons of historical data. Prophet deals with missing data and trend changes and can often adapt to deviations. It allows users to make more accurate forecasts faster than other time series forecasting strategies, requiring very little computer time. Prophet is at the level of other models and quickly generates predictions in seconds. This tool can be used to generate accurate weather forecasts even from incomplete or black data without manual work. In addition, the Prophet has many "human" seasons of the week and year [28,29].

As a powerful tool for Python and R released in 2017 by Facebook, Prophet models time series datasets with trends, seasonality, and holidays. Prophet takes a few seconds to fit the model with tunable parameters, and it is represented by the Formula (7) [30]:

$$y(t) = g(t) + s(t) + h(t) + \epsilon_t \tag{7}$$

The equation provides a comprehensive prediction formula for the Prophet forecasting model, wherein the anticipated outcome, y(t), is determined by the linear or logistic equation, g(t); seasonality based on the chosen period, such as yearly, monthly, or daily, is denoted as s(t); holiday-related anomalies are denoted as h(t); and unforeseen errors are denoted as ϵ_t. The model encompasses multiple parameters that can be fine-tuned to enhance forecasting accuracy. Depending on the intended use, the model can be classified as linear or logistic. Linear models normalize outliers and do not impose a maximum or minimum threshold. Conversely, logistic models are suitable for saturated forecasts that require defining the highest and lowest values [30].

3.4.3. Autoregressive Integrated Moving Average (ARIMA)

ARIMA, a classic statistical model, uses patterns such as trends and seasonality to predict future scores in a series. It is a generalized version of the ARMA model specially designed to handle non-stationary time series. Unlike the ARMA model, which assumes stationarity of the analyzed time series, non-stationary time series must first undergo a transformation process to remove seasonality and trends through finite-point differentiation. A stationary time series is a combination of signal and noise. The ARIMA model separates the time signal from the noise and gives its forecast for a later time point. As indicated by the method's acronym, its structural components are the following [31,32]:

AR for autoregression: a regression model that uses the dependence relationship between an observation and several lagged observations (model parameter p).

I for integration: calculating the differences between observations at different time points (model parameter d), aiming to make the time series stationary.

MA for moving average: this approach considers the dependence that may exist between observations and the error terms created when a moving average model is used on observations that have a time lag (model parameter q) [33].

One way to represent an AR model with order p, or AR (p), is through a linear process, as shown in Equation (8). The stationary variable is denoted by x and the constant by c. The autocorrelation coefficients at lags 1, 2, . . ., p are represented by $\varnothing$, while the residuals are the Gaussian white noise series with a mean of zero and a variance of σ [34].

$$x_t = c + \sum_{i=1}^{p} \varnothing_i x_{t-i} + \varepsilon_t \tag{8}$$

Equation (9) represents an MA (q) order model, wherein the θ terms denote the weights given to the current and previous values of a stochastic term in the time series. Here, μ is the expectation of x and is generally assumed to be zero, while θ equals one. We consider ε to be a Gaussian white noise series with a mean of zero and variance of σ [34].

$$x_t = \mu + \sum_{i=o}^{q} \theta_i \varepsilon_{t-i} \tag{9}$$

Equation (10) shows how these two models are combined to create an ARMA model of order (p, q), where $\varnothing \neq 0$, $\theta \neq 0$, and $\sigma > 0$. The parameters represent the AR and MA orders p and q, respectively. ARIMA forecasting, also known as Box and Jenkins forecasting, can handle non-stationary time series data due to its "integration" step. This step involves differencing the time series, converting a non-stationary time series into a stationary one [34].

$$x_t = c + \sum_{i=1}^{p} \varnothing_i x_{t-i} + \varepsilon_t + \sum_{i=o}^{q} \theta_i \varepsilon_{t-i} \tag{10}$$

3.4.4. ARIMA-LSTM Hybrid Model

The hybrid ARIMA-LSTM model is designed to capture the linear and nonlinear aspects of time series data. The time series must be stationary to apply the ARIMA model and predict future values. It should be checked with the Dickey–Fuller test to see if it is in place, and it should be performed if it is not already. Then, optimal parameters will be found to build the model, and finally, predictions will be made using the built model. LSTM works well for non-stationary parts of data as well as has relatively larger memory. The residuals obtained from ARIMA are fed into an LSTM model and trained to tap the pattern and predict the residuals for the next future period [35].

These two models have been chosen for their ability to break down a time series into linear and nonlinear trends, as expressed by Equation (11). In this equation, L_t illustrates the linear component of the time series at time step t. Also, N_t defines the nonlinear component, and ε_t represents the error term in the x_t time series [36].

$$x_t = L_t + N_t + \varepsilon_t \tag{11}$$

The reason for choosing different types of algorithms to conduct the research was to include the wide range of data found in cancer rate numbers and new case amounts and incidence rates with different qualities. LSTM networks provide flexibility in understanding long-term connected changes and complex patterns common in information. As a time-series analysis model, Prophet's ability to deal with unexpected values, missing data, and shifting trends is beneficial for the unpredictable nature of healthcare information, like cancer-related datasets. As a statistical analysis model, ARIMA is strong at examining and predicting linear sequences and is vital for ensuring that a complete analytical method can compare against more complex models.

3.5. Evaluation Metrics

This study selected a suite of evaluation metrics that best represent the models' forecasting accuracy, reliability, and applicability in a real-world context to comprehensively assess machine learning models, including LSTM, Prophet, and ARIMA, deployed in forecasting cancer incidence trends in Canada.

Different criteria, such as forecast error measurements, the speed of calculation, interpretability, and others, have been used to assess forecasting quality, where y is the measured value at time t. Forecast error measures or forecast accuracy are the most important in solving practical problems. Typically, the commonly used forecast error measurements are applied to estimate the quality of forecasting methods and choose the best forecasting mechanism for multiple objects. Despite their drawbacks, a set of "traditional" error measurements in every domain is applied. These error measurements are used as presets in domains despite the drawbacks. This section provides an analysis of existing and quite common forecast error measures that are used in forecasting. Measures are divided into groups according to the calculating method and value of error for a specific time t. The formula for calculating and the names of assessments are considered for each error measure [37].

3.5.1. Mean Absolute Error (MAE)

MAE measures the average magnitude of absolute errors between actual and predicted values. Lower MAE values indicate better accuracy. It is widely used in forecasting tasks because it provides an intuitive measure of prediction error in the same unit as the data.

Mean Absolute Error, is given by [37]:

$$MAE = \frac{1}{n}\sum_{i=1}^{n}|F_i - A_i|$$

where n is the number of observations, F_i is the forecasted value for observation i, and A_i is the actual value for observation i.

3.5.2. Mean Squared Error (MSE)

MSE calculates the average squared difference between actual and predicted values. MSE penalizes significant errors more heavily, making it useful for detecting significant deviations in predictions.

Mean Squared Error, is given by [37]:

$$MSE = \frac{1}{n}\sum_{i=1}^{n}(F_i - A_i)^2$$

where n is the number of observations, F_i is the forecasted value for observation i, and A_i is the actual value for observation i.

3.5.3. Root Mean Squared Error (RMSE)

RMSE is the square root of MSE, which provides an interpretable error value in the same unit as the target variable. RMSE is sensitive to large errors and is commonly used in forecasting applications to measure model performance.

Root Mean Squared Error is given by [37]:

$$RMSE = \sqrt{\frac{1}{n}\sum_{i=1}^{n}(F_i - A_i)^2}$$

where n is the number of observations, F_i is the forecasted value for observation i, and A_i is the actual value for observation i.

3.5.4. Mean Absolute Percentage Error (MAPE)

MAPE expresses the prediction error as a percentage of actual values, making it easier to interpret in relative terms. As it provides a percentage-based error measure, MAPE is particularly useful for comparing errors across datasets with different scales.

Mean Absolute Percentage Error is given by [37]:

$$MAPE = \frac{1}{n}\sum_{t=1}^{n}\left|\frac{A_i - F_i}{A_i}\right|$$

where n is the number of observations, F_i is the forecasted value for observation i, and A_i is the actual value for observation i.

3.5.5. Coefficient of Determination (R^2)

R^2 represents the proportion of variance in the dependent variable that is predictable from the independent variables.

The Coefficient of Determination is given by:

$$R^2 = 1 - \frac{RSS}{TSS}$$

R^2, or the coefficient of determination, is a widely used metric in regression analysis. It measures the proportion of the variance in the dependent variable that is predictable from the independent variables. However, it has limitations, such as being biased statistics and providing invalid results in the presence of measurement errors. Therefore, while R-squared is a valuable metric, it should be interpreted cautiously and in conjunction with other criteria [38]. It is widely used in regression and forecasting models to indicate how well the model explains the variability in the data. A value closer to 1 indicates a better fit.

R^2 is not always suitable for time series forecasting due to the complex nature of time series data and the potential for model uncertainty. Goel [39] highlights the need for hybrid models that can capture both linear and nonlinear components in time series data, suggesting that a single metric like R^2 may not adequately capture the predictive performance. Chatfield [40] further emphasizes the importance of considering model uncertainty in time series analysis, which can affect the accuracy of forecasts. Hewamalage [41] underscores the need for robust and efficient forecasting methods, indicating that R^2 may not be the most suitable metric in all cases. Lastly, Kim [42] discusses the impact of estimation error on forecast mean squared errors, which can also affect the reliability of R^2 in time series forecasting.

The limitations mentioned regarding the R^2 metric, such as potential bias and sensitivity to measurement errors, are intended to highlight practical issues related to real-world model interpretation and data quality considerations. Specifically, R^2 can be influenced by factors such as model specification, omitted variables, and data inaccuracies, rather than being inherently flawed mathematically. Therefore, R^2 values should always be interpreted with careful attention to these practical and contextual limitations, especially in complex forecasting scenarios.

4. Results

4.1. Performance of the Models

After deploying all models for every category, evaluation metrics were extracted to assess the models' performance. The results help us to choose the best models for categories. This section gives the error rates for each model for forecasting new cancer cases and incidence rates for 2022 to 2026 for different categories. The models were trained on data from 1992 to 2021.

It is important to note that negative R^2 values, as observed for the Prophet model in our analysis, indicate that the model does not improve predictive accuracy compared with a baseline mean-only (intercept-only) model. Such results do not inherently suggest that the Prophet model is incorrectly specified or invalid. Rather, these negative values highlight that, within the specific context of our forecasting problem, the Prophet model's predictive strength was comparatively weaker than the other evaluated models (ARIMA, LSTM, and Hybrid ARIMA-LSTM). Therefore, R^2 values, particularly negative ones, should be interpreted cautiously as indicators of relative model performance rather than absolute measures of model validity.

4.1.1. Error Rates for Geography Categories

Table 1 shows the error rates for new cancer cases and cancer incidence rates in geographical regions. The error rates have been interpreted to indicate the best models, which have been highlighted in bold and italic. The error rates show that the hybrid model performs the best in forecasting new cancer cases and cancer incidence rates for geographic regions.

Table 1. Error rates of geography regions for new cancer cases and cancer incidence rate.

Geography	Category	Model	MSE	MAE	RMSE	MAPE	R^2
Alberta	New Cancer Cases	ARIMA	0.0028	0.0377	0.0528	0.0444	0.6795
		LSTM	0.0028	0.0379	0.0527	0.0452	0.6905
		Hybrid	***0.0015***	***0.0344***	***0.0385***	***0.0402***	***0.8296***
		Prophet	0.0032	0.0509	0.0564	0.0596	0.3438
	Cancer Incidence Rate	ARIMA	0.0102	0.0629	0.1012	0.0786	0.0832
		LSTM	0.0081	0.0671	0.0907	0.0820	0.0898
		Hybrid	***0.0013***	***0.0293***	***0.0357***	***0.0315***	***0.8651***
		Prophet	0.0051	0.0568	0.0714	0.0656	0.3887
British Columbia	New Cancer Cases	ARIMA	0.0032	0.0383	0.0567	0.0468	0.6612
		LSTM	0.0028	0.0416	0.0525	0.0491	0.7100
		Hybrid	***0.0018***	***0.0317***	***0.0419***	***0.0382***	***0.8151***
		Prophet	0.0038	0.0544	0.0614	0.0665	0.3208
	Cancer Incidence Rate	ARIMA	0.0112	0.0816	0.0961	0.0935	0.0659
		LSTM	0.0091	0.0769	0.0954	0.0934	0.1547
		Hybrid	***0.0064***	***0.0628***	***0.0799***	***0.0766***	***0.3516***
		Prophet	0.0071	0.0595	0.0845	0.0765	0.0301
Manitoba	New Cancer Cases	ARIMA	0.0092	0.0762	0.0960	0.0844	0.4569
		LSTM	0.0047	0.0547	0.0687	0.0677	0.6866
		Hybrid	***0.0004***	***0.0169***	***0.0205***	***0.0199***	***0.9752***
		Prophet	0.0061	0.0583	0.0779	0.0661	0.5133
	Cancer Incidence Rate	ARIMA	0.0148	0.0910	0.1218	0.1202	0.1289
		LSTM	0.0054	0.0564	0.0732	0.0598	0.2090
		Hybrid	***0.0015***	***0.0240***	***0.0390***	***0.0279***	***0.8844***
		Prophet	0.0089	0.0877	0.1174	0.0922	−1.7234

Table 1. *Cont.*

Geography	Category	Model	MSE	MAE	RMSE	MAPE	R^2
New Brunswick	New Cancer Cases	ARIMA	0.0059	0.0705	0.0768	0.0835	0.3275
		LSTM	0.0038	0.0493	0.0619	0.0613	0.5627
		Hybrid	***0.0018***	***0.0258***	***0.0427***	***0.0343***	***0.7917***
		Prophet	0.0048	0.0594	0.0694	0.0726	0.4504
	Cancer Incidence Rate	ARIMA	0.0060	0.0605	0.0776	0.0657	0.4920
		LSTM	0.0023	0.0350	0.0480	0.0433	0.5112
		Hybrid	***0.0011***	***0.0252***	***0.0325***	***0.0281***	***0.7727***
		Prophet	0.0068	0.0741	0.0823	0.0851	−1.1331
Newfoundland and Labrador	New Cancer Cases	ARIMA	0.0062	0.0634	0.0790	0.0748	0.2867
		LSTM	0.0155	0.0778	0.1244	0.0997	0.6262
		Hybrid	***0.0003***	***0.0141***	***0.0169***	***0.0154***	***0.9763***
		Prophet	0.0122	0.0816	0.1105	0.0895	−2.8241
	Cancer Incidence Rate	ARIMA	0.0060	0.0658	0.0776	0.0718	0.3345
		LSTM	0.0119	0.0692	0.1093	0.0844	0.7782
		Hybrid	***0.0007***	***0.0211***	***0.0274***	***0.0222***	***0.9157***
		Prophet	0.0109	0.0766	0.1046	0.0819	−0.3781
Northwest Territories	New Cancer Cases	ARIMA	0.0194	0.1343	0.1394	0.1676	0.1355
		LSTM	0.0128	0.0908	0.1132	0.1170	0.6193
		Hybrid	***0.0052***	***0.0601***	***0.0721***	***0.0842***	***0.8061***
		Prophet	0.0252	0.1397	0.1589	0.1923	0.1366
	Cancer Incidence Rate	ARIMA	0.0200	0.0995	0.1414	0.1293	0.07207
		LSTM	0.0164	0.0809	0.1279	0.1113	0.2239
		Hybrid	***0.0076***	***0.0672***	***0.0869***	***0.0922***	***0.5949***
		Prophet	0.0155	0.1101	0.1245	0.1375	0.3650
Nova Scotia	New Cancer Cases	ARIMA	0.0062	0.0634	0.0790	0.0748	0.2867
		LSTM	0.0004	0.0163	0.0206	0.0119	0.7926
		Hybrid	***0.0002***	***0.0118***	***0.0139***	***0.0125***	***0.8699***
		Prophet	0.0091	0.0694	0.0951	0.0767	0.4746
	Cancer Incidence Rate	ARIMA	0.0054	0.0661	0.0737	0.0780	0.6996
		LSTM	0.0087	0.0866	0.0939	0.0960	0.3972
		Hybrid	***0.0003***	***0.0145***	***0.0165***	***0.0164***	***0.9188***
		Prophet	0.0058	0.0641	0.0990	0.0735	−1.7068
Nunavut	New Cancer Cases	ARIMA	0.0038	0.0379	0.0617	0.0826	0.3726
		LSTM	0.0030	0.0431	0.0549	0.0744	0.9006
		Hybrid	***0.0022***	***0.0289***	***0.0469***	***0.0557***	***0.9356***
		Prophet	0.0309	0.1348	0.1757	0.2021	0.2435
	Cancer Incidence Rate	ARIMA	0.0010	0.0255	0.0260	0.0566	0.4159
		LSTM	0.0041	0.0373	0.0640	0.0837	0.7505
		Hybrid	***0.0009***	***0.0233***	***0.0298***	***0.0422***	***0.9471***
		Prophet	0.0231	0.1117	0.1521	0.1067	0.1507
Ontario	New Cancer Cases	ARIMA	0.0081	0.0614	0.0901	0.0693	0.3200
		LSTM	0.0043	0.0496	0.0658	0.0563	0.2001
		Hybrid	***0.0019***	***0.0283***	***0.0436***	***0.0329***	***0.6904***
		Prophet	0.0035	0.0517	0.0589	0.0570	0.1763
	Cancer Incidence Rate	ARIMA	0.0191	0.0910	0.1083	0.0936	0.55701
		LSTM	0.0107	0.0631	0.1035	0.0840	0.4479
		Hybrid	***0.0021***	***0.0344***	***0.0459***	***0.0388***	***0.6580***
		Prophet	0.0128	0.1011	0.1212	0.1162	−0.5615

Table 1. *Cont.*

Geography	Category	Model	MSE	MAE	RMSE	MAPE	R^2
Prince Edward Island	New Cancer Cases	ARIMA	0.0110	0.0776	0.1047	0.0879	0.3742
		LSTM	0.0187	0.0693	0.1368	0.0784	0.1700
		Hybrid	***0.0036***	***0.0451***	***0.0604***	***0.0632***	***0.8212***
		Prophet	0.0227	0.1229	0.1507	0.1065	0.2397
	Cancer Incidence Rate	ARIMA	0.0059	0.0588	0.0767	0.0613	0.1394
		LSTM	0.0039	0.0623	0.0626	0.0654	0.1945
		Hybrid	***0.0035***	***0.0469***	***0.0590***	***0.0532***	***0.2424***
		Prophet	0.0181	0.1059	0.1347	0.1042	−2.7544
Quebec	New Cancer Cases	ARIMA	0.0084	0.0511	0.0919	0.0558	0.1893
		LSTM	0.0020	0.0398	0.0444	0.0440	0.5558
		Hybrid	***0.0006***	***0.0242***	***0.0250***	***0.0260***	***0.5084***
		Prophet	0.0052	0.0488	0.0719	0.0522	−0.6552
	Cancer Incidence Rate	ARIMA	0.0007	0.0250	0.0267	0.0271	0.2899
		LSTM	0.0012	0.0353	0.0408	0.0996	0.6675
		Hybrid	***0.0005***	***0.0161***	***0.0231***	***0.0207***	***0.8603***
		Prophet	0.0112	0.0918	0.1061	0.1077	−3.3572
Saskatchewan	New Cancer Cases	ARIMA	0.0115	0.0741	0.1075	0.0958	0.4375
		LSTM	0.0111	0.0865	0.1052	0.1005	0.1892
		Hybrid	***0.0048***	***0.0486***	***0.0691***	***0.0607***	***0.3505***
		Prophet	0.0086	0.0688	0.0929	0.0845	0.2633
	Cancer Incidence Rate	ARIMA	0.0179	0.1095	0.1340	0.1652	0.1713
		LSTM	0.0208	0.1249	0.1442	0.1869	0.3781
		Hybrid	***0.0122***	***0.0716***	***0.1103***	***0.0965***	***0.2076***
		Prophet	0.0143	0.0848	0.1194	0.1119	−0.5023
Yukon	New Cancer Cases	ARIMA	0.0106	0.0862	0.1030	0.1074	0.5719
		LSTM	0.0160	0.1135	0.1145	0.0911	0.8823
		Hybrid	***0.0026***	***0.0344***	***0.0513***	***0.0449***	***0.8793***
		Prophet	0.0137	0.1021	0.1169	0.1293	0.3063
	Cancer Incidence Rate	ARIMA	0.0205	0.1055	0.1432	0.1283	0.3311
		LSTM	0.0044	0.0361	0.0664	0.0483	0.8559
		Hybrid	***0.0016***	***0.0311***	***0.0395***	***0.0451***	***0.9427***
		Prophet	0.0263	0.1244	0.1621	0.1606	−1.1203

4.1.2. Error Rates for Age Categories

Table 2 shows the error rates for new cancer cases and cancer incidence rates in age group categories. The error rates have been interpreted to indicate the best models, indicated by bold and italic highlights. The error rates show that the hybrid model performs the best in forecasting new cancer cases and cancer incidence rates for age group categories.

Table 2. Error rates of age group categories for new cancer cases and cancer incidence rate.

Age Group	Category	Model	MSE	MAE	RMSE	MAPE	R^2
0 to 04 years	New Cancer Cases	ARIMA	0.0186	0.1079	0.1362	0.1765	0.1522
		LSTM	0.0198	0.1249	0.1407	0.2338	0.4500
		Hybrid	***0.0178***	***0.1267***	***0.1333***	***0.2349***	***0.1454***
		Prophet	0.1187	0.2956	0.3445	0.6277	−6.2204
	Cancer Incidence Rate	ARIMA	0.0019	0.0343	0.0436	0.0956	0.2485
		LSTM	0.0080	0.0689	0.0896	0.1696	0.1359
		Hybrid	***0.0003***	***0.0124***	***0.0169***	***0.0270***	***0.1520***
		Prophet	0.0961	0.2822	0.3100	0.2458	−1.9227

Table 2. *Cont.*

Age Group	Category	Model	MSE	MAE	RMSE	MAPE	R^2
05 to 09 years	New Cancer Cases	ARIMA	0.0445	0.1901	0.2108	0.4117	0.1155
		LSTM	0.0554	0.2000	0.2353	0.4075	0.0097
		Hybrid	***0.0237***	***0.1442***	***0.1541***	***0.3136***	***0.3751***
		Prophet	0.1057	0.2656	0.3251	0.4799	−2.0613
	Cancer Incidence Rate	ARIMA	0.0020	0.0417	0.0453	0.0712	0.2856
		LSTM	0.0018	0.0310	0.0420	0.0497	0.3977
		Hybrid	***0.0010***	***0.0280***	***0.0319***	***0.0344***	***0.1493***
		Prophet	0.0148	0.0859	0.1215	0.1345	−1.4655
10 to 14 years	New Cancer Cases	ARIMA	0.0112	0.0929	0.1056	0.1679	0.0206
		LSTM	0.0140	0.1061	0.1183	0.1846	0.0688
		Hybrid	***0.0101***	***0.0845***	***0.1004***	***0.1504***	***0.0770***
		Prophet	0.0273	0.143	0.1652	0.1652	−0.9431
	Cancer Incidence Rate	ARIMA	0.0058	0.0572	0.0761	0.1240	0.3283
		LSTM	0.0079	0.0639	0.0890	0.1169	0.2946
		Hybrid	***0.0029***	***0.0456***	***0.0537***	***0.0632***	***0.6257***
		Prophet	0.0317	0.1619	0.1780	0.2154	−1.0946
15 to 19 years	New Cancer Cases	ARIMA	0.0257	0.1459	0.1571	0.1969	0.0586
		LSTM	0.0270	0.1365	0.1642	0.1046	0.1821
		Hybrid	***0.0256***	***0.1341***	***0.1601***	***0.1792***	***0.2258***
		Prophet	0.0769	0.2243	0.2774	0.3919	−0.6949
	Cancer Incidence Rate	ARIMA	0.0019	0.0428	0.0443	0.0536	0.2529
		LSTM	0.0215	0.1133	0.1467	0.1521	0.2127
		Hybrid	***0.0012***	***0.0264***	***0.0348***	***0.0279***	***0.3815***
		Prophet	0.0293	0.1462	0.1711	0.1793	−0.5151
20 to 24 years	New Cancer Cases	ARIMA	0.0082	0.0584	0.0909	0.0682	0.2217
		LSTM	0.0135	0.1071	0.1160	0.1310	0.5725
		Hybrid	***0.0018***	***0.0361***	***0.0420***	***0.0436***	***0.8290***
		Prophet	0.0256	0.1309	0.1601	0.1498	−2.2898
	Cancer Incidence Rate	ARIMA	0.0045	0.0517	0.0675	0.0704	0.2005
		LSTM	0.0147	0.1144	0.1214	0.1427	0.4443
		Hybrid	***0.0021***	***0.0352***	***0.0453***	***0.0392***	***0.4128***
		Prophet	0.0319	0.1595	0.1784	0.2025	−1.7085
25 to 29 years	New Cancer Cases	ARIMA	0.0091	0.0931	0.0999	0.1045	1.5091
		LSTM	0.0045	0.0501	0.0672	0.0660	0.5181
		Hybrid	***0.0039***	***0.0465***	***0.0625***	***0.0620***	***0.6534***
		Prophet	0.0207	0.1293	0.1440	0.1597	−1.8633
	Cancer Incidence Rate	ARIMA	0.0017	0.0407	0.0413	0.0447	0.6333
		LSTM	0.0104	0.0715	0.1020	0.0866	0.3196
		Hybrid	***0.0002***	***0.0130***	***0.0143***	***0.0154***	***0.5169***
		Prophet	0.0103	0.0776	0.1016	0.0942	−0.162
30 to 34 years	New Cancer Cases	ARIMA	0.0212	0.1211	0.1457	0.1536	0.2017
		LSTM	0.0134	0.0966	0.1159	0.1141	0.1338
		Hybrid	***0.0079***	***0.0721***	***0.0889***	***0.0849***	***0.1797***
		Prophet	0.3214	0.2738	0.3214	0.3220	−1.5855
	Cancer Incidence Rate	ARIMA	0.0015	0.0367	0.0396	0.0447	0.2534
		LSTM	0.0164	0.1075	0.1282	0.1244	0.4915
		Hybrid	***0.0004***	***0.0170***	***0.0205***	***0.0198***	***0.4139***
		Prophet	0.0185	0.1128	0.1360	0.1310	−0.6678

Table 2. *Cont.*

Age Group	Category	Model	MSE	MAE	RMSE	MAPE	R^2
35 to 39 years	New Cancer Cases	ARIMA	0.0040	0.0504	0.0635	0.0698	0.8737
		LSTM	0.0115	0.0984	0.1070	0.1378	0.5311
		Hybrid	***0.0039***	***0.0484***	***0.0627***	***0.0679***	***0.8771***
		Prophet	0.0052	0.0602	0.0724	0.0865	0.7172
	Cancer Incidence Rate	ARIMA	0.0029	0.0438	0.0543	0.0494	0.5215
		LSTM	0.0114	0.1009	0.1065	0.1131	0.0491
		Hybrid	***0.0014***	***0.0282***	***0.0368***	***0.0310***	***0.2678***
		Prophet	0.0254	0.1307	0.1594	0.1395	−0.3627
40 to 44 years	New Cancer Cases	ARIMA	0.0077	0.1023	0.1329	0.1390	0.6226
		LSTM	0.0036	0.0574	0.0598	0.0685	0.4477
		Hybrid	***0.0015***	***0.0331***	***0.0391***	***0.0371***	***0.5223***
		Prophet	0.0200	0.1269	0.1416	0.1641	0.1681
	Cancer Incidence Rate	ARIMA	0.0024	0.0466	0.0499	0.0540	0.1890
		LSTM	0.0098	0.0893	0.0990	0.0981	0.1507
		Hybrid	***0.0001***	***0.0072***	***0.0105***	***0.0074***	***0.2190***
		Prophet	0.0112	0.0855	0.1058	0.1006	−1.7236
45 to 49 years	New Cancer Cases	ARIMA	0.0070	0.0592	0.0835	0.0989	0.8396
		LSTM	0.0035	0.0545	0.0590	0.0900	0.2453
		Hybrid	***0.0020***	***0.0370***	***0.0450***	***0.0613***	***0.7002***
		Prophet	0.0554	0.1919	0.2355	0.1978	−0.3463
	Cancer Incidence Rate	ARIMA	0.0067	0.0566	0.0823	0.1302	0.2436
		LSTM	0.0122	0.0805	0.1106	0.1737	0.0910
		Hybrid	***0.0001***	***0.0084***	***0.0100***	***0.0174***	***0.9899***
		Prophet	0.0135	0.0998	0.1286	0.2087	−1.6021
50 to 54 years	New Cancer Cases	ARIMA	0.0053	0.0660	0.0727	0.0903	0.3711
		LSTM	0.0055	0.0491	0.0742	0.0736	0.2727
		Hybrid	***0.0020***	***0.0328***	***0.0448***	***0.0444***	***0.8250***
		Prophet	0.1113	0.3037	0.3336	0.3778	−0.7868
	Cancer Incidence Rate	ARIMA	0.0002	0.0137	0.0144	0.0355	0.4636
		LSTM	0.0074	0.0578	0.0859	0.1351	0.2222
		Hybrid	***0.0001***	***0.0034***	***0.0039***	***0.0098***	***0.9734***
		Prophet	0.0320	0.1613	0.1790	0.1922	−3.2580
55 to 59 years	New Cancer Cases	ARIMA	0.0053	0.0542	0.0726	0.0574	0.6032
		LSTM	0.0056	0.0504	0.0750	0.0578	1.2721
		Hybrid	***0.0023***	***0.0368***	***0.0475***	***0.0401***	***0.1101***
		Prophet	0.0230	0.1342	0.1518	0.1448	−1.794
	Cancer Incidence Rate	ARIMA	0.0068	0.0542	0.0829	0.0341	0.4939
		LSTM	0.0043	0.0483	0.0655	0.0897	0.6194
		Hybrid	***0.0002***	***0.0112***	***0.0150***	***0.0292***	***0.7621***
		Prophet	0.0122	0.0926	0.1106	0.1004	−0.8536
60 to 64 years	New Cancer Cases	ARIMA	0.0044	0.0595	0.0665	0.0642	0.7781
		LSTM	0.0034	0.0463	0.0586	0.0510	0.2373
		Hybrid	***0.0023***	***0.0231***	***0.0481***	***0.0262***	***0.5316***
		Prophet	0.0026	0.0406	0.0513	0.0462	0.6347
	Cancer Incidence Rate	ARIMA	0.0048	0.0639	0.0739	0.0402	0.4163
		LSTM	0.0093	0.0861	0.0963	0.0426	0.5478
		Hybrid	***0.0002***	***0.0142***	***0.0150***	***0.0182***	***0.5654***
		Prophet	0.0119	0.0987	0.1103	0.0743	0.2763

Table 2. *Cont.*

Age Group	Category	Model	MSE	MAE	RMSE	MAPE	R^2
65 to 69 years	New Cancer Cases	ARIMA	0.0083	0.0662	0.0914	0.0772	0.3804
		LSTM	0.0071	0.0643	0.0840	0.0786	0.2028
		Hybrid	***0.0030***	***0.0473***	***0.0546***	***0.0546***	***0.6826***
		Prophet	0.0434	0.1977	0.2083	0.1373	−7.8478
	Cancer Incidence Rate	ARIMA	0.0049	0.0701	0.0867	0.0423	0.7709
		LSTM	0.0008	0.0226	0.0278	0.0313	0.3561
		Hybrid	***0.0001***	***0.0070***	***0.0083***	***0.0235***	***0.6739***
		Prophet	0.0069	0.0612	0.0845	0.0679	0.5764
70 to 74 years	New Cancer Cases	ARIMA	0.0000	0.0806	0.0892	0.0931	0.2429
		LSTM	0.0039	0.0520	0.0627	0.0634	0.8156
		Hybrid	***0.0031***	***0.0459***	***0.0559***	***0.0620***	***0.8845***
		Prophet	0.0579	0.2302	0.2409	0.1138	−2.4798
	Cancer Incidence Rate	ARIMA	0.0001	0.0101	0.0116	0.0327	0.4240
		LSTM	0.0045	0.0498	0.0672	0.1582	−0.4997
		Hybrid	***0.0001***	***0.0086***	***0.0117***	***0.0275***	***0.2875***
		Prophet	0.0056	0.0725	0.0935	0.2287	−1.1505
75 to 79 years	New Cancer Cases	ARIMA	0.0035	0.0524	0.0592	0.0669	0.7772
		LSTM	0.0061	0.0757	0.0778	0.0964	0.5426
		Hybrid	***0.0033***	***0.0512***	***0.0572***	***0.0584***	***0.5831***
		Prophet	0.0054	0.0633	0.0732	0.0903	0.4110
	Cancer Incidence Rate	ARIMA	0.0018	0.0218	0.0422	0.0563	0.0188
		LSTM	0.0023	0.0326	0.0479	0.0835	0.3755
		Hybrid	***0.0010***	***0.0205***	***0.0316***	***0.0465***	***0.4501***
		Prophet	0.0125	0.0835	0.11201	0.0843	0.5386
80 to 84 years	New Cancer Cases	ARIMA	0.0023	0.0442	0.0476	0.0462	0.9672
		LSTM	0.0024	0.0407	0.0485	0.0428	0.7745
		Hybrid	***0.0007***	***0.0196***	***0.0261***	***0.0210***	***0.8385***
		Prophet	0.0267	0.0500	0.0634	0.0575	0.1867
	Cancer Incidence Rate	ARIMA	0.0013	0.0358	0.0363	0.0623	0.2378
		LSTM	0.0042	0.0620	0.0650	0.1096	0.5701
		Hybrid	***0.0002***	***0.0126***	***0.0154***	***0.0130***	***0.6267***
		Prophet	0.0076	0.0694	0.0869	0.1163	0.5425
85 to 89 years	New Cancer Cases	ARIMA	0.0040	0.0524	0.0629	0.0538	0.2693
		LSTM	0.0023	0.0398	0.0480	0.0425	0.1433
		Hybrid	***0.0019***	***0.0355***	***0.0432***	***0.0376***	***0.1592***
		Prophet	0.0056	0.0568	0.0745	0.0601	−1.6369
	Cancer Incidence Rate	ARIMA	0.0093	0.0950	0.0963	0.2053	0.0619
		LSTM	0.0105	0.0884	0.1027	0.2135	0.2379
		Hybrid	***0.0014***	***0.0286***	***0.0375***	***0.0650***	***0.2018***
		Prophet	0.0192	0.1139	0.1386	0.1236	8.1164
90 years and over	New Cancer Cases	ARIMA	0.0099	0.0671	0.0995	0.0737	4.7627
		LSTM	0.0094	0.0799	0.0969	0.0894	1.5906
		Hybrid	***0.0032***	***0.0479***	***0.0564***	***0.0536***	***0.4497***
		Prophet	0.0182	0.1257	0.1350	0.1387	−2.9161
	Cancer Incidence Rate	ARIMA	0.0011	0.0258	0.0338	0.0560	0.5235
		LSTM	0.0037	0.0450	0.0607	0.0956	0.4617
		Hybrid	***0.0003***	***0.0155***	***0.0184***	***0.0327***	***0.6609***
		Prophet	0.0076	0.0714	0.0874	0.0755	−0.6405

4.1.3. Error Rates for Sex Categories

Table 3 shows the error rates for new cancer cases and cancer incidence rate in sex categories. The error rates have been interpreted to indicate the best models, which have been highlighted in bold. The error rates show that the LSTM model performs the best in forecasting new cancer cases for sex categories.

Table 3. Error rates of sex-based categories for new cancer cases and cancer incidence rate.

Sex	Category	Model	MSE	MAE	RMSE	MAPE	R^2
Males	New Cancer Cases	ARIMA	0.0061	0.0506	0.0781	0.0552	0.0908
		LSTM	***0.0023***	***0.0219***	***0.0481***	***0.0244***	***0.5148***
		Hybrid	0.0029	0.0364	0.0537	0.0399	0.3304
		Prophet	0.0031	0.0433	0.0557	0.0478	0.4621
	Cancer Incidence Rate	ARIMA	0.0069	0.0728	0.0833	0.0772	0.1768
		LSTM	***0.0022***	***0.0415***	***0.0465***	***0.0454***	***0.0470***
		Hybrid	0.0036	0.0491	0.0600	0.0530	0.0662
		Prophet	0.0093	0.0827	0.0967	0.08276	−1.8708
Females	New Cancer Cases	ARIMA	0.0055	0.0484	0.0740	0.0529	0.4091
		LSTM	***0.0019***	***0.0248***	***0.0436***	***0.0288***	***0.3378***
		Hybrid	0.0019	0.0259	0.0437	0.0292	0.3402
		Prophet	0.0021	0.0338	0.0463	0.0377	0.5566
	Cancer Incidence Rate	ARIMA	0.0058	0.0714	0.0761	0.0714	0.1504
		LSTM	***0.0017***	***0.0324***	***0.0413***	***0.0329***	***0.2201***
		Hybrid	0.0045	0.0606	0.0672	0.0626	0.8291
		Prophet	0.0065	0.0582	0.0805	0.0587	−0.1023
Both Sexes	New Cancer Cases	ARIMA	0.0054	0.0445	0.0741	0.0489	0.5487
		LSTM	***0.0021***	***0.0226***	***0.0454***	***0.0258***	***0.4082***
		Hybrid	0.0024	0.0297	0.0493	0.0330	0.3410
		Prophet	0.0032	0.0478	0.0562	0.0532	0.3917
	Cancer Incidence Rate	ARIMA	0.0036	0.0520	0.0603	0.0532	0.0001
		LSTM	***0.0013***	***0.0292***	***0.0366***	***0.0301***	***0.0165***
		Hybrid	0.0038	0.0562	0.0618	0.0592	0.3813
		Prophet	0.0075	0.0679	0.0867	0.0703	−0.6117

4.2. Forecasting New Cancer Cases and Incidence Rate

Among the other models, the hybrid model is the optimum model for predicting the values for geography categories from 2022 to 2026. Table 4 shows the results extracted from the mentioned model.

Table 4. Predicted number of new cancer cases and cancer incidence rates by regions in Canada.

Geography/Predicted Years		**2022**	**2023**	**2024**	**2025**	**2026**
Alberta	New Cancer Cases	23,907	24,387	24,702	24,975	25,927
	Cancer Incidence Rate	443.8	462.2	461.7	433.7	458.9
British Columbia	New Cancer Cases	31,801	32,438	32,729	32,728	33,456
	Cancer Incidence Rate	531.3	539.5	540.6	537.9	545.7
Manitoba	New Cancer Cases	8181	8300	8374	8418	8530
	Cancer Incidence Rate	505.3	516.0	517.2	513.1	509.3
New Brunswick	New Cancer Cases	5959	5999	6033	6076	6187
	Cancer Incidence Rate	656.8	657.3	648.5	647.9	662.2
Newfoundland and Labrador	New Cancer Cases	4171	4116	4062	3976	4012
	Cancer Incidence Rate	693.4	690.7	678.8	650.3	596.1
Northwest Territories	New Cancer Cases	241	237	244	240	263
	Cancer Incidence Rate	389.0	400.4	396.4	375.7	341.8

Table 4. *Cont.*

Geography/Predicted Years		2022	2023	2024	2025	2026
Nova Scotia	New Cancer Cases	7467	7434	7445	7511	7562
	Cancer Incidence Rate	693.5	674.2	652.9	652.6	653.8
Nunavut	New Cancer Cases	84	79	77	79	81
	Cancer Incidence Rate	200.1	196.7	188.3	179.4	173.0
Ontario	New Cancer Cases	94,677	94,763	94,975	95,398	97,951
	Cancer Incidence Rate	582.2	573.6	555.0	545.0	543.7
Prince Edward Island	New Cancer Cases	1102	1111	1157	1161	1181
	Cancer Incidence Rate	620.0	620.8	626.4	602.0	636.9
Quebec	New Cancer Cases	63,803	63,841	63,932	64,073	64,264
	Cancer Incidence Rate	675.7	668.7	669.5	671.8	670.4
Saskatchewan	New Cancer Cases	6585	6636	6666	6624	6716
	Cancer Incidence Rate	491.8	495.5	496.5	494.9	493.7
Yukon	New Cancer Cases	199	198	188	183	188
	Cancer Incidence Rate	445.4	464.5	445.8	393.0	333.6

Compared with the other models, the hybrid model is the optimum model for predicting the values for age group categories from 2022 to 2026. Table 5 demonstrates the results extracted from the model mentioned.

Table 5. Predicted number of new cancer cases and cancer incidence rate by age groups in Canada.

Age Group/Predicted Years		2022	2023	2024	2025	2026
0 to 4 years	New Cancer Cases	453	454	452	450	450
	Cancer Incidence Rate	23.2	23.4	23.4	23.4	23.4
5 to 9 years	New Cancer Cases	280	270	265	264	266
	Cancer Incidence Rate	13.8	13.9	13.8	13.8	13.8
10 to 14 years	New Cancer Cases	286	290	291	286	290
	Cancer Incidence Rate	13.2	13.5	13.3	13.4	13.5
15 to 19 years	New Cancer Cases	534	531	535	537	530
	Cancer Incidence Rate	24.4	24.1	24.1	24.1	24.2
20 to 24 years	New Cancer Cases	937	929	936	930	935
	Cancer Incidence Rate	36.4	35.7	35.8	35.9	35.9
25 to 29 years	New Cancer Cases	1605	1625	1633	1665	1715
	Cancer Incidence Rate	59.6	60.1	60.4	60.5	60.3
30 to 34 years	New Cancer Cases	2514	2526	2536	2545	2555
	Cancer Incidence Rate	91.4	90.9	90.7	91.1	91.5
35 to 39 years	New Cancer Cases	3960	4040	4073	4095	4179
	Cancer Incidence Rate	137.6	136.9	135.8	135.5	136.0
40 to 44 years	New Cancer Cases	5660	5678	5705	5732	5808
	Cancer Incidence Rate	210.2	210.4	210.1	209.5	209.3
45 to 49 years	New Cancer Cases	8595	8489	8379	8287	8234
	Cancer Incidence Rate	315.5	314.2	315.8	316.5	315.9

Table 5. *Cont.*

Age Group/Predicted Years		2022	2023	2024	2025	2026
50 to 54 years	New Cancer Cases	15,325	14,930	14,509	14,018	13,488
	Cancer Incidence Rate	509.6	510.0	510.6	510.9	510.9
55 to 59 years	New Cancer Cases	22,931	22,845	22,740	22,576	22,228
	Cancer Incidence Rate	775.0	775.4	774.7	774.8	774.6
60 to 64 years	New Cancer Cases	32,186	32,419	32,481	32,641	33,517
	Cancer Incidence Rate	1140.0	1144.1	1142.8	1139.6	1140.5
65 to 69 years	New Cancer Cases	38,617	39,032	39,397	39,965	41,398
	Cancer Incidence Rate	1604.8	1608.2	1604.8	1603.0	1603.0
70 to 74 years	New Cancer Cases	39,764	40,584	41,431	42,145	43,771
	Cancer Incidence Rate	2040.0	2037.9	2037.4	2033.9	2031.8
75 to 79 years	New Cancer Cases	31,024	31,431	31,890	32,303	33,313
	Cancer Incidence Rate	2362.2	2369.2	2372.2	2372.2	2368.4
80 to 84 years	New Cancer Cases	22,494	22,578	22,682	22,787	22,883
	Cancer Incidence Rate	2590.6	2591.1	2590.8	2588.9	2586.9
85 to 89 years	New Cancer Cases	14,756	15,094	15,181	15,342	15,602
	Cancer Incidence Rate	2667.2	2671.3	2671.5	2672.3	2674.6
90 years and above	New Cancer Cases	8185	8311	8432	8550	8685
	Cancer Incidence Rate	2446.3	2449.3	2444.8	2437.5	2440.8

Compared with the other models, the LSTM model is the best model for forecasting the values for sex-based categories from 2022 to 2026. Table 6 shows the results extracted from the model mentioned.

Table 6. Predicted number of new cancer cases and cancer incidence rate by sex in Canada.

Sex/Predicted Years		2022	2023	2024	2025	2026
Males	New Cancer Cases	129,012	129,515	130,009	131,690	133,088
	Cancer Incidence Rate	600.6	598.9	599.7	600.8	602.3
Females	New Cancer Cases	119,514	120,428	121,119	121,614	123,904
	Cancer Incidence Rate	540.1	539.2	537.3	534.4	530.6
Both Sexes	New Cancer Cases	244,007	244,941	245,242	245,051	248,705
	Cancer Incidence Rate	567.6	566.3	565.3	563.8	561.8

4.3. Visualization Insights

Figures 2–4 visually show the results of forecasted new cancer cases from 2022 to 2026 for regions, age groups, and sex, respectively.

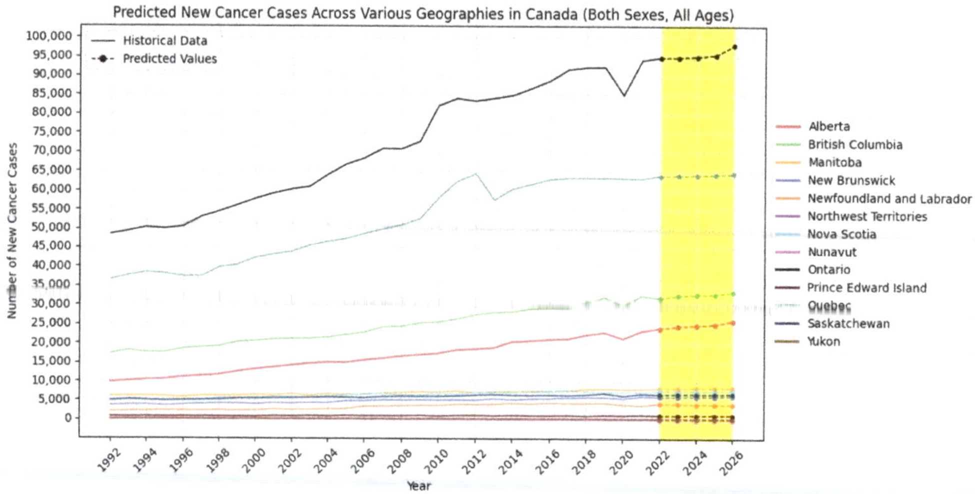

Figure 2. Forecasted new cancer cases across various regions in Canada (the yellow-shaded area shows the predicted values).

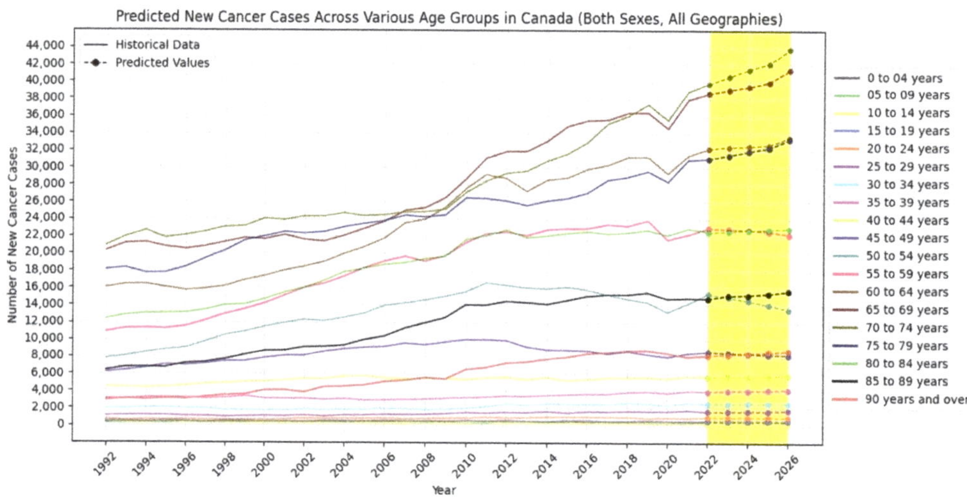

Figure 3. Forecasted new cancer cases across various age groups in Canada (the yellow-shaded area shows the predicted values).

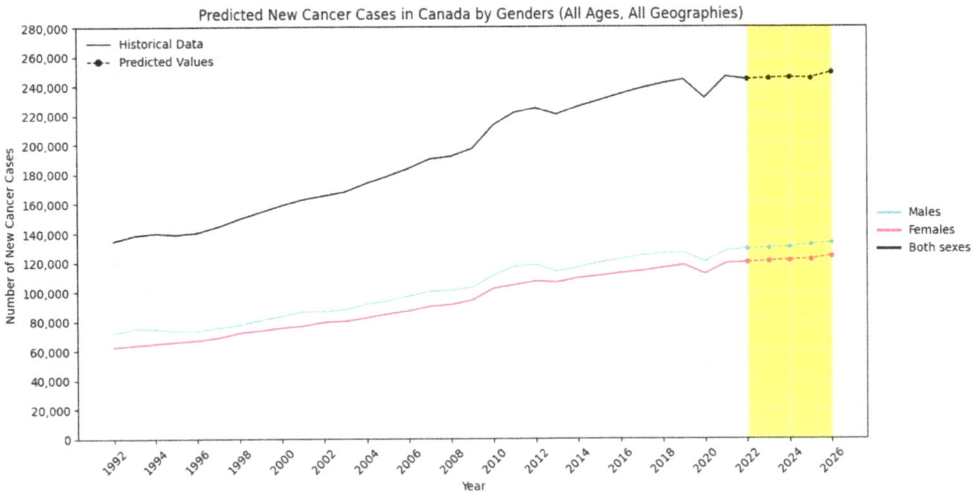

Figure 4. Forecasted new cancer cases in Canada by sexes (the yellow-shaded area shows the predicted values).

Also, Figures 5–7 visually show the results of the forecasted cancer incidence rate per 100,000 people from 2022 to 2026 for regions, age groups, and sexes, respectively.

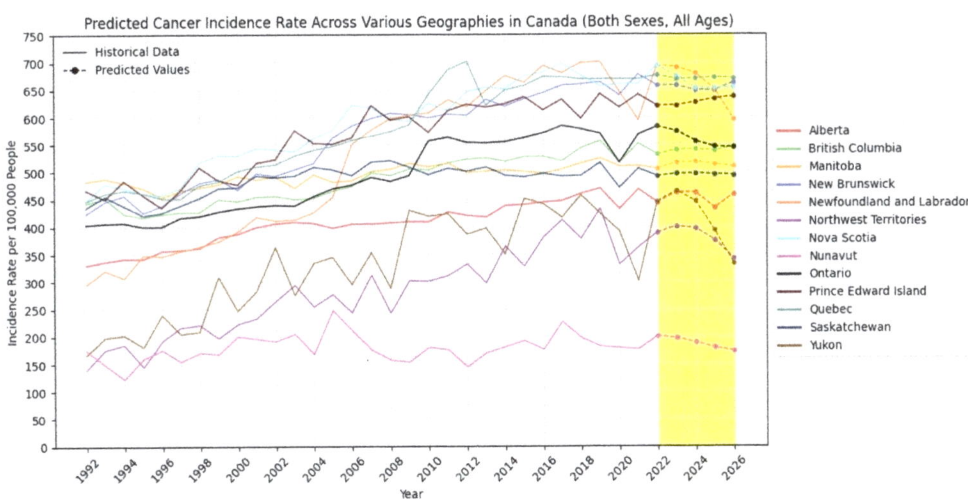

Figure 5. Forecasted cancer incidence rate per 100,000 people across various regions in Canada (the yellow-shaded area shows the predicted values).

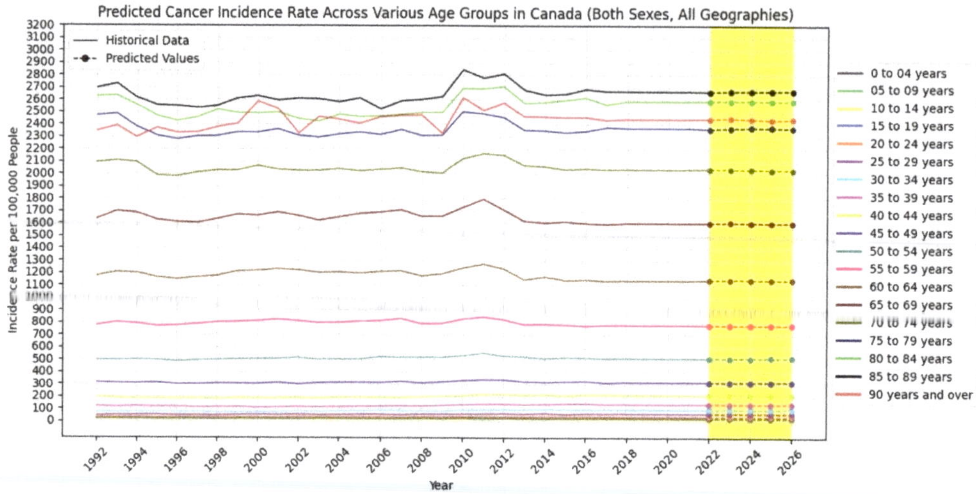

Figure 6. Forecasted cancer incidence rate per 100,000 people across various age groups in Canada (the yellow-shaded area shows the predicted values).

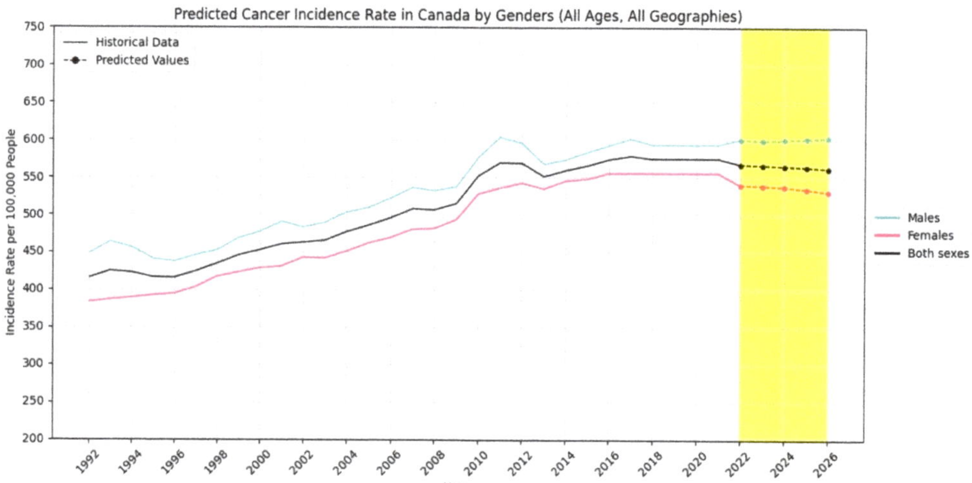

Figure 7. Forecasted cancer incidence rate per 100,000 people in Canada by sex (the yellow-shaded area shows the predicted values).

5. Discussion

The findings of this study align with previous research on cancer incidence forecasting in Canada but extend existing methodologies by incorporating machine learning (ML) models to enhance predictive accuracy. Past studies, such as those by Brenner et al. [16–18], have relied heavily on statistical models like CANPROJ, which use age-period-cohort (APC) frameworks to extrapolate trends. While effective in capturing historical linear patterns, such models assume that past trends will continue predictably, limiting their ability to reflect complex, nonlinear dynamics in cancer data. In contrast, the machine learning models used in this study, particularly the hybrid ARIMA-LSTM model, are adaptive and data-driven, capable of learning from fluctuations and underlying patterns that may not follow a strict statistical progression.

For instance, Brenner et al. projected new cancer cases up to 2024 using historical data and demographic adjustments. Our approach not only extends these projections to 2026, offering a more updated outlook, but also improves accuracy by integrating deep learning with statistical time series models. The hybrid ARIMA-LSTM model consistently yielded lower error rates than other models, demonstrating that this combined approach effectively captures both linear and nonlinear trends in cancer incidence forecasting.

The analysis reveals distinct patterns and trends across sex, geography, and age groups. Males exhibit a steady increase in both new cancer cases and incidence rates, while females experience a rise in absolute cases but a decline in incidence rates.

The observed trend in female cancer incidence—where absolute cancer cases are increasing while incidence rates are declining—suggests demographic shifts, notably population growth and aging, rather than improvements in cancer treatments alone. Additionally, improvements in screening programs and early detection efforts (such as breast and cervical cancer screening) documented in the existing literature likely play a role in stabilizing or reducing incidence rates for certain cancer types.

Brenner et al. confirmed that despite an overall decline in cancer incidence and mortality rates, Canada is expected to see an increase in new cancer cases and deaths in 2024, primarily due to its growing and aging population. While advancements in prevention, screening, and treatment have mitigated the effects of certain cancers, these near-term projections emphasize the ongoing burden cancer may pose to individuals and the Canadian healthcare system [18].

Geographically, regions like Alberta, British Columbia, Ontario, and Quebec show increasing cancer cases and incidence rates, indicating a growing cancer burden. In contrast, provinces such as Newfoundland and Labrador demonstrate a declining trend, possibly reflecting effective local cancer control measures or public health strategies. Age-wise, cancer incidence remains stable among children but increases significantly among middle-aged and older adults, especially in individuals aged 75 and above.

These findings underscore the need for targeted public health interventions explicitly tailored to demographic groups and geographic regions showing an increased cancer burden. The steady rise in cancer cases among older adults and specific provinces highlights the importance of developing age-specific and region-specific cancer prevention and control strategies. Meanwhile, stability in pediatric cancer incidence suggests that existing pediatric cancer strategies may be effective but require sustained support.

Given the complexity of cancer incidence trends, selecting an accurate forecasting model is critical for public health planning. An evaluation of model performance reveals that the hybrid ARIMA-LSTM model consistently achieves the lowest error rates across most geographic and age group categories, making it the most suitable choice for cancer incidence forecasting. This model outperforms the ARIMA, LSTM, and Prophet models in key accuracy metrics, including MAE, MSE, RMSE, MAPE, and R^2.

5.1. Model Performance Across Demographics and Regions

Geographic performance: The hybrid ARIMA-LSTM model yields significantly lower RMSE values across multiple provinces, with R^2 values exceeding 0.80 in most cases, indicating strong predictive accuracy. In contrast, the Prophet model exhibits the highest error rates, often producing negative R^2 values, suggesting poor model fit.

Age group performance: The hybrid model provides the most accurate predictions for middle-aged and older adults (50+ years), achieving the lowest MAPE and RMSE values. In contrast, the Prophet model underperforms in most age categories.

Gender performance: While the hybrid model excels in most categories, LSTM performs best in gender-based forecasting, particularly for male and female cancer incidence rates, as indicated by its superior MAE and RMSE values.

The hybrid ARIMA-LSTM model's superior performance is attributed to its ability to capture both linear and nonlinear trends in cancer incidence data. ARIMA alone is well suited for handling linear trends but struggles with complex patterns, whereas LSTM excels in capturing long-term dependencies. By integrating these approaches, the hybrid model effectively mitigates their individual limitations, resulting in more accurate and reliable cancer incidence forecasts.

5.2. Implications for Public Health and Cancer Prevention

The findings highlight the critical role of advanced forecasting models in improving cancer prevention and resource allocation strategies. Rising incidence rates in middle-aged and older adults necessitate robust screening programs and preventive measures tailored to these demographics. Similarly, region-specific public health initiatives that address unique risk factors are essential to mitigating the cancer burden. By leveraging accurate forecasting models, policymakers and healthcare professionals can develop more effective intervention strategies, optimize resource allocation, and ultimately improve cancer outcomes across diverse populations.

Our study provides a foundation for further integrating AI-driven forecasting models in epidemiological research. Future research could explore ensemble methods, combining traditional epidemiological models (e.g., APC) with deep learning architectures to refine cancer incidence predictions further. Additionally, incorporating real-time clinical and genetic data could enhance prediction accuracy and improve personalized cancer risk assessments.

5.3. Limitations

One of the key limitations of this study is the imputation of Quebec's cancer incidence data after 2017 due to the absence of official records. While we employed a multiple imputation approach to enhance accuracy and capture uncertainty, projections remain dependent on historical trends and national averages rather than direct registry data. The variability in imputed estimates reflects the inherent uncertainty in forecasting missing data. Future studies should integrate officially updated Quebec data when available to refine predictive models further and validate imputed estimates.

Also, this study analyzes cancer incidence as a whole, whereas prevention programs typically target specific cancers. Future research should extend this analysis to individual cancer types, allowing for a more detailed examination of how prevention efforts impact site-specific cancer trends.

Moreover, our study assumes that biological and environmental factors primarily drive cancer incidence trends, but access to healthcare services plays a crucial role in early detection and diagnosis. Screening disparities, specialist availability, and healthcare system delays may introduce biases in observed cancer incidence rates across age groups and regions. Future studies should incorporate healthcare accessibility indices to better quantify the role of healthcare infrastructure in shaping cancer trends.

Author Contributions: Conceptualization, E.K. and K.P.; methodology, E.K. and K.P.; software, E.K.; validation, E.K. and K.P.; formal analysis, E.K.; investigation, E.K.; resources, E.K. and K.P.; data curation, E.K.; writing—original draft preparation, E.K.; writing—review and editing, E.K. and K.P.; visualization, E.K.; supervision, K.P.; project administration, K.P.; funding acquisition, K.P. All authors have read and agreed to the published version of the manuscript.

Funding: This research received no external funding.

Data Availability Statement: The original data presented in the study are openly available in the Statistics Canada portal, published on 31 January 2024 at this link https://www150.statcan.gc.ca/n1/daily-quotidien/240131/dq240131d-eng.htm.

Conflicts of Interest: The authors declare no conflicts of interest.

References

1. Kibbe, W.A.; Klemm, J.D.; Quackenbush, J. Cancer Informatics: New Tools for a Data-Driven Age in Cancer Research. *Cancer Res.* **2017**, *77*, e1–e2. [CrossRef] [PubMed]
2. Biemar, F.; Foti, M. Global progress against cancer—Challenges and opportunities. *Cancer Biol. Med.* **2013**, *10*, 183–186. [CrossRef] [PubMed]
3. Sikora, K. Developing a global strategy for cancer. *Eur. J. Cancer* **1999**, *35*, 24–31. [CrossRef] [PubMed]
4. Ivanović, M.; Radovanović, M. Modern machine learning techniques and their applications. In *Electronics, Communications and Networks IV*; CRC Press: Boca Raton, FL, USA, 2015. [CrossRef]
5. Rathor, A.; Gyanchandani, M. A review at Machine Learning algorithms targeting big data challenges. In Proceedings of the 2017 International Conference on Electrical, Electronics, Communication, Computer, and Optimization Techniques (ICEECCOT), Mysuru, India, 15–16 December 2017; pp. 1–7. [CrossRef]
6. Nguyen, G.T.; Dlugolinsky, S.; Bobák, M.; Tran, V.D.; López García, Á.; Heredia, I.; Malík, P.; Hluchý, L. Machine Learning and Deep Learning frameworks and libraries for large-scale data mining: A survey. *Artif. Intell. Rev.* **2019**, *52*, 77–124. [CrossRef]
7. Udousoro, I.C. Machine Learning: A Review. *Semicond. Sci. Inf. Devices* **2020**, *2*, 5–14. [CrossRef]
8. Verma, M.; Khoury, M.J.; Ioannidis, J.P. Opportunities and Challenges for Selected Emerging Technologies in Cancer Epidemiology: Mitochondrial, Epigenomic, Metabolomic, and Telomerase Profiling. *Cancer Epidemiol. Biomark. Prev.* **2012**, *22*, 189–200. [CrossRef]
9. Berger, M.L.; Curtis, M.D.; Smith, G.; Harnett, J.; Abernethy, A.P. Opportunities and challenges in leveraging electronic health record data in oncology. *Future Oncol.* **2016**, *12*, 1261–1274. [CrossRef]
10. Gupta, S.; Gupta, A.; Kumar, Y. Artificial intelligence techniques in Cancer research: Opportunities and challenges. In Proceedings of the 2021 International Conference on Technological Advancements and Innovations (ICTAI), Tashkent, Uzbekistan, 10–12 November 2021; pp. 411–416. [CrossRef]
11. Schlick, C.J.; Castle, J.P.; Bentrem, D.J. Utilizing Big Data in Cancer Care. *Surg. Oncol. Clin. N. Am.* **2018**, *27*, 641–652. [CrossRef]
12. Shweta; Riya; Kumar, A. Cancer Prediction Using Machine Learning Algorithm. *Int. J. Sci. Res. (IJSR)* **2022**, *11*, 873–875. [CrossRef]
13. Kaur, I.; Doja, M.N.; Ahmad, T. Data mining and machine learning in cancer survival research: An overview and future recommendations. *J. Biomed. Inform.* **2022**, *128*, 104026. [CrossRef]
14. Shruti Trivedi, N.K. Predictive Analytics in Healthcare using Machine Learning. In Proceedings of the 2023 14th International Conference on Computing Communication and Networking Technologies (ICCCNT), Delhi, India, 6–8 July 2023; pp. 1–5. [CrossRef]
15. Meropol, N.J.; Donegan, J.; Rich, A.S. Progress in the Application of Machine Learning Algorithms to Cancer Research and Care. *JAMA Netw. Open* **2021**, *4*, e2116063. [CrossRef] [PubMed]
16. Brenner, D.R.; Poirier, A.; Woods, R.R.; Ellison, L.F.; Billette, J.M.; Demers, A.A.; Zhang, S.X.; Yao, C.; Finley, C.; Fitzgerald, N.; et al. Canadian Cancer Statistics Advisory Committee. Projected estimates of cancer in Canada in 2022. *CMAJ* **2022**, *194*, E601–E607. [CrossRef] [PubMed] [PubMed Central]
17. Brenner, D.R.; Weir, H.K.; Demers, A.A.; Ellison, L.F.; Louzado, C.; Shaw, A.; Turner, D.; Woods, R.R.; Smith, L.M. Projected estimates of cancer in Canada in 2020. *Can. Med. Assoc. J.* **2020**, *192*, E199–E205. [CrossRef] [PubMed]
18. Brenner, D.R.; Gillis, J.; Demers, A.A.; Ellison, L.F.; Billette, J.-M.; Zhang, S.X.; Liu, J.L.; Woods, R.R.; Finley, C.; Fitzgerald, N.; et al. Projected estimates of cancer in Canada in 2024. *Can. Med. Assoc. J.* **2024**, *196*, E615–E623. [CrossRef]
19. Table 13-10-0394-01: Leading Causes of Death, Total Population, by Age Group. Statistics Canada: Ottawa, ON, Canada, 2025. Available online: https://www150.statcan.gc.ca/t1/tbl1/en/tv.action?pid=1310039401 (accessed on 4 August 2018).
20. Canadian Cancer Statistics Advisory Committee in Collaboration with the Canadian Cancer Society Statistics Canada and the Public Health Agency of Canada. *Canadian Cancer Statistics*; Canadian Cancer Society: Toronto, ON, Canada, 2021. Available online: www.cancer.ca/Canadian-Cancer-Statistics-2021-EN (accessed on 28 March 2022).
21. Xie, L.; Semenciw, R.; Mery, L. Cancer incidence in Canada: Trends and projections (1983–2032). *Health Promot. Chronic Dis. Prev. Can.* **2015**, *35* (Suppl. S1), 2–186. [CrossRef]
22. de Oliveira, C.; Weir, S.; Rangrej, J.; Krahn, M.D.; Mittmann, N.; Hoch, J.S.; Chan, K.K.W.; Peacock, S. The economic burden of cancer care in Canada: A population-based cost study. *CMAJ Open* **2018**, *6*, E1–E10. [CrossRef]
23. Qiu, Z.; Hatcher, J. *Cancer Projection Analytical Network Working Team CANPROJ: The Rpackage of Cancer Projection Methods Based on Generalized Linear Models for Age Period/or Cohort Version, I*; Alberta Health Services: Edmonton, AB, Canada, 2013.

24. Government of Canada, S.C. Cancer Incidence in Canada, 2021. The Daily. Available online: https://www150.statcan.gc.ca/n1/daily-quotidien/240131/dq240131d-eng.htm (accessed on 31 January 2024).
25. Government of Canada, S.C. *Canadian Cancer Registry—Age-Standardization: Incidence*; Government of Canada, Statistics Canada: Ottawa, ON, Canada, 2025. Available online: https://www.statcan.gc.ca/en/statistical-programs/document/3207_D12_V4 (accessed on 17 November 2021).
26. Hochreiter, S.; Schmidhuber, J. Long short-term memory. *Neural Comput.* **1997**, *9*, 1735–1780. [CrossRef]
27. Emmert-Streib, F.; Yang, Z.; Feng, H.; Tripathi, S.; Dehmer, M. An Introductory Review of Deep Learning for Prediction Models with Big Data. *Front. Artif. Intell.* **2020**, *3*, 4. [CrossRef]
28. Kaninde, S.; Mahajan, M.; Janghale, A.; Joshi, B. Stock Price Prediction using Facebook Prophet. *ITM Web Conf.* **2022**, *44*, 3060. [CrossRef]
29. Korstanje, J. The Prophet Model. In *Advanced Forecasting with Python*; Apress: New York, NY, USA, 2021. [CrossRef]
30. Shen, J.; Valagolam, D.; McCalla, S. Prophet forecasting model: A machine learning approach to predict the concentration of air pollutants ($PM_{2.5}$, PM_{10}, O_3, NO_2, SO_2, CO) in Seoul, South Korea. *PeerJ* **2020**, *8*, e9961. [CrossRef]
31. Rundo, F.; Trenta, F.; di Stallo, A.L.; Battiato, S. Machine learning for quantitative finance applications: A survey. *Appl. Sci.* **2019**, *9*, 5574. [CrossRef]
32. Siami-Namini, S.; Tavakoli, N.; Namin, A.S. A comparison of ARIMA and LSTM in forecasting time series. In Proceedings of the 2018 17th IEEE International Conference on Machine Learning and Applications (ICMLA), Orlando, FL, USA, 17–20 December 2018; pp. 1394–1401.
33. Kontopoulou, V.I.; Panagopoulos, A.D.; Kakkos, I.; Matsopoulos, G.K. A Review of ARIMA vs. Machine Learning Approaches for Time Series Forecasting in Data Driven Networks. *Future Internet* **2023**, *15*, 255. [CrossRef]
34. Sima, S.N.; Akbar, S.N. Forecasting Economics and Financial Time Series: ARIMA vs. LSTM. *arXiv* **2018**, arXiv:1803.06386. [CrossRef]
35. Kulshreshtha, S.; Vijayalakshmi, A. An ARIMA-LSTM hybrid model for stock market prediction using live data. *J. Eng. Sci. Technol. Rev.* **2020**, *13*, 117–123. [CrossRef]
36. Zhang, G.P. Time series forecasting using a hybrid ARIMA and neural network model. *Neurocomputing* **2003**, *50*, 159–175. [CrossRef]
37. Maxim, S.; Adriaan, B.; Shcherbakova, N.L.; Anton, T.; Janovsky, T.A.; Kamaev, V.A. A survey of forecast error measures. *World Appl. Sci. J.* **2013**, *24*, 171–176.
38. Cheng, C.; Shalabh Garg, G. Coefficient of determination for multiple measurement error models. *J. Multivar. Anal.* **2014**, *126*, 137–152. [CrossRef]
39. Goel, H.; Melnyk, I.; Banerjee, A. R2N2: Residual Recurrent Neural Networks for Multivariate Time Series Forecasting. *arXiv* **2017**, arXiv:1709.03159.
40. Chatfield, C. Model uncertainty and forecast accuracy. *J. Forecast.* **1996**, *15*, 495–508. [CrossRef]
41. Hewamalage, H.; Bergmeir, C.; Bandara, K. Recurrent Neural Networks for Time Series Forecasting: Current Status and Future Directions. *arXiv* **2019**, arXiv:1909.00590. [CrossRef]
42. Kim, T.; Leybourne, S.J.; Newbold, P. Asymptotic mean-squared forecast error when an autoregression with linear trend is fitted to data generated by an I(0) or I(1) process. *J. Time Ser. Anal.* **2004**, *25*, 583–602. [CrossRef]

algorithms

MDPI

Article

Early Risk Prediction in Acute Aortic Syndrome on Clinical Data Using Machine Learning

Mehdi Tavafi [1], Kalpdrum Passi [1,*] and Robert Ohle [2]

1 School of Engineering & Computer Science, Laurentian University, Sudbury, ON P3E 2C6, Canada; mtavafi@laurentian.ca
2 Department of Emergency Medicine, Health Science North Research Institute, Northern Ontario School of Medicine, Sudbury, ON P3E 5J1, Canada; rohle@hsnsudbury.ca
* Correspondence: kpassi@laurentian.ca

Abstract: This study explores machine learning's potential for early Acute Aortic Syndrome (AAS) prediction by integrating and cleaning extensive clinical datasets from 68 emergency departments in the USA, covering the medical histories of nearly 150,000 patients from 2021 to 2022. Utilizing various data-splitting strategies and classifiers, the research constructs predictive models and addresses dataset size limitations, achieving an exceptional accuracy of 99.3% with the Relief feature method and random forest classifier, facilitating further research on AAS and other cardiovascular diseases.

Keywords: machine learning; acute aortic syndrome (AAS); clinical data; SMOTE method; feature extraction; Principal Component Analysis (PCA); relief method; correlation-based feature selection (CFS)

1. Introduction

Acute Aortic Syndrome (AAS) encompasses a spectrum of life-threatening conditions, including Acute Aortic Dissection (AAD), Intramural Hematoma (IMH), and Penetrating Aortic Ulcer (PAU) [1]. AAD involves a tear in the inner layer of the aortic wall; IMH entails bleeding within the aortic wall, without a clear tear in the inner layer; and PAU refers to a defect or ulceration in the aortic wall penetrating deeper layers, as indicated in Figure 1 below. Various risk factors, including hypertension and atherosclerosis, are associated with these subtypes [2,3].

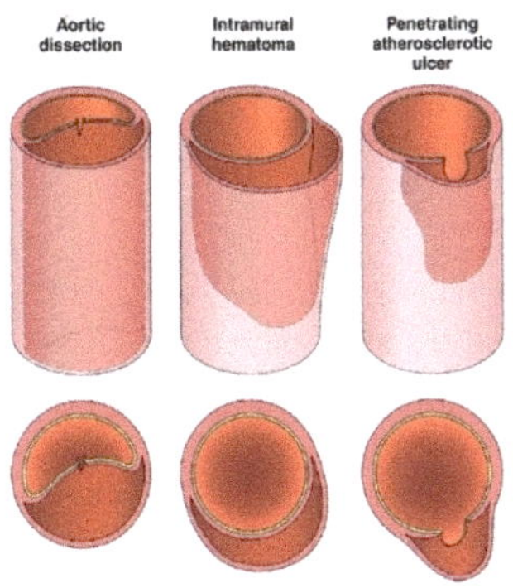

Figure 1. Anatomy of the aorta and pathogenesis of Acute Aortic Syndrome [3].

Characterized by defects in the aortic wall, AAS poses the imminent risk of vessel obstruction or rupture, often manifesting through symptoms such as chest pain [3]. High blood pressure and genetic factors are commonly associated with AAS [1]. Symptoms include intense pain, often resembling a heart attack [1,4]. Prompt diagnosis, typically through imaging techniques, is crucial. A compromised aortic wall can lead to severe complications, underscoring the urgency of addressing AAS [3]. The incidence of AAS in the general population ranges from 3.5 to 6.0 cases per 100,000 patient-years, with higher rates observed among individuals aged 64 to 74 years and those aged 75 years and older [5,6].

Diagnosing AAS presents a multifaceted challenge due to its diverse clinical presentations and the absence of standardized diagnostic criteria [3,7]. This diagnostic uncertainty contributes to delays in treatment, emphasizing the critical need for improved diagnostic approaches [8]. Machine learning, a branch of artificial intelligence, has emerged as a promising tool in healthcare, offering the potential to enhance diagnostic accuracy and patient outcomes [9,10].

Recognizing the gap in diagnostic guidance, this paper leverages a comprehensive dataset integrating clinical records from 68 emergency departments across the USA, encompassing medical histories of nearly 150,000 patients from 2021 to 2022. By exploring the utility of machine learning techniques, the study aims to develop predictive models for identifying patients at risk of AAS. Through systematic review and analysis of diagnostic accuracy methodologies, this research seeks to elucidate critical factors influencing AAS diagnosis and facilitate the development of clinical decision support systems. Ultimately, the objective is to expedite AAS diagnosis and improve patient care in emergency settings.

1.1. Machine Learning and Deep Learning in Acute Aortic Syndrome

Machine learning is revolutionizing the detection and classification of Acute Aortic Syndrome (AAS) through medical imaging interpretation and clinical data analysis. Here is how it's making an impact:

1.1.1. Medical Imaging Interpretation

- Computed Tomography (CT) Scans: Algorithms analyze CT scans to detect subtle patterns of AAS, learning from extensive datasets to improve accuracy [11].
- Magnetic Resonance Imaging (MRI): Similar to CT scans, algorithms analyze MRI images to recognize AAS features, enhancing subtype identification [12].

1.1.2. Clinical Variable and Results Analysis

- Risk Prediction Models: Models integrate clinical variables and imaging results to predict AAS risk, leveraging data patterns for accurate risk estimation [13].
- Integration of Multimodal Data: Machine learning integrates information from diverse sources for comprehensive AAS detection and classification [13].

2. Literature Review of AAS

In studies related to AAS and its subsets, such as Acute Aortic Dissection (AAD) criteria, the key measure of success is primarily assessed through the Area Under the Receiver Operating Characteristic (ROC) Curve (AUC), along with sensitivity and specificity. Analyzing these parameters allows for a comprehensive statistical evaluation of the results in the below-mentioned research studies and facilitates meaningful comparisons between them.

In some research, the choice of methodology for predicting AAS is influenced by the type of dataset sources available. Some studies utilize Computed Tomography (CT) Scans and Magnetic Resonance Imaging (MRI), while others combine clinical variables and CT images. As a result, researchers adopt a hybrid approach, incorporating both clinical and imaging data. Additionally, some studies concentrate specifically on clinical measurements and demographic data, employing machine learning techniques. Various researchers utilize a diverse array of machine learning strategies to analyze these datasets.

2.1. Prediction of AAS by Machine Learning Techniques

In prior investigations focusing on AAS, researchers adopted varied methodologies to collect data. Some studies relied on immediate medical experiment results and demographic data from patients arriving at emergency departments, while others concentrated on patients admitted to hospitals, incorporating more detailed parameters and epidemiological experiment results. Certain studies utilized standard data entry forms, capturing extensive information on patient demographics, history, clinical presentations, physical findings, imaging study results, and patient outcomes, including mortality.

In October 2020, Duceau et al. [13] applied machine learning methods to prehospital research, involving 976 patients. Their study focused on prehospital triage and utilized 27 variables and patient characteristics. Two prediction models for AAS were formulated, employing logistic regression and an ensemble machine learning approach named Super Learner (SL). Under-triage, representing the percentage of AAS patients not transported to the specialized aortic center, and over-triage, indicating the percentage of patients with alternative diagnoses transported to the specialized aortic center, were key parameters studied. For internal validation, Duceau et al. employed five-fold cross-validation in their respective studies. The SL algorithm demonstrated superior performance in predicting AAS, attributed to its ability to comprehend intricate relationships and patterns within the data. The enhanced predictive accuracy of the SL algorithm was evident in its higher AUC value of 0.73 compared to the logistic regression model's 0.67 in the validation cohort, indicating superior predictive capabilities.

In Huo et al.'s [14] study, initially considering 526 patients, 34 cases were excluded from the analysis, resulting in a final population size of 492. The study utilized Correlation-Based Feature Selection (CFS) to choose a subset of attributes most relevant for classification, considering each feature's utility in predicting the class and addressing intercorrelations among them. Huo et al. applied 10-fold cross-validation during hyperparameter tuning for advanced machine learning models in the training data. In their study, the Bayesian Network outperformed five other methods, achieving a superior AUC value of 0.857. This underscores the effectiveness of the Bayesian Network in their research.

Wu et al. [15] achieved the highest AUC for predicting in-hospital rupture of type A aortic dissection using the random forest technique. The research retrospectively evaluated 1133 consecutive patients diagnosed with Thoracic Aortic Aneurysm and Dissection (TAAD), employing the random forest method. A notable finding from the research was the exceptional performance of the random forest classification model, achieving an outstanding AUC of 0.994 for the training dataset and AUC of 0.752 for testing. This remarkable result indicates an exceptional discrimination ability in the training dataset, accompanied by sensitivity of 51.4% and a specificity of 94.5%. These metrics collectively emphasize the robust predictive capabilities of the model, highlighting its effectiveness in accurately distinguishing and classifying cases within the context of TAAD.

Guo et al. [16] conducted a thorough research study involving 1344 patients diagnosed with acute aortic dissection, comprising 1071 survivors and 273 non-survivors. The study utilized five machine learning models, including logistic regression, decision tree, K-Nearest Neighbor, Gaussian Naive Bayes, and Extreme Gradient Boosting (XGBoost), to predict in-hospital mortality risk. Among these models, the XGBoost model demonstrated remarkable performance, with the highest mean AUC of 0.927 across 10 iterations. The study revealed that the XGBoost model was an effective approach for generating accurate and early predictions of in-hospital mortality in patients with AAD. Evaluation metrics further reinforced XGBoost's superiority, showing high accuracy at 0.918 and robust values for sensitivity, specificity, positive predictive value, and negative predictive value.

In Wu et al.'s [17] study, continuous variables were presented as mean ± standard deviation, and categorical variables as frequencies and percentages. A decision tree, utilizing demographic and clinical data from the training set, reveals distinct risk profiles for various aortic dissection types. A nomogram based on logistic regression analysis established a scoring system using 23 selected variables. The data were randomly divided into training (80%) and testing (20%) sets, with missing values imputed using the median of recorded measurements. This pragmatic strategy ensured effective model training and testing, offering insights into model performance on unseen data while addressing missing values. The study explored various machine learning techniques, with the XGBoost model demonstrating the highest accuracy and robustness. Shapley Additive explanations analysis highlighted factors such as Stanford type A, maximum aortic diameter > 5.5 cm, high variability in HR, high variability in diastolic BP, and involvement of the aortic arch impacting in-hospital deaths before surgery.

Lin et al.'s study [18] showcased the impressive performance of a Convolutional Neural Network (CNN) model in predicting acute type A aortic dissection rupture. The CNN achieved a remarkable AUC of 0.99, along with notable sensitivity (93%) and specificity (90%). The investigation identified age, gender, specific biomarkers, and aortic morphological parameters as independent predictors for acute type A aortic dissection rupture, emphasizing the CNN's efficacy in accurately predicting and identifying potential risk factors. Notably, both random forests and CNN outperformed logistic regression (LR) in predicting acute type A aortic dissection risk, while the Support Vector Machine (SVM) demonstrated inferior performance compared to LR.

2.2. Literature Review Summary

In summary, the reviewed studies collectively advance the refinement of diagnostic and predictive models for AAS, demonstrating progress across diverse methodologies. The emphasis on the AUC in comparing diagnostic performance underscores the effectiveness of notable models like XGBoost and random forest, indicating their accuracy in predicting and classifying cases. These findings contribute to a comprehensive understanding of factors influencing outcomes and risk estimation in Acute Aortic Syndrome and its subsets.

The survey's notable discovery was the impressive AUC of 0.99 achieved using the CNN in predicting the risk of Acute Aortic Dissection rupture [16]. The dataset was strategically divided, with 70% designated for training and 30% for testing, enhancing the robustness of the model evaluation. Specifically, for predicting AAS, the highest AUC recorded was 0.974, accompanied by a notable 91.8% sensitivity, utilizing the multivariate logistic regression [19].

In the domain of AAS research, the study with the smallest patient cohort, as indicated in Table 1, is associated with Morello et al. [20], conducted in 2023. This investigation focused on the identification and analysis of 128 cases of AAS evaluated in two emergency departments. On the contrary, the study with the largest patient cohort encountered in this research on AAS is McLatchie et al.'s [21], conducted in 2023. Initially centered on the identification and analysis of cases in three UK emergency departments, this study expanded to include 5548 patients and considered 44 variables, providing a comprehensive exploration of the subject.

Table 1. Related work summary.

Ref.	Variable	Sample Size	Preprocessing	Methods	Results
B. Duceau [13]	32	976	5-fold cross-validation	Logistic regression Super Learner (SL)	AUC: 0.73 Sensitivity: 99% Specificity: 18%
D. Huo [14]	15	492	CFS feature selection 10-fold cross-validation	Bayesian Network, Naive Bayes, SMO J48 (decision tree)	AUC: 0.857 Sensitivity: 93.1% Specificity: 70.2%
J. Wu [15]	16	1133	Divided the sample into training (70%) and testing (30%) data	Random forest	AUC: 0.752 Sensitivity: 99% Specificity: 51.4%
T. Guo [16]	41	1344	Treatment Encoding Type of AAD and Gender Encoding Binary Feature Encoding 10-fold cross-validation	Logistic regression Decision tree Extreme Gradient Boosting Nearest neighbor Gaussian Naive Bayes	AUC: 0.927 Sensitivity: 72.9% Specificity: 96.6% Accuracy: 0.918
Z. Wu [17]	23	380	Divided the sample into training (80%) and testing (20%) data	Logistic regression Decision tree Extreme Gradient Boosting Random Forest (RF) Support Vector Machine (SVM)	AUC: 0.926 Sensitivity: 85% Specificity: 93%
Y. Lin [18]	10	200	Shapiro–Wilk test used to determine normal distribution. Normal distribution data presented as (Mean SD), compared with *t*-tests. Non-normal distribution data presented as median (M) and interquartile range, compared by two independent-sample rank-sum tests.	Logistic regression Random Forest SVM CNN	AUC: 0.99 Sensitivity: 93% Specificity: 90% Accuracy: 0.90
F. Tong [19]	22	638	Patients categorized into subgroups based on the onset time (<2 h and ≥2 h). *t*-test, Mann–Whitney U test, or Chi-square test used for normally distributed continuous variables, non-normally distributed continuous variables, and categorical variables, respectively.	Multivariate logistic regression	AUC: 0.974 Sensitivity: 91.8% Specificity: 91.3%
F. Morello [20]	35	128	Pretest Probability Assessment Median D-dimer levels compared between patients with non-AAS and alternative diagnoses	ADD-RS Plus D-dimer	AUC: 0.74 Sensitivity: 65% Specificity: 83%
R. McLatchie [21]	44	5548	Constructing exact binomial 80% confidence intervals around key proportions. Handling missing data in the calculation of performance indices for clinical decision tools (CDTs).	Multicenter observational EDs assessing for potential AAS, using both prospective and retrospective recruitment, with anonymized patient data collection	AUC: 0.958 Sensitivity: 95% Specificity: 97%

Table 1. *Cont.*

Ref.	Variable	Sample Size	Preprocessing	Methods	Results
D. Wang [22]	17	1298	Internal validation: 5-fold cross-validation	Logistic regression	AUC: 0.838 Sensitivity: 84% Specificity: 91% Accuracy: 0.94
R. Ohle [23]	17	1340	Continuous variables presented as means ± standard deviation. Categorical variables presented as frequencies and percentages. Two-sided chi-square or Fisher's exact test.	ADDRS, RIPP Von Kodolitsch AORTAs LOVY	AUC: 0.828 Sensitivity: 99.7% Specificity: 53%
R. Gorla [24]	17	376	Continuous variables presented as means ± standard deviation; categorical variables presented as frequencies and percentages	ROC analysis used to determine the sensitivity and specificity of D-d at the cutoff value of 0.5 mg/L	AUC: 0.91 Sensitivity: 97.6% Specificity: 63.2%
L. Deng [25]	12	462	Categorical data described as numbers and percentages. Continuous data displayed as mean with standard deviation (SD) or median with interquartile range	ADD-RS plus D-dimer	AUC: 0.911 Sensitivity: 93.1% Specificity: 70.2%
F. Morello [26]	19	313	Categorical variables reported as proportions plus 95% confidence interval (CI). Mann–Whitney U test for non-parametric continuous variables. Kruskal–Wallis with post hoc Dunn's multiple comparison test for independent samples. Pearson's $\chi 2$ test for categorical variables.	Logistic regression	AUC: 0.92 Sensitivity: 95.20% Specificity: 46.60%
D. Song [27]	7	558	Chi-square test used for categorical variables. Normality tests performed for continuous variables.	Multivariate logistic regression	AUC: 0.928 Sensitivity: 100% Specificity: 67.8%
F. Fu [28]	23	630	Two-tailed Student's *t*-test $\chi 2$ test employed for categorical variables. Independent sample Mann–Whitney U test used for non-normally distributed data.	Logistic regression	AUC: 0.919 Sensitivity: 89.3% Specificity: 80.6%
F. Morello [29]	12	3330	Feature coefficient and heat maps	Multivariable logistic regression	AUC: 0.729 Sensitivity: 100% Specificity: 43.1%
L. Xing [30]	5	569	Internal validation: 20 repetitions of 10-fold cross-validation External validation	Multivariate logistic regression SPSS set $p < 0.05$	AUC: 0.833 Sensitivity: 91% Specificity: 87%

One limitation observed in the above-mentioned studies is the absence of a sample size calculation. This study recognizes the importance of having at least 10 events for each predictor parameter when developing prediction models, as small sample sizes can compromise statistical power and the reliability of predictive models. However, this comprehensive thesis addresses this limitation by incorporating a substantial total sample size of 148,707 cases with 42 clinical variables' data that will be explained more in the next section, which is about the data. This marks a significant transition into the realm of big data compared to earlier, smaller studies in the field of Acute Aortic Syndrome (AAS). Significantly, this extensive dataset also holds potential applicability for predicting various heart diseases beyond AAS.

3. Roadmap

In this section, Figure 2 is designed to provide a visual roadmap outlining the steps of the project, including cleaning, preprocessing, and implementation. This roadmap serves to enhance understanding and facilitate the follow-through of the project's implementation process.

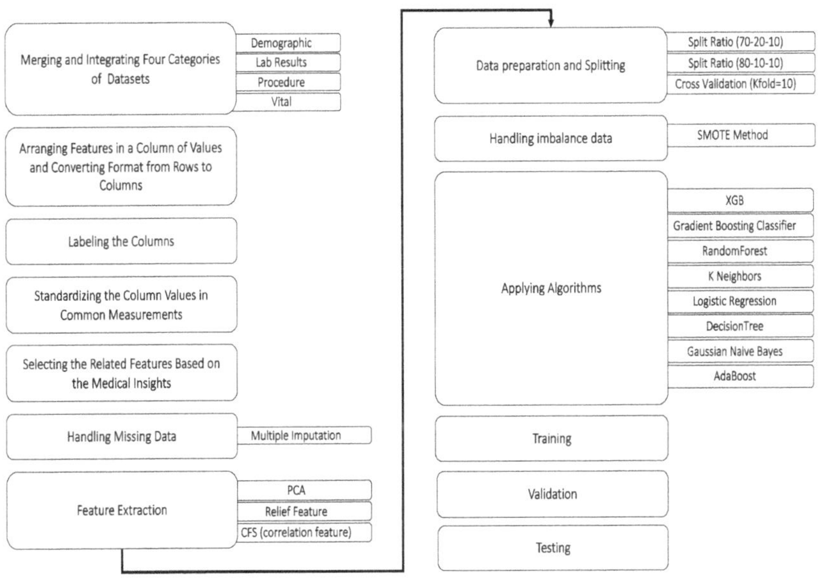

Figure 2. Project process and roadmap.

4. Clinical Dataset

Clinical datasets in Acute Aortic Syndrome (AAS) are indispensable reservoirs of patient information that significantly contribute to advancing our comprehension of this intricate cardiovascular ailment. These datasets comprise a wide array of clinical histories, imaging results, laboratory tests, and treatment outcomes [14], offering a comprehensive overview of AAS presentations. Leveraging the richness of these datasets allows for discerning patterns, identifying risk factors, and tailoring diagnostic and therapeutic approaches to individual patients [1,15]. Meticulous data integration, cleaning, and analysis enable clinicians to derive valuable insights into various facets of AAS, facilitating early detection, risk prediction, and personalized patient care [15,16].

The dynamic utilization of clinical datasets in AAS research involves continuous refinement and analysis to uncover hidden patterns and enhance diagnostic and treatment strategies. By employing advanced computational techniques, including machine learning, to extract meaningful information from these datasets, clinicians are empowered to make evidence-based decisions and formulate effective treatment plans [1,15]. This iterative process of data analysis and refinement not only contributes to the scientific understanding of AAS but also drives ongoing progress in heart medicine, enabling clinicians to better predict, diagnose, and manage this life-threatening cardiovascular condition in emergency department settings.

4.1. Structure of Dataset

This study utilizes a diverse array of clinical datasets from emergency departments (EDs) in hospitals, focusing on patients with and without Acute Aortic Syndrome (AAS). These datasets, gathered from 150 EDs in Canada and the USA between 2021 and 2022, provide a detailed overview of patients' physiological conditions, diagnostic patterns, and disposition outcomes.

The dataset was organized into separate files, with each patient assigned a unique visit UID. In Table 2, the numbers of files, columns, and rows, and unique visit UIDs in each of the four categories of files are visible.

Table 2. Dataset overview.

Categories	No. of Files	No. of Columns	No. of Rows	Unique-UID
Demographic	11	6	335,201	146,114
Procedure	15	3	308,828	109,756
Lab result	15	5	4,202,716	92,892
Vital	15	4	1,048,575	57,465
Total	56	18	5,895,320	**148,707**

4.1.1. Demographic Dataset

This dataset includes demographic information, such as age and gender, for both non-AAS and AAS patient groups, as depicted in Table 3. Specifically, a gender imbalance is evident within the AAS group, with males constituting 65.1% compared to females, at 34.9%, suggesting gender-specific trends in AAS. The presence of missing data underscores the importance of ensuring analysis reliability. Furthermore, Figure 3 and Table 3 highlight that 46.5% of AAS patients fall within the 60–80-year-old age range, emphasizing the prevalence of this condition among older demographics. Meanwhile, the disposition outcomes column offers insights into patients' final healthcare status, encompassing discharge, admission, transfer, and mortality, reflecting the diverse scenarios encountered within the ED setting for both non-AAS and AAS groups. Additionally, the chief complaint column details the primary reasons for seeking medical attention, notably focusing on chest pain symptoms. Further analysis elucidates the prevalence and severity of chest pain within the AAS group, emphasizing the importance of comprehensive symptom assessment in addressing healthcare needs. These combined analyses provide valuable insights into demographic characteristics, disposition outcomes, diagnosis patterns, and symptom profiles within both patient populations.

The comparison of gender distributions between patients without and with AAS reveals noteworthy findings. In the absence of Acute Aortic Syndrome (AAS) (Figure 4), the gender distribution is relatively balanced, with women at 54.13% and men at 45.87%. However, in the presence of AAS (Figure 5), there is a significant shift, indicating a higher proportion of male patients at 65.12%, with females comprising 34.88%. This gender disparity suggests that AAS may exhibit gender-specific patterns or predispositions. Further investigation into the underlying factors contributing to this gender-related difference could provide valuable insights into the characteristics and risk factors associated with Acute Aortic Syndrome in different demographic groups.

Table 3. Demographics dataset details.

Demographics	Non-AAS (n = 148,578)		AAS (n = 129)	
	Count	**Percentage**	**Count**	**Percentage**
Age				
<18	4848	3.3%	0	0%
18–40	50,328	33.9%	11	8.5%
40–60	50,796	34.2%	40	31%
60–80	32,691	22%	60	46.5%
80+	7322	4.9%	18	14%
Missing data	2593	1.7%	0	0%
Gender				
Male	66,960	45.1%	84	65.1%
Female	79,025	53.2%	45	34.9%
Missing data	2593	1.7%	0	0%

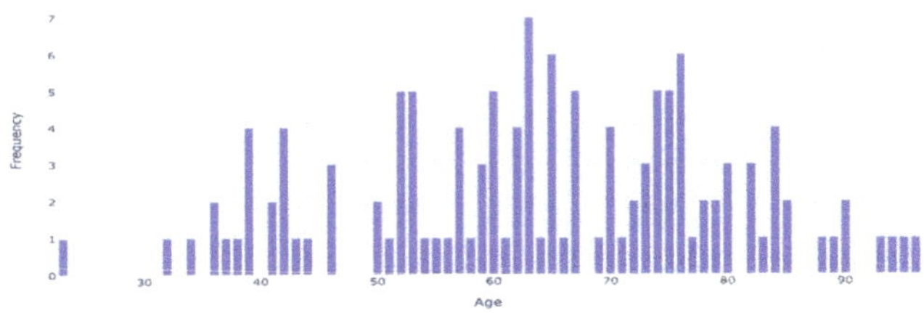

Figure 3. Age frequency distribution of patients with AAS.

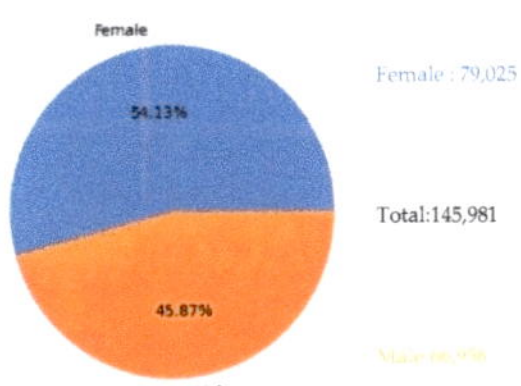

Figure 4. Age distribution of non-AAS patients.

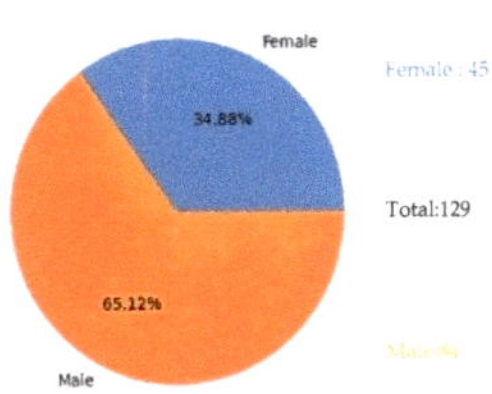

Figure 5. Age distribution of patients with AAS.

4.1.2. Lab Results Dataset

This dataset encompasses measurements of biomarkers and biochemical parameters obtained from blood samples, including D-dimer, hemoglobin, and troponin levels. It offers valuable insights into patients' physiological profiles and provides markers for potential clotting abnormalities and cardiac injury associated with AAS.

Table 4 provides data on troponin levels in the lab results dataset for both the non-AAS (148,578 individuals) and AAS (129 individuals) groups. Troponin is a protein associated with heart muscle contraction, and its levels in the blood can indicate cardiac injury. The unit for troponin measurement is nanograms per liter (ng/L).

Table 4. Troponin analysis.

Lab Results	Non-AAS (n = 148,578)		AAS (n = 129)	
	Count	Percentage	Count	Percentage
Troponin (ng/mL)				
0–1	55,172	37.13%	54	41.86%
1–3	2888	1.94%	1	0.78%
3–8	5879	3.96%	7	5.43%
8–12	1192	0.80%	4	3.10%
12–15	419	0.28%	1	0.78%
15–25	626	0.42%	2	1.55%
25–50	464	0.31%	1	0.78%
50–80	124	0.08%	0	0%
80–130	47	0.03%	1	0.78%
Missing data	81,755	55%	58	45%

In the non-AAS group, the average troponin level is 2 ng/L, while in the AAS group, it slightly rises to 4 ng/L. The examination of troponin level distribution across various ranges reveals differences between the two groups. For example, in the 0–1 ng/L range, a higher percentage of individuals is observed in the AAS group (41.86%) compared to the non-AAS group (37.13%). Additionally, the proportion of individuals with troponin levels in the 15–25 ng/L range is higher in the AAS group (1.55%) than in the non-AAS group (0.42%).

The table also underscores the presence of missing data, with 55% of individuals in the non-AAS group and 45% in the AAS group lacking recorded troponin values.

4.1.3. Vital Signs Dataset

This part of the dataset includes measurements of essential health indicators, such as blood pressure, body temperature, and pulse rate. It provides insights into patients' overall health status and helps monitor physiological parameters relevant to AAS diagnosis and management.

Table 5 offers a summary of diastolic blood pressure (Diastolic-BP) measurements in both the non-AAS (148,578 individuals) and AAS (129 individuals) groups within the vitals dataset. The unit for diastolic blood pressure is millimeters of mercury (mmHg). Diastolic blood pressure signifies the pressure in the arteries when the heart is at rest between beats.

Table 5. Diastolic-BP analysis.

Vitals	Non-AAS (n = 148,578)		AAS (n = 129)	
	Count	Percentage	Count	Percentage
Diastolic-BP (mmHg)				
0–30	64	0.04%	2	1.55%
30–60	7237	4.87%	13	10.08%
60–90	29,903	20.13%	14	10.85%
90–120	13,963	9.40%	25	19.38%
120–150	3954	2.66%	1	0.78%
150–180	839	0.56%	0	0%
180–240	70	0.05%	1	0.78%
>240	1	0%	0	0%
Missing data	92,547	62%	73	56.6%

In the non-AAS group, the average diastolic blood pressure is 85 mmHg, while in the AAS group, it is slightly lower at 83 mmHg. The table illustrates the distribution of diastolic blood pressure across different ranges for both groups. For instance, in the 60–90 mmHg range, a higher percentage of individuals is observed in the non-AAS group (20.13%) compared to the AAS group (10.85%). Conversely, in the 90–120 mmHg range, the AAS group has a higher percentage (19.38%) than the non-AAS group (9.40%).

Moreover, the table highlights the presence of missing data, with 62% of individuals in the non-AAS group and 56.6% in the AAS group lacking recorded diastolic blood pressure values. Addressing missing data is crucial for a comprehensive analysis of blood pressure patterns, especially in the context of aortic dissection.

Table 6 presents a summary of systolic blood pressure (Systolic-BP) measurements in both the non-AAS (148,578 individuals) and AAS (129 individuals) groups within the vitals dataset. The unit for systolic blood pressure is millimeters of mercury (mmHg). Systolic blood pressure denotes the maximum pressure in the arteries during a heartbeat.

Table 6. Systolic-BP analysis.

Vitals	Non-AAS (n = 148,578)		AAS (n = 129)	
	Count	Percentage	Count	Percentage
Systolic-BP (mmHg)				
0–30	283	0.19%	0	0%
30–60	1471	0.99%	3	2.33%
60–90	3884	2.61%	2	1.55%
90–120	22,176	14.93%	32	24.81%
120–150	22,618	15.22%	10	7.75%
150–180	4941	3.33%	5	3.88%
180–240	571	0.38%	4	3.10%
>240	4	0.003%	0	0%
Missing data	92,881	63%	73	56.6%

In the non-AAS group, the average systolic blood pressure is 121 mmHg, and in the AAS group, it is slightly lower, at 118 mmHg. The table illustrates the distribution of systolic blood pressure across different ranges for both groups. For instance, in the 90–120 mmHg range, the AAS group has a higher percentage (24.81%) compared to the non-AAS group (14.93%). On the other hand, in the 120–150 mmHg range, the non-AAS group has a higher percentage (15.22%) than the AAS group (7.75%).

Additionally, the table indicates the presence of missing data, with 63% of individuals in the non-AAS group and 56.6% in the AAS group lacking recorded systolic blood pressure values. Addressing missing data is crucial for a comprehensive analysis of blood pressure patterns, particularly in the context of aortic dissection.

4.1.4. Procedure Dataset

In this segment of the dataset, there are 15 individual files, each with three columns—Visit-UID, procedure code, and procedure description—collecting information about various medical procedures carried out on patients. In preparation for analysis, rows with similar medical details were grouped by assigning them new titles or brief abbreviations. This arrangement enhances the structure of the dataset, making the analysis of medical procedures more efficient. This organized structure aids in obtaining a clearer understanding of patient categories with AAS and assists in identifying which procedures were conducted or overlooked during their hospital stay.

4.2. Data Preprocessing and Standardization

There are integral steps aimed at enhancing the reliability and interpretability of analyses. This involves standardizing units, ensuring consistency in labeling, and addressing missing data. The standardized datasets enable meaningful comparisons and correlations across various hospitals and patient populations. The implementation of preprocessing before integrating separate datasets entails cleaning, organizing, and standardizing the individual datasets. This stage is crucial to ensure that the data are in a suitable and uniform format for seamless integration. Common preprocessing tasks include handling missing values, addressing outliers, standardizing units or scales, and resolving inconsistencies in data formats. Through these preprocessing steps, the quality, reliability, and compatibility of the individual datasets are enhanced, laying the foundation for a more accurate and coherent analysis upon integration.

4.3. Missing Data

Missing data are a common challenge in medical research, especially in cardiovascular health studies, where participant withdrawal can reduce sample sizes. Missingness refers to absent information, which can introduce bias and reduce analysis efficiency. Understanding the reasons behind missing data, known as missingness mechanisms, is crucial for accurate analyses. There are three main mechanisms: MCAR (missing completely at random), MAR (missing at random), and MNAR (missing not at random) [31,32].

To address missing data, various methods are available, each with its advantages and limitations. These include Complete Case Analysis, Mean or Median Imputation, Regression Imputation, Multiple Imputation (MI), and others. MI is favored for its ability to account for uncertainty by creating multiple datasets with varied imputed values.

In this research, Multiple Imputation by Chained Equations (MICE) was chosen due to its robustness and ability to provide reliable results in the presence of missing data. The imputation principle involves estimating or replacing missing values based on statistical techniques to minimize bias and preserve the dataset's statistical properties. Multiple Imputation by Chained Equations (MICE) is an iterative method where missing values are imputed by modeling each incomplete variable conditional on the observed values of other variables. This approach generates multiple imputed datasets, which are analyzed separately and then combined to account for imputation uncertainty [33]. The choice of imputation method depends on factors like data distribution and relationships. For categorical variables with no discernible relationships, MICE is suitable. It imputes missing values by modeling each variable with missing data as a function of other variables, iteratively updating imputed values until convergence is reached.

4.3.1. Missing-Data Mechanisms

Various factors can result in missing data, and it is crucial to acknowledge them. The choice of methods to address missing data in statistical analysis relies on assumptions about the underlying mechanisms, emphasizing the importance of understanding the reasons behind missing data [31,32]. Table 7 categorizes missing-data mechanisms for predictors into three types: MCAR (missing completely at random), MAR (missing at random), and MNAR (missing not at random). It outlines the scenarios associated with each mechanism, providing a foundational understanding for selecting suitable methods to address missing data in statistical analyses.

Based on the characteristics and relationships among our dataset values, the choice between imputation methods is determined. In the case of a dataset where variables are neither continuous nor correlated, the selection of an appropriate imputation technique becomes crucial. Specifically, when dealing with non-continuous variables that exhibit no discernible relationships, Multiple Imputation by Chained Equations (MICE) emerges as a suitable option. It is particularly well-suited for handling missing values in categorical variables, allowing for the estimation of probabilities associated with certain events.

Table 7. Types of missing-data mechanisms for predictors.

Label	Missing Mechanism	Description
MCAR	Missing completely at random	Administrative errors, accidents
MAR	Missing at random	Missingness related to known patient characteristics, time, or place ("MAR on x"), or to the outcome ("MAR on y")
MNAR	Missing not at random	Missingness related to the value of the predictor or to variables not available in the analysis

4.3.2. Multiple Imputation by Chained Equations (MICE)

This method involves imputing missing values in a dataset by modeling each incomplete variable conditional on the observed values of the other variables. The imputation equations are created for each variable with missing data. The general idea is to perform imputation in a series of steps, with each step updating one variable at a time. This process is iterated until convergence. The imputation models can vary depending on the nature of the variables (continuous, categorical, etc.) and the assumptions you make about the data [33].

Multiple Imputation by Chained Equations (MICE) is an iterative imputation method that imputes missing values in a dataset by modeling each variable with missing data as a function of other variables. The method is based on the idea of imputing missing values multiple times, creating multiple datasets with plausible imputed values. These datasets are then analyzed separately, and the results are combined to account for the uncertainty introduced by the imputation process [34].

The general equation for imputing a missing value in MICE can be described as follows:

$$Y_i^m = \mu_i + \epsilon_i^m$$

where Y_i^m represents the imputed value for the missing data in a variable, i, that m-th imputed dataset; μ_i is the predicted value for the missing data; and ϵ_i^m is a random error term sampled from the distribution of the residuals of the predictive model [35].

The MICE algorithm proceeds through multiple cycles, where each cycle involves updating the imputed values for each variable based on the imputed values of other variables. This process is repeated until convergence, and the final imputed values are obtained by combining the results from all imputed datasets [36].

In this study, we used IterativeImputer from the scikit-learn library, which implements MICE for imputing missing data. This method employs a Bayesian Ridge Regression model to predict missing values iteratively. In each iteration, the model imputes missing values for each feature in the dataset, taking into account the correlation between features. By default, it uses 10 iterations to converge, though this can be adjusted. The imputed data are then combined, ensuring that the variability introduced by the imputation process is incorporated into the final analysis.

4.4. Balancing Data with SMOTE

To address the imbalance challenge in the dataset, with only 129 positive cases among 148,578 negative cases, the Synthetic Minority Oversampling Technique (SMOTE) was employed.

4.4.1. What Is SMOTE

SMOTE stands for Synthetic Minority Oversampling Technique. It is a popular method used to address class imbalance in machine learning datasets, particularly in classification tasks. Class imbalance occurs when one class (the minority class) is significantly underrepresented compared to the others (the majority classes).

The main goal of SMOTE is to balance the class distribution by generating synthetic samples for the minority class. In this study, SMOTE was applied to address the imbalance between positive and negative cases of Acute Aortic Syndrome (AAS). With only 129 positive cases among 148,578 negative cases, the dataset faced an imbalance challenge. By generating synthetic samples of the minority class, SMOTE ensured that the predictive model is not biased toward the majority class. This improved the model's ability to accurately identify both positive and negative cases of AAS, thereby enhancing its predictive performance.

4.4.2. Application of SMOTE

In this study, as shown in Figure 6, the dataset initially exhibited a significant class imbalance, with only 129 positive AAS cases compared to 148,578 negative cases. This imbalance posed a challenge for model training, as it could lead to biased predictions favoring the majority class. In the graph, the minority class is depicted as a small cluster of orange data points, while the majority class appears as a dense cluster of blue points.

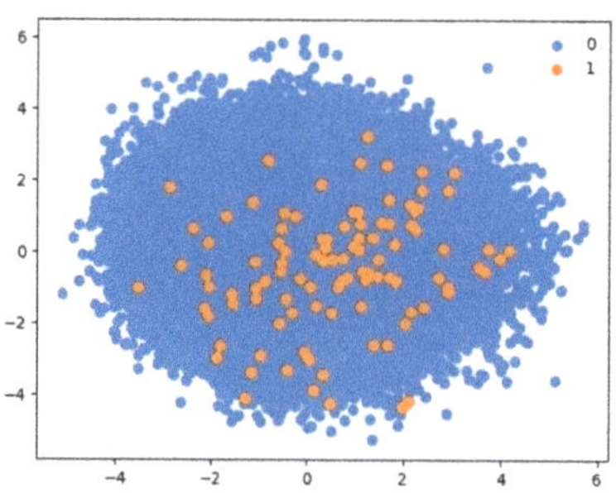

Figure 6. Dataset before applying SMOTE.

To address this, we applied the Synthetic Minority Oversampling Technique (SMOTE) using k = 5 nearest neighbors with the imbalanced-learn Python library. SMOTE generates synthetic samples for the minority class, helping to balance the class distribution. As illustrated in Figure 7, the minority class becomes better represented after SMOTE is applied, reducing bias in the model and improving overall prediction performance. This balanced dataset contributes to the model's ability to more accurately identify AAS cases and generalize effectively.

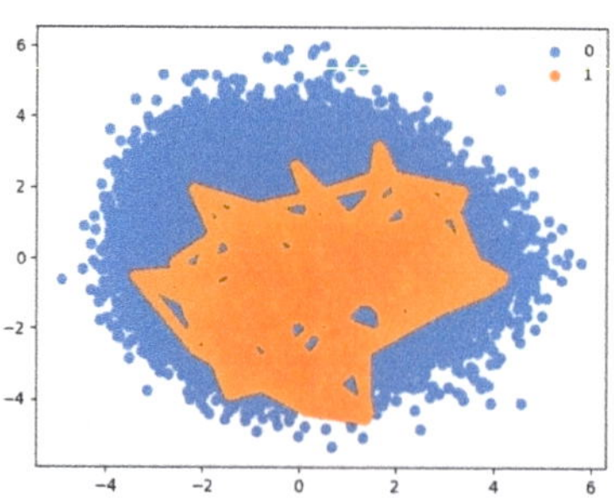

Figure 7. Dataset after applying SMOTE.

4.5. Data Loading and Exploration

The process of loading and exploring clinical datasets in Python involves utilizing key libraries such as Pandas, NumPy, Scikit-learn, and Stats models. These libraries enable efficient data manipulation, numerical operations, visualization, machine learning tasks, and statistical modeling. By leveraging demographic information, researchers can gain insights into the distribution of the population across different age groups and genders, forming the basis for exploring patterns and trends within the dataset. This analysis facilitates a comprehensive understanding of the dataset's diversity and composition, ultimately contributing to valuable insights for medical research and healthcare decision-making. After cleaning and preprocessing the data, and based on medical knowledge and a review of the relevant literature, 26 of the most relevant variables were selected from the initial 139, as shown in Table 8. These selected variables are illustrated in Table 3 below and serve as inputs for the classifiers and machine learning methods used in this study.

Table 8. Input variables.

	Variables	Unit
1	AAS	
2	AGE	year
3	GENDER	M and F
4	D-DIMER	ng/mL
5	HBA1C	Percentage
6	HEMOGLOBIN	g/dL
7	ABSOLUTE_LYMPHOCYTE_COUNT	K/μL
8	LYMPHOCYTE_PERCENTAGE	Percentage
9	NEUTROPHIL_ABSOULTE	
10	PLATELET_COUNT	K/μL
11	HIGH_SENSITIVITY_TROPONIN T_2HOUR	ng/L
12	TROPONIN I	ng/L
13	TROPONIN T	ng/L
14	TROPONIN T_INTERPRETATION	
15	DIASTOLIC BP	mmHg
16	SYESTOLIC BP	mmHg
17	GLASGOW_COME_SCORE	
18	HEART_RATE_MONITORED	bpm
19	HEIGHT	cm
20	PAIN SCORE	
21	PULSE OX	Percentage
22	PULSE RATE	bpm
23	RESPIRATORY RATE	bar/min
24	TEMPRETURE C	Centigrade
25	WEIGHT_KILOGRAM	kilogram
26	BODY_MASS_INDEX	kg/m^2

The selected features reflect a comprehensive combination of demographic, physiological, and biochemical indicators that are clinically relevant to the early identification and prediction of Acute Aortic Syndrome (AAS). Here is a brief overview of their significance:

- Age (years): Age is a major risk factor for AAS, as vascular elasticity decreases and aortic wall fragility increases with age.
- Gender (M and F): AAS tends to be more common in males, but outcomes may vary by gender, making it a relevant predictive variable.
- D-dimer (ng/mL): Elevated D-dimer levels indicate active clot formation and breakdown, often present in AAS due to aortic wall disruption.
- HBA1C (%): Reflects long-term glucose control; poorly managed diabetes is associated with vascular damage, which may contribute to aortic pathology.
- Hemoglobin (g/dL): Low levels can indicate bleeding or anemia, while high levels may be associated with increased blood viscosity and cardiovascular strain.
- Absolute lymphocyte count/lymphocyte percentage: These can reflect immune response or systemic inflammation, which may be indirectly linked to vascular injury.
- Neutrophil absolute: High neutrophil counts often reflect inflammation or acute stress response, commonly seen in serious cardiovascular events.
- Platelet count (K/µL): Platelets play a role in clotting, and abnormal levels could signal systemic inflammation or coagulopathy relevant to AAS.
- Troponins (ng/L): Elevated levels, especially high-sensitivity troponin, indicate myocardial injury, which may occur with or mimic AAS.
- Blood pressure (mmHg): Both systolic and diastolic pressures are critical, as hypertension is a key risk factor and exacerbating condition in AAS.
- Glasgow Coma Score: While less directly related, altered consciousness could indicate severe hemodynamic compromise.
- Heart rate, pulse rate (bpm), respiratory rate (bar/min), and temperature (°C): Vital signs reflect the patient's immediate physiological state, with abnormal values often seen in AAS due to pain, shock, or cardiovascular strain.
- Height, weight, and body mass index (BMI): Obesity and body composition affect cardiovascular health and aortic structure.
- Pain score: Chest or back pain is a hallmark symptom of AAS, often described as sudden and severe.
- Pulse Ox (oxygen saturation%): May decrease in cases where AAS compromises circulation or causes secondary cardiac issues.

These features were chosen not only for their statistical contribution but also for their pathophysiological relevance to AAS. The combination of these indicators provides a comprehensive profile that supports robust model performance and clinical applicability.

5. Method

As depicted in Figure 2 within the project roadmap, the initial step involves addressing missing data. Following this, the interquartile range (IQR) method is employed to assess data spread and identify outliers, refining the dataset for subsequent analysis. Subsequently, the focus shifts to feature extraction, aiming to simplify and transform the dataset by selecting essential variables. Various feature extraction methods, such as PCA, Relief feature selection, and CFS, are utilized to manage data complexity and streamline information, ultimately facilitating more efficient analysis and interpretation.

5.1. Feature Extraction

To handle the complexity and high dimensionality of our clinical dataset—which includes demographic information, vital signs, lab results, and cardiovascular-related procedures—we applied three complementary feature extraction techniques: Principal Component Analysis (PCA), Relief with SelectKBest, and Correlation-Based Feature Selection (CFS).

- PCA helped reduce dimensionality by transforming correlated features into a smaller set of uncorrelated components. This was particularly helpful for compressing lab and vital-sign data without significant loss of information, improving model efficiency and reducing overfitting.
- Relief with SelectKBest was used to identify and retain features most relevant for distinguishing between AAS and non-AAS cases. It works well for clinical data by emphasizing variables that strongly separate the target classes, such as key biomarkers and physiological indicators.
- CFS was applied to select a subset of features that are highly correlated with the target variable (AAS) while minimizing redundancy between features. This ensures that the model benefits from meaningful inputs without duplicating information.

By combining these methods, we aimed to extract the most informative and non-redundant features, allowing our models to focus on the variables that matter most. This process not only streamlined the dataset for training and evaluation but also supported a deeper understanding of the clinical variables that play a significant role in predicting Acute Aortic Syndrome.

5.2. Classifiers

In this study, as illustrated in Figure 2, a variety of classification algorithms were employed to address the diagnostic challenges associated with AAS. These classifiers include random forest (RF), logistic regression (LR), Gradient Boosting Classifier (G-Boost), Extreme Gradient Boosting (XGB), K-Nearest Neighbors (KNNs), decision trees, Gaussian Naive Bayes (Gaussian-NB), and AdaBoost. Each algorithm offers unique capabilities in handling the complexity of clinical data and extracting valuable insights for accurate AAS diagnosis. The application of these classifiers aims to establish a comprehensive framework for categorizing patients and assisting clinicians in making informed decisions regarding AAS diagnosis and management.

One widely employed technique is random forest (RF), recognized for its ensemble learning approach, which constructs multiple decision trees on random subsets of features and data points. By mitigating overfitting and enhancing generalization, random forest offers robustness and insightful feature importance analysis.

Logistic regression (LR) stands out as a straightforward, yet powerful algorithm suited for binary classification tasks. It estimates probabilities based on predictor variables, providing interpretability and effectiveness.

Gradient Boosting Classifier (G-Boost) sequentially combines weak learners, refining predictions through gradient descent optimization. Its iterative approach allows it to capture intricate data patterns, making it valuable for tasks like diagnosing AAS. Similarly, Extreme Gradient Boosting (XGB) merges decision trees with regularization techniques, offering high performance and interpretability, especially in handling numerical clinical features for AAS diagnosis.

K-Nearest Neighbor (KNN) classifies instances based on the majority class of their nearest neighbors, proving valuable for assessing complex clinical manifestations and determining the likelihood of AAS based on similar cases. Decision trees provide hierarchical decision-making, capturing non-linear relationships within data, essential for understanding AAS diagnostic logic and interpreting predictive factors.

Gaussian Naive Bayes leverages Bayes' theorem and assumes feature independence, making it efficient for handling numerical clinical variables and aiding in probabilistic classification for AAS diagnosis.

Lastly, AdaBoost sequentially trains weak learners, emphasizing challenging instances to improve accuracy iteratively, contributing to more accurate classification outcomes in AAS diagnosis. Overall, these classification methods offer diverse approaches to handling AAS diagnostic challenges, providing valuable insights and accurate predictions based on clinical data.

In addition, we selected widely used machine learning algorithms, such as random forest, XGBoost, Gradient Boosting, and logistic regression, based on their strong performance in similar medical prediction tasks. To improve model performance, we used grid search with 10-fold cross-validation for hyperparameter tuning. For example, in random forest, we tested different numbers of trees (from 50 to 500) and tree depths (5 to 20). For XGBoost, we adjusted learning rates (0.01 to 0.2) and tree depths (3 to 10). These tuning steps helped us find the best model settings for our dataset.

We have conducted a basic statistical analysis to compare the performance of the different classification models used in our study. We calculated the mean accuracy and 95% confidence intervals (CI) for each classifier using 10-fold cross validation.

Here are the results of our statistical comparison:

- Random forest (RF): Mean accuracy = 99.2%, CI = [99.1%, 99.3%].
- Decision trees (DT): Mean accuracy = 98.9%, CI = [98.7%, 99.1%].
- K-Nearest Neighbors (KNN): Mean accuracy = 98.2%, CI = [98.1%, 98.4%].
- Extreme Gradient Boosting (XGB): Mean accuracy = 93.9%, CI = [88.7%, 99.0%]
- Gradient Boosting (G-Boost): Mean accuracy = 91.5%, CI = [85.7%, 97.2%]
- AdaBoost: Mean accuracy = 83.4%, CI = [78.9%, 87.8%].
- Logistic regression (LR): Mean accuracy = 71.6%, CI = [70.6%, 72.6%]
- Gaussian Naive Bayes (Gaussian-NB): Mean accuracy = 70.8%, CI = [69.4%, 72.2%]

The results indicate that random forest, decision trees, and K-Nearest Neighbors achieved the highest performance, with random forest slightly outperforming the others. In contrast, logistic regression and Gaussian Naive Bayes had the lowest accuracy, with relatively narrow confidence intervals, suggesting more consistent but lower predictive power.

5.3. Evaluation Metrics

In this study, the performance of classification models for diagnosing AAS is evaluated using a set of metrics. The evaluation metrics employed include accuracy, specificity, sensitivity (recall), Area Under the Curve (AUC), precision, and the F1-score. These metrics provide comprehensive insights into the performance of the classification models, allowing for a thorough assessment of their effectiveness in accurately identifying AAS cases.

Accuracy measures overall model performance, specificity assesses the model's ability to correctly identify true negatives, and sensitivity evaluates the model's capability to capture true positives. The AUC reflects the model's discriminative ability across various thresholds, while precision quantifies the accuracy of positive predictions. The F1-score provides a balanced measure of precision and recall. These metrics collectively provide insights into the reliability and effectiveness of classification models in diagnosing AAS, aiding clinicians in decision-making.

6. Results

In this study, following the roadmap outlined in Figure 2, the dataset underwent partitioning into three sets: a training set and a combined validation and test set. Two splitting formats were applied: an 80-10-10 split and a 70-20-10 split. These splits allocate proportions of the dataset for training, validation, and testing purposes, facilitating robust model development and evaluation. In the 80-10-10 split, 80% of the data constituted the training set, while the remaining 20% were further divided into 10% for validation and 10% for testing. Similarly, in the 70-20-10 split, 70% of the data were allocated to the training set, and the remaining 20% were split into 10% for validation and 10% for testing.

Additionally, Stratified K-Fold Cross-Validation was employed in this study, specifically utilizing a 10-fold Stratified Cross-Validation approach. This methodology involved partitioning the dataset into ten distinct subsets or "folds". The model underwent training ten times, with each iteration using nine folds for training and reserving the remaining fold for testing. Stratification ensured that each fold accurately represented the complete dataset, maintaining consistent proportions of class labels. This approach provided a reliable assessment of the model's generalization ability while preserving a balanced distribution of classes across each fold.

In the dataset, there were 129 positive cases of AAS and 148,578 non-AAS cases. After handling missing and imbalanced data, and applying machine learning methods, the Relief feature method combined with random forest on an 80:10:10 splitting strategy consistently outperformed other combinations, demonstrating superior accuracy, sensitivity, and specificity (99.3%, 99.5%, and 99.3%, respectively). The identified top ten important features through Relief feature extraction, including age, troponin levels, and temperature, offer crucial insights into AAS prediction, enhancing diagnostic accuracy and improving patient outcomes in emergency departments.

The following top results in Table 9 were observed in analyzing various classifiers and feature selection methods, considering accuracy, sensitivity, and specificity as key criteria. The table below presents the best results among all the methods applied.

Table 9. Models results.

Splitting Strategy	Feature Selection	Class	Precision	F1-Score	Accuracy	Sensitivity	Specificity	AUC
10-fold cross-val.	PCA	RF	0.984	**0.991**	**0.991**	**1**	0.982	**1**
SR 70:20:10	PCA	RF	0.987	0.99	0.99	0.993	0.987	**1**
SR 80:10:10	PCA	RF	**0.987**	0.99	0.99	0.993	**0.987**	**1**
10-fold cross-val.	CFS	RF	0.986	**0.993**	0.987	0.997	0.986	0.997
10-fold cross-val.	CFS	DT	0.982	0.99	0.987	**0.998**	0.982	0.997
SR 70:20:10	CFS	RF	0.992	0.992	**0.989**	**0.998**	**0.992**	**1**
SR 80:10:10	CFS	RF	**0.993**	0.99	0.987	0.978	0.984	**1**
10-fold cross-val.	Relief F	XGB	0.984	0.991	0.991	**0.995**	0.983	**1**
10-fold cross-val.	Relief F	RF	0.986	**0.992**	0.992	0.991	0.986	**1**
SR 70:20:10	Relief F	RF	0.987	**0.992**	0.992	0.993	0.992	**1**
SR 80:10:10	Relief F	RF	**0.991**	0.986	**0.993**	**0.995**	**0.993**	**1**

Based on the analysis, both the CFS and Relief feature methods demonstrate slightly better performance compared to PCA, as indicated by their highest values for accuracy, sensitivity, and specificity across various classifiers and scenarios. However, the Relief feature method combined with random forest on the SR 80:10:10 splitting strategy emerges as the most consistently high-performing combination, with an accuracy of 0.993, sensitivity of 0.995, specificity of 0.993, and AUC of 1.000.

6.1. Feature Importance Analysis with Relief Feature Selection

In Table 10 and Figure 8, the values correspond to the feature importance obtained using the Relief feature selection method. Each feature is represented, along with its importance value. The importance values range from highest to lowest, with age having the highest importance value of 0.1516 and gender having the lowest importance value of 0.0033. The bar graph provides a visual representation of these importance values, with the color gradient ranging from black for the most significant feature to yellow for the least significant feature, aiding in the interpretation of feature importance.

Table 10. Top 10 important features of the Relief method.

Features Name	Importance Value
Age	0.1516
Troponin	0.1471
Temperature	0.1285
Weight—kilogram	0.124
Height—cm	0.1115
Respiratory rate	0.1092
Body mass index	0.085
Pulse Ox	0.0722
Pain score	0.0676
Gender	0.0033

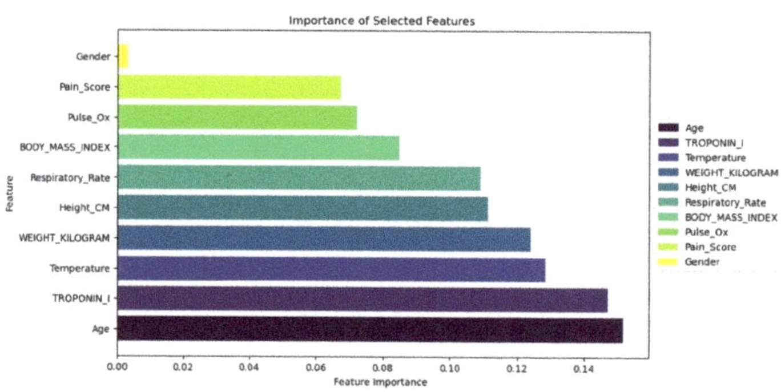

Figure 8. Top 10 important features with Relief method.

The top ten important features identified through the Relief feature extraction method, as depicted in Figure 8, offer valuable insights into potential risk factors and indicators associated with AAS. These features include age, troponin levels, temperature, weight, height, respiratory rate, BMI, pulse oximetry readings, pain score assessments, and gender. Leveraging these key features in predictive models enhances the diagnosis and prognosis processes in emergency departments, ultimately improving patient outcomes and resource allocation strategies. By incorporating these significant features into predictive models, healthcare professionals can make more informed decisions, leading to better patient care and management of AAS cases.

6.2. Discussion

In comparison to the prior literature on the prediction of Acute Aortic Syndromes (AAS) using machine learning and Deep leaning techniques, our study presents notable advancements in methodology, data handling, and scale. Duceau et al. [13] employed logistic regression and the Super Learner (SL) ensemble method, with SL achieving an AUC of 0.73 using 5-fold cross-validation on a dataset comprising 976 patients, including 609 positive cases.

Huo et al. [14] implemented Correlation-Based Feature Selection (CFS) and identified the Bayesian Network as the most effective model, achieving an AUC of 0.857 with a sample size of 492. Similarly, Wu et al. [15] explored the predictive value of D-dimer and radiographic features using both multivariate logistic regression and random forest models. Their study, conducted on 558 patients with 93 positive cases, reported an AUC of 0.994 for the random forest model in predicting in-hospital rupture of type A aortic dissection.

Guo et al. [16] demonstrated the predictive capability of the XGBoost algorithm in assessing in-hospital mortality risk among AAS patients, achieving an AUC of 0.927. They further validated XGBoost's performance using 10-fold cross-validation on a dataset of 1344 patients, where it outperformed other models in terms of accuracy and robustness.

Lin et al. [18] applied a Convolutional Neural Network (CNN) to predict rupture risk in acute type A aortic dissection, achieving an AUC of 0.99. However, the model was trained and validated on a relatively small dataset of 200 patients, which may limit its generalizability.

In contrast, our study integrates a broad range of preprocessing techniques, including multiple imputation (MICE) for handling missing data; Synthetic Minority Oversampling Technique (SMOTE) for class imbalance; and various feature selection methods, such as Relief. Multiple machine learning classifiers were evaluated, and the optimal combination—Relief feature selection with random forest—achieved superior performance with an AUC of 1.0 and accuracy of 99.3%. This comprehensive pipeline allowed us to effectively model a real-world, high-dimensional, and imbalanced clinical dataset.

Moreover, the scale of our dataset represents a significant contribution to the field. While the largest sample size identified in the previous literature was 5548 patients in the study by McLatchie [21], our integrated dataset comprises 148,707 patient records collected from 68 emergency departments. Of these, 148,578 patients were non-AAS cases, while 129 were confirmed AAS cases. This extensive dataset not only enhances the statistical power of our analysis but also provides a valuable foundation for future research in AAS prediction and broader cardiovascular risk modeling.

The scale of this research dataset represents a substantial contribution to the field of AAS prediction. As shown in Figure 9, which compares sample sizes across related studies, the largest previously reported dataset included 5548 patients in the study by McLatchie [21]. In contrast, our integrated dataset comprises 148,707 patient records collected from 68 emergency departments, including 129 confirmed AAS cases and 148,578 non-AAS cases. This significant increase in sample size not only strengthens the statistical power of our findings but also enhances the generalizability and clinical relevance of our machine learning models. Moreover, this extensive dataset provides a valuable resource for future research on AAS detection and broader cardiovascular risk prediction.

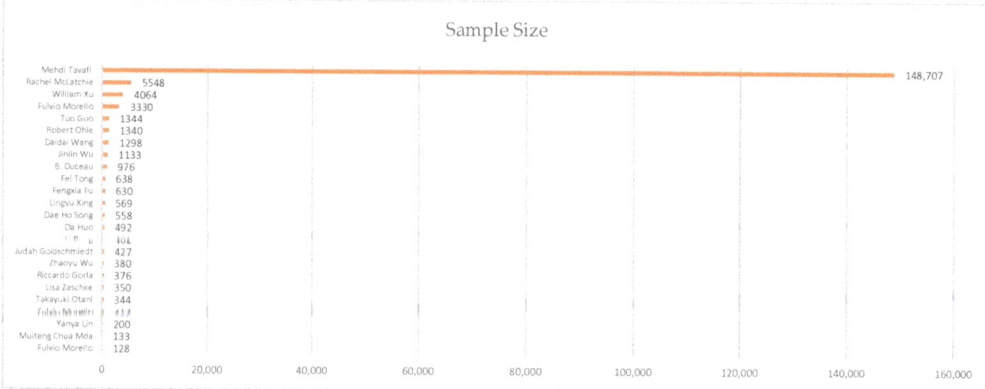

Figure 9. Sample size comparison.

7. Conclusions

One of the main aims of this research was to gather and clean a large clinical dataset focused on cardiovascular health, with the intention of making it useful for studies like ours. During the data preparation phase, we encountered missing values, which we handled using the Multiple Imputation by Chained Equations (MICE) method. Due to class distribution imbalance in the dataset, the SMOTE technique was used to address underrepresented classes.

Different forms of selection of three features were employed using Principal Component Analysis (PCA), Correlational-Based feature selection (CFS), and Relief feature, with each one providing its own advantages. Therefore, an evaluation was conducted on each selected method based on the outcome, using different approaches to determine the optimal one.

The selected features were tested against eight classification algorithms, which include Gradient Boosting, Extreme Gradient Boosting (XGB), random forest, logistic regression, K-Nearest Neighbors, decision tree, Gaussian Naive Bayes, and AdaBoost. The models were evaluated based on accuracy, AUC, precision, F1-score, sensitivity, and specificity, which reflect the model performance.

One particularly relevant study is that by B. Duceau et al. [13], who focused on prehospital triage of AAS using machine learning. Their approach employed 5-fold cross-validation and a Super Learner model, achieving a ROC of 0.87 and sensitivity of 0.99 using a dataset of 976 hospital admissions, of which 609 were confirmed AAS cases.

In this study, we used a data-splitting strategy that allocated 80% for training, 10% for testing, and 10% for validation. By combining this with the Relief F feature selection method and a random forest classifier, we achieved impressive results: 99.3% accuracy, 0.995 sensitivity, and 0.993 specificity, among others. This setup outperformed all the other models we tested and showed a remarkable predictive ability compared to previous research. The differences in performance across various feature selection methods really underscore how crucial it is to choose the right mix of feature selection and classification techniques that fit the dataset and the predictive task at hand. For context, one of the other standout results in the existing literature comes from Y. Lin et al. [18], who reported an accuracy of 90%, with sensitivity and specificity values of 0.93 and 0.90, respectively, using a Convolutional Neural Network (CNN). Their research pinpointed age, sex, certain biomarkers, and the aorta's morphological parameters as key independent predictors for rupture in Acute Type A Aortic Dissection (ATAAD). In our analysis, we evaluated 25 features and identified the most significant predictors through a thorough feature ranking process. The top-ranked variables included age, troponin levels, temperature, weight, height, and respiratory rate. Interestingly, gender also played a notable role, coming in tenth in terms of importance. These results highlight the clinical significance of regularly collected vital signs and biochemical markers in aiding the early detection of AAS in emergency-department scenarios.

In short, regarding sample size, this study compiled an impressive clinical dataset featuring 148,707 patient records related to various cardiovascular diseases. It showcased the potential of machine learning as a game-changer for early AAS prediction in the emergency department. However, there is still a need for more research to refine these techniques and validate the findings using different classifiers or methods. By offering such a large dataset, this study sets the stage for future exploration in this area, aiming to develop effective tools for the early detection and management of AAS.

8. Future Work

For future work, the methodologies and findings of this study could be extended to leverage this integrated dataset for the prediction of other cardiovascular diseases and diverse datasets. The techniques employed in this research, specifically in the realms of data preprocessing, feature extraction, and machine learning model application, offer opportunities for further refinement and optimization.

Additionally, the potential for handling imbalanced data could be explored using the ADASYN (Adaptive Synthetic Sampling) technique as an alternative to SMOTE, aiming to address dataset imbalances more effectively.

Moreover, future research endeavors could explore the incorporation of advanced machine learning models, such as deep learning, to obtain more comprehensive results and potentially enhance predictive capabilities. This expansion into cutting-edge methodologies could contribute to a deeper understanding of the dataset and improve the overall effectiveness of predictive models.

Author Contributions: Conceptualization, M.T. and K.P.; methodology, M.T. and K.P.; software, M.T.; validation, M.T. and K.P.; formal analysis, M.T.; investigation, M.T.; resources, M.T. and R.O.; data curation, M.T. and R.O.; writing—original draft preparation, M.T. and K.P.; writing—review and editing, M.T.; visualization, M.T.; supervision, K.P. and R.O.; project administration, M.T.; All authors have read and agreed to the published version of the manuscript.

Funding: This research received no external funding.

Data Availability Statement: Data is available on request.

Conflicts of Interest: The authors declare no conflict of interest.

References

1. Nienaber, C.A.; Powell, J.T. Management of acute aortic syndromes. *Eur. Heart J.* **2012**, *33*, 26–35. [CrossRef] [PubMed]
2. Vilacosta, I.; Román, J.A.S.; di Bartolomeo, R.; Eagle, K.; Estrera, A.L.; Ferrera, C.; Kaji, S.; Nienaber, C.A.; Riambau, V.; Schäfers, H.-J.; et al. Acute Aortic Syndrome Revisited. *J. Am. Coll. Cardiol.* **2021**, *78*, 2106–2125. [CrossRef] [PubMed]
3. Isselbacher, E.M.; Preventza, O.; Iii, J.H.B.; Augoustides, J.G.; Beck, A.W.; Bolen, M.A.; Braverman, A.C.; Bray, B.E.; Brown-Zimmerman, M.M.; Chen, E.P.; et al. 2022 ACC/AHA Guideline for the Diagnosis and Management of Aortic Disease. *J. Am. Coll. Cardiol.* **2022**, *80*, e223–e393. [CrossRef] [PubMed]
4. Allen, B.D.; Bergmann, L.L. Current Concepts in Acute Aortic Syndrome. *Adv. Clin. Radiol.* **2021**, *3*, 139–151. [CrossRef]
5. Mussa, F.F.; Horton, J.D.; Moridzadeh, R.; Nicholson, J.; Trimarchi, S.; Eagle, K.A. Acute Aortic Dissection and Intramural Hematoma: A Systematic Review. *JAMA* **2016**, *316*, 754–763. [CrossRef]
6. Clouse, W.D.; Hallett, J.W.; Schaff, H.V.; Spittell, P.C.; Rowland, C.M.; Ilstrup, D.M.; Melton, L.J. Acute Aortic Dissection: Population-Based Incidence Compared with Degenerative Aortic Aneurysm Rupture. *Mayo Clin. Proc.* **2004**, *79*, 176–180. [CrossRef]

7. Morello, F.; Santoro, M.; Fargion, A.T.; Grifoni, S.; Nazerian, P. Diagnosis and management of acute aortic syndromes in the emergency department. *Intern. Emerg. Med.* **2021**, *16*, 171–181. [CrossRef]
8. Ohle, R.; Savage, D.W.; McIsaac, S.; Yadav, K.; Caswell, J.; Conlon, M. Epidemiology, mortality and miss rate of acute aortic syndrome in Ontario, Canada: A population-based study. *Can. J. Emerg. Med.* **2023**, *25*, 57–64. [CrossRef]
9. Subhan, S.; Malik, J.; Haq, A.U.; Qadeer, M.S.; Zaidi, S.M.J.; Orooj, F.; Zaman, H.; Mehmoodi, A.; Majeedi, U. Role of Artificial Intelligence and Machine Learning in Interventional Cardiology. *Curr. Probl. Cardiol.* **2023**, *48*, 101698. [CrossRef]
10. El Naqa, I.; Murphy, M.J. What Is Machine Learning? In *Machine Learning in Radiation Oncology*; El Naqa, I., Li, R., Murphy, M.J., Eds.; Springer International Publishing: Cham, Switzerland, 2015; pp. 3–11. [CrossRef]
11. Ma, Z.; Jin, L.; Zhang, L.; Yang, Y.; Tang, Y.; Gao, P.; Sun, Y.; Li, M. Diagnosis of Acute Aortic Syndromes on Non-Contrast CT Images with Radiomics-Based Machine Learning. *Biology* **2023**, *12*, 337. [CrossRef]
12. Grist, T.; Rubin, G.D. Acute Aortic Syndrome: State-of-the-Art Diagnostic Imaging. In *Diseases of the Chest and Heart 2015–2018*; Hodler, J., Von Schulthess, G.K., Kubik-Huch, R.A., Zollikofer, C.L., Eds.; Springer: Milan, Italy, 2015; pp. 149–156. [CrossRef]
13. Duceau, B.; Alsac, J.; Bellenfant, F.; Mailloux, A.; Champigneulle, B.; Favé, G.; Neuschwander, A.; El Batti, S.; Cholley, B.; Achouh, P.; et al. Prehospital triage of acute aortic syndrome using a machine learning algorithm. *Br. J. Surg.* **2020**, *107*, 995–1003. [CrossRef] [PubMed]
14. Huo, D.; Kou, B.; Zhou, Z.; Lv, M. A machine learning model to classify aortic dissection patients in the early diagnosis phase. *Sci. Rep.* **2019**, *9*, 2701. [CrossRef] [PubMed]
15. Wu, J.; Qiu, J.; Xie, E.; Jiang, W.; Zhao, R.; Qiu, J.; Zafar, M.A.; Huang, Y.; Yu, C. Predicting in-hospital rupture of type A aortic dissection using random forest. *J. Thorac. Dis.* **2019**, *11*, 4634–4646. [CrossRef] [PubMed]
16. Guo, T.; Fang, Z.; Yang, G.; Zhou, Y.; Ding, N.; Peng, W.; Gong, X.; He, H.; Pan, X.; Chai, X. Machine Learning Models for Predicting In-Hospital Mortality in Acute Aortic Dissection Patients. *Front. Cardiovasc. Med.* **2021**, *8*, 727773. [CrossRef]
17. Wu, Z.; Li, Y.; Xu, Z.; Liu, H.; Liu, K.; Qiu, P.; Chen, T.; Lu, X. Prediction of preoperative in-hospital mortality rate in patients with acute aortic dissection by machine learning: A two-centre, retrospective cohort study. *BMJ Open* **2023**, *13*, e066782. [CrossRef]
18. Lin, Y.; Hu, J.; Xu, R.; Wu, S.; Ma, F.; Liu, H.; Xie, Y.; Li, X. Application of Logistic Regression and Artificial Intelligence in the Risk Prediction of Acute Aortic Dissection Rupture. *J. Clin. Med.* **2022**, *12*, 179. [CrossRef]
19. Tong, F.; Wang, Y.; Sun, Z. Development and validation of nomogram models to discriminate between acute aortic syndromes and non-ST-elevation myocardial infarction during troponin-blind period. *Front. Cardiovasc. Med.* **2023**, *10*, 1077712. [CrossRef]
20. Morello, F.; Santoro, M.; Giachino, F.; Caciolli, F.; Capretti, E.; Castelli, M.; Pivetta, E.; Nazerian, P.; Lupia, E. Pre-Test Probability Assessment and D-Dimer Based Evaluation in Patients with Previous Acute Aortic Syndrome. *Medicina* **2023**, *59*, 548. [CrossRef]
21. McLatchie, R.; Reed, M.J.; Freeman, N.; Parker, R.A.; Wilson, S.; Goodacre, S.; Cowan, A.; Boyle, J.; Clarke, B.; Clarke, E. Diagnosis of Acute Aortic Syndrome in the Emergency Department (DAShED) study: An observational cohort study of people attending the emergency department with symptoms consistent with acute aortic syndrome. *Emerg. Med. J.* **2023**, *41*, 136–144. [CrossRef]
22. Wang, D.; Zhang, H.; Du, L.; Zhai, Q.; Hu, G.; Gao, W.; Zhang, A.; Wang, S.; Hao, Y.; Shang, K.; et al. Early Prediction Model of Acute Aortic Syndrome Mortality in Emergency Departments. *Int. J. Gen. Med.* **2022**, *15*, 3779–3788. [CrossRef]
23. Ohle, R.; McIsaac, S.; Van Drusen, M.; Regis, A.; Montpellier, O.; Ludgate, M.; Bodunde, O.; Savage, D.W.; Yadav, K. Evaluation of the Canadian Clinical Practice Guidelines Risk Prediction Tool for Acute Aortic Syndrome: The RIPP Score. *Emerg. Med. Int.* **2023**, *2023*, 1–7. [CrossRef] [PubMed]
24. Gorla, R.; Erbel, R.; Kahlert, P.; Tsagakis, K.; Jakob, H.; Mahabadi, A.-A.; Schlosser, T.; Eggebrecht, H.; Bossone, E.; Jánosi, R.A. Accuracy of a diagnostic strategy combining aortic dissection detection risk score and D-dimer levels in patients with suspected acute aortic syndrome. *Eur. Heart J. Acute Cardiovasc. Care* **2017**, *6*, 371–378. [CrossRef] [PubMed]
25. Deng, L.; Xia, Q.; Diao, L.; Lin, F.; Cao, Y.; Han, H.; Song, M. Aortic Dissection Detection Risk Score and D-Dimer for Acute Aortic Syndromes in the Chinese Population: Exploration of Optimal Thresholds and Integrated Diagnostic Value. *J. Cardiovasc. Transl. Res.* **2023**, *16*, 886–895. [CrossRef] [PubMed]
26. Morello, F.; Oddi, M.; Cavalot, G.; Ianniello, A.; Giachino, F.; Nazerian, P.; Battista, S.; Magnino, C.; Tizzani, M.; Settanni, F.; et al. Prospective diagnostic and prognostic study of copeptin in suspected acute aortic syndromes. *Sci. Rep.* **2018**, *8*, 16713. [CrossRef]
27. Song, D.H.; Choi, J.H.; Lee, J.Y. Predicting acute aortic syndrome using aortic dissection detection risk score, D-dimer, and X-ray. *Heliyon* **2023**, *9*, e20578. [CrossRef]
28. Fu, F.; Wang, X.; Shi, M.; Li, Y.; Xiao, Z.; Xu, X.; Jing, L.; Meng, F. Acute aortic syndrome risk stratification score: A new risk assessment tool. *Preprint* **2023**. [CrossRef]
29. Morello, F.; Bima, P.; Pivetta, E.; Santoro, M.; Catini, E.; Casanova, B.; Leidel, B.A.; Soeiro, A.d.M.; Nestelberger, T.; Mueller, C.; et al. Development and Validation of a Simplified Probability Assessment Score Integrated with Age-Adjusted d-Dimer for Diagnosis of Acute Aortic Syndromes. *J. Am. Heart Assoc.* **2021**, *10*, e018425. [CrossRef]
30. Xing, L.; Zhou, Y.; Han, Y.; Chen, C.; Dong, Z.; Zheng, X.; Chen, D.; Yu, Y.; Liao, F.; Guo, S.; et al. Simple Death Risk Models to Predict In-hospital Outcomes in Acute Aortic Dissection in Emergency Department. *Front. Med.* **2022**, *9*, 890567. [CrossRef]
31. Little, R.; Rubin, D. *Statistical Analysis with Missing Data*, 2nd ed.; Wiley: Hoboken, NJ, USA, 2014.

32. Rubin, D.B. Inference and missing data. *Biometrika* **1976**, *63*, 581–592. [CrossRef]
33. Gibson, S.J.; Narendra, A.; Dainotti, M.G.; Bogdan, M.; Pollo, A.; Poliszczuk, A.; Rinaldi, E.; Liodakis, I. Using Multivariate Imputation by Chained Equations to Predict Redshifts of Active Galactic Nuclei. *Front. Astron. Space Sci.* **2022**, *9*, 836215. [CrossRef]
34. Steyerberg, E.W. Clinical Prediction Models. In *Statistics for Biology and Health*; Springer: New York, NY, USA, 2009. [CrossRef]
35. Carpenter, J.R.; Kenward, M.G. *Multiple Imputation and Its Application*, 1st ed.; Wiley: Hoboken, NJ, USA, 2013. [CrossRef]
36. Van Buuren, S. *Flexible Imputation of Missing Data*; Chapman & Hall/CRC: Boca Raton, FL, USA, 2012.

algorithms

MDPI

Article

Prompt Once, Segment Everything: Leveraging SAM 2 Potential for Infinite Medical Image Segmentation with a Single Prompt

Juan D. Gutiérrez [1,*], Emilio Delgado [2], Carlos Breuer [2], José M. Conejero [2] and Roberto Rodriguez-Echeverria [2]

[1] Department of Electronics and Computer Science, Universidad de Santiago de Compostela, Rúa Benigno Ledo, 27002 Lugo, Spain
[2] Instituto de Investigación en Tecnologías Informáticas Aplicadas (INTIA), Universidad de Extremadura, Av. Universidad s/n, 10003 Cáceres, Spain; edm@unex.es (E.D.); cbc@unex.es (C.B.); chemacm@unex.es (J.M.C.); rre@unex.es (R.R.-E.)
* Correspondence: juandiego.gutierrez@usc.es

Abstract: Semantic segmentation of medical images holds significant potential for enhancing diagnostic and surgical procedures. Radiology specialists can benefit from automated segmentation tools that facilitate identifying and isolating regions of interest in medical scans. Nevertheless, to obtain precise results, sophisticated deep learning models tailored to this specific task must be developed and trained, a capability not universally accessible. Segment Anything Model (SAM) 2 is a foundational model designed for image and video segmentation tasks, built on its predecessor, SAM. This paper introduces a novel approach leveraging SAM 2's video segmentation capabilities to reduce the prompts required to segment an entire volume of medical images. The study first compares SAM and SAM 2's performance in medical image segmentation. Evaluation metrics such as the Jaccard index and Dice score are used to measure precision and segmentation quality. Then, our novel approach is introduced. Statistical tests include comparing precision gains and computational efficiency, focusing on the trade-off between resource use and segmentation time. The results show that SAM 2 achieves an average improvement of 1.76% in the Jaccard index and 1.49% in the Dice score compared to SAM, albeit with a ten-fold increase in segmentation time. Our novel approach to segmentation reduces the number of prompts needed to segment a volume of medical images by 99.95%. We demonstrate that it is possible to segment all the slices of a volume and, even more, of a whole dataset, with a single prompt, achieving results comparable to those obtained by state-of-the-art models explicitly trained for this task. Our approach simplifies the segmentation process, allowing specialists to devote more time to other tasks. The hardware and personnel requirements to obtain these results are much lower than those needed to train a deep learning model from scratch or to modify the behavior of an existing one using model modification techniques.

Keywords: image segmentation; deep learning; zero-shot learning; medical imaging; foundation models

1. Introduction

Image segmentation is a crucial problem in the field of computer vision [1]. The objective is to partition an image into meaningful segments, each corresponding to different objects or regions of interest within the image. This task involves classifying every pixel in an image to its corresponding category, thus enabling more detailed analysis and interpretation of visual data. Image segmentation is fundamental in various applications, such as object detection, scene understanding, and automated image editing.

The segmentation problem becomes even more critical in medical imaging due to its potential impact on patient care. Medical image segmentation involves identifying and isolating regions of interest in images obtained from medical scans, such as X-rays, Magnetic Resonance Imaging (MRI), Computed Tomography (CT), or ultrasound. These regions may correspond to anatomical structures, pathological areas, or other clinically relevant features. Accurate segmentation in medical images is essential for tasks such as tumor detection, organ delineation, and treatment planning. Advances in medical image segmentation, often driven by deep learning techniques, are paving the way for more accurate and efficient diagnostic tools, ultimately enhancing the quality of patient care [2–4]. While deep learning techniques are highly effective for various tasks, including image segmentation, training, and fine-tuning, they require substantial computational and personnel resources [5]. Furthermore, the time needed to achieve functional results is considerable. However, medical cost prediction is essential in the current healthcare environment, where resources are limited, and the demand for medical services is increasing [6].

In 2023, Meta (https://ai.facebook.com/, accessed on 6 March 2025) introduced SAM, a foundational model designed for image segmentation tasks [7]. Since its release, SAM has been the focus of multiple research efforts. In 2024, Meta took this breakthrough model a step further with the release of SAM 2 [8]. Also, as a foundation model, SAM 2's main advantage over its predecessor is its ability to extend segmentation capabilities to video. This is achieved through a memory module that enables the model to track objects across frames, processing the individual images that make up a video. As with SAM, Meta continues its commitment to the open-source community by publicly releasing both the SAM 2 model and its corresponding dataset. They are distributed under the Apache License, which permits users to freely use, modify, and share the software, even for commercial purposes, provided that proper attribution is given and license notices are preserved.

In our previous work [9], we demonstrated that the results of a foundation model like SAM can be substantially improved by applying techniques that do not require significant computational power, dedicated teams of experts, or massive additional datasets. Combining the model's capabilities with a novel prompting technique, we were able to segment medical images with a minimum number of prompts, achieving results comparable to those obtained by state-of-the-art models explicitly trained for this task. We had to provide prompts for all the slices of a medical image volume. If the volume contained 250 slices, SAM needed a prompt for each. Although prompts can be automatically generated, they depend on the geometric characteristics of the object to be segmented, so the prompt generation algorithm needs to be adapted to every segmentation target (organ or lesion). This task has development and maintenance costs, as the results need to be monitored to ensure the quality of the generated prompts, and the algorithm needs to be updated if the results are not satisfactory. Specialists could manually provide prompts, but this also has personnel costs. We intend to drastically reduce all those costs by providing a library of prototypical prompts for every segmentation task so we can let the specialists devote their time to other, more critical tasks since the segmentation process is considerably simplified. In addition, the hardware and personnel requirements to obtain these results are much lower than those needed to train a deep learning model from scratch or to modify the behavior of an existing one using model modification techniques. These results would go even further if, instead of segmenting all the slices of a volume, it was sufficient to segment just one slice, and the model would propagate the segmentation to the rest of the slices.

In this paper, we try to answer two main research questions: (1) how much, if anything, does SAM 2 improve the performance of SAM in the medical image segmentation tasks? (2) Can we leverage SAM 2 video segmentation capabilities for medical image segmentation to reduce further the number of prompts needed to segment a volume of medical images? Since the publication of SAM, the scientific community has been interested in its performance in medical image segmentation tasks. Many papers have been published investigating its performance in this field. Studying the differences between SAM and SAM 2 when segmenting medical images can be a fundamental resource that other researchers can use to determine whether or not to use this new version in their research, given the vast amount of effort applied to build on SAM's segmentation capabilities in this direction. Before exploring whether we can leverage SAM 2's video segmentation capabilities to reduce the number of prompts needed to segment medical image volumes, we must first determine whether SAM 2 performs at least as well as SAM in the medical image segmentation task. If SAM 2 does not offer performance improvements, investigating its video segmentation capabilities would be irrelevant. While a comprehensive, modality-specific performance analysis of SAM 2 is beyond the scope of this study, we also include an exploratory evaluation that offers initial insights into its applicability and effectiveness across different imaging modalities and anatomical regions.

The structure of this paper is organized as follows. In Section 2, we review the related works that have been published on the topic of medical image segmentation using SAM and compare them with our approach. Section 3 details the methodology behind our experiments, including the datasets utilized, the operation of segmentation with SAM 2, the preprocessing steps applied to images and videos, the data inputs required by SAM 2, and the metrics employed to evaluate segmentation quality. Section 4 compares the experimental results obtained using SAM and SAM 2 and assesses the new segmentation technique's performance. These findings are further discussed in Section 5, where specific aspects and nuances are explored in greater depth. Finally, Section 6 offers an in-depth analysis of the results and proposes potential directions for future research.

2. Related Works

In [10], the authors presented MedSAM, a fine-tuned SAM model for medical image segmentation that outperforms the default model in 3D and 2D. The Medical SAM Adapter (Med-SA), introduced in [11], enhances SAM specifically for medical image segmentation by incorporating domain-specific medical knowledge and a light adaptation technique. Such is the interest in the application of SAM to the field of medical image segmentation that [12] focuses on presenting a comprehensive overview of the efforts applied to improve the efficacy of SAM in said task. This model was later extended in 2024 with the release of SAM 2, an advanced version capable of segmenting images and videos [8].

Foundation models like SAM are trained on vast datasets. They are versatile tools that can be integrated into various tasks across domains. A notable feature of this kind of model is its zero-shot transfer capability, which allows it to perform segmentation in domains for which it was not explicitly trained [13]. The strength of these models lies in their ability to generalize across tasks, thanks to the extensive training data and the model's capacity to learn abstract features and latent representations, enabling the model to execute tasks accurately, even when encountering previously unseen data. However, each time the specialist needs to segment an image using these tools, there is an inherited cost associated with prompting the same object every time. In the particular case of the medical image segmentation task, this is a downside, as specialist time is a scarce and valuable resource in this domain. This work aims to reduce specialist effort as much as possible.

Wu et al. [14] propose a "One-Prompt Segmentation" paradigm that bridges interactive and one-shot methods for medical image segmentation. Their approach utilizes a single prompted image to generalize segmentation across unseen tasks without requiring retraining. This is achieved through the integration of a "One-Prompt Former", a module designed to efficiently incorporate template features into the segmentation process. Trained on 64 medical datasets and evaluated on 14 unseen datasets, the method demonstrates robust generalization capabilities. However, its reliance on four distinct prompt types (clicks, bounding boxes, doodles, and segmentation masks) for different anatomical structures necessitates user interaction for each dataset, potentially increasing the complexity of clinical deployment.

SAM 2 has attracted considerable interest in the field of medical image segmentation. It has been applied to achieve remarkable results in the segmentation of complex anatomical structures like ocular CT scans, as demonstrated by [15], and in liver CT images [16]. Both studies utilized refined medical SAM 2 models to achieve these advancements. Medical SAM 2 was introduced by Zhu et al. [17]. It leverages SAM 2's video segmentation framework to process medical imaging data, including unordered 2D slices and 3D volumes. The key innovation lies in a self-sorting memory bank that dynamically selects and organizes embeddings based on confidence scores and dissimilarity measures. This mechanism enhances segmentation consistency and generalization by prioritizing the most informative embeddings, irrespective of their temporal order. The framework achieves significant performance gains across a wide range of benchmarks.

In contrast, our method avoids user-dependent prompt customization, as seen in [14], and complex memory mechanisms, as in [17]. Instead, we employ a single, generalized prompt per dataset, effectively minimizing user interaction while maintaining strong segmentation performance across diverse datasets. By structuring medical volumes as bidirectional, video-like sequences rather than ordering frames based on embedding scores or dissimilarity measures, we leverage SAM 2's capabilities without incurring excessive computational demands. This approach strikes a pragmatic balance between segmentation quality and generalization for clinical applications. Additionally, our automated prompt generation is tailored to specific tasks using an example image frame and its associated mask, further reducing the need for manual intervention.

3. Methods

3.1. Experimental Setup

In order to answer the research questions, a series of tests have to be carried out. All the tests use the same setup to ensure a fair comparison between the models. The experiments run on an Acer Predator Helios 300 laptop (Acer Inc., New Taipei City, Taiwan) with a 12-core Intel Core i7-10750H 2.60 GHz CPU, 32 GB of RAM, and an NVIDIA GeForce RTX 2070 GPU with 8 GB of GDDR6 memory. The laptop runs Windows 11 with Ubuntu 24.04 LTS via Windows Subsystem for Linux (WSL). It has Python 3.12.4, PyTorch 2.3.1, and CUDA 12.1.0 installed. The experiments use the same configuration for both models to maintain consistency and fairness in the comparison.

We intentionally chose a consumer laptop instead of a high-end computing system to evaluate the models' performance in a real-world scenario that is more accessible to general users, particularly to medical professionals who work with systems featuring diverse hardware configurations depending on the specific hospital or healthcare facility. This decision allows us to assess whether these models can be efficiently deployed on consumer-grade hardware, which is crucial for wider adoption in practical settings. Furthermore, considering that medical images contain sensitive patient data, it is essential to ensure that segmentation processes can be executed on dedicated medical hardware systems. By using a typical consumer laptop, we aim to demonstrate the feasibility of running advanced medical image segmentation models on affordable and widely available equipment rather than on specialized servers that may not be as readily accessible.

Different pre-trained checkpoints are available for each model. Table 1 contains the names of the models and their respective sizes for reference, with the chosen models' checkpoints in bold. The greater the size of the model, the better it performs. The choice to test SAM is ViT-L, as the laptop's GPU cannot load the ViT-H checkpoints due to its GPU memory limitations. However, in the case of SAM 2, the large version of the model can run without problems. Although the test machine cannot run the best version of SAM, it can run the best version of SAM 2. Note that the best SAM 2 model size is 28.14% smaller than the best SAM model and 64.99% smaller than the one used for the comparison.

Table 1. Model checkpoint sizes (chosen checkpoints in bold).

SAM		SAM 2	
Name	**Size**	**Name**	**Size**
ViT-H	2.4 GB	**Large**	**856.4 MB**
ViT-L	**1.2 GB**	Base+	308.5 MB
ViT-B	357.7 MB	Small	175.8 MB
		Tiny	148.7 MB

3.2. Datasets

To assess SAM 2's performance in segmenting medical images, compare it with the original SAM, and test our proposed approach to medical image segmentation, we selected two widely recognized public lung datasets, one comprising axial lung scans and the other containing frontal chest X-rays, ensuring representation of both image modalities in our experiments. These datasets were chosen due to their accessibility, publication status, and frequent use in previous scientific studies, underscoring their significance in comparative research. Furthermore, they are the same datasets used in our previous work [9], allowing for a direct comparison between the models. Image dimensions are described in width × height.

Both datasets provide lung masks verified by radiology specialists, ensuring the availability of well-labeled data for research. The first dataset (COVID-19) includes 20 axial lung scans [18], divided into two subsets: Coronacases (see Figure 1a) and Radiopaedia (see Figure 1b). The quality of the CT slices in the Coronacases subset is superior to that of the Radiopaedia subset, the latter being composed of cone beam CTs with lower resolution, hence the disparity in quality. Moreover, while the Coronacases subset consists exclusively of 512 px × 512 px slices, the Radiopaedia subset is more varied, including 829,630 px × 630 px slices and 110,630 px × 401 px slices. Coronacase CT scans in this dataset average 258.1 slices, while Radiopaedia averages 93.9, providing 3520 slices for evaluating SAM 2's performance. This dataset is also utilized to evaluate the performance of DMDF-Net, as reported by Owais et al. [19]. The differences between these two kinds of CT make them ideal for a separate study so that they will be treated as different datasets during this work.

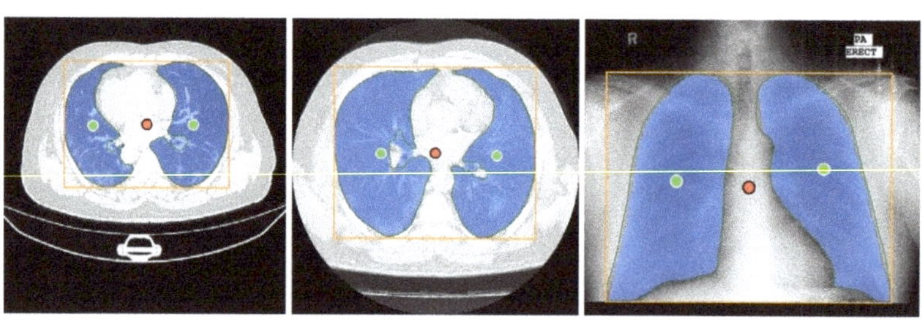

(**a**) Coronacases subset. (**b**) Radiopaedia subset. (**c**) Montgomery dataset.

Figure 1. Prediction examples (yellow box: target location; green circles: lung centers; red circle: background).

The second dataset (Montgomery) comprises 138 frontal chest X-rays [20], provided in Portable Network Graphics (PNG) format, along with corresponding left and right lung masks (see Figure 1c). Chen et al. [21] used this dataset, referred to as Montgomery after the collection site in Montgomery County, MD, USA, to evaluate the performance of TransAttUnet. This dataset contains 414,892 px × 4020 px slices and 4020 px × 4892 px slices.

Dataset Diversity

A well-defined evaluation dataset is essential for ensuring unbiased and generalizable results. This section addresses potential concerns regarding dataset diversity by detailing the representativeness of the test data, including variations in patient demographics and disease types, while also providing a comprehensive description of the data sources.

The COVID-19 dataset [18] is derived from the volumes folder (https://academictorrents.com/details/136ffddd0959108becb2b3a86630bec049fcb0ff, accessed on 6 March 2025) within the COVID-19 image dataset collection [22]. Its primary contribution lies in providing high-quality labels for objects of interest created by experienced radiologists. The data sources are detailed in [22] and include reputable platforms such as Radiopaedia (https://radiopaedia.org/, accessed on 6 March 2025) and Coronacases (https://coronacases.org/, accessed on 6 March 2025). As its name suggests, the dataset specifically includes COVID-19 cases.

The Montgomery dataset [20] was collected in collaboration with the Department of Health and Human Services, Montgomery County, MD, USA. In addition to medical images, the dataset authors provide manually segmented lung masks. These segmentations were performed under the supervision of a radiologist, following anatomical landmarks. The dataset includes tuberculosis cases from a screening program conducted in Montgomery County.

Although both datasets are anonymized to protect patient privacy, their curators have provided certain demographic information. Figure 2 shows the sex and age distribution for these datasets.

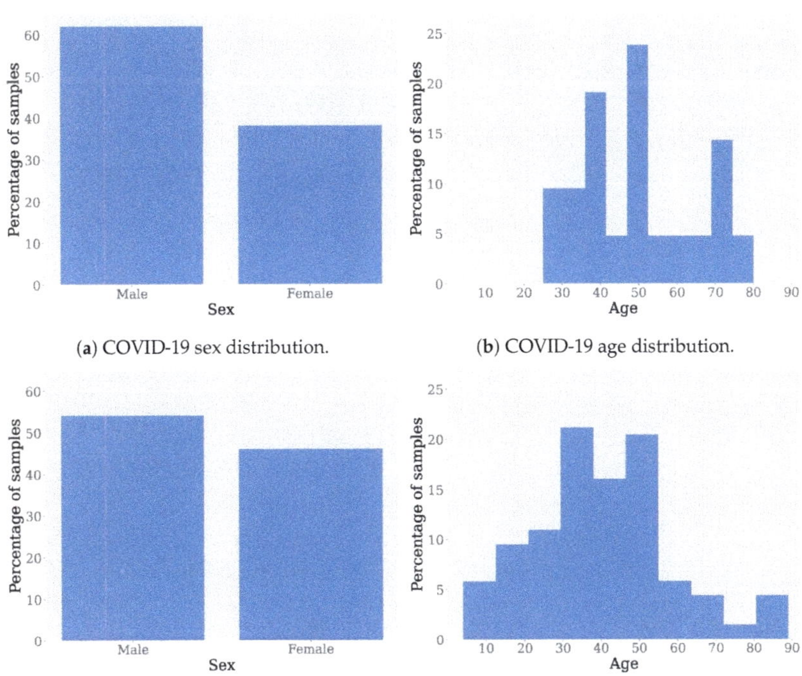

(**a**) COVID-19 sex distribution. (**b**) COVID-19 age distribution.

(**c**) Montgomery sex distribution. (**d**) Montgomery age distribution.

Figure 2. Sex and age distribution in COVID-19 and Montgomery datasets.

The sex distribution in the COVID-19 and Montgomery datasets is not perfectly balanced but remains relatively close to an even split, according to the data provided in their respective publications. Specifically, the COVID-19 dataset consists of 61.90% male and 38.10% female cases, while the Montgomery dataset includes 45.99% male and 54.01% female cases.

The age distribution in the COVID-19 dataset is skewed toward middle-aged and older individuals, with samples between 25 and 80 years old and prominent peaks around 40, 50, and 70 years old. This suggests a focus on conditions prevalent in middle-aged and elderly populations. In contrast, the Montgomery dataset exhibits a broader and more evenly distributed age range, spanning from young (10s and 20s) to elderly individuals (80s and 90s). The distribution shows noticeable peaks around 30 and 55 years old, indicating a more balanced representation across different age groups. While the COVID-19 dataset is particularly suited for studying diseases that predominantly affect middle-aged and older adults, the Montgomery dataset allows for broader generalization across diverse age demographics.

3.3. Comparison Between SAM and SAM 2

SAM [7], a foundation model developed by Meta AI Research, is designed to segment all distinct objects in an image without user interaction. Its architecture is depicted in Figure 3a. The model employs an autonomous segmentation approach to generate masks that delineate objects within the image. However, SAM also supports flexible prompts, such as point coordinates or bounding boxes, to refine segmentation results. These prompts do not crop the input image but rather guide the model's attention to specific regions, enabling iterative refinements based on user input.

SAM 2 [8] builds upon the success of its predecessor, SAM, by extending segmentation capabilities to video. Its architecture is depicted in Figure 3b. The model initially identifies and segments objects in the first frame of a video based on user-provided prompts, generating a set of masks for each identifiable object. These prompts may include point coordinates or bounding boxes that indicate where the target object is likely located (positive points for the foreground) or where it is absent (negative points for the background). Notably, the bounding box does not crop the input image but instead guides the model's focus. This process can be iteratively refined until the segmentation results are satisfactory. Once the desired segmentation is achieved in the first frame, SAM 2 propagates these prompts across the video, enabling object tracking in subsequent frames. The model retains the flexibility of various prompt types, ensuring an interactive experience that enhances precision and adaptability.

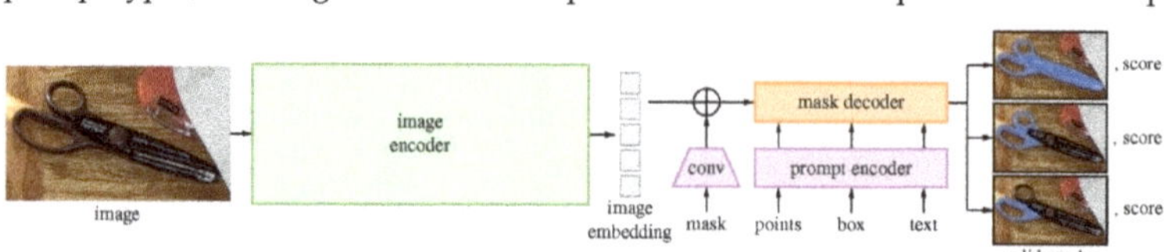

(a) SAM architecture.

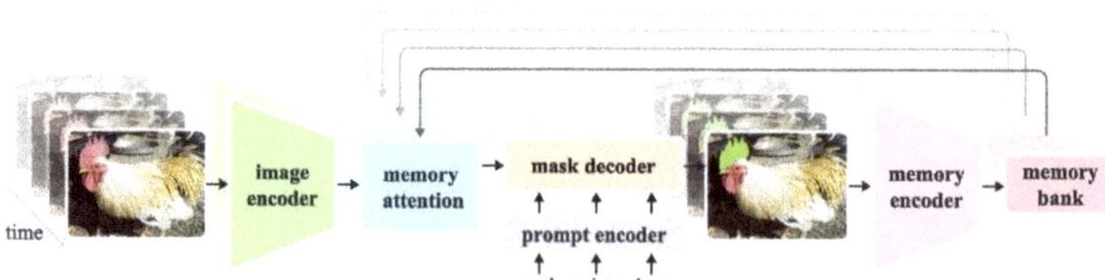

(b) SAM 2 architecture.

Figure 3. SAM [7] vs. SAM 2 [8] architecture.

The primary architectural difference between SAM and SAM 2 stems from the distinct tasks they are designed to address: SAM segments objects in static images, whereas SAM 2 extends segmentation across video frames. While SAM focuses solely on image segmentation, SAM 2 introduces a temporal component, allowing it to process a sequence of images, effectively forming a video. To capture the relationships between frames, the memory encoder's output is stored in a memory bank. This memory bank, together with a memory attention mechanism, maintains object segmentation continuity across frames. In addition to generating segmentation masks, SAM estimates a confidence score for its results based on the Jaccard index. When SAM 2 tracks objects across frames, it further provides an estimated occlusion score for each detected object, enhancing its ability to handle object persistence and visibility changes.

Given an input image, SAM 2 is capable of autonomously identifying and segmenting the various elements it contains. This process produces a series of masks, each corresponding to a potential object within the image. These masks may overlap when multiple candidate regions are present. Alternatively, users can guide the segmentation using *flexible prompts*, which help refine the results. These prompts can consist of point coordinates or bounding boxes indicating where the target object is located (positive prompts or foreground) or where it is not (negative prompts or background). Importantly, the bounding box does not crop the image; it merely instructs SAM 2 where to focus its attention.

In this study, the selected prompting approach combines minimal point coordinates within a bounding box. This method is intended to simulate an interactive tool where a specialist might begin by drawing a bounding box around the lungs, then marking the areas to be segmented (i.e., the lungs), and finally, indicating parts of the background to be excluded. Figure 1 illustrates two examples of this approach using different CT slices: one from each subset of the selected dataset (Coronacases and Radiopaedia) and a chest X-ray. The orange box encompasses all the masks generated for the current slice. The green circles denote a point near the center of each lung. In contrast, the red circle identifies the background, indicating a region that should not be considered part of the lungs.

3.4. Image Processing

The datasets utilized in this study consist of medical images in various formats. Even when the formats overlap, the characteristics of each sample differ. This section examines the unique attributes of each dataset. It outlines the necessary steps to standardize them into a standard format.

CT scans and corresponding masks in the CT dataset are stored in Neuroimaging Informatics Technology Initiative (NIfTI) format (https://nifti.nimh.nih.gov/, accessed on 6 March 2025). Since SAM cannot process this format directly, it is first converted to a more suitable format for this study.

Each CT scan comprises multiple slices representing axial samples taken from the patient. Each slice consists of values arranged in a two-dimensional matrix of rows and columns. These values, known as Hounsfield Units (HUs), indicate the attenuation of X-rays as they pass through different materials, with distilled water serving as the reference [23]. The values typically range from $[-1000, +1000]$. Depending on the anatomical region under study and the nature of the tissues involved, a contrast enhancement technique known as *windowing* [24] may be beneficial. This process requires knowledge of the window's width and level. The window width determines which attenuation values are of interest, while the window level specifies the center of the window. When windowing is applied, all values below and above the specified width are disregarded. In the dataset used, the Coronacases CT volumes have not been windowed, whereas the Radiopaedia volumes have already undergone this process. Therefore, the Coronacases volumes are appropriately windowed to ensure consistency across the dataset. Finally, all CT slices are converted to grayscale, with each pixel assigned a value between 0 and 255.

In contrast, X-rays do not utilize HUs. Instead, they produce images in which the brightness or darkness of the pixels reflects the degree of X-ray absorption by different tissues. Consequently, no preprocessing steps are required for the chest X-ray dataset.

At this point, all images are in a standardized format and ready for further processing by the original SAM but not yet by SAM 2.

3.5. Video Processing

Unlike the original SAM, which processed each image independently, SAM 2 can process videos. However, video processing is carried out in a particular way. To allow SAM 2 to process a video, it must first be converted into a sequence of independent frames. This means the model operates on a series of individual images that happen to be temporally ordered. The user is responsible for converting the video file into independent frames in JPEG or PNG format. The key difference is that SAM 2, unlike the previous version of the model, includes a memory module that keeps track of segmentations from previous frames, allowing it to improve the segmentation of the current one. Ultimately, this enables SAM 2 to track objects throughout a scene.

A video is a sequence of images, each representing a frame. The frames have a temporal relation, as they are shown in succession. In the medical imaging domain, a volume is a sequence of slices, each representing a frame. Although there is no temporal relation between the slices, there is a spatial relation, as they are part of the same volume. This spatial relation can be transformed into a temporal one if the initial slice is considered the first frame of the video, the second slice the second frame, and so on. This transformation allows us to take advantage of SAM 2's memory and try to reduce the number of prompts needed to segment a volume.

Figure 4a shows a summary of the proposed prompt reduction process. For reference, Figure 4b shows a summary of the segmentation process proposed in our previous work [9], using SAM instead of SAM 2. The first step is to convert the different frames of the video to be segmented to the Joint Photographic Experts Group (JPEG) format. The second step is dividing the video into two parts, using what we have called a *seed frame*. If given the chance to choose a single slice as the best representation of a whole volume, the specialist would likely select one of the central slices. The slices closer to the start and end of the volume are less likely to contain the organ to be segmented in its entirety. For the tests performed in this study, we are choosing the central slice of the volume as the seed frame. Given the dataset's characteristics, would this choice be the most appropriate? To answer this question, we analyze the spatial distribution of the Jaccard Index and Dice Score for the Coronacases and Radiopaedia datasets using SAM, as the outcomes of this analysis will be used to support the selection of the middle slice as the seed for the SAM 2 video segmentation process. The results can be seen in Figure 5. The X-axis represents the normalized slice position, as each volume has a different number of slices. The Y-axis represents the metric value (Jaccard Index or Dice Score) for the given dataset. The average metric value is marked with a red dotted line, while the position of the central slice is marked with a vertical solid blue line. The 1% percentile of the metric is marked with an orange range, while the 2% percentile is marked with a yellow range. In the Coronacases dataset, any slice inside the 1% percentile of the metric would be a good candidate, making it an appropriate choice for the seed frame. In this case, the central slice is inside that range. On the other hand, the Radiopaedia dataset shows different behavior. The 1% percentile of the metric is displaced to the right of the center slice because of the dataset's characteristics. However, the central slice is still inside the 2% percentile of the metric, making it a good candidate for the seed frame.

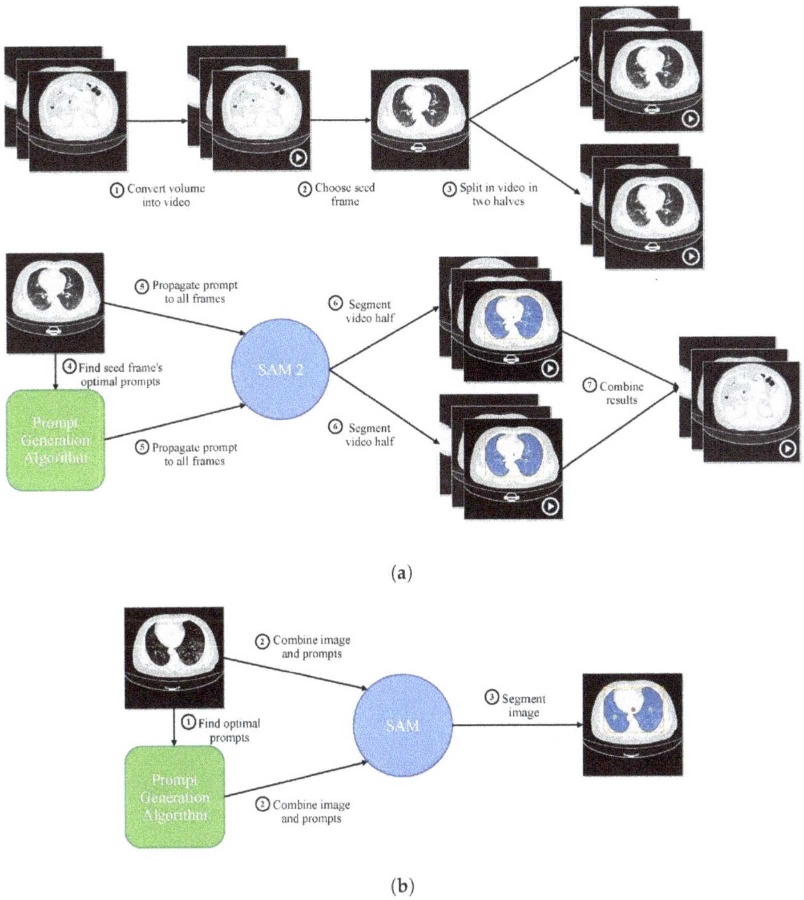

Figure 4. Proposed segmentation process. (**a**) Proposed segmentation process using SAM 2. (**b**) Previously proposed segmentation process using SAM [9].

We will make the central slice shared by both halves of the video, and it will be the first frame. Using this seed frame and moving backward through the volume's slices, we create the first half of the video that SAM 2 will process. Similarly, by moving forward in time, we create the second half of the video. In this way, SAM 2 can use the memory of the segmentation of previous slices to improve the current slice segmentation.

Our prompting algorithm [9] selects the prompt to segment the seed frame. The selection process for determining prompt points begins with identifying the contours within the mask. Initially, a bounding box encompassing all mask contours for the seed frame is established, followed by identifying the centroid of each mask contour. However, due to the irregular shape of the lungs, the centroid may occasionally fall outside the mask boundary. To address this, the centroid is adjusted by using it as a seed to find intersections on the X and Y axes with the mask. The centroid is then repositioned to the intersection's midpoint, which contains the most points, ensuring it is placed within the mask. This adjustment is applied even when the centroid is inside the mask to ensure it is more accurately centered within the corresponding mask. A negative prompt is also included, representing the center of the frame. Once segmented, SAM 2 can propagate the segmentation to the rest of the frames of the two halves of the video.

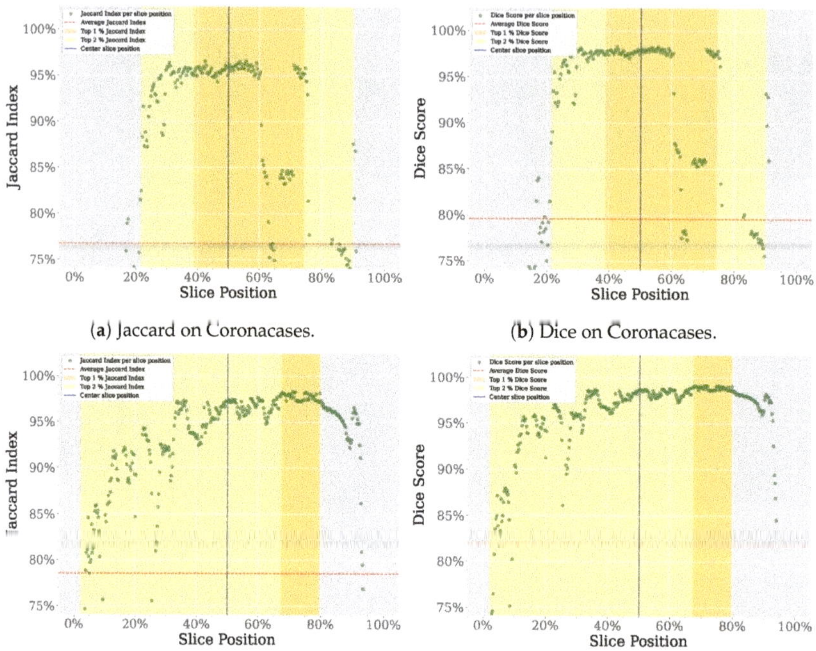

(**a**) Jaccard on Coronacases. (**b**) Dice on Coronacases.

(**c**) Jaccard on Radiopaedia. (**d**) Dice on Radiopaedia.

Figure 5. Spatial distribution of segmentation metrics using SAM, with emphasis on the central slice.

In the case of the Montgomery dataset samples, there is no temporal relation between the slices since they are independent chest radiographs belonging to different patients. However, there is a spatial relation since the nature of these samples is similar. In this case, we can also take advantage of SAM 2 memory to improve the segmentation of the radiographs.

Assuming a folder with the slices in JPEG format exists, Algorithm 1 shows the algorithm for dividing the slices into two parts, selecting the seed, adding the prompts needed for the seed frame, propagating them to the rest of the slices, and combining the results.

3.6. Metrics

The effectiveness of SAM 2's segmentation results will be evaluated using the Jaccard index (JCI) Equation (1) and the Dice score (DSC) Equation (2). These metrics are widely employed to assess the similarity between A and B images.

$$JCI(A,B) = \frac{|A \cap B|}{|A \cup B|}, \tag{1}$$

$$DSC(A,B) = \frac{2|A \cap B|}{|A| + |B|}. \tag{2}$$

Müller et al. [25] argue that both the Jaccard index and the Dice score are reliable and accurate metrics for evaluating the automatic segmentation of medical images. The Dice score offers a balanced perspective by considering both recall and precision. At the same time, the Jaccard index imposes a stricter penalty for under- or over-segmentation, making it particularly valuable when a high level of segmentation accuracy is essential. More information about these metrics can be found in [9].

Algorithm 1 Video processing algorithm.

```
Require: video exists
Require: video frames > 0

  half_1, half_2 ← SplitVideo(video)
  results_1 ← ProcessVideo(half_1)
  results_2 ← ProcessVideo(half_2)
  result ← JoinResults(results_1, results_2)

  function SPLITVIDEO(video)
      frames ← length(video)
      seed frame ← ⌊frames/2⌋
      copy frames 0 to seed frame to half_1
      reverse frame order in half_1
      copy frames seed frame to end to half_2
  end function

  function PROCESSVIDEO(video)
      prompts ← GetPrompts(seed frame)
      segment seed frame with prompts
      propagate segmentation through video
      save results
  end function

  function JOINRESULTS(results_1, results_2)
      reverse results order in results_1
      delete seed frame results in results_1
      join results_1 and results_2
  end function
```

4. Results

This section presents the results of the experiments conducted to answer the research questions posed in this work: (1) how much, if anything, does SAM 2 improve the performance of SAM in medical image segmentation tasks? (2) Can we leverage SAM 2 video segmentation capabilities for medical image segmentation to reduce further the number of prompts needed to segment a volume of medical images? Each of these research questions is addressed in a separate subsection.

4.1. SAM vs. SAM 2

SAM 2 is a generalization of SAM to the video domain. It processes video frames one at a time. It has a memory attention module that provides access to the previous memories of the target object. When applied to images, the memory is empty, and the model behaves like SAM. In another paper [8], the authors claim that SAM 2 delivers better performance under said conditions than SAM on image segmentation benchmarks while being six times faster. We want to test if SAM 2 can also improve the performance of SAM on medical image segmentation tasks, comparing both models on the same datasets we used in our previous work [9].

4.1.1. Segmentation Performance

A comparison across the three datasets used in our previous work is shown in Figure 6.

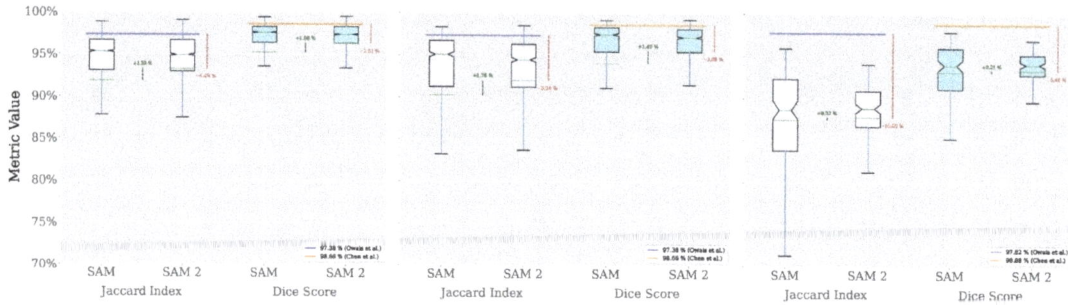

(a) Coronacases. (b) Radiopaedia. (c) Montgomery.

Figure 6. Segmentation comparison (Owais et al. [19], Chen et al. [21]).

The results show that SAM 2 outperforms SAM in all cases. The improvement is more significant in the Radiopaedia dataset, where the average Jaccard index increases by 1.76% and the average Dice score by 1.49%. In the Coronacases dataset, the improvement is similar, with the Jaccard index increasing by 1.39% and the Dice score by 1.08%. The Montgomery dataset shows a more modest improvement, at most half a percentage point in both metrics.

However, the improvement is most notable in the results' distribution. Figure 6 shows that average values are closer to the median in each case, and the variance is lower, which means that SAM 2 is more consistent in its performance than SAM. Table 2 confirms it, showing that the standard deviation is lower for SAM 2 in all cases.

Table 2. SAM 2's segmentation results (delta from SAM).

	Coronacases		Radiopaedia		Montgomery	
	Jaccard Index	**Dice Score**	**Jaccard Index**	**Dice Score**	**Jaccard Index**	**Dice Score**
Minimum	12.81% (+4.37)	22.71% (+7.15)	14.32% (+8.05)	25.05% (+13.26)	65.16% (+3.57)	78.91% (+2.67)
Maximum	99.05% (+0.21)	99.52% (+0.10)	98.52% (+0.19)	99.26% (+ 0.10)	94.07% (−1.87)	96.65% (−0.98)
Average	93.29% (+1.39)	96.35% (+1.08)	92.04% (+1.76)	95.57% (+ 1.49)	87.77% (+0.32)	93.40% (+0.21)
Std Dev	7.16% (−4.29)	4.81% (−3.75)	8.82% (−5.27)	6.18% (− 4.83)	5.21% (−0.88)	3.13% (−0.47)

In Table 3, the performance of various state-of-the-art Deep Learning (DL) models in the lung segmentation task is compared with that of SAM 2. The results of SAM are also included for reference. The performance reported by Owais et al. [19] was obtained using the same CT dataset as in this study. Their DMDF-Net achieved a Jaccard index of 97.38% and a Dice score of 98.66%, whereas SAM 2 obtained a Jaccard index of 92.66% and a Dice score of 95.96%. Similarly, Chen et al. [21] used the same X-ray dataset as this work. Their TransAttUnet model achieved a Jaccard index of 97.82% and a Dice score of 98.88%, whereas SAM 2 obtained a Jaccard index of 87.77% and a Dice score of 93.40%. In both cases, the custom models outperformed SAM 2. However, it is important to highlight that, despite not being specifically trained on medical images, SAM 2 produced results that were relatively close to those of domain-specific solutions. Notably, SAM 2 consistently outperformed SAM across all instances.

Table 3. Segmentation performance of SAM 2 vs. state-of-the-art medical image segmentation models.

	Jaccard Index	SAM (Delta)	SAM 2 (Delta)	Dice Score	SAM (Delta)	SAM 2 (Delta)
Owais et al. [19]	97.38%	91.09% (−6.29)	92.66% (−4.72)	98.66%	94.68% (−3.98)	95.96% (−2.70)
Chen et al. [21]	97.82%	87.45% (−10.37)	87.77% (−10.05)	98.88%	93.19% (−5.69)	93.40% (−5.48)

Although the Jaccard index and Dice score are suitable performance measures, comparing the execution time of SAM 2 with state-of-the-art models provides additional insight into its overall efficiency. Table 4 presents a comparison of the execution times of SAM 2 and the model proposed by Owais et al., with SAM included for reference. In the row corresponding to Owais et al., the execution times for SAM 2 and SAM represent the average time required to segment both the Coronacases and Radiopaedia samples. Execution time data for the model by Chen et al. are not available. Hu et al. [26] are also included in this comparison. In the row corresponding to Hu et al., the execution times for SAM 2 and SAM reflect the time required to segment samples from the Coronacases, Radiopaedia, and Montgomery datasets. The model by Owais et al. is capable of processing a single image in 0.039 s, while SAM 2 requires 0.0685 s. However, as discussed in Section 4.1.6, the time required for an expert to manually segment a medical image is measured in minutes. Hu et al. report a processing time of approximately 11.2 s per image, in which case SAM 2 demonstrates a significant advantage in execution speed.

Table 4. Execution time of SAM 2 vs. state-of-the-art medical image segmentation models.

	Execution Time (s)	SAM (Delta)	SAM 2 (Delta)
Owais et al. [19]	0.039	0.876 (+0.837)	0.685 (+0.646)
Hu et al. [26]	11.2	0.96 (−10.24)	0.81 (−10.39)

4.1.2. Model Performance Deltas

Focusing on improvement differences, or deltas, instead of absolute values could shed more light on this comparison. The distribution of these deltas for each dataset and metric appears in Figure 7, without outliers. These deltas are shown in Table 2 in parentheses.

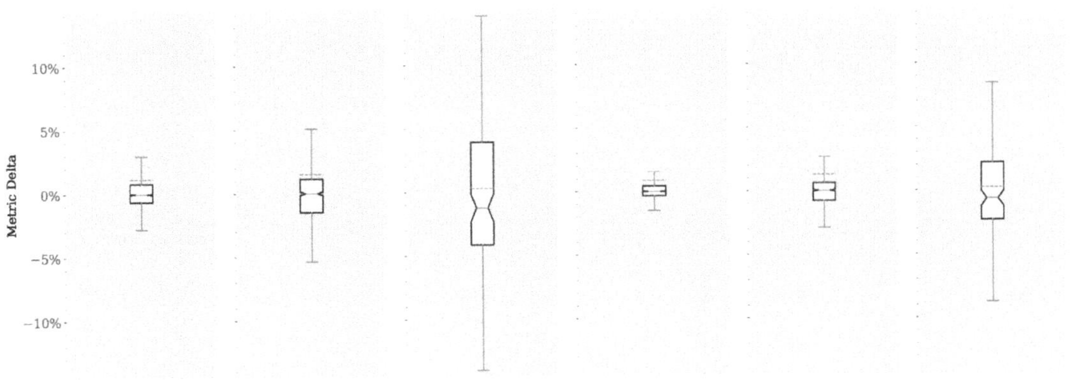

(a) (b) (c) (d) (e) (f)

Figure 7. SAM 2 vs. SAM segmentation delta comparison. (**a**) CoronacasesJaccard index. (**b**) Radiopaedia Jaccard index. (**c**) Montgomery Jaccard index. (**d**) Coronacases Dice score. (**e**) Radiopaedia Dice score. (**f**) Montgomery Dice score.

Coronacases and Radiopaedia deltas for both metrics are centered around zero, suggesting that the central tendency of the delta values is neutral, with no significant overall increase or decrease. However, the Montgomery dataset shows a slight negative skew (around 1%), indicating that the improvement in this dataset is more extreme than in the other two.

The Interquartile Range (IQR), represented by the box, is small for Coronacases and Radiopaedia deltas for both metrics. It shows that the middle 50% of the data lies close to ±1%. The whiskers extend close to ±3% except in the Jaccard index for Radiopedia, which is close to ±5%, suggesting that the changes are relatively small for better and worse segmentation results. Again, Montgomery shows a more significant delta, with the IQR extending close to ±5% and the whiskers close to ±15% Jaccard index, and close to ±3% and the whiskers close to ±10% Dice score, reinforcing a more significant improvement in this dataset.

The notch around the median suggests that we can be 95% confident that the actual median lies within this notch. The notch does not overlap with the ends of the box, suggesting that the median is distinct and significantly different from the IQR endpoints.

Overall, the Jaccard index changes for the Coronacases and Radiopaedia datasets appear to be centered around zero, with a small degree of variability and no significant outliers. The distribution is relatively symmetric and well-behaved.

In any case, the box plots appear symmetric around the median, indicating that the distribution of the delta values is relatively balanced. A slightly more prolonged whisker at the upper end might suggest a minor positive skew. This skew is reinforced by the average value (represented by the discontinuous green line) being consistently higher than the median (represented by the solid green line) in every instance.

4.1.3. Outliers Analysis

Leaving the outliers out of the plot maintains the focus on the main distribution of the data. However, it is essential to note that the outliers are not necessarily errors or anomalies in the data. They could be valid data points that are more extreme than the rest. In this case, they represent the most significant improvements (and declines) in the segmentation results. The last step in analyzing these data would be to investigate these outliers. Figure 8 shows the normalized deltas for each dataset and metric, sorted from best to worst values.

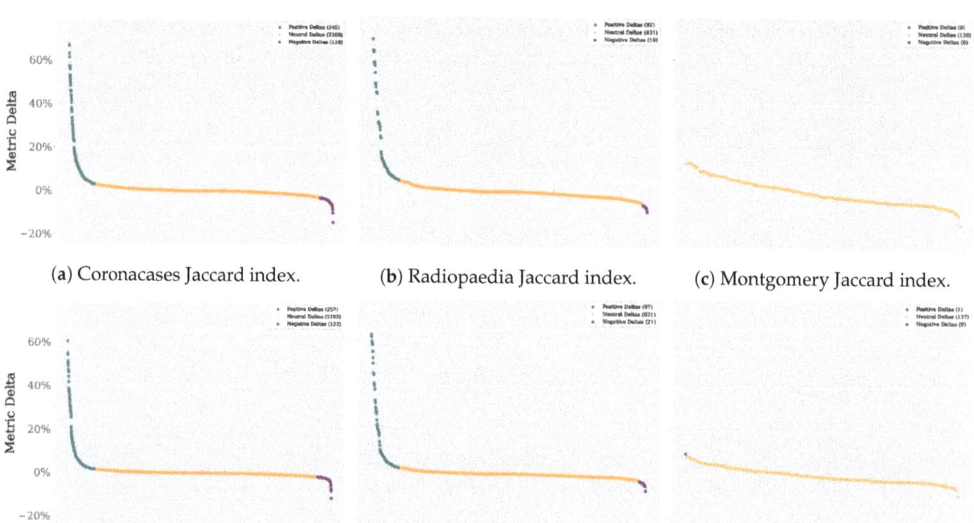

(**a**) Coronacases Jaccard index. (**b**) Radiopaedia Jaccard index. (**c**) Montgomery Jaccard index.

(**d**) Coronacases Dice score. (**e**) Radiopaedia Dice score. (**f**) Montgomery Dice score.

Figure 8. SAM 2 vs. SAM deltas in descending order.

The Coronacases and Radiopaedia datasets show many extremely positive deltas for the Jaccard index and Dice score. Although extreme negative deltas exist, they are less frequent. Most deltas are close to zero, meaning the results will remain the same. However, the odds of improvement are higher than the odds of decline. The Montgomery dataset, on the other hand, shows no outliers for both metrics because the improvements are less infrequent than in the other two datasets. Most deltas are positive, meaning the odds of performance improvement are higher than the odds of decline.

SAM 2 improves SAM performance because the model segments are better. There is no correlation between the size of the masks and model performance. The Pearson correlation coefficient is close to 0.20 for both the Jaccard index and Dice score when testing the Coronacases and Radiopaedia datasets and around 0.07 when testing the Montgomery dataset. These low values mean there is no linear correlation between the mask size and the delta values.

4.1.4. Best and Worst Deltas

For illustrative purposes, Figure 9 shows samples of the best and worst deltas for each dataset and metric. The improvement is quite notable in some cases, such as the Coronacases or Radiopaedia examples. The Montgomery improvement is also significant.

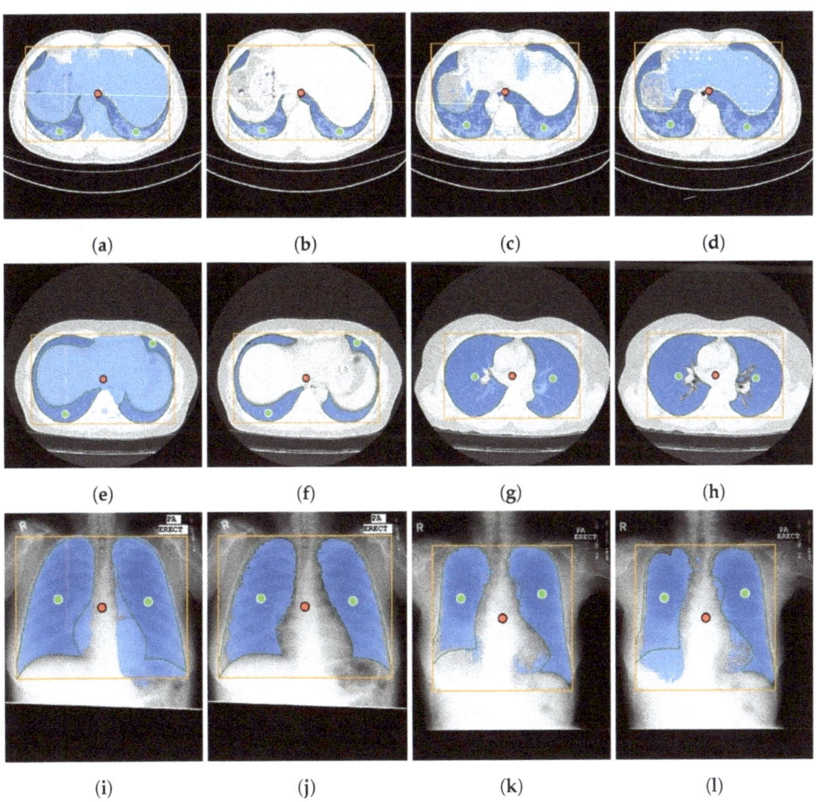

Figure 9. Best and worst delta examples (Jaccard index delta and Dice score delta). (**a**) Coronacases (SAM). (**b**) Coronacases improvement (SAM 2) (67.12% and 60.44%). (**c**) Coronacases (SAM). (**d**) Coronacases decline (SAM 2) (−32.58% and −26.08%). (**e**) Radiopaedia (SAM). (**f**) Radiopaedia improvement (SAM 2) (62.72% and 54.81%). (**g**) Radiopaedia (SAM). (**h**) Radiopaedia decline (SAM 2) (−08.80% and −04.81%). (**i**) Montgomery (SAM). (**j**) Montgomery improvement (SAM 2) (13.89% and 08.47%). (**k**) Montgomery (SAM). (**l**) Montgomery decline (SAM 2) (−13.99% and −08.77%).

4.1.5. Execution Time

Lastly, we compare the execution time of the models. Figure 10a shows the execution time comparison between SAM and SAM 2. The execution time is lower for SAM 2, as the authors of the model claim. However, the most significant improvement occurs during the embedding generation phase, particularly in the image-loading process. Consequently, SAM 2 achieves a lower segmentation time than SAM. When processing a single image only once, SAM 2 is faster than SAM. However, when performing multiple segmentation operations over the same image, SAM 2 would take more time than SAM in each iteration. These results make sense, as SAM 2 prediction architecture is more complex than SAM's, primarily due to its incorporation of a memory bank to enhance contextual understanding across segmentations. This additional structure improves segmentation consistency and adaptability across related images but also introduces additional computational overhead, particularly in data transfer and memory access times. Consequently, this increased architectural complexity likely contributes to the higher input/output latency and reduced overall throughput. Even when SAM 2 is operating in 2D segmentation mode, tensor propagation through its architecture remains necessary, further impacting processing efficiency. This suggests a trade-off between improved segmentation performance and real time execution speed.

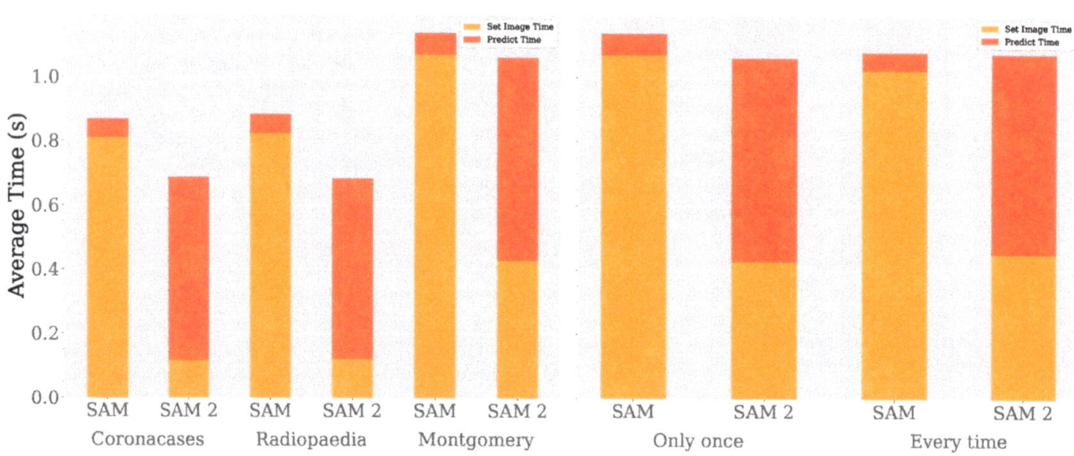

(**a**) Execution time comparison. (**b**) Operation mode time comparison.

Figure 10. SAM vs SAM 2 time analysis.

While evaluating SAM 2 performance, we found that SAM and SAM 2 behave differently depending on how they are executed. Figure 10b shows these differences.

The first two columns represent the time it takes to segment the Montgomery dataset when model is loaded only once. In contrast, the second two columns correspond to the scenario where the model is reloaded before processing each image, repeatedly segmenting the same image instead of the entire dataset. These results show that, in order to get the most out of SAM 2, the model should be loaded only once and then used to process all images. Otherwise, SAM and SAM 2 will take the same time to segment the images. Keeping this limitation in mind could speed the segmentation process up considerably when trying different prompts over the same image.

4.1.6. Impact of SAM 2 on Clinical Workflows

Manual segmentation of medical images is a time-intensive process that requires the intervention of highly experienced specialists. Recent studies have evaluated the time required to segment anatomical structures in various types of medical images. For instance, in the segmentation of 100 images from nine different modalities, three doctors with over 10 years of experience performed the annotation, requiring an average time of 4.27 min per image [27]. Similarly, in another study in which they used COVID-19 images obtained via CT, the manual segmentation of a CT scan consisting of 250 slices took a total time of 400 ± 45 min, which translates to an average of 1.6 min per slice [28]. This process was conducted in three phases: preliminary annotations were performed by junior specialists, then refined by more experienced radiologists, and finally, verified by a senior radiologist.

The integration of SAM in medical image segmentation has significantly reduced annotation time without compromising segmentation quality. In the annotation of medical images across various modalities, SAM decreased the average annotation time from 4.27 to 2.96 min per image while also improving annotation quality, as measured by the Human Correction Effort (HCE) index [27], decreasing the HCE value from 5.07 to 4.80. Likewise, in the study of COVID-19 images in CT, where manual segmentation of a single slice took an average of 1.6 min [28], SAM reduced this time to ~1 s per slice, as illustrated in Figure 10, representing a reduction of over 96%. These findings highlight that incorporating SAM into medical image segmentation not only enhances process efficiency but also alleviates the annotation workload for specialists.

Although the prediction time of SAM 2 is approximately ten times higher than that of SAM, the total segmentation time in both cases is ~1 s. This implies that, within the segmentation process carried out by the medical specialist, which may take several minutes, the impact of SAM 2's segmentation time is negligible. It is important to emphasize that after SAM 2 automatically segments the image, the medical specialist must refine the segmentation outcome obtained by the model based on their expert knowledge and the specific clinical context. In this regard, SAM 2 cannot replace the experience of medical professionals in annotation or diagnostic processes; rather, it serves as an assistive tool that streamlines their workflow, reduces annotation time, and enhances the quality of segmented images through its segmentation capabilities.

4.1.7. Hypothesis Test

A paired *t*-test was performed to determine if the differences between SAM and SAM 2 were statistically significant, as the segmentation results came from the same set of images segmented by both systems. The results are shown in Table 5 and Figure 11.

Table 5. SAM vs SAM 2 paired t-tests.

	Coronacases		Radiopaedia		Montgomery	
	Jaccard	**Dice**	**Jaccard**	**Dice**	**Jaccard**	**Dice**
T-statistic	−9.00	−8.70	−5.60	−5.58	−0.68	−0.76
***p*-value**	4.72×10^{-19}	6.38×10^{-18}	2.97×10^{-8}	3.36×10^{-8}	0.498	0.447
Result	Reject	Reject	Reject	Reject	Fail to reject	Fail to reject

The analysis of the results reveals that SAM 2 consistently outperforms SAM in the Coronacases and Radiopaedia datasets, as indicated by highly significant p-values across both the Jaccard and Dice metrics. The t-statistics are strongly negative, confirming SAM 2's superior performance in these cases. However, in the Montgomery dataset, the results show no significant difference between SAM and SAM 2, with p-values well above the typical threshold for significance. This indicates that the two systems perform similarly on this dataset, suggesting that SAM 2's advantages may be less pronounced in specific contexts. While SAM 2 shows robust improvements in most cases, its performance relative to SAM may vary depending on the dataset.

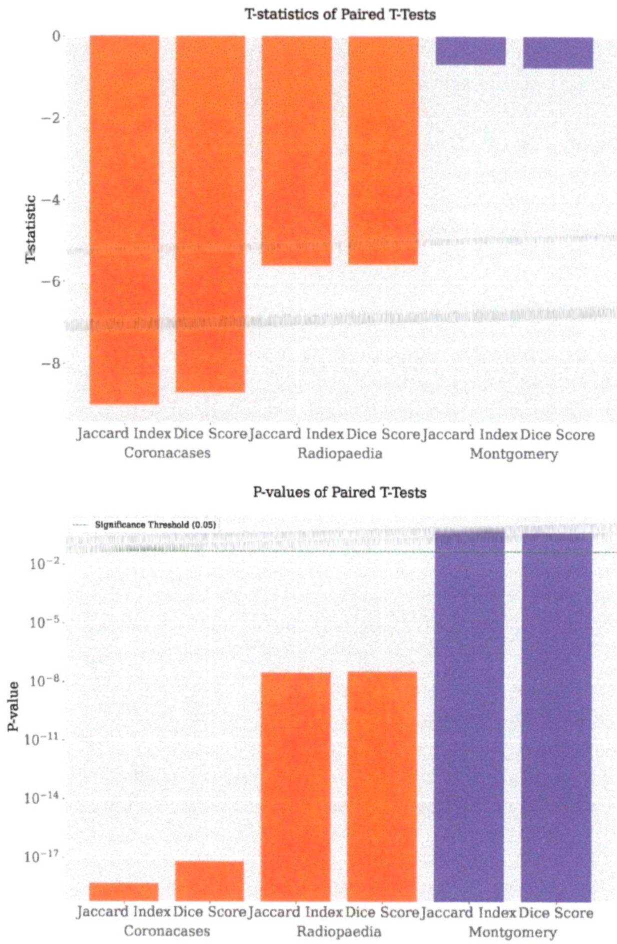

Figure 11. Hypothesis tests.

With these results, we can conclude that SAM 2 improves SAM performance in medical image segmentation tasks. Given these results, it is safe to test SAM 2 in a more challenging scenario, such as video segmentation, knowing that it will not behave worse than SAM.

4.2. SAM 2 Video Segmentation for Image Volumes

Figure 12 shows the results of the video segmentation tests described in Section 3.5 in a box plot format. Table 6 shows the exact values of the results. Only the Coronacases and Radiopaedia datasets are shown, as the Montgomery dataset is not structured in volumes. Each Montgomery's sample is an independent X-ray, with no time relation between them. The X-axis compares the results of SAM and SAM 2 for the Jaccard index and the Dice score. While SAM needs one prompt for each slice to achieve these results, with our proposed technique, SAM 2 only needs one prompt for the whole volume. The Coronacases dataset has 10 volumes and 2156 slices with their corresponding mask. With SAM, we would need 2156 prompts to segment the whole dataset. However, with SAM 2, we only need 10 prompts, one for each volume. The Y-axis shows the values of each metric. Each box plot represents the distribution of the results for each dataset and metric. The boxes are paired per metric. The outliers are not shown in the plot. The median value is shown as a solid green horizontal line inside the box, while the average is dashed. The notch around the median represents the 95% confidence interval. The state-of-the-art results are shown as a horizontal line atop each box. The delta between different model versions is shown as a green vertical dashed line between the boxes. The delta between the model and the state-of-the-art results is shown as a dashed red line at the right of each pair of boxes.

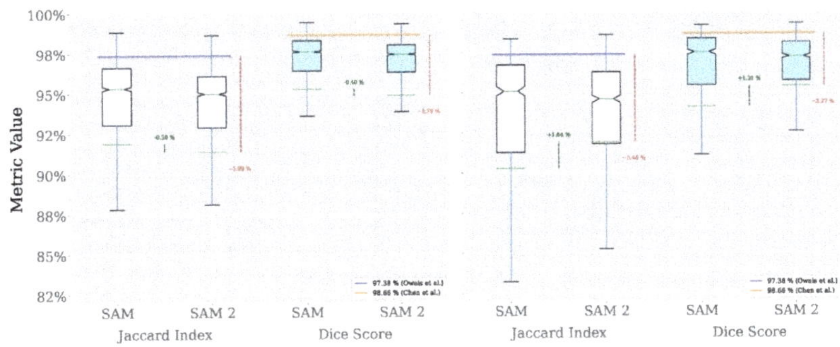

(**a**) Coronacases. (**b**) Radiopaedia.

Figure 12. Video results (Owais et al. [19], Chen et al. [21]).

Table 6. SAM 2 video's segmentation results (delta from SAM).

	Coronacases		Radiopaedia	
	Jaccard Index	**Dice Score**	**Jaccard Index**	**Dice Score**
Minimum	0.32% (−8.11%)	0.65% (−14.92%)	6.01% (−0.26%)	11.34% (−0.46%)
Maximum	98.63% (−0.21%)	99.31% (−0.11%)	98.56% (+0.23%)	99.28% (+0.12%)
Average	91.39% (−0.50%)	94.87% (−0.40%)	91.92% (+1.64%)	95.39% (+1.31%)
Std Dev	12.26% (+0.81%)	10.07% (+1.52%)	10.07% (−4.02%)	7.68% (−3.33%)

When comparing the results in the Coronacases dataset, SAM 2's results are slightly worse than SAM's. The average Jaccard index is 0.50% lower, and the average Dice score is 0.50% lower. In both cases, this decrease is below the 0.50% threshold. However, the distribution of values with SAM 2 is more compact than with SAM.

On the other hand, the Radiopaedia dataset shows a different behavior. Results are slightly better with SAM 2 than with SAM. The average Jaccard index is 1.64% higher, and the average Dice score is 1.31% higher. Again, the distribution of values with SAM 2 is more compact than with SAM.

Could we use a single prototypical seed prompt for the whole dataset, further reducing the prompting effort and creating a library of prototypical prompts for the medical image segmentation tasks? For this test, we used the seed prompt from the first volume of each dataset to segment the rest of the volumes in that dataset. For illustrative purposes, Figure 13 shows the seed prompt chosen for each dataset (Figure 13a,c) from the first volume, side by side with the seed prompt they are replacing from the second volume (Figure 13b,d). Although they are not identical, they share some fundamental characteristics resembling the same anatomical structure, like the rough shape and location of the lungs and the heart, the image's appearance, and its dimensions.

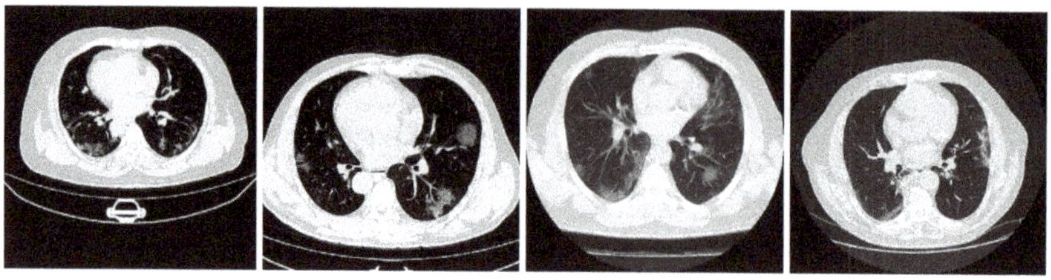

(a) (b) (c) (d)

Figure 13. Shared seed video results. (**a**) Coronacases shared seed. (**b**) Coronacases proper seed. (**c**) Radiopaedia shared seed. (**d**) Radiopaedia proper seed.

The results are shown in Figure 14. When processing the Coroncases dataset, the Jaccard index and the Dice score show an improvement of 0.60% and 0.40%, respectively. The Radiopaedia datasets result in a decrease of 0.18% and 0.16% for the Jaccard index and the Dice score, respectively. In both cases, the results are very similar to the ones obtained when using the seed prompt from the same volume. For the 2156 masks in the Coronacases dataset, using a single seed prompt would reduce the number of prompts needed to segment the volume to one. That is a 99.95% reduction in prompts needed to segment the volume. This previous test shows that the model can successfully segment all the volumes in a dataset using a single, representative seed prompt taken from one of the volumes, drastically reducing the number of prompts needed to segment the dataset (e.g., from 2156 to 10 in the Coronacases dataset).

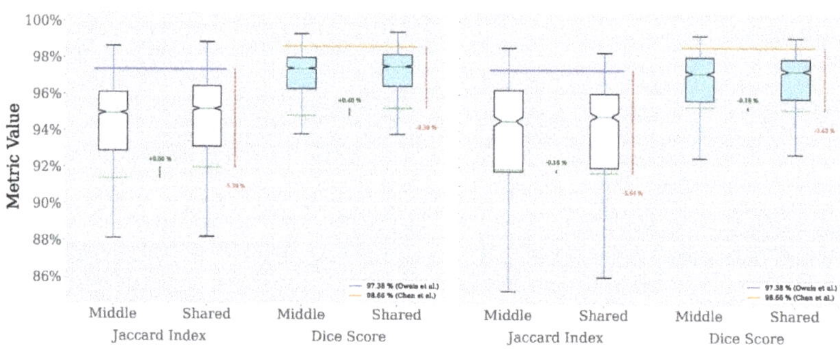

(**a**) Coronacases. (**b**) Radiopaedia.

Figure 14. Shared seed video results (Owais et al. [19], Chen et al. [21]).

4.3. *Exploratory Analysis of Spleen MRI Segmentation*

The primary objective of this study is to compare segmentation efficacy and prompting strategies within lung CT and X-ray datasets. This focus is motivated by the fact that CT and X-ray are among the most commonly used imaging modalities in radiological workflows. Additionally, it enables direct benchmarking against previously published studies, including our own prior work. Nevertheless, in this section, we briefly explore the applicability of SAM-based models to other imaging modalities and anatomical regions. This is not intended as an exhaustive evaluation across all modalities or organs but rather as a preliminary step to inform future research directions. In particular, we analyze the segmentation capabilities of SAM and SAM 2 on spleen MRI images.

For this exploratory analysis, we selected the clinical abdominal organ segmentation dataset AMOS [29], which comprises 500 CT and 100 MRI volumes. Each of these volumes includes multiple segmentation labels corresponding to various abdominal organs, such as the spleen. We chose the spleen as the segmentation target to assess the performance of an organ different from the lungs and MRI to evaluate the models on a modality distinct from the CT data used in the primary comparison. The spleen's relatively simple morphology and lack of pronounced concavities make it a suitable candidate for this exploratory segmentation task. To evaluate the segmentation performance of SAM and SAM 2 specifically on MRI data, we selected 14 volumes labeled as MRI. To ensure representativeness and reduce potential biases related to MRI acquisition devices, we further narrowed the selection to a subset of 8 volumes acquired using a Siemens Ingenia scanner.

Figure 15 shows an example of an MRI slice from the AMOS dataset, illustrating the spleen segmentation result produced by SAM 2.

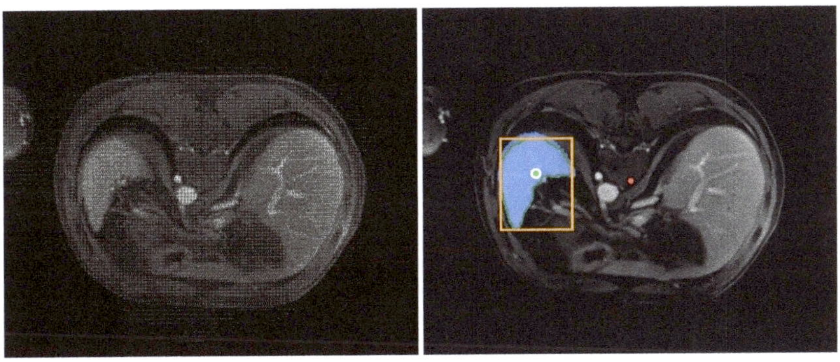

(**a**) MRI slice. (**b**) Prompt and spleen segmentation.

Figure 15. MRI prediction example.

The segmentation methodology follows the approach described previously in Sections 3.4 and 3.5. In this exploratory evaluation, we assessed four segmentation configurations. First, we applied SAM with individual prompts provided for every slice across the eight selected MRI volumes. Second, we evaluated SAM 2 using the same per-slice prompting strategy. Third, we tested a propagation-based approach with SAM 2, where segmentation was initialized using a single prompt on the central slice of each volume. Finally, we explored a variant of this propagation-based strategy in which the seed prompt was shared across all volumes, aiming to further reduce the prompting effort by using a single prompt for the entire dataset.

Figure 16 summarizes the MRI segmentation performance of SAM and SAM 2 on the AMOS dataset. On the one hand, the X-axis in Figure 16a compares the performance of SAM and SAM 2 in image processing mode using the Jaccard index and Dice score. On the other hand, Figure 16b compares the performance of SAM 2 in video processing mode, using either the middle slice of each volume as a seed prompt or a shared seed prompt for the entire dataset. For this subset of the dataset, which includes eight volumes and a total of 1633 slices, SAM requires 1633 prompts to achieve complete segmentation, whereas SAM 2 in video processing mode reduces this requirement to only 8 prompts, one per volume for the middle-slice seed and one for the entire dataset in the shared-seed configuration. The Y-axis displays the corresponding metric values, with each box representing the distribution per dataset and metric. Outliers are omitted for clarity. Solid horizontal green lines denote median values, dashed horizontal lines indicate mean values, and notches represent 95% confidence intervals. Horizontal reference lines correspond to state-of-the-art performance: the blue line indicates the Jaccard index (0.94) achieved by a multi-class, multi-modal nnU-Net on spleen MRI images [30], while the orange line marks the Dice score (0.977) achieved by the TransDiffSeg model when segmenting spleen MRI images [31]. It is worth noting that, while the Dice score benchmark is based on the AMOS dataset, the Jaccard index reference is drawn from a different one. Vertical dashed green lines indicate performance differences between model versions, and vertical dashed red lines highlight deviations from the state-of-the-art baselines.

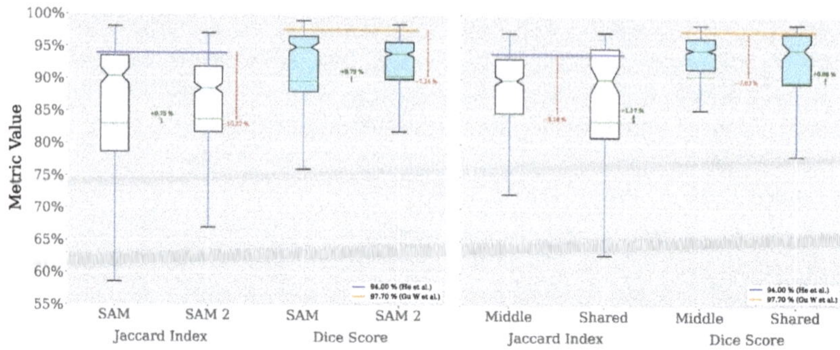

(**a**) SAM vs. SAM 2 image processing. (**b**) SAM 2 video processing shared seed.

Figure 16. Video results (He et al. [30], Gu W. et al. [31]).

In this exploratory evaluation on spleen MRI segmentation, the highest average performance was achieved using the video processing mode of SAM 2, where the middle slice of each volume was used as the seed frame. This configuration yielded a mean Dice score of 0.9067, representing a decline of 7.03% compared to the state-of-the-art Dice value of 0.977 reported by TransDiffSeg [31]. Similarly, the mean Jaccard index reached 0.8481, corresponding to a decline of 9.18% relative to the benchmark Jaccard index of 0.94 obtained by a multi-modal nnU-Net [30].

The same configuration used for lung segmentation was employed without modification, and no preprocessing was performed on the MRI volumes, as this analysis was intended to be exploratory. Because neither the prompt was tailored to MRI images nor any additional preprocessing was applied, the gap between the Dice and Jaccard scores obtained with this approach and those of the state-of-the-art increased from 3.27 and 5.39 percentage points, respectively, in the best-performing lung segmentation configuration to 7.03 and 9.19 in the best-performing spleen segmentation configuration. These findings suggest that the prompting strategy and segmentation approach proposed in this study can be effectively transferred to different imaging modalities and anatomical targets, delivering competitive results with minimal adaptation.

Despite these differences, the results are promising, especially considering that (1) the models were not fine-tuned for this specific task, (2) unlike the lung CT images, no preprocessing was applied to the MRI data, and (3) the prompting strategy was not adapted to the target organ or imaging modality. Nevertheless, although a comprehensive, modality-specific performance analysis of SAM 2 is beyond the scope of this work, this exploratory section offers initial insights into its applicability and effectiveness for SAM-based segmentation tasks beyond the lung CT and X-ray data analyzed in the primary comparative study.

5. Discussion

Medical image segmentation is critical in clinical applications, such as diagnosis and treatment planning. Ever since computers have been able to work in image processing, this task has been attempted to be automated. The application of artificial intelligence to this task has been a priority since its resurgence at the turn of the century [32]. Recent advances in deep learning have significantly improved the accuracy and efficiency of segmentation methods, particularly those that require minimal user input.

Deep learning-based interactive segmentation methods, such as those incorporating Convolutional Neural Network (CNN)s with user inputs like bounding boxes and scribbles like [33], have demonstrated increased accuracy and robustness, especially for previously unseen objects. Due to their zero-shot learning features, these methods require fewer user interactions and less time than traditional methods.

Techniques such as geodesic distance transforms and resolution-preserving networks further improve the accuracy of interactive segmentation by refining the initial automatic segmentations with minimal user intervention [34].

A deep learning-based interactive segmentation method that achieves accurate results with fewer user interactions is proposed in [35]. The authors claim their method consumes less time and generalizes well to previously unseen objects in medical images. In order to do so, they first encode user-provided interior margin points via a CNN to achieve a good initial segmentation result of both previously seen and unseen objects. Then, an information fusion method combines the initial segmentation with a few additional user clicks to refine the segmentation.

Knowledge distillation techniques have been employed to transfer knowledge from large, well-trained networks for medical image segmentation to smaller, lightweight networks. This approach maintains high segmentation accuracy while significantly reducing computational complexity and storage requirements. To cite just one example, [36] improved a lightweight network's segmentation capability by up to 32.6%.

The integration of SAM 2 into clinical workflows, particularly in radiotherapy, aligns with the increasing demand for efficiency and precision in oncology. Radiotherapy is a complex, multi-step process involving imaging acquisition, contouring of anatomical structures, treatment planning, delivery, and follow-up, requiring significant expertise and coordination among specialists [37]. In resource-constrained settings, many of these steps remain highly manual and time-consuming. SAM 2 could support the automation and standardization of critical stages such as segmentation and verification, thereby reducing clinicians' workload and enhancing treatment consistency. By accelerating processes like image acquisition and contouring, SAM 2 may also help minimize the time patients spend undergoing imaging procedures, thus reducing discomfort and limiting unnecessary exposure to ionizing radiation. This fits into a broader trend toward the adoption of AI-based tools [38], such as those developed in initiatives like Medical Open Network for AI (MONAI) [39] or Open Health Imaging Foundation Viewer (OHIF) [40], which are being successfully integrated into image-based workflows to improve diagnostic accuracy and therapeutic planning.

We aim to enable specialists to perform medical image segmentation with as little interaction as possible at the lowest possible cost. All the work mentioned in this section has one thing in common: the need for considerable resources to develop, reproduce, or use it. In order to develop deep learning networks, it is necessary to have a team of professionals dedicated exclusively to it, with access to first-rate data and computational resources. Fine-tuning an existing neural network is less demanding than creating one from scratch. However, it is still a process within the reach of a few.

For those who need these resources, the task of segmenting medical images becomes a slow and tedious process, requiring the intervention of a medical imaging specialist throughout the process. The proposal of this work is an evolution of our previous one [9]. The segmentation of each image was performed with a minimum number of prompts. Our current proposal provides a single prompt to segment all images from the same source with an accuracy close to that obtained by state-of-the-art models trained explicitly for this task. The specialist's task is reduced to monitoring the results to ensure the quality of the results, being able to devote more time to other, more critical tasks.

The results of using SAM 2 to segment an entire volume, or a whole dataset, of medical images using a single set of prompts and a reference frame that can then be propagated to the rest of the frames are very promising. Compared to SAM, SAM 2 yields very similar results in quality. In the case of the Coronacases dataset, the decrease in the quality of the results is minimal. In the case of the Radiopaedia dataset, the results improve. This difference in results is consistent with those obtained in the first experiment (see Table 1). The average results obtained with SAM 2 were better in both datasets. However, the improvement was more significant in the Radiopaedia dataset. The nature of the data is a key factor in the segmentation result if one wants to compare the results between SAM and SAM 2.

The video processing algorithm proposed in this work has similarities with the prompts selection algorithm presented in our previous work. Both proposals manage to improve the results of the medical image segmentation task without altering the essence of the segmentation, and they do so efficiently. In this case, if we ignore the segmentation task handled by SAM 2, the computational complexity of the proposed algorithm would be linear $O(n)$, where n is the number of images in the volume. Therefore, no significant computational burden is being added to the segmentation process.

The results shown in Figure 12 show that SAM 2 video segmentation results are similar to SAM image segmentation results. To achieve these results in our experiments, SAM needs one set of prompts for each slice (two positive, one negative, and a bounding box), while SAM 2 needs only a single set of these prompts for the whole volume. Each volume starts and ends with slices that have no corresponding mask, so the CT machine can capture the whole organ (e.g., the lungs) in the image.

When using SAM 2's prompt propagation features, its behavior in these start and end extremes of the volume is worse than SAM's. Notice how the metric minimum values are far lower with SAM 2 than with SAM in Table 6. Even though the model is not able to segment the frames closer to the extremes of the volumes, where the area to segment is smaller, SAM 2 is still able to segment the rest of the volume with a single set of prompts while maintaining very similar global results. In the Coronacases dataset, SAM 2 cannot propagate the prompt only in three slices of the whole dataset. As a consequence, it loses track of the object twice at the start and once at the end of a volume. In the Radiopaedia, it happens four times: twice at the start and twice at the end of the volume.

Although there exists a slight decline in the Coronacases dataset results, it is greatly compensated by the difference in the number of prompts needed to segment each volume. Using SAM would require 2156 prompts, one for each slice. However, SAM 2 would require only 10 prompts, one for each of the 10 volumes, as the model can propagate the seed frame segmentation through the whole volume. That is a 99.54% reduction in prompts needed to segment the volume. Moreover, when using a single seed prompt for the whole dataset, the number of prompts needed to segment the volume is reduced to one. That is a 99.95% reduction in prompts needed to segment the volume. In both instances, the results are very similar to those obtained using one prompt for each slice. These results justify the development of a system that allows radiology specialists to select a single representative frame of a given machine to segment the rest of the frames of the same machine. These results justify the development of a prototypical prompt library for medical image segmentation that allows radiology specialists to select a single representative frame of a given machine to segment the rest of the frames of the same machine.

5.1. Limitations

While this study compares SAM 2 and SAM's performance when segmenting medical images and introduces a novel approach to segmenting medical image volumes, several limitations should be acknowledged. Firstly, although the study primarily focused on a single medical image segmentation task, namely lung segmentation, we have included an exploratory analysis of spleen segmentation in MRI data. This preliminary evaluation provides valuable initial insights into the applicability of the proposed methods beyond the lung and across different imaging modalities. Although it does not constitute a comprehensive assessment, it demonstrates that the results of SAM 2 improve upon those of SAM. The generalizability of the findings to a broader range of organs and imaging modalities still needs to be thoroughly tested. Future work should explore applying the proposed methods to additional segmentation tasks to determine their broader applicability. Secondly, the study employed only one prompt configuration, consisting of a bounding box with two positive points and one negative point. This configuration was chosen for its simplicity and effectiveness in lung segmentation, as demonstrated in our previous work [9], and was retained unchanged in the exploratory spleen MRI analysis. However, the performance and adaptability of other prompt configurations were not explored, potentially limiting the method's robustness and flexibility in more complex segmentation scenarios. Finally, the datasets used in this study contained COVID-19 lesions, which introduces a degree of specificity to the results. COVID-19 lesions may introduce unique challenges or biases that do not occur in other lung pathologies. Future studies should validate the approach on a broader range of lung conditions to ensure its applicability across diverse clinical scenarios. These limitations suggest clear lines for future research to enhance the generalizability and robustness of the findings presented in this study.

5.2. *Requirements for Training Segmentation Models*

As noted in Section 1, training segmentation models for medical imaging demands substantial computational resources, specialized expertise, and significant financial investment. Recent studies have highlighted these challenges.

For instance, DMDF-Net [19], a dual multiscale dilated fusion network, was designed for segmenting COVID-19 lesions in lung CT scans. The model was trained on the MosMed [41] and COVID-19-CT-Seg [18] datasets (70 CT scans totaling 5569 images). Training was conducted over 15 epochs with a batch size of eight and a learning rate of 0.001, utilizing an NVIDIA GTX 1070 GPU. The total estimated project cost, covering dataset curation, model architecture design, model training and evaluation, and personnel expenses, including three engineers, amounted to EUR 61,500 over six months. This estimate is based on the average annual salary of a Machine Learning Engineer in Spain, approximately EUR 41,000 (https://www.glassdoor.es/Salaries/spain-machine-learning-engineer-salary-SRCH_IL.0,5_IN219_KO6,31.htm?countryRedirect=true, accessed on 12 March 2025).

Similarly, TransAttUnet [21], a multi-level attention-guided U-Net incorporating transformer-based mechanisms, was developed for medical image segmentation. The model was trained on 4255 images from the ISIC-2018 [42], JSRT [43], Montgomery [20], NIH [44], Clean-CC-CCII [45], Bowl [46], and GLaS [47] datasets. Training was conducted over 100 epochs with a batch size of four and a learning rate of 0.0001, utilizing an NVIDIA Titan XP GPU. Given that this project required a team of five engineers, the estimated cost amounted to EUR 102,500 over six months, using the same salary reference.

Another example is a Mask R-CNN-based approach [26] for lung CT segmentation, trained on a dataset of 1265 ground-truth images. The model was trained using an NVIDIA GTX 1050 Ti GPU. The total expenditure for this project amounted to 101,600 € over six months, underscoring the substantial costs associated with prolonged training and hyperparameter optimization. Assuming a team of four engineers, personnel costs alone would be approximately EUR 82,000, according to the previously cited salary benchmark.

Furthermore, DS-TransUNet [48], a Residual U-Net designed for medical image segmentation, was trained on the LUNA, VESSEL12 [49], and HUG-ILD [50] datasets (11,325 images). Training was conducted over 50 epochs with a batch size of eight and a learning rate of 0.0001, utilizing an NVIDIA GTX 1060 GPU. This project involved six engineers, resulting in an estimated personnel cost of EUR 123,000 over six months, following the salary estimate previously discussed.

Moreover, the time required to achieve functional results is considerable. Training and refining foundational models, such as SAM2, demands a large number of GPUs and extensive datasets to achieve optimal performance. For instance, MedSAM2, the SAM2 fine-tuned model for medical applications, utilized 64 NVIDIA A100 GPUs for distributed training [17]. This setup highlights the challenges in resource allocation and underscores the necessity of optimizing efficiency in segmentation models.

These studies highlight the substantial computational demands, dataset requirements, and financial commitments associated with training segmentation models. In contrast, our proposed approach leverages pretrained segmentation models alongside advanced prompting strategies, significantly reducing both computational and development costs. Rather than training complex architectures from scratch, we optimize segmentation tasks through efficient model adaptation, minimizing GPU utilization and eliminating the need for large-scale dataset curation. This strategy offers a cost-effective, scalable, and accessible alternative for medical image segmentation.

6. Conclusions

In this paper, we compared SAM 2 with SAM in medical image segmentation tasks. Regardless of our first impulses, new is not necessarily better. When deciding between SAM or SAM 2, consider precision, responsiveness, and computing resources. In particular, SAM 2 is the way to go if the best precision when segmenting medical images is required. It usually provides the same results as SAM but is better on average. In our tests, SAM 2 results get up to an average 1.76% improvement in the Jaccard index, a 1.49% improvement in the Dice Score, and a better standard deviation for both metrics, getting even closer to the state-of-the-art solutions than SAM does. However, SAM is still the best choice in a pipeline where responsiveness is critical. After processing the image to get its embeddings, SAM can predict a mask in around 61 ms. In comparison, SAM 2 takes around 588 ms to perform the same task, which is approximately ten times slower. The threshold for users to feel that the system reacts instantaneously to their actions is 100 ms [51]. SAM is below this threshold, while SAM 2 is above it. If computing resources are scarce, SAM 2 is the best choice. The best SAM 2 model is smaller than the best SAM model. At the same time, the computing time for a single prediction is faster on average.

Furthermore, we presented a new medical image segmentation technique that uses a single seed prompt to segment a whole volume, further reducing the number of prompts needed to perform the task in 99.54% of the Coronacases dataset. The results are very close to the ones obtained when using one prompt for each slice, with practically no difference in the metrics used to measure the differences. Besides, we have also shown that the model is able to segment all the volumes in a dataset using a single, representative seed prompt taken from one of the volumes. In this case, the reduction in the number of prompts needed to segment the volume is 99.95% in the Coronacases dataset. This new technique could be used to virtually reduce the number of prompts needed to segment a volume up to 100%, allowing us to choose a representative seed prompt for images with similar characteristics, thus achieving infinite segmentation results with a single prompt.

In future work, given the results obtained in this paper, we plan to test our segmentation technique in a case study in a hospital, integrating it into a segmentation tool. It would be interesting to study whether we can automate the creation of the artificial seed iteratively while the machine is working. Moreover, as part of this clinical implementation, future research will involve evaluating how the segmentation results influence clinical decision-making and patient outcomes. This will include potential collaborations with radiology experts to gain deeper insights into the practical utility of the developed techniques, thus ensuring that the segmentation tool can be effectively integrated into real-world medical workflows. These steps are crucial in translating the technical advancements of SAM 2 into practical solutions that improve clinical practices and patient care.

We will also test the technique in other medical image segmentation tasks, such as tumor segmentation, to see if the results are similar. The results obtained in this paper suggest that SAM 2 can recognize objects in images, even if they are rudimentary, and transfer that knowledge to other images. What are the characteristics of the images that allow the model to do this? How far can we refine these seed frames to make them more representative of the whole volume? Data augmentation techniques could be used to generalize the seed prompt to meet certain desirable characteristics. We have also evaluated our approach to medical imaging modalities beyond CT and X-rays, such as MRI, with promising results. Extending this evaluation to other common modalities, such as Ultrasound Sonography (USG), would further test the robustness of our method. Moreover, given the growing importance of Hyperspectral Imaging (HSI) in medical diagnostics [52], we plan to include this modality in our future benchmarking efforts. Lastly, it is essential to consider the extent to which our improvements can enhance SAM 2 results. The existence of a potential ceiling value beyond which further improvements may be unreachable could be examined. This limit would likely be influenced by various factors that require thorough investigation.

Author Contributions: All authors contributed equally to the conception, design, implementation, and writing of this paper. All authors have read and agreed to the published version of the manuscript.

Funding: This work was supported by Grant CPP2021-008491 funded by MICIU/AEI/10.13039/501100011033 and by the European Union NextGeneration EU/PRTR.

Data Availability Statement: The source code used to reproduce the analyses and results in this paper is available at https://github.com/i3uex/prompt_once_segment_everything_code (accessed on 10 April 2025).

Conflicts of Interest: The authors declare that they have no known competing financial interests or personal relationships that could have appeared to influence the work reported in this paper.

References

1. Szeliski, R. *Computer Vision: Algorithms and Applications*; Springer Nature: Berlin/Heidelberg, Germany, 2022.
2. Nieto-del-Amor, F.; Ye-Lin, Y.; Monfort-Ortiz, R.; Diago-Almela, V.J.; Modrego-Pardo, F.; Martinez-de-Juan, J.L.; Hao, D.; Prats-Boluda, G. Automatic Semantic Segmentation of EHG Recordings by Deep Learning: An Approach to a Screening Tool for Use in Clinical Practice. *Comput. Methods Programs Biomed.* **2024**, *254*, 108317. [CrossRef]
3. Wang, G.; Luo, X.; Gu, R.; Yang, S.; Qu, Y.; Zhai, S.; Zhao, Q.; Li, K.; Zhang, S. PyMIC: A Deep Learning Toolkit for Annotation-Efficient Medical Image Segmentation. *Comput. Methods Programs Biomed.* **2023**, *231*, 107398. [CrossRef]
4. Mikhailov, I.; Chauveau, B.; Bourdel, N.; Bartoli, A. A Deep Learning-Based Interactive Medical Image Segmentation Framework with Sequential Memory. *Comput. Methods Programs Biomed.* **2024**, *245*, 108038. [CrossRef]
5. Klemetti, A.; Raatikainen, M.; Myllyaho, L.; Mikkonen, T.; Nurminen, J.K. Systematic Literature Review on Cost-Efficient Deep Learning. *IEEE Access* **2023**, *11*, 90158–90180. [CrossRef]
6. Sandoval Serrano, D.R.; Rincón, J.C.; Mejía-Restrepo, J.; Núñez-Valdez, E.R.; García-Díaz, V. Forecast of Medical Costs in Health Companies Using Models Based on Advanced Analytics. *Algorithms* **2022**, *15*, 106. [CrossRef]
7. Kirillov, A.; Mintun, E.; Ravi, N.; Mao, H.; Rolland, C.; Gustafson, L.; Xiao, T.; Whitehead, S.; Berg, A.C.; Lo, W.Y.; et al. Segment Anything. *arXiv* **2023**, arXiv:2304.02643 . [CrossRef]
8. Ravi, N.; Gabeur, V.; Hu, Y.T.; Hu, R.; Ryali, C.; Ma, T.; Khedr, H.; Rädle, R.; Rolland, C.; Gustafson, L.; et al. SAM 2: Segment Anything in Images and Videos. *arXiv* **2024**, arXiv:2408.00714.

9. Gutiérrez, J.D.; Rodriguez-Echeverria, R.; Delgado, E.; Rodrigo, M.Á.S.; Sanchez-Figueroa, F. No More Training: SAM's Zero-Shot Transfer Capabilities for Cost-Efficient Medical Image Segmentation. *IEEE Access* **2024**, *12*, 24205–24216. [CrossRef]
10. Ma, J.; Wang, B. Segment Anything in Medical Images. *arXiv* **2023**, arXiv:2304.12306. [CrossRef]
11. Wu, J.; Ji, W.; Liu, Y.; Fu, H.; Xu, M.; Xu, Y.; Jin, Y. Medical SAM Adapter: Adapting Segment Anything Model for Medical Image Segmentation. *arXiv* **2023**, arXiv:2304.12620. http://arxiv.org/abs/2304.12620. [CrossRef]
12. Zhang, Y.; Shen, Z.; Jiao, R. Segment Anything Model for Medical Image Segmentation: Current Applications and Future Directions. *Comput. Biol. Med.* **2024**, *171*, 108238. [CrossRef]
13. Chang, M.W.; Ratinov, L.; Roth, D.; Srikumar, V. Importance of Semantic Representation: Dataless Classification. In Proceedings of the AAAI, AAAI'08, Chicago, IL, USA, 13–17 July 2008; Volume 2, pp. 830–835.
14. Wu, J.; Xu, M. One-Prompt to Segment All Medical Images. In Proceedings of the IEEE/CVF Conference on Computer Vision and Pattern Recognition (CVPR), Seattle, WA, USA, 17–21 June 2024.
15. Kulyabin, M.; Zhdanov, A.; Pershin, A.; Sokolov, G.; Nikiforova, A.; Ronkin, M.; Borisov, V.; Maier, A. Segment Anything in Optical Coherence Tomography: SAM 2 for Volumetric Segmentation of Retinal Biomarkers. *Bioengineering* **2024**, *11*, 940. [CrossRef] [PubMed]
16. Kong, L.; Huang, M.; Zhang, L.; Chan, L.W.C. Enhancing Diagnostic Images to Improve the Performance of the Segment Anything Model in Medical Image Segmentation. *Bioengineering* **2024**, *11*, 270. [CrossRef] [PubMed]
17. Zhu, J.; Qi, Y.; Wu, J. Medical SAM 2: Segment Medical Images as Video via Segment Anything Model 2. *arXiv* **2024**, arXiv:2408.00874. . [CrossRef]
18. Jun, M.; Cheng, G.; Yixin, W.; Xingle, A.; Jiantao, G.; Ziqi, Y.; Minqing, Z.; Xin, L.; Xueyuan, D.; Shucheng, C.; et al. *COVID-19 CT Lung and Infection Segmentation Dataset*; Zenodo: Genève, Switzerland, 2020. [CrossRef]
19. Owais, M.; Baek, N.R.; Park, K.R. DMDF-Net: Dual Multiscale Dilated Fusion Network for Accurate Segmentation of Lesions Related to COVID-19 in Lung Radiographic Scans. *Expert Syst. Appl.* **2022**, *202*, 117360. [CrossRef]
20. Jaeger, S.; Candemir, S.; Antani, S.; Wáng, Y.X.J.; Lu, P.X.; Thoma, G. Two Public Chest X-ray Datasets for Computer-Aided Screening of Pulmonary Diseases. *Quant. Imaging Med. Surg.* **2014**, *4*, 475. [CrossRef]
21. Chen, B.; Liu, Y.; Zhang, Z.; Lu, G.; Kong, A.W.K. TransAttUnet: Multi-level Attention-guided U-Net with Transformer for Medical Image Segmentation. *arXiv* **2022**, arXiv:2107.05274. [CrossRef]
22. Cohen, J.P.; Morrison, P.; Dao, L. COVID-19 Image Data Collection. *arXiv* **2020**, arXiv:2003.11597. [CrossRef]
23. Dance, D.R.; Christofides, S.; Maidment, A.D.A.; McLean, I.D.; Ng, K.H. *Diagnostic Radiology Physics*; Non-Serial Publications; International Atomic Energy Agency: Vienna, Austria, 2014.
24. Tidwell, A.S. Advanced Imaging Concepts: A Pictorial Glossary of CT and MRI Technology. *Clin. Tech. Small Anim. Pract.* **1999**, *14*, 65–111. [CrossRef]
25. Müller, D.; Soto-Rey, I.; Kramer, F. Towards a Guideline for Evaluation Metrics in Medical Image Segmentation. *BMC Res. Notes* **2022**, *15*, 210. [CrossRef]
26. Hu, Q.; De F. Souza, L.F.; Holanda, G.B.; Alves, S.S.; Dos S. Silva, F.H.; Han, T.; Rebouças Filho, P.P. An Effective Approach for CT Lung Segmentation Using Mask Region-Based Convolutional Neural Networks. *Artif. Intell. Med.* **2020**, *103*, 101792. [CrossRef]
27. Huang, Y.; Yang, X.; Liu, L.; Zhou, H.; Chang, A.; Zhou, X.; Chen, R.; Yu, J.; Chen, J.; Chen, C.; et al. Segment Anything Model for Medical Images? *Med. Image Anal.* **2024**, *92*, 103061. [CrossRef] [PubMed]
28. Ma, J.; Wang, Y.; An, X.; Ge, C.; Yu, Z.; Chen, J.; Zhu, Q.; Dong, G.; He, J.; He, Z.; et al. Toward Data-efficient Learning: A Benchmark for COVID-19 CT Lung and Infection Segmentation. *Med. Phys.* **2021**, *48*, 1197–1210. [CrossRef]
29. Ji, Y.; Bai, H.; Ge, C.; Yang, J.; Zhu, Y.; Zhang, R.; Li, Z.; Zhanng, L.; Ma, W.; Wan, X.; et al. Amos: A Large-Scale Abdominal Multi-Organ Benchmark for Versatile Medical Image Segmentation. *Adv. Neural Inf. Process. Syst.* **2022**, *35*, 36722–36732. [CrossRef]
30. He, X.; Hu, Z.; Dev, H.; Romano, D.J.; Sharbatdaran, A.; Raza, S.I.; Wang, S.J.; Teichman, K.; Shih, G.; Chevalier, J.M.; et al. Test Retest Reproducibility of Organ Volume Measurements in ADPKD Using 3D Multimodality Deep Learning. *Acad. Radiol.* **2024**, *31*, 889–899. [CrossRef]
31. Gu, W.; Zhang, G.; Ju, R.; Wang, S.; Li, Y.; Liang, T.; Guo, W.; Gong, Z. TransDiffSeg: Transformer-Based Conditional Diffusion Segmentation Model for Abdominal Multi-Objective. *J. Imaging Inform. Med.* **2024**, *38*, 262–280. [CrossRef]
32. Pham, D.; Xu, C.; Prince, J.L. Current Methods in Medical Image Segmentation. *Annu. Rev. Biomed. Eng.* **2000**, *2*, 315–337. [CrossRef]
33. Wang, G.; Li, W.; Zuluaga, M.A.; Pratt, R.; Patel, P.; Aertsen, M.; Doel, T.; David, A.; Deprest, J.; Ourselin, S.; et al. Interactive Medical Image Segmentation Using Deep Learning with Image-Specific Fine Tuning. *IEEE Trans. Med. Imaging* **2017**, *37*, 1562–1573. [CrossRef] [PubMed]
34. Wang, G.; Zuluaga, M.A.; Li, W.; Pratt, R.; Patel, P.; Aertsen, M.; Doel, T.; David, A.; Deprest, J.; Ourselin, S.; et al. DeepIGeoS: A Deep Interactive Geodesic Framework for Medical Image Segmentation. *IEEE Trans. Pattern Anal. Mach. Intell.* **2017**, *41*, 1559–1572. [CrossRef]

35. Luo, X.; Wang, G.; Song, T.; Zhang, J.; Aertsen, M.; Deprest, J.; Ourselin, S.; Vercauteren, T.K.M.; Zhang, S. MIDeepSeg: Minimally Interactive Segmentation of Unseen Objects from Medical Images Using Deep Learning. *Med. Image Anal.* **2021**, *72*, 102102. [CrossRef]
36. Qin, D.; Bu, J.; Liu, Z.; Shen, X.; Zhou, S.; Gu, J.J.; Wang, Z.; Wu, L.; Dai, H.F. Efficient Medical Image Segmentation Based on Knowledge Distillation. *IEEE Trans. Med. Imaging* **2021**, *40*, 3820–3831. [CrossRef]
37. Gupta, V.; Erdal, B.; Ramirez, C.; Floca, R.; Genereaux, B.; Bryson, S.; Bridge, C.; Kleesiek, J.; Nensa, F.; Braren, R.; et al. Current State of Community-Driven Radiological AI Deployment in Medical Imaging. *JMIR AI* **2024**, *3*, e55833. [CrossRef] [PubMed]
38. Vandewinckele, L.; Claessens, M.; Dinkla, A.; Brouwer, C.; Crijns, W.; Verellen, D.; Van Elmpt, W. Overview of Artificial Intelligence-Based Applications in Radiotherapy: Recommendations for Implementation and Quality Assurance. *Radiother. Oncol.* **2020**, *153*, 55–66. [CrossRef] [PubMed]
39. MONAI Consortium. *MONAI: Medical Open Network for AI*; Zenodo: Genève, Switzerland, 2024. [CrossRef]
40. Ziegler, E.; Urban, T.; Brown, D.; Petts, J.; Pieper, S.D.; Lewis, R.; Hafey, C.; Harris, G.J. Open Health Imaging Foundation Viewer: An Extensible Open-Source Framework for Building Web-Based Imaging Applications to Support Cancer Research. *JCO Clin. Cancer Inform.* **2020**, *4*, 336–345. [CrossRef]
41. Morozov, S.; Andreychenko, A.; Pavlov, N.; Vladzymyrskyy, A.; Ledikhova, N.; Gombolevskiy, V.; Blokhin, I.; Gelezhe, P.; Gonchar, A.; Chernina, V.Y. MosMedData: Chest CT Scans with COVID-19 Related Findings Dataset. *arXiv* **2020**, arXiv:2005.06465. [CrossRef]
42. Codella, N.; Rotemberg, V.; Tschandl, P.; Celebi, M.E.; Dusza, S.; Gutman, D.; Helba, B.; Kalloo, A.; Liopyris, K.; Marchetti, M.; et al. Skin Lesion Analysis Toward Melanoma Detection 2018: A Challenge Hosted by the International Skin Imaging Collaboration (ISIC). *arXiv* **2019**, arXiv:cs/1902.03368. . [CrossRef]
43. Shiraishi, J.; Katsuragawa, S.; Ikezoe, J.; Matsumoto, T.; Kobayashi, T.; Komatsu, K.i.; Matsui, M.; Fujita, H.; Kodera, Y.; Doi, K. Development of a Digital Image Database for Chest Radiographs With and Without a Lung Nodule: Receiver Operating Characteristic Analysis of Radiologists' Detection of Pulmonary Nodules. *Am. J. Roentgenol.* **2000**, *174*, 71–74. [CrossRef]
44. Tang, Y.B.; Tang, Y.X.; Xiao, J.; Summers, R.M. XLSor: A Robust and Accurate Lung Segmentor on Chest X-Rays Using Criss-Cross Attention and Customized Radiorealistic Abnormalities Generation. In Proceedings of the 2nd International Conference on Medical Imaging with Deep Learning. PMLR, London, UK, 8–10 July 2019; pp. 457–467.
45. He, X.; Wang, S.; Chu, X.; Shi, S.; Tang, J.; Liu, X.; Yan, C.; Zhang, J.; Ding, G. Automated Model Design and Benchmarking of Deep Learning Models for COVID-19 Detection with Chest CT Scans. *Proc. AAAI Conf. Artif. Intell.* **2021**, *35*, 4821–4829. [CrossRef]
46. Caicedo, J.C.; Goodman, A.; Karhohs, K.W.; Cimini, B.A.; Ackerman, J.; Haghighi, M.; Heng, C.; Becker, T.; Doan, M.; McQuin, C.; et al. Nucleus Segmentation across Imaging Experiments: The 2018 Data Science Bowl. *Nat. Methods* **2019**, *16*, 1247–1253. [CrossRef]
47. Malík, P.; Knapová, K.; Krištofík, Š. Instance Segmentation Model Created from Three Semantic Segmentations of Mask, Boundary and Centroid Pixels Verified on GlaS Dataset. In Proceedings of the 2020 Federated Conference on Computer Science and Information Systems, Sofia, Bulgaria, 6–9 September 2020, pp. 569–576. [CrossRef]
48. Khanna, A.; Londhe, N.D.; Gupta, S.; Semwal, A. A Deep Residual U-Net Convolutional Neural Network for Automated Lung Segmentation in Computed Tomography Images. *Biocybern. Biomed. Eng.* **2020**, *40*, 1314–1327. [CrossRef]
49. Rudyanto, R.D.; Kerkstra, S.; van Rikxoort, E.M.; Fetita, C.; Brillet, P.Y.; Lefevre, C.; Xue, W.; Zhu, X.; Liang, J.; Öksüz, İ.; et al. Comparing Algorithms for Automated Vessel Segmentation in Computed Tomography Scans of the Lung: The VESSEL12 Study. *Med. Image Anal.* **2014**, *18*, 1217–1232. [CrossRef]
50. Depeursinge, A.; Vargas, A.; Platon, A.; Geissbuhler, A.; Poletti, P.A.; Müller, H. Building a Reference Multimedia Database for Interstitial Lung Diseases. *Comput. Med. Imaging Graph.* **2012**, *36*, 227–238. [CrossRef] [PubMed]
51. Nielsen, J. Chapter 5: Usability Heuristics. In *Usability Engineering*; Morgan Kaufmann: Burlington, MA, USA, 1994; pp. 115–164.
52. Lai, C.L.; Karmakar, R.; Mukundan, A.; Natarajan, R.K.; Lu, S.C.; Wang, C.Y.; Wang, H.C. Advancing Hyperspectral Imaging and Machine Learning Tools toward Clinical Adoption in Tissue Diagnostics: A Comprehensive Review. *APL Bioeng.* **2024**, *8*, 041504. [CrossRef]

algorithms

MDPI

Article

AI Under Attack: Metric-Driven Analysis of Cybersecurity Threats in Deep Learning Models for Healthcare Applications

Sarfraz Brohi * and Qurat-ul-ain Mastoi

School of Computing and Creative Technologies, University of the West of England, Bristol BS16 1QY, UK; qurat-ul-ain.mastoi@uwe.ac.uk

* Correspondence: sarfraz.brohi@uwe.ac.uk

Abstract: Incorporating Artificial Intelligence (AI) in healthcare has transformed disease diagnosis and treatment by offering unprecedented benefits. However, it has also revealed critical cybersecurity vulnerabilities in Deep Learning (DL) models, which raise significant risks to patient safety and their trust in AI-driven applications. Existing studies primarily focus on theoretical vulnerabilities or specific attack types, leaving a gap in understanding the practical implications of multiple attack scenarios on healthcare AI. In this paper, we provide a comprehensive analysis of key attack vectors, including adversarial attacks, such as the gradient-based Fast Gradient Sign Method (FGSM), evasion attacks (perturbation-based), and data poisoning, which threaten the reliability of DL models, with a specific focus on breast cancer detection. We propose the Healthcare AI Vulnerability Assessment Algorithm (HAVA) that systematically simulates these attacks, calculates the Post-Attack Vulnerability Index (PAVI), and quantitatively evaluates their impacts. Our findings revealed that the adversarial FGSM and evasion attacks significantly reduced model accuracy from 97.36% to 61.40% (PAVI: 0.385965) and 62.28% (PAVI: 0.377193), respectively, demonstrating their severe impact on performance, but data poisoning had a milder effect, retaining 89.47% accuracy (PAVI: 0.105263). The confusion matrices also revealed a higher rate of false positives in the adversarial FGSM and evasion attacks than more balanced misclassification patterns observed in data poisoning. By proposing a unified framework for quantifying and analyzing these post-attack vulnerabilities, this research contributes to formulating resilient AI models for critical domains where accuracy and reliability are important.

Keywords: healthcare AI; Deep Learning (DL); vulnerable AI; breast cancer detection; adversarial attacks; Post-Attack Vulnerability Index (PAVI); mitigation workflow

1. Introduction

Artificial intelligence (AI) has revolutionized various industries, and healthcare has emerged as one of the most transformative fields for its application. AI-powered systems are widely used for disease diagnosis, process automation, and supporting clinical decision-making [1–4]. Deep learning (DL), which is considered a subset of AI, has demonstrated exceptional efficacy in medical imaging tasks by enabling the precise classification and diagnosis of diseases such as breast cancer. DL models have been proven instrumental in analyzing digitized images of Fine-Needle Aspiration (FNA) biopsies and can be applied to perceive valuable insights that enhance clinical decision-making and patient outcomes [5,6].

Despite their potential, DL models in healthcare are not resilient against cybersecurity threats. Adversarial, data poisoning, and adversarial evasion attacks pose severe risks to the reliability of AI systems and patient safety. Adversarial attacks introduce subtle imperceptible perturbations in the input data to mislead the models into making incorrect predictions [7,8]. A variation of the adversarial attack, called the evasion attack, targets the model during inference by introducing perturbations that bypass detection thresholds without altering the model's structure or training data. Data poisoning attacks alter training datasets by injecting malicious samples to compromise a model's learning process and degrade its performance [9,10]. In healthcare, such attacks pose severe risks because misclassifications or tampering with diagnoses can result in delayed treatments, unnecessary procedures, or even harm to the patient [11–13]. For example, an adversarial attack on breast cancer detection systems can misclassify malignant cells as benign, delaying life-saving treatments.

Recent efforts have focused on developing novel frameworks to enhance the resilience of DL models. Studies have highlighted using federated learning to mitigate data poisoning by decentralizing model training to reduce the risk of malicious data corruption [14]. Integrating adversarially robust training algorithms has been proposed to improve the model's reliability against gradient-based attacks such as the Fast Gradient Sign Method (FGSM) [15]. Explainable AI techniques have also gained attention in identifying threats by elucidating decision pathways in complex DL models, enabling researchers to pinpoint areas vulnerable to exploitation [16].

In this research, we propose the Healthcare AI Vulnerability Assessment Algorithm (HAVA), which integrates multiple features, simulates multiple attacks and computes performance metrics and the Post-Attack Vulnerability Index (PAVI) for attack analysis and mitigation assistance. By contextualizing the severity of performance degradation, HAVA provides a link between identifying theoretical vulnerabilities and implementing real-world defenses. Through this research, we have produced the following key contributions:

1. Comprehensive analysis of FGSM, data poisoning and evasion attacks to offer a holistic view of the cybersecurity threats faced by DL models in healthcare.
2. Introduction of the PAVI as a core feature of the HAVA to standardize quantification and comparison of DL model vulnerabilities across different attack scenarios.
3. Empirical evaluation of the impact of these attacks on a DL model trained with the Wisconsin Diagnostic Breast Cancer (WDBC) dataset to provide actionable insights into the model vulnerabilities.
4. Provision of actionable recommendations and customized defense strategies based on visualizations and comparative analyses generated by the HAVA, focusing on improving the reliability of AI applications in healthcare.

This paper is organized as follows. Section 2 reviews related works and identifies gaps in the existing research. Section 3 outlines the research materials and methods containing the dataset description, preprocessing, and mathematical representation of the classification model and attacks. Section 4 provides and explains the HAVA. Section 5 presents our experimental results and discussion of post-attack analysis, mitigation workflow, contextualizing vulnerability, and guiding actionable insights. Section 6 concludes this research with a brief and critical discussion of the findings.

2. Related Works

The vulnerability of DL models to cybersecurity threats has been a critical area of research, particularly in high-stakes domains such as healthcare. Szegedy et al. [17] demonstrated the weakness of DL models against adversarial attacks, where imperceptible perturbations lead to incorrect predictions. Goodfellow et al. [18] introduced the FGSM. They provided an efficient approach for generating adversarial examples and highlighting the fragility of DL models to gradient-based attacks.

Finlayson et al. [13] demonstrated how adversarial attacks misclassify malignant tumors as benign. Such incidents can delay life-saving treatments. Sorin et al. [19] identified the risks of adversarial attacks in radiology and emphasized the need for domain-specific defenses in healthcare applications. Albattah and Rassam [20] highlighted the vulnerability of Convolutional Long Short-Term Memory (ConvLSTM) models to adversarial attacks. Yang et al. [21] explored adversarial attacks on Large Language Models (LLMs) in medical applications. Newaz et al. [22] demonstrated how attacks could disrupt system functionality and lead to erroneous medical decisions.

Data poisoning represents another significant threat. Malicious samples introduced into the training dataset can compromise the model's integrity through this attack. Aljanahi et al. [23] highlighted the potential for data poisoning to inject biases, thus reducing the model's reliability and jeopardizing patient outcomes. Verde et al. [24] showed that even minimal poisoning levels can destabilize machine learning models. They stressed advanced anomaly detection methods to safeguard critical systems. Evasion attacks that can exploit model decision thresholds to bypass detection have also gained attention. Muthalagu et al. [10] investigated the vulnerabilities of DL models to such attacks and proposed adaptive defense mechanisms that leverage real-time model monitoring. These findings demonstrate the dynamic nature of evasion attacks and their challenges to static defense strategies.

Several defense mechanisms have been developed to mitigate these threats. Adversarial training has emerged as a prominent technique to enhance robustness by incorporating adversarial examples into the training process [18]. Noise-filtering and feature-smoothing approaches have also been explored to counter adversarial and evasion attacks [25]. Hong et al. [26] proposed applying differentially private learning to adjust model training to dynamically reduce poisoned data's impact. However, these approaches often face trade-offs between computational efficiency and model resilience that limit their practical applicability in resource-constrained healthcare settings.

Despite the emerging research and developments, there are critical gaps in this area of research. To the best of our knowledge, and based on extensive research in AI security, there is a significant lack of studies focused on vulnerability assessments in DL models for healthcare using post-attack analysis. While studies such as Atmane and Ahmad [27] and Zou et al. [28] have explored adversarial threats and vulnerabilities in AI systems, these works do not provide a quantifiable approach to evaluating the vulnerabilities of DL models. Consequently, the existing literature highlights a gap our research seeks to address.

By introducing a novel framework for post-attack analysis and quantifying vulnerabilities through the PAVI, the HAVA offers a unique and systematic approach to this critical area of research. The current research lacks a unified framework for evaluating multiple attack vectors and their collective impact on DL models. Additionally, traditional evaluation metrics, such as accuracy and confusion matrices, fail to contextualize the relative severity of attacks. Due to this, it has become difficult to prioritize defenses effectively. To address these gaps, we designed and implemented the HAVA. Unlike previous approaches, the HAVA integrates attack simulations, performance metrics, and the PAVI to provide a comprehensive and quantitative evaluation framework. By applying the HAVA to breast cancer detection, this research integrates theoretical vulnerability analysis with pragmatic approaches to enable the development of more resilient AI-driven healthcare applications.

3. Materials and Methods

This study utilized the WDBC dataset retrieved from the UCI Machine Learning Repository [29,30]. The dataset contains 569 observations with 30 numerical features derived from digitized images of Fine-Needle Aspiration biopsies. These features include the standard error, mean, and worst values of attributes such as texture, radius, and perimeter. This dataset was chosen for its widespread use in evaluating AI-based diagnostic systems, balanced representation of benign and malignant cases, and relevance to healthcare applications. Feature selection was performed using the Scikit-learn library in Python. Initially, 15 key features were identified using the univariate selection method. Further refinement was performed, where we evaluated all the features and retained only those selected by at least two methods from Logistic Regression, Best-First Search, and Random Forest. This resulted in the final 14 most relevant features, as shown in Table 1.

We performed data preprocessing by scaling all the features to a range of 0 to 1, using a StandardScaler to ensure consistency. The dataset was divided into training (80%) and testing (20%) subsets to preserve the class distribution. We carried out the experiments using Python 3.12.3 alongside several libraries to handle data preprocessing, model building, and evaluation. We used TensorFlow.keras from TensorFlow 2.17.0 and Scikit-learn 1.5.0 to develop and train the DL models for tasks like data splitting, scaling, and implementing the MLP classifier. Data manipulation was performed using NumPy 1.26.4 and Pandas 2.2.2, and visualisations were created with Matplotlib 3.9.1 and Seaborn 0.13.2. The WDBC dataset was obtained using the ucimlrepo library.

Table 1. Selected features using univariate and multi-method selection techniques.

No.	Univariate Selection	Multi-Method Selection
1	radius mean	concave points worst
2	compactness worst	texture mean
3	radius worst	perimeter mean
4	texture mean	concavity worst
5	perimeter mean	concavity mean
6	area se	perimeter worst
7	area worst	area se
8	perimeter se	texture worst
9	texture worst	radius worst
10	perimeter worst	concave points mean
11	concavity worst	area worst
12	concave points worst	smoothness worst
13	concavity mean	area mean
14	area mean	radius mean
15	radius se	

All our experiments were executed on a system powered by an Intel(R) Core(TM) i7-10850H CPU running at 2.70 GHz, with 32 GB of RAM and an NVIDIA GeForce RTX 2070 GPU featuring 8 GB of dedicated memory. The system operated on Windows 11 Education (64-bit). This hardware setup ensured sufficient computational resources for training the models and efficiently running adversarial attack simulations. For a better understanding of our research, we have provided a list of the important symbols used in this research with their descriptions, in Table 2:

Table 2. List of symbols used in the manuscript.

Symbol	Meaning
$Z^{(l)}$	Weighted input to the l-th layer of the neural network.
$a^{(l)}$	Activation output of the l-th layer of the neural network.
$W^{(l)}$	Weight matrix for the l-th layer of the neural network.
$b^{(l)}$	Bias vector for the l-th layer of the neural network.

Table 2. *Cont.*

Symbol	Meaning
f	Activation function (e.g., ReLU, Logistic, Tanh) applied to compute the layer output.
y	True label of the input sample.
$\hat{y}$	Predicted probability of the input sample.
$J(\theta)$	Cross-entropy loss function for optimizing the model parameters.
x_{adv}	Adversarial example generated using the FGSM method.
x	Original input data.
ϵ	Magnitude of the perturbation applied in FGSM attack.
$\nabla_x J$	Gradient of the loss function with respect to the input x.
$N(0, \sigma^2)$	Gaussian noise with mean 0 and variance σ^2, used in evasion attacks.
$PAVI$	Post-Attack Vulnerability Index; quantifies the relative degradation in model performance.

3.1. The Classification Model

A Multi-Layer Perceptron (MLP) was employed as the classification model. The MLP was chosen for its ability to model complex and non-linear relationships. An MLP is ideal for highly precise tasks such as breast cancer classification. The MLP consisted of multiple layers. Each layer performed the following operations:

$$z^{(l)} = W^{(l)} a^{(l-1)} + b^{(l)} \tag{1}$$

$$a^{(l)} = f(z^{(l)}) \tag{2}$$

where $W^{(l)}$ represents the weights, $b^{(l)}$ the biases and f the activation function. We applied ReLU [31], Logistic and Tanh activation functions for the hidden layers. The output layer used the sigmoid function, which produced a probability score for binary classification:

$$\hat{y} = \sigma(z) = \frac{1}{1 + e^{-z}} \tag{3}$$

The model's parameters were optimized using the cross-entropy loss function:

$$J(\theta) = -\frac{1}{m} \sum_{i=1}^{m} \left[y^{(i)} \log \hat{y}^{(i)} + (1 - y^{(i)}) \log(1 - \hat{y}^{(i)}) \right] \tag{4}$$

where $y^{(i)}$ is the true label, $\hat{y}^{(i)}$ is the predicted probability and m is the number of samples.

3.2. Simulated Attacks

We simulated three cybersecurity attacks: adversarial FGSM, data poisoning, and adversarial evasion. Each attack type exploited distinct model vulnerabilities to reflect real-world threats to healthcare applications.

3.2.1. Adversarial Fast Gradient Sign Method (FGSM) Attack

Adversarial examples were generated using the FGSM [18]. Perturbations were crafted to exploit the gradient of the loss function:

$$x_{\text{adv}} = x + \epsilon \cdot \text{sign}(\nabla_x J(x, y)) \tag{5}$$

where x is the input data, ϵ is the perturbation magnitude, $J(x, y)$ is the cross-entropy loss function and $\nabla_x J$ represents its gradient with respect to x. This method highlighted the model's sensitivity to minor but carefully crafted input changes that could lead to significant misclassifications.

3.2.2. Data Poisoning Attack

Data poisoning involves injecting mislabeled or corrupted samples into the training set to degrade model performance. In this study, $\alpha\%$, i.e., 10% of training labels were randomly flipped by following the approach of Biggio et al. [32]. This process is defined as:

$$D_{\text{poison}} = \{(x_i, \hat{y}_i) \mid \hat{y}_i = 1 - y_i \text{ for } i \in \mathcal{P}, \hat{y}_i = y_i \text{ otherwise}\} \tag{6}$$

where D_{poison} is the poisoned dataset, y_i is the original label for sample x_i, and $\mathcal{P}$ represents the subset of indices selected for poisoning. This attack compromised the model's generalisation ability by introducing contradictory patterns into the training data.

3.2.3. Adversarial Evasion Attack

The adversarial evasion attack targeted the model's inference stage by introducing small perturbations to the input data for effectively bypassing decision thresholds. We added Gaussian noise to the test data, which is defined as:

$$x_{\text{evasion}} = x + \mathcal{N}(0, \sigma^2) \tag{7}$$

where $\mathcal{N}(0, \sigma^2)$ represents Gaussian noise with mean 0 and variance σ^2. This technique evaluated the model's ability to handle noisy or corrupted inputs and reflected challenges encountered in real-world scenarios.

4. Healthcare AI Vulnerability Assessment Algorithm (HAVA)

Algorithm 1, the HAVA, provided a structured framework for evaluating the robustness of the DL model against the abovementioned cybersecurity attacks. The HAVA not only simulated and evaluated multiple attack types but also introduced the PAVI to quantify the severity of the performance degradation. The PAVI could assist in seeking actionable insights to help with defense prioritization. The high-level workflow of the HAVA is shown in Figure 1.

The process began with data preprocessing, where we normalized the input data to ensure consistent scaling across features. We carefully split the data into training and testing subsets to maintain class distribution. The DL model was trained on the preprocessed data, and its baseline performance was evaluated using accuracy and a confusion matrix. We stratified the dataset during the train–test split to maintain balanced class distributions between the training and testing subsets, and we carefully evaluated the model's performance on a separate test set, ensuring no data leakage occurred between the training and testing phases to minimize overfitting. The algorithm then systematically launched all the attacks to assess the model's resilience. The HAVA computed each attack's resulting accuracy, as well as the PAVI and confusion matrix, to capture the performance impact.

A key feature of the HAVA is the introduction of the PAVI, which quantifies the relative drop in accuracy under each attack scenario as a percentage of the baseline accuracy. This metric provides a clear and quantitative measure of the model's attack vulnerability. The algorithm outputs the computed accuracy, PAVI and confusion matrices for all scenarios, which provides a comprehensive view of the model's vulnerabilities by considering the baseline and post-attack accuracy degradation. This systematic approach allowed for a detailed analysis of the DL model's robustness to highlight areas that required improvements to mitigate cybersecurity risks effectively. Unlike traditional metrics, which measure accuracy, the PAVI provides a nuanced understanding of a model's vulnerabilities by evaluating the relative severity of performance degradation after an attack. It does not predict vulnerabilities beforehand but serves as a critical tool for assessing the post-attack impact and guiding future defensive strategies. By identifying and quantifying vulnerabilities through the PAVI, the HAVA enables researchers to design targeted defense mechanisms, such as adversarial training or data augmentation tailored to specific attack scenarios.

Algorithm 1: Healthcare AI Vulnerability Assessment Algorithm (HAVA)

Input: D: Dataset; ϵ: Perturbation magnitude for adversarial FGSM/evasion attacks; α: Poisoning fraction; M: Model architecture (Multi-Layer Perceptron)

Output: Accuracy (Acc), Post-Attack Vulnerability Index ($PAVI$), Confusion Matrix (CM)

Process:

1. **Data Preprocessing**
   (a) Normalize D using StandardScaler to scale all features to the range $[0,1]$.
   (b) Split D into training (D_{train}) and testing (D_{test}) subsets using stratified sampling to preserve class distribution.
2. **Baseline Model Training and Evaluation**
   (a) Train the model M on D_{train} using a binary cross-entropy loss function.
   (b) Evaluate M on D_{test} to compute baseline accuracy $Acc_{original}$ and confusion matrix $CM_{original}$.
3. **Attack Simulations and Evaluations**
   (a) **Adversarial FGSM Attack**
   - Generate adversarial samples D_{adv} using the FGSM:

$$D_{adv} = D_{test} + \epsilon \cdot \text{sign}(\nabla_x J(D_{test}, y)),$$

   where J is the loss function and $\nabla_x J$ represents its gradient with respect to the input.
   - Evaluate M on D_{adv} to compute accuracy Acc_{adv} and confusion matrix CM_{adv}.

   (b) **Data Poisoning Attack**
   - Inject mislabeled samples $(\alpha \cdot D_{train})$ into D_{train} to create D_{poison}.
   - Retrain M on D_{poison} and evaluate on D_{test} to compute accuracy Acc_{poison} and confusion matrix CM_{poison}.

   (c) **Adversarial Evasion Attack**
   - Add Gaussian noise to generate evasion samples:

$$D_{evasion} = D_{test} + \mathcal{N}(0, \sigma^2),$$

   where $\mathcal{N}$ represents Gaussian noise with mean 0 and variance σ^2.
   - Evaluate M on $D_{evasion}$ to compute accuracy $Acc_{evasion}$ and confusion matrix $CM_{evasion}$.
4. **Vulnerability Assessment**
   Compute the Post-Attack Vulnerability Index (PAVI) for each attack scenario:

$$PAVI = \frac{Acc_{original} - Acc_{attack}}{Acc_{original}} \times 100,$$

   where Acc_{attack} refers to the accuracy after each attack.

return *Acc, PAVI and CM for all scenarios.*

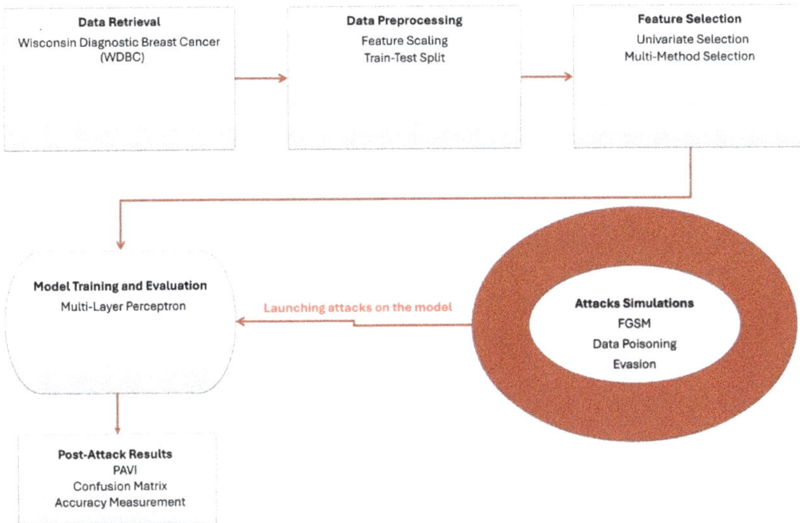

Figure 1. A high-level workflow of the HAVA.

5. Results and Discussion

We trained the MLP classifier for 120 epochs by recording accuracy and loss at each step. The training process demonstrated strong convergence, with accuracy increasing from 90.55% in Epoch 1 to 99.12% in Epoch 120, as shown in Figure 2. The model learned efficiently, with rapid improvement in early epochs, and maintained stable optimization in later stages. The training loss, as represented in Figure 3, decreased consistently. It started at 0.6300 and reached 0.0318, which confirms that the model effectively minimizes errors. The smooth decline in loss and the low gap between training accuracy (99.12%) and test accuracy (97.36%) indicate that the model generalizes well without overfitting.

To evaluate the model's robustness, three cybersecurity attacks were simulated, which included the adversarial FGSM with a perturbation magnitude of $\epsilon = 0.1$, data poisoning (random label flipping of 10% of training labels) and adversarial evasion using Gaussian noise addition with a variance of $\sigma^2 = 0.05$. The model's performance was quantified using accuracy, confusion matrices and the PAVI to understand and mitigate vulnerabilities.

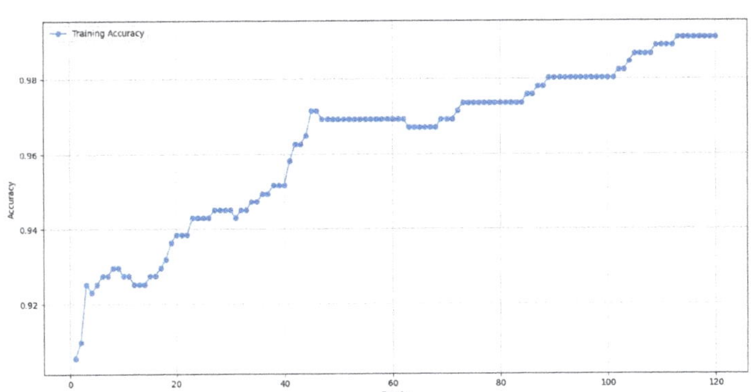

Figure 2. Training accuracy over epochs.

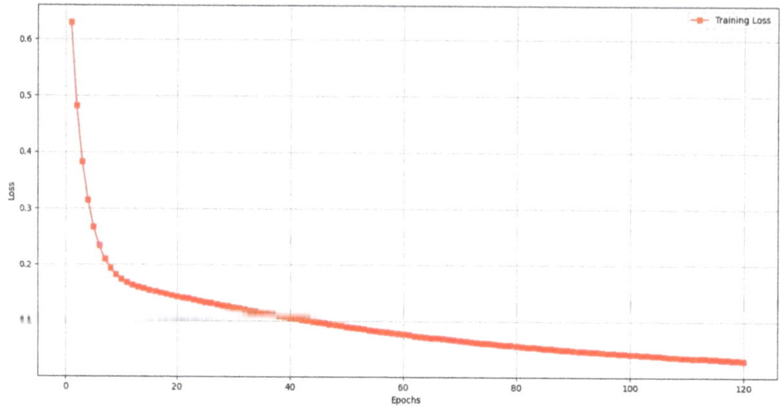

Figure 3. Training loss over epochs.

5.1. Quantifying Post-Attack Impact for Iterative Improvement

The ability to quantify post-attack impact using the PAVI is an essential element of the HAVA. Unlike traditional accuracy metrics, which only capture absolute performance degradation, the PAVI contextualizes the severity of these losses by relating them to the model's baseline reliability. For instance, as shown in Figure 4 and Table 3, the adversarial FGSM and adversarial evasion attacks reduced accuracy from 97.36% to 61.40% and 62.28%, respectively. These attacks yielded a high PAVI of 38.60% and 37.72%, indicating a substantial compromise in the model's performance. In contrast, data poisoning caused a milder reduction to 89.47% accuracy and a low PAVI of 10.53%. This standardized metric enables a nuanced comparison across attack types and facilitates identifying vulnerabilities that demand immediate intervention. Without the PAVI, the relative impact of different attacks could be misinterpreted, especially when working with models of high baseline accuracies.

The HAVA leverages these insights for iterative improvement by integrating the feedback from the PAVI evaluations into the model development cycle. For example, a high PAVI for adversarial FGSM attacks highlights the need to prioritize adversarial training in subsequent iterations. Similarly, a lower PAVI for data poisoning suggests that less resource-intensive defenses, such as anomaly detection or federated learning, may suffice. During the mitigation workflow, discussed in the subsection below, this iterative process allows developers and cybersecurity researchers to focus resources on the most critical vulnerabilities to optimize the balance between resilience and computational efficiency.

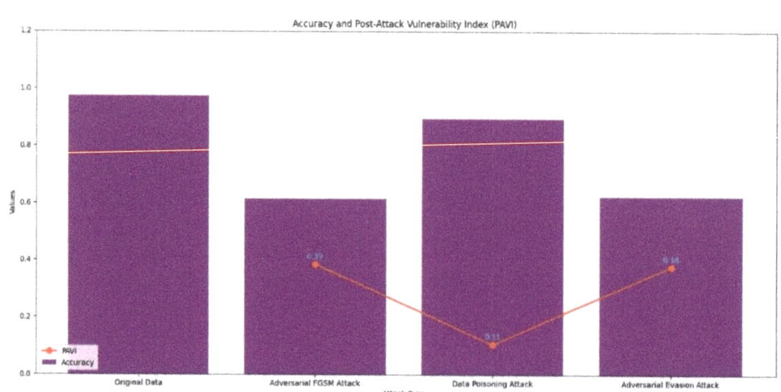

Figure 4. Model accuracy with the PAVI: original vs. attacks.

5.2. Mitigation Workflow

The HAVA plays an integral role in the broader mitigation workflow for AI models in healthcare. The workflow typically comprises four stages: attack simulation and evaluation, prioritization of defenses, testing and validation, and iterative improvement.

5.2.1. Attack Simulation and Evaluation

The HAVA systematically introduces the adversarial FGSM, data poisoning and adversarial evasion attacks, and it quantifies their impact through the PAVI. This step provides a clear understanding of which attack types pose the greatest threat to the model's reliability.

5.2.2. Prioritization of Defenses

By identifying attack types with the highest PAVI values, the HAVA enables researchers to prioritize targeted defenses. For instance, adversarial training and feature smoothing might be deployed to address adversarial attacks, while federated learning could mitigate the effects of data poisoning.

5.2.3. Testing and Validation

The algorithm supports rigorous testing of defense mechanisms by re-evaluating the model under simulated attacks post-defense integration. The PAVI provides a consistent benchmark to measure the effectiveness of these defenses to ensure that improvements are both meaningful and quantifiable.

5.2.4. Iterative Improvement

Insights from PAVI evaluations can be fed back into the new development cycles to enable continuous refinement of the model and its defenses. This life cycle approach ensures that AI models remain resilient against evolving cybersecurity threats, which is crucial for dynamic domains like healthcare.

5.3. Contextualizing Vulnerability and Guiding Actionable Insights

Our findings highlighted the varied impact of different attack types on model performance. The adversarial FGSM and evasion attacks resulted in high false positive rates, as shown in Figure 5. In real-world scenarios, such incidents can lead to unnecessary biopsies, wasting resources, and causing patient distress. Conversely, data poisoning gradually erodes diagnostic reliability without inducing drastic performance drops. This type of impact can undermine trust over time. The PAVI contextualizes these vulnerabilities by translating them into actionable insights. For instance, high PAVI values associated with adversarial attacks underscore the urgency of integrating adversarially robust training. In contrast, lower PAVI values for data poisoning suggest a focus on proactive data integrity measures.

By quantifying the relative severity of performance degradation, the HAVA guides the development of tailored defenses that address specific vulnerabilities. The algorithm's holistic evaluation of attack impacts and defense effectiveness ensures that AI systems in healthcare can be continuously improved rather than discarded after compromise.

The utility of the PAVI in healthcare can be exemplified through a breast cancer diagnostic system. Suppose adversarial attacks cause a PAVI of 38.60%, resulting in a significant misclassification of malignant cells as benign. This outcome directly jeopardizes patient outcomes by delaying life-saving treatments. By identifying adversarial attacks as the primary vulnerability, the PAVI enables the prioritization of adversarial training during model re-training. Subsequently, testing and validation confirm whether the mitigation strategy reduces the PAVI to acceptable levels, such as below 10%. This iterative refinement ensures the AI model's safety and reliability in real-world applications to safeguard patients' health and maintain trust in AI-driven diagnostics.

The PAVI's importance is particularly pronounced in healthcare, where diagnostic errors have life-altering consequences. For example, high PAVI values under adversarial attacks could prompt the implementation of adversarial training to mitigate the misclassification of malignant cells as benign to prevent delayed treatments. Similarly, PAVI's insights into adversarial evasion attack vulnerabilities could inspire the development of noise-resistant input preprocessing techniques to reduce false positives that lead to unnecessary medical interventions. By integrating the PAVI into mitigation workflows, the HAVA empowers researchers and practitioners to create resilient AI systems capable of navigating real-world deployment challenges. We assume that the HAVA and the PAVI can be customized and applied by future research works according to their requirements. For example, a model's PAVI can be categorized into low, medium and high by setting a range of values considering its criticality.

The future work in this domain faces challenges and opportunities. Future research could expand on this work by developing and integrating advanced defense mechanisms, such as adversarial training, federated learning, and privacy-preserving techniques by considering the HAVA framework. Testing the HAVA across diverse medical imaging datasets and conditions will also ensure its scalability and applicability in real-world scenarios. While this study focused on the PAVI as a holistic measure of model robustness, future work could incorporate additional performance metrics, such as precision, recall, and F1 score, to comprehensively evaluate model performance under different attack scenarios.

Table 3. Comparison of accuracy, PAVI and confusion matrices.

Attack Type	Accuracy	PAVI	Confusion Matrix
Original data	0.973684	N/A	TN = 70, FP = 2, FN = 1, TP = 41
Adversarial FGSM attack	0.614035	0.385965	TN = 28, FP = 44, FN = 0, TP = 42
Data-poisoning attack	0.894737	0.105263	TN = 63, FP = 9, FN = 3, TP = 39
Adversarial evasion attack	0.622807	0.377193	TN = 29, FP = 43, FN = 0, TP = 42

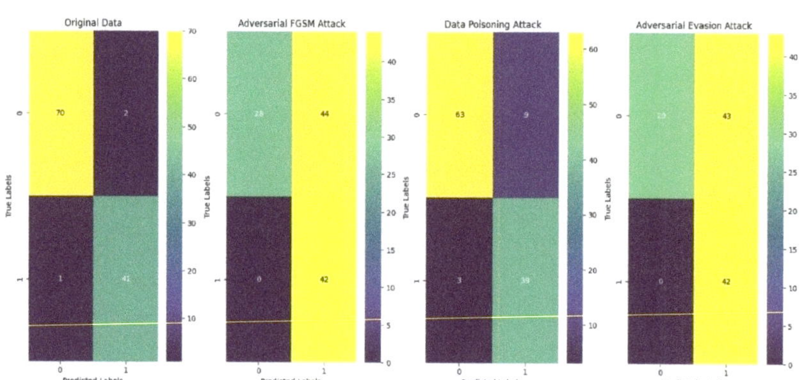

Figure 5. Model confusion matrices: original vs. attacks.

Future efforts could also explore defense strategies to mitigate the vulnerabilities identified in this study. For instance, adversarial defenses, such as input preprocessing, defensive distillation, and ensemble modeling, could be integrated with the HAVA to strengthen the resilience of DL models in healthcare applications. Explainable AI (XAI) models, including SHapley Additive exPlanations (SHAP), Local Interpretable Model-agnostic Explanations

(LIME), and Saliency Maps, could also play an integral role in the detection of adversarial attacks. Moreover, research could address a key gap by performing a sensitivity analysis to quantify the relationship between attack magnitudes, such as varying ϵ or σ^2, and their impact on model performance and the PAVI. Understanding this relationship would help researchers and practitioners better assess the robustness of AI models under different levels of adversarial stress, paving the way for more resilient AI systems.

Recent advancements in this domain have started focusing on cybersecurity attacks and vulnerabilities, particularly concerning LLMs [33]. Atmane and Ahmad [27] comprehensively analyzed the vulnerabilities of LLMs and highlighted the need for advanced safeguards to mitigate adversarial risks. Zou et al. [28] explored transferable adversarial attacks and demonstrated how misaligned models remain vulnerable to universal perturbations that compromise their decision-making processes. Liu et al. [34] emphasized the potential of adversarial training to bolster the resilience of LLMs. They provided a framework that could inspire similar approaches in the context of DL models for healthcare. These studies suggest that extending defense mechanisms to healthcare applications can bridge the gap between theoretical advancements in LLM safety and their practical deployment in high-stakes scenarios.

6. Conclusions

By simulating and evaluating adversarial FGSM, data-poisoning and adversarial evasion attacks, this study has demonstrated the varying degrees to which these threats compromise a model's performance, which can result in significant accuracy drops and increased false classification rates. The introduction of the HAVA with the PAVI provides a comprehensive framework for quantifying and assessing the impact of multiple attack vectors on DL models.

The PAVI contextualizes the severity of performance degradation, and provides a standardized means to quantify a model's vulnerabilities relative to its baseline accuracy. For example, the adversarial FGSM and evasion attacks, characterized by high PAVI values, emphasize the need for defenses such as adversarial training and noise-resistant preprocessing. Conversely, with its relatively low PAVI, data poisoning suggests resource-efficient measures such as federated learning. These insights transform post-attack impacts into a foundation for targeted mitigation efforts to ensure continuous improvement of AI models in dynamic healthcare environments.

Our findings have significant implications for healthcare applications, where errors induced by attacks can lead to delayed treatments, unnecessary medical interventions, or the erosion of trust in AI systems. By emphasising diagnostic accuracy and cybersecurity, the HAVA serves as a bridge that translates theoretical vulnerabilities into actionable defense strategies to ensure that AI models in healthcare are high-performing and resilient to evolving threats.

Author Contributions: S.B. conceptualized the study; Q.-u.-a.M. handled the data collection and preprocessing tasks; data analysis and result interpretation were performed by both S.B. and Q.-u.-a.M.; data visualization was led by S.B.; Q.-u.-a.M. reviewed related works and both authors identified the research gaps; S.B. designed and implemented the HAVA; S.B. and Q.-u.-a.M. drafted the manuscript; experimentation was carried out by S.B. and Q.-u.-a.M.; administrative coordination and documentation support were provided by S.B., with S.B. also serving as the corresponding author. All authors have read and agreed to the published version of the manuscript.

Funding: This research received no external funding.

Data Availability Statement: The dataset analyzed in this study is publicly available and can be retrieved from the source in reference [29].

Conflicts of Interest: The authors declare no conflicts of interest.

References

1. Heng, W.W.; Abdul-Kadir, N.A. Deep Learning and Explainable Machine Learning on Hair Disease Detection. In Proceedings of the 2023 IEEE 5th Eurasia Conference on Biomedical Engineering, Healthcare and Sustainability (ECBIOS), Tainan, Taiwan, 2–4 June 2023; pp. 150–153. [CrossRef]
2. Niteesh, K.R.; Pooja, T.S. Application of Deep Learning in Detection of various Hepatic Disease Classification Using H & E Stained Liver Tissue Biopsy. In Proceedings of the 2024 2nd International Conference on Artificial Intelligence and Machine Learning Applications Theme: Healthcare and Internet of Things (AIMLA), Namakkal, India, 15–16 March 2024; pp. 1–6. [CrossRef]
3. Bouali, L.Y.; Boucetta, I.; Bekkouch, I.E.I.; Bouache, M.; Mazouzi, S. An Image Dataset for Lung Disease Detection and Classification. In Proceedings of the 2021 International Conference on Theoretical and Applicative Aspects of Computer Science (ICTAACS), Skikda, Algeria, 15–16 December 2021; pp. 1–6. [CrossRef]
4. Mastoi, Q.; Latif, S.; Brohi, S.; Ahmad, J.; Alqhatani, A.; Alshehri, M.S.; Al Mazroa, A.; Ullah, R. Explainable AI in medical imaging: An interpretable and collaborative federated learning model for brain tumor classification. *Front. Oncol.* **2025**, *15*, 1535478. [CrossRef]
5. Murty, P.S.R.C.; Anuradha, C.; Naidu, P.A.; Mandru, D.; Ashok, M.; Atheeswaran, A.; Rajeswaran, N.; Saravanan, V. Integrative hybrid deep learning for enhanced breast cancer diagnosis: Leveraging the Wisconsin Breast Cancer Database and the CBIS-DDSM dataset. *Sci. Rep.* **2024**, *14*, 26287. [CrossRef] [PubMed]
6. Alshayeji, H.; Ellethy, H.; Abed, S.; Gupta, R. Computer-aided detection of breast cancer on the Wisconsin dataset: An artificial neural networks approach. *Biomed. Signal Process. Control* **2022**, *71*, 103141. [CrossRef]
7. Jain, A.; Sangeeta, K.; Sadim, S.B.M.; Dwivedi, S.P.; Albawi, A. The Impact of Adversarial Attacks on Medical Imaging AI Systems. In Proceedings of the IEEE 13th International Conference on Communication Systems and Network Technologies (CSNT), Jabalpur, India, 6–7 April 2024; pp. 362–367. [CrossRef]
8. Akhtar, N.; Mian, A. Threat of adversarial attacks on deep learning in computer vision: A survey. *IEEE Access* **2018**, *6*, 14410–14430. [CrossRef]
9. Biggio, B.; Roli, F. Wild patterns: Ten years after the rise of adversarial machine learning. *Pattern Recognit.* **2018**, *84*, 317–331. [CrossRef]
10. Muthalagu, R.; Malik, J.A.; Pawar, P.M. Detection and prevention of evasion attacks on machine learning models. *Expert Syst. Appl.* **2025**, *266*, 126044. [CrossRef]
11. Tsai, M.J.; Lin, P.Y.; Lee, M.E. Adversarial Attacks on Medical Image Classification. *Cancers* **2023**, *15*, 4228. [CrossRef] [PubMed] [PubMed Central]
12. Muoka, G.W.; Yi, D.; Ukwuoma, C.C.; Mutale, A.; Ejiyi, C.J.; Mzee, A.K.; Gyarteng, E.S.A.; Alqahtani, A.; Al-antari, M.A. A Comprehensive Review and Analysis of Deep Learning-Based Medical Image Adversarial Attack and Defense. *Mathematics* **2023**, *11*, 4272. [CrossRef]
13. Finlayson, S.G.; Bowers, J.D.; Ito, J.; Zittrain, J.L.; Beam, A.L.; Kohane, I.S. Adversarial attacks on medical machine learning. *Science* **2019**, *363*, 1287–1289. [CrossRef]
14. Yang, Q.; Liu, Y.; Chen, T.; Tong, Y. Federated Machine Learning: Concept and Applications. *ACM Trans. Intell. Syst. Technol.* **2019**, *10*, 2. [CrossRef]
15. Javed, H.; El-Sappagh, S.; Abuhmed, T. Robustness in deep learning models for medical diagnostics: Security and adversarial challenges towards robust AI applications. *Artif. Intell. Rev.* **2025**, *58*, 12. [CrossRef]
16. Mutalib, N.; Sabri, A.; Wahab, A.; Abdullah, E.; AlDahoul, N. Explainable deep learning approach for advanced persistent threats (APTs) detection in cybersecurity: A review. *Artif. Intell. Rev.* **2024**, *57*, 297. [CrossRef]
17. Szegedy, C.; Zaremba, W.; Sutskever, I.; Bruna, J.; Erhan, D.; Goodfellow, I.; Fergus, R. Intriguing properties of neural networks. *arXiv* **2014**, arXiv:1312.6199. [CrossRef]
18. Goodfellow, I.J.; Shlens, J.; Szegedy, C. Explaining and harnessing adversarial examples. *arXiv* **2015**, arXiv:1412.6572. [CrossRef]
19. Sorin, V.; Soffer, S.; Glicksberg, B.S.; Barash, Y.; Konen, E.; Klang, E. Adversarial attacks in radiology—A systematic review. *Eur. J. Radiol.* **2023**, *167*, 111085. [CrossRef]
20. Albattah, A.; Rassam, M.A. Detection of Adversarial Attacks against the Hybrid Convolutional Long Short-Term Memory Deep Learning Technique for Healthcare Monitoring Applications. *Appl. Sci.* **2023**, *13*, 6807. [CrossRef]
21. Yang, Y.; Jin, Q.; Huang, F.; Lu, Z. Adversarial Attacks on Large Language Models in Medicine. *arXiv* **2024**, arXiv:2406.12259. [CrossRef]
22. Newaz, A.I.; Haque, N.I.; Sikder, A.K.; Rahman, M.A.; Uluagac, A.S. Adversarial Attacks to Machine Learning-Based Smart Healthcare Systems. In Proceedings of the GLOBECOM 2020—2020 IEEE Global Communications Conference, Taipei, Taiwan, 7–11 December 2020; pp. 1–6. [CrossRef]

23. Aljanabi, M.; Omran, A.H.; Mijwil, M.M.; Abotaleb, M.; El-kenawy, E.-S.M.; Mohammed, S.Y. Data poisoning: Issues, challenges, and needs. In Proceedings of the 7th IET Smart Cities Symposium (SCS 2023), Manama, Bahrain, 3–5 December 2023. [CrossRef]
24. Verde, L.; Marulli, F.; Marrone, S. Exploring the Impact of Data Poisoning Attacks on Machine Learning Model Reliability. *Procedia Comput. Sci.* **2021**, *192*, 1184–1193. [CrossRef]
25. Xu, W.; Evans, D.; Qi, Y. Feature squeezing: Detecting adversarial examples in deep neural networks. In Proceedings of the 2018 Network and Distributed Systems Security Symposium (NDSS), San Diego, CA, USA, 18–21 February 2018; pp. 1–15.
26. Hong, S.; Chandrasekaran, V.; Kaya, Y.; Dumitraş, T.; Papernot, N. On the Effectiveness of Mitigating Data Poisoning Attacks with Gradient Shaping. *arXiv* **2020**, arXiv:2002.11497. [CrossRef]
27. Atmane, B.; Ahmad, W. On the Validity of Traditional Vulnerability Scoring Systems for Adversarial Attacks against LLMs. *arXiv* **2024**, arXiv:2309.12345. [CrossRef]
28. Zou, A.; Wang, Z.; Carlini, N.; Nasr, M.; Kolter, J.Z.; Fredrikson, M. Universal and Transferable Adversarial Attacks on Aligned Language Models. *arXiv* **2023**, arXiv:2307.15043. [CrossRef]
29. Wolberg, W.; Mangasarian, O.; Street, N.; Street, W. Breast Cancer Wisconsin (Diagnostic). 1995. Available online: https://archive.ics.uci.edu/dataset/17/breast+cancer+wisconsin+diagnostic (accessed on 9 January 2025).
30. Street, W.N.; Wolberg, W.H.; Mangasarian, O.L. Nuclear feature extraction for breast tumor diagnosis. *Biomed. Image Process. Biomed. Vis.* **1993**, *1905*, 861–870. [CrossRef]
31. Nair, V.; Hinton, G.E. Rectified linear units improve restricted Boltzmann machines. In Proceedings of the 27th International Conference on Machine Learning (ICML-10), Haifa, Israel, 21–24 June 2010; pp. 807–814.
32. Biggio, B.; Nelson, B.; Laskov, P. Poisoning attacks against support vector machines. In Proceedings of the 29th International Conference on Machine Learning (ICML-12), Edinburgh, Scotland, 26 June–1 July 2012; pp. 1467–1474.
33. Hamid, R.; Brohi, S. A Review of Large Language Models in Healthcare: Taxonomy, Threats, Vulnerabilities, and Framework. *Big Data Cogn. Comput.* **2024**, *8*, 161. [CrossRef]
34. Liu, X.; Cheng, H.; He, P.; Chen, W.; Wang, Y.; Poon, H.; Gao, J. Adversarial Training for Large Neural Language Models. *arXiv* **2020**, arXiv:2004.08994. [CrossRef]

algorithms

MDPI

Article

Text-Guided Synthesis in Medical Multimedia Retrieval: A Framework for Enhanced Colonoscopy Image Classification and Segmentation

Ojonugwa Oluwafemi Ejiga Peter [1], Opeyemi Taiwo Adeniran [2], Adetokunbo MacGregor John-Otumu [3], Fahmi Khalifa [2] and Md Mahmudur Rahman [1,*]

[1] Department of Computer Science, School of Computer, Mathematical and Natural Sciences, Morgan State University, Baltimore, MD 21251, USA; ojeji1@morgan.edu

[2] Department of Electrical and Computer Engineering, Morgan State University, Baltimore, MD 21251, USA; opade7@morgan.edu (O.T.A.); fahmi.khalifa@morgan.edu (F.K.)

[3] Department of Information Technology, Federal University of Technology Owerri, Owerri 460116, Imo State, Nigeria; adetokunbo.johnotumu@futo.edu.ng

* Correspondence: md.rahman@morgan.edu

Abstract: The lack of extensive, varied, and thoroughly annotated datasets impedes the advancement of artificial intelligence (AI) for medical applications, especially colorectal cancer detection. Models trained with limited diversity often display biases, especially when utilized on disadvantaged groups. Generative models (e.g., DALL-E 2, Vector-Quantized Generative Adversarial Network (VQ-GAN)) have been used to generate images but not colonoscopy data for intelligent data augmentation. This study developed an effective method for producing synthetic colonoscopy image data, which can be used to train advanced medical diagnostic models for robust colorectal cancer detection and treatment. Text-to-image synthesis was performed using fine-tuned Visual Large Language Models (LLMs). Stable Diffusion and DreamBooth Low-Rank Adaptation produce images that look authentic, with an average Inception score of 2.36 across three datasets. The validation accuracy of various classification models Big Transfer (BiT), Fixed Resolution Residual Next Generation Network (FixResNeXt), and Efficient Neural Network (EfficientNet) were 92%, 91%, and 86%, respectively. Vision Transformer (ViT) and Data-Efficient Image Transformers (DeiT) had an accuracy rate of 93%. Secondly, for the segmentation of polyps, the ground truth masks are generated using Segment Anything Model (SAM). Then, five segmentation models (U-Net, Pyramid Scene Parsing Network (PSNet), Feature Pyramid Network (FPN), Link Network (LinkNet), and Multi-scale Attention Network (MANet)) were adopted. FPN produced excellent results, with an Intersection Over Union (IoU) of 0.64, an F1 score of 0.78, a recall of 0.75, and a Dice coefficient of 0.77. This demonstrates strong performance in terms of both segmentation accuracy and overlap metrics, with particularly robust results in balanced detection capability as shown by the high F1 score and Dice coefficient. This highlights how AI-generated medical images can improve colonoscopy analysis, which is critical for early colorectal cancer detection.

Keywords: medical imaging synthesis; polyp detection; text-to-image generation; image segmentation; generative AI; medical image synthesis; colorectal cancer detection; data augmentation; synthetic colonoscopy images; text-to-image generation; DreamBooth; Stable Diffusion; Low-Rank Adaptation (LoRA); polyp segmentation; Feature Pyramid Network; Vision Transformer; Segment Anything Model; medical diagnostic models; healthcare AI

1. Introduction

Artificial intelligence (AI) has initiated substantial transformations in the analysis of medical imaging. In gastroenterology, the scientific study of the health and diseases of the stomach, small intestine, colon, and rectum, AI-assisted colonoscopy has shown the potential to improve the diagnosis of colon cancer and reduce the incidence of colorectal cancer (CRC) [1]. The efficacy of artificial intelligence models is fundamentally dependent on the quantity and quality of training image data for colon cancer. A fundamental drawback in the advancement of successful models for medical imaging and image interpretation is the lack of sufficient training and testing data. The challenges of generating large datasets include privacy concerns, invasive methodologies, and the labor-intensive nature of professional data annotation [2].

The absence of extensive, varied, and thoroughly annotated datasets hinders the training and development of sophisticated AI-assisted colonoscopy technologies [3,4]. The inaccessibility of data in this context leads to the creation of severely defective AI models or algorithms with intrinsic bias when used for vulnerable populations [5]. The scarcity of ample high-quality training data undermines AI's efficacy in improving the identification and prevention of colorectal cancer, particularly among groups facing health care disparities. Like prior research, there has been an effort to utilize generative adversarial networks (GANs) for the synthesis of text-to-image mapping, among other methodologies [6–8]. Recent evaluations have emphasized the refinement of large language models based on vision, including Stable Diffusion (SD), Contrastive Language-Image Pre-training (CLIP), and DreamBooth + Low-Rank Adaptation (DB+LoRa), for the creation of medical images [9]. However, the application of these algorithms to generate a comprehensive array of high-quality colonoscopy images remains unexplored. The issue is the lack of a robust framework for generating synthetic colonoscopy images to enhance training data for more effective diagnostic algorithms.

Researchers are exploring various approaches (GANs, VQGAN, CLIP, Bootstrapping Language-Image Pre-training (BLIP)) to address these issues by improving and diversifying medical imaging databases [10–12]. This study examines the use of artificial intelligence for text-to-image synthesis and intelligent data augmentation to improve AI models and promote demographic equity. Inception score (IS) and Fréchet Inception Distance (FID) are utilized to evaluate synthetic images generated by fine-tuning the SD, CLIP and DB + LoRa models. In addition, advanced classification models such as BiT, ViT, FixResNeXt, EfficientNet, and DeiT are employed to train the generated images. Assessments of these models are based on standard metrics, including the F1 score, accuracy, precision, recall, and Area Under Curve (AUC), among others. All of this manifests itself as a structured plan to improve the standards of imaging and medical diagnosis.

2. Related Work

In recent years, artificial intelligence has demonstrated potential in medical image processing, improving the precision and efficacy of various diagnostic procedures, including colonoscopy [1]. Recent advances in AI for medical imaging have shown promising developments in various approaches. Pengxiao et al. [13] introduced X. Latent-based Diffusion Model for Long-tailed Recognition (LDMLR), which addresses long-tailed recognition challenges through latent-based diffusion models. Du et al. [14] developed Adaptive Refinement Semantic Diffusion Models (ArSDM), focusing on the scarcity of annotated medical image data through adaptive refinement semantic diffusion. Earlier work by Ku et al. [15] established TextControlGAN to improve image quality with text control. In 2024, Ejiga Peter et al. [9] conducted a comparative analysis of multiple approaches, including CLIP and Stable Diffusion, while Iqbal et al. [16] developed a Conditional Generative Adversarial Network (GAN) for facial expressions.

In the specific domain of gastrointestinal imaging, several notable contributions emerged. Shin et al. [17] and Qadir et al. [18] implemented Convolutional Neural Network (CNN)-based approaches for polyp detection, while Dong et al. [19] introduced a transformer-based solution. Clinical applications have shown remarkable progress, with Repici et al. [20] demonstrating the efficacy of GI-Genius in colonoscopy and Kudo et al. [21] developing EndoBRAIN for polyp detection. Zhou et al. [22] contributed ENDOANGEL for real-time assessment, while Mahmood et al. [23] focused on depth estimation in endoscopy. Goceri [24] provided a comprehensive review of data augmentation techniques across different medical imaging modalities. This work investigates generative artificial intelligence in the context of colonoscopy imaging interpretation, specifically focusing on text-to-image generation and advanced data augmentation techniques. Early detection during colonoscopy is crucial to avert colon cancer, a major global health problem [5].

Kim et al. [3] investigated the generation of synthetic image data within a scientific framework, specifically focusing on medical image diagnostics and laboratory techniques, using the OpenAI DALL-E 3. However, the model exhibited low precision due to intrinsic bias within the system. They additionally examined the ethical implications of producing synthetic data. This research was constrained by the lack of an iterative generation process, which included erroneous or extraneous features, duplication of existing images, and reliance on proxy features. In a similar vein, Yang et al. [25] created an AI-generated image model to serve as a data source for synthetic data. Upon thorough examination, Yang et al. [25] employed CovNets and transformer-based models. Convolutional neural network models, such as ResNet-50 and ResNet-101, demonstrate substantial improvements. Transformers demonstrate improvements in ViT-S/16, DeiT-S, and DeiT-B. The larger versions typically exhibit superior overall performance. Our strategy emphasizes text-to-image synthesis utilizing fine-tuned Large Language models for the development of synthetic colonoscopy images and Classification models for polyp detection, facilitating the early identification of colorectal cancer.

Cao et al. [26] examined AI-generated content (AIGC) and its historical evolution from Generative Adversarial Networks (GANs) to contemporary ChatGPT, emphasizing the unimodality and multimodality of generative AI models. Bandi et al. [27] conducted a survey of various GAN-based designs for AIGC and examined the fundamental needs for the development of AIGC, including the input–output format of the model, the evaluation metrics, and the associated obstacles. However, the analyses presented in both [26] and Bandi et al. [27] were purely theoretical and devoid of practical application; therefore, our research transcends qualitative examination by incorporating the practical implementation of AIGC with cutting-edge models such as SD. Bendel [28] examined image synthesis (image production) from an ethical perspective. Elements of creation can also facilitate destruction, which is why Bendel [28] advocated the ethical application of generative AI in image synthesis. The significant potential of image synthesis models entails a considerable duty to guarantee ethical utilization. Bendel [28] used the Midjourney, SD, and DALL-E2 models to analyze the topic from the point of view of risk and opportunity. In a comparable context, Ray et al. [28] addressed the meticulous supervision required to realize the potential of generative AI in precise medical diagnostics and neurointerventional surgery while mitigating the risk of encountering pitfalls. Both works lack practical application and are purely theoretical. However, ethical considerations were implemented during the construction and testing of the models in our research.

Derevyanko et al. [29] conducted a comparative examination of SD, Midjourney, and DALL-E, advocating for their implementation due to their educational use. The study demonstrated that neural network applications can improve the teaching of students in design-related fields. Mahmood et al. Al [23] developed a depth estimator utilizing an extensive dataset of synthetic images produced through a precise forward model of an endoscope and an anatomically accurate colon. Their studies revealed the following enhancements in porcine colon data: an 88% improvement in Structural Similarity Index Measure (SSIM) for depth estimation, a 48% improvement in SSIM for phantom colon data depth estimation, and approximately a 125% improvement compared to the prior dictionary learning method. Additional validation of various medical imaging tasks and modalities would enhance the broader application.

Iqbal et al. [16] developed a synthetic image generation model using Conditional GAN for single-sample face images. The research achieved an initial accuracy of 76% on individual neutral images and a final accuracy of 99% after the fine-tuning of synthetic expressions, representing a 23% improvement over the original accuracy recorded. This method presents possibilities to address the difficulty of Single Sample Per Person (SSPP) in facial recognition systems. However, it is limited solely to variations in expression and can necessitate the integration of additional motions to capture other forms of facial alterations for applicability in different contexts.

Du et al. [14] used the Adaptive refinement semantic diffusion model for the synthesis of colonoscopy images. Polyp segmentation exhibited the greatest enhancement with PraNet (6.0% mDice, 5.7% mIoU), succeeded by SANet and Polyp-PVT. CenterNet demonstrated the most significant gain in average precision (9.1%) and the greatest improvement in the F1 score (6.1%) for the diagnosis of polyps. The research indicates that the use of synthetic images generated by ArSDM for training significantly enhances the results in both polyp segmentation and detection tasks. The methodology effectively addresses weakly annotated medical imaging data.

Ku et al. [15] present a novel methodology for text-to-image synthesis that improves image quality and adherence to textual descriptions compared to previous methods. Compared to the Caltech-UCSD Birds-200-2011 (CUB) dataset, the model improved the Inception score by 17.6% and decreased the Fréchet Inception Distance by 36.6% relative to the GAN-INT-CLS model based on cGAN. The model is limited to bird images at a relatively low resolution (128 × 128) and was assessed only on a single dataset, CUB.

Ejiga Peter et al. [9] employed three methodologies for medical image synthesis: DB + LoRA, fine-tuned SD, and CLIP. They analyzed numerous advanced strategies and tackled the need for dynamic generation of medical images from textual descriptions. The models were evaluated using single-center and multicenter datasets. SD beat other Fréchet Inception Distance techniques. The highest multicenter score of 0.064 indicated excellent image quality. DB + LoRA outperformed CLIP (1.568) and SD (2.362) in the initial score. SD produced diversified and high-quality images efficiently, beating FID and competing in IS. Their analysis did not evaluate the images generated clinically or diagnostically. The research shows the potential of AI-generated medical imaging, but it also stresses the need for clinical trials and ethical considerations.

Sanchez et al. [30] explored how deep learning has improved colonoscopy polyp identification. The CNN is the most popular architecture for end-to-end applications; hybrid methods are less popular. The biggest issues are large, annotated datasets and inconsistent evaluation metrics. Their research shows that these methods can improve the identification of adenoma but require clinical validation. Standardization of assessment methods, semisupervised learning, elimination of Histogram of Displacement (HD) colonoscopy images, and improved access to large public datasets can result.

Goceri [24] conducted an extensive evaluation of data enhancement methodologies for medical imaging. The efficacy of augmentation techniques varies according to the specific medical imaging modality used. Shearing and translation proved to be most effective for brain Magnetic Resonance Imaging (MRI), lung Computed Tomography (CT), and breast mammography, but noise-based methods often faltered. The most precise components of brain MRI were translation, shearing, and rotation, with an accuracy of 88.24%. Translation by shearing exhibited optimal performance on lung CT at 85.74%. Translation, shearing, and rotation were the most beneficial for breast mammography (83.34%). The results for color shift, sharpening, and contrast modification were most pronounced in the classification of the eye fundus, with a precision of 88.21%. Shearing and noise performed poorly, but the combinations performed better. Fundus images had the greatest improvement in color and contrast. GAN-based methods are more diverse, yet suffer from gradient vanishing [31,32]. The assessment stresses image categorization and the selection of task-related augmentation techniques.

Wang et al. [33] used deep learning in real time to identify colonoscopy polyps. In addition to 27,113 images and videos, 1290 patient records confirmed findings. The approach performed well in datasets, with per-image sensitivity from 88.24% to 94.38% and specificity from 95.40% to 95.92%. Please note that the confirmed polyp videos were 100% sensitive. The gadget can handle 25 frames per second with low latency for real-time clinical applications. This method allows endoscopists to test their polyp-detecting skills.

This pilot study by Misawa et al. [34] evaluates a computer-aided detection (CADe) system for the real-time identification of polyps during colonoscopy. Although previous CADe systems were capable of recognizing over 90% static images and 70% videos, the extract failed to include the performance characteristics of the system. Expanding datasets and including video-based analysis could improve the practical importance of this research. The absence of performance metrics in the passage is concerning. The initiative aims to reduce human error in polyp detection, thus improving adenoma diagnosis and perhaps decreasing the rates of colorectal cancer in intervals.

Dong et al. [19] used Polyp-olyp Pyramid Vision Transformer(PVT) and a transformer encoder that incorporates Context Feature Module (CFM), Cross-interaction Module (CIM), and SAM segment polyps, achieving a score of 0.900 Dice and 0.833 IoU on the Endoscene dataset, surpassing previous approaches in five datasets. The models appear to be resilient to variations in appearance, tiny objects, and rotation, demonstrating strong performance on hitherto unseen data. The limits of polyps are difficult to see due to overlapping light and shadow, as well as numerous false positives from the reflection point. The model surpasses polyp segmentation techniques in recommended colonoscopy applications.

Guo et al. [35] introduced Dilated ResFCN and SE-Unet, two innovative fully convolutional neural network (FCNN) architectures for the segmentation of colonoscopy polyps. The average Dice score was 0.8343, the standard deviation was 0.1837, and only three polyps were overlooked. The strategies mentioned above secured victories in the Gastrointestinal Image ANAlysis (GIANA) tournaments in 2017 and 2018. The study was beneficial; however, the temporal dependencies of colonoscopy records should enhance future research.

Qadr et al. [18] used Mask R-CNN to identify and segment colonoscopy polyps to reduce the physician 25% missed rate. Multiple CNN feature extractors and additional training data were evaluated to construct Mask R-CNN. An ensemble method for enhancement was proposed. The segmentation of the leading model was performed on the 2015 Medical Image Computing and Computer Assisted Intervention (MICCAI) dataset, with the following results: recall 72.59%, accuracy 80%, Dice coefficient 70.42%, and Jaccard index 61.24%. The study elucidates the trade-offs between model complexity and dataset quality for better polyp identification and segmentation. The results are promising, but automated polyp recognition should be improved.

Borgli et al. [36] tested CNN architectures for gastrointestinal endoscopy using 110,079 images and 374 movies for multiclass classification. Size, diversity, segmentation masks, and bounding boxes help, but class imbalance and interobserver variability hurt. ResNet-152 and DenseNet-161 achieved amazing results with microaveraged F1 scores of 0.910, macroaverages of 0.617, and Matthews Correlation Coefficients of 0.902. Despite its appeal, the model struggled to distinguish esophagitis from ulcerative colitis. The material is suitable for AI-assisted gastrointestinal endoscopic diagnostic tools; however, classification accuracy needs to be improved.

Kudo et al. [21] used a large training dataset to test EndoBRAIN, an AI system that detects colorectal polyps from endocytoscopic images. The model outperformed the trainee and professional endoscopists in stained image analysis with 96.9% sensitivity, 100% specificity, and 98% precision. Size and various imaging modalities are benefits, but retrospective design and Japanese center concentration are weaknesses. EndoBRAIN's 100% positive and 94.6% negative predictive scores improve colorectal polyp diagnosis. More prospective trials are needed to prove that AI can improve endoscopic diagnostics.

Zhou et al. [22] developed ENDOANGEL, a deep convolutional neural network-based method to assess the quality of intestinal preparation through precise image and video analysis. This model surpassed human endoscopists, achieving 93.33% accuracy on conventional images and 80.00% accuracy on bubble images. The video examination demonstrated an accuracy of 89.04%. The benefits of ENDOANGEL include an objective and consistent evaluation, immediate colonoscopy scoring, and enhanced image and video quality. The study had limitations, including the use of retrospective data collection for training and restricted video assessment. The reproducible evaluation of intestinal preparation as a continuous variable during colonoscopy withdrawal is an innovative approach that enhances the potential to improve colonoscopy results and standardize the evaluation of stool preparation quality.

The literature review shows that AI for colonoscopy analysis, particularly polyp detection and categorization, has advanced. However, significant gaps and constraints remain due to the bias of the models resulting from the reduced variability of the training dataset [3,25]. Some studies have examined novel AI-generative systems for the generation of medical images [9,14]. The lack of comprehensive systems that incorporate segmentation, classification, and image creation for colonoscopy analysis [14,25] and the lack of studies on artificial data augmentation and model fairness among demographic groups [30] are major problems. The study is expected to contribute significantly to AI-assisted colonoscopy analysis, as these prospects fit with the research objectives and questions.

3. Materials and Methods

The research technique employs a complete framework for the interpretation of medical images, with a specific emphasis on colonoscopy imaging. This framework incorporates three fundamental components: image production and augmentation, classification, and segmentation, utilizing cutting-edge deep learning models to establish a resilient system for colonoscopy image processing and analysis. Our methodology integrates contemporary artificial intelligence tools with conventional medical imaging practices to improve the detection and categorization of polyps in colonoscopy images, as seen in Figure 1. Originally trained on the LAION-5B dataset [37], the SD model offers a wealth of information from a wide spectrum of image-text combinations. Comprising 5.85 billion CLIP-filtered image-text pairs (2.3 billion English samples, 2.2 billion from more than 100 additional languages) and 1 billion with language-agnostic text, LAION5B is a vast collection.

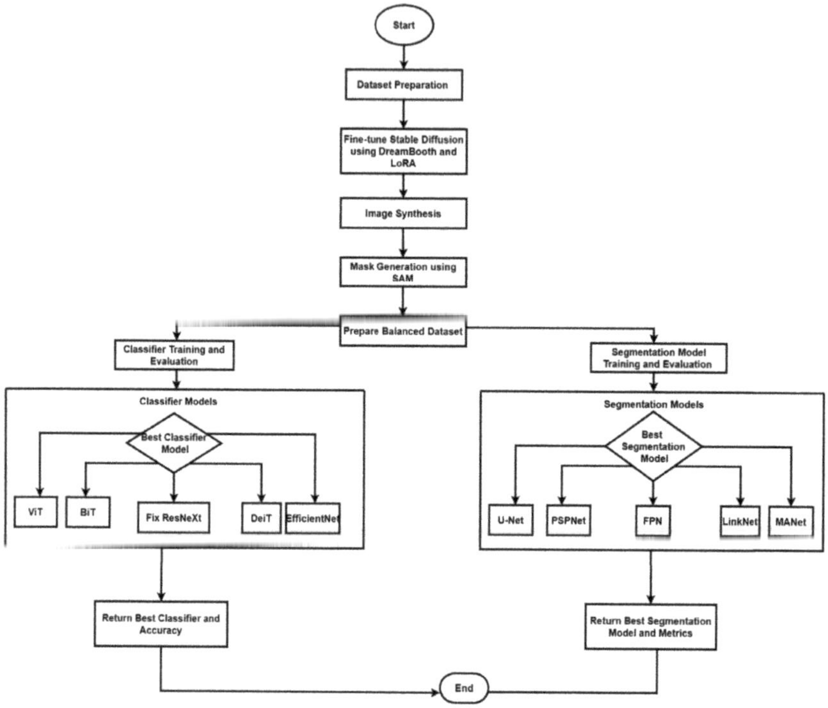

Figure 1. Comprehensive flow diagram of the research methodology, illustrating the sequential process from dataset preparation through model development and evaluation.

3.1. Dataset Description

The study uses the Conference and Labs of the Evaluation Forum (CLEF) dataset for the image generation task, which contains 2000 colonoscopy images paired with 20,242 training prompts and 5000 non-image test prompts to train and evaluate CLIP, SD, and DB LoRa. Research evaluates the ability of models to generate medical images from textual descriptions [9]. This study uses a dataset of 15,428 images classified into three main groups. The initial dataset comprises 5914 images obtained from reputable medical imaging repositories that include the CLEF Image [38], Cerebral Palsy-Comprehensive Health Index of Limb Disorders (CP-CHILD) [39], and binary polyp data [40]. To enhance the diversity and robustness of the dataset, we sampled 1800 synthetic images using fine-tuned Stable Diffusion and created 7714 augmented images through various data augmentation methods. The Classification Model Dataset contains 2946 original polyp and 2967 polyp images, supplemented with 900 polyp and non-polyp synthetic images. When combined with the original dataset, this creates an augmented dataset of 3846 non-polyp and 3867 polyp images, enhancing the diversity and balance of the training data. The complete dataset is partitioned using a 70-20-10 split ratio for training, testing, and validation, respectively, ensuring an equitable distribution of polyp and non-polyp images in each segment to promote impartial model training and assessment. The 70:20:10 split allocates 70% for training data to learn patterns, 20% for validation to adjust hyperparameters and prevent overfitting, and 10% for testing to evaluate the performance of the final model. This balanced ratio ensures sufficient training while maintaining independent validation and testing sets.

For the image segmentation task, the dataset contains 1824 images distributed in four distinct folders. The real-world data are stored in two folders: *real_images*, which contains 612 original colonoscopy images, and *real_masks*, which contain their corresponding 612 segmentation masks. The synthetic data, generated using Fine-tuned Stable Diffusion and DreamBooth LoRa, are organized in *mdpi_syn* with 300 synthetic colonoscopy images and *mdpi_masks* with their 300 corresponding segmentation masks.

The image generation pipeline uses stable diffusion 1.5, obtained by Hugging Face (Hugging Face, New York, USA), as its principal model. The system employs two advanced fine-tuning methodologies: DreamBooth (DB) for subject-specific customization and Low-Rank Adaptation (LoRA) for efficient parameter modifications. Our training parameters used a 4-step batch size with 8-bit Adam optimization, integrating gradient checkpointing and bfloat16 precision. The training procedure executes for 1000 iterations utilizing logit normal weighting to guarantee optimal convergence. To improve contextual awareness and the quality of image formation, we used the Contrastive Language Image Pre-training (CLIP) method, using its zero shot transfer abilities and natural language supervision attributes. See Figure 2.

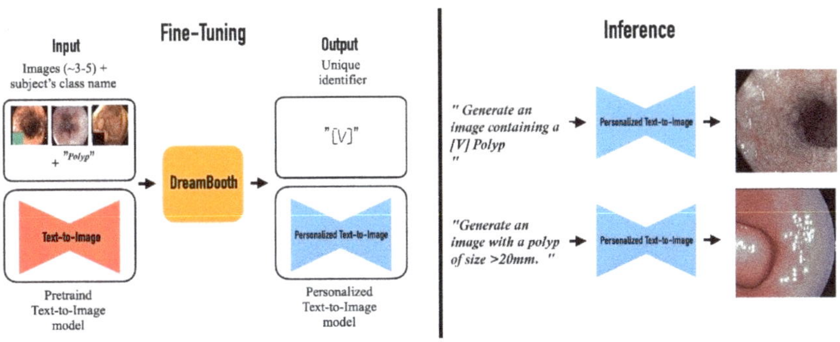

Figure 2. DB fine-tunes text-to-image model with few polyp images to generate personalized colonoscopy images.

3.2. Training Pipeline

The image processing pipeline starts with a thorough standardization procedure, in which all images are resized to 256 × 256 pixels with LANCZOS resampling, subsequently converting them to RGB color space. Resizing to 256 × 256 ensures consistent memory usage and fixed network inputs while preserving features for subsequent 224 × 224 random cropping during training. All images are stored in PNG format to preserve image quality through lossless compression. The training set is subjected to further augmentation techniques, including color jittering, random rotation of ±15 degrees, random horizontal flipping, and random scaled cropping to 224 × 224 pixels. The model sees slightly different versions of the same image during training, improving its robustness and generalization capabilities. All images are subsequently normalized using standard ImageNet normalization parameters and processed in batches via PyTorch python library DataLoader with a batch size of 32 for optimal training efficiency. Pytorch was created from Facebook's AI Research lab (FAIR), Menlo Park, California, USA. PyTorch 2.2.x was used in this research.

We executed and assessed five cutting-edge models for classification tasks: Vision Transformer (ViT), Big Transfer (BiT), FixResNeXt, Data-efficient Image Transformer (DeiT) and EfficientNet. Each model possesses distinct advantages for the classification challenge, with transformers that deliver strong feature extraction skills and convolutional networks that facilitate effective spatial relationship processing. The segmentation component of our approach employs five distinct architectures, U-Net, PSPNet, Feature Pyramid Network (FPN), LinkNet, and MANet. The models were chosen for their demonstrated efficacy in segmenting medical images and their ability to address the unique problems posed by colonoscopy images.

The training methodology utilizes the AdamW optimizer with weight decay and Cross Entropy Loss as a loss function. To avoid overfitting and guarantee optimal model performance, we established an early stopping mechanism based on the plateau of validation loss, consistently retaining the best validation model weights during the training phase. This method guarantees that our models preserve their generalizability while attaining superior performance on the designated task. The binary cross-entropy loss function for classification is defined as

$$L_{\text{BCE}} = -\frac{1}{N}\sum_{i=1}^{N}[y_i \log(\hat{y}_i) + (1-y_i)\log(1-\hat{y}_i)] \quad (1)$$

where N represents the number of samples, y_i is the true label, and $\hat{y}_i$ is the predicted probability for the positive class. For the LoRA adaptation process, the weight matrix transformation is computed as:

$$W = W_0 + BA = W_0 + \Delta W \quad (2)$$

where W_0 represents the original weight matrix, B and A are low-rank decomposition matrices and ΔW is the update matrix. The Dice coefficient, used for evaluating segmentation performance, is calculated as:

$$\text{Dice} = \frac{2|X \cap Y|}{|X| + |Y|} = \frac{2\text{TP}}{2\text{TP} + \text{FP} + \text{FN}} \quad (3)$$

where X and Y represent the predicted segmentation masks and ground truth, respectively, TP denotes true positives, FP denotes false positives and FN denotes false negatives. Our evaluation approach integrates many metrics to thoroughly evaluate distinct facets of the system's performance. The quality of images is assessed by the Inception score (IS) and Fréchet Inception Distance (FID), which offer quantifiable metrics for the caliber of synthetic image synthesis. Classification performance is evaluated using many metrics, such as accuracy, precision, recall (sensitivity), F1 score, and area under the ROC curve (AUC-ROC). For segmentation tasks, we assess quality by Intersection over Union (IoU), Dice coefficient, Peak Signal-to-Noise Ratio (PSNR), and Structural Similarity Index (SSIM), guaranteeing a comprehensive evaluation of segmentation precision and dependability [41–47]. The CLEF data comprise text-image pairs, as seen in Figure 3.

Figure 3 displays image-text pairs in which a number of descriptive text prompts are paired with each colonoscopy image. In addition to having distinct labels (such as 064086616.png and 040086376.png), each image features a set of text questions that offer several approaches to describing or creating comparable medical situations. This pairing structure produces a comprehensive dataset with detailed descriptions of every medical image from various textual perspectives. The instructions in each image addresses a variety of topics related to the medical scene, from identifying locations and image features to describing apparent instruments and discoveries. This creates a rich image–text relationship in which a single medical image is connected to multiple relevant text descriptions, each highlighting different aspects of the same clinical scenario.

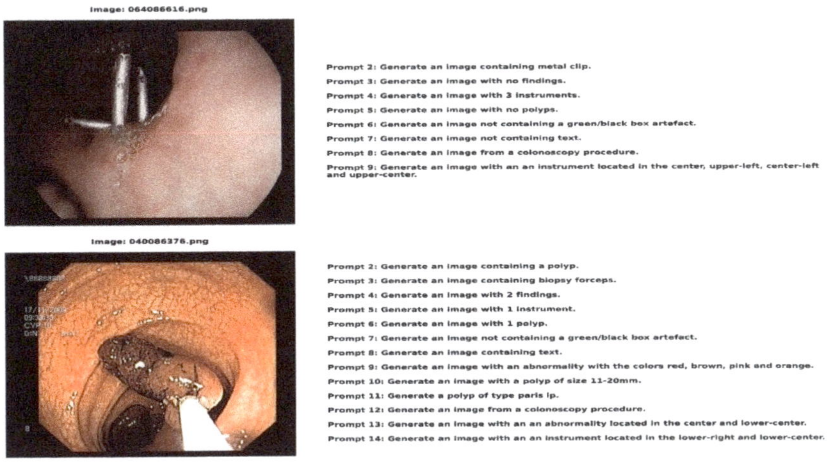

Figure 3. The dataset shows image–text pairs where each colonoscopy image is matched with multiple descriptive text prompt images.

3.3. *Algorithm*

The preprocessing pipeline coordinates the data preprocessing process through a strategic multihierarchical procedure. The first step is to turn the file that contains image locations and prompts into a structured framework using the pandas library by sorting out the data for polyps and non-polyps. This becomes the structural format of organized data that can feed other pre-processing and training model data stages. In the data partitioning process, random shuffling is used to have equal distribution over training, testing, and validation. The images are analyzed using the Python Imaging Library and each step of the pipeline is designed to support different classification models to achieve the best performance. The process of synthesizing colonoscopy images and training classification and segmentation models is formalized in Algorithm 1.

This algorithm presents the complete pipeline of our methodology, from data preparation through model training and evaluation. The algorithm takes as input colonoscopy images, custom prompts, and pre-trained models and outputs the best performing classifier and segmentation model along with their respective performance metrics. Each function in the algorithm represents a distinct phase in our pipeline, with the main process divided into the data preparation, synthesis, classification training, and segmentation model training stages. For reproducibility and convenience in the case of further investigations of this topic, all code, including models, training procedure scripts, and assessment schemes—is committed to the repository [48]. The datasets included in this study are available through their respective platforms, CLEF [38], CP-CHILD [39], and binary polyp data [40]. The synthesized images produced and their associated prompts can be accessed in [48]. The repository contains a detailed documentation of all implementation specifics, including hyperparameters and model setups, to facilitate the replication of our results and the advancement of the approach.

Algorithm 1 Colonoscopy Image analysis through text-to-image synthesis using generative AI

1. **Input:** Colonoscopy images, Custom prompts, Pre-trained Stable Diffusion 1.5, SAM model
2. **Output:** Best classifier C, Accuracy Acc, Best segmentation model S, Performance $Perf$
3. Dataset Preparation:
    - (a) $D_{orig} \leftarrow$ PrepareDataset (images, prompts)
    - (b) $G_{ft} \leftarrow$ FineTuneStable (Diffusion 1.5, D_{orig})
    - (c) $D_{syn} \leftarrow$ SynthesizeImages (G_{ft}, prompts, 5000)
    - (d) $D_{syn\_mask} \leftarrow$ GenerateMasks (D_{syn}, SAM)
    - (e) $D_{bal} \leftarrow$ SampleBalancedDataset (D_{orig}, D_{syn_mask}, 1000)
4. Classifier Training:
    - (a) **for** each M in {ViT, BiT, FixResNeXt, DeiT, EfficientNet} **do**
        - i. $C_M \leftarrow$ TrainClassifier (M, D_{bal})
        - ii. $Acc_M \leftarrow$ EvaluateClassifier (C_M, D_{bal})
5. Segmentation Model Training:
    - (a) **for** each S in {U-Net, PSPNet, FPN, LinkNet, MANet} **do**
        - i. $S_{trained} \leftarrow$ TrainSegmentation (S, D_{bal})
        - ii. $Perf_S \leftarrow$ EvaluateSegmentation ($S_{trained}$, D_{bal})
6. **return** Best classifier C, Accuracy Acc, Best segmentation model S, Performance $Perf$

Helper Functions:

FineTune (G, D):	Fine-tune model using DreamBooth and LoRA
SynthesizeImages (G, prompts, n):	Generate n images using G
GenerateMasks (D, SAM):	Generate masks for images in D using SAM
TrainClassifier (M, D):	Train classifier M on dataset D
EvaluateClassifier (C, D):	Evaluate classifier C
TrainSegmentation (S, D):	Train segmentation model S on dataset D
EvaluateSegmentation (S, D):	Evaluate segmentation model S

3.4. Software and Hardware Requirements

Python 3.10 programming language was used to implement all algorithms. The code was developed and executed using Anaconda 2023.09 distribution for environment management, Google Colab Pro (subscription-based), and Vertex Workbench 1.11 cloud platforms. We utilized various libraries including accelerate 0.16.0, PyTorch 2.0.1, torchvision 0.15.2, transformers 4.25.1, huggingface hub 0.15.1, diffusers 0.14.0, xformers 0.0.20, and bitsandbytes 0.37.0. Computations were performed on high-performance hardware: g2-standard-48 machines (4 NVIDIA L4 GPUs, 48 vCPUs, 192 GB RAM) and a 40 GB NVIDIA A100 GPU. The system utilized 83.5 GB of total RAM (with 2.2 GB utilized during the experiments) and 40.0 GB of GPU RAM, with a storage capacity of 235.7 GB (100 GB data disk + 150 GB boot disk). With pretrained Stable Diffusion 1.5 and SAM models for image synthesis and segmentation, this configuration facilitated a complete colonoscopy analysis pipeline that was evaluated using a variety of classifier architectures (ViT, BiT, FixResNeXt, DeiT, EfficientNet) and segmentation models (U-Net, PSPNet, FPN, LinkNet, MANet).

4. Results

The results and a discussion of the research are presented in this chapter, which details both software and hardware specifications. Table 1 presents a comparison of performance metrics (FID scores and average inception scores) in three different models (CLIP, SD and DB + LoRa) in three different datasets (single, multi and both). The FID scores range from

0.06 to 0.12, with SD showing the best performance (lowest FID scores) in all datasets. For Inception scores (IS avg), DB + LoRa consistently achieves the highest values (2.36), followed by SD (2.33), while CLIP shows the lowest IS avg (1.57). Each model maintains consistent performance across different datasets, with only minor variations in FID scores.

Table 1. Performance comparison of different models across datasets. The evaluation metrics include FID score (lower is better) and Inception score (IS) measurements, including average (avg), standard deviation (std), and median (med) values.

Dataset	Model	FID	IS avg	IS std	IS med
single	CLIP	0.11	1.57	0.03	1.56
multi	CLIP	0.11	1.57	0.03	1.56
both	CLIP	0.12	1.57	0.03	1.56
single	SD	0.06	2.33	0.07	2.34
multi	SD	0.06	2.33	0.07	2.34
both	SD	0.07	2.33	0.07	2.34
single	DB+LoRa	0.11	2.36	0.05	2.36
multi	DB+LoRa	0.07	2.36	0.05	2.36
both	DB+LoRa	0.08	2.36	0.05	2.36

Table 2 presents a detailed evaluation of model performance using Inception Score Groups (G1-G10) in three different models (CLIP, SD, and DB+LoRa) and three dataset configurations (single, multi, and both).

Table 2. Detailed Inception score evaluation across different groups (G1-G10) for each model and dataset combination. Groups represent different aspects of image quality assessment, showing model consistency across evaluation dimensions.

Dataset	Model	G1	G2	G3	G4	G5	G6	G7	G8	G9	G10
single	CLIP	1.56	1.55	1.55	1.57	1.55	1.55	1.54	1.54	1.56	1.51
multi	CLIP	1.56	1.55	1.55	1.57	1.55	1.55	1.54	1.54	1.56	1.51
both	CLIP	1.56	1.55	1.55	1.57	1.55	1.55	1.54	1.54	1.56	1.51
single	SD	2.37	2.40	2.40	2.39	2.24	2.26	2.31	2.22	2.25	2.77
multi	SD	2.37	2.40	2.40	2.39	2.24	2.26	2.31	2.22	2.25	2.77
both	SD	2.37	2.40	2.40	2.39	2.24	2.26	2.31	2.22	2.25	2.77
single	DB+LoRa	2.35	2.27	2.39	2.41	2.31	2.33	2.34	2.36	2.46	2.38
multi	DB+LoRa	2.35	2.27	2.39	2.41	2.31	2.33	2.34	2.36	2.46	2.38
both	DB+LoRa	2.35	2.27	2.39	2.41	2.31	2.33	2.34	2.36	2.46	2.38

The scores show that CLIP consistently maintains lower values (around 1.51–1.57) across all groups, while SD and DB+LoRa achieve higher scores (ranging from 2.22–2.77). In particular, SD shows greater variability with peaks in G2–G4 (≈ 2.40) and G10 (2.77), while DB+LoRa demonstrates more stable performance between groups with slight improvements in G4 (2.41) and G9 (2.46).

4.1. Image Generation Results

The synthesized images were measured using the inception score and the Fréchet Inception Distance. Among the three models, CLIP has the highest Fréchet FID score: 0.114 for 0.128 and 0.124 for three (3) datasets [9]. These higher ratings indicate poorer image quality and realism as CLIP-generated images seem less like real photos than other models. Figure 4 shows the final image. The higher FID score for the multicenter dataset indicates that CLIP struggles to create realistic images when trained on a diverse dataset from numerous medical facilities. High FID scores indicate that in this case, CLIP is not the best approach to obtain high-quality medical images. The images in Figure 4 demonstrate

CLIP's capability to generate synthetic colonoscopy images from textual descriptions, though with notable quality limitations when trained on diverse medical facility datasets.

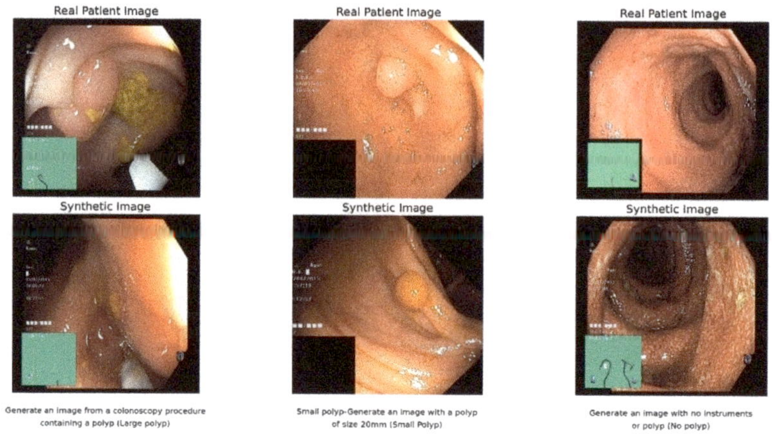

Figure 4. CLIP text to image based colonoscopy image generation. Comparison between real patient colonoscopy images (**top** row) and synthetic images generated using CLIP (**bottom** row) based on text prompts. **Left**: Generation of a large polyp. **Center**: Generation of a small 20mm polyp. **Right**: Generation of a normal colon view without instruments or polyps.

The implementation combines Stable Diffusion pre-trained, DreamBooth, and LoRA for the synthesis of colonoscopy images, optimized with a resolution of 512 pixels, a learning rate of $1 \times e^{-4}$, and specialized medical prompts. This architecture efficiently handles medical imaging complexity while minimizing computational resources through LoRA's targeted modifications and DreamBooth's instance-specific adaptations. Indicating better image quality and realism, the lowest FID scores for fine-tuned SD are "0.099" (single center), "0.064" (multicenter), and "0.067" (combined datasets) [9]. The reduced score of the multicenter dataset implies better performance of healthcare facilities. Although somewhat inferior to fine-tuned DB + LoRa, SD offers a high amount of visual diversity and quality, averaging "2.33" in all datasets. The consistency of SD across datasets shows its ability to function regardless of the data source. In general, fine-tuned SD produces high-quality, diversified medical images. Figure 5 shows the synthetic images that demonstrate SD's ability to generate diverse high-quality medical images with FID scores of 0.064–0.099 across different datasets, showing consistent performance regardless of data source.

The FID scores of "0.11" (single center), "0.073" (multicenter), and "0.076" (combined datasets) obtained by fine-tuning DB + LoRa show a high level of image quality and accuracy. With a wider range of training data, the multicenter score is more favorable. However, scores are higher than for SD, which has been fine-tuned, indicating a good level of quality overall. Regardless of the data source, the Inception score of "2.36" remains constant across all datasets, indicating strong image diversity and quality [9]. Figure 6 shows the result of the text-to-image synthesis using DB and LoRa. The synthetic images demonstrate the model's ability to generate colonoscopy images in response to specific text prompts, with each pair showing the relationship between real patient images and their synthetic counterparts.

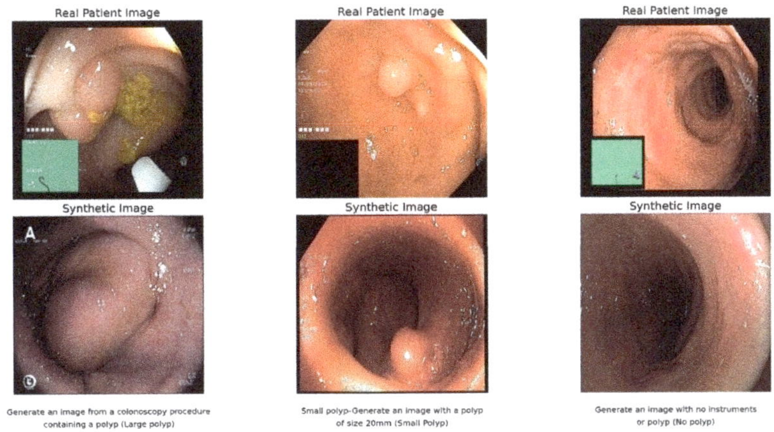

Figure 5. Fine-tuned SD text-to-image-based colonoscopy image generation. Comparison between real patient colonoscopy images (**top** row) and synthetic images generated using fine-tuned Stable Diffusion (**bottom** row). The image pairs show three scenarios: (**left**) a large polyp visualization, (**center**) a small 20mm polyp, and (**right**) normal colon without instruments or polyps.

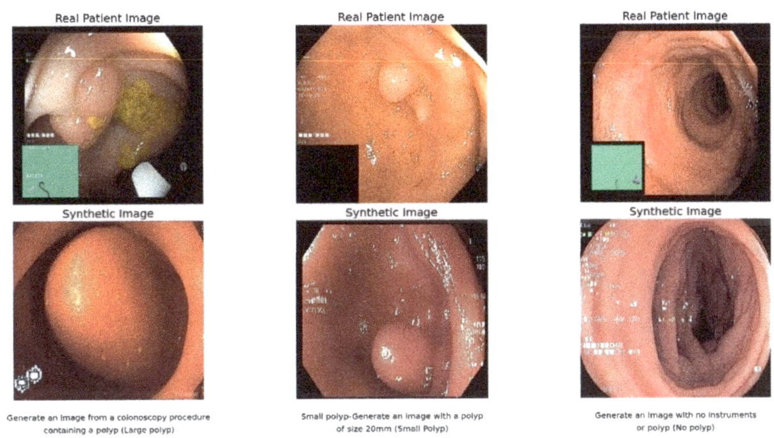

Figure 6. DB and LoRa text-to-image-based colonoscopy image generation. Comparison of real patient colonoscopy images (**top** row) with synthetic images generated using DB and LoRa models (**bottom** row). Three clinical scenarios are presented: (**left**) colonoscopy procedure showing a large polyp, (**center**) visualization of a small 20mm polyp, and (**right**) normal colon view without instruments or polyps.

In terms of image variety and value, these scores are slightly better than those of SD. Fine-tuned SD achieves higher FID scores, but fine-tuned DB + LoRA strikes a better balance between diversity and realism, potentially making it the best choice for medical imaging tasks that require high-quality and diverse image generation.

4.2. Model Comparison

Figures 7 and 8 show the evaluation of each visual generative AI model in terms of FID and IS in three datasets.

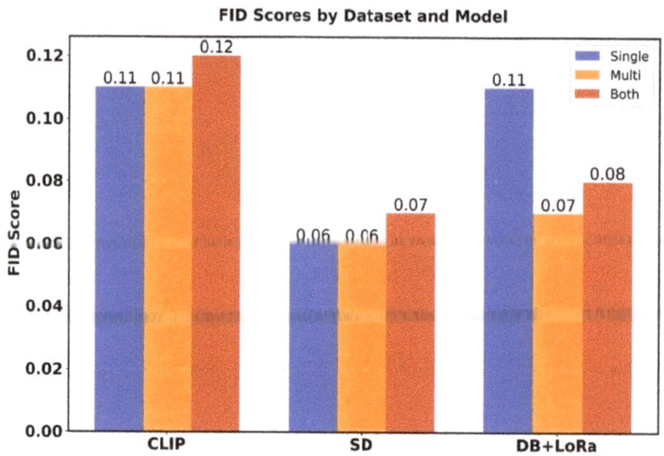

Figure 7. FID comparison across three models and three datasets.

While fine-tuned DB and LoRa produce high quality, lifelike images, fine-tuned SD beats CLIP and fine-tuned DB in generating such images. Its superiority is shown by producing the lowest FID values among all tests. With an average Inception score of 2.36, the DB + LoRa model ranks highest followed by fine-tuned SD, with an average of 2.33. The average starting score for CLIP is the lowest. However, fine-tuned DB + LoRA achieves a better balance between diversity and realism, so it may be the perfect solution for medical imaging positions that require both high-quality and diverse image generation.

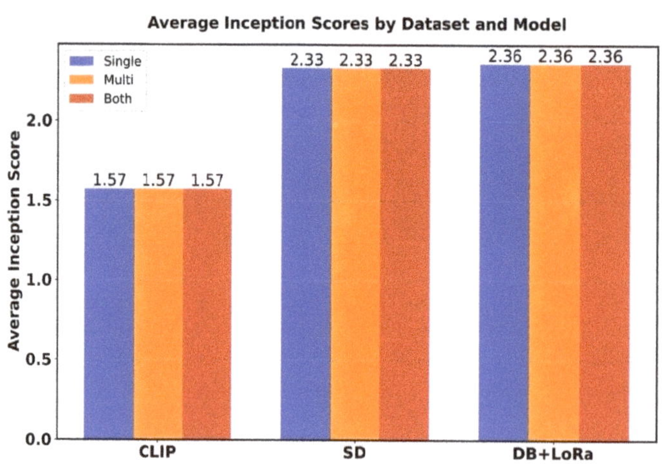

Figure 8. IS comparison across three models and three datasets.

4.3. Image Segmentation Results

This section comprises two primary tasks, namely image mask generation and image segmentation. The dataset contains 1824 images: 612 real colonoscopy images with masks and 300 synthetic images with masks. A pretrained faster R-CNN with ResNet50 backbone first classifies and localizes polyp regions using bounding boxes, which then guide the SAM model for precise mask generation. Image masks were created for shapes identified with the Segment Anything Model (SAM) [49]. The technique starts with initializing SAM with a pre-trained checkpoint and finds circles and outlines in the input image that mimic polyps.

Input points are produced along the boundary of every form found. Figure 9 shows the location of the polyp in both real and AI-generated endoscopic views, highlighting the similarity between actual and synthetic medical imaging data. Following mask generation with the Segment Anything Model (SAM), we performed manual visual screening of all masks generated. This validation process involved systematic examination of each image–mask pair to verify accuracy and alignment with anatomical boundaries. Masks that exhibited inaccuracies or did not properly delineate the target structures were excluded from further analysis, ensuring that the dataset contained only precisely segmented regions for subsequent processing. For model training and evaluation, a standard 80:20 train–test split was applied. This approach ensures robust model development by allocating 80% of the data for training and reserving 20% for independent testing, allowing for a comprehensive assessment of the performance and generalizability of the segmentation models.

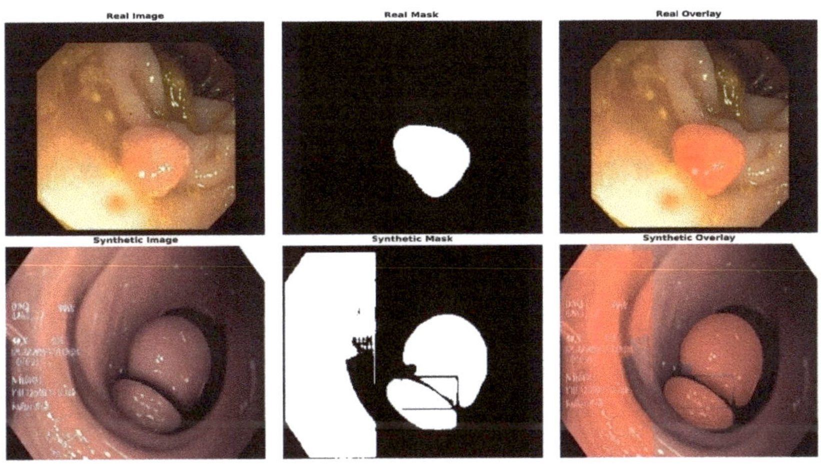

Figure 9. Comparison of real and synthetic colonoscopy images with polyp detection. Top row shows a real colonoscopy image with its corresponding binary mask and region overlay. Bottom row displays a synthetic colonoscopy image with its binary mask and region overlay.

The analyses of the five segmentation models showed that the metrics had varying effects on each model's performance. With the highest IoU (0.65), UNet showed strong performance in many metrics, particularly achieving the highest recall (0.85) and Dice coefficient (0.78). FPN demonstrated solid results with the highest precision (0.77) and PSNR (7.21). LinkNet achieved the highest F1 score (0.78) among all models, although its other metrics were comparable to its peers. PSPNet showed slightly lower overall performance, with the lowest IoU (0.63) and PSNR (6.64). MANet's performance was middle of the pack across most metrics, with values generally similar to FPN and LinkNet. Regarding structural similarity, all models showed relatively low SSIM scores ranging from 0.44 to 0.49, with UNet and FPN tied for the highest at 0.49. The PSNR values were consistently in the range of 6–7 in all models, with the FPN achieving the highest at 7.21.

Figures 10 and 11 show the segmentation findings for real and synthetic colonoscopy image polyp images.

A pink growth is shown against a crimson intestinal lining in the original photograph. The real mask displays the polyp area as white. The segmentation of the UNet is shown in black on the expected mask. Green indicates a valid identification, red indicates a missing area, and yellow indicates a false positive. The overlay contrasts the results. UNet accurately depicts the polyp's form and position but overestimates its size, especially around the edges. UNet's multiscale feature recognition and over-segmentation are shown here. Perhaps fine-tuning or postprocessing could sharpen edges. The results of this study are shown in Table 3. Table 3 shows the Dice coefficients. The five segmentation algorithms were thoroughly evaluated using the synthetic colonoscopy dataset, yielding the following results: UNet demonstrated better overall performance, achieving the highest scores in IoU (0.65), F1 score (0.76), and Dice coefficient (0.78), as seen in Table 3.

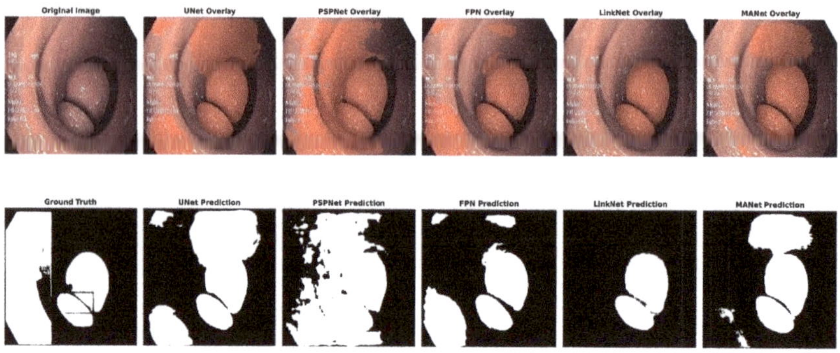

Figure 10. Comparison of polyp segmentation performance across different deep learning architectures. Top row shows overlay visualizations on the original (synthetic) colonoscopy image, while bottom row presents binary mask predictions. From left to right: original image, UNet, PSPNet, FPN, LinkNet, and MANet segmentation results, with ground truth mask for reference. The overlays (red regions) and binary predictions demonstrate varying segmentation accuracies and boundary detection capabilities across the different network architectures.

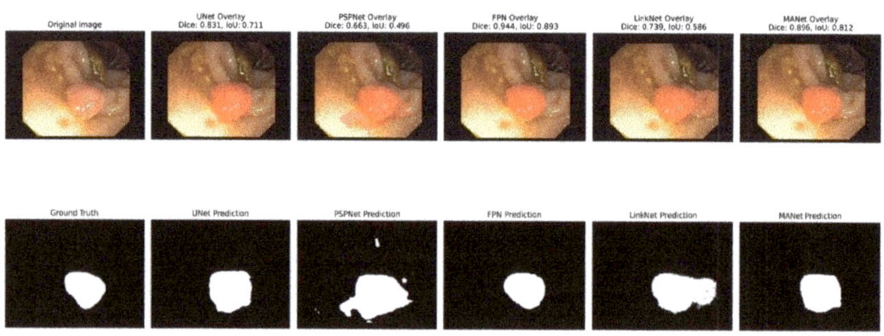

Figure 11. Comparison of polyp segmentation performance across different deep learning architectures. Top row shows the original (real) endoscopic image with model overlay predictions in red (UNet, PSPNet, FPN, LinkNet, and MANet). Bottom row displays the corresponding binary segmentation masks, with ground truth (leftmost) and model predictions, demonstrating the relative accuracy of each architecture in polyp region identification and boundary delineation.

Table 3. Comprehensive performance evaluation of segmentation models with results demonstrating varying capabilities across different architectures with UNet achieving superior performance in most metrics.

Model	IoU	F1 Score	Precision	Recall	PSNR	SSIM	Dice Coef.
UNet [50]	0.65	0.76	0.74	0.85	7.05	0.49	0.78
PSPNet [51]	0.63	0.76	0.71	0.84	6.64	0.44	0.77
FPN [52]	0.64	0.77	0.77	0.78	7.21	0.49	0.77
LinkNet [53]	0.64	0.78	0.73	0.83	7.01	0.47	0.77
MANet [54]	0.64	0.77	0.75	0.80	7.07	0.48	0.77

The models demonstrate consistently strong performance with minimal variation across metrics. UNet achieves a notably higher IoU of 0.65 compared to 0.63–0.64 for other models, indicating superior segmentation accuracy. The Dice coefficients range from 0.77 to 0.78, indicating an excellent overlap between predicted and ground truth segmentations. LinkNet shows the highest F1 score at 0.78, while FPN achieves the best PSNR at 7.21. SSIM values range from 0.44 to 0.49, with UNet and FPN tied for the highest structural similarity. Precision varies from 0.71 to 0.77, and recall ranges from 0.78 to 0.85, demonstrating a good balance between accuracy and completeness across all architectures. The result demonstrates a significant improvement over the results from [55].

4.4. Image Classification Results

The dataset used for classification consists of three sources: the original image dataset contains 1184 test images, 4138 training images, and 592 validation images; the synthetic image dataset has 358 test images, 1260 training images, and 182 validation images; and the augmented dataset comprises 1542 test images, 5398 training images, and 774 validation images. Advanced classification models, including ViT, BiT, FixResNeXt, DeiT, and EfficientNet, were trained using images generated from this investigation. Conventional metrics were used to evaluate these models. This comprehensive strategy aims to improve medical diagnosis and imaging technology. Figure 12 illustrates a 5 × 2 grid of original colonoscopy data randomly selected. Figure 13 illustrates the results of the models based on the original data.

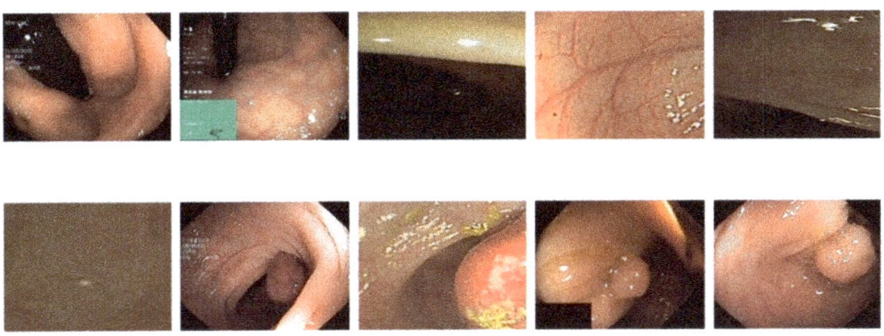

Figure 12. Endoscopic views from a colonoscopy procedure showing various segments and mucosal patterns of the colon interior.

EfficientNet has a pronounced superiority in all performance criteria used. Each metric confirmed that EfficientNet has one of the highest validation accuracy values of 97% and an F1 measures of 96.79% and is superior to all the models used. FixResNeXt was slightly less successful with a maximum validation accuracy of 86% and an F1 score of 85.95%. ViT's results are the second best of all networks, although they are far less impressive than EfficientNet's 96.79% AUC ratings.

Loss measurements shed more light on this discrepancy in performance: FixResNeXt has a validation loss of 0.36, while the remaining models have even higher levels of loss. The validation loss of EfficientNet is 0.11, making it the best performing model. Precision and recall also retain the same traits and are presented as follows. Validation precision and recall of EfficientNet: 96.8%, 96.8%; validation of the second best model, FixResNeXt: 86.2%, 85.9%. Specifically, most of the models demonstrate low discrepancies between the training and validation performance. EfficientNet demonstrates better adaptability to the data of this set, as well as higher efficiency in terms of all scores. The large accuracy margin points to the fact that the EfficientNet architecture is learning features and patterns in the data that other architectures are unable to, thereby making EfficientNet suitable for tasks such as the ones used in this initial dataset.

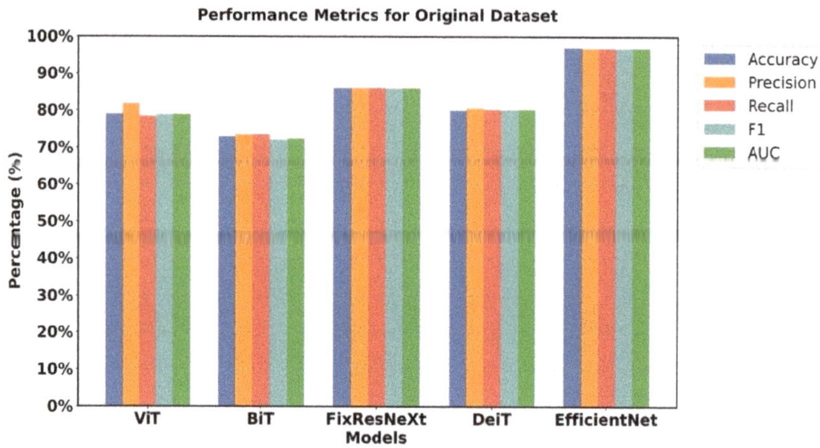

Figure 13. Performance comparison of deep learning and transformer-based models across multiple evaluation metrics, showing EfficientNet achieving superior performance across all measures on the original image dataset.

Figure 14 shows a 5 × 2 grid of randomly sampled synthetic colonoscopy data. Looking at the metrics in Figure 15, EfficientNet is smoother in almost all metrics, although not as dominant as it was with the initial data.

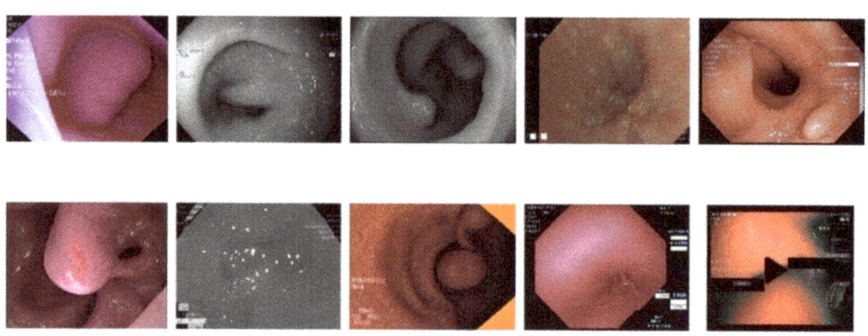

Figure 14. Synthetic endoscopic images generated to simulate various views and conditions encountered during medical endoscopy procedures.

The percentage accuracy of the training was 80 %, the accuracy of the validation was 79 %, and the F1 scores for the training and validation were 79.9% and 79.1%, respectively, which are comparatively lower than the scores obtained on the original data. Other models demonstrate better relative performance, specifically based on the metrics from the validation sets. FixResNeXt takes second place with the best validation accuracy of 71%, and an F1 score of 70.8%. BiT achieved a fantastic validation precision of 75.64% and ViT achieved a validation precision of 75.47%, which is higher than the training precisions of 64.98% and 61.46%, respectively.

Loss metrics further illustrate the narrowed gap: FixResNeXt's 0.58 loss and other models' losses are much closer to the validation loss of 0.5133, which belongs to EfficientNet.

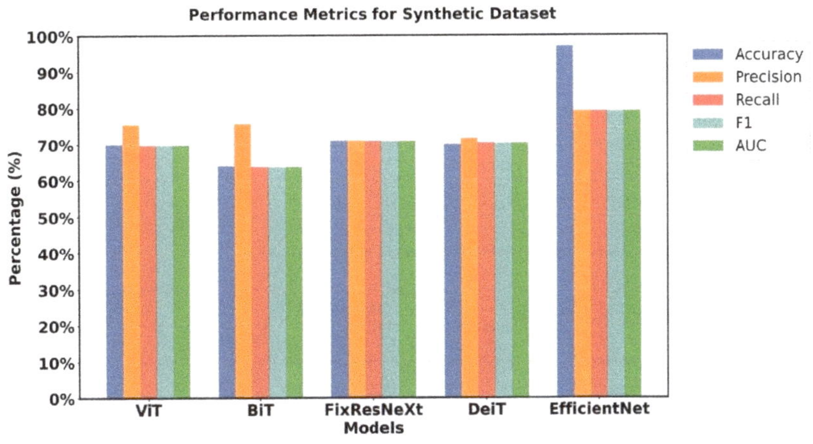

Figure 15. Performance evaluation of five deep learning and transformer-based models on AI-generated colonoscopy data, demonstrating generally lower but more consistent performance across models compared to original data, with EfficientNet maintaining superior accuracy but showing more metric variation.

An evaluation of overall performance highlights the fact that, with most models obtaining percentage scores within the range of 60–70% for the different evaluation criteria, synthetic data seem more difficult. This results from heightened complexity, variety, and noise in the synthetic data production process. The results indicate that the performance discrepancies between the models and the synthetic data stem from possible deficiencies not present in the actual data. Synthetic data may effectively enhance the evaluation of a model's robustness and its ability to generalize to novel occurrences.

Figure 16 shows a 5 $\times$ 5 grid of randomly sampled augmented colonoscopy data (combination of original and synthetic data). The augmented dataset causes a significant reversal in the performance of the various models and shows the variation in the data characteristics that affect the model performance. In this case, DeiT and ViT are the best that demonstrate high accuracy and F1 score, as well as the lowest error rate. Training precision of 98% was achieved, with a validation accuracy of 93%, while F1 scores achieved 97.94% in training and 92.89% in validation. The DeiT has shown the following performance, which shows a great improvement compared to the previous models. ViT achieved 93% validation accuracy and a 92.51% F1 score; in contrast, BiT achieved 92% validation accuracy with a 92.38% F1 score. This shows that the augmented dataset is well suited for transformer-based architectures.

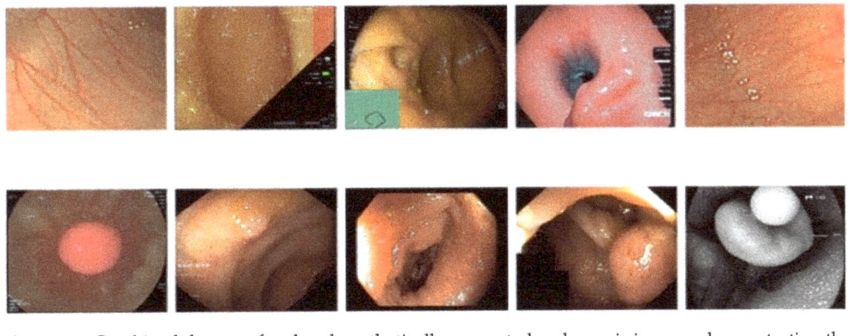

Figure 16. Combined dataset of real and synthetically generated endoscopic images, demonstrating the visual similarity between actual endoscopic findings and artificially generated medical imaging data.

In contrast, EfficientNet outperformed all other models in the previous datasets but has the lowest validation in this case, which is a precision score 86%. This change in the improvement rate is stark and underlines the importance of specific dataset attributes for model effectiveness. Loss metrics also point to these performance changes. Figure 17 shows that DeiT validation loss is 0.20, which is less than Efficient Net's 0.38 and the opposite of what has been seen in previous datasets. Relative performance can also be seen in the AUC scores, where DeiT achieved 92.90%, while EfficientNet achieved 86.05%.

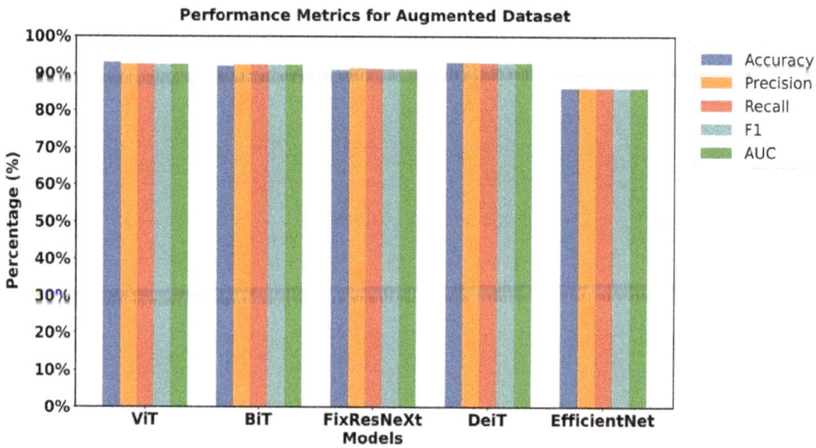

Figure 17. Performance evaluation of deep learning models on an augmented endoscopic dataset, showing substantially improved and more uniform performance across all models and metrics compared to both original and synthetic datasets, with most models achieving approximately 90% across all evaluation measures.

One unique feature of the intelligent data results is that most models had validation scores greater than 90% (EfficientNet not included). Training and validation performance are also closely matched for the top models with relatively little gap. For example, the training accuracy of 98% compared to the validation accuracy of 93% shows that DeiT and ViT have great generalization as seen in Figure 17.

These results indicate that the intelligent dataset contains distinguishable patterns, which makes transformer-based models highly effective. The high overall scores, as well as the proximity to the training validation performance, indicate that this dataset is more 'teachable' in gross terms, but with certain attributes that tend to benefit a given architectural design. This scenario shows that the structure of the model should correspond to the type of data and the qualitative difference that occurs in the work of the model in different sets.

This research captures major variations in the performance of the various models. Looking at the performance of the models in the original dataset, EfficientNet has the highest accuracy score and the highest F1 score (97% accuracy, 96.79% F1). FixResNeXt comes next in a short time, followed by other models that range from at most 75–80% on most of the metrics.

In the case of the synthetic dataset, overall model performances were comparatively lower than those achieved on the original dataset. EfficientNet retains a sample advantage over FixRexNet, although the score boundaries are significantly lower (79% validation accuracy). The performance difference decreases with FixResNeXt and VIT as close competitors, but there are differences in the validation precision: 71% for FixResNeXt and 75.47% for VIT, as seen in Figures 18 and 19.

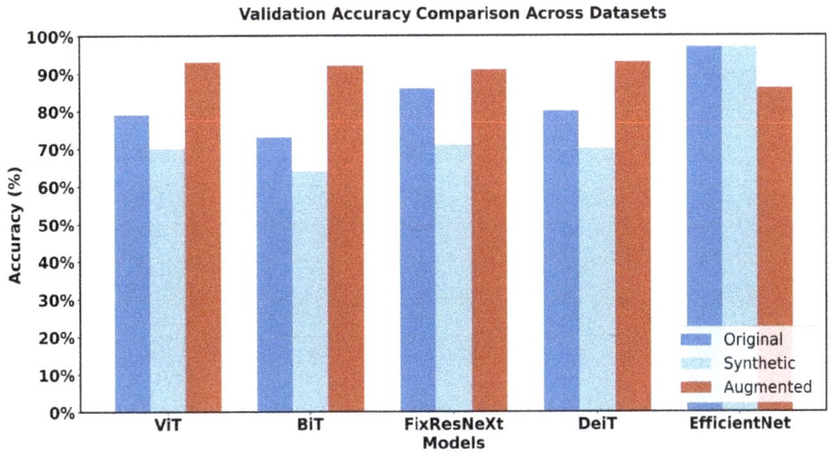

Figure 18. Validated accuracy comparison across the 3 datasets.

The augmented dataset shows a complete transition. The result shows that ViT and DeiT are the most accurate models with a validation accuracy of 93% and having the highest f1 score of 92.89%.

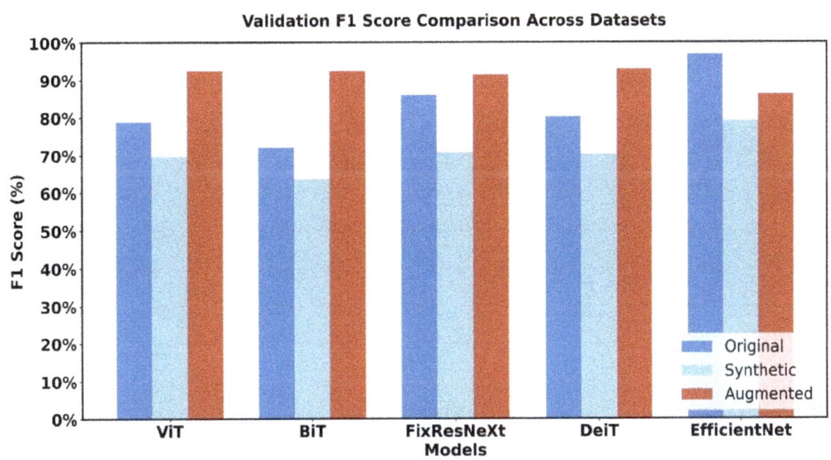

Figure 19. Validated F1 Score comparison across the 3 datasets.

The other two architectures, FixResNeXt and BiT, follow slightly behind ViT and DeiT. In contrast, here the validation metrics look worse for the accuracy of EfficientNet (86%). In particular, most customer variants demonstrate improved accuracy in the augmented dataset compared to the synthetic and original datasets, thus containing more learnable patterns. The Vision Transformer (ViT) demonstrates remarkable proficiency in polyp detection in both real and synthetic colonoscopy images, as shown in the figure. The model, trained on an augmented dataset that combined real colonoscopy images and synthetic data generated through fine-tuned Stable Diffusion, processes the input images by dividing them into fixed-size patches that are linearly embedded and processed through transformer encoder blocks. This training approach enables the ViT to learn robust features common to both real and synthetic polyps, preventing overfitting to specific real-world image characteristics. The model's effectiveness is evident in its high-confidence predictions:

accurately identifying a subtle polyp in the real image with 0.95 confidence and a more prominent polyp in the synthetic image with 0.99 confidence. The ViT generates appropriate bounding boxes in both cases, a smaller and precise box for the real polyp and a larger box that encompasses the full structure of the synthetic polyp, validating the effectiveness of synthetic data enhancement in medical image analysis, as seen in Figure 20.

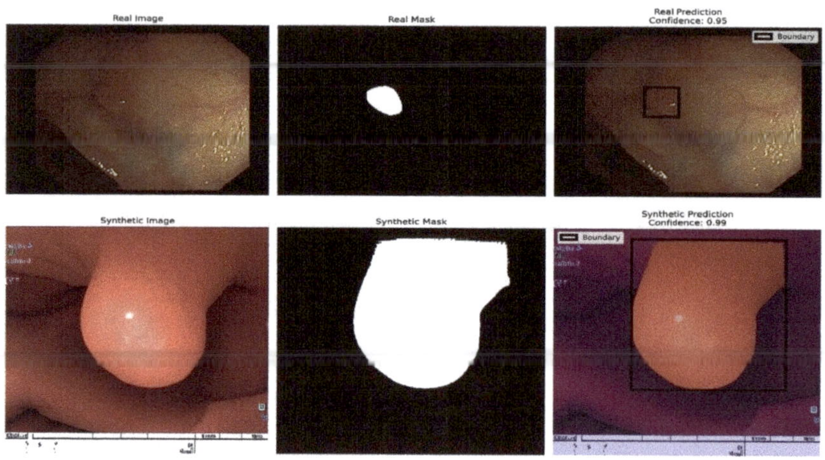

Figure 20. Visual comparison of ViT-based polyp detection performance on real and synthetic colonoscopy images, demonstrating high confidence predictions (0.95 and 0.99, respectively) with accurate boundary box localization.

The difference between training and validation scores, which affect a model's capacity to generalize, is the smallest for the augmented dataset. By comparing the outcomes, the results show that EfficientNet, one of the most variable networks, performs worst in intelligent dataset but better in the original dataset. Conversely, in the augmented dataset, the transformer-based structure (DeiT, ViT) performs much better overall. Intelligent Data Augmentation produced the best overall results for the following reasons:

1. **High Performance**
   The augmented dataset demonstrated exceptional performance, consistently achieving accuracy metrics above 92% in different models and evaluation metrics. This indicates robust and reliable model behavior across various architectural implementations.
2. **Performance Consistency**
   A notable pattern emerged in the comparative analysis. The original dataset showed inconsistent performance, with only one model achieving high accuracy (EfficientNet with 97% validation accuracy). The synthetic dataset consistently showed lower performance across all models. In contrast, the augmented dataset maintained consistently high performance across multiple architectures, indicating improved data quality and representation.
3. **Strong Generalization**
   The minimal gap between training and validation accuracy in the augmented dataset (typically within 2-3 percentage points) indicates effective knowledge transfer, reduced overfitting, and robust model generalization capabilities.
4. **Architecture-Agnostic Performance**
   Unlike the original and synthetic datasets, which showed significant performance variations between different architectures, the augmented dataset demonstrated more

balanced performance. This indicates reduced architecture-specific bias in the learning process.

5. **Enhanced Model Applicability**
The consistent high performance across diverse architectural approaches indicates that the knowledge extracted from the augmented dataset is more universally applicable. The learned features are more generalizable across different model architectures, and the dataset provides robust training signals for various deep learning approaches.

Although the score accrued from the initial dataset was the maximum (97% for EfficientNet), intelligent data offered the highest precision of performance with model consistency and generic precision. This makes it the most valuable from a machine learning perspective because in addition to offering a clear separation for analyzing the data, it can also inform the best choice for model selection and could translate to superior accuracy in real-world applications.

5. Discussion

This study created a novel strategy to address the lack of medical imaging data, especially when it comes to colonoscopy operations for underrepresented groups. The main objective of the study was to improve the detection models of CRC by combining various data augmentation approaches with sophisticated machine learning and deep learning techniques to synthesize colonoscopy images. To produce realistic artificial colonoscopy images, the researchers modified and improved several visual generative AI models, such as CLIP, Stable Diffusion (SD), and DreamBooth (DB) with LoRA. The Fréchet Inception Distance and Inception score were used to thoroughly assess the quality of these produced images. The research used several models for image classification tasks, including EfficientNet, FixResNeXt, Big Transfer, Vision Transformer, and Data-efficient Image Transformers. The study used original, augmented, and synthetic datasets for testing and training. And also for image segmentation tasks, the study implemented U-Net, PSNet, FPN, LinkNet, and MANet. With lower FID scores across all datasets, the results showed that DreamBooth in conjunction with LoRA created the most realistic photos. ViT and DeiT models achieved 93% validation precision and 92.89% F1 scores in classification tasks, according to the expanded dataset. This showed that creating synthetic images from high-quality data can improve model performance and generalizability across various demographic subgroups.

The CLIP, SD, and DB LoRa models were all successfully used for colonoscopy image generation in the study. Fine-tuned SD and DB LoRa produced the lowest FID scores for the datasets in terms of image originality and quality. The adapted models achieved optimal results when generating several images of synthetic colonoscopy. Inception scores were used to prove the diversity and realism of the generated image. DB LoRa received the highest average IS value of 2.36 for all datasets, indicating good image variety and quality. The quality and clinical usefulness of the images generated have therefore been quantitatively assessed using FID and IS metrics. The FID scores remained below 15 while the IS values were above 2 in all different datasets, which is an indication of the high quality and diversification of the images synthesized. The researchers were able to train and test the ViT, BiT, FixResNeXt, DeiT, and EfficientNet models using synthetic, original, and augmented data. The augmented data strengthened the results in addition to obtaining a higher validation precision with ViT and DeiT both having a precision of 93% and an F1 score of 92.89%, which means that synthetic data enhancement is effective. For the image segmentation task, the study adopted and assessed the performance of U-Net, PSNet, FPN, LinkNet, and MANet. FPN produced excellent results, with an IoU of 0.64, an F1 score of 0.78, a recall of 0.75, and a Dice coefficient of 0.77.

This study clearly showed both improved performance and fairness of the model with augmented synthetic data. The augmented dataset performed steadily better than the original and synthetic datasets for all models and measures, indicating lower bias and better generalization. All research objectives were met systematically, indicating general research contributions in the areas of synthetic image generation, improved model performance, and possible elimination of bias when using AI-enabled analysis of colonoscopy images. By improving AI-based colonoscopy screening with improved training datasets, this study significantly reduces health disparities in CRC therapy outcomes. In addition to demonstrating how artificial data augmentation can improve the effectiveness and equity of AI models for polyp recognition and classification, this study advances the field of generative AI in medical imaging. The innovative approach to medical picture synthesis, extensive evaluation techniques, improved model performance, and important implications for healthcare equity are just a few of its strengths. This study extensively evaluated a number of state-of-the-art models in a variety of fields and showed increased validation accuracy using better datasets. However, this study also has drawbacks, especially when it comes to a thorough clinical validation and moral issues around the use of artificial data in healthcare settings, which need further investigation before practical implementation.

6. Conclusions

In conclusion, this work has shown that generative AI, text-to-image synthesis, and intelligent data augmentation can be applied to overcome limitations arising from a limited number of colonoscopy images and data bias. This study demonstrated a novel way to generate a diverse and realistic number of synthetic colonoscopy images that could reflect a rather wide range of patients by improving state-of-the-art models such as CLIP, DB LoRa and SD. The comparative analysis of these synthetic images computed via FID and IS metrics, as well as the outcome of classification and segmentation models trained to utilize augmented datasets, prove the critical enhancements in AI model effectiveness and non-bias. The proposed augmentation method using original and synthetic images showed better performance than original and purely synthetic datasets for several models and evaluation metrics. This study helps address the problem of minority representation in both the identification and treatment of CRC by improving the training datasets of AI-supported colonoscopy technologies. It also pushes the point of generative AI in analyzing colonoscopy and medical imaging at large, moving with more than colonoscopy applications. However, some limitations must be investigated in subsequent studies, for example, the requirement for clinical evaluation of synthesized images and some ethical concerns about incorporating AI-generated medical data. However, this work sets a robust framework upon which future studies can build to enhance the efficiency of applying artificial intelligence to the analysis of medical images and to overcome disparities affecting health in different countries. This study recommends the use of augmented datasets in AI model training for colonoscopy assistance tools, as synthetic image generation has produced promising results. Augmented data sets improve developer resources, model accuracy, and generalization while also reducing discrimination caused by the underrepresentation of racial minorities in medical imaging data. A notable limitation of this study is the absence of human evaluation through blinded evaluation. Future work would benefit from having experienced medical professionals perform blinded comparisons between real and synthetic colonoscopy images. This expert evaluation would provide valuable information on the clinical viability of the generated images and help validate whether the synthetic data could effectively supplement medical training datasets. Clinical validation studies in real world settings are critical to determining the effectiveness of these methods and addressing potential risks before deployment. Future research should focus on large-scale clinical validation of AI models trained on augmented datasets, the development of ethical guidelines for the use of synthetic medical images in clinical and training settings, and the application of synthetic data augmentation techniques to other medical imaging modalities besides colonoscopy. General implementation requires careful consideration of practical challenges, approval processes, and integration into existing ones.

Author Contributions: Conceptualization, O.O.E.P., O.T.A. and M.M.R.; methodology, M.M.R., F.K., O.O.E.P. and A.M.J.-O.; software, O.O.E.P.; validation, O.O.E.P., F.K. and M.M.R.; formal analysis, O.O.E.P.; investigation, O.O.E.P.; resources, F.K. and M.M.R.; data curation, O.O.E.P. and M.M.R.; writing—original draft preparation, F.K., M.M.R. and O.O.E.P.; writing—review and editing, O.T.A., A.M.J.-O., F.K. and M.M.R.; visualization, O.O.E.P. and O.T.A.; supervision, F.K. and M.M.R.; project administration, F.K. and M.M.R.; funding acquisition, F.K. and M.M.R. All authors have read and agreed to the published version of the manuscript.

Funding: This work is supported in part by the National Science Foundation (NSF) under Grant No. 2131307, "CISE-MSI: DP: IIS: III: Deep Learning-Based Automated Concept and Caption Generation of Medical Images Towards Developing an Effective Decision Support System", and in part by the Office of the Director, National Institutes of Health (NIH) Common Fund under Award No. 1OT2OD032581-01. The content is solely the responsibility of the authors and does not necessarily represent the official views of AIM-AHEAD, the NIH, or any other funding agencies.

Institutional Review Board Statement: Not applicable.

Informed Consent Statement: This work used publicly available data.

Data Availability Statement: The data presented in this study are openly available. The source code and implementation details can be found at https://github.com/Ejigsonpeter/Text-Guided-Synthesis-for-Colon-Cancer-Screening/tree/main (accessed on 20 January 2025). The datasets used in this study are accessible through secure cloud storage. The complete dataset collection is available at https://drive.google.com/drive/folders/12WrV0W1ULOrhfWy8TxAwLHDfqg9iiIna?usp=sharing (accessed on 20 October 2024). The synthetic dataset, original dataset, augmented dataset, and CLEF dataset can be accessed through their respective repositories [https://drive.google.com/file/d/1PXiYVGK6Mv3cLe0xNbf1e5VsFdUbuTq8/view?usp=sharing, https://drive.google.com/file/d/1eqdnWFhXp1afbj62JNc7QGkEkNzVAolF/view?usp=sharing, https://drive.google.com/file/d/1TzA-_La1vub8TM8PHnC5uUDF33wZNw0J/view?usp=sharing, https://drive.google.com/file/d/1_6coUaFtFmMDSITcDiviaESl-5rESfDm/view?usp=sharing (accessed on 20 November 2024)].

Conflicts of Interest: The authors declare no conflicts of interest.

Abbreviations

The following abbreviations are used in this manuscript:

AI	Artificial Intelligence
AIGC	AI-Generated Content
ArSDM	Arbitrary-Style Diffusion Model
AUC	Area Under the Curve
BiT	Big Transfer
BLIP	Bootstrapping Language-Image Pre-training
CADe	Computer-Aided Detection
CFM	Cross Fusion Module
cGAN	Conditional Generative Adversarial Network
CIM	Cross Interaction Module
CLIP	Contrastive Language-Image Pre-Training
CNN	Convolutional Neural Network

CRC	Colorectal Cancer
DB	DreamBooth
DeiT	Data-Efficient Image Transformers
DL	Deep Learning
DR	Adenoma Detecting Rate
FCNN	Fully Convolutional Neural Network
FID	Fréchet Inception Distance
FPN	Feature Pyramid Network
GANs	Generative Adversarial Networks
HD	High Definition
IS	Inception Score
LDM	Latent Diffusion Model
LinkNet	Link Network
LoRA	Low-Rank Adaptation
MANet	Multi-Scale Attention Network
Mask R-CNN	Mask Region-based Convolutional Neural Network
mDice	Mean Dice Coefficient
mIoU	Mean Intersection over Union
ML	Machine Learning
Polyp-PVT	Polyp Pyramid Vision Transformer
PRISMA	Preferred Reporting Items for Systematic Reviews and Meta-Analyses
PSPNet	Pyramid Scene Parsing Network
SAM	Spatial Attention Module
SD	Stable Diffusion
SSPP	Single Sample Per Person
U-Net	U-Shaped Network
VQGAN	Vector-Quantized Generative Adversarial Network

References

1. Wang, P.; Berzin, T.M.; Brown, J.R.G.; Bharadwaj, S.; Becq, A.; Xiao, X.; Liu, P.; Li, L.; Song, Y.; Zhang, D.; et al. Real-time automatic detection system increases colonoscopic polyp and adenoma detection rates: A prospective randomised controlled study. *Gut* **2019**, *68*, 1813–1819. [CrossRef] [PubMed]
2. Bernal, J.; Tajkbaksh, N.; Sanchez, F.J.; Matuszewski, B.J.; Chen, H.; Yu, L.; Angermann, Q.; Romain, O.; Rustad, B.; Balasingham, I.; et al. Comparative Validation of Polyp Detection Methods in Video Colonoscopy: Results from the MICCAI 2015 Endoscopic Vision Challenge. *IEEE Trans. Med. Imaging* **2017**, *36*, 1231–1249. [CrossRef] [PubMed]
3. Kim, J.J.H.; Um, R.S.; Lee, J.W.Y.; Ajilore, O. Generative AI can fabricate advanced scientific visualizations: Ethical implications and strategic mitigation framework. *AI Ethics* **2024**. [CrossRef]
4. Videau, M.; Knizev, N.; Leite, A.; Schoenauer, M.; Teytaud, O. Interactive Latent Diffusion Model. In *Proceedings of the Genetic and Evolutionary Computation Conference*; ACM: New York, NY, USA, 2023; pp. 586–596. [CrossRef]
5. Bray, F.; Ferlay, J.; Soerjomataram, I.; Siegel, R.L.; Torre, L.A.; Jemal, A. Global cancer statistics 2018: GLOBOCAN estimates of incidence and mortality worldwide for 36 cancers in 185 countries. *CA Cancer J. Clin.* **2018**, *68*, 394–424. [CrossRef]
6. Alhabeeb, S.K.; Al-Shargabi, A.A. Text-to-Image Synthesis with Generative Models: Methods, Datasets, Performance Metrics, Challenges, and Future Direction. *IEEE Access* **2024**, *12*, 24412–24427. [CrossRef]
7. Tan, Y.X.; Lee, C.P.; Mai, N.; Lim, K.M.; Lim, J.Y.; Alqahtani, A. Recent Advances in Text-to-Image Synthesis: Approaches, Datasets and Future Research Prospects. *IEEE Access* **2023**, *11*, 88099–88115. [CrossRef]
8. Iglesias, G.; Talavera, E.; Díaz-Álvarez, A. A survey on GANs for computer vision: Recent research, analysis and taxonomy. *Comput. Sci. Rev.* **2023**, *48*, 100553. [CrossRef]
9. Ejiga Peter, O.O.; Rahman, M.M.; Khalifa, F. Advancing AI-Powered Medical Image Synthesis: Insights from MedVQA-GI Challenge Using CLIP, Fine-Tuned Stable Diffusion, and Dream-Booth + LoRA. Conference and Labs of the Evaluation Forum. 2024. Available online: https://ceur-ws.org/Vol-3740/paper-145.pdf (accessed on 12 December 2024).
10. Najjar, R. Redefining Radiology: A Review of Artificial Intelligence Integration in Medical Imaging. *Diagnostics* **2023**, *13*, 2760. [CrossRef]

11. Alnaggar, O.A.M.F.; Jagadale, B.N.; Saif, M.A.N.; Ghaleb, O.A.; Ahmed, A.A.; Aqlan, H.A.A.; Al-Ariki, H.D.E. Efficient artificial intelligence approaches for medical image processing in healthcare: Comprehensive review, taxonomy, and analysis. *Artif. Intell. Rev.* **2024**, *57*, 221. [CrossRef]
12. Arora, A.; Alderman, J.E.; Palmer, J.; Ganapathi, S.; Laws, E.; Mccradden, M.D.; Oakden-Rayner, L.; Pfohl, S.R.; Ghassemi, M.; McKay, F.; et al. The value of standards for health datasets in artificial intelligence-based applications. *Nat. Med.* **2023**, *29*, 2929–2938. [CrossRef]
13. Han, P.; Ye, C.; Zhou, J.; Zhang, J.; Hong, J.; Li, X. Latent-based Diffusion Model for Long-tailed Recognition. In Proceedings of the IEEE/CVF Conference on Computer Vision and Pattern Recognition Workshops, Seattle, WA, USA, 17–18 June 2024.
14. Du, Y.; Jiang, Y.; Tan, S.; Wu, X.; Dou, Q.; Li, Z.; Li, G.; Wan, X. ArSDM: Colonoscopy Images Synthesis with Adaptive Refinement Semantic Diffusion Models. In Proceedings of the Medical Image Computing and Computer Assisted Intervention—MICCAI 2023, Vancouver, BC, Canada, 8–12 October 2023. [CrossRef]
15. Ku, H.; Lee, M. TextControlGAN: Text-to-Image Synthesis with Controllable Generative Adversarial Networks. *Appl. Sci.* **2023**, *13*, 5098. [CrossRef]
16. Iqbal, M.A.; Jadoon, W.; Kim, S.K. Synthetic Image Generation Using Conditional GAN-Provided Single-Sample Face Image. *Appl. Sci.* **2024**, *14*, 5049. [CrossRef]
17. Shin, Y.; Qadir, H.A.; Aabakken, L.; Bergsland, J.; Balasingham, I. Automatic Colon Polyp Detection using Region based Deep CNN and Post Learning Approaches. *IEEE Access* **2019**, *6*, 40950–40962. [CrossRef]
18. Qadir, H.A.; Shin, Y.; Solhusvik, J.; Bergsland, J.; Aabakken, L.; Balasingham, I. Polyp Detection and Segmentation using Mask R-CNN: Does a Deeper Feature Extractor CNN Always Perform Better? In Proceedings of the International Symposium on Medical Information and Communication Technology (ISMICT), Oslo, Norway, 8–10 May 2019; pp. 1–6. [CrossRef]
19. Dong, B.; Wang, W.; Fan, D.-P.; Li, J.; Fu, H.; Shao, L. Polyp-PVT: Polyp Segmentation with Pyramid Vision Transformers. *arXiv* **2021**, arXiv:2108.06932. [CrossRef]
20. Repici, A.; Badalamenti, M.; Maselli, R.; Correale, L.; Radaelli, F.; Rondonotti, E.; Ferrara, E.; Spadaccini, M.; Alkandari, A.; Fugazza, A.; et al. Efficacy of Real-Time Computer-Aided Detection of Colorectal Neoplasia in a Randomized Trial. *Gastroenterology* **2020**, *159*, 512–520.e7. [CrossRef]
21. Kudo, S.E.; Misawa, M.; Mori, Y.; Hotta, K.; Ohtsuka, K.; Ikematsu, H.; Saito, Y.; Takeda, K.; Nakamura, H.; Ichimasa, K.; et al. Artificial Intelligence-assisted System Improves Endoscopic Identification of Colorectal Neoplasms. *Clin. Gastroenterol. Hepatol.* **2020**, *18*, 1874–1881.e2. [CrossRef]
22. Zhou, J.; Wu, L.; Wan, X.; Shen, L.; Liu, J.; Zhang, J.; Jiang, X.; Wang, Z.; Yu, S.; Kang, J.; et al. A novel artificial intelligence system for the assessment of bowel preparation (with video). *Gastrointest Endosc* **2020**, *91*, 428–435.e2. [CrossRef]
23. Mahmood, F.; Chen, R.; Durr, N.J. Unsupervised Reverse Domain Adaptation for Synthetic Medical Images via Adversarial Training. *IEEE Trans. Med. Imaging* **2018**, *37*, 2572–2581. [CrossRef] [PubMed]
24. Goceri, E. Medical image data augmentation: Techniques, comparisons and interpretations. *Artif. Intell. Rev.* **2023**, *56*, 12561–12605. [CrossRef]
25. Yang, Z.; Zhan, F.; Liu, K.; Xu, M.; Lu, S. AI-Generated Images as Data Source: The Dawn of Synthetic Era. *arXiv* **2023**. [CrossRef]
26. Cao, Y.; Li, S.; Liu, Y.; Yan, Z.; Dai, Y.; Yu, P.S.; Sun, L. A Comprehensive Survey of AI-Generated Content (AIGC): A History of Generative AI from GAN to ChatGPT. *arXiv* **2023**. [CrossRef]
27. Bandi, A.; Adapa, P.V.S.R.; Kuchi, Y.E.V.P.K. The Power of Generative AI: A Review of Requirements, Models, Input–Output Formats, Evaluation Metrics, and Challenges. *Future Internet* **2023**, *15*, 260. [CrossRef]
28. Bendel, O. Image synthesis from an ethical perspective. *AI Soc.* **2023**. [CrossRef]
29. Derevyanko, N.; Zalevska, O. Comparative analysis of neural networks Midjourney, Stable Diffusion, and DALL-E and ways of their implementation in the educational process of students of design specialities. *Pedagog. Psychol.* **2023**, *9*, 36–44. [CrossRef]
30. Sánchez-Peralta, L.F.; Bote-Curiel, L.; Picón, A.; Sánchez-Margallo, F.M.; Pagador, J.B. Deep learning to find colorectal polyps in colonoscopy: A systematic literature review. *Artif. Intell. Med.* **2020**, *108*, 101923. [CrossRef] [PubMed]
31. Salimans, T.; Goodfellow, I.; Zaremba, W.; Cheung, V.; Radford, A.; Chen, X. Improved Techniques for Training GANs. In *Advances in Neural Information Processing Systems*; Lee, D., Sugiyama, M., Luxburg, U., Guyon, I., Garnett, R., Eds.; Curran Associates, Inc.: Red Hook, NY, USA, 2016.
32. Heusel, M.; Ramsauer, H.; Unterthiner, T.; Nessler, B.; Hochreiter, S. GANs Trained by a Two Time-Scale Update Rule Converge to a Local Nash Equilibrium. In *Advances in Neural Information Processing Systems*; Guyon, I., Von Luxburg, U., Bengio, S., Wallach, H., Fergus, R., Vishwanathan, S., Garnett, R., Eds.; Curran Associates, Inc.: Red Hook, NY, USA, 2017.
33. Wang, P.; Xiao, X.; Glissen Brown, J.R.; Berzin, T.M.; Tu, M.; Xiong, F.; Hu, X.; Liu, P.; Song, Y.; Zhang, D.; et al. Development and validation of a deep-learning algorithm for the detection of polyps during colonoscopy. *Nat. Biomed. Eng.* **2018**, *2*, 741–748. [CrossRef]

34. Misawa, M.; Kudo, S.E.; Mori, Y.; Cho, T.; Kataoka, S.; Yamauchi, A.; Ogawa, Y.; Maeda, Y.; Takeda, K.; Ichimasa, K.; et al. Artificial Intelligence-Assisted Polyp Detection for Colonoscopy: Initial Experience. *Gastroenterology* **2018**, *154*, 2027–2029.e3. [CrossRef]
35. Guo, Y.; Bernal, J.; Matuszewski, B.J. Polyp Segmentation with Fully Convolutional Deep Neural Networks—Extended Evaluation Study. *J. Imaging* **2020**, *6*, 69. [CrossRef]
36. Borgli, H.; Thambawita, V.; Smedsrud, P.H.; Hicks, S.; Jha, D.; Eskeland, S.L.; Randel, K.R.; Pogorelov, K.; Lux, M.; Nguyen, D.T.D.; et al. HyperKvasir, a comprehensive multi-class image and video dataset for gastrointestinal endoscopy. *Sci. Data* **2020**, *7*, 283. [CrossRef]
37. Beaumont, R. LAION-5B: A New Era of Open Large-Scale Multi-Modal Datasets. 2022. Available online: https://laion.ai/blog/laion-5b/ (accessed on 15 December 2024).
38. Hicks, S.; Storås, A.; Halvorsen, P.; De Lange, T.; Riegler, M.; Thambawita, V. Overview of ImageCLEFmedical 2023—Medical Visual Question Answering for Gastrointestinal Tract. 2023. Available online: https://ceur-ws.org/Vol-3497/paper-107.pdf (accessed on 15 December 2024).
39. Wang, W.; Tian, J. CP-CHILD Records the Colonoscopy Data. figshare 2020. Available online: https://figshare.com/articles/dataset/CP-CHILD_zip/12554042?file=23383508 (accessed on 15 December 2024).
40. Rahman, M.S. Binary Polyps Classification. 2024. Available online: https://www.kaggle.com/datasets/mdsahilurrahman71/binary-polyps-classification?resource=download (accessed on 15 December 2024).
41. Chicco, D.; Jurman, G. The advantages of the Matthews correlation coefficient (MCC) over F1 score and accuracy in binary classification evaluation. *BMC Genom.* **2020**, *21*, 6. [CrossRef]
42. Fawcett, T. An introduction to ROC analysis. *Pattern Recognit. Lett.* **2006**, *27*, 861–874. [CrossRef]
43. Rezatofighi, H.; Tsoi, N.; Gwak, J.; Sadeghian, A.; Reid, I.; Savarese, S. Generalized Intersection Over Union: A Metric and A Loss for Bounding Box Regression. In Proceedings of the IEEE/CVF Conference on Computer Vision and Pattern Recognition (CVPR), Long Beach, CA, USA, 15–20 June 2019; pp. 658–666. [CrossRef]
44. Powers, D.M.W. Evaluation: From precision, recall and F-measure to ROC, informedness, markedness and correlation. *arXiv* **2020**, arXiv:2010.16061.
45. Hore, A.; Ziou, D. Image Quality Metrics: PSNR vs. SSIM. In Proceedings of the International Conference on Pattern Recognition, Istanbul, Turkey, 23–26 August 2010; pp. 2366–2369. [CrossRef]
46. Wang, Z.; Bovik, A.C.; Sheikh, H.R.; Simoncelli, E.P. Image Quality Assessment: From Error Visibility to Structural Similarity. *IEEE Trans. Image Process.* **2004**, *13*, 600–612. [CrossRef] [PubMed]
47. Taha, A.A.; Hanbury, A. Metrics for evaluating 3D medical image segmentation: Analysis, selection, and tool. *BMC Med. Imaging* **2015**, *15*, 29. [CrossRef] [PubMed]
48. Ejiga, P.O.; Oluwafemi, O. Text-Guided Synthesis for Colon Cancer Screening. GitHub Repository. 2024. Available online: https://github.com/Ejigsonpeter/Text-Guided-Synthesis-for-Colon-Cancer-Screening (accessed on 15 December 2024).
49. HuggingFace. Mask Generation. 2024. Available online: https://huggingface.co/docs/transformers/tasks/mask_generation (accessed on 15 December 2024).
50. Ronneberger, O.; Fischer, P.; Brox, T. U-Net: Convolutional networks for biomedical image segmentation. *arXiv* **2015**. [CrossRef]
51. Zhao, H.; Shi, J.; Qi, X.; Wang, X.; Jia, J. Pyramid Scene Parsing Network. *arXiv* **2017**. [CrossRef]
52. Lin, T.; Dollár, P.; Girshick, R.; He, K.; Hariharan, B.; Belongie, S. Feature Pyramid Networks for Object Detection. *arXiv* **2016**. [CrossRef]
53. Chaurasia, A.; Culurciello, E. LinkNet: Exploiting encoder representations for efficient semantic segmentation. In Proceedings of the IEEE Visual Communications and Image Processing (VCIP), St. Petersburg, FL, USA, 10–13 December 2017. Available online: https://arxiv.org/abs/1707.03718 (accessed on 15 December 2024).
54. Safari, F.; Savić, I.; Kunze, H.; Ernst, J.; Gillis, D. A Review of AI-based MANET Routing Protocols. In Proceedings of the 2023 19th International Conference on Wireless and Mobile Computing, Networking and Communications (WiMob), Montreal, QC, Canada, 21–23 June 2023; pp. 43–50. [CrossRef]
55. Ejiga Peter, O.O. Advancing Colonoscopy Analysis Through Text-to-Image Synthesis Using Generative AI for Intelligent Data Augmentation, Image Classification, and Segmentation. 2024. Available online: https://www.proquest.com/openview/9a3add722e60af686957df5383de11f5/1?pq-origsite=gscholar&cbl=18750&diss=y (accessed on 8 January 2025).

algorithms

MDPI

Article

Edge Detection Attention Module in Pure Vision Transformer for Low-Dose X-Ray Computed Tomography Image Denoising

Luella Marcos [1], Paul Babyn [2] and Javad Alirezaie [1,*]

[1] Department of Electrical, Computer and Biomedical Engineering, Toronto Metropolitan University, Toronto, ON M5B 2K3, Canada
[2] Department of Medical Imaging, University of Saskatchewan, Saskatoon, SK S7N 0W8, Canada
* Correspondence: javad@torontomu.ca

Abstract: X-ray computed tomography (CT) is vital for medical diagnostics, but frequent radiation exposure raises concerns, driving the adoption of low-dose CT (LDCT) to mitigate risks. However, LDCT often introduces noise, compromising diagnostic accuracy. This paper proposes a pure vision transformer (PViT) for LDCT denoising, enhanced with a gradient–Laplacian attention module (GLAM) to improve edge preservation and fine structural detail reconstruction. The model's robustness was validated across five diverse datasets (piglet, head, abdomen, chest, thoracic), demonstrating consistent performance in preserving anatomical structures. Extensive ablation studies on attention configurations and loss functions further substantiated the contributions of each module. Quantitative evaluation using PSNR and SSIM, alongside radiologist assessment, confirmed significant noise suppression and sharper anatomical boundaries, particularly in regions with fine details such as organ interfaces and bone structures. Additionally, in benchmark comparisons against state-of-the-art LDCT models (RED-CNN, TED-Net, DSC-GAN, DRL-EMP) and traditional methods (BM3D), the model exhibited lower parameter and stable training performance. These findings highlight the model's robustness, efficiency, and clinical applicability, making it a promising solution for improving LDCT image quality while maintaining computational efficiency.

Keywords: gradient–Laplacian attention modules; low-dose CT denoising; deep learning; medical image processing; machine learning; vision transformers

1. Introduction

In the field of medical imaging, X-ray computed tomography (CT) plays a crucial role in diagnosing a wide range of conditions. However, the cumulative frequent exposure to radiation is a significant concern, prompting the need for low-dose computed tomography (LDCT) [1,2]. While LDCT reduces radiation exposure, it often results in noisy, low-quality images, which can compromise diagnostic accuracy. To address this, image denoising techniques are essential to enhance the quality of LDCT images while preserving critical anatomical structures [2]. Traditional low-dose computed tomography (LDCT) denoising methods are divided into several key categories: filter-based, model-based, transform-domain, and statistical methods. These methods each have unique strengths but also face specific limitations in maintaining an optimal balance between noise reduction and image detail retention, particularly in modern clinical settings.

Filter-based methods such as Gaussian, median, and bilateral filtering reduce noise by smoothing or averaging pixel intensities but differ in how they handle edges [3]. Gaussian filtering, for instance, reduces noise by averaging pixel values, though it often blurs fine details, which limits its suitability for highly detailed LDCT images [4]. Recent advancements like adaptive filtering [4,5] adjust filter strength based on image regions, improving edge preservation and reducing oversmoothing. However, adaptive filters may still struggle in regions with high noise levels, where detail is lost due to excessive smoothing in non-homogeneous areas. Approaches like non-local means (NLMs) [6,7], anisotropic diffusion [8], and total variation (TV) minimization [4] are designed to maintain image structure while reducing noise. NLM denoising, for example, compares and averages similar pixel patches across the image, as demonstrated by Zhang et al. [9], who modified NLMs to improve denoising in LDCT images. While effective, this approach is computationally intensive, limiting its efficiency in real-time applications, especially for large datasets. Anisotropic diffusion, another model-based technique, diffuses noise differently across regions to retain edges while smoothing uniform areas [10], but it can amplify artifacts in areas with low contrast, impacting diagnostic accuracy [8]. TV minimization, a popular choice for iterative reconstruction, reduces noise by minimizing image gradients [11]. He et al. [12] presented a TV-based method optimized for LDCT imaging, which retains edges well; however, this method can lead to staircase artifacts, particularly in areas with smooth gradients. Transform-domain methods decompose the image into wavelet or frequency components, making it easier to filter out noise selectively [13]. Wavelet transform denoising, for instance, decomposes an image into wavelet coefficients and selectively thresholds these coefficients to remove noise. Li et al. [14] improved on traditional wavelet methods with a multi-scale adaptive thresholding approach, which enhances detail preservation by handling noise at various frequencies. Despite their benefits, wavelet-based methods often require tuning across multiple scales, making them computationally complex and difficult to adapt for heterogeneous noise patterns, a limitation highlighted in Li et al.'s work. Fourier transform denoising, which uses frequency-based filtering, is also widely applied but can inadvertently blur details by removing high-frequency noise components indiscriminately, reducing diagnostic value in areas with high texture or detail [15]. Statistical denoising relies on probabilistic models to distinguish between noise and useful signals. Techniques such as K-SVD (sparse representation) utilize dictionary learning to construct a sparse, noise-free representation of the image [16]. The K-SVD method is adaptable and effective for LDCT, particularly in low-contrast areas; however, it can fail in high-noise or high-contrast regions where the learned basis functions may inadequately represent essential details. Bayesian estimation models, including maximum a posteriori (MAP) estimations, apply statistical priors to separate noise from signal [17]. While MAP estimation can yield high-quality denoising results, it relies heavily on accurate prior models, and incorrect priors can lead to oversmoothing, reducing the visibility of small or subtle structures. These studies reveal that while traditional denoising methods offer significant noise reduction capabilities for LDCT, each has inherent limitations. Recent model improvements attempt to address these issues, but achieving a perfect balance among noise reduction, computational efficiency, and detail retention remains an ongoing challenge.

Recently, deep learning models have emerged as powerful tools in medical image processing. Vision transformers (ViTs) offer a promising alternative to convolution-based networks by leveraging self-attention mechanisms to capture the long-range dependencies in images [18]. This study serves as the continuation of the paper by the authors, with the use of a pure vision transformer (PViT)-based architecture [19]. However, directly applying ViTs to LDCT denoising introduces challenges in accurately retaining fine structural details and edges, as shown in Figure 1. Comparing Figure 1b with the denoised image in Figure 1c using PViT alone, it is evident that the anatomical details within the highlighted blue region of interest are not well preserved. This discrepancy arises primarily from PViT's limited ability to enhance fine structural details and detect subtle edge variations in low-dose CT images. Therefore, this paper primarily addresses the mentioned limitation by implementing an edge detection attention module. The used gradient and Laplacian filters, integrated into an attention module, are designed to enhance edge information by capturing both first- and second-order derivatives, detecting changes in the boundaries and textural details of the image, thus improving the representation of critical anatomical boundaries in the CT images. By combining attention mechanisms with these edge detectors, the PViT model aims to deliver high-quality, denoised LDCT images with greater edge consistency. The contributions of this paper are as follows:

1. There have been few transformer-based studies for LDCT denoising, so we aimed to address this gap by introducing a novel pure vision transformer with an edge detection attention module.
2. We leveraged the concept of edge detection attention modules in vision transformers that target the preservation of CT image edges and textural details.
3. We investigated the effectiveness of each edge detection attention module in LDCT denoising by performing ablation experiments using various kernels, datasets, and objective functions.
4. Benchmark testing with state-of-the-art LDCT denoising models was also performed to compare the proposed model with the recent developments in the LDCT denoising task in the research community.

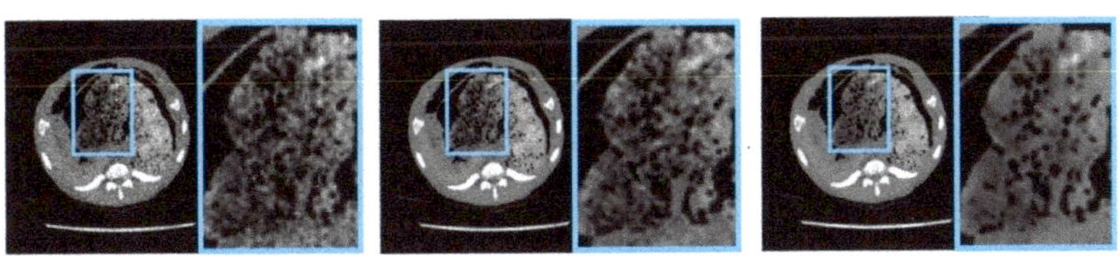

(a) (b) (c)

Figure 1. Not-well-preserved anatomical details in the highlighted blue ROI, produced using a pure vision transformer for LDCT denoising. Image generated from running the PViT model in [19] using the piglet dataset for this study. (**a**) Piglet LDCT (15 mAs) slice. (**b**) Piglet NDCT (300 mAs) slice. (**c**) Generated output from PViT.

2. Materials and Methods

2.1. System Model

The innovation of this work lies in the multi-head self-attention module of the pure vision transformer (PViT) for LDCT denoising, as developed in [19], incorporating a Noise2Neighbours reshaping module. Figure 2 shows the enhanced PViT structure, which originally used a multi-scale dot product operation for its multi-head self attention (MHSA) modules, as illustrated in Figure 3a, being replaced with the proposed gradient–Laplacian attention module (GLAM) displayed in Figure 3b, which is discussed further in the next section. The overall framework of the system used in the experiment follows a UNet framework, which is composed of the PViT blocks in Figure 2.

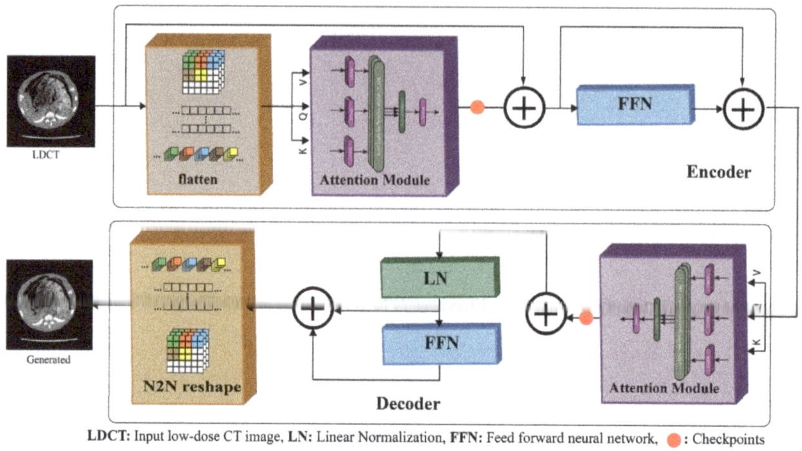

Figure 2. Pure transformer block for LDCT denoising with the integration of gradient–Laplacian attention module.

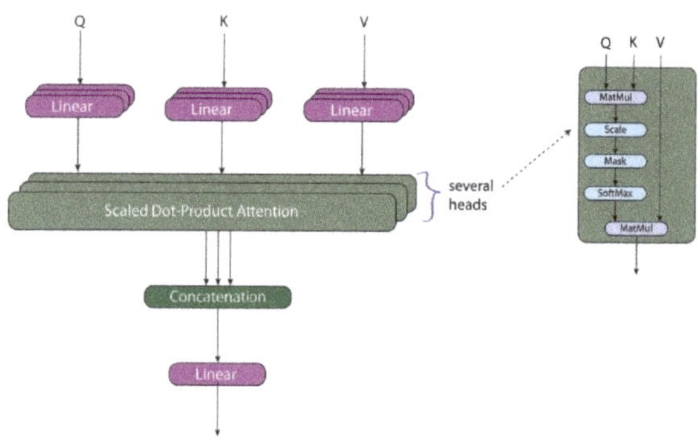

(**a**)

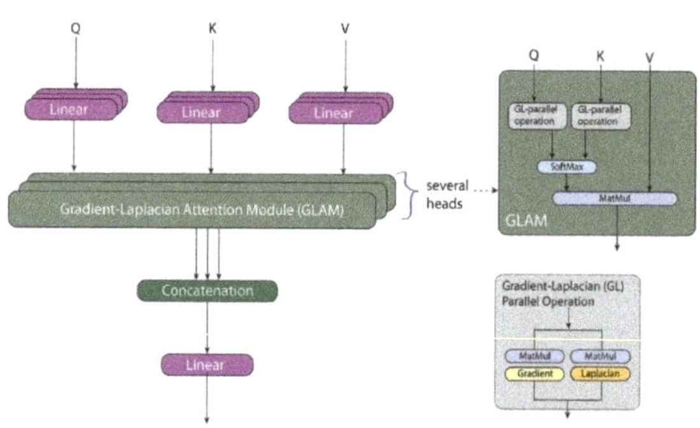

(**b**)

Figure 3. Attention modules in the pure vision transformer for LDCT denoising. (**a**) Multi-head self attention module for PViT. (**b**) Proposed gradient–Laplacian attention module for PViT.

2.2. Gradient–Laplacian Attention Module

Yan, Fang and Qiao [20] introduced a U-shaped transformer containing Sobel pixel attention and channel attention modules for LDCT denoising. Their experiment mainly focused on the architecture of the internal structure of their dual-attention block: (i) series vs. (ii) parallel. Unlike the common multi-head self attention (MHSA) for the PViT in Figure 3a, we propose the use of a parallel dual attention block that focuses on the use of a gradient and Laplacian operation, as shown in Figure 3b.

We compute the edge map for the input feature map X using gradient kernels, G_i, which includes horizontal, vertical, and diagonal edge detection variation to allow detecting image edges in multiple directions. For the Laplacian operator, we use an 8-neighbor Laplacian kernel for a stronger edge detection, L_8, instead of the typical 3×3 kernel, L_3, to compute the second-order derivative in capturing regions with abrupt intensity changes. Equation (1) defines the computation of the edge magnitude map M using both gradient and Laplacian operators:

$$M = \sqrt{\sum (X \times G_i)^2 + (X \times L_8)^2} \tag{1}$$

where X represents the input feature map that undergoes edge detection. The gradient kernels G_i (where i denotes the directions: horizontal, vertical, and diagonal variations) allow for detecting edges in multiple directions. The Laplacian operator is applied using an 8-neighbor Laplacian kernel (L_8) instead of the standard 3×3 kernel (L_3), providing stronger edge detection by capturing higher-order intensity variations.

The resulting edge map M is used within the gradient–Laplacian attention module (GLAM) to refine attention weights, emphasizing the structural details in the transformer's self-attention mechanism. It is important to note that X in this equation is not the attention score matrix QK^T; rather, it is the feature representation upon which edge detection is performed before computing attention weights.

Hence, the overall attention module using only the proposed edge detection gradient–Laplacian kernels is as follows:

$$Attention(Q, K, V, M) = softmax\left(\frac{QK^T + \beta M}{\sqrt{d_k}}\right)V \tag{2}$$

where β balances the contribution of all edge directions in the attention modules as the model is being trained.

Figure 4 shows how each filter highlights or detects the edges of the image edges and image texture at the marked checkpoints on the system design in Figure 2. Please note that, at these checkpoints, an N2N reshaping module is applied in order to see the actual feature map of the whole CT image and not just the patched images. The gradient operator emphasizes gradient-based edge detection by capturing directional changes in intensity—such as vertical, horizontal, and diagonal edges. This makes it particularly effective in detecting sharp transitions between regions of different densities or intensities, such as the boundaries between bones and soft tissues in CT images. The Laplacian operator, on the other hand, highlights areas of rapid intensity change by focusing on second-order derivatives, effectively enhancing fine details in the image and preserving subtle features like small structures and textures that might otherwise be lost during denoising. Further discussion about the results is provided in Section 3, including quantitative results.

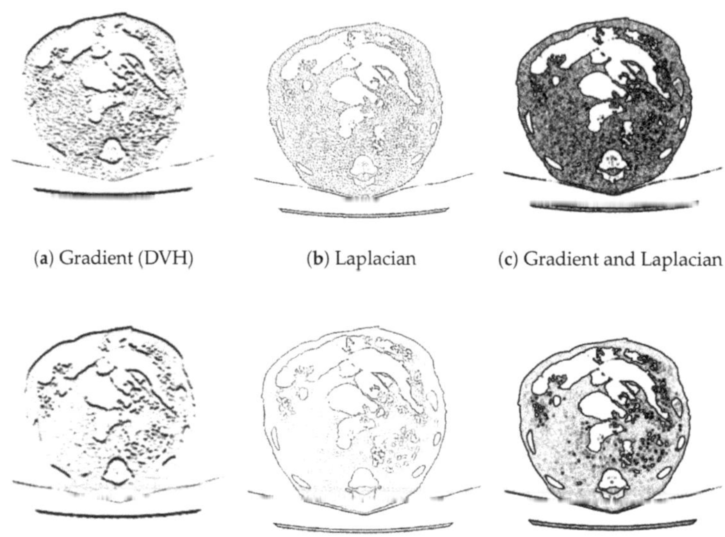

(**a**) Gradient (DVH) (**b**) Laplacian (**c**) Gradient and Laplacian

(**d**) Gradient (DVH) (**e**) Laplacian (**f**) Gradient and Laplacian

Figure 4. Edge enhancement at each upsampling and downsampling checkpoint labeled in Figure 2 using different filters in the attention module. (**a–c**) The feature maps generated from checkpoint at the encoder; (**d–f**) the feature maps generated from the checkpoint at the decoder.

2.3. Evaluation Metrics and Loss Functions

Evaluating the effectiveness of LDCT denoising methods is crucial, and using metrics like Peak Signal-to-Noise Ratio (PSNR), Mean Squared Error (MSE), and Structural Similarity Index Measure (SSIM) are important for assessing both the quantitative and qualitative aspects of denoised images. Each metric provides distinct insights, which together give a more comprehensive evaluation. As for the objective functions used, using thr Mean Squared Error (MSE) and the Structural Dissimilarity Index Measure (DSSIM) as loss functions can be effective in LDCT denoising because they offer complementary advantages in training deep learning models.

The Peak Signal-to-Noise Ratio (PSNR) is widely used to measure the similarity between an original high-quality image (usually the normal-dose CT) and the denoised image. The PSNR is calculated based on the ratio of the maximum pixel intensity to the noise power, measured in decibels (dB) [21], shown mathematically in Equation (3). A higher PSNR value typically indicates less noise and closer resemblance to the reference image. However, the PSNR alone does not account for perceptual quality, such as structural details and textures, which are crucial in medical imaging. Therefore, the PSNR is often used alongside other metrics.

$$PSNR(x,y) = 10\log_{10}\frac{(\max(x_j))^2}{MSE} \tag{3}$$

The SSIM is one of the most significant metrics for LDCT denoising as it considers human visual perception, focusing on structural similarity, luminance, and contrast. SSIM values range from 0 to 1, with values closer to 1 indicating high structural similarity to the reference image [22]. This is calculated as in Equation (4). The SSIM of denoised image (x) and the reference NDCT image (y) can be calculated using Equation (4), where μ is the mean, σ is the sample deviation, σ_{xy} stands for the sample covariance, while $\alpha, \beta, \gamma \geq 0$ and $\alpha, \beta, \gamma > 0$ are used for controlling the luminance, contrast, and structure similarities between the two images. The SSIM is particularly relevant in medical imaging because preserving anatomical structures is crucial for accurate diagnosis. Unlike the PSNR and MSE, the SSIM gives more weight to perceptual quality, making it a better metric for assessing how well a denoised image retains essential details.

$$\begin{aligned} SSIM(x,y) &= \frac{(2\mu_x\mu_y + c_1)(2\sigma_{xy} + c_2)}{(\mu_x^2 + \mu_y^2 + c1)(\sigma_x^2 + \sigma_y^2 + c_2)} \\ &= \left(\frac{2\mu_x\mu_y}{\mu_x^2 + \mu_y^2}\right)^{\alpha} \left(\frac{2\sigma_{xy}}{\sigma_x^2 + \sigma_y^2}\right)^{\beta} \left(\frac{\sigma_{xy}}{\sigma_x\sigma_y}\right)^{\gamma} \end{aligned} \tag{4}$$

The standard error of the mean (SEM) can also be used to calculate the uncertainty of a result. This can be calculated using the expression in (5), where σ is the standard deviation, and $\hat{N}$ is the mean [23].

$$SEM = \frac{\sigma}{\sqrt{\hat{N}}} \tag{5}$$

The MSE calculates the average squared differences between predicted pixel values and target values, penalizing larger errors more heavily. This makes it highly effective for ensuring pixel-wise accuracy in reconstructed images. In the context of LDCT denoising, the MSE is straightforward to implement, calculated by applying Equation (6), and works well for minimizing noise while encouraging the model to match the intensities of the normal-dose reference image y_i. However, the MSE focuses only on pixel differences and does not account for human perceptual quality, so it may lead to overly smooth results that miss important structural details.

$$L_{MSE}(\theta) = \frac{1}{N}\sum_{i=1}^{N} \|f(x_i;\theta) - y_i\|_F^2. \tag{6}$$

The Structural Dissimilarity Index Measure (DSSIM) as a loss function is derived from the Structural Similarity Index Measure (SSIM). It focuses on structural dissimilarity rather than pixel-wise error, as calculated in Equation (7). Unlike the MSE, the DSSIM penalizes loss in structural features, like edges and textures, by assessing differences in luminance, contrast, and structural composition. Using the DSSIM as a loss function helps the model preserve anatomical structures, which is crucial for diagnostic accuracy in medical images. It also aligns better with human perception, as small pixel differences matter less than overall structural integrity. However, the DSSIM alone can overlook intensity accuracy and may not perform as well in areas without strong structural patterns, making it useful in combination with other loss terms.

$$L_{DSSIM}(\theta) = \frac{1}{N}\sum_{i=1}^{N}(1 - SSIM(f(x_i;\theta) - y_i))/2 \tag{7}$$

Perceptual loss (PL) is calculated using the last four blocks of the VGG16-pretrained network [24]. Unlike the MSE, perceptual loss takes high-level features into consideration, which accurately models the human visual system due to its ability to learn the features. The feature maps, ϕ_i, are extracted from the last convolutional layer in blocks $i = 1,2,3,4$ of the VGG16 with size $h_i \times w_i \times d_i$, which can be expressed as

$$L_{PL}(x,y) = \sum_{i=1}^{N} \frac{1}{h_i w_i d_i} \|\phi_i(x) - \phi_i(y)\|^2 \tag{8}$$

The overall proposed loss function can be calculated as follows, where γ represents the contribution of each loss function depending on how the model is being trained. To determine the optimal balance, we conducted ablation studies with different loss weightings, which is discussed in Section 4.

$$L(\theta) = \gamma_1 L_{MSE}(\theta) + \gamma_2 L_{DSSIM}(\theta) + \gamma_3 L_{PL}(\theta) \quad (9)$$

2.4. Dataset & Training Details

Five different datasets of 512 × 512 NDCT–LDCT image pairs were used for this experiment. The piglet dataset and the thoracic dataset were from Yi and Babyn [25], and the abdomen, chest dataset, and the head dataset were obtained from the Cancer Imaging Archive (TCIA) Mayo Clinic [26]. Table 1 below shows the X-ray current dose used for obtaining the images. These images were in the form of Digital Imaging and Communications in Medicine (DICOM) files, which included metadata such as the image pixel size and medical information about the patient. For data preparation, the CT images were calibrated to the standard Hounsfield unit (HU), which refers to the specific substance being observed in the image. In this experiment, the calibration method was the same as in [27]. For this experiment, Hounsfield unit (HU) windowing was applied. Table 1 also shows a summary of the window level (WL) and window width (WW) for each dataset normalization. The dataset partition used for this experiment was 60% training, 30% validation, and 10% testing for each type of dataset. It is also important to note that all data in this work were analyzed in 2D slices, and all the models were trained for 150 epochs using the Adam optimizer with a learning rate of 0.0001, decay steps of 0.5, rate of 0.9, and batch sizes of 4–8. The experiments were carried using Pytorch and Tensorflow-Keras API on a Windows operating system with an Intel(R) Core(TM)i7-10700k CPU @2.90 GHz processor (Santa Clara, CA, USA), and NVIDIA GeForce RTX 3070 and 1080 (Santa Clara, CA, USA).

Table 1. Dataset X-ray current information and Hounsfield unit [HU] windowing for normalization.

Dataset	NDCT	LDCT	WL [HU]	WW [HU]
Piglet	300 mAs	15 mAs	40	400
Thoracic	480 mAs	60 mAs	−650 to −700	1500 to 2000
Abdomen	502 mAs	498 mAs	40	40
Chest	712 mAs	690 mAs	40	400
Head	202 mAs	180 mAs	30 to 50	80 to 100

3. Results

The results in Tables 2–6 provide a detailed quantitative comparison of different low-dose CT (LDCT) denoising models, including the pure vision transformer (PViT) and its variations utilizing attention modules and loss functions. The uncertainty values, provided as standard errors of the mean (SEMs), give us deeper insight into the consistency of these models in producing denoised images. To strengthen the validity of the proposed model and its variations, we also compared their results with the following benchmark models: (i) traditional BM3D [28]; (ii) convolution-based denoising networks, RED-CNN and DRL-E-MP [27]; (iii) hybrid convolution-transformer based model TED-Net [29]; and, finally, (iv) a recent generative denoising network, DSC-GAN [30]. Figures 5 and 6 illustrate visual comparisons and training trends for the piglet dataset. Similarly, Figures 7 and 8 present results for the thoracic dataset, while Figures 9 and 10 correspond to the head dataset. For the abdomen dataset, Figures 11 and 12 provide the respective visual comparisons and training trends. Finally, Figures 13 and 14 showcase the results for the chest dataset.

Table 2. Piglet Dataset. Average SSIM and PSNR with No. of parameters using two transformer blocks for the PViT model variants (GAM: gradient attention module, LAM: Laplacian attention module, GLAM: gradient–Laplacian attention module) and variants of the loss functions (MSE, SSIM, PL, proposed: MSE + SSIM + PL) used for the training (150 epochs). Uncertainties were calculated using SEM.

Model	SSIM ↑	PSNR ↑	#Param	Training Time
LDCT	0.6152 ± 0.0023	25.12 ± 0.03	—	—
PViT	0.9631 ± 0.0015	43.34 ± 0.02	1.68 M	15 min
GAM-PViT (DVH)	0.9730 ± 0.0011	43.62 ± 0.01	1.66 M	15 min
LAM-PViT	0.9622 ± 0.0017	42.12 ± 0.03	1.66 M	15 min
GLAM-PViT (MSE)	0.9728 ± 0.0013	43.51 ± 0.02	1.70 M	18 min
GLAM-PViT (SSIM)	0.9727 ± 0.0015	43.49 ± 0.02	1.71 M	18 min
GLAM-PViT (PL)	0.9732 ± 0.0010	43.62 ± 0.01	1.75 M	20 min
GLAM-PViT (proposed)	0.9756 ± 0.0010	43.84 ± 0.01	1.82 M	30 min
Benchmark 1: RED-CNN	0.9321 ± 0.0021	39.68 ± 0.04	3.33 M	50 min
Benchmark 2: TED-Net	0.9536 ± 0.0019	43.15 ± 0.03	3.28 M	80 min
Benchmark 3: DSC-GAN	0.9602 ± 0.0018	42.23 ± 0.03	4.16 M	120 min
Benchmark 4: BM3D *	0.8263 ± 0.0027	36.55 ± 0.04	n/a	60 min
Benchmark 5: DRLEMP	0.9529 ± 0.0018	41.66 ± 0.03	2.80 M	60 min

↑ Higher SSIM/PSNR values indicates more accurate denoised image. * BM3D involves algorithmic parameters and settings (e.g., block size, search window size, thresholding parameters) that can be tuned, but these are not learned from data in the same manner as neural network weights.

Table 3. Thoracic dataset. Average SSIM and PSNR with No. of parameters using two transformer blocks for the PViT model variants (GAM: gradient attention module, LAM: Laplacian attention module, GLAM: gradient–Laplacian attention module) and variants of the loss functions (MSE, SSIM, PL, proposed: MSE + SSIM + PL) used for the training (100 epochs). Uncertainties were calculated using standard error of the mean (SEM).

Model	SSIM ↑	PSNR ↑	#Param	Training Time
LDCT	0.2617 ± 0.0028	19.75 ± 0.03	—	—
PViT	0.6651 ± 0.0019	31.26 ± 0.02	1.68 M	15 min
GAM-PViT (DVH)	0.6712 ± 0.0015	32.11 ± 0.01	1.66 M	15 min
LAM-PViT	0.6601 ± 0.0019	29.81 ± 0.03	1.66 M	15 min
GLAM-PViT (MSE)	0.6756 ± 0.0014	32.36 ± 0.02	1.70 M	18 min
GLAM-PViT (SSIM)	0.6742 ± 0.0015	32.25 ± 0.02	1.71 M	18 min
GLAM-PViT (PL)	0.6769 ± 0.0013	32.43 ± 0.01	1.75 M	20 min
GLAM-PViT (proposed)	0.6788 ± 0.0012	32.92 ± 0.01	1.82 M	30 min
Benchmark 1: RED-CNN	0.4926 ± 0.0030	26.85 ± 0.04	3.33 M	50 min
Benchmark 2: TED-Net	0.6231 ± 0.0024	30.28 ± 0.03	3.28 M	80 min
Benchmark 3: DSC-GAN	0.6433 ± 0.0021	29.25 ± 0.03	4.16 M	120 min
Benchmark 4: BM3D *	0.4621 ± 0.0035	26.85 ± 0.04	n/a	60 min
Benchmark 5: DRLEMP	0.5283 ± 0.0028	27.31 ± 0.04	2.80 M	60 min

↑ Higher SSIM/PSNR values indicates more accurate denoised image. * BM3D involves algorithmic parameters and settings (e.g., block size, search window size, thresholding parameters) that can be tuned, but these are not learned from data in the same manner as neural network weights.

Table 4. Head dataset. Average SSIM and PSNR with No. of Parameters using two transformer blocks for the PViT model variants (GAM: gradient attention module, LAM: Laplacian attention module, GLAM: gradient–Laplacian attention module) and variants of the loss functions (MSE, SSIM, PL, proposed: MSE + SSIM + PL) used for the training (100 epochs). Uncertainties were calculated using standard error of the mean (SEM).

Model	SSIM ↑	PSNR ↑	#Param	Training Time
LDCT	0.2264 ± 0.015	30.43 ± 0.08	—	—
PViT	0.6888 ± 0.010	42.66 ± 0.07	1.68 M	15 min
GAM-PViT (DVH)	0.6811 ± 0.005	43.04 ± 0.07	1.66 M	15 min
LAM-PViT	0.6504 ± 0.015	41.68 ± 0.09	1.66 M	15 min
GLAM-PViT (MSE)	0.6820 ± 0.007	43.23 ± 0.06	1.70 M	18 min
GLAM-PViT (SSIM)	0.6822 ± 0.007	43.21 ± 0.08	1.71 M	18 min
GLAM-PViT (PL)	0.6813 ± 0.005	44.02 ± 0.05	1.75 M	20 min
GLAM-PViT (proposed)	0.6893 ± 0.005	44.16 ± 0.04	1.82 M	30 min
Benchmark 1: RED-CNN	0.4721 ± 0.012	36.88 ± 0.10	3.33 M	50 min
Benchmark 2: TED-Net	0.5713 ± 0.010	41.75 ± 0.07	3.28 M	80 min
Benchmark 3: DSC-GAN	0.5632 ± 0.015	39.62 ± 0.08	4.16 M	120 min
Benchmark 4: BM3D *	0.3156 ± 0.015	34.21 ± 0.09	n/a	60 min
Benchmark 5: DRLEMP	0.4893 ± 0.015	38.64 ± 0.08	2.80 M	60 min

↑ Higher SSIM/PSNR values indicates more accurate denoised image. * BM3D involves algorithmic parameters and settings (e.g., block size, search window size, thresholding parameters) that can be tuned, but these are not learned from data in the same manner as neural network weights.

Table 5. Abdomen dataset. Average SSIM and PSNR with No. of parameters using two transformer blocks for the PViT model variants (GAM: gradient attention module, LAM: Laplacian attention module, GLAM: gradient–Laplacian attention module) and variants of the loss functions (MSE, SSIM, PL, proposed: MSE + SSIM + PL) used for the training (100 epochs). Uncertainties were calculated using standard error of the mean (SEM).

Model	SSIM ↑	PSNR ↑	#Param	Training Time
LDCT	0.6234 ± 0.0035	30.14 ± 0.05	—	—
PViT	0.8609 ± 0.0012	41.21 ± 0.08	1.68 M	15 min
GAM-PViT (DVH)	0.8421 ± 0.0025	38.23 ± 0.08	1.66 M	15 min
LAM-PViT	0.8613 ± 0.0018	40.66 ± 0.06	1.66 M	15 min
GLAM-PViT (MSE)	0.8428 ± 0.0022	39.05 ± 0.07	1.70 M	18 min
GLAM-PViT (SSIM)	0.8452 ± 0.0019	39.16 ± 0.10	1.71 M	18 min
GLAM-PViT (PL)	0.8645 ± 0.0010	40.28 ± 0.05	1.75 M	20 min
GLAM-PViT (proposed)	0.8742 ± 0.0009	43.25 ± 0.03	1.82 M	30 min
Benchmark 1: RED-CNN	0.8413 ± 0.0030	36.92 ± 0.09	3.33 M	50 min
Benchmark 2: TED-Net	0.8603 ± 0.0016	41.03 ± 0.07	3.28 M	80 min
Benchmark 3: DSC-GAN	0.8524 ± 0.0025	40.35 ± 0.08	4.16 M	120 min
Benchmark 4: BM3D *	0.8152 ± 0.0040	34.27 ± 0.10	n/a	60 min
Benchmark 5: DRLEMP	0.8579 ± 0.0020	37.64 ± 0.06	2.80 M	60 min

↑ Higher SSIM/PSNR values indicates more accurate denoised image. * BM3D involves algorithmic parameters and settings (e.g., block size, search window size, thresholding parameters) that can be tuned, but these are not learned from data in the same manner as neural network weights.

Table 6. Chest dataset. Average SSIM and PSNR with No. of parameters using two transformer blocks for the PViT model variants (GAM: gradient attention module, LAM: Laplacian attention module, GLAM: gradient–Laplacian attention module), and variants of the loss functions (MSE, SSIM, PL, proposed: MSE + SSIM + PL) used for the training (100 epochs). Uncertainties were calculated using standard error of the mean (SEM).

Model	SSIM ↑	PSNR ↑	#Param	Training Time
LDCT	0.3489 ± 0.0040	26.32 ± 0.08	—	—
PViT	0.7932 ± 0.0015	36.19 ± 0.05	1.68 M	15 min
GAM-PViT (DVH)	0.8064 ± 0.0025	34.72 ± 0.06	1.66 M	15 min
LAM-PViT	0.8107 ± 0.0010	35.28 ± 0.05	1.66 M	15 min
GLAM-PViT (MSE)	0.8012 ± 0.0035	34.17 ± 0.09	1.70 M	18 min
GLAM-PViT (SSIM)	0.8056 ± 0.0028	35.19 ± 0.03	1.71 M	18 min
GLAM-PViT (PL)	0.8124 ± 0.0018	35.82 ± 0.04	1.75 M	20 min
GLAM-PViT (proposed)	0.8224 ± 0.0010	36.71 ± 0.02	1.82 M	30 min
Benchmark 1: RED-CNN	0.6423 ± 0.0035	29.63 ± 0.10	3.33 M	50 min
Benchmark 2: TED-Net	0.7725 ± 0.0020	34.92 ± 0.07	3.28 M	80 min
Benchmark 3: DSC-GAN	0.6234 ± 0.0045	33.25 ± 0.06	4.16 M	120 min
Benchmark 4: BM3D *	0.5673 ± 0.0050	27.31 ± 0.09	n/a	60 min
Benchmark 5: DRLEMP	0.6636 ± 0.0030	31.33 ± 0.05	2.80 M	60 min

↑ Higher SSIM/PSNR values indicates more accurate denoised image. * BM3D involves algorithmic parameters and settings (e.g., block size, search window size, thresholding parameters) that can be tuned, but these are not learned from data in the same manner as neural network weights.

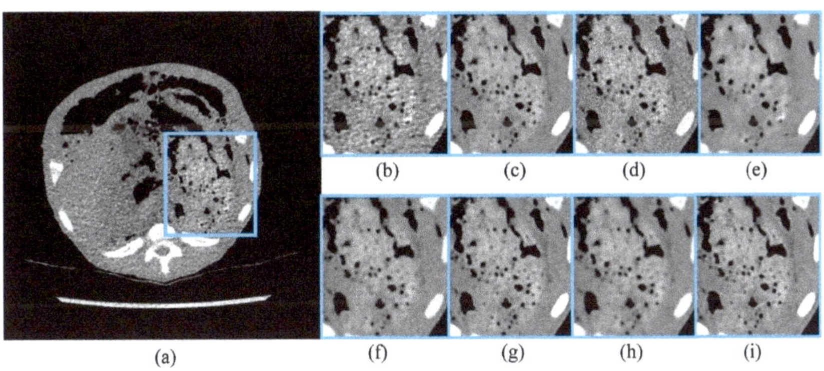

Figure 5. Benchmark test visual results for piglet data: (**a**) input LDCT image reference with blue ROI, (**b**) ROI of LDCT image, (**c**) ROI of NDCT image, and ROI of output image using (**d**) RED-CNN, (**e**) PViT, (**f**) DSC-GAN, (**g**) DRLEMP, (**h**)TED-Net, (**i**) GLAM-PViT.

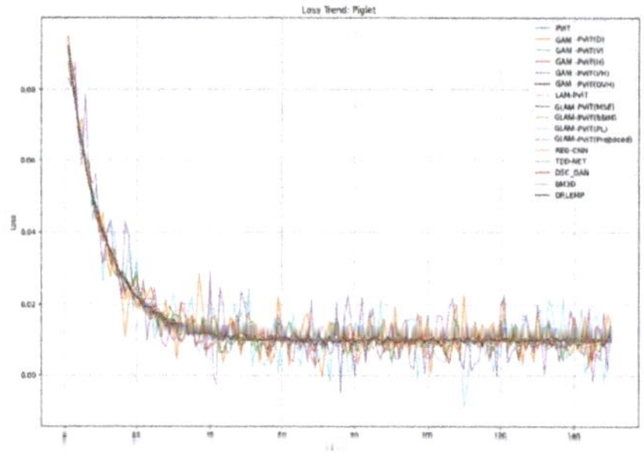

(**a**)

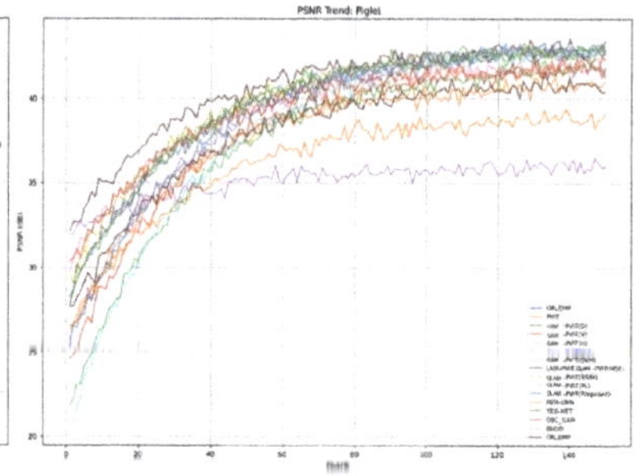

(**b**)

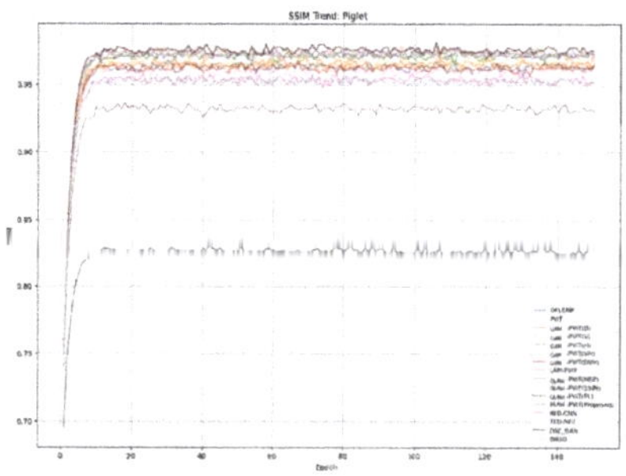

(**c**)

Figure 6. Loss, PSNR, and SSIM trend over 150 epochs using piglet dataset. (**a**) Loss. (**b**) PSNR. (**c**) SSIM.

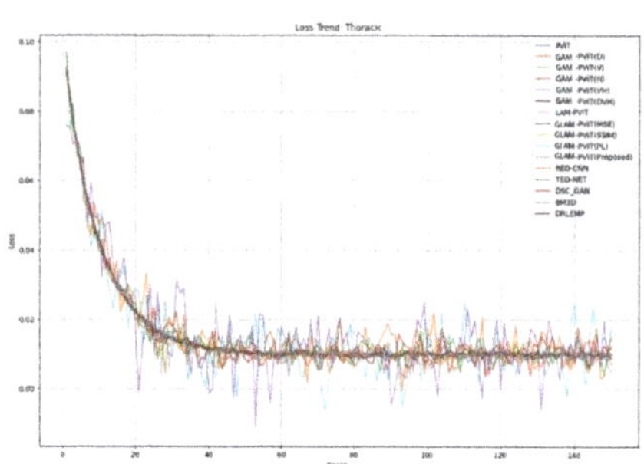

(**a**)

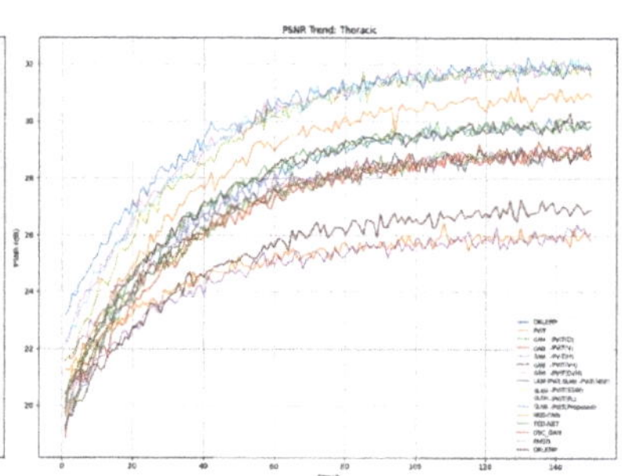

(**b**)

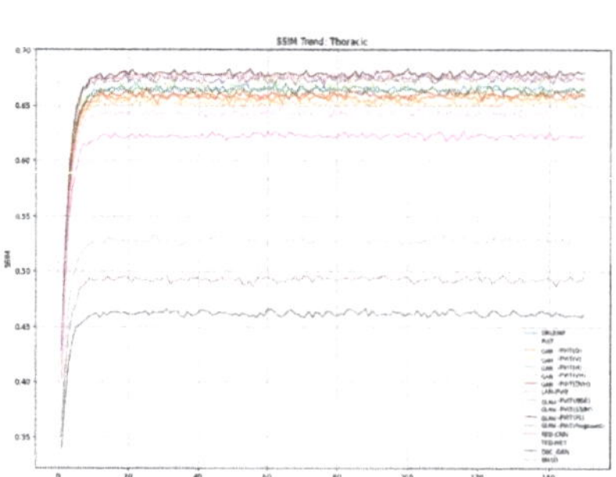

(**c**)

Figure 7. PSNR and SSIM trend over 150 epochs using thoracic dataset. (**a**) Loss. (**b**) PSNR. (**c**) SSIM.

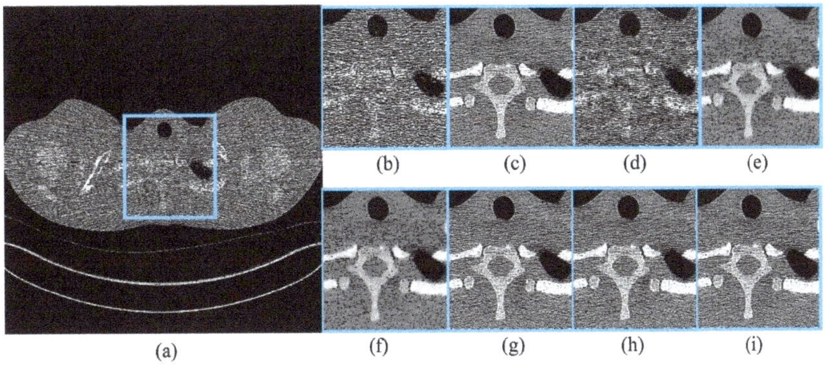

Figure 8. Benchmark test visual results for thoracic data: (**a**) input LDCT image reference with blue ROI, (**b**) ROI of LDCT image, (**c**) ROI of NDCT image, and ROI of output image using (**d**) RED-CNN, (**e**) PViT, (**f**) DSC-GAN, (**g**) DRLEMP, (**h**) TED-Net, (**i**) GLAM-PViT.

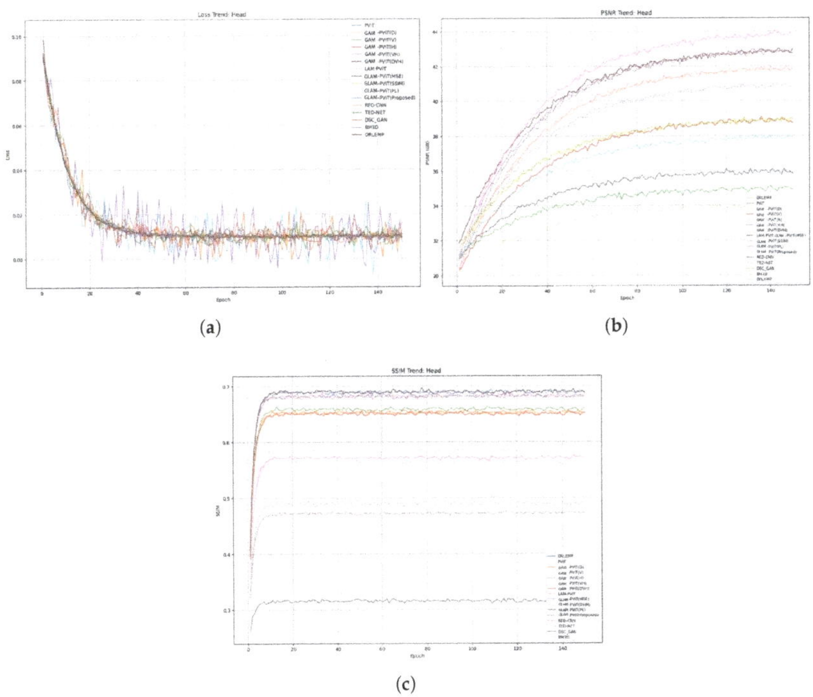

Figure 9. PSNR and SSIM trend over 150 epochs using head dataset. (**a**) Loss. (**b**) PSNR. (**c**) SSIM.

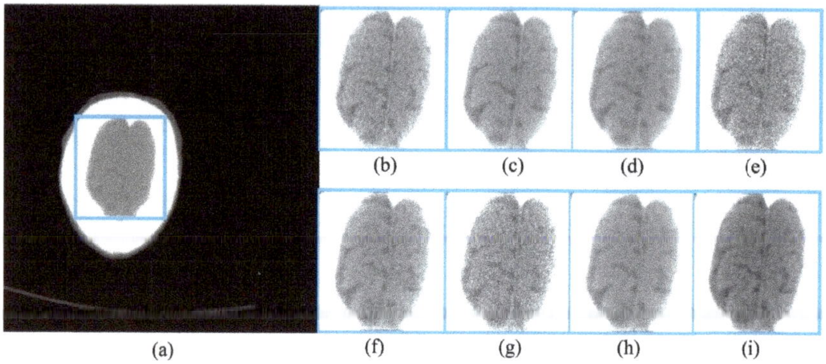

Figure 10. Benchmark test visual results for dead data: (**a**) input LDCT image reference with blue ROI, (**b**) ROI of LDCT image, (**c**) ROI of NDCT image, and ROI of output image using (**d**) RED-CNN, (**e**) PViT, (**f**) DSC-GAN, (**g**) DRLEMP, (**h**) TED-Net, (**i**) GLAM-PViT.

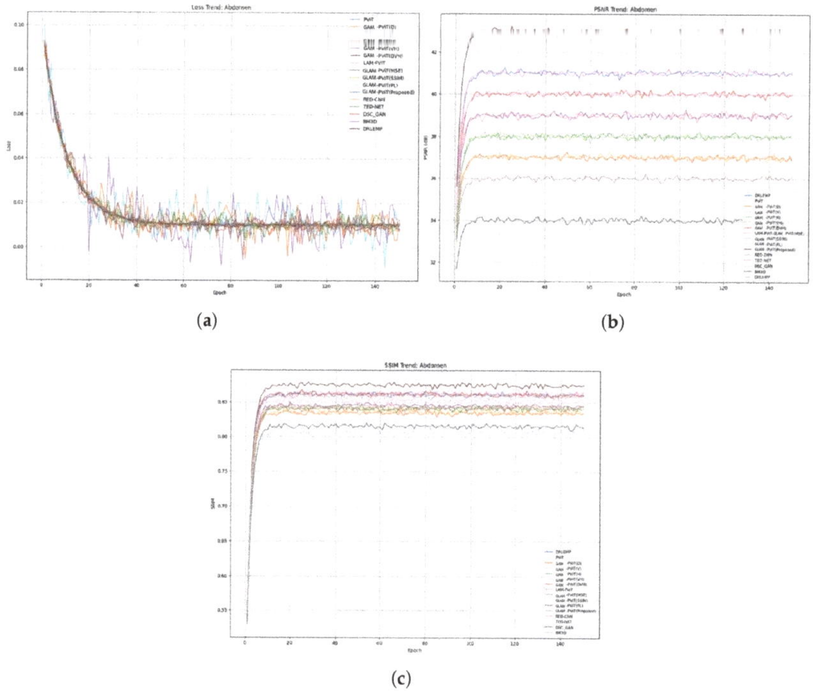

Figure 11. PSNR and SSIM trend over 150 epochs using abdomen dataset. (**a**) Loss. (**b**) PSNR. (**c**) SSIM.

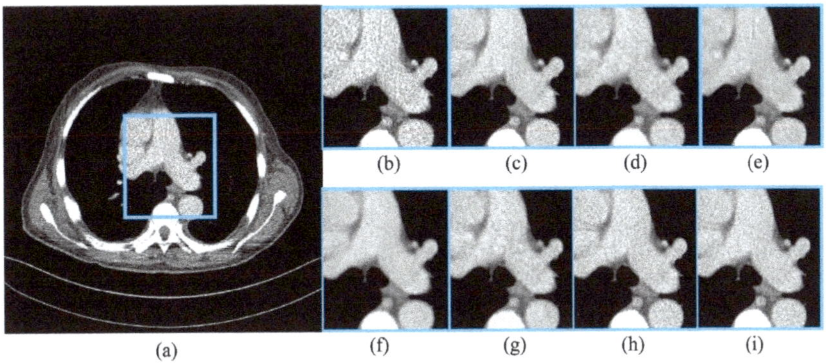

Figure 12. Benchmark test visual results for abdomen data: (a) input LDCT image reference with blue ROI, (b) ROI of LDCT image, (c) ROI of NDCT image, and ROI of output image using (d) RED-CNN, (e) PViT, (f) DSC-GAN, (g) DRLEMP, (h) TED-Net, (i) GLAM-PViT.

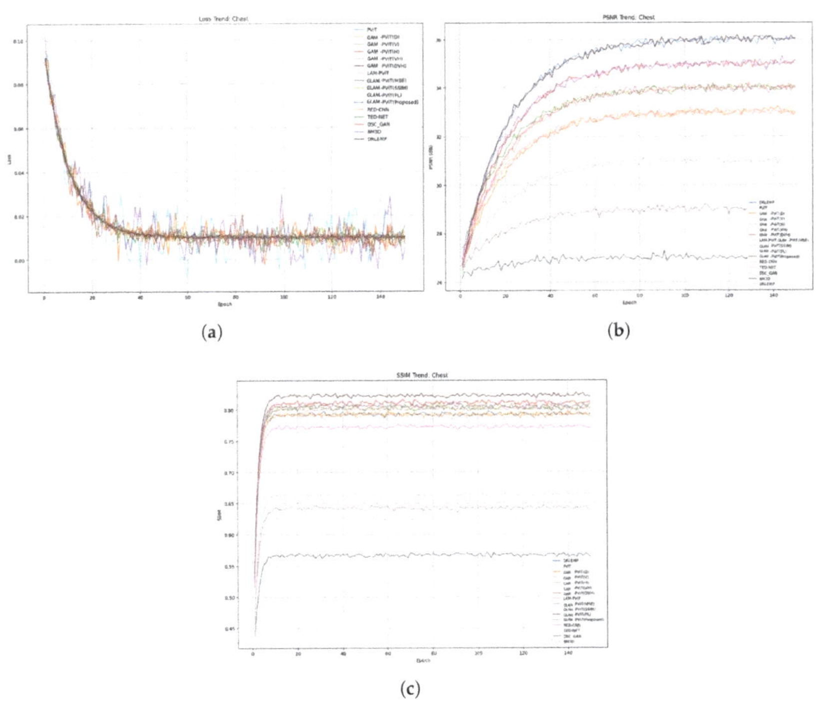

Figure 13. PSNR and SSIM trend over 150 epochs using chest dataset. (a) Loss. (b) PSNR. (c) SSIM.

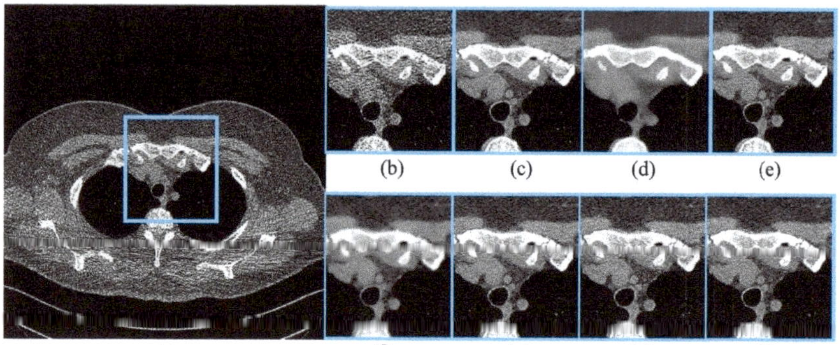

Figure 14. Benchmark test visual results for chest data: (**a**) input LDCT image reference with blue ROI, (**b**) ROI of LDCT image, (**c**) ROI of NDCT image, and ROI of output image using (**d**) RED-CNN, (**e**) PViT, (**f**) DSC-GAN, (**g**) DRLEMP, (**h**) TED-Net, (**i**) GLAM-PViT.

4. Discussion

4.1. Optimal Balance for Loss Function

To determine the optimal weighting strategy, we conducted ablation studies using each loss function individually and analyzed their influence on noise suppression and structural detail preservation.

Our results revealed that MSE loss alone, despite its effectiveness in reducing pixel-wise errors, often led to oversmoothed reconstructions, potentially obscuring fine anatomical details. In contrast, the DSSIM loss significantly improved edge preservation and contrast by penalizing structural inconsistencies, ensuring that organ boundaries and fine textures were more accurately reconstructed. Additionally, PL loss contributed to perceptually realistic restorations by utilizing high-level feature similarities rather than solely relying on pixel-wise accuracy. These observations align with prior studies demonstrating that structural and perceptual losses play a key role in preserving the diagnostic information in LDCT imaging. Based on these insights, we adopted a detail-preserving loss weighting strategy with $\gamma_1 = 0.2, \gamma_2 = 0.4, \gamma_3 = 0.4$. This configuration prioritizes the DSSIM and PL over the MSE, effectively balancing noise suppression and anatomical structure retention. Benchmark comparisons further validated the effectiveness of this approach, as GLAM-PViT outperformed state-of-the-art models (RED-CNN, TED-Net, DSC-GAN, DRL-EMP, BM3D) in preserving fine details while maintaining high PSNR and SSIM scores.

4.2. Piglet Dataset

The baseline piglet LDCT images exhibit poor quality (SSIM: 0.6152, PSNR: 25.12) with significant noise. The PViT model achieves a marked improvement (SSIM: 0.9631, PSNR: 43.34) with low uncertainty, demonstrating robust denoising capability. Gradient attention modules (GAMs) further enhance performance, with the diagonal-vertical-horizontal (DVH) configuration achieving the highest SSIM (0.9730) and PSNR (43.62) with low uncertainty. The gradient–Laplacian attention module (GLAM) paired with a combined loss function (MSE + SSIM + PL) delivers the best results (SSIM: 0.9756, PSNR: 43.84) with consistency, outperforming benchmark models like RED-CNN, TED-Net, and DSC-GAN.

4.3. Thoracic Dataset

The thoracic dataset starts with poorer baseline image quality (SSIM: 0.2617, PSNR: 19.75) than the piglet dataset. The PViT model achieves improvements (SSIM: 0.6651, PSNR:

31.26), though the denoising results are less pronounced compared to the piglet dataset. GAM-PViT (DVH) achieves an SSIM of 0.6712 and a PSNR of 32.11, reflecting moderate enhancement. The GLAM-PViT model with the proposed loss function yields the best performance (SSIM: 0.6788, PSNR: 32.92), showcasing its ability to handle more complex noise patterns. Despite these challenges, GLAM-PViT remains competitive and consistent across varied noise levels.

4.4. Head Dataset

The baseline head dataset images (SSIM: 0.2264, PSNR: 30.43) suffer from significant structural artifacts. The PViT model achieves notable improvements (SSIM: 0.6888, PSNR: 42.66), performing better than on thoracic data but falling short of the piglet results. GAM-PViT (DVH) and LAM-PViT show further enhancement, with GLAM-PViT providing the best results (SSIM: 0.6893, PSNR: 44.16). These results highlight the effectiveness of combining attention mechanisms and a tailored loss function for addressing the structural artifacts and noise in head CT images.

4.5. Abdomen Dataset

The baseline abdomen dataset images (SSIM: 0.6234, PSNR: 30.14) show moderate noise levels. The PViT model achieves significant improvement (SSIM: 0.8609, PSNR: 41.21), outperforming the head and thoracic datasets. GAM-PViT (DVH) shows modest gains, while LAM-PViT (SSIM: 0.8613, PSNR: 40.66) provides superior edge and contour preservation. The GLAM-PViT model with the combined loss function achieves the highest performance (SSIM: 0.8742, PSNR: 43.25), underscoring the model's robustness in handling moderate noise and preserving structural integrity.

4.6. Comparison Across Datasets

The PViT variants consistently outperform the traditional models, such as RED-CNN, TED-Net, and DSC-GAN, on all datasets. The GLAM-PViT model with the proposed loss function delivers the best denoising results, achieving high SSIM and PSNR values with low uncertainty. The performance variations across datasets reflect the differences in noise complexity and structural features, with the piglet and abdomen datasets showing better results compared to the thoracic and head datasets. This demonstrates the adaptability of GLAM-PViT to diverse noise patterns and anatomical structures.

4.7. Training Performance

Figures 6, 7, 9, 11 and 13 provide insights into the performance, convergence behavior, and the generalization ability of the models. For the loss trends (Figures 6a, 7a, 9a, 11a, and 13a), the steady decrease indicates stable training and convergence, which can be observed in the GLAM-PViT (proposed), TED-NET, PViT and DRLEMP models. In contrast, GLAM-PViT (PL), BM3D, DSC-GAN, and RED-CNN show a downward trend with sudden oscillations, which indicate instability. Similar patterns were observed on each dataset.

Next, regarding the PSNR trends (Figures 6b, 7b, 9b, 11b and 13b), slight fluctuations can be noticed for all the models, which indicate sensitivity to noise. Despite this discrepancy, the GLAM-PViT (proposed), TED-NET, DRLEMP, attention module, and loss function variants of the proposed model show an early steeper PSNR improvement as well as a consistently higher PSNR and stabilize without a decline. These behaviors indicate a strong denoiser model and higher training efficiency. The traditional modesl, BM3D, CNN-based model, and RED-CNN, lag behind the other models.

Lastly, for the SSIM trends (Figures 6c, 7c, 9c, 11c and 13c) of all the models, slight fluctuations can also be observed, which could indicate instability in texture preservation. Similar to the PSNR trends, the transformer-based models including the proposed model still show a steady increase and a significantly higher SSIM while maintaining the PSNR, meaning that these models have better perceptual quality.

4.8. Visual and Clinical Implications

The visual results confirm that the proposed GLAM-PViT model produces cleaner, sharper images with reduced noise and artifacts. These improvements make the images diagnostically useful, closely resembling high-dose CT scans. The low uncertainties across datasets ensure consistent performance, highlighting the model's robustness for clinical applications.

While numerous unsupervised denoising models, such as Noise2Self [31] and Patch2Self [32], have demonstrated strong performance in self-supervised noise learning, our study followed a supervised approach, leveraging paired LDCT–NDCT data to train a model with explicit noise-to-clean mappings. This allows for more precise noise suppression and structural preservation compared to unsupervised methods, which rely on statistical assumptions about noise. However, exploring hybrid or self-supervised approaches for LDCT denoising remains an interesting avenue for future research, particularly for scenarios where paired training data are scarce.

5. Conclusions

The proposed gradient–Laplacian attention module (GLAM), integrated into the vision transformer (PViT) network, significantly enhanced edge detection and detail preservation across all datasets (piglet, head, abdomen, chest, and thoracic) by sharpening image edges during the denoising process. This improvement stems from the combined use of Sobel and Laplacian filters, each focusing on distinct edge characteristics. A series of ablation studies validated the effectiveness of the proposed network. First, we compared the performance of the baseline PViT using traditional MHSA with various attention mechanisms, including GAM-PViT (diagonal, vertical, horizontal, VH, DVH), LAM-PViT, and the proposed GLAM-PViT. Next, we evaluated the proposed loss function with different combinations—MSE, SSIM, PL, and MSE+SSIM+PL—to determine optimal performance. Benchmark comparisons were then conducted with state-of-the-art denoising models (RED-CNN, TED-Net, DSC-GAN, BM3D, and DRLEMP) to assess the proposed model's competitiveness.

The results indicate that leveraging transformer-based models for denoising in low-dose CT imaging can enhance diagnostic accuracy, potentially benefiting patient care across various medical fields. This approach shows particular promise in cancer diagnostics, where early tumor detection, accurate lesion segmentation, staging, and treatment planning are critical. Integrating these models into clinical workflows could reduce false positives and negatives, streamline interpretation, support large-scale screening, and stimulate further advancements in medical imaging research.

Author Contributions: The authors confirm contribution to this paper as follows: study conception: J.A. and P.B.; methodology and investigation: L.M.; data curation: P.B.; analysis and interpretation of results: L.M., J.A., and P.B.; draft manuscript preparation: L.M.; review and editing: J.A. and P.B.; funding acquisition: J.A. All authors have read and agreed to the published version of this manuscript.

Funding: This research was supported by an NSERC Discovery grant RGPIN-202004441 that was awarded to Javad Alirezaie.

Data Availability Statement: The data (thoracic, chest, abdomen, and head) used for this study are openly available from the The Cancer Imaging Archive (TCIA): https://doi.org/10.7937/9NPB-2637 (accessed on 26 February 2025). The Piglet dataset was provided by Dr. Paul Babyn; further inquiries can be directed to the corresponding author.

Acknowledgments: The authors would like to thank Cynthia McCollough, the Mayo Clinic, and the American Association of Physicists in Medicine for making the CT data available for this study.

Conflicts of Interest: The authors declare no conflicts of interest.

References

1. Shin, E.; Lee, S.; Kang, H.; Kim, J.; Kim, K.; Youn, H.; Jin, Y.W.; Seo, S.; Youn, B. Organ-specific Effects of Low Dose Radiation Exposure: A Comprehensive Review. *Front. Genet.* **2020**, *11*, 566244. [CrossRef] [PubMed]
2. Zhang, J.; Gong, W.; Ye, L.; Wang, F.; Shangguan, Z.; Cheng, Y. A Review of deep learning methods for denoising of medical low-dose CT images. *Comput. Biol. Med.* **2024**, *171*, 108112. [CrossRef]
3. Tun, M.T.; Sugiura, Y.; Shimamura, T. Poisson–Gaussian Noise Removal for Low-Dose CT Images by Integrating Noisy Image Patch and Impulse Response of Low-Pass Filter in CNN. *J. Signal Process.* **2024**, *28*, 57–67. [CrossRef]
4. Li, Z.; Liu, Y.; Zhang, P.; Lu, J.; Ren, S.; Gui, Z. Adaptive Weighted Total Variation Expansion and Gaussian curvature Guided Low-dose CT Image Denoising Network. *Biomed. Signal Process. Control* **2024**, *94*, 106329. [CrossRef]
5. Hu, Y.; Ren, J.; Yang, J.; Bai, R.; Liu, J. Noise Reduction by Adaptive-sin Filtering for Retinal OCT Images. *Sci. Rep.* **2021**, *11*, 19498. [CrossRef] [PubMed]
6. Lepcha, D.C.; Dogra, A.; Goyal, B.; Goyal, V.; Kukreja, V.; Bavirisetti, D.P. A Constructive Non-local Means Algorithm for Low-dose Computed Tomography Denoising with Morphological Residual Processing. *PLoS ONE* **2023**, *18*, e0291911. [CrossRef]
7. Chyophel Lepcha, D.; Goyal, B.; Dogra, A. Low-dose CT Image Denoising using Sparse 3D Transformation with Probabilistic Non-local Means for Clinical Applications. *Imaging Sci. J.* **2023**, *71*, 97–109. [CrossRef]
8. Wang, L.; Liu, Y.; Wu, R.; Liu, Y.; Yan, R.; Ren, S.; Gui, Z. Image Processing for Low-dose CT via Novel Anisotropic Fourth-order Diffusion Model. *IEEE Access* **2022**, *10*, 50114–50124. [CrossRef]
9. Zhang, P.; Liu, Y.; Gui, Z.; Chen, Y.; Jia, L. A Region-adaptive Non-local Denoising Algorithm for Low-dose Computed Tomography Images. *Math. Biosci. Eng.* **2023**, *20*, 2831–2846. [CrossRef]
10. Vasu, G.T.; Palanisamy, P. CT and MRI Multi-modal Medical Image Fusion using Weight-Optimized Anisotropic Diffusion Filtering. *Soft Comput.* **2023**, *27*, 9105–9117. [CrossRef]
11. Wang, Z.; Ma, F.; Ji, P.; Fu, C. Image Denoising Based on an Improved Wavelet Threshold and Total Variation Model. In Proceedings of the International Conference on Intelligent Computing, Tianjin, China, 5–8 August 2024; Springer: Singapore, 2024; pp. 142–154.
12. He, Y.; Zeng, L.; Chen, W.; Gong, C.; Shen, Z. Bilateral Weighted Relative Total Variation for Low-Dose CT Reconstruction. *J. Digit. Imaging* **2023**, *36*, 458–467. [CrossRef] [PubMed]
13. Zhou, Y.; Kong, Z.; Huang, T.; Ahn, E.; Li, H.; Ding, L. WaveletDFDS-Net: A Dual Forward Denoising Stream Network for Low-Dose CT Noise Reduction. *Electronics* **2024**, *13*, 1906. [CrossRef]
14. Li, Z.; Liu, Y.; Shu, H.; Lu, J.; Kang, J.; Chen, Y.; Gui, Z. Multi-scale Feature Fusion Network for Low-dose CT Denoising. *J. Digit. Imaging* **2023**, *36*, 1808–1825. [CrossRef]
15. Zhang, Y.; Yang, X.; Gong, G.; Meng, X.; Wang, X.; Zhang, Z. FMUnet: Frequency Feature Enhancement Multi-level U-Net for Low-Dose CT Denoising with a Real Collected LDCT Image Dataset. In Proceedings of the International Conference on Intelligent Computing, Tianjin, China, 5–8 August 2024; Springer: Singapore, 2024; pp. 172–183.
16. Elad, M.; Aharon, M. Image Denoising via Sparse and Redundant Representations Over Learned Dictionaries. *IEEE Trans. Image Process.* **2006**, *15*, 3736–3745. [CrossRef] [PubMed]
17. Gao, Y.; Lu, S.; Shi, Y.; Chang, S.; Zhang, H.; Hou, W.; Li, L.; Liang, Z. A Joint-parameter Estimation and Bayesian Reconstruction Approach to Low-dose CT. *Sensors* **2023**, *23*, 1374. [CrossRef]
18. Dosovitskiy, A.; Beyer, L.; Kolesnikov, A.; Weissenborn, D.; Zhai, X.; Unterthiner, T.; Dehghani, M.; Minderer, M.; Heigold, G.; Gelly, S.; et al. An Image is Worth 16x16 Words: Transformers for Image Recognition at Scale. In Proceedings of the International Conference on Learning Representations (ICLR), Vienna, Austria, 4 May 2021.
19. Marcos, L.; Babyn, P.; Alirezaie, J. Pure Vision Transformer (CT-ViT) with Noise2Neighbors Interpolation for Low-Dose CT Image Denoising. *J. Imaging Inform. Med.* **2024**, *37*, 2669–2687. [CrossRef]
20. Yan, H.; Fang, C.; Qiao, Z. A Multi-Attention Uformer for Low-Lose CT Image Denoising. *Signal Image Video Process.* **2024**, *18*, 1429–1442. [CrossRef]
21. Kim, W.; Jeon, S.Y.; Byun, G.; Yoo, H.; Choi, J.H. A Systematic Review of Deep Learning-based Denoising for Low-dose Computed Tomography from a Perceptual Quality Perspective. *Biomed. Eng. Lett.* **2024**, *14*, 1153–1173. [CrossRef]
22. Zubair, M.; Rais, H.M.; Al-Tashi, Q.; Ullah, F.; Faheeem, M.; Khan, A.A. Enabling Predication of the Deep Learning Algorithms for Low-Dose CT Scan Image Denoising Models: A Systematic Literature Review. *IEEE Access* **2024**, *12*, 79025–79050. [CrossRef]
23. Barde, M.P.; Barde, P.J. What to use to express the variability of data: Standard deviation or standard error of mean? *Perspect. Clin. Res.* **2012**, *3*, 113–116. [CrossRef]

24. Simonyan, K.; Zisserman, A. Very Deep Convolutional Networks for Large-Scale Image Recognition. *arXiv* **2014**, arXiv:1409.1556.
25. Yi, X.; Babyn, P. Sharpness-Aware Low Dose CT Denoising Using Conditional Generative Adversarial Network. *J. Digit. Imaging* **2018**, *31*, 655–669. [CrossRef] [PubMed]
26. McCollough, C.; Chen, B.; Holmes, D.; III Duan, X.; Yu, Z.; Yu, L.; Leng, S.; Fletcher, J. *Data from Low Dose CT Image and Projection Data [Data Set]*; The Cancer Imaging Archive: Rochester, MN, USA; 2021. [CrossRef]
27. Gholizadeh-Ansari, M.; Alirezaie, J.; Babyn, P. Deep Learning for Low-Dose CT Denoising using Perceptual Loss and Edge Detection Layer. *J. Digit. Imaging* **2019**, *33*, 505–514. [CrossRef] [PubMed]
28. Makinen, Y.; Azzari, L.; Foi, A. Collaborative Filtering of Correlated Noise: Exact Transform-Domain Variance for Improved Shrinkage and Patch Matching. *IEEE Trans. Image Process.* **2020**, *29*, 8339–8354. [CrossRef]
29. Wang, D.; Wu, Z.; Yu, H. TED-Net: Convolution-Free T2T Vision Transformer-Based Encoder-Decoder Dilation Network for Low-Dose CT Denoising. In *Machine Learning in Medical Imaging*; Springer: Cham, Switherland, 2021; pp. 416–425. [CrossRef]
30. Zhao, F.; Liu, M.; Gao, Z.; Jiang, X.; Wang, R.; Zhang, L. Dual-scale similarity-guided cycle generative adversarial network for unsupervised low-dose CT denoising. *Comput. Biol. Med.* **2023**, *161*, 107029. [CrossRef]
31. Batson, J.; Royer, L. Noise2self: Blind denoising by self-supervision. In Proceedings of the International Conference on Machine Learning, Long Beach, CA, USA, 9–15 June 2019; pp. 524–533.
32. Fadnavis, S.; Chowdhury, A.; Batson, J.; Drineas, P.; Garyfallidis, E. Patch2Self2: Self-supervised Denoising on Coresets via Matrix Sketching. In Proceedings of the IEEE/CVF Conference on Computer Vision and Pattern Recognition, Seattle, WA, USA, 16–22 June 2024; pp. 27641–27651.

algorithms

MDPI

Review

Using Wearable Technology to Detect, Monitor, and Predict Major Depressive Disorder—A Scoping Review and Introductory Text for Clinical Professionals

Quinty Walschots [1], Milan Zarchev [2,3], Maurits Unkel [4] and Astrid Kamperman [2,3,*]

[1] Faculty of Medicine, Leiden University, P.O. Box 9500, 2300 RA Leiden, The Netherlands; quintywalschots@gmail.com

[2] Department of Psychiatry, Epidemiological and Social Psychiatric Research Institute (ESPRi), Erasmus MC, University Medical Center Rotterdam, P.O. Box 2040, 3000 CA Rotterdam, The Netherlands; m.zarchev@erasmusmc.nl

[3] Department of Psychiatry, Erasmus MC, University Medical Center Rotterdam, P.O. Box 2040, 3000 CA Rotterdam, The Netherlands

[4] Department of Neuroscience, Erasmus MC, University Medical Center Rotterdam, P.O. Box 2040, 3000 CA Rotterdam, The Netherlands; m.unkel@erasmusmc.nl

* Correspondence: a.kamperman@erasmusmc.nl

Abstract: The rising popularity of wearable devices allows for extensive and unobtrusive collection of personal health data for extended periods of time. Recent studies have used machine learning to create predictive algorithms to assess symptoms of major depressive disorder (MDD) based on these data. This review evaluates the clinical relevance of these models. Studies were selected to represent the range of methodologies and applications of wearables for MDD algorithms, with a focus on wrist-worn devices. The reviewed studies demonstrated that wearable-based algorithms were able to predict symptoms of MDD with considerable accuracy. These models may be used in the clinic to complement the monitoring of treatments or to facilitate early intervention in high-risk populations. In a preventative context, they could prompt users to seek help for earlier intervention and better clinical outcomes. However, the lack of standardized methodologies and variation in which performance metrics are reported complicates direct comparisons between studies. Issues with reproducibility, overfitting, small sample sizes, and limited population demographics also limit the generalizability of findings. As such, wearable-based algorithms show considerable promise for predicting and monitoring MDD, but there is significant room for improvement before this promise can be fulfilled.

Keywords: depression; wearables; prediction; mental healthcare

1. Introduction

In the past two decades, there has been increasing interest in wearable technology [1,2]. These wearables include any type of technology one can wear on their person, such as pedometers, headphones, and virtual reality headsets. The category of smartwatches is the most common, making up roughly 30% of all wearables [3]. The FitBit and Apple Watch are prominent examples. With smartwatches, it is possible to collect a wide variety of data points about the user's health, such as heart rate and physical activity. Their displays or companion apps make these data easily accessible for the user. There is a rising interest in monitoring personal fitness and mental health [4]. However, mobile mood-tracking apps are often used infrequently, and users tend to avoid entering negative moods [5]. Wearables allow for continuous collection of a large variety of detailed information and have previously been used to identify what emotions the user is experiencing [6,7]. Furthermore, wearables can collect these data while remaining unobtrusive, making them especially suitable for long-term measurements with minimal impact on the user. The use of wearables in mental health care has been a topic of interest for some time. While existing reviews focus on exploring the various wearable sensors and features that can inform predictive models [8–11], this review focuses more on the practical applications and their feasibility. Specifically, this review aims to evaluate the role of wearables in a clinical setting, in particular, how they may be used to identify and monitor symptoms of major depressive disorder (MDD) in a way that is accessible to both researchers and clinical professionals.

1.1. Major Depressive Disorder

Major depressive disorder (MDD) is one of the most prevalent mood disorders worldwide, affecting an estimated 280 million people (3.8% of the population) as reported in 2023 [12]. In reality, these numbers may be even higher, as it is not uncommon for MDD to stay undiagnosed [13]. Furthermore, MDD is becoming more prevalent as its global burden has increased by more than 50% compared to 35 years ago [14]. It is characterized by persistent feelings of sadness and hopelessness, as well as a generally depressed mood and anhedonia. For detailed diagnostic criteria, refer to the Diagnostic and Statistical Manual of Mental Disorders (DSM-5) [15]. Diagnosis and monitoring of MDD rely heavily on subjective and retrospective reports by the patient or observations made by others. Wearables offer a method to relate depressive symptoms to objective measures and monitor their development over time. Furthermore, they offer additional insights to the casual user about their own mental health, which could prompt them to seek professional help at earlier time points. This could help reduce the number of undiagnosed patients as well as facilitate earlier diagnosis or intervention, which is typically associated with better treatment outcomes and reduces the burden of the disease both emotionally and financially [16]. Recent studies have been looking into how wearable technology may be used for such a purpose.

1.2. Measurable Features of MDD

While there is no single or definitive cause for MDD, disruptions of several biological processes have been related to the disease. One prominent example is the circadian clock. Using external time cues, this system modulates certain processes in the body (most notably the sleep-wake cycle) to follow a roughly 24 h rhythm [17]. It has been widely reported that the circadian clock is disrupted in patients with depression, as reflected, among other things, by the prevalence of insomnia and disrupted sleep reported by this population [18,19]. Another major regulatory mechanism found to be disrupted in MDD is the hypothalamic pituitary adrenal (HPA) axis [20,21]. This system is crucial for stress adaptation and is normally activated in response to emotional or physical stressors [22]. The HPA axis is involved in the regulation of blood pressure, metabolism, and the fight–flight response, which in turn may increase heart rate, body temperature, and perspiration when activated [23–25].

Both the circadian clock and the HPA axis involve physiological processes that can be measured using sensors available in most wearables. Accelerometers can further measure physical activity, which can also be used to quantify dimensions of sleep. Existing research has shown that depressed patients generally spend more time sedentary compared to healthy controls [26], and people with lower activity levels are more likely to show signs of depression [27]. The level of physical activity has been found to increase as treatment progresses, making it a promising feature for monitoring depressive symptoms [28,29]. Furthermore, the activity of patients was found to be shifted towards later in the day, with a dampened diurnal amplitude [30]. Photoplethysmogram (PPG) sensors can measure heart rate. Measured heart rate, and specifically lowered heart rate variability (HRV), has been found to be associated with poor sleep and increased risk of depressive symptoms, and HRV was found to increase following successful treatment [31,32]. Additionally, there appears to be a relation between HRV and disease severity, as the reduction in HRV was found to be more prominent when depressive symptoms were worse [33,34]. Electrodermal activity (EDA) sensors can measure perspiration. Multiple studies have found reduced

EDA in depressed patients [35–37], and one even claimed to be able to differentiate between depressed and non-depressed individuals within their population based on whether skin conductance was above or below a certain threshold [38]. Finally, many smartwatches include temperature sensors. Body temperature is commonly elevated in patients with depression [39–42]. This was related to the circadian rhythm, as it was specifically the nocturnal core temperature [39,40] and evening peripheral temperature [42] that were higher in depressed patients compared to non-depressed participants. As such, these two well-understood mechanisms are often invoked to explain why it might be possible to predict mood from wearables in theory. It should be noted, however, that these studies identified associations between isolated physiological features and depression. Individually, these associations are too small to meaningfully predict a complex psychological outcome such as depression in a broader population. Instead, we found that studies aiming to predict depression typically combine a number of these features in an attempt to model the intricacies of how they interact.

1.3. Introduction to Predictive Algorithms

Research on the prediction of depression makes use of technical jargon unique to the machine learning literature. A brief discussion of commonly encountered concepts is thus needed to cover some recurring terms and methods. In general, a predictive algorithm is the predetermined set of computer instructions for how the data will be processed to ultimately come to the desired predictions. To assess how successful an algorithm is, a measure of the true outcome is measured when possible, or a gold standard within the expert field is used as the "ground truth" or ideal expected result. The goal for the prediction is to be as close as possible to this ground truth. For example, the ground truth of whether a person is depressed can be assessed by a clinician or, somewhat less optimally, by a screener survey, independently from the algorithm. The time between the last collected data and the predicted outcome can vary and is henceforth referred to as the prediction horizon.

After the instructions are coded, the model is trained. This is typically conducted using cross-validation, randomly splitting the data into folds of training and testing sets. For each fold, model parameters are optimized iteratively by exploring combinations of features. The model trained on each training set will predict the outcome found in each test set. Very little input is required at this stage. To conclude the training, the parameters for all folds are integrated into a unified model. The quality of this unified model is then assessed by applying it to yet-unused data that were put aside from the start and comparing the predictions to the ground truth. Cross-validation is a crucial tool to prevent overfitting. This happens when the model is so fine-tuned to the training data that it loses generalizability to new populations [43]. Other ways to minimize the chances of overfitting include regularization and feature selection.

The exact way model performance is assessed depends on the type of prediction it makes. For classification models, performance is commonly assessed using the error matrix and accompanying area under the receiver operator characteristic (AUROC) curve. The error matrix is built up of true (T)/false (F) positives (P)/negatives (N). Then, sensitivity (TP/(TP + FN)), i.e., the proportion of positive cases correctly predicted, and specificity (TN/(TN + FP)), i.e., the proportion of negative cases correctly predicted, are formulated to create the ROC. We obtain the AUROC by taking the integral of this curve, which ranges between 0 and 1, where 0 would mean all outcomes wrongly classified, 0.5 would mean no discriminatory power or similar to random guessing, and 1 would mean all correctly classified. For regression models, to assess performance with AUROC, a threshold is set on the outcome scale to define everything above as positive and below as negative. When no gold standard is present, relative quality measures such as the mean square error and variations on it are used. Generally, the lower the relative quality measure, the better a given model is able to fit a dataset.

Finally, one should be aware of the fundamental difference between the statistical modeling encountered in classical epidemiological research and the predictive modeling in wearables research. In classical epidemiology, we build models to remove bias from specific estimates, which we then interpret individually in terms of direction and effect size [44,45]. These interpretations often rely on statistical assumptions about the data. In predictive modeling, the focus is instead exclusively on achieving more accurate predictions as measured by the metrics described above. Biased relationships are not a problem and can paradoxically be exploited for the purpose of better prediction [46]. Individual associations are irrelevant, as only the performance of all the variables taken together is assessed. Prioritizing predictive performance allows for very flexible models to exploit both the smallest associations and the most complex interactions in the data without the need for strict statistical assumptions. This flexibility comes at the cost of interpretability, meaning it is not always clear exactly how variables interact with each other to produce the observed results [47]. For instance, a Random Forest algorithm combines logical decision trees to show exactly which features and their values were used to classify a sample, whereas non-linear or complex algorithms are more like a black box. Predictive modelers thus have to make a trade—they can build sophisticated algorithms to predict mental health outcomes from wearable technology, but they surrender the ability to understand *how* physiological features might relate to depression.

2. Search Method

To select papers that describe studies that focused on the use of wearables to predict the presence and severity of depressive symptoms, we conducted a search in PubMed (from the time of inception to June 2023) using the following terms: "wearables", "depression", "predictive algorithms", and variations of these terms. In addition, the reference lists of selected papers were checked for relevant publications. We chose PubMed in particular because the articles found in this database likely reflect best what clinical research professionals will encounter when looking to research the applications of wearables in healthcare. We included original research studies. Review studies were considered not eligible. We considered studies written in English only. Given the scoping nature of this review, the list of included studies is not comprehensive but instead represents the range of methodologies and applications of wearables in this field of research. As such, studies were included if they met each of the following three criteria: (1) using a predictive algorithm to (2) detect or predict depressive symptoms according to clinical standards using (3) data collected using a wearable device. Furthermore, wearables were selected to be wrist-worn and feasible to be used in day-to-day life. Studies using smartphone data were not excluded as long as wrist-worn wearable data were used as well. The reasoning behind this was that the requirement for smartphones would not significantly hinder practical implementation due to the wide availability of smartphones to the general public. Any algorithm training method was acceptable as long as the reported aim was to detect or predict symptoms of depression using wearable data. This includes algorithms detecting current depression or symptom severity, as well as the prediction of future symptom severity or onset of depression. In-person clinical interviews with a mental health care professional (i.e., a psychiatrist or resident) constituted the current gold standard for diagnosis and were therefore preferred as ground truth. In order to maintain our focus on clinical depression, studies that instead used screeners to determine true mood were only included if classifications were made using the clinical cut-off scores.

3. Results

A total of 15 studies were selected for the current review. An overview of all included studies can be found in Table 1. Among the collected studies, there was substantial diversity in the populations that were recruited and how the ground truth was determined. Additionally, the studies varied considerably in how the wearables were used to predict depression. More specifically, we noticed that a wide array of different features was selected using diverse types and brands of wearables. Also, we found a variety of prediction goals and ground truth determination methods. An overview of these methodological differences, along with the reported quality of each resulting algorithm, can be found in Table 2. The following sections highlight the exemplary methodological features that emerged from this set of studies in more detail.

Table 1. Overview of the selected studies.

Reference	Title	Population (Baseline)	Duration of Study Period
Bai et al., 2021 [48]	Tracking and Monitoring Mood Stability of Patients With Major Depressive Disorder by Machine Learning Models Using Passive Digital Data: Prospective Naturalistic Multicenter Study	261 outpatients with MDD	12 weeks
Chikersal et al., 2021 [49]	Detecting Depression And Predicting Its Onset Using Longitudinal Symptoms Captured By Passive Sensing: A Machine Learning Approach With Robust Feature Selection	138 college students (20 ≥ mild MDD, 118 HC at baseline)	16 weeks (1 semester)
Cho et al., 2019 [50]	Mood Prediction of Patients With Mood Disorders by Machine Learning Using Passive Digital Phenotypes Based on the Circadian Rhythm: Prospective Observational Cohort Study	55 (18 MDD, 18 BD-I, 19 BD-II)	2003 days total, over a 2-year study period
Ghandeharioun et al., 2017 [51]	Objective Assessment of Depressive Symptoms with Machine Learning and Wearable Sensors Data	12 patients with MDD	8 weeks
Griffiths et al., 2022 [52]	Investigation Of Physical Activity, Sleep, And Mental Health Recovery In Treatment Resistant Depression (TRD) Patients Receiving Repetitive Transcranial Magnetic Stimulation (rTMS) Treatment	17 patients with TRD	5 weeks
Horowitz et al., 2022 [53]	Using Machine Learning With Intensive Longitudinal Data To Predict Depression And Suicidal Ideation Among Medical Interns Over Time	2459 first-year training physicians (7.9% MDD, 3.6% suicidal ideation at baseline)	92 days
Kim et al., 2019 [54]	Depression Prediction by Using Ecological Momentary Assessment, Actiwatch Data, and Machine Learning: Observational Study on Older Adults Living Alone	47 elderly (≥mild symptoms of MDD, baseline SGDS ≥ 5)	14 days
Lee et al., 2022 [55]	Prediction Of Impending Mood Episode Recurrence Using Real-Time Digital Phenotypes In Major Depression And Bipolar Disorders In South Korea: A Prospective Nationwide Cohort Study	95 patients with MDD	23,459 days total over a 4 year study period.

Table 1. *Cont.*

Reference	Title	Population (Baseline)	Duration of Study Period
Lu et al., 2018 [56]	Joint Modeling of Heterogeneous Sensing Data for Depression Assessment via Multitask Learning	103 college students (39, 64 HC)	3 months
Mahendran et al., 2019 [57]	Sensor-Assisted Weighted Average Ensemble Model for Detecting Major Depressive Disorder	450 (with complaints of mood swings)	7 days
Makhmutova et al., 2022 [58]	Predicting Changes In Depression Severity Using The PSYCHE-D (Prediction Of Severity Change-Depression) Model Involving Person-Generated Health Data: Longitudinal Case-Control Observational Study	4036 (38.7% HC/minimal symptoms, 61.3% ≥ mild symptoms; 20.7% with severity change after 3 months)	3 months
Mullick et al., 2022 [59]	Predicting Depression in Adolescents Using Mobile and Wearable Sensors: Multimodal Machine Learning–Based Exploratory Study	55 adolescents (≥mild MDD)	24 weeks
Pedrelli et al., 2020 [60]	Monitoring Changes in Depression Severity Using Wearable and Mobile Sensors	31 (with MDD)	8 weeks
Rykov et al., 2021 [61]	Digital Biomarkers for Depression Screening With Wearable Devices: Cross-sectional Study With Machine Learning Modeling	267 (110 ≥ mild MDD/157 HC)	14 days, consecutive
Tazawa et al., 2020 [62]	Evaluating Depression With Multimodal Wristband-Type Wearable Device: Screening And Assessing Patient Severity Utilizing Machine-Learning	86 (30 ≥ mild MDD, 15 BD, 41 HC)	5250 days

BD (-I/II) = Bipolar Disorder (type I/II). HC = Healthy controls. MDD = Major Depressive Disorder. SGDS = Short Geriatric Depression Scale. TRD = Treatment-Resistant Depression.

Table 2. Details of study setups and results.

Reference	Wearable Specifications	Predictive Features	Prediction Outcome	Ground Truth Determination	Quality Measures (Best Model)
Bai et al., 2021 [48]	Mi band-2 Smartphone: OS n.s.	Activity Sleep Heart rate Phone usage	Detect current mood state (stable/swinging)	Change in PHQ-9 score over time more or less than 5 points, and score above the cut-off of 11 (≥moderate depression) or below 5 (remission)	Accuracy ranges [1] = 75.64–84.27% Sensitivity ranges [1] = 85.33–93.33%
Chikersal et al., 2021 [49]	FitBit Flex 2 Smartphone: Android, iOS	Activity Sleep Location Phone use	Predict post-semester depression (depression yes/no)	BDI-II above or below the cut-off of 14 for ≥mild depression	Accuracy = 81.3% F1 = 0.75
			Predict post-semester change in severity (symptoms worsened, yes/no)	Did the BDI-II level (minimal, mild, moderate, severe) change, yes or no	Accuracy = 88.1% F1 = 0.81

Table 2. *Cont.*

Reference	Wearable Specifications	Predictive Features	Prediction Outcome	Ground Truth Determination	Quality Measures (Best Model)
Cho et al., 2019 [50]	FitBit Charge HR or 2 Smartphone: Android, OS n.s.	Activity Sleep Heart rate Light exposure	Predict future mood state (stable/biased)	Mood state classification based on mood score distribution within the study population. 'Biased' for the highest 30%, 'stable' for the lowest 70%.	Accuracy = 67% Sensitivity = 39% Specificity = 74% AUC = 0.67
			Predict future mood episodes (occurs yes/no)	Mood episodes were identified retrospectively by the clinician based on interview and eMoodchart app data (app developed by research group)	Accuracy = 73.1% Sensitivity = 67.2% Specificity = 63.7% AUC = 0.79
Ghandeharioun et al., 2017 [51]	Empatica E4 wristband (both wrists) Smartphone: Android	EDA Temperature Sleep Activity Phone use Location	Predict the current HDRS-17 score	Biweekly HDRS-17	RMSE = 4.5
Griffiths et al., 2022 [52]	FitBit: model n.s.	Activity Sleep	Detect current depression severity (severe yes/no)	PHQ-9 above or below the clinical cut-off of 20 for severe depression	Accuracy = 82% Sensitivity = 82% Specificity = 81% F1 = 0.81
Horowitz et al., 2022 [53]	FitBit Charge 4	Daily mood Activity Sleep Heart rate	Predict end-of-quarter depression (yes/no)	PHQ-9 above or below the cut-off of 10 for ≥moderate depression	AUC = 0.749 All variables: AUC = 0.750
			Predict end-of-quarter suicidal ideation (present yes/no)	Based on the final question of PHQ-9, yes or no	AUC = 0.736 All variables: AUC = 0.699
Kim et al., 2019 [54]	Actiwatch Spectrum PRO	Activity Sleep Light exposure EMA	Detect current depression (depressed yes/no)	Classified as depressed if HDRS ≥ 8 (mild) and SGDS ≥ 7 (mild or worse)	Accuracy = 91% Sensitivity = 88% Specificity = 94% F1 = 0.90 AUC = 0.96
Lee et al., 2022 [55]	FitBit Charge HR, or 2, or 3 Smartphone: Android, iOS, possibly other OS n.s.	Activity Sleep Heart rate Light exposure	Predict future mood episodes (occurs yes/no)	Mood episodes were identified retrospectively by the clinician based on interview and eMoodchart app data (app developed by research group)	Accuracy = 93.8% Sensitivity = 91.5% Specificity = 94.3% AUC = 97.3%
Lu et al., 2018 [56]	FitBit Charge HR Smartphone: Android, iOS	Heart rate Activity Sleep Location	Predict the current QIDS score	Self-reported QIDS score	4-task model: R2 = 0.36 F1 = 0.77
			Predict current symptom severity level (which category as rated by a clinician)	Only if diagnosed by the clinician at baseline through interview per DSM-5 and QIDS: severity categorized by the clinician (stable, mild, moderate, severe)	

Table 2. *Cont.*

Reference	Wearable Specifications	Predictive Features	Prediction Outcome	Ground Truth Determination	Quality Measures (Best Model)
Mahendran et al., 2019 [57]	Mi band-3	Selected 9 questions of the HDRS-21 Activity	Detect current depression (depressed yes/no)	HDRS-21	Accuracy = 99.01% Sensitivity = 98.4% Specificity = 98.87% F1 = 0.98 PPV = 97.54%
Makhmutova et al., 2022 [58]	FitBit: model n.s.	PHQ-9 (true and predicted) Lifestyle Changes Activity Sleep	Predict current PHQ-9 score	PHQ-9 measured at three-month intervals	Quadratic weighted Cohen κ = 0.476 Adjacent accuracy = 77.6%
			Detect change in severity (change since three months ago yes/no)	PHQ-9 severity level is categorized according to clinical cut-offs (minimal, mild, moderate, moderately severe, severe)	Sensitivity = 55.4% Specificity = 65.3% AUPRC = 0.31
Mullick et al., 2022 [59]	FitBit Inspire HR; software version 1.84.5 Smartphone: Android, iOS	Heart rate Sleep Steps Phone use Location	Predict current PHQ-9 score	Weekly PHQ-9	MAE = 2.39 MSE = 10.28 MAPE = 0.27 RMSE = 2.83
			Detect change in severity level (how many PHQ-9 points up/down)	PHQ-9 severity levels determined with clinical cut-offs (minimal, mild, moderate, moderately severe, severe)	MAE = 3.12 MSE = 20.14 MAPE = 7.16 RMSE = 4.48
Pedrelli et al., 2020 [60]	Empatica E4 wristbands (both wrists) Smartphone: Android	EDA Heart rate Activity Phone use	Predict the current HDRS-17 score	HDRS-17 score derived from biweekly HDRS-28 measurements	MAE = 4.08 RMSE = 5.35 R = 0.56
Rykov et al., 2021 [61]	FitBit Charge 2	Activity Sleep Circadian rhythms	Detect current depression (depressed yes/no)	Depression is classified based on PHQ-9 with a cut-off of 8 (mild or worse)	Accuracy = 80% Sensitivity = 82% Specificity = 78%
Tazawa et al., 2020 [62]	Silmee W20 wristband	Activity Sleep Heart rate Skin temperature UV light exposure	Detect current depression	Assessed by a clinician using HDRS-17, MADRS, or YMRS, and self-reported BDI-II and PSQI.	Accuracy = 76% Sensitivity = 73% Specificity = 79%
			Predict the current HDRS-17 score	HDRS-17 by clinician	R = 0.61 R2 = 0.37 MAE = 4.94

AUC = Area Under Curve. AUPRC = Area Under Precision Recall Curve. BDI-II = Beck Depression Inventory-II. DSM-5: Diagnostic and Statistical Manual of Mental Disorders, 5th edition. EDA = Electrodermal Activity. EMA = Ecological Momentary Assessment. HDRS-17/21 = Hamilton Depression Rating Scale with 17 or 21 items. MADRS = Montgomery Åsberg Depression Rating Scale. MAE = Mean Absolute Error. MAPE = Mean Absolute Percentage Error. MSE = Mean Squared Error. n.s. = not specified. OS = Operating system. PHQ-9 = Patient Health Questionnaire-9. PPV = Positive Predictive Value. PSQI = Pitsburg Sleep Quality Index. QIDS = Quick Inventory of Depressive Symptomatology. RMSE = Root Mean Square Error. SGDS = Short Geriatric Depression Scale. UV = Ultraviolet. YMRS = Young Mania Rating Scale. [1] Multiple models were made to distinguish between different subgroups. The reported ranges encompass the quality measures of the best model for each distinction.

3.1. Variation in Available Predictive Features

Wearables are able to collect vast amounts of personal data, and most studies use different combinations of the same commonly selected features. For wearables, these include activity (often measured as a number of steps or time in motion), sleep (derived from activity), and heart rate. When smartphones were used, additional features commonly included phone use (apps, communication) and location. However, some research groups utilized less common features. For example, Chikersal et al. [49] used Bluetooth to infer how many different people the user met. Based on how frequently devices were scanned to be in proximity, devices were categorized as "self" (most frequently scanned) and "other" (less frequently scanned). Moreover, as the study population consisted entirely of college students who lived on campus, common locations on campus were labeled and visits to these locations were tracked. Both features offered additional insight into the social network and activities of the participants. These types of features are difficult to translate to the general public but could be interesting in targeting populations that spend the majority of their time frequenting the same general area.

Ghandeharioun et al. [51] had each participant wear two Empatica E4 wristbands, one on each wrist. This allowed consideration of the symmetry of electrodermal activity between the left and right wrist. The number of skin conductance responses and magnitude of EDA showed stronger asymmetry on days when mental health was poor. The study population was small, so these results should be considered preliminary. A follow-up study with a slightly larger sample size used the same two-wristband approach and found that two of the top ten features were related to EDA, particularly the left/right asymmetry [60]. For practical application, two wristbands are less convenient for the user, but EDA asymmetry in depression may still be interesting to investigate for short-term application or from a fundamental research perspective.

Less commonly, survey data were included as a feature alongside wearable data. For example, one study used a selection of nine Hamilton Depression Rating Scale (HDRS)-21 questions in addition to wearable activity data to predict HDRS-21 scores. This produced an incredibly accurate model (99% accuracy), but this should be considered with caution as using part of the ground truth to predict the ground truth likely inflated the accuracy [57]. Another study first created an algorithm using a combination of wearable-collected sleep data, patient demographic and lifestyle survey data, and Patient Health Questionnaire (PHQ)-9 data to predict PHQ-9 severity levels in between survey moments. The static demographic data were found to be most important for this prediction. A second algorithm then used all available data to predict the PHQ-9 score 3 months after baseline. The previously predicted PHQ-9 development was one of the most important features of this second algorithm. The authors acknowledged that the need for surveys should be minimized to optimize future applications of such algorithms [58].

3.2. Feature Selection

From the wide variety of available features, each study makes a selection of features to use for their model. Consumer-grade wearables differ in the amount and sophistication of sensors they can provide, which is the first limiting factor researchers encounter in which features they select. However, sometimes, pre-existing hypotheses about the underlying mechanisms of depression also influence feature selection. For example, Cho et al. [50] and Lee et al. [55] chose to look specifically at features involving the circadian rhythm. Alternatively, data-driven approaches can be applied for selection. An often necessary first step in this process is to remove features that are heavily correlated with each other and thus provide redundant information [57–59]. Another data-driven approach is to create several model iterations using different selections of features and choosing the selection that results in the best prediction accuracy. This method was used, for example, by Griffiths et al. [52], to choose how many features to include in their model. After identifying the features with the highest importance, they created models using different numbers of features (top 5, top 10, etc.). As determined by cross-validation, the model using the top

10 features performed best, letting them predict symptom severity with up to 82% accuracy. Similarly, Pedrelli et al. [60] made models using different groups of features (smartphone only, wearable only, or both) to estimate HDRS scores. They then used two cross-validation approaches. The first simulated the tracking of single patients by using the first weeks for training and the last weeks for testing. The second focused on generalizability, splitting the participants into a training and test group. They found the smartphone-only model to be more accurate for the more personalized approach, whereas the wearable-only model allowed for better generalizability.

It is important to also realize how feature selection can lead to overfitting when conducted incorrectly. For example, Kim et al. [54] first classified their population as either depressed or not depressed, then compared these two groups and selected the features that were most predictive for classifying individuals. Since it is not reported otherwise, it must be assumed they made this comparison without first splitting the data into a training and test group. While these features may be particularly relevant within this population, it is impossible to know whether this would be the same in a new and unseen population. In a similar manner, Rykov et al. [61] explicitly state they based their feature selection on the statistical associations found over the entire sample. This again greatly compromises generalizability to new populations.

3.3. Prediction Outcomes and Horizons

A predictive algorithm can be used in many ways to anticipate depressive symptoms. Variation may lie in the type of outcome that is predicted or the prediction horizon. The prediction outcome may be a continuous score indicating symptom severity or a categorical outcome classifying by either depression diagnosis (yes or no) or clinical cut-off (above or below a clinical cut-off). With a smaller prediction horizon, a model may predict whether symptoms are being experienced in the present moment or whether symptoms have changed over recent weeks. With a larger prediction horizon, a model may predict whether depressive symptoms will change in the near future or even whether they will arise several weeks in advance. Each of these outcomes can be useful as long as the appropriate context is considered.

The following will highlight some studies to exemplify the various options. Firstly, Ghandeharioun et al. [51] looked at a continuous outcome, aiming to predict daily HDRS-17 scores for a period of 8 weeks. Predicting daily mood scores this way may be useful for more detailed symptom tracking in between regular treatment visits. Conversely, Griffiths et al. [52] used a binary outcome, as their model predicted whether the current PHQ-9 scores of patients with treatment-resistant depression (TRD) were above or below the clinical cut-off (PHQ-9 $\geq$ 20) for severe depression. Such a binary outcome reduces nuance but makes interpretability more direct in the clinic. In fact, in clinical practice, the category is often sufficient without knowing an exact severity score. The authors note that this type of prediction for symptom monitoring is likely redundant for TRD patients due to their frequent in-person monitoring. However, with some adjustments, predicting on which side of the clinical cut-off patients fall can be useful for monitoring treatment progress, for example.

Bai et al. [48] investigated the binary outcome of whether symptoms changed over time. This was classified based on the difference between the highest and lowest of three consecutive PHQ-9 scores, measured at least one week apart. The distinction was made primarily between swinging mood (symptom change) and stable mood (no symptom change), and groups were further specified as moderate or drastic swing and stable remission or depression for a total of four outcome groups. A plethora of models were created that decided which of two groups an individual belonged in, each using different features and algorithm training methods. A major disadvantage of this method is that each model assumes a binary outcome (e.g., stable depression or moderate swing), thereby ignoring the possibility that the individual belongs to one of the other groups (e.g., stable remission). The highest accuracy was reached with models deciding between stable remission and moderate swing and between stable remission and drastic swing. These particular models may be useful for patients known to be in stable remission who wish to be alerted early of potential relapses.

Exploring a slightly larger prediction horizon, Cho et al. [50] aimed to predict mood states and impending mood episodes in patients with pre-existing mood disorders (MDD, Bipolar disorder type I/II). The algorithm used 18 days' worth of data to predict mood state and occurrence of mood episodes over the following three days. The ground truth was determined using the absolute mood score (AMS) as self-reported in the eMoodChart app that was newly designed for this study. The ground truth distinction between stable (neutral) and biased (depressed, manic, hypomanic) was made using AMS percentiles rather than cut-off scores. For example, the best model considered the mood state of the 30% highest AMS to be biased and the lowest 70% to be stable. As such, the distinction relies on group distribution rather than true mood score. The occurrence of mood episodes was instead confirmed through in-person interviews, as is the clinical standard. A similar study was conducted by the same group with a larger sample size [55]. They predicted mood episodes over the same prediction horizon, removing the reliance on AMS distribution for the ground truth. The reported accuracy for predicting depressive episodes in MDD patients was very high. However, for lack of reporting otherwise, presumably, all recorded episodes were used for retrospective feature selection, resulting in overfitting. The prediction of impending mood episodes a few days before they occur would give patients forewarning, allowing them to contact their clinician and be better prepared to deal with the episode.

Further expanding the prediction horizon, Chikersal et al. [49] aimed to predict symptoms of depression several weeks in advance. Specifically, over the course of a 16-week study period, two binary outcomes were predicted each week using the data available at that time: whether participants would have depression at the final check-up and whether their symptoms then would be worse compared to baseline. Depression and worsening symptoms were predicted with acceptable accuracy (> 80%) up to 9 and 14 weeks in advance, respectively. A caveat is that no mood data were collected outside of the Beck Depression Inventory-II (BDI-II) at the start and end of the 16-week study period, so it is unknown when exactly symptoms started developing. As such, it is unclear exactly how far in advance the model is able to predict the onset of depression. However, because it is unlikely that all 36 new cases would have been classified as newly depressed after the first two weeks, it is safe to assume that the number of cases was indeed predicted correctly several weeks in advance. A major benefit of predicting this far in advance is that these passive sensing models may be able to pick up on early signs of depression that participants themselves may not be aware of yet and that would, therefore, be missed through regular self-reported measures. This allows earlier detection and, most importantly, the possibility of earlier intervention.

Similarly, Horowitz et al. [53] also aimed to predict whether depression occurred several weeks in advance. Specifically, the two outcomes they predicted were the presence of depression and suicidal ideation at the end of a quarter (13 weeks). Each day, a new iteration of the models was made using the data available up to that time. To predict depression with an acceptable accuracy (AUC > 0.7), a minimum of two weeks' worth of data was needed, whereas prediction of suicidal ideation required at least 7 weeks' worth of data. Predicting participants' mood status was thus possible 6–11 weeks in advance. Model variations were created that used only the mood variables based on the self-reported daily mood scores or using all variables, including mood and wearable data. For predicting depression, accuracy was comparable across variations, while suicidal ideation was predicted slightly better using only mood variables. This implies wearable data are not necessary for accurate predictions as long as participants submit mood data. However, a major benefit of wearables is that they do not require user input and are, therefore, less obtrusive than daily mood surveys.

3.4. The Duration of Data Collection

Aside from feature selection and prediction outcomes, another interesting consideration is that different prediction outcomes require different durations of data collection. Since most studies only looked at a single type of outcome, this was not typically investigated in a direct manner. Tazawa et al. [62] did look at two outcomes. First to detect current depression (binary), and second to predict current severity score (continuous). They compared algorithms using 3 and 7 days' worth of data to investigate if a longer period was beneficial. While the prediction of depression showed no difference, the severity score was predicted significantly better with 7 days' worth of data. This implies that more complex predictions (continuous score as opposed to binary classification) may particularly benefit from the additional measurements. As mentioned before, Chikersal et al. [49] also looked at two types of predictions and found that predicting the onset of depression required 7 weeks' worth of data, whereas predicting worsening symptoms only required a minimum of 2 weeks. In a similar comparison, Horowitz et al. [53] found that predicting future depression was accurate after only 2 weeks, whereas suicidal ideation was not accurately predicted until 7 weeks' worth of data were available. The difference in time needed to predict future depression is likely due to the different model training methods and feature selection used, which both heavily influence the data requirements. In the current review, not enough studies focus on this aspect to draw a conclusion on how much data is required for specific types of predictions. Nonetheless, it is advisable to remember that some predictions and algorithm training methods benefit from longer periods of data collection. A practical consideration when making such a model should, therefore, be whether that duration is suitable for the model's intended application.

3.5. Types of Machine Learning Models (Ensemble vs. Single Type)

There are many ways of training a predictive algorithm. Some examples include linear regression, decision trees, or gradient boosting. Additionally, it is possible to combine several training models into an ensemble model. Such ensemble models have been found by multiple studies to have superior accuracy when compared to single-type models. For example, Lu et al. [56] used multitask learning to create their predictive algorithms that made two predictions: the current Quick Inventory of Depressive Symptomatology (QIDS) score for all participants (healthy and depressed) and the current severity of depressive symptoms for patients. The tasks for the multitask models were based on the type of prediction, (1) QIDS score, and (2) severity, as well as the operating system of the user's smartphone, (1) iOS and (2) Android. Two-task models each did one type of prediction for the two different operating systems, and four-task models combined QIDS score and severity prediction for both operating systems. Overall, the multitask models outperformed the single-task ones, and the four-task models generally performed better than the two-task models, showing the potential of combined predictive models to enhance each other. Additionally, the models using FitBit and smartphone data performed slightly better than those using smartphone data alone, showing that the wearable data can also improve the predictive capabilities of these models.

Another study that used a combination of different training methods was conducted by Mahendran et al. [57]. The algorithms that were compared used logistic regression, random forest, and a weighted average ensemble that combined the two. The accuracy reported for logistic regression and for random forest was generally high, but they found the weighted average ensemble model to be the most accurate of all. As mentioned earlier, the accuracy may be inflated due to the use of some HDRS-21 data to predict HDRS-21 scores, but this was the case for all three model variations. As such, this study again indicates that ensemble models can improve predictive quality. While the accuracy of ensemble models seems better than that of singular models, they also come with some disadvantages. Firstly, more complex models require more computing power and resources, which may not be available or desirable. Secondly, the increasing complexity of a model increases the risk of overfitting, whereas simpler models are more robust. Finally, due to the complexity of ensemble models, it is much more difficult to rationalize and understand how predictions are made compared to single-type models. Depending on the data complexity and prediction goal, a fitting model complexity should be chosen.

3.6. Common Limitations

Finally, while wearables offer a lot of potential and many of the discussed models can predict depressive symptoms with impressive accuracy, it is also important to go over a number of common limitations and pitfalls that should be avoided when further researching this topic. Some of these have been mentioned throughout the previous sections. First, when best practices are not followed, there is a high risk of overfitting a model during feature selection, thus limiting generalizability [54,55,61]. Second, multiple studies used very small groups of participants, which is also likely to limit generalizability [50–52,54,59,60]. Third, some models relied on active user input through mood-scoring apps or surveys [53,54,57]. This directly conflicts with one of the main strengths of wearables: the ability to collect data without active user contribution. Fourth, none of the studies reviewed tested their model on independently collected validation datasets, thus increasing the risk of bias. This is an issue also highlighted in a recent review of models using smartphone data to predict depression [63]. These limitations combined make it highly likely that the impressive results observed in individual studies might fall short if the algorithms were applied to the real world. The following section will discuss some common limitations found in the reviewed studies, as well as general limitations that need to be considered when researching wearable predictive models.

One of these recurring limitations was that study populations had limited generalizability due to the overrepresentation of certain demographics. For example, many studies used populations that were predominantly female [51,52,56,58–61]. Additionally, people over the age of 65 were only included in a single study [54]. This is unfortunate, as this type of research may be particularly useful for the elderly population, which is at an increased risk of experiencing depression [64]. Lastly, most studies looked at participants who were predominantly White [56,58–60] or Asian [48,54,61,62], whereas Black people were in the minority if they were included at all. The latter is especially relevant because one of the common wearable sensors, the photoplethysmography (PPG) sensor, relies on how green light is absorbed by the skin and blood flowing underneath to measure heart rate. The accuracy of this sensor was found to be dependent on skin color, with less accuracy for darker skin tones [65]. Moreover, the fact that Black people are often underrepresented in validation studies is a systemic issue that should be taken into account when considering the use of wearables for health tracking in these populations.

Some other methodological challenges include the lack of standard protocols due to the novelty of this type of research. This is illustrated by the fact that many studies use different methods to establish the ground truth. Some relied on mood-scoring methods newly designed for their study [50], others used in-person visits with a psychiatrist [62], and the majority used one or more in-person or self-reported questionnaires such as the Hamilton Depression Rating Scale, Patient Health Questionnaire-9, or Beck Depression Inventory-II [49,54,58]. This large variety of methods complicates direct comparisons between studies. The reporting of methodological details is not always clear and complete. For example, the model of the wearable is not always specified [52,58], and the operating systems of smartphones used are not always disclosed [48,50,55]. Similarly, the way the predictive quality of the algorithms is reported also varies. In part, this is because binary classifications are simply assessed in a different way than when the outcome is a numeric score. However, even within the same types of predictions, the reported quality outcomes vary. This makes direct comparisons especially complicated when common measures (e.g., specificity, F1-score, mean absolute error) are not reported [48,51,56]. The variability in methods and reporting quality has been reported on before in more detail [66]. A last note on the methods is that patients are commonly not considered as separate individuals but rather as a collection of data that can be compiled with all the other patients' data into one big dataset for the algorithm to analyze [55,56]. Alternatively, it also occurred that repeated measurements from the same patient were pooled together and treated as independent observations [58,62]. This can artificially increase the sample size and mislead the certainty with which algorithms make predictions about personal trajectories. It should finally be noted that the search strategy for this review did not include databases focused on computer science or engineering and instead used PubMed as the primary database in order to reflect the studies clinical research professionals would most likely encounter. Readers should be aware that this has likely led to the exclusion of interesting articles written with different disciplinary backgrounds and with potentially different approaches and limitations.

A final practical consideration is that the companies that make these consumer-grade wearables are continuously updating their models and releasing new versions of them. While new versions presumably are of similar or improved quality, this does add another factor that can vary when comparing the results of different studies. Additionally, not all studies specify which version they used and instead only report the brand of the device [52,58].

4. Discussion

The papers reviewed here altogether indicate wearable data have a lot of potential to be used for the detection, monitoring, and prediction of depressive symptoms. These predictions can be used for a wide variety of purposes, ranging from monitoring existing symptoms to facilitating early interventions. Exactly how much data is needed varies for each of these purposes and should be fine-tuned to the type of prediction a given model aims to make. Models can be made with diverse complexity, and more complex models tend to be slightly more accurate. However, simpler models are less likely to be overfitted, and these predictions are easier to grasp by humans. Certain types of wearable features (e.g., activity, sleep) were frequently used in the literature to successfully predict depression outcomes, although novel features (e.g., electrodermal activity, phone use) were also occasionally encountered. These features hold the potential to either better tune model predictions or inspire new directions altogether in research on how depression operates.

Application of Wearables in Mental Health Care

The widespread application of wearables in mental healthcare is the obvious end goal for this type of research. However, there are a number of real-world complexities yet to be solved. To start with, wearables collect massive amounts of personal data, which usually means they are reliant on cloud storage and capacity. This not only requires a lot of resources but can also have a significant environmental impact [67]. Moreover, the collection, transmission, and storage of large amounts of personal data need to meet a high standard of data security [68,69]. Similarly, there is the non-trivial issue of data privacy, which is an important ethical consideration but also a deciding factor for whether patients would trust these types of algorithms enough to use them [70,71]. There would be much to gain by independent systematic evaluation of the many different data collectors and health apps, preferably through international collaboration [72]. Finally, from a socioeconomic point of view, it is important to consider that access to wearables is not universal, and the accessibility of predictive algorithms is based in large part on the user's economic status and insurance. There is also considerable sampling and selection bias, as health-conscious people are more likely to participate in both studies and applications [73]. It should be noted that the US Food and Drug Administration (FDA) has outlined plans to regulate artificial intelligence and machine learning algorithms for health applications [74]. Their primary focus is to ensure that algorithms implemented in healthcare are explainable, transparent, secure to cyberattacks, and not biased towards certain sociodemographic groups. It remains to be seen how future academic research on mental healthcare responds to institutional regulation on wearables and machine learning.

Given the importance of the doctor–patient relationship, it is unlikely that wearables will ever fully replace the diagnosis by a clinician [75]. Instead, wearables may prove more useful as a complementary tool. For example, they could be used to monitor recovery progress in between visits and for early detection of relapse for patients with a previous diagnosis. By contrast, algorithms that predict the future onset of depression several weeks in advance seem able to detect physiological or behavioral traits indicating prodromal symptoms of depression, symptoms that go under the radar of traditional diagnoses. Since both reviewed studies with a longer prediction horizon looked at highly specific populations they considered to be higher risk [49,53], it would be interesting to initially apply these models to specific groups of at-risk individuals. The reviewed studies both looked at first-year medical students or trainees, but other groups could include people who are grieving or who have recently become unemployed [76,77]. Predicting this far in advance is admittedly a much less common approach in research, so there is still a lot of progress to be made in this direction, but the results so far are promising.

Alternatively, a more research-focused approach can also be explored. Most studies simply observe which features are used by the algorithm, and some do report which features have the biggest predictive value for the model. A question that is often left open is why these features are so informative. This is a very interesting and unexplored area of research that may provide novel insights into the underlying mechanisms of depression. Furthermore, these important features could potentially inspire new or more personalized interventions. For example, if a patient is classified as depressed based most importantly on their excessive late-night activity, they might benefit from a treatment that focuses more on their sleeping habits. However, the efficacy of this approach is merely speculative, as no studies were found looking at such personalized treatment adjustments.

5. Conclusions

All in all, the fact remains that the algorithms were able to predict depressive symptoms with better accuracy than purely random prediction. Even with the noted limitations, these are promising results. The use of consumer-grade wearables and machine learning in this manner is still a very novel approach that still has a long way to go before any of the widespread applications mentioned above would be feasible. Improvement is especially constructive in the development of more standardized methods and clearer guidelines for conducting and reporting these kinds of studies. This would naturally improve reproducibility, comparability across studies, and, most importantly, the predictive quality and validity of the models. The next steps would include larger-scale studies, ideally proportionally more studies with longer prediction horizons, an exploration of potential intervention strategies, and more focus on the research implications of these algorithms in order to truly reach the full potential of wearable technology in mental health care.

Author Contributions: Conceptualization, Q.W. and A.K.; methodology, Q.W., M.Z., M.U. and A.K.; validation, M.Z. and M.U.; investigation, Q.W.; data curation, Q.W.; writing—original draft preparation, Q.W. and A.K.; writing—review and editing, Q.W., M.Z., M.U. and A.K.; supervision, A.K. All authors have read and agreed to the published version of the manuscript.

Funding: Astrid Kamperman and Milan Zarchev are funded by the Epidemiological and Social Psychiatric Research Institute (ESPRi), a consortium of academic and non-academic research groups at the following institutes of mental health care (GGz): Parnassia Psychiatric Institute Antes, GGz Breburg, GGz Delfland, GGz Westelijk Noord-Brabant and Yulius.

Data Availability Statement: The original contributions presented in the study are included in the article; further inquiries can be directed to the corresponding author.

Conflicts of Interest: The authors declare no conflicts of interest.

References

1. Omura, J.D.; Carlson, S.A.; Paul, P.; Watson, K.B.; Fulton, J.E. National physical activity surveillance: Users of wearable activity monitors as a potential data source. *Prev. Med. Rep.* **2017**, 5, 124–126. [CrossRef] [PubMed]

2. Thompson, W.R. Worldwide Survey Of Fitness Trends For 2019. *ACSM's Health Fit. J.* **2018**, *22*, 10–17. [CrossRef]
3. Wearables—Statistics & Facts. Available online: https://www.statista.com/topics/1556/wearable-technology/-topicOverview (accessed on 10 May 2023).
4. Cruz, S.; Lu, C.; Ulloa, M.; Redding, A.; Hester, J.; Jacobs, M. Perceptions of Wearable Health Tools Post the COVID-19 Emergency in Low-Income Latin Communities: Qualitative Study. *JMIR Mhealth Uhealth* **2024**, *12*, e50826. [CrossRef] [PubMed]
5. Schueller, S.M.; Neary, M.; Lai, J.; Epstein, D.A. Understanding People's Use of and Perspectives on Mood-Tracking Apps: Interview Study. *JMIR Ment. Health* **2021**, *8*, e29368. [CrossRef]
6. Saganowski, S.; Dutkowiak, A.; Dziadek, A.; Dzieżyc, M.; Komoszyńska, J.; Michalska, W.; Polak, A.; Ujma, M.; Kazienko, P. Emotion Recognition Using Wearables: A Systematic Literature Review—Work-in-progress. In Proceedings of the 2020 IEEE International Conference on Pervasive Computing and Communications Workshops (PerCom Workshops), Austin, TX, USA, 23–27 March 2020.
7. Shu, L.; Yu, Y.; Chen, W.; Hua, H.; Li, Q.; Jin, J.; Xu, X. Wearable Emotion Recognition Using Heart Rate Data from a Smart Bracelet. *Sensors* **2020**, *20*, 718. [CrossRef]
8. Abd-Alrazaq, A.; AlSaad, R.; Aziz, S.; Ahmed, A.; Denecke, K.; Househ, M.; Farooq, F.; Sheikh, J. Wearable Artificial Intelligence for Anxiety and Depression: Scoping Review. *J. Med. Internet Res.* **2023**, *25*, e42672. [CrossRef]
9. Ahmed, A.; Aziz, S.; Alzubaidi, M.; Schneider, J.; Irshaidat, S.; Abu Serhan, H.; Abd-Alrazaq, A.; Solaiman, B.; Househ, M. Wearable devices for anxiety & depression: A scoping review. *Comput. Methods Programs Biomed. Update* **2023**, *3*, 100095. [CrossRef]
10. Kang, M.; Chai, K. Wearable Sensing Systems for Monitoring Mental Health. *Sensors* **2022**, *22*, 994. [CrossRef] [PubMed]
11. Lee, S.; Kim, H.; Park, M.J.; Jeon, H.J. Current Advances in Wearable Devices and Their Sensors in Patients with Depression. *Front. Psychiatry* **2021**, *12*, 672347. [CrossRef]
12. Depressive Disorder (Depression). Available online: https://www.who.int/news-room/fact-sheets/detail/depression (accessed on 15 May 2023).
13. Williams, S.Z.; Chung, G.S.; Muennig, P.A. Undiagnosed depression: A community diagnosis. *SSM Popul. Health* **2017**, *3*, 633–638. [CrossRef]
14. Liu, Q.; He, H.; Yang, J.; Feng, X.; Zhao, F.; Lyu, J. Changes in the global burden of depression from 1990 to 2017: Findings from the Global Burden of Disease study. *J. Psychiatr. Res.* **2020**, *126*, 134–140. [CrossRef] [PubMed]
15. *Diagnostic and Statistical Manual of Mental Disorders: DSM-5™*, 5th ed.; American Psychiatric Publishing, a Division of American Psychiatric Association: Washington, DC, USA, 2013.
16. Halfin, A. Depression: The benefits of early and appropriate treatment. *Am. J. Manag. Care* **2007**, *13*, S92–S97. [PubMed]
17. Vitaterna, M.H.; Takahashi, J.S.; Turek, F.W. Overview of circadian rhythms. *Alcohol Res. Health* **2001**, *25*, 85–93. [PubMed]
18. Boyce, P.; Barriball, E. Circadian rhythms and depression. *Aust. Fam. Physician* **2010**, *39*, 307–310.
19. Soria, V.; Urretavizcaya, M. Circadian rhythms and depression. *Actas Esp. Psiquiatr.* **2009**, *37*, 222–232.
20. Coppen, A.; Abou-Saleh, M.; Milln, P.; Metcalfe, M.; Harwood, J.; Bailey, J. Dexamethasone suppression test in depression and other psychiatric illness. *Br. J. Psychiatry* **1983**, *142*, 498–504. [CrossRef]
21. Green, H.S.; Kane, J.M. The dexamethasone suppression test in depression. *Clin. Neuropharmacol.* **1983**, *6*, 7–24. [CrossRef]
22. Tsigos, C.; Chrousos, G.P. Hypothalamic-pituitary-adrenal axis, neuroendocrine factors and stress. *J. Psychosom. Res.* **2002**, *53*, 865–871. [CrossRef]
23. The Connection between Anxiety and Body Temperature. Available online: https://www.calmclinic.com/anxiety/symptoms/body-temperature (accessed on 22 June 2023).
24. Cortisol. Available online: https://my.clevelandclinic.org/health/articles/22187-cortisol (accessed on 22 June 2023).
25. Vedder, H. Physiology of the Hypothalamic-Pituitary-Adrenocortical Axis. In *NeuroImmune Biology*, 1st ed.; Rey, A.D., Chrousos, G., Besedovsky, H., Eds.; Elsevier: Amsterdam, The Netherlands, 2008; Volume 7, pp. 154–196.
26. Helgadóttir, B.; Forsell, Y.; Ekblom, Ö. Physical activity patterns of people affected by depressive and anxiety disorders as measured by accelerometers: A cross-sectional study. *PLoS ONE* **2015**, *10*, e0115894. [CrossRef]
27. De Mello, M.T.; de Aquino Lemos, V.; Antunes, H.K.M.; Bittencourt, L.; Santos-Silva, R.; Tufik, S. Relationship between physical activity and depression and anxiety symptoms: A population study. *J. Affect. Disord.* **2013**, *149*, 241–246. [CrossRef]
28. Raoux, N.; Benoit, O.; Dantchev, N.; Denise, P.; Franc, B.; Alliale, J.-F.; Widlöcher, D. Circadian pattern of motor activity in major depressed patients undergoing antidepressant therapy: Relationship between actigraphic measures and clinical course. *Psychiatry Res.* **1994**, *52*, 85–98. [CrossRef] [PubMed]
29. Todder, D.; Caliskan, S.; Baune, B.T. Longitudinal changes of day-time and night-time gross motor activity in clinical responders and non-responders of major depression. *World J. Biol. Psychiatry* **2009**, *10*, 276–284. [CrossRef] [PubMed]
30. Minaeva, O.; Booij, S.H.; Lamers, F.; Antypa, N.; Schoevers, R.A.; Wichers, M.; Riese, H. Level and timing of physical activity during normal daily life in depressed and non-depressed individuals. *Transl. Psychiatry* **2020**, *10*, 259. [CrossRef] [PubMed]
31. Balogh, S.; Booij, S.H.; Lamers, F.; Antypa, N.; Schoevers, R.A.; Wichers, M.; Riese, H. Increases in heart rate variability with successful treatment in patients with major depressive disorder. *Psychopharmacol. Bull.* **1993**, *29*, 201–206.
32. da Estrela, C.; McGrath, J.; Booij, L.; Gouin, J.-P. Heart Rate Variability, Sleep Quality, and Depression in the Context of Chronic Stress. *Ann. Behav. Med.* **2021**, *55*, 155–164. [CrossRef]

33. Agelink, M.W.; Boz, C.; Ullrich, H.; Andrich, J. Relationship between major depression and heart rate variability.: Clinical consequences and implications for antidepressive treatment. *Psychiatry Res.* **2002**, *113*, 139–149. [CrossRef]
34. Kemp, A.H.; Quintana, D.S.; Gray, M.A.; Felmingham, K.L.; Brown, K.; Gatt, J.M. Impact of Depression and Antidepressant Treatment on Heart Rate Variability: A Review and Meta-Analysis. *Biol. Psychiatry* **2010**, *67*, 1067–1074. [CrossRef]
35. Iacono, W.G.; Lykken, D.T.; Peloquin, L.J.; Lumry, A.E.; Valentine, R.H.; Tuason, V.B. Electrodermal activity in euthymic unipolar and bipolar affective disorders. A possible marker for depression. *Arch. Gen. Psychiatry* **1983**, *40*, 557–565. [CrossRef]
36. Mestanikova, A.; Ondrejka, I.; Mestanik, M.; Hrtanek, I.; Snircova, E.; Tonhajzerova, I. Electrodermal Activity in Adolescent Depression. *Adv. Exp. Med. Biol.* **2016**, *935*, 83–88. [CrossRef]
37. Storrie, M.C.; Doerr, H.O.; Johnson, M.H. Skin conductance characteristics of depressed subjects before and after therapeutic intervention. *J. Nerv. Ment. Dis.* **1981**, *169*, 176–179. [CrossRef]
38. Ward, N.G.; Doerr, H.O. Skin conductance. A potentially sensitive and specific marker for depression. *J. Nerv. Ment. Dis.* **1986**, *174*, 553–559. [CrossRef] [PubMed]
39. Avery, D.H.; Shah, S.H.; Eder, D.N.; Wildschindtz, G. Nocturnal sweating and temperature in depression. *Acta Psychiatr. Scand.* **1999**, *100*, 295–301. [CrossRef]
40. Avery, D.H.; Wildschiødtz, G.; Rafaelsen, O.J. Nocturnal temperature in affective disorder. *J. Affect. Disord.* **1982**, *4*, 61–71. [CrossRef]
41. Rausch, J.L.; Johnson, M.; Corley, K.; Hobby, H.; Shendarkar, N.; Fei, Y.; Ganapathy, V.; Leibach, F. Depressed patients have higher body temperature: 5-HT transporter long promoter region effects. *Neuropsychobiology* **2003**, *47*, 120–127. [CrossRef] [PubMed]
42. Tocchetto, B.F.; Ramalho, L.; Zortea, M.; Bruck, S.M.; Tomedi, R.B.; Alves, R.L.; da Silva Torres, I.L.; Fregni, F.; Caumo, W. Peripheral body temperature rhythm as a marker of the severity of depression symptoms in fibromyalgia. *Biol. Psychol.* **2023**, *177*, 108494. [CrossRef] [PubMed]
43. Molnar, C.; Freiesleben, T. *Supervised Machine Learning for Science: How to Stop Worrying and Love Your Black Box*, 1st ed.; Bookdown, 2024; Available online: https://ml-science-book.com/ (accessed on 24 April 2024).
44. Breiman, L. Statistical Modeling: The Two Cultures (with comments and a rejoinder by the author). *Stat. Sci.* **2001**, *16*, 199–231. [CrossRef]
45. Hernán, M.A.; Hsu, J.; Healy, B. A Second Chance to Get Causal Inference Right: A Classification of Data Science Tasks. *CHANCE* **2019**, *32*, 42–49. [CrossRef]
46. Yarkoni, T.; Westfall, J. Choosing Prediction Over Explanation in Psychology: Lessons From Machine Learning. *Perspect. Psychol. Sci.* **2017**, *12*, 1100–1122. [CrossRef]
47. Molnar, C. *Interpretable Machine Learning: A Guide for Making Black Box Models Explainable*, 2nd ed.; Bookdown, 2022; Available online: https://christophm.github.io/interpretable-ml-book (accessed on 24 April 2024).
48. Bai, R.; Xiao, L.; Guo, Y.; Zhu, X.; Li, N.; Wang, Y.; Chen, Q.; Feng, L.; Wang, Y.; Yu, X.; et al. Tracking and Monitoring Mood Stability of Patients With Major Depressive Disorder by Machine Learning Models Using Passive Digital Data: Prospective Naturalistic Multicenter Study. *JMIR Mhealth Uhealth* **2021**, *9*, e24365. [CrossRef]
49. Chikersal, P.; Doryab, A.; Tumminia, M.; Villalba, D.K.; Dutcher, J.M.; Liu, X.; Cohen, S.; Creswell, K.G.; Mankoff, J.; Creswell, J.D.; et al. Detecting Depression and Predicting its Onset Using Longitudinal Symptoms Captured by Passive Sensing: A Machine Learning Approach with Robust Feature Selection. *ACM Trans. Comput.-Hum. Interact.* **2021**, *28*, 3. [CrossRef]
50. Cho, C.H.; Lee, T.; Kim, M.-G.; In, H.P.; Kim, L.; Lee, H.-J. Mood Prediction of Patients With Mood Disorders by Machine Learning Using Passive Digital Phenotypes Based on the Circadian Rhythm: Prospective Observational Cohort Study. *J. Med. Internet Res.* **2019**, *21*, e11029. [CrossRef] [PubMed]
51. Ghandeharioun, A.; Fedor, S.; Sangermano, L.; Ionescu, D.; Alpert, J.; Dale, C.; Sontag, D.; Picard, R. Objective assessment of depressive symptoms with machine learning and wearable sensors data. In Proceedings of the 2017 Seventh International Conference on Affective Computing and Intelligent Interaction (ACII), San Antonio, TX, USA, 23–26 October 2017.
52. Griffiths, C.; da Silva, K.M.; Leathlean, C.; Jiang, H.; Ang, C.S.; Searle, R. Investigation of physical activity, sleep, and mental health recovery in treatment resistant depression (TRD) patients receiving repetitive transcranial magnetic stimulation (rTMS) treatment. *J. Affect. Disord. Rep.* **2022**, *8*, 100337. [CrossRef]
53. Horwitz, A.G.; Kentopp, S.D.; Cleary, J.; Ross, K.; Wu, Z.; Sen, S.; Czyz, E.K. Using machine learning with intensive longitudinal data to predict depression and suicidal ideation among medical interns over time. *Psychol. Med.* **2022**, *53*, 5778–5785. [CrossRef]
54. Kim, H.; Lee, S.; Lee, S.; Hong, S.; Kang, H.; Kim, N. Depression Prediction by Using Ecological Momentary Assessment, Actiwatch Data, and Machine Learning: Observational Study on Older Adults Living Alone. *JMIR Mhealth Uhealth* **2019**, *7*, e14149. [CrossRef] [PubMed]
55. Lee, H.J.; Cho, C.-H.; Lee, T.; Jeong, J.; Yeom, J.W.; Kim, S.; Jeon, S.; Seo, J.Y.; Moon, E.; Baek, J.H.; et al. Prediction of impending mood episode recurrence using real-time digital phenotypes in major depression and bipolar disorders in South Korea: A prospective nationwide cohort study. *Psychol. Med.* **2022**, *53*, 5636–5644. [CrossRef]
56. Lu, J.; Shang, C.; Yue, C.; Morillo, R.; Ware, S.; Kamath, J.; Bamis, A.; Russell, A.; Wang, B.; Bi, J. Joint Modeling of Heterogeneous Sensing Data for Depression Assessment via Multi-task Learning. *Proc. ACM Interact. Mob. Wearable Ubiquitous Technol.* **2018**, *2*, 21. [CrossRef]
57. Mahendran, N.; Vincent, D.R.; Srinivasan, K.; Chang, C.-Y.; Garg, A.; Gao, L.; Reina, D.G. Sensor-Assisted Weighted Average Ensemble Model for Detecting Major Depressive Disorder. *Sensors* **2019**, *19*, 4822. [CrossRef] [PubMed]

58. Makhmutova, M.; Kainkaryam, R.; Ferreira, M.; Min, J.; Jaggi, M.; Clay, I. Predicting Changes in Depression Severity Using the PSYCHE-D (Prediction of Severity Change-Depression) Model Involving Person-Generated Health Data: Longitudinal Case-Control Observational Study. *JMIR Mhealth Uhealth* **2022**, *10*, e34148. [CrossRef]
59. Mullick, T.; Radovic, A.; Shaaban, S.; Doryab, A. Predicting Depression in Adolescents Using Mobile and Wearable Sensors: Multimodal Machine Learning-Based Exploratory Study. *JMIR Form. Res.* **2022**, *6*, e35807. [CrossRef]
60. Pedrelli, P.; Fedor, S.; Ghandeharioun, A.; Howe, E.; Ionescu, D.F.; Bhathena, D.; Fisher, L.B.; Cusin, C.; Nyer, M.; Yeung, A.; et al. Monitoring Changes in Depression Severity Using Wearable and Mobile Sensors. *Front. Psychiatry* **2020**, *11*, 584711. [CrossRef]
61. Rykov, Y.; Thach, T.-Q.; Bojic, I.; Christopoulos, G.; Car, J. Digital Biomarkers for Depression Screening With Wearable Devices: Cross-sectional Study With Machine Learning Modelling. *JMIR Mhealth Uhealth* **2021**, *9*, e24872. [CrossRef] [PubMed]
62. Tazawa, Y.; Liang, K.-C.; Yoshimura, M.; Kitazawa, M.; Kaise, Y.; Takamiya, A.; Kishi, A.; Horigome, T.; Mitsukura, Y.; Mimura, M.; et al. Evaluating depression with multimodal wristband-type wearable device: Screening and assessing patient severity utilizing machine-learning. *Heliyon* **2020**, *6*, e03274. [CrossRef] [PubMed]
63. Leaning, I.E.; Ikani, N.; Savage, H.S.; Leow, A.; Beckmann, C.; Ruhé, H.G.; Marquand, A.F. From smartphone data to clinically relevant predictions: A systematic review of digital phenotyping methods in depression. *Neurosci. Biobehav. Rev.* **2024**, *158*, 105541. [CrossRef]
64. Depression and Older Adults. Available online: https://www.nia.nih.gov/health/depression-and-older-adults (accessed on 10 September 2023).
65. Colvonen, P.J.; DeYoung, P.N.; Bosompra, N.-O.; Owens, R.L. Limiting racial disparities and bias for wearable devices in health science research. *Sleep* **2020**, *43*, zsaa159. [CrossRef]
66. De Angel, V.; Lewis, S.; White, K.; Oetzmann, C.; Leightley, D.; Oprea, E.; Lavelle, G.; Matcham, F.; Pace, A.; Mohr, D.C.; et al. Digital health tools for the passive monitoring of depression: A systematic review of methods. *NPJ Digit. Med.* **2022**, *5*, 3. [CrossRef] [PubMed]
67. Powell, D.; Godfrey, A. Considerations for integrating wearables into the everyday healthcare practice. *npj Digit. Med.* **2023**, *6*, 70. [CrossRef]
68. Gerke, S.; Minssen, T.; Cohen, I.G. Ethical and Legal Challenges of Artificial Intelligence-Driven Healthcare. In *Artificial Intelligence in Healthcare*, 1st ed.; Bohr, A., Memarzadeh, K., Eds.; Elsevier: Amsterdam, The Netherlands, 2020; ISBN 9780128184387. [CrossRef]
69. Silva-Trujillo, A.G.; González, M.J.G.; Pérez, L.P.R.; Villalba, L.J.G. Cybersecurity Analysis of Wearable Devices: Smartwatches Passive Attack. *Sensors* **2023**, *23*, 5438. [CrossRef]
70. Sui, A.; Sui, W.; Liu, S.; Rhodes, R. Ethical considerations for the use of consumer wearables in health research. *Digit. Health* **2023**, *9*, 20552076231153740. [CrossRef]
71. Ford, E.; Curlewis, K.; Wongkoblap, A.; Curcin, V. Public Opinions on Using Social Media Content to Identify Users With Depression and Target Mental Health Care Advertising: Mixed Methods Survey. *JMIR Ment. Health* **2019**, *6*, e12942. [CrossRef]
72. Essén, A.; Stern, A.D.; Haase, C.B.; Car, J.; Greaves, F.; Paparova, D.; Vandeput, S.; Wehrens, R.; Bates, D.W. Health app policy: International comparison of nine countries' approaches. *NPJ Digit. Med.* **2022**, *5*, 31. [CrossRef]
73. Smuck, M.; Odonkor, C.A.; Wilt, J.K.; Schmidt, N.; Swiernik, M.A. The emerging clinical role of wearables: Factors for successful implementation in healthcare. *NPJ Digit. Med.* **2021**, *4*, 45. [CrossRef] [PubMed]
74. Food and Drug Administration (FDA). *Artificial Intelligence & Medical Products: How CBER, CDER, CDRH, and OCP Are Working Together*; FDA: Silver Spring, MD, USA, 2024.
75. Zafar, F.; Alam, L.F.; Vivas, R.R.; Wang, J.; Whei, S.J.; Mehmood, S.; Sadeghzadegan, A.; Lakkimsetti, M.; Nazir, Z. The Role of Artificial Intelligence in Identifying Depression and Anxiety: A Comprehensive Literature Review. *Cureus* **2024**, *16*, e56472. [CrossRef] [PubMed]
76. Blomqvist, S.; Högnäs, R.S.; Virtanen, M.; LaMontagne, A.D.; Hanson, L.L.M. Job loss and job instability during the COVID-19 pandemic and the risk of depression and anxiety among Swedish employees. *SSM Popul. Health* **2023**, *22*, 101424. [CrossRef]
77. Zisook, S.; Shear, K. Grief and bereavement: What psychiatrists need to know. *World Psychiatry* **2009**, *8*, 67–74. [CrossRef] [PubMed]

algorithms

MDPI

Article

An Efficient AdaBoost Algorithm for Enhancing Skin Cancer Detection and Classification

Seham Gamil [1], Feng Zeng [1,*], Moath Alrifaey [2], Muhammad Asim [3,4] and Naveed Ahmad [5]

[1] School of Computer Science and Engineering, Central South University, Changsha 410083, China; sehamgameel7@gmail.com
[2] Department of Mechanical and Manufacturing Engineering, Faculty of Engineering, Universiti Putra Malaysia, Serdang 43400, Malaysia; eng.alrifaiy2005@gmail.com
[3] Center of Excellence in Quantum and Intelligent Computing, Prince Sultan University, Riyadh 11586, Saudi Arabia; masim@psu.edu.sa
[4] EIAS Data Science Lab, College of Computer and Information Sciences, Prince Sultan University, Riyadh 11586, Saudi Arabia
[5] College of Computer and Information Sciences, Prince Sultan University, Riyadh 11586, Saudi Arabia; nahmed@psu.edu.sa
* Correspondence: fengzeng@csu.edu.cn

Abstract: Skin cancer is a prevalent and perilous form of cancer and presents significant diagnostic challenges due to its high costs, dependence on medical experts, and time-consuming procedures. The existing diagnostic process is inefficient and expensive, requiring extensive medical expertise and time. To tackle these issues, researchers have explored the application of artificial intelligence (AI) tools, particularly machine learning techniques such as shallow and deep learning, to enhance the diagnostic process for skin cancer. These tools employ computer algorithms and deep neural networks to identify and categorize skin cancer. However, accurately distinguishing between skin cancer and benign tumors remains challenging, necessitating the extraction of pertinent features from image data for classification. This study addresses these challenges by employing Principal Component Analysis (PCA), a dimensionality-reduction approach, to extract relevant features from skin images. Additionally, accurately classifying skin images into malignant and benign categories presents another obstacle. To improve accuracy, the AdaBoost algorithm is utilized, which amalgamates weak classification models into a robust classifier with high accuracy. This research introduces a novel approach to skin cancer diagnosis by integrating Principal Component Analysis (PCA), AdaBoost, and EfficientNet B0, leveraging artificial intelligence (AI) tools. The novelty lies in the combination of these techniques to develop a robust and accurate system for skin cancer classification. The advantage of this approach is its ability to significantly reduce costs, minimize reliance on medical experts, and expedite the diagnostic process. The developed model achieved an accuracy of 93.00% using the DermIS dataset and demonstrated excellent precision, recall, and F1-score values, confirming its ability to correctly classify skin lesions as malignant or benign. Additionally, the model achieved an accuracy of 91.00% using the ISIC dataset, which is widely recognized for its comprehensive collection of annotated dermoscopic images, providing a robust foundation for training and validation. These advancements have the potential to significantly enhance the efficiency and accuracy of skin cancer diagnosis and classification. Ultimately, the integration of AI tools and techniques in skin cancer diagnosis can lead to cost reduction and improved patient outcomes, benefiting both patients and healthcare providers.

Keywords: skin cancer diagnosis; machine learning; Convolutional Neural Network (CNN); adaptive boosting algorithm (AdaBoost); principal component analysis (PCA); Support Vector Machine (SVM)

1. Introduction

Artificial intelligence (AI) and machine learning (ML) have transformed numerous fields by emulating human cognitive abilities and enhancing performance through algorithms driven by data. Within the healthcare domain, AI and ML have demonstrated great potential in disease detection, diagnosis, and treatment. In dermatology, these technologies have been particularly valuable in analyzing visually complex and diverse skin diseases. However, despite these advancements, the detection and classification of skin cancer remain significant research challenges in the fields of medical image analysis and computer-aided diagnosis. Early detection of skin cancer is vital for improving patient outcomes, underscoring the critical need for automated methods for detection and classification [1].

Skin cancer, specifically melanoma, is a prevalent and dangerous form of cancer that exhibits an increasing incidence compared to other types [2]. Melanoma originates in melanocytes, leading to skin darkening, and can manifest in various colors and shades [3]. Its aggressive spread makes it highly hazardous and potentially fatal. These factors emphasize the urgent requirement for effective methods of detection and classification.

Accurate identification of skin diseases, including melanoma, is crucial for successful treatment, and machine learning methods have emerged as valuable tools for prognosis. However, the diverse characteristics of melanoma pose challenges to its precise extraction. Manual detection of skin cancer necessitates a comprehensive understanding of various types and features, while early detection using discriminatory features remains complex. Advanced techniques are therefore necessary to automate the extraction of relevant features.

This study aims to leverage the Principal Component Analysis (PCA) algorithm for extracting relevant features in skin cancer detection. Additionally, accurately classifying skin images into malignant and benign categories presents an additional challenge, which is addressed through the utilization of the AdaBoost algorithm as an ensemble classifier technique. AdaBoost enhances classification accuracy by iteratively training classifiers with low individual performance and combining their predictions through weighted voting.

Our approach addresses the challenges associated with skin cancer detection and classification by incorporating advanced techniques and algorithms. Consequently, this paper has the following contributions:

The primary contributions of this work involve the development of an efficient and accurate model for classifying and detecting skin cancer based on the CNN model. This model offers several key features and benefits:

1. To evaluate machine learning algorithms and select one model based on its best performance in predicting skin cancer.
2. To design a model that can automatically extract discriminative features without human expert intervention.
3. To build an ensemble classifier with an AdaBoost algorithm to improve performance.

The rest of the paper is structured as follows: Section 2 presents a concise summary of the related work conducted in the field of skin cancer diagnosis. In Section 3, the proposed methodology for detecting and classifying skin cancer is presented. In Section 4, the experimental results are illustrated. Finally, Section 5 encompasses the conclusions and future work.

2. Related Work

Cancer is one of the leading causes of deaths in the last two decades. It is either diagnosed malignant or benign [1]. Skin cancer is the most frequent cancer in humans, and its rate is increasing intensely worldwide [2]. Every year, more than 46,000 new cases are recorded in the United Kingdom [4]. Early identification is critical for boosting survival chances, with one study reporting a 90% reduced mortality rate for early-stage skin cancer. However, the present biopsy procedure for diagnosis is laborious and time-consuming. Fortunately, computer technologies provide a viable answer by making it faster, simpler, and more economical to detect skin cancer indications. These systems use clinical pictures and machine learning algorithms to conduct early assessments of suspected skin disorders.

Melanoma skin cancer is the most serious and fatal disease in the family of skin cancer diseases [3]. According to studies, the incidence of skin cancer is growing year after year in comparison to various types of cancer [5]. Melanoma, an among the most prevalent kinds of skin cancer, involves melanocytes, cells on the skin's surface that produce pigmentation [6]. It can appear in a variety of dark tints and colors, including rose pink, royal purple, blue, and even colorless [7]. Melanoma's aggressive nature and tendency to spread quickly make it highly dangerous and potentially lethal. Melanoma can appear anywhere on the body; however, it most commonly occurs on the rear of the lower limbs [8]. Skin cancer death rates can be considerably reduced with timely identification and early diagnosis [7,8]. As a result, the early detection and classification of skin cancer are crucial. Dermatologists noted that melanoma may spread to several sites and organs of the human body [9]. As a result, melanoma is the most serious type of skin cancer. As a result, despite its rarity, it is far and away the leading cause of death [10]. The rising frequency of skin cancer can be due to prolonged and direct sun exposure, which can cause the development of both benign and malignant tumors.

Melanoma and nevi are both melanocytic tumors, which can lead physicians to misclassify patients based only on visual inspection [11]. Early diagnosis is critical since there is a greater likelihood of successful therapy in the early stages of the disease. However, visual variables such as eye tiredness might impede effective diagnosis, frequently resulting in inaccurate lesion detection [12]. Identifying skin cancer early improves the odds of effective therapy. However, distinguishing between malignant and benign skin lesions and precisely diagnosing skin cancer at these early stages can be difficult. This is because skin lesions commonly resemble one another. Melanoma's early development features are similar to those of other benign moles, making it difficult for even experienced dermatologists to distinguish between what is malignant and what is benign [13].

Researchers are currently examining and evaluating different deep learning algorithms to detect skin diseases. In a study, five machine learning algorithms, namely Random Forest, Kernel SVM, Naive Bayes, Logistic Regression, and Convolutional Neural Networks, were utilized to diagnose skin disorders [14]. According to the results, the Convolutional Neural Network model displayed the best performance in identifying diseases based on the confusion matrix. Another group of researchers proposed an AI system based on neural networks, which involved extracting features during image collection and utilizing a feed-forward neural network for classification. In a separate study, six alternative data mining methods were recommended to classify different types of skin diseases. Additionally, an ensemble approach combining Bagging, AdaBoost, and Gradient Boosting classifiers was developed, demonstrating higher accuracy and effectiveness in detecting skin diseases [14]. Furthermore, the authors introduced an artificial intelligence technique for skin cancer detection that employed image processing and a deep neural network [15]. The approach included segmenting the affected region, extracting its features using image processing, and utilizing a Convolutional Neural Network for prediction. The training and testing accuracy achieved were 93.77% and 89.5%, respectively. Finally, researchers presented an adaptable federated machine learning model for diagnosing various skin disorders. This model incorporated Dermoscopy and global intelligence (server) and exhibited improved accuracy in diagnosing skin conditions [16].

Mustafa and Kimura [17] proposed an automated method for detecting skin cancer, specifically melanoma, from photographs of affected skin regions. Their aim was to achieve higher precision by utilizing a small set of features. The images were initially divided into the relevant lesions, and then 15 features were extracted using techniques from image processing and computer vision. To implement the system, they employed a nonlinear Support Vector Machine (SVM) with a Gaussian radial basis function (RBF) kernel. The study involved a dataset of 200 photos, and the results showed that only six criteria were necessary for accurately identifying melanoma. The system achieved an accuracy of 86.67% using the optimal parameters.

Daghrir et al. [18] introduced a hybrid approach that combined a Convolutional Neural Network (CNN) with two classical machine learning techniques, specifically K-nearest neighbors (KNN) and Support Vector Machines (SVM). They collected a dataset of 640 lesion images from the International Skin Imaging Collaboration (ISIC) archive, using 512 images for training and the remaining 128 images for testing. The CNN architecture comprised 9 layers, including 3 convolutional layers, 3 max pooling layers, 2 dropout layers, and a fully connected layer for prediction. Various preprocessing techniques, such as the Otsu method, filters, and the morphological snake's method, were employed. The final classification involved all three algorithms, with a majority vote. This hybrid approach achieved an accuracy of 88.4%. Specifically, the CNN achieved the highest accuracy of 85.5% individually, followed by the SVM with a second-best accuracy of 71.8%.

Esteva et al. [19] devised a method to classify universal skin diseases by fine-tuning the VGG16 and VGG19 architectures for training their networks. Their network attained a Top-1 classification accuracy of 60.0% and a Top-3 classification accuracy of 80.3%. These outcomes demonstrated a substantial improvement compared to existing methods in their experiments. The researchers further advocated for the adoption of a similar approach to enhance classification outcomes in skin disease detection.

Nasr-Esfahani et al. [20] developed their own CNN that encompassed preprocessing, feature extraction, and classification functions. They employed a dataset of 170 nondermoscopic images obtained from the digital image archive of the Department of Dermatology at the University Medical Center Groningen (UMCG). To enhance the training process, the dataset was augmented, resulting in a total of 6120 original and synthesized images. Various preprocessing techniques, including illumination correction, mask generation, and Gaussian filtering, were applied. The CNN architecture consisted of an input layer, followed by alternating layers of convolution and max-pooling, culminating in a fully connected layer. The objective was to classify between two classes, melanoma and nevus. The proposed model achieved an accuracy of 81% with a specificity rate of 80%.

Jenitha et al. [21] conducted a study where pre-processed images from a medical database were employed as input for three different machine learning algorithms: K-nearest neighbors (KNN), Support Vector Machines (SVM), and Convolutional Neural Networks (CNN). The objective of the classification task was to assign images to either the cancerous or noncancerous class. The dataset consisted of 1000 lesion images obtained from a medical institute. The data were divided into three subsets: training data, testing data, and validation data. In this study, the KNN algorithm achieved an accuracy of 80%.

Shah et al. [22] presented an innovative method for classifying skin cancer based on texture and color features. Their system was designed to aid pathologists in determining the specific type of skin cancer. To evaluate the effectiveness of their approach, they utilized a benchmark image database containing 225 skin cancer images. The accuracy obtained using the K-nearest neighbors (KNN) classifier was 85%, which was slightly lower compared to the accuracy achieved with the Support Vector Machine (SVM) and Convolutional Neural Network (CNN) classifiers.

Yuan et al. [23] developed a decision-based support system aimed at assisting in the early diagnosis of skin cancer. The main focus of the system was to utilize texture information exclusively to predict whether skin lesions were benign or malignant. To enhance generalization error rates and computational efficiency, a three-layer system based on SVM was employed. To validate their approach, a binary class benchmark classifier was used. They trained an SVM with a polynomial kernel of various degrees on a dataset of 2000 samples. By identifying the malignancy in skin lesion images, they found that a degree 4 polynomial yielded optimal results, achieving a standard accuracy rate of 70%.

Ashafuddula and Islam [24] developed an automated deep learning system for classifying melanoma and nevus moles using high-intensity pixel values from lesion images. The model achieved notable performance metrics, including an accuracy of 92.58%, sensitivity of 93.76%, specificity of 91.56%, and precision of 90.68%. However, the study has several limitations, such as reliance on a specific dataset, which may limit the model's generalizability to other datasets or diverse populations. Additionally, the model's focus on high-intensity pixel values may overlook other important features like texture and shape. The study also lacks extensive real-world validation and faces challenges in model interpretability, which are crucial for clinical adoption. Addressing these limitations through broader validation, incorporating diverse features, and enhancing interpretability could improve the model's robustness and facilitate its use in clinical settings.

Yang et al. [25] developed a hybrid system combining machine learning and computerized adaptive testing (CAT) based on the Rasch model to classify skin cancer using data from the HAM10000 and ISIC 2019 datasets. Despite its promising results, the study has several limitations. These include its reliance on specific datasets, which may limit the model's generalizability to other populations. The incremental learning approach requires careful data integration management to avoid model degradation. Additionally, challenges in model interpretability and the need for extensive real-world validation are significant hurdles for clinical adoption. Addressing these issues through broader validation, incorporating diverse data, and enhancing interpretability is crucial for ensuring the model's robustness and practical applicability in clinical settings.

Dondapati et al. [26] developed a system to classify skin cancer using CNNs, evaluated on datasets like HAM10000 and ISIC 2019. Despite achieving high classification accuracy, the study faces several limitations. These include reliance on specific datasets that may limit generalizability to other populations, substantial computational resource requirements, and the need for high-quality annotated data. The performance inconsistency across different skin lesion types highlights challenges with class imbalance and dataset diversity. Additionally, the interpretability of CNN models remains a significant hurdle for clinical adoption, as clinicians need to understand and trust the model's decisions.

Zareen et al. [27] developed a system that utilizes hybrid texture features for skin cancer classification. The study demonstrated the effectiveness of combining texture features with machine learning techniques to improve classification accuracy. However, the study has several limitations. The reliance on specific datasets may affect the generalizability of the model to other populations or real-world clinical settings. Additionally, while the hybrid texture features improve classification accuracy, the computational complexity and resource requirements may be high. The need for high-quality, annotated datasets is also a significant challenge, as these may not always be readily available. Furthermore, the interpretability of the machine learning models remains a critical issue, which is essential for clinical adoption. Addressing these limitations through the use of more diverse datasets, optimizing computational efficiency, and enhancing model interpretability is crucial for improving the robustness and practical applicability of the proposed system.

3. Materials and Methods

Self-learning algorithms are enabled by models inspired by the human brain. These models let machines to learn from data and gradually enhance their performance over time. Machine learning algorithms have grown in relevance across a wide range of industries, including healthcare. They are very useful for identifying disorders by utilizing medical databases. Many firms use these tools to forecast diseases early on and improve medical diagnostics. This study seeks to overcome the issues involved with skin cancer diagnosis and categorization by establishing a complete strategy.

This research focuses on addressing the challenges associated with skin cancer detection and classification by developing a comprehensive approach. The motivation behind the research is to improve the accuracy, efficiency, and accessibility of skin cancer diagnosis by incorporating advanced techniques and algorithms. The research builds on the Efficient Net B0 model, which is noted for its lightweight construction and strong picture categorization performance. To assess the effectiveness of our approach, we compare the performance of the Efficient Net B0 model with other widely used models, including EfficientNet B7, VGG-16, and AlexNet. These models represent state-of-the-art architectures in the field of image classification. The comparison encompasses evaluation metrics such as accuracy, precision, recall, and F1-score. Transfer learning is used to utilize pre-trained weights and improve skin cancer-classification accuracy. The Principal Component Analysis (PCA) technique is used for feature extraction, which reduces dataset dimensionality while keeping key properties. This helps to capture underlying information, simplify calculations, and decrease overfitting. The Adaboost technique improves classification accuracy by iteratively training weak classifiers and applying greater weights to misclassified examples. The combined strength of numerous weak classifiers improves overall performance and overcomes difficulties in correctly categorizing skin lesions. For classification and prediction, the model utilizes SVM, a supervised learning algorithm that creates a hyperplane to separate different classes in the dataset. By mapping the input data into a higher-dimensional space and finding the optimal hyperplane, SVM maximally separates the classes. As shown in Figure 1, the model architecture consists of multiple algorithms working in tandem to achieve robust and accurate skin cancer diagnosis.

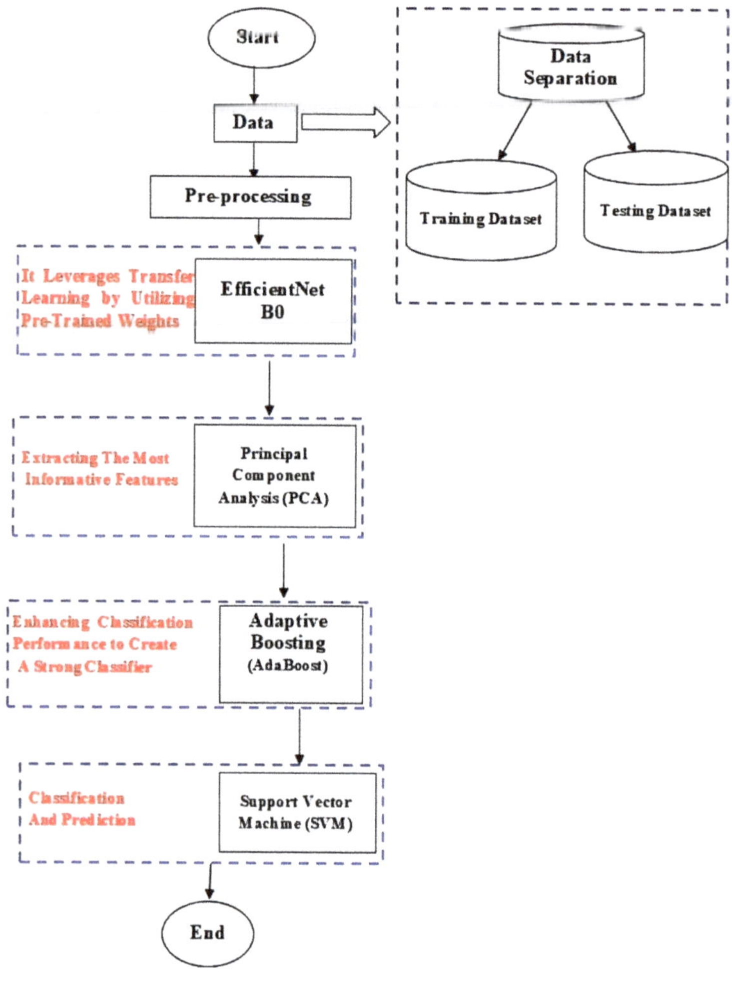

Figure 1. Our proposed model.

Through our research, we aim to develop a robust and accurate skin cancer diagnosis and categorization system by combining the power of the Efficient Net B0 model, PCA algorithm, Adaboost algorithm, and SVM algorithm. The use of these new approaches has the ability to enhance early detection, increase diagnosis accuracy, and eventually contribute to better treatment results for people with skin cancer.

3.1. Convolutional Neural Networks (CNNs)

CNNs are deep learning models developed to analyze visual data such as photos and movies. They are made up of many layers that extract hierarchical features using convolution, pooling, and nonlinear activation. CNNs are modeled after the visual processing systems seen in the human brain. The convolutional layer is the central component, capturing local patterns with learnable filters. Pooling levels down the sample while maintaining key information adds complexity, as do non-linear activation functions. Fully connected layers complete the final classification or regression operation, which is frequently followed by a SoftMax activation function for multi-class classification. CNNs learn optimum parameters via backpropagation and gradient descent to optimize a loss function. Large annotated datasets are essential for successful training. CNNs learn optimum parameters via backpropagation and gradient descent to optimize a loss function. Large annotated datasets are essential for successful training. CNNs excel at autonomously learning hierarchical representations and abstract features, making them extremely useful in computer vision applications. CNNs have revolutionized medical image analysis by extracting relevant characteristics that enable effective classification, segmentation, and detection. They have transformed medical image analysis and contributed to substantial progress.

3.2. *EfficientNet B0 Model*

The EfficientNet B0 model is a lightweight CNN design that performs well in image categorization. It is part of the EfficientNet family, which includes increasingly complicated models. EfficientNet B0 balances accuracy and computing economy by consistently scaling its breadth, depth, and resolution. Its design incorporates convolutional, pooling, and fully connected layers, which allow it to learn hierarchical representations from input pictures. During training, methods like backpropagation and gradient descent are used to improve the model parameters. It is often trained on large-scale picture datasets, such as ImageNet, to obtain generalizable features. Once trained, the EfficientNet B0 model may be used to perform various image-classification tasks, such as identifying skin cancer, by determining the probability distribution across classes. Its usefulness stems from its ability to retain accuracy while remaining computationally efficient.

3.3. *Principal Component Analysis (PCA)*

The curse of dimensionality refers to the difficulties that come when working with datasets that have a large number of dimensions. It makes it difficult to generate statistically significant findings, increases overfitting, takes longer to compute, and reduces accuracy in machine learning models. This issue is addressed using feature engineering approaches such as feature selection and extraction. PCA is a widely used dimensionality-reduction approach that uses an orthogonal transformation to convert correlated variables into uncorrelated ones. It detects primary components, captures the highest variation in the data, and decreases dimensionality while keeping key patterns, as shown in Algorithm 1. Using PCA in skin cancer-classification procedures improves efficiency and efficacy by lowering computing complexity and the risk of overfitting. PCA works by preprocessing the data, calculating the covariance matrix, conducting eigen decomposition, selecting principal components based on eigenvalues, and projection the data onto the chosen components. It enhances data visualization, computational efficiency, and the effectiveness of machine learning algorithms by collecting useful aspects. PCA is a strong feature extraction approach that minimizes dimensionality while maintaining crucial properties.

Here is how PCA works to extract features:

1. Data preprocessing: Initially, the input data are preprocessed by shifting them to a mean of zero. This step ensures that the data are centered on the mean. The preprocessed data are then grouped into matrix X, which has n samples and m variables. This matrix is typically referred to as X and has dimensions ($n \times m$).
2. Mean calculation: We determine the mean for each variable across all samples. The mean vector has dimensions of $1 \times m$
3. Calculate the covariance matrix: It quantifies the associations between various characteristics in the dataset, revealing how they co-vary with one another. The covariance

matrix is generated from preprocessed data and represents the connections between variables. The following formula is used to determine each element in the matrix.

$$\text{cov}(x, y) = (1/(n-1)) \times \Sigma\, ((x\_i - \text{mean}(x)) \times (y\_i - \text{mean}(y))) \quad (1)$$

4. Eigen decomposition: The covariance matrix is decomposed to obtain its eigenvectors and eigenvalues. The resulting eigenvectors reflect the primary components, which encapsulate the data's key patterns. The associated eigenvalues indicate the amount of variation explained by each major component. During the eigen decomposition procedure, the covariance matrix is divided into eigenvectors and eigenvalues. Eigenvalue decomposition and Singular Value Decomposition (SVD) are typical techniques for obtaining these eigenvectors and eigenvalues.
5. Selecting principal components: The corresponding eigenvalues are used to calculate the principal components. The eigenvalues are arranged in descending sequence, with the top k eigenvalues chosen as principal components. PCA reduces the dimensionality of the data by identifying the top k main components. These main components are orthogonal to one another, implying they are uncorrelated. This quality enables PCA to reduce duplicate and less useful elements while focusing on the most important ones.
6. Feature projection: The original data are projected onto the chosen primary components to produce a lower-dimensional representation. This projection effectively converts the data to a new feature space, with each dimension representing a primary component. This is accomplished by multiplying the transposed eigenvector matrix by the preprocessed data matrix (X).

Overall, PCA is an effective feature extraction approach that reduces the dimensionality of data while retaining its key properties. By identifying the most important features, PCA improves data visualization and computational efficiency, in addition to the effectiveness of subsequent machine learning techniques. The Pseudo Code of PCA is presented in Algorithm 1.

Algorithm 1. The Pseudo Code of Principal Component Analysis (PCA) Algorithm

```
Input: Data matrix X of size (n × p)
    where n is the number of samples and p is the number of features
    Number of components k (k <= p)
Steps:
1. Standardize the data:
   Compute the mean of each feature
        mean_X = mean(X, axis = 0)
   Subtract the mean from each feature value to center the data
        X_centered = X − mean_X
2. Compute the covariance matrix of the centered data:
   Covariance matrix C = (1 / (n − 1)) × (X_centeredT × X_centered)
3. Compute the eigenvalues and eigenvectors of the covariance matrix:
   Eigenvalues λ and eigenvectors V of C such that C × V = λ × V
4. Sort the eigenvalues and their corresponding eigenvectors in descending order:
   Sort eigenvalues λ in descending order
   Reorder the eigenvectors V accordingly
5. Select the top k eigenvectors to form a new matrix W:
   W = (v1, v2,..., vk) where vi is the i-th eigenvector
6. Transform the original data to the new subspace:
   Principal components Z = X_centered × W
7. Compute the explained variance:
   Total variance = sum(λ)
   Explained variance for each principal component = (λ / total_variance)
8. Extract the most informative features:
   Calculate the contribution of each original feature to the principal components:
      feature_contributions = | W |
9. Output the principal components return Z, explained variance, and feature contributions.
```

3.4. Adaptive Boosting (AdaBoost) Algorithm

AdaBoost, which stands for "adaptive boosting", AdaBoost, or "adaptive boosting" is a well-known machine learning algorithm used for binary classification. It combines many weak classifiers to form a stronger classifier. Its core principle is to award larger weights to misclassified samples. This technique seeks to correct misclassifications in succeeding rounds, eventually resulting in the right classifications. The Pseudo Code of AdaBoost Algorithm is presented in Algorithm 2.

The working principles of Adaboost are stated below:

1. Weight initialization: At the start, each sample in the dataset is given an equal weight.

   Weights for each sample: $\frac{1}{N}$
   Number of training instances: N

2. Training weak classifiers: Training samples are trained on classifiers, and the overall error of the model is determined as

$$\Sigma \text{ (weights of erroneously categorized samples)}$$

3. Calculating classifier weight: The weight of each weak classifier is determined by its performance. A classifier that performs better receives more weight.

   The basic classifier's performance is computed using the formula:

$$\text{Performance} = \frac{1}{2} \times \log \frac{1 - \text{Total Error}}{\text{Total Error}} \quad (2)$$

4. Weight updating: This provides for a reduction in the weight of correctly identified samples while raising the weight of wrongly categorized ones.

   New weights for misclassified samples:

$$\text{New Weight} = \text{Old Weight} \times e^{\text{performance}} \quad (3)$$

   To calculate new weights for successfully identified samples, multiply the old weight by

$$\text{New Weight} = \text{Old Weight} \times e^{-\text{performance}} \quad (4)$$

5. Combining weak classifiers: The weak classifiers are combined by assigning weights to them based on their performance. These weights determine the contribution of each classifier to the final prediction.
6. Making predictions: The final strong classifier is constructed by integrating the predictions of all weak classifiers. The forecast is produced based on the weighted majority vote of the weak classifiers.

Algorithm 2. The Pseudo Code of AdaBoost Algorithm

Initialize the weights of training : $w[i] = 1/N$, is the number of trainings
for $= t = 1$ ***to*** T
    $h_t = (D_n, w_t)$ — base classifier
    $\varepsilon_t = \sum_{i=1}^{n} w_{t,i} * (h_t(x_i) \neq y_i)$ — weighted error of the base classifier
    $\alpha_t = \frac{1}{2} \log\left(\frac{1-\varepsilon_t}{\varepsilon_t}\right)$ — coefficient of the base classifier
for $i = 1$ ***to*** n — re-weighting the training points
  if $h_t\ (x_i) \neq y_i$ **then** — error
      $w_{t+1,i} = \frac{w_{i,t}}{2\varepsilon_t}$ — weight increase
  else — correct classification
      $w_{t+1,i} = \frac{w_{i,t}}{2(1-\varepsilon_t)}$ — weight decrease
return $h_t(x) = \sum_{t=1}^{T} \alpha_t\, h_t(x)$ — weighted "vote" of base classifier produces (strong classifier)

3.5. Support Vector Machines (SVM)

SVM is a widely and commonly used machine learning technique for classification. As shown in Algorithm 3, it works by determining the best margin for separating distinct types of data. SVM uses kernel functions to handle both linearly and non-linearly separable data. Its goal is to optimize the margin between classes while accurately categorizing data points. SVM is a strong supervised learning classifier that can be applied to both binary and multi-class classification applications.

SVM have a hierarchical foundation made up of several layers. SVM is fundamentally made up of a training dataset, a training method, and a model structure. The training data consist of input characteristics and their related classifications, and the method uses support vectors to establish the ideal margin. The model structure includes information about the margin, support vectors, and feature weights. SVM sublayers contain the kernel function, which converts input to a higher-dimensional space for linear separation. Support vectors, which are critical for decision boundaries, are the data points that come closest to the margin. The decision margin defines the distance between the support vectors and the decision boundaries, with the goal of maximizing it. During classification, the trained SVM model is used to classify fresh data by translating it into a high-dimensional space and analyzing its location relative to the model's margins and bounds.

In addition to its layered architecture, the SVM algorithm is enhanced with the inclusion of a pseudo code snippet, as detailed in Algorithm 3. This pseudo code provides a structured representation of the algorithmic steps involved in SVM classification. Additional layers of SVM, such as the direct inference extension and the multi-class SVM layer, further contribute to its classification efficiency and handling of multi-class classification issues.

Algorithm 3. The Pseudo Code of SVM Algorithm

```
Inputs:
    X: Training matrix (each row represents a training sample)
    y: Corresponding classifications (values can be +1 or −1)
    C: Penalty parameter (measures the allowance for errors)
    epsilon: A small value for stopping criterion (convergence threshold)
    max_iterations: The maximum number of iterations
Steps:
1. Initialize parameters:
       Set weights w to zeros
       Set bias b to zero
       Set iteration counter t to 0
2. Repeat until convergence or reaching the maximum number of iterations:
       Increment t by 1
       For each training sample (x_i, y_i) in X, y:
         Compute the margin : margin = y_i * (dot_product(w, x_i) + b)
         If margin < 1:
           Compute the gradient of the loss function with respect to
            w : gradient = w − C * (y_i * x_i)
           Compute the gradient of the loss function with respect to
                     b: gradient_b = −C * y_i − Update weights:
       w = w − (1 / t) * gradient_w − Update bias : b = b − (1 / t) * gradient_b
     Return w, b
```

3.6. Dataset

The International Skin Imaging Collaboration (ISIC (and DermIS datasets were chosen for their comprehensive and diverse collection of skin cancer images, which are essential for developing a generalized model. By incorporating these datasets, we ensured that our model could effectively classify a wide range of skin lesion types and conditions. These datasets serve as crucial resources for training and testing machine learning models, especially those based on CNNs. By leveraging these datasets, researchers and practitioners can successfully extract unique features and improve the accuracy of skin cancer-classification algorithms. They are indispensable tools for enhancing the performance of machine learning algorithms used in diagnosing skin cancer.

We divided the dataset into 10 equal parts (folds). For each fold, 9 parts were used for training the model, and the remaining part was used for testing. This process was repeated 10 times, each time using a different fold for testing and the remaining folds for training. By averaging the results across all folds, we obtained a comprehensive and unbiased evaluation of the model's performance. As shown in Figure 2, the images used in this study include both melanoma and benign skin lesions, which are critical for training the model to distinguish between different types of skin conditions. Figure 2a illustrates a melanoma image, while Figure 2b shows a benign image.

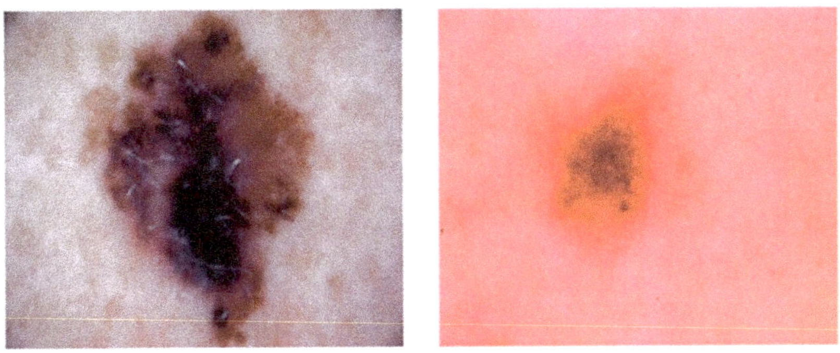

(a) (b)

Figure 2. Images of a skin lesion. (**a**) Melanoma image. (**b**) Benign image.

4. Experimental Results

When evaluating the efficiency of a classification model, relying solely on accuracy can be inadequate. Therefore, we assessed the efficiency of our skin cancer classifier using various metrics, including accuracy, precision, recall, F1 score, and support. Additionally, we utilized a Confusion Matrix to account for the number of correct and incorrect predictions, providing a comprehensive evaluation of the model's performance. To measure the performance in a multi-class classification task, we calculated the average accuracy, recall, and F1 score.

These metrics were calculated using the mean and standard deviation across multiple cross-validation folds to ensure robustness and reliability. We employed 10-fold cross-validation to classify skin cancer using the ISIC and DERMIS datasets. Cross-validation is a robust statistical method that enhances the reliability and generalizability of machine learning models by preventing overfitting and ensuring performance consistency. This technique involves dividing the dataset into multiple folds (in our case, 10-fold cross-validation), training the model on 80% of the data, and validating it on the remaining 20%. By averaging the results across all folds, we obtained a comprehensive and unbiased evaluation of the model's performance. Using both the ISIC and DERMIS datasets further validated the robustness and effectiveness of our model across different data sources, ensuring a reliable classification of skin cancer.

4.1. Evaluation Metrics for Performance

Several performance indicators, including accuracy, sensitivity, specificity, precision, and the F1-score, are used to evaluate the efficacy of various approaches for identifying skin cancer. These measurements are computed using the true positive (TP), false positive (FP), false negative (FN), and true negative (TN) values. Performance metrics are critical for assessing the success of a model. After the model has been trained on the existing data, performance measurements are used to assess its ability to properly categorize fresh, unseen data that were not included in the training process. To evaluate a model's performance, numerous formulae are employed to determine key metrics including as sensitivity, accuracy, precision, recall, and F1 score.

These formulae are as follows:

1. Sensitivity: Also known as the true positive rate, is computed by dividing the number of true positive (TP) predictions by the total number of true positives and false negatives (FN). The following formula is used to calculate sensitivity:

$$\text{Sensitivity (TP)} = \frac{\text{TP}}{\text{TP} + \text{FN}} \quad (5)$$

2. (Specificity) true negative rate: The true negative rate is determined by dividing the number of true negative (TN) predictions by the sum of TN and FP.

   The formula for specificity is given below:

$$\text{Sensitivity (TN)} = \frac{\text{TN}}{\text{TN} + \text{FP}} \quad (6)$$

3. Accuracy: is calculated by dividing the sum of true positives and true negatives by the total number of samples.

   The accuracy formula is as follows:

$$\text{Accuracy} = \frac{\text{Tp} + \text{TN}}{\text{Tp} + \text{TN} + \text{FP} + \text{FN}} \quad (7)$$

4. Precision: The amount of genuine positive predictions is divided by the sum of true positives and false positives.

   Precision is calculated using the formula below:

$$\text{Precision} = \frac{\text{TP}}{\text{TP} + \text{FP}} \quad (8)$$

5. Recall (Sensitivity): To calculate recall, divide the number of true positive predictions by the sum of true positives and false negatives to compute recall.

   The recall formula is as follows:

$$\text{Recall} = \frac{\text{TP}}{\text{TP} + \text{FN}} \quad (9)$$

6. F1 Score: This metric combines precision and recall. It is calculated using the harmonic mean of accuracy and recall, assigning equal weight to both measures.

   The F1 score is calculated using the formula below:

$$\text{F1 Score} = 2\left(\frac{\text{Precision} \times \text{Recall}}{\text{Precision} + \text{Recal}}\right) \quad (10)$$

These formulas provide a quantitative assessment of the model's performance by comparing its capacity to accurately classify data and discriminate between true positives, true negatives, false positives, and false negatives.

4.2. Evaluation Metrics of the Algorithms and Classifiers That Were Applied in the Proposed Model

In our study, we conducted a comparative analysis of four classification algorithms (SVM, Random Forest, Neural Network, and Decision Tree) for skin cancer classification. We evaluated their performance using metrics such as accuracy, precision, recall, and

F1-score. These metrics were calculated using the mean and standard deviation across multiple cross-validation folds to ensure robustness and reliability of the results.

4.2.1. Performance Evaluation of Classification Algorithms

Table 1 displays the mean and standard deviation of accuracy, precision, recall, and F1-score for each classification algorithm on the ISIC dataset and DermIS.

Table 1. Performance metrics of classification algorithms for ISIC dataset.

Classification Algorithms	Accuracy	Precision	Recall	F1-Score
EfficientNetB0-PCA DT	90.40 ± 2.62	90.55 ± 2.59	90.46 ± 2.60	90.41 ± 2.61
EfficientNetB0-PCA RF	90.92 ± 2.23	91.04 ± 2.22	91.04 ± 2.20	90.85 ± 2.21
EfficientNetB0-PCA NN	90.93 ± 2.16	91.17 ± 2.34	90.96 ± 2.17	90.93 ± 2.16
EfficientNetB0-PCASVM	91.00 ± 2.11	91.06 ± 2.14	91.04 ± 2.12	91.04 ± 2.14

Table 1 presents the performance metrics for four classification algorithms evaluated for skin cancer classification using the ISIC dataset. The models compared include EfficientNetB0 with PCA followed by Decision Tree (DT), Random Forest (RF), Neural Network (NN), and SVM. The EfficientNetB0-PCA DT model achieved an accuracy of 90.40% with a standard deviation of 2.62%, while the EfficientNetB0-PCA RF model showed a slightly better performance with an accuracy of 90.92% and a standard deviation of 2.23%. The EfficientNetB0-PCA NN model achieved a mean accuracy of 90.93% with a standard deviation of 2.16%, demonstrating high precision and stability. The EfficientNetB0-PCA SVM model achieved the highest accuracy of 91.00% with the lowest standard deviation of 2.11%, indicating the best overall performance and stability among the models compared. The metrics are reported as "mean ± standard deviation" to provide insight into the average performance and variability across different cross-validation folds, ensuring a robust comparison and highlighting the reliability of the model in classifying skin cancer. This approach emphasizes the effectiveness of using EfficientNetB0 for feature extraction combined with PCA for dimensionality reduction and demonstrates that the SVM classifier outperforms other classifiers in this setup.

These results clearly show that EfficientNetB0-PCA SVM outperforms the other classification algorithms in terms of accuracy, precision, recall, and F1-score for skin cancer classification using the ISIC dataset. As shown in Figure 3, The graphical plot highlights the comparative performance of each model, where EfficientNetB0-PCA SVM consistently achieves the highest metrics across all evaluation criteria. The bar representing the SVM model is noticeably higher, indicating superior accuracy (91.00 ± 2.11%) and demonstrating the least variability, which underscores its reliability and robustness in classification tasks. In contrast, the Decision Tree model, despite its simplicity, shows the lowest performance with an accuracy of 90.40 ± 2.62%, indicating higher variability and less stability. The Random Forest and Neural Network models perform better than the Decision Tree but still fall short compared to the SVM model. The precision, recall, and F1-score metrics follow a similar trend, reinforcing the conclusion that the SVM model provides a more balanced and consistent performance. This visualization effectively communicates the advantage of using EfficientNetB0-PCA SVM, making it a promising candidate for accurate and reliable skin cancer classification.

Table 2 provides a comparison of the performance of various classification algorithms in our model by showing their mean accuracy, standard deviation, precision, recall, and F1-score, all expressed as percentages. The EfficientNetB0-PCA NN classifier achieved a mean accuracy of 92.60% with a standard deviation of 1.89%, indicating strong and consistent performance. Its precision, recall, and F1-score were also high, with mean values of 92.845%, 92.579%, and 92.845%, respectively, and low standard deviations. The EfficientNetB0-PCA RF classifier had a slightly lower mean accuracy of 91.88% and a standard deviation of 2.03%. Its precision and F1-score were 92.106%, and recall was 91.855%, showing reliable but slightly less consistent performance compared to the NN model. The

EfficientNetB0-PCA DT classifier had the lowest performance, with a mean accuracy of 91.38% and a higher standard deviation of 2.76%. Its precision, recall, and F1-score followed the same trend, with values of 91.676%, 91.348%, and 91.676%, respectively, indicating more variability in performance. EfficientNetB0-PCA SVM stood out with the highest mean accuracy of 93.00% and the lowest standard deviation of 1.70%, reflecting excellent and consistent performance. Its precision, recall, and F1-score were also the highest among all algorithms, with values of 93.185%, 92.975%, and 93.185%, respectively, and the lowest standard deviations, highlighting the robustness and reliability of this classifier. In summary, EfficientNetB0-PCA SVM surpasses other classifiers in terms of accuracy, precision, recall, and F1-score, with the additional advantage of lower performance variability, making it an exceptionally reliable choice for classification tasks in our model.

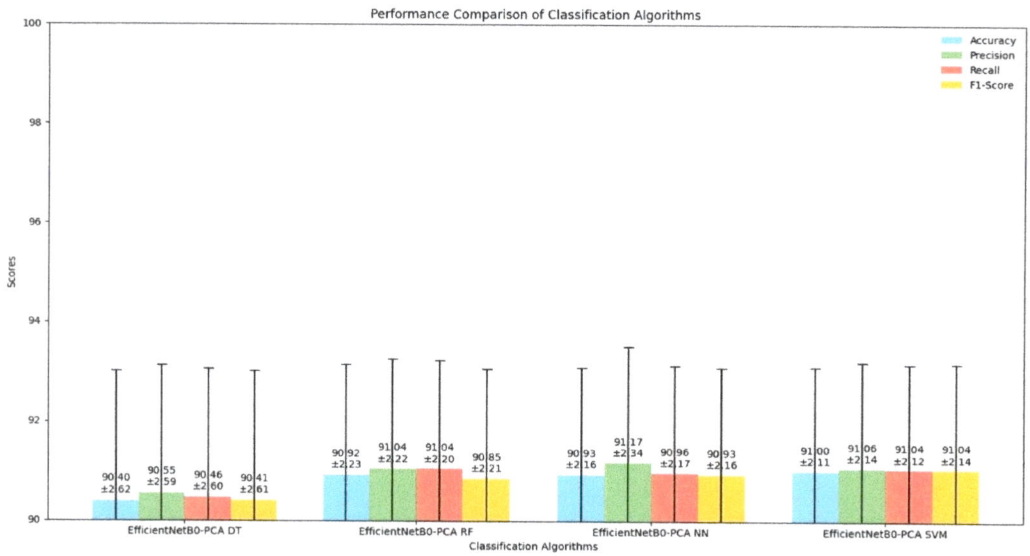

Figure 3. Visualization of the performance metrics for algorithms classifiers.

Table 2. Performance metrics of classification algorithms for DermIS dataset.

Classification Algorithms	Accuracy	Precision	Recall	F1-Score
EfficientNetB0-PCA DT	91.38 ± 2.76	91.676 ± 2.820	91.348 ± 2.903	91.676 ± 2.820
EfficientNetB0-PCA RF	91.88 ± 2.03	92.106 ± 2.046	91.855 ± 2.144	92.106 ± 2.046
EfficientNetB0-PCA NN	92.60 ± 1.89	92.845 ± 2.023	92.579 ± 1.974	92.845 ± 2.023
EfficientNetB0-PCASVM	93.00 ± 1.70	93.185 ± 1.825	92.975 ± 1.797	93.185 ± 1.825

Based on our results, the performance metrics provide an overview of how each algorithm classifier performed in our model, as depicted in Figure 4. The EfficientNetB0-PCA SVM classifier had the best overall performance, followed by EfficientNetB0-PCA RF and EfficientNetB0-PCA NN, while the EfficientNetB0-PCA DT classifier performed somewhat worse. The experimental findings clearly show that the EfficientNetB0-PCA SVM classifier beat the other methods in terms of accuracy, precision, recall, and the F1-score. As a result, we elected to use EfficientNetB0-PCA SVM algorithms in our model to identify and classify skin cancers. The excellent accuracy, as well as the balanced precision and recall values, demonstrate EfficientNetB0-PCA SVM's ability to effectively detect cases of skin cancer.

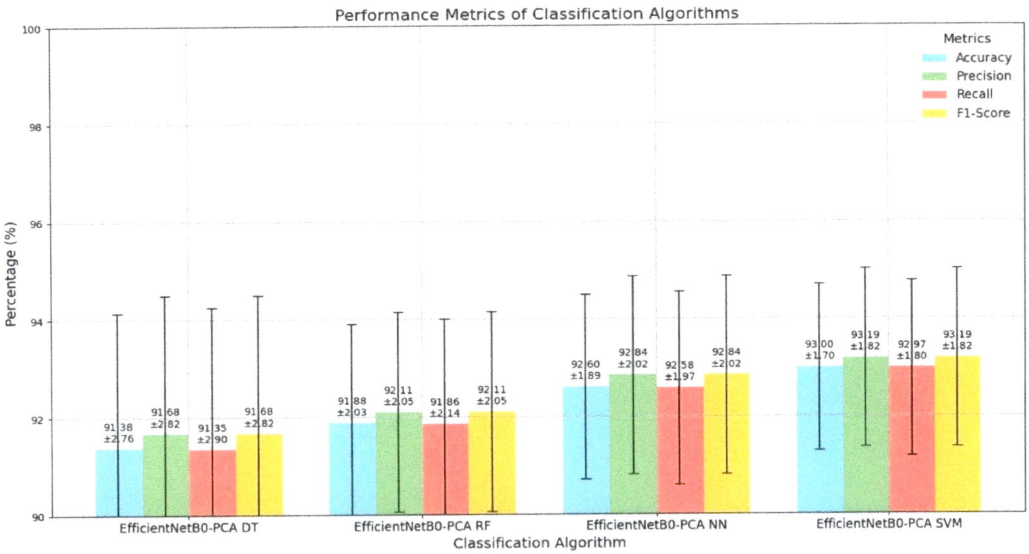

Figure 4. Visualization of the performance metrics for algorithms classifiers.

The comparison study provided us with useful insights into the performance of several algorithms, which influenced our decision to choose the EfficientNetB0-PCA SVM classifier for skin cancer diagnosis and categorization. The experimental results showed how each model and algorithm combination performed in terms of accuracy, precision, recall, F1 score, and support. Our goal in comparing these results was to discover the most powerful algorithm that delivers high accuracy in skin cancer categorization.

4.2.2. Statistical Analysis: *T*-Test Results

To assess the statistical significance of the differences between the performance of various classification algorithms, we conducted pairwise T-tests on the accuracy results obtained from 10-fold cross-validation.

The results presented in Table 3, showing no statistically significant differences between the classification algorithms (DT, NN, RF, SVM) using EfficientNetB0-PCA on the ISIC dataset, can be interpreted as positive. This indicates that multiple algorithms are effective for this task, providing flexibility and robustness in model selection. Researchers and practitioners can choose any of these models based on other factors such as computational efficiency, ease of implementation, or specific application requirements, without worrying about significant performance discrepancies.

Table 3. Statistical analysis of classification algorithms for ISIC dataset.

Classification Algorithms	T-Statistic	*p*-Value
EfficientNetB0-PCA (DT vs. NN)	−0.466	0.647
EfficientNetB0-PCA (DT vs. RF)	−0.451	0.657
EfficientNetB0-PCA (DT vs. SVM)	−0.530	0.602
EfficientNetB0-PCA (NN vs. RF)	0.011	0.992
EfficientNetB0-PCA (NN vs. SVM)	−0.067	0.948
EfficientNetB0-PCA (RF vs. SVM)	−0.076	0.940

The statistical analysis of classification algorithms for the DermIS dataset using EfficientNetB0-PCA, as shown in Table 4, reveals no statistically significant differences between the compared pairs of algorithms. The T-statistic and P-value for each comparison

(DT vs. NN, DT vs. RF, DT vs. SVM, NN vs. RF, NN vs. SVM, and RF vs. SVM) indicate that Decision Tree (DT), Neural Network (NN), Random Forest (RF), and SVM perform similarly on the DermIS dataset. This lack of significant differences suggests that these algorithms are equally effective for this task, allowing flexibility in choosing any of them based on other considerations such as computational efficiency or ease of implementation, without concern for substantial performance variations.

Table 4. Statistical analysis of classification algorithms for DermIS dataset.

Classification Algorithms	T-Statistic	p-Value
EfficientNetB0-PCA (DT vs. NN)	−1.0966	0.2873
EfficientNetB0-PCA (DT vs. RF)	−0.4370	0.6673
EfficientNetB0-PCA (DT vs. SVM)	−1.5033	0.1501
EfficientNetB0-PCA (NN vs. R)	0.7823	0.4442
EfficientNetB0-PCA (NN vs. SVM)	−0.4720	0.6426
EfficientNetB0-PCA (RF vs. SVM)	−1.2742	0.2188

4.2.3. Mean Accuracy and Confidence Intervals of Classification Algorithms

This section presents the mean accuracy and the associated 95% confidence intervals for various classification models. Mean accuracy indicates the overall effectiveness of each model in correctly classifying the data. The 95% confidence intervals show the range within which the true accuracy. This takes into account the variability in the model's performance across different data subsets, providing a clearer understanding of the model's reliability and stability.

Table 5 presents the analysis of classification algorithms for the DermIS dataset using EfficientNetB0-PCA, as shown by the mean accuracy and 95% confidence intervals, demonstrates that all four models—Decision Tree (DT), Random Forest (RF), Neural Network (NN), and SVM—perform at a high level with comparable accuracy. The mean accuracies are 90.40% for DT, 90.92% for RF, 90.93% for NN, and 91.00% for SVM. The overlapping confidence intervals indicate no significant differences between their performances, suggesting that any of these algorithms can be effectively used for this classification task, providing flexibility in model selection based on other considerations such as computational resources or ease of implementation.

Table 5. Mean accuracy and confidence intervals of classification algorithms for ISIC dataset.

Classification Algorithms	Mean Accuracy (%)	95% Confidence Intervals (%)
EfficientNetB0-PCA DT	90.40%	(88.42%, 92.38%)
EfficientNetB0-PCA RF	90.92%	(89.24%, 92.60%)
EfficientNetB0-PCA NN	90.93%	(89.30%, 92.56%)
EfficientNetB0-PCA SVM	91.00%	(89.41%, 92.59%)

Table 6 shows the analysis of classification algorithms for the DermIS dataset using EfficientNetB0-PCA, demonstrating high performance across all models: DT (91.38%), RF (91.88%), NN (92.60%), and SVM (93.00%). The overlapping 95% confidence intervals indicate no significant performance differences, suggesting that any of these models can be effectively used for this task.

Table 6. Mean accuracy and confidence intervals of classification algorithms for DemIS dataset.

Classification Algorithms	Mean Accuracy (%)	95% Confidence Intervals (%)
EfficientNetB0-PCA DT	91.38	(89.29, 93.46)
EfficientNetB0-PCA RF	91.88	(90.34, 93.41)
EfficientNetB0-PCA NN	92.60	(91.17, 94.03)
EfficientNetB0-PCA SVM	93.00	(91.72, 94.28)

4.3. Evaluation Metrics of the Proposed Model with State-of-the-Art Pre-Trained Techniques

In Table 7, we compare our suggest model's performance with other state-of-the-art approaches. The table showcases the results of different classifiers applied to the DermIS dataset, using the SVM technique, and reports their corresponding accuracy scores.

Table 7. Comparative of proposed model with state-of-the-art models.

Classifier	Dataset	Technique	Accuracy
Amelard et al. [28]	DermIS	SVM	86.00
Almansour et al. [29]	DermIS	SVM	90.00
Farooq et al. [30]	DermIS	SVM	80.00
Priya Natha [31]	ISIC	SVM	86.9
A Abdelhafeez [32]	ISIC	SVM	85.74
Proposed model	ISIC	SVM	91.00
Proposed model	DermIS	SVM	93.00

In the study conducted by Amelard et al. [28], a classifier was developed for the DermIS dataset, achieving an accuracy of 86%. Similarly, Almansour et al. [29] introduced another classifier on the same dataset, obtaining an accuracy of 90%. Additionally, Farooq et al. [30] presented their classifier for the DermIS dataset, obtaining an accuracy of 80%. Priya Natha [31] worked on the ISIC dataset using an SVM classifier and achieved an accuracy of 86.9%, while A Abdelhafeez [32] reached 85.74% accuracy on the ISIC dataset using the same technique.

In contrast, our proposed model achieved an impressive accuracy of 93% on the DermIS dataset and 91.00% on the ISIC dataset. These results clearly indicate that our proposed model exceeds the state-of-the-art models presented by Amelard et al. [28], Almansour et al. [29], Farooq et al. [30], Priya Natha [31], and A Abdelhafeez [32] in terms of accuracy for both the DermIS and ISIC dataset.

5. Conclusions

In conclusion, the implementation of AI techniques such as CNNs, transfer learning, PCA, and AdaBoost shows great promise in revolutionizing skin cancer diagnosis and classification. These techniques enable accurate detection and classification, enhancing diagnostic efficiency. Transfer learning with CNNs effectively extracts features from skin lesion images, while PCA and AdaBoost improve the accuracy and reliability of classification models. Integrating SVM and other algorithms with AI further boosts accuracy with large datasets. However, this study acknowledges limitations, including potential biases, annotation variations, and data imbalances. Future work should address these gaps by expanding datasets to include diverse skin types, incorporating non-dermoscopic images, and integrating Vision Transformers into AI tools. Vision Transformers could be optimized for handling challenges like irregular shapes and diverse textures in skin cancer images, providing valuable insights and improving the interpretability and generalization of AI-assisted diagnostics. These advancements can lead to cost reductions and improved patient outcomes, benefiting both patients and healthcare providers.

Author Contributions: Conceptualization, S.G., F.Z., M.A. (Muhammad Asim) and M.A. (Moath Alrifaey); Data curation, M.A. (Muhammad Asim), N.A. and M.A. (Moath Alrifaey); Formal analysis, N.A. and M.A. (Muhammad Asim); Funding acquisition, M.A. (Muhammad Asim) and N.A.; Investigation, M.A. (Muhammad Asim), M.A. (Moath Alrifaey) and N.A.; Methodology, S.G., F.Z. and M.A. (Muhammad Asim); Project administration, F.Z. and M.A. (Moath Alrifaey); Resources, F.Z., M.A. (Moath Alrifaey) and N.A.; Software, S.G.; Supervision, F.Z.; Validation, N.A., M.A. (Moath Alrifaey) and N.A.; Visualization, S.G. and N.A.; Writing—original draft, S.G.; Writing—review & editing, F.Z., M.A. (Muhammad Asim), N.A. and M.A. (Moath Alrifaey). All authors have read and agreed to the published version of the manuscript.

Funding: This research was supported by the EIAS Data Science & Blockchain Lab at Prince Sultan University, Riyadh, Saudi Arabia. The authors would like to thank Prince Sultan University for paying the APC of this article.

Data Availability Statement: Data can be shared upon reasonable request from corresponding author.

Acknowledgments: The authors would like to thank Prince Sultan University for their support.

Conflicts of Interest: The authors declare no conflicts of interest.

References

1. Saba, T.; Khan, M.A.; Rehman, A.; Marie-Sainte, S.L. Region extraction and classification of skin cancer: A heterogeneous framework of deep CNN features fusion and reduction. *J. Med. Syst.* **2019**, *43*, 289. [CrossRef]
2. Saba, T. Computer vision for microscopic skin cancer diagnosis using handcrafted and non-handcrafted features. *Microsc. Res. Tech.* **2021**, *84*, 1272–1283. [CrossRef]
3. Nawaz, M.; Mehmood, Z.; Nazir, T.; Naqvi, R.A.; Rehman, A.; Iqbal, M.; Saba, T. Skin cancer detection from dermoscopic images using deep learning and fuzzy k-means clustering. *Microsc. Res. Tech.* **2022**, *85*, 339–351. [CrossRef] [PubMed]
4. Van Bodegraven, B.; Vernon, S.; Eversfield, C.; Board, R.; Craig, P.; Gran, S.; Harwood, C.A.; Keohane, S.; Levell, N.J.; Matin, R.N. 'Get Data Out'Skin: National cancer registry incidence and survival rates for all registered skin tumour groups for 2013–2019 in England. *Br. J. Dermatol.* **2023**, *188*, 777–784. [CrossRef] [PubMed]
5. Kong, B.; Sun, S.; Wang, X.; Song, Q.; Zhang, S. Invasive cancer detection utilizing compressed Convolutional Neural Network and transfer learning. In Proceedings of the 2018 International Conference on Medical Image Computing and Computer-Assisted Intervention, Granada, Spain, 16–20 September 2018; pp. 156–164.
6. Zhang, Y.; Wang, S.; Phillips, P.; Dong, Z.; Ji, G.; Yang, J. Detection of Alzheimer's disease and mild cognitive impairment based on structural volumetric MR images using 3D-DWT and WTA-KSVM trained by PSOTVAC. *Biomed. Signal Process. Control* **2015**, *21*, 58–73. [CrossRef]
7. Kasmi, R.; Mokrani, K. Classification of malignant melanoma and benign skin lesions: Implementation of automatic ABCD rule. *IET Image Process.* **2016**, *10*, 448–455. [CrossRef]
8. Friedman, R.J.; Rigel, D.S.; Kopf, A.W. Early detection of malignant melanoma: The role of physician examination and self-examination of the skin. *CA Cancer J. Clin.* **1985**, *35*, 130–151. [CrossRef] [PubMed]
9. Hosny, K.M.; Kassem, M.A.; Fouad, M.M. Classification of skin lesions into seven classes using transfer learning with AlexNet. *J. Digit. Imaging* **2020**, *33*, 1325–1334. [CrossRef] [PubMed]
10. Leiter, U.; Garbe, C. Epidemiology of melanoma and nonmelanoma skin cancer—The role of sunlight. In *Sunlight, Vitam D and Skin Cancer*; Springer: New York, NY, USA, 2008; pp. 89–103.
11. Burdick, J.; Marques, O.; Weinthal, J.; Furht, B. Rethinking skin lesion segmentation in a convolutional classifier. *J. Digit. Imaging* **2018**, *31*, 435–440. [CrossRef] [PubMed]
12. Stoecker, W.V.; Chiang, C.-S.; Moss, R.H. Texture in skin images: Comparison of three methods to determine smoothness. *Comput. Med. Imaging Graph.* **1992**, *16*, 179–190. [CrossRef] [PubMed]
13. Trufant, J.; Jones, E. Skin cancer for primary care. In *Common Dermatologic Conditions in Primary Care*; Humana Press: Totowa, NJ, USA, 2019; pp. 171–208.
14. Lakhani, P.; Sundaram, B. Deep learning at chest radiography: Automated classification of pulmonary tuberculosis by using Convolutional Neural Networks. *Radiology* **2017**, *284*, 574–582. [CrossRef] [PubMed]
15. Zoph, B.; Vasudevan, V.; Shlens, J.; Le, Q.V. Learning transferable architectures for scalable image recognition. In Proceedings of the 2018 IEEE Conference on Computer Vision and Pattern Recognition, Salt Lake City, UT, USA, 18–23 June 2018; pp. 8697–8710.
16. Zhu, J.-Y.; Park, T.; Isola, P.; Efros, A.A. Unpaired image-to-image translation using cycle-consistent adversarial networks. In Proceedings of the 2017 IEEE International Conference on Computer Vision, Venice, Italy, 22–29 October 2017; pp. 2223–2232.
17. Mustafa, S.; Kimura, A. A SVM-based diagnosis of melanoma using only useful image features. In Proceedings of the 2018 International Workshop on Advanced Image Technology (IWAIT), Chiang Mai, Thailand, 7–9 January 2018; pp. 1–4.
18. Daghrir, J.; Tlig, L.; Bouchouicha, M.; Sayadi, M. Melanoma skin cancer detection using deep learning and classical machine learning techniques: A hybrid approach. In Proceedings of the 2020 5th International Conference on Advanced Technologies for Signal and Image Processing (ATSIP), Sousse, Tunisia, 2–5 September 2020; pp. 1–5.
19. Esteva, A.; Kuprel, B.; Novoa, R.A.; Ko, J.; Swetter, S.M.; Blau, H.M.; Thrun, S. Dermatologist-level classification of skin cancer with deep neural networks. *Nature* **2017**, *542*, 115–118. [CrossRef] [PubMed]
20. Nasr-Esfahani, E.; Samavi, S.; Karimi, N.; Soroushmehr, S.M.R.; Jafari, M.H.; Ward, K.; Najarian, K. Melanoma detection by analysis of clinical images using Convolutional Neural Network. In Proceedings of the 2016 38th Annual International Conference of the 2016 IEEE Engineering in Medicine and Biology Society (EMBC), Orlando, FL, USA, 16–20 August 2016; pp. 1373–1376.
21. Jenitha, A.; Amrutha, G.; Kishore, K.; Rohan, K.; Sagar, S.; KGF, K.I. Skin Cancer Recognition and Detection Using Machine Learning Algorithm. In Proceedings of the First International Conference on Advanced Scientific Innovation in Science, Engineering and Technology, ICASISET 2020, Chennai, India, 16–17 May 2020; European Alliance for Innovation: Bratislava, Slovakia, 2021; p. 122.

22. Shah, V.V.; Mirani, S.J.; Nanavati, Y.V.; Narayanan, V.; Pereira, S.I. Stock market prediction using neural networks. *Int. J. Soft Comput. Eng.* **2016**, *6*, 86–89.
23. Yuan, X.; Yang, Z.; Zouridakis, G.; Mullani, N. SVM-based Texture Classification and Application to Early Melanoma Detection. In Proceedings of the 2006 International Conference of the IEEE Engineering in Medicine and Biology Society, New York, NY, USA, 30 August–3 September 2006; pp. 4775–4778. [CrossRef]
24. Ashafuddula, N.; Islam, R. Melanoma skin cancer and nevus mole classification using intensity value estimation with Convolutional Neural Network. *arXiv* **2022**, arXiv:2209.15465. [CrossRef]
25. Yang, T.-Y.; Chien, T.-W.; Lai, F.-J. Web-based skin cancer assessment and classification using machine learning and mobile computerized adaptive testing in a Rasch Model: Development study. *JMIR Med. Inform.* **2022**, *10*, e33006. [CrossRef] [PubMed]
26. Dondapati, R.D.; Sivaprakasam, T.; Kumar, K.V. Dermatological Decision Support Systems using CNN for Binary Classification. *Eng. Technol. Appl. Sci. Res.* **2024**, *14*, 14240–14247. [CrossRef]
27. Zareen, S.S.; Sun, G.; Li, Y.; Qadri, S.; Qadri, S.U. *A Machine Vision Approach for Classification of Skin Cancer Using Hybrid Texture Features*; SSRN: Rochester, NY, USA, 2022.
28. Amelard, R.; Wong, A.; Clausi, D.A. Extracting high-level intuitive features (HLIF) for classifying skin lesions using standard camera images. In Proceedings of the 2012 Ninth Conference on Computer and Robot Vision, Toronto, ON, Canada, 28–30 May 2012; pp. 396–403.
29. Almansour, E.; Jaffar, M.A. Classification of Dermoscopic skin cancer images using color and hybrid texture features. *Int. J. Comput. Sci. Netw. Secur.* **2016**, *16*, 135–139.
30. Farooq, M.A.; Azhar, M.A.M.; Raza, R.H. Automatic lesion detection system (ALDS) for skin cancer classification using SVM and neural classifiers. In Proceedings of the 2016 IEEE 16th International Conference on Bioinformatics and Bioengineering (BIBE), Taichung, Taiwan, 31 October–2 November 2016; pp. 301–308.
31. Natha, P.; Pothuraju, R. Skin cancer detection using machine learning classification models. *Preprints* **2023**, 2023110248. [CrossRef]
32. Abdelhafeez, A.; Mohamed, H.K.; Maher, A.; Khalil, N.A. A novel approach toward skin cancer classification through fused deep features and neutrosophic environment. *Front. Public Health* **2023**, *11*, 1123581. [CrossRef] [PubMed]

MDPI AG
Grosspeteranlage 5
4052 Basel
Switzerland
Tel.: +41 61 683 77 34

Algorithms Editorial Office
E-mail: algorithms@mdpi.com
www.mdpi.com/journal/algorithms

www.ingramcontent.com/pod-product-compliance
Lightning Source LLC
Chambersburg PA
CBHW061547220926
51850CB00005B/276
* 9 7 8 3 7 2 5 8 6 5 0 6 2 *